Richard Wright

THE AMERICAN CRITICAL TRADITION 6
M. Thomas Inge, *General Editor*

Richard Wright

The Critical Reception

Edited with an Introduction by
John M. Reilly

Burt Franklin & Co., Inc.

For Joyce

Library of Congress Cataloging in Publication Data

Main entry under title:
Richard Wright: the critical reception.
(The American critical tradition)
Includes index.
1. Wright, Richard, 1908–1960—Criticism and
interpretation—Addresses, essays, lectures.
I. Reilly, John M.
PS3545.R815Z82 813′.5′2 78-5476
ISBN 0-89102-110-8 (cloth)
0-89102-126-4 (paper)
Manufactured in the United States of America

Acknowledgments and permissions
are listed on pages xliii–xlvii
which constitute an extension of the
copyright page for the purposes
of notice.

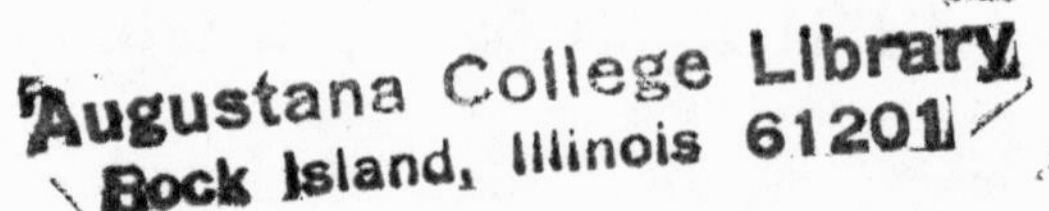

General Editor's Preface

When we speak of a writer's reputation in critical terms, we should recognize that he actually has two: the response of book reviewers and critics during his own lifetime to each of his works as it was published, and the retrospective evaluation of his achievement by literary historians and academic critics in the decades after his career is concluded. The primary concern of modern scholarship has been the latter, on the assumption that the passage of time is essential before a writer's achievement can be objectively viewed and assessed. The purpose of the volumes in the American Critical Tradition series, however, is to provide overviews of the critical reputations earned by major American authors in their own times. Such overviews are necessary before the full impact of a writer's influence can be properly evaluated and an understanding of how he related to his contemporary cultural milieu achieved.

The few efforts hitherto made in summarizing a writer's contemporary critical standing have usually been based on a reading of sample reviews or vague impressions retained by veterans of the era. Seldom have literary historians gone back to locate and read all or most of the comment elicited by a career in progress. In the present volumes, the editors have sought to unearth every known review of each book in the contemporary newspapers, journals, and periodicals, and to demonstrate the critical response chronologically through reprint, excerpt, or summary. Exhaustive checklists of reviews not included in the text are appended to each chapter, and the editor has provided an introduction summarizing the major trends observable in the criticism. The results not only elucidate the writer's career, but they reveal as well intellectual patterns in book reviewing and the reception of serious writing by the American reading public. Each volume is, therefore, a combined literary chronicle and reference work of a type previously unavailable.

M. Thomas Inge
General Editor

Contents

Introduction

For many in Richard Wright's audience the author's person is as much a fascination as are his works. How can it be, they wonder, that this man, who was born in poverty and subject to racial oppression in his childhood and youth, became a famous novelist? Wright himself thought the question important, for in chapter thirteen of his autobiography *Black Boy,* he related the events that led to his literary awakening. One morning in Memphis he read a newspaper editorial denouncing H. L. Mencken. Feeling a vague sympathy for the white writer who had earned the scorn normally directed at blacks, he sought the help of an Irish Catholic, also reviled by southerners, in getting copies of Mencken's books from the public library. The white man's library card and a note forged by Wright to the librarian saying "Will you please let this nigger boy have some books by H. L. Mencken?" secured him copies of *A Book of Prefaces* and *Prejudices*. That night Wright began to read the books in his rented room. He was startled. The lucid, raging style was that of a man fighting by words. "Could words be weapons?" he asked himself. "Well, yes, for here they were. Then, maybe, perhaps, I could use them as a weapon?" Guilt about his intellectual violation of caste arrangements made Wright fearful that a difference in his outward manner would betray him, but within himself he was forever changed by the passion for literature awakened that night by reading Mencken. As he read such books as Sinclair Lewis' *Main Street* (it was the first serious novel he tried), Theodore Dreiser's *Jennie Gerhardt* and *Sister Carrie*, and other works praised by Mencken, Wright found "nothing less than a sense of life itself." All his experience had shaped him for the realism and naturalism of modern fiction, and he could not read enough of it.

The step from reading realistic literature to writing it remained to be taken, but there is no doubt that Wright intended his account of the discovery of Mencken and modern literature to represent his call to a literary vocation. As such, it is an effective literary device. A long period of development is compressed by the mature author of the autobiography into a brief time in which the painfully sensitive and lonely youth finds that the power of the written word promises him a field for his talents and a way of overcoming social oppression. The paradigm of *Black Boy* appears clearly in the episode. The self-determining personality conflicts with the enormous force of the social and material environment. Racism and poverty nearly shape Wright's destiny, but within himself he finds the capacity for creativity.

The paradigm of Wright's narrative exemplifies one of our culture's basic conceptions of reality. Readers fascinated by the achievement of Richard Wright share with him a wonder about the relationship of society and the individual's psychology. Wright and his readers acknowledge environmental necessities, described for example by literary naturalism; yet, they also know the possibilities of self-realization. Indeed, it is fundamental to our culture that we are preoccupied with finding the significance of experience by reconciling the conflicting interpretations of environmental determinism and self-determination. Wright gave unusual power to this interpretive conflict in his fiction, as readers of *Native Son* are aware. His public career also exemplified the pattern: besides being a creative artist Wright also served as a spokesman for the American blacks and later for the Third World people whose collective experience in history he understood through analogy with his own personal life. Inevitably, then, the paradigm of determinism and self-direction that informs Richard Wright's art, giving it both subject and structure, also provides the framework within which his readers seek to understand his work. To outline this framework was the job of Wright's reviewers; the present task of criticism is to explain Wright and his work with the aid of those earlier reviewers' commentaries.

Wright served his literary apprenticeship during the ten years he spent in Chicago between 1927 and 1937. He had felt the first call to literature, the interest in the writings of Mencken, while still a teen-aged youth in Memphis. However, he was in his twenties when he undertook the extensive reading of modern authors and of social science, the contemplation of life, and the formal experiments necessary for him to determine his literary purpose. At that time much of his energy, like that of many another southern migrant and child of the working class, had to be devoted to the struggle for economic and physical survival. While doing menial jobs in cafés, selling burial insurance, and working as a temporary postal employee, Wright began drafting short stories. He also became acquainted with other young people who had an interest in books. One of his stories, a Gothic frame tale entitled "Superstition," was printed in *Abbott's Monthly Magazine,* a journal read by the large black popular audience of Chicago. This story was strictly a potboiler, though indicative of Wright's life-long interest in the popular thriller genres.

He began writing about his serious interests shortly after he accepted an invitation to visit the John Reed Club meeting rooms in 1933. This event was as significant to Wright as his earlier visit to the Memphis public library, and again he wrote an account, in "I Tried to Be a Communist," symbolizing its place in his career. At his first Reed Club meeting Wright met people he would know for years to come and "who were to form the first sustained relationships in my life." Excited by the devotion they showed to their political and artistic cause, Wright lay awake in his bed after that first meeting reading the magazines his new friends had given him. The magazines conveyed the similarity of experience among people of all lands and made Wright believe that he could overcome the sense of helplessness he felt as an American black. In the activity of the political left he might find a home for himself, and in revolutionary expression he might find a valuable role for his understanding of experience. Feeling at once that he had found a definite audience he "wrote a wild, crude poem in free verse, coining images of black hands playing, working, holding bayonets, stiffening finally in death." That poem was undoubtedly "I Have Seen Black Hands," published the following June (1934) in *New Masses.* Wright's description of the Reed Club meeting, like the Mencken incident, also foreshortens the process of his development, but still it is a fact that he threw himself fully into Reed Club activities. He became an officer of the club in 1933, joined the Communist party the same year, contributed poems to *New Masses,* and published revolutionary verse in the middle western Reed Club magazines *Anvil* and *Left Front.*

Though he would later have difficulties with party policies, Wright's entry into left-wing literary life released within him great creative energy. By the end of 1935 he had published additional poems and a sketch in *New Masses;* had seen his verse appear in *International Literature,* the multilingual organ of the International Union of Revolutionary Writers, where he also received critical attention in an article linking him with Langston Hughes and Sterling Brown; and had drafted the story that would become "Big Boy Leaves Home." Moreover, he had written one novel and part of another. The completed novel was rejected by several publishers in 1935 and 1936 and did not appear until after Wright's death when it came out under the title *Lawd Today,* but still the young Wright earned a reputation on the left as an author with promise. Some of the acclaim derived from the desire among progressive literary people to encourage black authors for political reasons. Nevertheless, Wright made the most of the opportunity it afforded him. When he was invited to sign the call for a national American Writers Congress, he willingly added his name to a list that included Nelson Algren, Kenneth Burke, Malcolm Cowley, Theodore Dreiser, James T. Farrell, Langston Hughes, Lincoln Steffens, and Nathaniel West. At the congress the Reed Clubs were disbanded, but the meetings concluded with the founding of the League of American Writers. Richard Wright was one of the members of the national council.

In 1937 Wright passed an examination for a permanent job with the post office, but psychologically he was ready to try making his living as a writer. So he went to New York, first as a delegate to the second American Writers Congress and then to live as a permanent resident. Soon he became a journalist on the *Daily Worker*—director of the Harlem Bureau—and almost at once he joined in broader literary activity. He planned and edited the journal *New Challenge,* which lasted only long enough to publish his first extended theoretical piece, "Blueprint for Negro Writing." He wrote an autobiographical sketch, "The Ethics of Living Jim Crow," for *American Stuff* (1937), the anthology of the Federal Writers Project, and contributed reviews and a story, "Silt," to *New Masses.*

By the end of the year Wright had achieved success to match his promise. *Story* magazine sponsored a contest open to all members of the Federal Writers Project who had not previously published a book. Wright submitted "Big Boy Leaves Home" and three other stories he had written in Chicago. The stories were united by their common subject, the violence of racist terror, and by the thematic development of collective response to that terror manifest in the progression from Big Boy's flight in the first story to the Reverend Taylor's triumph in the last, "Fire and Cloud." The contest judges—Sinclair Lewis, Harry Scherman, and Lewis Gannett—chose Wright's manuscript for first prize. His apprenticeship was complete.

Story published "Fire and Cloud" in its March 1938 issue and arranged with Harper's to publish the full manuscript under the title *Uncle Tom's Children.* The contest guaranteed critical attention for the volume and provided most reviewers with their lead paragraphs. Thus, Herschel Brickell in the *New York Evening Post* overcame his doubts that Wright's revelations of the South would serve any useful purpose by quoting Lewis Gannett's comment on the stories: "They sing as well as sear." Brickell also observed that Wright had avoided the usual stereotypes in writing of blacks, a point that some black reviewers themselves chose to stress. For example, in *The Nation,* Sterling Brown praised the book as one written from within black experience telling a truth about the South that "has not often been within the covers of a book." Marvel Cooke writing in the *New York Amsterdam News* found the use of dialect in the stories masterful. Cooke also explicitly identified a political purpose in the volume, saying it was "the most exciting proletarian literature produced during the past twelve months" and a cry for immediate anti-lynching legislation as well as an encouragement of unity among black and white workers.

Black response was less than unanimously favorable, though. Zora Neale Hurston, whose own novel *Their Eyes Were Watching God* Wright had condemned in *New Masses* for employing ministrel show stereotypes, described Wright's stories in the *Saturday Review of Literature* as examples of unrelieved hatred. She, too, saw politics in the volume. What was new in the stories, she said, was wish fulfillment: "The hero suffers but he gets his man." And this was all in the service of the Communist solution for injustice—that is, "state responsibility for everything and individual responsibility for nothing, not even feeding one's self. And march!"

Other negative comments seemed motivated by defensiveness about the white South. Malcolm Purcell, Jr., in the *Macon Telegraph* doubted that Wright any longer retained a clear picture of the South, since he unfairly related incidents too rare to indict southern mores. James Saxon Childers, writing in the *Birmingham New Age-Herald,* worried that the unrelieved venom of Wright's stories, evident in the fact that blacks were portrayed as innocent victims, would hinder the improvement of conditions desired by honorable persons of both races.

Most reviews of *Uncle Tom's Children,* however, were decidedly favorable, even enthusiastic. Lewis Gannett in the *New York Herald-Tribune* revealed the opinion that led him to vote for Wright in the *Story* magazine contest by calling the work "part of a new American history." The reviewer for the *Dallas Morning News* applauded the departure from stereotype, and, while commenting that characters were more typical than individualized, concluded that much should be expected of Wright in the future. Ardent literary approval appeared in Robert Van Gelder's comparison of Wright to Hemingway *(New York Times Book Review);* in Allen Maxwell's judgment that Wright's style was in the tradition of Steinbeck's terseness as was his gradual progression through intensifying emotional stages without sacrifice of narrative to "message" *(Southwest Review);* and in Fred T. Marsh's suggestion that *Uncle Tom's Children* might well win another prize—the Pulitzer *(New York Herald Tribune Books).*

Many reviewers joined Cooke, Hurston, Purcell, and Childers in commenting on the politics of the stories. For instance, Malcolm Cowley in the *New Republic* accepted as valid both Wright's indication that violence was endemic in the South and his fictionalized representation of the Communist slogan of black and white unity in "Fire and Cloud." Surprisingly, though, the critics on the left played down Wright's politics in favor of discussion of his artistry. Granville Hicks in *New Masses* naturally found that Wright's stories strengthened the literature of the left but singled out for approval the emotional complexity of "Long Black Song" and disapproved Wright's tendency to race ahead before carefully completing the construction of his narratives. Alan Calmer in the *Daily Worker* also gave his attention to narrative style, finding that the pace and descriptions dovetailed perfectly. Calmer's admonition to Wright was that he should dig more deeply into his material in order to set events into a fuller social perspective. He saw "Fire and Cloud" as an example of this prescription fulfilled. It can be surmised that Calmer's criticism had its effect on Wright, for when he published an expanded edition of *Uncle Tom's Children* in 1940 it included an introduction, "The Ethics of Living Jim Crow," and concluded with the story "Bright and Morning Star," two pieces that explicitly broadened the social context. James T. Farrell had a particular affinity for Wright, since both men carefully worked to guard the integrity of their writing from the influence of political immediacy. This affinity seemed evident in the review Farrell wrote for *Partisan Review* where he praised *Uncle Tom's Children* for its exemplary realism at a time when "fables and allegories" had become the fashion.

An immediate consequence of the success of *Uncle Tom's Children* was that Wright became a public figure in New York. He was honored at the convention of the Communist party, invited to speak before community meetings, and urged to participate more actively in the League of American Writers. In April 1938 the Book Union selected his book for distribution to its members and in May he became a literary editor for *New Masses*.

Also, he wrote. The "Portrait of Harlem" in *New York Panorama,* a publication in the American Guides Series of the Federal Writers Project was Wright's work. The story "Bright and Morning Star" appeared in *New Masses* in May. At the same time, he was writing another novel. In the spring of 1939, he received a Guggenheim fellowship, which he used to complete this novel and to begin a new one. The completed work was *Native Son*. After the manuscript was accepted by Harper's, it was sent to the Book-of-the-Month Club which planned to make it a selection for the fall of 1939. Publication was delayed, but the book finally appeared on March 1, 1940 and it was to make Wright once and for all an important American author. Harper's reported sales of 200,000 copies before the end of the month, and *Native Son* was number one on the best-seller list by April 1, 1940.

Reviewers could not fail to respond in some way to the novel's literary quality, for it was character portrayal, the control of point of view, and plot construction that convinced readers of the truth in Wright's vision of American life. The careful merger of social and personal detail produced the compelling symbol called Bigger Thomas and the tragic dynamics of his fictional career. Yet to read *Native Son* was to become oblivious to the author's craft, which created a style that was nearly a transparent medium. Critics of the book, therefore, testified to its literary merit mainly by indirection as they remarked upon its power to disturb a reader, measured Bigger by the criterion of plausibility, and compared Wright's story to social reality.

Henry Seidel Canby's essay for the *Book-of-the-Month Club News* promised readers the unique experience of entering the mind of a contemporary black man. Lewis Gannett's in the *New York Herald Tribune* agreed that the book was a novelty—indeed something terrifyingly new in American fiction—rooted in truth by the fact that Bigger Thomas was the man "Richard Wright just missed becoming." Harry Hansen in the *New York World-Telegram* cautioned that the horror of the story was less than a summary of the plot would suggest because the author had his heart in the tale. In contrast, Jonathan Daniels wrote in the *Saturday Review of Literature* that the book gained force from the irresistible objectivity that drew one into the story and delivered one's sympathies to Bigger. Milton Rugoff in the *New York Herald Tribune* developed this idea by observing that the intensely sensational criminal story was rooted in authentic environmental sources. The tendency to generalize Bigger was completed by the review in *Time,* which explained Timestyle that the sensations of the story "only pull the trigger of author Wright's bigger story—the murderous potentialities of the whole U.S. Negro problem."

The character of Bigger Thomas also interested others: Margaret Marshall applauded in *The Nation* Wright's boldness in choosing as his "hero" a "bad nigger"; Theophilus Lewis in *Interracial Review* found significance in Wright's reversal of a newspaper crime story in order to feature the criminal's point of view; and Sterling Brown declared in *Opportunity* that the novel's greatest achievement was Wright's probing of the consciousness of the outcast. The *Chicago Defender* concurred by describing Bigger's story as "a penetrating, realistic, clinical examination of a raw, open wound which is yet bleeding."

Malcolm Cowley, who had strongly approved Wright's social theme in *Uncle Tom's Children,* was equally positive about *Native Son.* Writing in the *New Republic* he said that the lawyer Boris Max's description of America as separate black and white nations was accurate. However, he found Max's plea for Bigger's individual life thematically weakening, because, though Wright's intention may have been otherwise, Bigger's death was necessary for his conversion into a human rather than a strictly racial symbol. Further attention to Bigger came from Ben Davis, Jr., in the *Sunday Worker.* As a whole, Davis thought the book was a successful indictment of capitalist America's oppression of the black nation, but Wright was mistaken in overwriting Bigger into a symbol for that nation's people. Something was needed in the novel to indicate that the black masses generally were struggling against capitalism in a correct way.

Davis' lengthy review showed the importance *Native Son* had for the left-wing, but his doctrinaire comments failed to confront issues critical to literature. Much more successful as a left-wing consideration of the novel was the series of essays Samuel Sillen wrote for *New Masses.* In the first (March 5, 1940) Sillen called the novel a "brilliant analysis of the interplay of social and psychological factors in experience," which constituted the creation of a new mode of writing, neither exclusively naturalistic nor limited to psychology but rather a fusion of perspectives into "dramatic realism." Because *Native Son* seemed to place Wright in "the first ranks of American literature," Sillen followed his review with an article outlining the responses to Wright's revolutionary novel (April 23, 1940) and then with a lengthy response of his own (April 30, 1940) to the reviewers' tendency to isolate various parts of the novel from its total meaning. Finally, Sillen invited readers of *New Masses* to make their own comments, and a selection of these appeared on May 21, 1940. Without doubt Sillen's efforts on behalf of *Native Son* were the most critically stimulating the novel received. Of course, like other reviewers Sillen approached the book with criteria derived from his own social view, which at the time tended to coincide with those of Wright, but the value of the articles lay in Sillen's attention to problems of interpretation and his insistence on viewing the novel as an organic work; thus, he gave credence to the contention that Wright was important to *literature* as well as society.

Many reviewers expressed their convictions about Wright's literary importance in what might be considered the shorthand method of comparing *Native Son* to other prominent works. Malcolm Cowley and Benjamin Davis both compared the novel to Steinbeck's *Grapes of Wrath,* the sensation of the previous year. That comparison also occurred to Clifton Fadiman *(New Yorker),* who approved of Wright's ability to avoid facile determinism—an ability that reminded Fadiman of Dreiser's *An American Tragedy*. Dreiser's tragedy also seemed the apt comparison for Peter Monro Jack *(New York Times Book Review),* who qualified it by noting the startling difference in Wright's attribution of injustice to racial rather than to merely social factors. Edward Skillin, Jr. *(Commonweal),* carried the comparison between Clyde Griffiths' story and Bigger's throughout his review. Another likely parallel was developed by James W. Ivy in *The Crisis*. On the surface, he said, *Native Son* was another sensational crime story, but beneath the plot the analysis of Bigger's mind gave the story Dostoevskian sweep. Bigger ranked with Raskolnikov or one of the Brothers Karamazov. Wright's story was "the greatest novel written by an American Negro" and the author was "one of the great novelists of this generation."

Despite the general approval, few reviewers were unqualified in their praise. Margaret Marshall found that the rhetoric of Wright's style had a bookish quality, Sillen believed that the third part of the book relaxed the pace, Mary-Carter Roberts of the *Washington Star* thought the splendid story failed to demonstrate just how Bigger could be considered a victim, and Peter Monro Jack felt that Bigger was too articulate to sustain realism. With the exception of Roberts' criticism, the defects noted by these reviewers continue to occupy critics. The problems attendant upon Wright's choice of narrative voice and the orations of Max are subjects that must be treated by anyone who writes about *Native Son*. Issues raised by the decidedly negative reviews of 1940, however, are a mixed lot. Howard Mumford Jones in the *Boston Evening Transcript* agreed with the consensus that the plot seemed powerful on first reading, but on reflection he found it simply predictable melodrama without sufficient complexity to sustain interest or to deserve praise for its construction. The character of Bigger wavered between victim and amoral monster. As a result, the deterministic thesis lacked support. David Daiches summed up his objections to the novel for the *Partisan Review* by declaring that "Wright is trying to prove a normal thesis by an abnormal case." Like Jones, Daiches found the story too melodramatic, but he would have found no objection to the moral if Wright had led Bigger to a more plausible crime.

Jones and Daiches made points worth considering. That was hardly true of two other negative reviews, those by Burton Rascoe in *American Mercury* and David L. Cohn in *Atlantic Monthly*. Rascoe claimed he found it impossible to conceive of a worse novel. To make his point he announced three criteria for realistic fiction: the theme must be integral to the story rather than a detachable commentary, a character conceived as ignorant cannot have an analytic consciousness, nor should a character be portrayed as behaving in ways that are inconsistent with the conceivable behavior of the author. These could have been legitimate points for analysis of *Native Son,* but, rather than applying them to the novel, Rascoe applied them *ad hominem* by recounting a literary luncheon at which Wright appeared to have been consumed by hatred for the whites present, going so far as to say that he hoped they all would have a chance to meet the murderer Bigger Thomas. For Rascoe such a remark was insufferable but consistent with the moral of *Native Son* which justified loathsome behavior on the specious grounds that Bigger suffered hardships, the same as many another person had endured without becoming a killer. Cohn's criticism found Wright's offense in his false portrayal of the situation of the American blacks. Not only were things much better for blacks than Wright admitted, argued Cohn, but they were unlikely to become any better, because the racial problem was insoluble. The Anglo-Saxon social structure would never permit equality, so rather than espouse a hatred that overlooked what good whites had done for black people, Wright would be well advised to take the long view of history. What Wright did instead was take the unusual course for a novelist under review of sending vehement denunciations of the presumption of Rascoe and Cohn to *American Mercury* and *Atlantic Monthly*. Then, as if to forestall any further such criticism, he completed and published the essay "How Bigger Was Born" (originally a lecture, then published in *Saturday Review,* and finally issued as a pamphlet by Harper's) documenting the social sources for his conception of the violent protagonist of his novel.

Wright took a brief vacation after the publication of *Native Son*—his reply to Cohn was written from Mexico—but almost immediately thereafter he returned to the full schedule of a popular spokesman. Two literary projects that he undertook in 1940 and 1941 were closely related to *Native Son*. First he agreed to collaborate with Paul Green on a dramatization of that novel, which included some fundamental changes in the story. John Houseman, who produced the play, was particularly displeased with what he felt was Green's moralistic rewriting. Therefore, without Green's knowledge Houseman revised the play before it opened under the direction of Orson Welles at the St. James Theater in New York on March 25, 1941. Welles's direction made a splendidly effective drama, and the play ran for

114 performances in New York before it went on the road. In October 1942 it returned for a "revival" and finally closed in January 1943. Harper's published the play in 1941 with the subtitle *The Biography of a Young American*. This version, however, was Green's and not the text of the theatrical success.

Wright's second project for 1941 was the preparation of a written text to accompany Edwin Rosskam's selection of photographs of Afro-American life. The relatively new form of the photoessay had already produced such classics as Agee and Walker's *Let Us Now Praise Famous Men* and Margaret Bourke White and Erskine Caldwell's *You Have Seen Their Faces,* which both portrayed poor whites. Wright and Rosskam were to do a similar treatment of blacks. As Wright worked on the project, traveling to Chicago to use Horace Cayton's files on the black urban experience and to Washington, D.C., with Rosskam to study the photo archives of the Agriculture Department, he planned his essay as a folk history. The theme of the history, actually a broadly impressionistic statement in its execution, projected the experience Wright himself knew of migration from the rural South to the great northern cities. Within the conceptual framework, Afro-Americans epitomize the modern experience in their passage from feudal slavery to technologically determined social relationships. In 1941 the theme offered Wright the chance for another creative portrayal of the unity between personally felt experience and history. In time the idea would also provide him with an interpretation of the emergence of the Third World.

The Viking Press book appeared in October 1941 under the title *12 Million Black Voices*. The reference to voices aptly announced Wright's effort to write the account of black experience in the collective first person. The review in the *Sunday Worker* singled out Wright's treatment of black Americans as a nation for special praise, adding that the book was "perhaps the first realistic, class-conscious narrative of the Negro people in the United States." The *Worker* reviewer quoted liberally from the text to demonstrate the deftness of Wright's prose but concluded in a manner reminiscent of Davis' *Worker* review of *Native Son* by listing among the book's shortcomings a failure to describe the black revolutionary tradition begun by slave revolts and continuing in the contemporary struggles around the Scottsboro case and Angelo Herndon. The review by Samuel Sillen in *New Masses* spared the prescriptive commentary and discussed the book with the same high level of comprehension shown in the series of essays on *Native Son*. To Sillen the book's impact came from its honesty and Wright's gifted representation of living speech; its profoundity came from the demonstration of the influence of economic and class factors on the ideas and emotions of people. Horace Cayton, writing for a black audience in the *Pittsburgh Courier,* gave the burden of his comment to assurance that the poetic imagery of Wright's narrative was grounded in empirically documented social fact and that his account of black life constituted an indispensable frame of reference for the study of race relatons. Another black critic, L. D. Reddick, directed his remarks to the audience of the *Jewish Survey*. He encouraged them to read *12 Million Black Voices* as a justification for mutual appreciation, rather than apathy or antipathy, among social minorities.

Newspapers with large white circulations were generally content to note the book's appearance and to describe its contents. Reviews in at least two prestigious "journals of opinion," however, discussed the book's purpose. George Streator in *Commonweal* granted the right of any author to write propaganda, but declared that Wright's Marxian text made him uneasy because in it he found an inclination to racial separatism that seemed related to the ferocity of Toussaint L'Ouverture. In *The Nation* Charles Curtis Munz disputed the subtitle's description of the book as a folk history, claiming that the history was cursory, the attention to folk culture slight. Instead, Munz said, the book was a defiant assertion that Uncle Tom was dead and a promise that blacks were determined to take their rightful place in America. This, Munz concluded in contrast to Streator, was propaganda all to the good.

In view of Wright's political involvement with the left, and the encouragement he found there, a brief paragraph near the end of the *Sunday Worker* review of *12 Million Black Voices* is of particular interest. Throughout the review the author was intent on using the opportunity to reiterate a correct point of view on the "Negro Question"; in this paragraph the reviewer related its connection to the European war. "Written before the character of the war had changed," the reviewer said, "and before America's national existence was placed in such dire peril" Wright's book "does not touch upon the stake of the Negroes in the battle to crush Hitler." The attempt to excuse Wright's neglect of the new party position reminds us that even though Wright could not foresee this change in the line, he was still actively supporting the policies of the CPUSA. Throughout the period of the German-Soviet pact he contributed speeches and essays on the irrelevance of a capitalist war to the interests of black people, just as he had earlier joined with other members of the League of American Writers in denouncing fascism. In fact, the German invastion of the Soviet Union on June 22, 1941, took place five days after his article "Not My People's War" had been published in *New Masses*. Wright did his best to act out his Marxist convictions within the party structure without compromise to his literary writing, a distinction between politics and literature not appreciated by the *Worker*. After 1941 the effort to keep the distinction became more difficult for Wright. When he wrote about his political experiences in the portion of his autobiography published as "I Tried to Be a Communist" he was inclined to say his break with the party began as early as 1936, but such articles as "Not My People's War" indicate that the break occurred later. According to Wright's biographer Michel Fabre, the break with the party took place quietly in 1942, without public notice being taken until Wright himself made it an issue.

Earlier Wright had needed the stimulation and approval provided by the left-wing, but with the security of three successful books to his credit, he required little additional encouragement to pursue creative projects. Between 1942 and 1944 he wrote extensive outlines and sections of two novels which remain incomplete or unpublished, completed the manuscript of "The Man Who Lived Underground" (sections published in *Accent* in 1942 and Edwin Seaver's annual *Cross-Section* in 1944), wrote a film script on the Fisk Jubilee Singers and pursued ideas for other films, planned an anthology of Afro-American literature, and prepared the prospectus for a new magazine. The most demanding and deeply felt project, however, was the autobiography, tentatively titled "American Hunger," which he completed at the end of 1943.

Originally, "American Hunger" told Wright's story up until his departure from Chicago for New York in 1937. Edward C. Aswell, Wright's editor at Harper's, suggested ending the book with his departure for Chicago from Memphis instead. Wright agreed and wrote some additional paragraphs for the conclusion. After designation as a Book-of-the-Month Club selection, the volume appeared in 1945 under the newly chosen title *Black Boy*.

Everything seemed to come together to make *Black Boy* Richard Wright's greatest popular success, as it continues to be to the present day. Acclaim for his previous works had built a receptive audience for his writings. The autobiographical form of his new book indicated it would give the truth about American racial experience directly, without the mediation of fictional plot and characters, and that truth promised to satisfy the readers' curiosity about the emergence of Richard Wright from his background of deprivation. Almost at once *Black Boy* went on the best-seller list. From April to June it was number one, and it stayed on the list throughout the year. When Harper's had printed half a million copies, a contractual arrangement with World Publishing Company guaranteed further distribution.

First reviews set the pattern of describing *Black Boy* as an impressive condemnation of American racism. The *Omaha World-Herald* called it "a stinging indictment of race prejudice and a ringing challenge to democracy," and Orville Prescott in the *New York Times* saw it as "a story from America's own lower depths." For Prescott the dreadful emotional effect of the book lay in the author's determination to omit nothing painful from the story. Other reviewers agreed about the painful effect, especially upon white readers. Amy Croughton in the *Rochester Times-Union* told her readers that their heartstrings would be wrung by the story, but it would be a slap in the face to whites who had never felt anything but friendship toward blacks. Still, the knowledge brought with the slap would be of benefit she thought. Frank McAllister of the *Atlanta Journal* said *Black Boy* would test the feeling of many whites that they knew the Negro. The idea of a challenge to white assumptions was repeated in the *Fort Worth Star-Telegram*. George Streator, who had been uneasy about the racial exclusivity he had discerned in *12 Million Black Voices*, now saw Wright contributing to further black emancipation in a book that would inform even sensitive Jews and Catholics of their involvement in oppression (*Commonweal*). Ray Gibbons (*Advance*) paralleled the enlightening effect of Wright's book with a classic predecessor: "Little Eva needled the North into violent hatred of slavery. Perhaps Richard can stab the South broad awake." In *Opportunity* Patsy Graves concentrated on Wright's description of the psychodynamics of the black experience and saw the strength of the book in the fact that it bluntly asked the question: How long will America continue to inflict such psychic wounds? E. Bruce Thompson in the *Journal of Mississippi History* wrote, as had McAllister, from a southern perspective and described the real tragedy of the book as the evidence of denial of basic human dignity to blacks by their native region.

In commenting on the general theme of *Black Boy* several of these reviewers briefly raised the issue of the representativeness of Wright's life, thereby opening the inquiry into how he happened to become an author in the first place. Prescott found it obvious that Wright's story was not typical because he felt his isolation more keenly than did other blacks. McAllister saw uniqueness in the fact that Wright did escape from routine oppression. Croughton made a point of saying the book could not explain the man Richard Wright had become. Other reviewers made Wright's uniqueness their central consideration. Lewis Gannett (*New York Herald Tribune*) said the book left one asking how Wright had escaped the conditions he described. The answer? An innate sense of dignity made him fight back. Lillian Smith (*PM*), however, could not find in Wright's telling of his story an indication of what experiences raised him above the unprepossessing influences he described. In a speculation which soon proved to be prophetic R. L. Duffus (*New York Times Book Review*) wondered how Wright's creativity was distorted or shaped by his southern life and how it might have fared in a more genial social climate such as in France. Marshall Bragdon in the *Springfield Sunday Union Republican* thought the atypical depth of Wright's psychic injuries was the result of his unusual sensitivity, but that it had been exaggerated in *Black Boy* in order "to wake up white America."

More than a few reviewers suggested that the atypicality they saw in Wright's story was damaging to both the book and his cause. W. T. Winston in *Best Sellers* granted Wright's achievement of vivid recall, but said the narrative showed immaturity in the author's "naive egotism" and his failure to provide the historical background that would account for, but not excuse, racial prejudice. Several prominent black reviewers also criticized the personal selectivity of *Black Boy* with, of course, a meaning distinct from Winston's. Ben Burns of the *Chicago Defender* agreed with Wright's advocates that he deservedly commanded the largest white audience of any black author, but he described *Black Boy* as the story of a "self-centered, anti-social rebel." In the *New York Herald Tribune Weekly Book Review* W. E. B. Du Bois carried the observation of Wright's selectivity in narration to the point of concern that *Black Boy* bore little relation to truth. Parts of the work were effective, but the frequent passages of commentary on black life in general—nearly all negative—and the absence from the book of any blacks with redeeming qualities made the work as a whole unconvincing. Theophilus Lewis, who regularly reviewed Wright in Roman Catholic journals and consistently objected to his violent plotting, wrote in *America* that *Black Boy* had value as a tract illustrating the evil of prejudice which forces individuals into flight. As an autobiography, however, it failed due to a lack of plausible motivation for the precocious behavior of the protagonist. Beatrice M. Murphy devoted her review in *Pulse* to pointing out inconsistencies in the narrative that she claimed revealed implausible action and to arguing that the family behavior Wright described as so damaging at least had explanations he failed to give. In part because of such faults the book was shocking, as Wright's work always was. But why, Murphy wondered, should a black author use his pen as a sword to stab his people in the back?

In contradiction to Burns, Du Bois, Lewis, and Murphy there were at least three notable reviews by blacks that gave *Black Boy* unreserved praise and at the same time worked to demonstrate that the book was not at all atypical in its record of experience. James W. Ivy in *The Crisis* summarized the book at length to support an assertion that Wright's portrayal of life was balanced and that "to argue as some have done, that the Negroes sketched by Wright are not typical of even the illiterate and ignorant southern peon is mere speciousness and a dodging of the issue posed by the sort of segregated living described." Another notable refutation was written by Wright's friend Horace Cayton as a long essay in *Twice-a-Year*. Cayton explicated the complex of fear-hate-fear functioning in the psychology of Afro-Americans and praised all of Wright's work for the care with which he incorporated such scientific concepts. Ralph Ellison, who also knew Wright and his literary practice intimately, chose to explain *Black Boy*'s connection with life by describing the homology of Wright's autobiography and the popular black cultural form of the blues in the *Antioch Review*.

The editors of *Negro Story* published parallel reviews considering the pertinence of race to the understanding of *Black Boy*. In the first review Richard Bentley (the pseudonym adopted by Alice C. Browning, publisher of the magazine) argued that only a black could appreciate the life of Richard Wright, whether or not it was a totally accurate account, because only a black would have felt the indignities Wright dramatized. F. K. Richter conceded in the second review that the book lost something by the extreme self-interest of the author but found that its value was overwhelmingly the result of its applicability to any minority experience.

Like those who took *Black Boy* as an indictment of white racism, many reviewers saw Wright's autobiography, even without the aid of such concepts as Cayton introduced, as a record of collective experience. John Cournos in the *Philadelphia Bulletin* asserted that the book was a true story of life learned in experience rather than in the study. M. C. R. in the *Washington Star* evidently found those parts of *Black Boy* to which some other reviewers objected—descriptions of family life and ignorance—to be indications that Wright could write objectively. Harry Salpeter *(Congress Weekly)* singled out the reported instances of black anti-Semitism as demonstrable proof of the appalling moral climate Wright described, and J. M. Braude *(Chicago Jewish Forum)* applied what he had learned from *Black Boy* to explain experiences he had working with youth in the courts. In the *Yale Review* Raymond Kennedy took the very abnormality of character, that other reviewers denounced, as evidence of *Black Boy*'s reality, for "Negroes as individuals and a group [are] rendered abnormal by their status and treatment."

Because of Wright's recent break with the Communist party, *Black Boy* was given none of the celebratory attention his previous works had received in the left-wing press. *New Masses,* however, did carry a review by Isidor Schneider. Despite a charge of self-justifying writing, Schneider's review made the useful point that the book helped explain Wright's characteristics as an author: choice of material, attitude toward people, and obsession with violence. Further attention to literary implications, without overt political overtones, appeared in reviews by Edward Weeks and Lionel Trilling. Weeks's contribution, in the *Atlantic Monthly,* to literary appreciation of the book lay in his observation of a similarity between *Black Boy* and the nineteenth-century fugitive slave narrative *Father Henson's Story*. Apart from Ralph Ellison's discussion of the blues pattern, this was the only attempt to relate *Black Boy* to Afro-American cultural tradition. Trilling's commentary in *The Nation* addressed itself explicitly to the problem of the relationship between determinism and self-realization. In Trilling's view *Black Boy* avoided the tendency of documentary autobiography to portray characters as victims. By exercise of great moral and intellectual imagination Wright denied readers the easy pleasure of pity. If Wright saw Trilling's review, surely he was pleased, because it focused directly on his literary "project" and even echoed Wright's earlier assertion in "How Bigger Was Born" that in writing *Native Son* he had resolved to permit no pity.

There was never any doubt of the unity of feeling between Wright's living and writing. Even reviewers who felt he disparaged blacks collectively in his books attributed the cause to his personal responses to racial discrimination. Regardless of his considerable popular and critical success as an author, it was unlikely he could ever be comfortable contending with subtle and overt racism. For that reason he was eager to travel for brief, if not permanent, escape from American racial practices. The opportunity came in 1946 following an exchange of correspondence with Gertrude Stein whose book *Wars I Have Seen* he had reviewed for *PM*. Stein had seen a copy of the review and a friendship by mail developed. She urged him to bring his wife and daughter for a stay in France. In May 1946 the Wrights left for an eight-month visit to Paris and England. During that time Wright met George Padmore, the Pan-African intellectual, and many of the French writers who had been impressed by his books. The attraction of a European life, full of intellectual stimulation of the sort he had once found in the John Reed Club and freedom from the day-to-day demands of racial "ethics," became so great that shortly after returning to the United States the Wrights made plans to go abroad permanently. The self-imposed exile that began in July 1947 was to last until Wright's death in 1960, a period of creativity for Wright longer than that in his native land. During those years he prepared and published eight of his books.

There has been much critical debate about the effect of exile on Wright's fiction, but the sojourn in Europe was without doubt invigorating to him as a person. Almost at once he found a place for himself with the African artists working in Paris for liberation from colonialism and discovered his affinity with the outlook of the Parisian existentialists. An existentialist outlook had been latent in *Black Boy* and "Early Days in Chicago," and overt in "The Man Who Lived Underground." Now Wright had available to him firsthand conceptual statements of the position. Similarly, identification with the cause of African anticolonialists was an extension of the premises of *12 Million Black Voices*. It was logical and exhilarating. For several years he was caught up in the adventure of entering a new stage of intellectual development and did very little work in fiction, spending his creative energy instead on such projects as his long-held dream to film *Native Son* in which he emphasized the felt unity of the story with his own biography by playing the role of Bigger Thomas. In 1952 he began to work diligently on the novel that was to be published as *The Outsider*.

The conception of this novel represented a critical stage in Wright's development. Evidence of the direction his thinking was taking had appeared in a series of letters published in Dorothy Norman's magazine *Twice-a-Year*. In the first, "A World View of the American Negro" (1946–47), he had described the fate of American blacks as a facet of the worldwide problem of colonial people drawn from their traditional culture into a modern one. The next two letters, published in 1948, discussed the onset of the cold war between the USSR and the United States, mirror images of each other. Neither popular initiative nor contending philosophies were the source of conflict, he had explained; rather, it was a fact that ideology and politics were now only means for manipulation of the masses caught amid a confusing combat of ruthless elites. The novel on which Wright worked in the early 1950s embodied these ideas in the story of an intellectual protagonist whose capacity to see into the real motives of contemporary history led him into relentlessly self-determined action. For Wright the story was an effort at philosophical fiction that would certify his whole intellectual development up to that time. His agent, Paul Reynolds, Jr., and his new editor at Harper's, John Fischer, asked for extensive revision of the manuscript in order to integrate the narrative with the discursive speeches which Wright used, as he had those of the lawyer Max in *Native Son,* to try and assure understanding in his readers. Wright, anxious to publish, accepted the suggestions and worked in good faith on revision. By March 1953 the book was ready.

To some reviewers the philosophy of Wright's new vision was exasperating. James N. Rhea in the *Providence Sunday Journal* called the book the worst novel he had ever read. Paradoxically he also found it interesting as a thriller, if one disregarded the symbolic trappings. Part of Rhea's displeasure was expressed by an opinion that was to become a common complaint among reviewers of Wright's exile writings. Wright, he said, was out of touch with race relations in America, so his black protagonist's career was fanciful. Melvin Altshuler in the *Washington Post* recognized the book's importance in Wright's development but found the concepts of the philosophical novel crass and sophomoric. The step from *Native Son* had been a long one and Wright needed to settle his attitude before he could write first-rate fiction from his new outlook. Sarah Patton Boyle, in the *Richmond Times Dispatch* noted that Wright described his novel as the first he had written without the burden of ideology, but, she wondered, what could a novel without a definitely positive philosophy have to say to anyone? Roland Sawyer in the *Christian Science Monitor* felt sure that this "fringe" work would never have been published except for Wright's established reputation. *Time* summed up Wright's career and the novel, concluding that *The Outsider* was a bore and asserting a preference for Ralph Ellison who recognized that his place was in America, his people's home, rather than in exile.

As if to respond to *Time*'s suggestion that it was necessary to choose a favorite black author, Harvey Curtis Webster wrote in the *New Leader* that beside *The Outsider* Ellison's *Invisible Man* "seems almost simple," and "all the other novels written by Negroes seem almost inconsequential." Webster approved highly of Wright's leading his protagonist, Cross Damon, to the discovery that "alone a man is nothing," because the process of the discovery revealed the development of a great writer's progress toward a theory of man in the universe. Few other reviewers were as rhapsodic as Webster, but Ralph deToledano, writing for the Classic Features Syndicate, agreed that Wright had achieved a mature voice and portrayed the figure of contemporary revolt, the nihilist, with "a passion and drive seldom encountered in contemporary novels." Gilbert Highet in *Harper's Magazine* thought the conception of the novel truly deserved the term "Dostoevskian." But he modified his approval of the book with a criticism relevant to the thematic paradigm of Wright's art: Cross's characterization violated realistic probability, since Wright converted him too rapidly from a poor, distracted man, subject to the direction of his environment, into a dispassionate intellectual seeking self-actualization.

Highet's concern with fictive failure in the novel was shared by other reviewers. For example, Saunders Redding in the *Baltimore Afro-American* also described the book's lack of realism. Partly, he said, this was due to the unfortunate consequences of Wright's interest in existentialism, a philosophy strictly introspective and insular, hardly the basis for dramatic action. Other critics, seeing the apparent gap between thematic passages and the dramatic narrative, sought terms other than "realistic novel" to describe *The Outsider.* Ted Poston in the *New York Post* said that, though the theme had interest, the work should not be taken as merely a philosophical treatise. It was a fast-moving, engrossing murder story. Marjorie Crow Hughes in *Commonweal* could not detach the philosophy from the form and thus determined to call the book a morality play. Even so, she found that while the form evoked the feeling of the chaotic present day, confusion extended to an implication that rationalism might understand chaos. Henry F. Winslow in *The Crisis* was one reviewer concerned with the novel's form whose enthusiasm matched Webster's. For him the appearance of Cross Damon in fiction was the long-awaited arrival of a contemporary tragic hero.

Two reviews of *The Outsider* by black critics were reminiscent of earlier responses to *Black Boy*. Both came out of a left-wing orientation. Lorraine Hansberry in *Freedom* saw the novel as a "disgusting spectacle" symbolizing not the reality of black life but Wright's philosophy of "nothingness." The evidence of the novel was that Wright had lost touch with his people; that he had lost his sense of the dignity of human struggle; that he had, in fact, become a purveyor of propaganda for the enemies of the Negro. Lloyd L. Brown writing in *Masses and Mainstream,* the successor to *New Masses,* claimed that Wright's highly touted ideas and philosophy were simply commercial "angles" for those who profit from retailing the notion that life is irrational.

In one way or another, all the reviewers of *The Outsider* considered it in connection with Wright's previous literary record. Some, like Lewis Vogler in the *San Francisco Chronicle* and R. F. Grady in *Best Sellers,* saw the subjective focus upon Cross Damon in the novel as a step beyond *Native Son.* Granville Hicks in the *New York Times Book Review* thought the story of Cross had the same demonic power of Wright's earlier fiction, now reinforced by the existential style of projective characterization. Hicks had qualifications to his opinion, but the thrust of his lengthy review was that *The Outsider* challenged "the modern mind as it has never been challenged before."

At nearly the same time as he finished *The Outsider,* Wright set to work on a novel that appeared to be an anomaly among his works, because it was so thoroughly Freudian. In *Savage Holiday* Wright diminished the cultural and social influences on character, that previously had been paramount in his description of social psychology, to tangential references. By so circumscribing psychodynamics, Wright seemed to depart from the Marxist conception of behavior determined in the last instance by social and production relationships. Again contrary to Marxism he seemed to assume a universal pattern of behavior rather than one historically conditioned. But Wright had long been interested in psychoanalytic theory, as for example in his portrayal of the dependent relationship of Cross Damon on his mother and the sensitivity to Oedipal patterns underlying the description of his own family relations in *Black Boy.* Equally as striking as the Freudianism of *Savage Holiday* was its exclusive concern with white characters without reference to caste conflict. This feature of the work coincided with Wright's belief, asserted as early as "How Bigger Was Born," that though his characters were black, what they became under pressure of existence might equally well happen to whites. Indeed, Cross Damon had been portrayed in such a way that his racial identity had relevance mainly as an advantage to him in recognizing the premises of human freedom. Moreover, Cross had also been conceived as a creature freed from the power of environment. Thus, the apparent anomalies of *Savage Holiday* represented further exploration by Wright of ideas he developed in his exile philosophy rather than reversal. *The Outsider* was an experimental search for a broader philosophy to underpin his writing, *Savage Holiday* was a consistent extension of this search.

Finally, in regard to *Savage Holiday,* it must be mentioned that one of the responses among American intellectuals to the cold war was a plea for literature that would not be divisive. Protest fiction seemed suspiciously subversive, though what was said was that protest fiction was dated and clumsy. The prescription for black authors was that they attempt to write universally, "racelessly." It would be wrong to imagine that Wright took such statements seriously. After all, in his Parisian milieu the best-known expositions on the failure of protest fiction were James Baldwin's essays "Everybody's Protest Novel" and "Many Thousands Gone," which denounced *Native Son.* Wright would hardly have been convinced by Baldwin's arguments. Still, it is possible that Wright anticipated that his own "raceless" novel would interest critics at this time. He was wrong, or, to be more accurate, he failed to realize that the book might not reach the notice of critics, which was precisely the case. He submitted the manuscript of *Savage Holiday* to both Harper's and World. Both rejected it, and it was finally published as a paperback original by Avon in 1954. It received no reviews.

Critics of the fiction Wright wrote about America during his exile—and he was to publish two more volumes—overstated the case when they asserted that he lost touch with the realities of experience in his native land. Still, it is true that a literary expatriate does not easily find an adequate subject for fiction abroad. Only after a decade did Wright begin to find it possible to set stories in Europe. This would be sufficient to create a crisis of imagination for any writer, but for Wright there was the additional fact that he, like many of the reviewers of *The Outsider,* was unsatisfied with Cross Damon's outlook. Wright became free of political dogma in exile. The basically Marxian convictions he retained made him immune to idealist philosophy. And he remained the product of his experiences: an alienated, rootless black man. Like his Cross Damon, his condition made him a "center of knowing," and for a while what he knew verged dangerously close to nihilism. It was not enough to sustain a person whose artistic identity had been the consequence of commitment to the interpretation of relationships between himself, others, and the social environment. He needed a compelling subject to create a new arc between his intellect and feeling, one that would revive in him an optimism of will, and he found it, when he needed it most, in the Third World.

The new subject resulted in the production of four books written within three years. All were nonfiction, each written in a way that combined analysis in terms of social concepts, the foundation he sought for his fiction of Afro-America, and a style of personal reportage akin to the sympathetic expression of *Black Boy*. The first of these books was undertaken with the encouragement of George Padmore, who was an associate of Kwame Nkrumah, then premier of the Gold Coast. With the financial support of Harper's, Wright spent three months in the Gold Coast during the summer of 1953. He traveled throughout the main populated areas, interviewed leaders, and spent some time as a tourist observing the life of traditional tribal people. Perhaps more clearly than ever before, Wright realized that he was a man in the tradition of Western rationalism whose African ancestry was mainly a matter of genealogical fact. His interest, therefore, was precisely in the matters of importance to a modern Westerner—that is, transformation of pre-industrial society and the political birth of a nation. And those are the themes which inform *Black Power,* the book he published in September 1954.

The most positive review of *Black Power* was written by Joyce Cary for *The Nation*. Cary, a veteran of the British African Service, assured readers that Wright had set his study of the Gold Coast properly in the context of the problem facing the African government: whether to maintain tribal organization or permit it to break down in the process of creating a modern state. Furthermore, he found Wright's descriptions of African life totally honest even to the extent of revealing his own inadequacy in coping with customs and mental attitudes so strange to him. Wright had chosen as the epigraph for his book a passage from Countee Cullen's poem "Heritage" including the line "What is Africa to me?" While the question was perfectly appropriate for an American black, to many reviewers Wright's preoccupation with his own responses to Africa invalidated his report politically. David E. Apter in the *Chicago Sunday Tribune Magazine of Books* accused Wright of shocking disregard for the well-being of Africans in his demand that they rush headlong into a Europeanized society. Richard Mourey of the *Hartford Courant* found it ironic that Wright should have approached Africans "with the same mental reservations the white man still entertains toward the American Negro." Fabian Udekwu of the *Catholic Interracialist* took particular issue with the open letter concluding *Black Power* in which Wright urged a forced draft direction of the African people, on the model of Leninist centralism. Neither this, said Udekwu, nor the versions of rugged individualism proposed by Western liberals would be appropriate for Africans who did not need the guidance of paternalistic foreigners to complete the anticolonial renaissance of their continent.

In contrast to those who thought Wright's political outlook too Western were several reviewers who found him insufficiently appreciative of the Western achievement in Africa. Michael Clark in the *New York Times Book Review* could not tolerate Wright's insistence that the Africans must go it alone in founding a modern state. To Clark this seemed no more than a projection of Wright's desire for racial revenge, or ignorant disregard of the possibility of such racial partnership of Africa and Europe as Clark claimed was emerging in the Francophone African countries. In the *Minneapolis Star,* John Chapman considered *Black Power* to be only a small slice of African life, because it failed to consider the colonialist side of the story. Bewilderment at the thought that colonialism had effects Wright claimed Africans must radically excise was expressed by Fred R. Conkling *(Fort Wayne News Sentinel)* in the question "What IS this black power?" The charge that Wright was biased was extended by Philip Harsham *(Louisville Courier-Journal* and *St. Louis Post-Dispatch)* and William Hugh Jansen *(Lexington Herald Leader)* well beyond politics. Harsham claimed that the chip on Wright's shoulder had grown to the size of a baobab tree and made his report on Britain's first self-governing African territory "one of the most subjective, most one-sided, and most emotional pieces of writing to be labeled non-fiction in many a moon." Jansen's remarks were more moderate. He granted the writing was honest and artful, but whatever value it had was accidental.

Many of the reviews alleging bias seemed to grow out of uneasiness about historical change in Africa, a change which called into doubt cherished assumptions of the West. The feeling was epitomized in the review R. T. Horchler contributed to *Best Sellers.* Horchler believed the reliability of Wright's study was damaged by his ignorance of such subjects as the role of Christianity and religion in Africa. Still, he admitted, the writing "draws the face of the West, not as it is, I pray, but as it looks to millions of people in the world: this is a deeply disturbing and depressing vision, but one good for us to know." Saunders Redding *(Baltimore Afro-American)* attempting an estimate of Wright's literary achievement in *Black Power* returned a negative verdict. Having repudiated communism and abjured existentialism, Redding wrote, Wright was adrift, as the confused structure and style of the report on Africa showed.

On the whole, response to *Black Power* in the United States was not approving, as the reviews demonstrate, but Wright seemed not to have been dismayed. His idea of himself as an engaged writer could still be readily projected into nonfiction. Perhaps in the nineteenth century one read fiction—say Dickens—for news about how people lived and for consideration of social problems, but the twentieth century had developed a journalism and popular social science for that purpose. Even though reviewers had expressed doubts about his African book, Wright could feel it spoke more directly than would have a novel, and it had not required the length or intimacy of experience that nurtures good fiction. It was perfectly natural that he should continue to present his thoughts about the fascinating subject of social reality in reportage.

Curiously, the book he undertook after *Black Power* was about Spain. During his friendship with Gertrude Stein in Paris she had told him he ought to go to Spain, because it would give him a look at a premodern society. So in 1954, as he cast about for the subject of another book, he decided to visit Spain and see for himself a country yet to undergo the social transformation that so engaged his mind. Paul Reynolds, Jr., arranged an advance from Harper's, and Wright went on a three-week trip to Spanish cities and then again returned in 1955. Between his trips to Spain, Wright learned of the forthcoming Afro-Asian conference to be held during 1955 in Bandung, Indonesia. He immediately resolved to go, since it would provide an ideal occasion for him to test his thesis that there was a common pattern of experience among people proceeding from a colonial state to independence. He secured funds for the trip from the Congress for Cultural Freedom, giving the congress the option of using some of his writing in their publications.

The book on the Bandung Conference, *The Color Curtain,* was composed rapidly from the lengthy summation of the results of a questionnaire Wright used for interviews, anecdotes about Western news reporters' views of the conference, some personal experiences in Indonesia, and commentary on the emergence of the new bloc of colored nations which included views he held prior to the trip. The Congress for Cultural Freedom published portions of the manuscript in *Encounter* and *Preuves,* and the book, rejected by Harper's, was published by World in March 1956. Wright then returned to work on the Spanish book and completed it about the middle of the year, in time for Harper's to publish it in February 1957.

Reviews of *The Color Curtain* were more favorable than those of *Black Power,* because in the context of the Bandung Conference Wright's style of personal discourse enforced an impression that he was decidedly a spokesman for the West. His anticommunist credentials had been certified by the inclusion of the essay on his personal experience with the Communist party in Richard Crossman's by then well-known book *The God That Failed,* and, in contrast to the militant letter which concluded *Black Power,* Wright ended *The Color Curtain* with a proposal for Western competition with communist and neutralist powers to win the friendship of the elites in emerging nations. His proposal seemed premised on the belief that if Western material aid were dispensed in Asia and Africa, intervention would nevertheless only be through the force of ideas. Though naive, the proposal made *The Color Curtain* congenial to those reading it as cold war prose. Tillman Durdin in the *New York Times Book Review,* for example, thought Wright showed insight by posing the problem facing Afro-Asian countries as a choice of whether they were to be brought out of backwardness "under the aegis of bloody Communist Totalitarianism or through wise and generous aid from the West that will link them with our free democratic system." A. T. Steele in the *New York Herald Tribune Book Review* concurred in words less aggressive.

Interestingly, Durdin's enthusiasm for Wright's style of reporting waned when he read of the great importance Wright believed the Afro-Asians gave to race. That, he thought, was overplayed. Similarly, Walter Simmons in the *Chicago Sunday Tribune Magazine of Books* found Wright's attribution of parallel significance to religion and race in the minds of Africans and Asians a dubious contention. Some reviewers, differently concerned with the cold war, were more general in their estimates of *The Color Curtain*. For example, Guy Wint wrote in *The Nation* that the book compelled one to be aware of "burning racial feelings," and Ellen Logue declared in *Books on Trial* that Wright brought amazing clarity to the problems addressed at the conference. Still others seemed able to disregard almost entirely the sentiments that had won Durdin and Steele's approval. Abner W. Berry interpreted the book in the *Daily Worker* as assurance that imperialism could never come to terms with the newly emerging Third World. Berry's review was a supplement to Herbert Aptheker's earlier notice of the book in the *Daily Worker,* which had emphasized Wright's anticommunism. Another review from the left, Charles Wisley's in *Masses and Mainstream,* coincided with Berry's in the assertion that Wright had performed a service in bringing the news of the imminent death of imperialism.

Reviews of *Pagan Spain* diverged in a manner similar to reviews of Wright's other reports. Positive views, such as one in the *Charlotte News* and one written by Jane A. B. Parker in the *Jackson Daily News* noted the novelty of the information Wright presented. For Parker the biggest eye-opener came in the discussion of sexual undertones in bullfighting and flamenco. The potential unpopularity of Wright's book was discussed by the *Dallas Times-Herald* review, which predicted that his treatment of Spanish religion would provoke defenders of the Church. The reviewer was right. Francis E. McMahon in *America* stated categorically that Wright's secularism made him unable to report fairly. Among the assumptions behind the secularism McMahon mentioned not only "rationalism, sentimental humanitarianism, sociological determinism," a formidable array, but also a "Freudian pan-sexualism" that gave the book a prurient tone. The negative review provided by R.P.O. to the *National Review* used mockery in place of McMahon's disdain to make a similar point. Wright's merchandise would be profitable, said the reviewer, because it provided titillation and a new mode for the liberal line. Spain would no longer be condemned for being Catholic, since Wright said it was not yet even Christian.

Again, negative reviews of *Pagan Spain* repeated the idea familiar from reviews of the earlier books that the report told more about Wright than about his purported subject. For Herbert L. Matthews *(New York Times Book Review)* that was precisely the value of the book, but for the *Washington Star* no interest in Wright's person could overcome the fact that his "patent bias and prejudice weaken all his findings."

All of Wright's previous books had been controversial, but always before Wright had been able to draw on what rhetoricians call "ethical proof," or the presumption of validity due to personal involvement in the topic. *Pagan Spain* conveyed no such proof to reviewers, or evidently to readers. With *Pagan Spain* controversy was largely confined to reviewers' predictions of its possibility, and sales of the book to the public were disappointing.

A summary statement of all the negative views of *Pagan Spain* appeared in the review contributed by Roi Ottley to the *Chicago Sunday Tribune Magazine of Books*. Wright, he said, lacked the reportorial talents and the understanding of foreign society necessary for accurate description. What made Ottley's review unusually interesting was the fact that he knew Wright well in Paris and evidently respected his abilities as a novelist. To synthesize his feelings about Wright, Ottley concluded the review by recommending that "Wright's gifts and insights as a novelist might be better served in reporting such dramas as now unfold in Montgomery, Tallahassee, and Clinton, Tenn. They are tailor made for his talents."

As his final volume of nonfiction Wright assembled four speeches he had composed during the 1950s in a collection published by Doubleday in 1957 entitled *White Man, Listen!* One speech, "Tradition and Industrialization," had been delivered at the time of the first Congress of Black Writers and Artists held in Paris in 1956; the others had been given as lectures to European audiences between 1950 and 1956. Each piece was a considered exposition of the concepts Wright had developed during his exile years about the culture and psychology of oppressed people. For Wright's career the volume illustrated his performance in the role of critical intellectual. The novelty of Wright's ideas was acknowledged by Saville R. Davis in the *Christian Science Monitor* and R. J. G. in the *San Francisco Chronicle*. That was encouraging, but even more so was the statement by Roi Ottley, again writing in the *Chicago Sunday Tribune Magazine of Books,* that this nonfiction work of Wright's was "the most trenchant prose he has written." Stanley Plastrik in *Dissent,* a journal Wright was associated with as a member of the editorial board, approved the courage of Wright's address to the white man but offered the caveat that his faith in Third World elites having the capacity and will to help themselves might have been misplaced in view of the widening gap between the rich and poor nations of the world. Thomas Berry in *The Sign* briefly noted Wright's self-assumed intellectual role in words that granted his seriousness while also expressing reservations: "With naive eighteenth century trust in 'reason,' he continues on with his prophetic mission. We read and wonder." Much less willing to grant Wright his role was Oscar Handlin who took the opportunity in a review in the *New York Times Book Review* to modify Wright's call for understanding of the colonial peoples with a remark reminiscent of interpretations of *The Color Curtain.* "The West . . . ," Handlin wrote "cannot overlook the tragic fact that it must rid itself of the errors of an earlier imperialism at the same time that it resists the aggressive encroachments of a totalitarian power hostile to the freedom of all peoples."

While working on the series of nonfictional books that occupied him after *The Outsider* and *Savage Holiday,* Wright did give thought to possible future works of fiction. In 1955 he wrote Paul Reynolds, Jr., about his ambitious plan for a series of writings that would go beyond the racial, class, sexual, and political factors that had formed the foundation of his previous work. The opening would be cast as a prose poem on natural behavior. This would link with the subject of *Savage Holiday,* repression, and then there would be a fiction about love between a European woman and an African man. There would be further volumes based on the career of Montezuma and another prose poem. The whole would be called *Celebration.* Many a writer proposes ambitious projects in mid-career, often in an attempt to stimulate creativity. By their nature such plans are abstract, projecting theme apart from rendition. For Wright it seems that his plan had little basis beyond the need to keep a connection with fiction. In any case, Reynolds, and Wright's former editor Edward Aswell, responded to the proposal unenthusiastically. Several years later, however, Wright conceived a more substantial idea for fiction, one that could draw again upon his autobiographical resources and relate narrative structure and style to the contingencies of historical experiences. This was to be a trilogy following a Mississippi black's growth to maturity in his homeland and his movement into the international setting of Paris. Wright completed the first volume, *The Long Dream,* then industriously persisted with the second volume, "Island of Hallucinations." Of the latter, only "Five Episodes" have been published; these in Herbert Hill's Knopf anthology *Soon, One Morning*. But the full text of *The Long Dream* was issued by Doubleday in 1958.

The Long Dream had much in common with the fiction Wright produced during his American period. Appropriately, it was dedicated to Aswell and Reynolds who had been his editor and agent during those years. Besides a setting within the community of southern blacks, the portrayal of the central character "Fishbelly" resembles that of Bigger Thomas and the Richard Wright of *Black Boy*. In distinction to his famous novel *Native Son* Wright depended in his new book exclusively on dramatic rendition without digression, though the narrative viewpoint was controlled as in the earlier works. With its anticipated sequels *The Long Dream* was to be a crystallization of Wright's fictional techniques and natural subject into a comprehensive *bildungsroman.* Again, like *Native Son,* Wright's new novel provided material for a New York play, this time under the hand of Ketti Frings, but the play failed and was withdrawn within five performances of its opening date, February 17, 1960.

Of course, by the time the play was produced reviews of the novel had long since appeared, and they had not been encouraging. In the *Saturday Review* Granville Hicks, who always had been fond of Wright's fiction, found the story faulted by melodrama of plot and inept style. Hicks reminded readers that Wright's forte was rendition of the feeling of alienation, but he feared that Wright did not understand that the strength of such rendition was not due to realistic craft and mistakenly continued to work as a surface realist. Robert Hatch in *The Nation* found *The Long Dream* illustrative of the artistic problem in all of Wright's work: he was a crusader rather than a writer. There was undoubted power in whatever Wright authored, said Hatch, and he took pains to illustrate what he meant, but denial of approval to Wright's craftsmanship at that point in his career meant his reputation was definitely in decline. During the exile years *Time* made no secret of hostility to Wright, and the review of *The Long Dream* granted truth of portrayal to the novel with one hand and took it away with the other in the statement that Wright's crude picture of black and white relations was written "as if nothing had changed since he grew up in Mississippi." The last point, denial of historical realism to Wright's novel, was amplified in three reviews by black critics. Ted Poston in the

New York Post found the real tragedy of the book not in the story of Fishbelly but in the fact that Wright had been away during "the most momentous decade in the life of his people" and showed "no awareness of what has happened to America—and even to Mississippi—during this decade." Saunders Redding put it this way in the *New York Times Book Review: "The Long Dream* proves that Wright has been away too long. Severing his cruel intimacy with the American environment, he has cut the umbilical cord through which his art was fed, and all that remains for it to feed on is memory, fading, of righteous love and anger. Come back, Dick Wright, to life again!" And Nick Aaron Ford in *Phylon* described Wright's newest fictional protest as a fight in "a battle that has already been conceded." The left critic who most severely criticized *The Long Dream* was Philip Bonosky of *Mainstream* who saw it as a self-evident failure, not because Wright had been away from America, but rather because he had succumbed to the futile idea that blacks like whites were "sick" and so social struggle had no purpose; flight alone seemed worthwhile.

In one of the few positive reviews of *The Long Dream* Maxwell Geismar of the *New York Herald Tribune Book Review* thought the sickness of which Bonosky complained was part of the reason Wright's novel exercised such "a morbid fascination"; it was a remarkably acute insight into the nightmarish life one experiences under racism. Despite Geismar, it was clear that reviewers were finding it hard to take Wright seriously any longer as an author worthy of the standing he had once enjoyed. His reputation was in decline and, as if to explain that the cause lay outside Wright's fiction, Charles Shapiro wrote the most remarkable statement of approval *The Long Dream* received. In the *New Republic* Shapiro lauded Wright because he went against the tide of literary taste in the 1950s and was conscious of doing so. Wright, he said, provided a field day for "those whose critical arrow points South, who worship peripheral discourse." Likewise those who were not precisely "new critics," but "whose literary maturity stems from the moment they enrolled in Lionel Trilling's classes and whose political wisdom consists in not having voted for Henry Wallace, will damn *The Long Dream* as naive, and, worst of all, as 'innocent.' " Shapiro's tone was harsh, but what he said was pertinent. Literary fashion among the establishment to which he alluded had had enough of the tradition of Dreiser, Steinbeck, *and* Wright. It was a time that has been described by Robert Bone in his study *The Negro Novel in America* as "The Revolt Against Protest."

Wright seemed undeterred in his literary plans by the reception of *The Long Dream*. He continued to work on "Island of Hallucinations," conceived yet another novel, and developed plans for a return to Africa, this time for extensive tours through both English and French colonial sectors. He also experimented, during periods of illness, with haiku, eventually writing enough of the poems to make it reasonable for him to consider publishing a volume of selections. As these projects were taking shape he collected a volume of his short stories, including examples of work he had written in the 1930s about southern black peasant life, "The Man Who Lived Underground," the autobiographical selection previously published as "Early Days in Chicago," two unpublished tales of the compulsions of American racial mores—one violent, the other comic—and two stories with foreign settings. He titled the collection *Eight Men* and in 1960 contracted with World for publication.

In November 1960 Richard Wright entered a clinic for a series of medical tests. It seemed merely routine for one who had suffered prolonged amoebic dysentery and had recently been ill with flu, but on November 28, 1960, he died of a heart attack at the age of fifty-two.

The publication of *Eight Men* in 1961, therefore, became an occasion for reviewers to sum up Wright's career. The best, most extensive appraisal was written by Irving Howe for the *New Republic*. Howe wrote movingly, as Shapiro in his review of *The Long Dream* had written sarcastically of the changed literary fashion that had left Wright "hardly read today by serious literary persons; his name barely known by the young," and for the benefit of the forgetful audience reminded them of Wright's career, to which *Eight Men* appeared a counterpart because it manifested a similar uneven restlessness indicating Wright's effort to keep learning and experimenting. In Howe's considered opinion Wright's main technical problem in later years had been conversion of his naturalism into "a more supple and terse instrument," as he had once done in "The Man Who Lived Underground," which put the concentration of detail required by naturalistic literature in service to "a radical, projective image." As for the qualities of his writing alleged to be faults by those no longer taking Wright seriously, Howe found them justified by the man's nature. The violence of the fiction which the accumulated weight of reviews indicated was obsessive was an inescapable part of Wright's experience and, therefore, inevitable content of his fictional reality. By extension of the argument from personal compulsion, Howe also reasoned that Wright's lack of attention to changes that had occurred in his native South was in a way justifiable, for feeling depends upon memory. What Wright remembered must have been for others also part of the presently felt past, regardless of recent material or social improvements.

Gloria Bramwell made her survey of Wright's career in *Midstream,* describing its leitmotiv as the representation of the guilt and fear at the core of minority experience, and the weakness of his writing as the tendency to intellectualize and thus attenuate his narratives. James Baldwin, who wrote of *Eight Men* in *The Reporter,* like most reviewers chose "The Man Who Lived Underground" as the outstanding story in the collection, but his expression of approval was at best a backhanded compliment to Wright. More than a decade before, Baldwin had severely condemned Wright's practice of social fiction. Despite critical defenses that had been made in Wright's behalf, it now seemed clear enough to Baldwin that he had been correct in his criticism because "Richard Wright was never, really, the social and polemical writer he took himself to be." Rather his talent "was an ability to convey inward states by means of externals." Saunders Redding produced two reviews of *Eight Men (New York Herald Tribune Book Review* and the *New Leader),* both of which repeated his opinion that exile had done Wright's work no good. Ted Poston of the *New York Post* repeated his concurrence. Two more negative reviews came from Lawrence Lee in the *Chicago Sunday Tribune Magazine of Books* and Richard Gilman in *Commonweal.* Lee found that Wright "continued to read all environments in the light of one from which he fled in his youth," and while he had just reason for anger about his youth, he had let uncontrolled self-pity mar his art ever since. Gilman denied any value whatsoever to Wright's fiction. "He was simply not a good writer, not even a competent one," and the acclaim he earned with *Native Son* had to do only with the accident of extraliterary excitement over the fact that Wright was a black. And that was the lowest point to which Wright's reputation ever sank.

The disregard for Wright observed by Howe and illustrated by Gilman began to be remedied in the 1960s. To be sure, this was the result at first of extraliterary history—the appearance of a black liberation movement in the United States—but then the disregard had been also a consequence of such events in extraliterary history as Wright's exile and changing literary taste. The new recognition among critics and intellectuals of a need for serious engagement of Afro-American culture redirected attention to Richard Wright and gave what appears to be new status to, at least, *Native Son* and *Black Boy.* Some small contribution toward reevaluation occurred when the text of Wright's unpublished first novel, *Lawd Today,* was printed by the Walker Company in 1963. Reviews were not numerous, and the views they expressed were familiar. For instance, Granville Hicks wrote in the *Saturday Review* of the lineage stretching from Dreiser through Farrell to Wright. Still, for all its evidence of apprentice work, a feature most reviewers noted, the appearance of *Lawd Today* was a low-voiced announcement of Wright's continued importance as an American author.

Now, fourteen years later, what promises to become a Richard Wright "revival" has begun with the publication by Harper & Row of the final section of Wright's famous autobiography, under the title *American Hunger;* and the announcement that the publishers intend to draw upon the Wright archive, recently acquired by the Beinecke Library of Yale University, for several more volumes, some of them perhaps previously unpublished.

Understandably, the publishers have encouraged readers to view the appearance of *American Hunger* as the result of a literary "find," since for the first time it presents in a single volume the section of *Black Boy* that

Wright deleted in 1944. In fact, however, all but a few pages of the book have been in print before. The greater part of the book, describing Wright's participation in the internecine affairs of the Communist party, appeared in "I Tried to Be a Communist," which was published in *Atlantic Monthly* seven months before *Black Boy* appeared, and reprinted in Richard Crossman's *The God That Failed*. Descriptions of Wright's experiences upon arrival in Chicago in 1927 appeared as "Early Days in Chicago" in Edwin Seaver's *Cross-Section* and then, retitled "The Man Who Went to Chicago," were published in Wright's collection *Eight Men*. In addition, the account of Wright's absurd time as a porter in a Chicago hospital was printed in *Harper's Magazine* under the title "What You Don't Know Won't Hurt You," and a few pages about the author's state of mind appeared in *Mademoiselle* magazine. Finally it might be noted that Constance Webb published a photo-offset pamphlet for private circulation in 1946 titled "A Hitherto Unpublished Manuscript by Richard Wright Being A Continuation of Black Boy." This included the entire text of the deleted section of *Black Boy* together with an essay by Webb; but, of course, it, too, had been preempted for priority of publication by the essays Wright carved out of his manuscript.

Despite this history of previous publications some reviewers of the 1977 volume of *American Hunger* treated the book as entirely new and speculated causes for its "suppression" in 1945. Robert Kirsch *(Los Angeles Times)* and Darryl Pinckney *(Village Voice)*, for example, felt that perhaps America was not then ready for such a somber view of racism in the North, especially since Wright had given the truncated *Black Boy* an ending that could be read as hopeful. Alden Whitman *(Chicago Tribune Book World)* guessed that the excision was meant to enhance the possibility of *Black Boy*'s selection by the Book-of-the-Month Club. Even Irving Howe, who had written frequently and ably on Wright, seemed unaware, at least for the moment, of the book's previous availability in scattered places and expressed irritation that we had to wait so long for this work from an important writer *(New York Times Book Review)*. Probably, then, it was a useful service for George Breitman to devote a large part of his commentary in *International Socialist Review* to an account of the publishing history of *American Hunger*.

Breitman's review also served to put Wright's treatment of the Communist party that he knew into the context of "third period" politics—that is, a time from 1928 to 1934 when the practice of the party was ultraleft. Breitman's perspective is that of the Fourth International (popularly known as Trotskyist). Other reviewers, from a wide range of perspectives, also focused attention chiefly on what Wright has to say about his communist experience in *American Hunger*. Jack Conroy, who is of Wright's generation and is himself a writer in radical circles, provided an account of his personal relationships with Wright for the *Chicago Daily News* and

Kansas City Star concluding that, though the narrative of Wright's troubles with the party is tedious, it cannot be doubted that participation in the Chicago John Reed Club was helpful to Wright. Michael Harrington, a democratic socialist, wrote in the *Chicago Sun-Times* that Wright's conflict with the Communist party was an essential experience in the creation of a great writer. Like Howe, Harrington also noted that Wright is remarkable for having gone through his experience without developing the hatred for communists so common among former party members. For Joseph Benson in the *Greensboro Daily News* Wright's story of communism was a purification meant to lay to rest the idea that he was "indoctrinated in Marxist ideology and felt its influence the rest of his life." Theodore Rosengarten also devoted his review in the *Washington Post Book World* to Wright's political story, but by constructing his summary as a conflict between the writer's needs and the party's demands he gave the narrative a generic pattern of tragedy.

Other reviewers, less concerned with the political story, chose to discuss *American Hunger* in terms of the autobiographical genre. Jerome W. Mondesire in the *Philadelphia Inquirer* described the book as episodic tests of Richard Wright resulting in the dismaying knowledge that expatriation from American racism was Wright's logical course of action. Edwin Warner in *Time* also observed the tests, stating that their consequence was Wright's liberation into a necessary loneliness. A grander, more consistently literary form to *American Hunger* was discerned by Irving Howe who described the book in the tradition of black autobiography: the hero, struggling to self-awareness, makes his life a symbol of its exploitation and becomes a spokesman for his people. In contrast to these reviewers, David Bradley in *Quest/77* baldly stated that *American Hunger,* like *Black Boy* before it, was not an autobiography at all, for it did not reveal the author. Rather, in its reflection of his cold-blooded intellectualism, the book presented the author as a prototype for protest fiction.

Some reviewers asserted their belief that publication of *American Hunger* will alter our understanding of Wright's canon. Kenneth Walker *(Washington Star)* and Frank Campenni *(Milwaukee Journal)* saw the significance of the new book as complementary to *Black Boy,* with the first volume showing a personal development and the second providing some of the historical context of black migration. To others, appearance of the book meant opportunity to study Wright in the context of black literature generally. Geoffrey Wolff in *New Times* examined the literary politics of relationships among Wright and Baldwin and Eldridge Cleaver, while Darryl Pinckney treated Wright's book as illustration of the peculiar position in black intellectual history he occupies because of his dissociation of racial culture from politics.

These latter review-essays are akin to contributions to Wright's secondary critical reputation, "the retrospective evaluation of his achievement by literary historians and academic critics." Their appearance immediately after publication of *American Hunger* suggests that critical study of Richard Wright will persist in the volume it has shown in the past ten years. If so, we may expect further study of the continuity of Wright's career. And, if a Wright "revival" does, indeed, come to pass aided by new publications, the most likely consequence will be recognition of the achievements of the exile years.

Still, whatever change occurs in the estimate of Richard Wright in American literary history, critics must continue to examine his perception of human personality in a social environment, define his style, and judge the validity of his conception of the prophetic experience of outsiders. All of these issues have been raised by his first reviewers, so if there is to be reevaluation of Wright in earnest it will come by extension of the first critical reception of his works.

This book is intended to record that early critical reception of Richard Wright's works upon their publication in the United States. Foreign reviews are omitted as are notices of the numerous translations of his work. The reviews selected for reprinting come from many sources, but an attempt has been made to balance illustration of broad response to the writings throughout the country by regular inclusion of reviews from major city dailies and prominent journals. Through them one can observe the themes that interested those critics who are usually thought of as influential, while they followed Wright's development. In addition, selections are included to demonstrate the evaluations that appeared in publications with special social, political, or religious points of view; thus, there are a number of fixed points within the critical writing to provide a means of marking the ups and downs of Wright's reputation.

Since dramatic reviews normally give primary attention to production and performance, none are included for dramatizations of *Native Son;* the film made of the novel; the play made from *The Long Dream;* or the adaptation Wright made of Louis Sapin's *Papa Bon Dieu* under the title *Daddy Goodness,* produced in New York by the Negro Ensemble Company in June 1968. Two notable reviews of books have also been left out because they are readily available in other publications: Ralph Ellison's review of *Black Boy,* "Richard Wright's Blues," which appears in Ellison's *Shadow and Act* (New York: Random House, 1964), and James Baldwin's review of *Eight Men,* accessible in *Nobody Knows My Name* (New York: Dial, 1961).

A chapter is allotted to each of Wright's book-length publications, except for *Savage Holiday*. Representative reviews are arranged in order of appearance. Most are complete as originally printed except for occasional elimination of plot summary, indicated by ellipses, when this is not an integral part of the author's argument, or omission of discussion of other author's books in combined reviews. Publication data and section headings within reviews have been eliminated. Where typographical errors occurred, they have been silently corrected.

The checklists of additional reviews at the end of each chapter provide help toward an exhaustive coverage of critical reception. Since I feel sure there are other reviews that I have been unable to locate, I invite users of this volume to bring them to the attention of the general editor or myself.

A book of this sort depends upon the work of many other scholars, and I wish to acknowledge the help I have found in the publications of Richard Abcarian, Russell C. Brignano, Jackson Bryer, Michel Fabre, Keneth Kinnamon, Edward Margolies, and Constance Webb. Fabre's *The Unfinished Quest of Richard Wright* (New York: Morrow, 1973) has been especially useful in establishing some of the facts and certifying the biographical chronology of this introduction. I could not have located many of the reviews without the generous help of Sally Williams of Harper & Row who made available to me the company's file of early reviews and Nahum Waxman who provided reviews of *American Hunger;* Regina Bailey, also at Harper & Row, found me a place to work through clippings and a firm able to provide the innumerable photocopies I needed. Thanks, too, go to the staff of the Schomburg Collection of Black Literature and History for giving me the use of the vertical files on Wright and rare copies of first editions to examine, and to the staff of the New York Public Library newspaper annex for helping me make efficient use of their resources. I am grateful for Herbert Aptheker's aid in securing permission to republish some significant reviews, and appreciative of the fine work of the photographers in the Educational Communications Center of the State University at Albany in preparing the title pages of Wright's books for reproduction. Finally, thanks go to my friend M. Thomas Inge who showed his characteristic generosity by encouraging me in this project as he has in others.

JOHN M. REILLY

Albany, New York
May 1978

Acknowledgments

The editor acknowledges the following newspapers, journals, and individuals for permission to reprint reviews: Countee Cullen, review of *Uncle Tom's Children* in *The African,* reprinted by permission of Ida M. Cullen. Saunders Redding, reviews of *The Outsider, Black Power, Pagan Spain* reprinted by permission of the Afro-American Newspaper Company of Baltimore and the author. Margot Jackson, "Black Power Is Strong Work," reprinted by permission of the *Akron Beacon Journal.* M. D. Reagan, "Violent Search for Freedom," and Francis E. McMahon, S. J., "Spain Through Secularist Spectacles," reprinted with permission of *America* 1953, 1957; all rights reserved, © 1953, 1957 by America Press, 106 W. 56 Street, New York, N.Y. 10019. Review of *Native Son* by Burton Rascoe from *American Mercury* (May 1940), pp. 113–116; reprinted by permission of *American Mercury,* P. O. Box 1306, Torrance, Calif. 90505. Eugene C. Holmes, review of *Uncle Tom's Children* reprinted by permission of *American Teacher.* Richard Lanmon, review of *Uncle Tom's Children,* and Frank McAllister, "Rejection, Rebellion, Aggression," reprinted by permission of the *Atlanta Journal* and *Constitution.* David L. Cohn, review of *Native Son;* Edward Weeks, "Bookshelf"; and Phoebe Adams, "The Wrong Road," copyright © May 1940, March 1945, May 1953 by The Atlantic Monthly Company, Boston, Mass.; reprinted with permission.

Marjorie B. Jones, "Life in Franco's Spain," reprinted by permission of *Baltimore Morning Sun.* Reviews from *Best Sellers* reprinted by permission of the journal. Review of *Uncle Tom's Children* from *Birmingham New Age Herald* reprinted by permission of the *Birmingham News.* Henry Seidel Canby, review of *Native Son,* and Joseph Gollomb, review of *Black Boy,* by permission of the Book-of-the-Month Club. Jeanne d'Ucel, review of *Black Power* from *Books Abroad,* Volume 29 #3, copyright by the University of Oklahoma Press, reprinted by permission. John Patrick O'Connell, "Confusion and Despair of a Twentieth Century Man"; Bob Senser, review of *Black Power;* Ellen Logue, review of *The Color Curtain;* Eva J. Ross, review of *Pagan Spain,* copyright © *Books on Trial,* published by the Thomas More Association, Chicago, Ill.; reprinted by permission. Edward A. Laycock, "Richard Wright Records Rebellion, Horror, and Despair of His Youth" reprinted by permission of the *Boston Globe.* Howard Mumford Jones, "Uneven Effect," from *Boston Evening Transcript,* reprinted by the courtesy of the author.

Review of *Black Boy* reprinted from *The Call* by permission of The Workmen's Circle. Bernard A. Tonnar, S.J., review of *Black Boy* reprinted from *Catholic Mirror* by permission of the *Denver Catholic Register,* The Reverend Joseph McSorley, review of *Native Son* from *Catholic World,* copyright Paulist Press, 1865 Broadway, New York, N.Y. 10023; reprinted by permission. Review of *Pagan Spain* reprinted by permission of the *Charlotte* (North Carolina) *News. Charm,* review of *Black Boy,* copyright © 1945 by Street & Smith Publications, Inc., Copyright © 1973 (renewed) by the Condé Nast Publications, Inc.; reprinted by permission. Review by G. E. C. of *Uncle Tom's Children* reprinted by permission of the *Chattanooga Times.* Jack Conroy, review of *American Hunger,* reprinted by permission of the *Chicago Daily News.* Review of *Native Son* and review by Ben Burns of *Black Boy* reprinted by courtesy of the *Chicago Defender.* Robert C. Marsh, review of *Pagan Spain* from "Two Writers Look at Spain," and Michael Harrington, review of *American Hunger* reprinted by courtesy of the *Chicago Sun-Times.* Reprinted by courtesy of the *Chicago Tribune:* Roi Ottley, "Wright Adds a New Monster to Gallery of Dispossessed," "He Should Stick to Fiction," "Reasoned Passion

Against Racism," and review of *The Long Dream;* David E. Apter, "A Negro's Dim View of Africa's Gold Coast"; Walter Simmons, "Arrested Case of Communism Looks at Asia"; Lawrence Lee, review of *Eight Men;* and Alden Whitman, review of *American Hunger.* John Field Mulholland, review of *12 Million Black Voices,* copyright 1942 Christian Century Foundation; reprinted by permission from the February 18, 1942, issue of *The Christian Century.* "Books in Brief"—review of *Native Son*—copyright 1940 Christian Century Foundation; reprinted by permission from the April 24, 1940, issue of *The Christian Century.* L. A. S., "One Negro's Life Story"; Roland Sawyer, "About a Monomaniac"; Joseph G. Harrison, review of *Pagan Spain;* Saville R. Davis, "Wright Speaks His Mind"; reprinted by permission from *The Christian Science Monitor,* © 1945, 1953, 1957, 1957 The Christian Science Publishing Society; all rights reserved. Frederick E. Ellis, review of *Pagan Spain,* reprinted by permission of *The Churchman.* Donald Urban, review of *The Outsider,* reprinted by permission of the *Cincinnati Enquirer* and the author. Ralph de Toledano, review of *The Outsider* for Classic Features, reprinted by permission of the author. Reprinted by permission of the Commonweal Publishing Co., Inc.; Edward Skillin, Jr., review of *Native Son;* George Streator, reviews of *12 Million Black Voices* and *Black Boy;* Marjorie Crow Hughes, "Anguish"; William Dunlea, "Wright's Continuing Protest"; and Richard Gilman, review of *Eight Men* from "The Immediate Misfortunes of Literacy." "A Negro's Boyhood" by Harry Salpeter, reprinted by permission of the American Jewish Congress from *Congress Weekly,* August 17, 1945, Vol. 12, No. 25, p. 12. James W. Ivy, review of *Native Son,* "American Hunger," and "Promise and Failure"; Henry F. Winslow, review of *Black Power* from "Beyond the Seas—An Uneasy World," "Forces of Fear," and "Nightmare Experiences" reprinted from *The Crisis* magazine with permission of Crisis Publishing Company. Review of *Lawd Today* by Doris Grumbach from *The Critic* © The Critic, published by the Thomas More Association, Chicago, Ill.; reprinted by permission. Reviews of *The Color Curtain* and *Pagan Spain* reprinted by permission of Current History, Inc.

"Vigorous Stories Portray Tragedy of Southern Negro," reprinted by permission of the *Dallas Morning News.* "Volume Destined for Controversy," reprinted by permission of the *Dallas Times Herald.* Carl Roberts, "Young Negro Writes of Own Race," reprinted by permission of the *Dayton Daily News.* Agnes M. Reeve, "Far Cry from Uncle Tom," and review of *Black Power* reprinted by permission of the *Dayton Journal Herald.* Stanley Plastrik, "Lonely Outsiders," reprinted by permission of *Dissent* magazine.

Daisy M. Kuhnes, review of *Black Boy* in *The Educational Forum,* Volume 9 (May 1945), pp. 481–482, reprinted by permission of Kappa Delta Pi, an honor society in education, P. O. Box A, West Lafayette, Ind. 47906, owners of the copyright. Edmund Fuller, review of *The Outsider* in *The Episcopal Church News,* reprinted by courtesy of the author. Herb Marynell, review of *American Hunger,* reprinted by permission of the *Evansville Press.*

Marion Hendy, review of *Uncle Tom's Children,* reprinted by courtesy of the *Florida Times-Union.* Fred R. Conkling, "Wright Sees Africa in Turmoil," reprinted by permission of the *Fort Wayne News Sentinel.* Review of *Black Boy* and Harold Monroe, "The Outsider Not Up to Par," reprinted by permission of *Fort Worth Star-Telegram.* Lorraine Hansberry, review of *The Outsider* in *Freedom* (April 1953), reprinted by permission of William Morris Agency, Inc., copyright © 1953 by Lorraine Hansberry. Max Eastman, "Man as a Promise," in *The Freeman,* reprinted by courtesy of the Foundation for Economic Education.

James R. Randall, review of *Black Power* and Joseph Benson, review of *American Hunger,* reprinted with permission of the *Greensboro Daily News.*

Gilbert Highet, "Mind-Forged Manacles," copyright 1953 by Harper's Magazine, reprinted by permission of the author from *Harper's Magazine* (May 1953), pp. 97–98. Richard Mourey, "Gold Coast Turmoil," reprinted by permission of the *Hartford Courant.* James Aswell, "Famed Negro Novelist Takes Look at Africa," reprinted by permission of the *Houston Chronicle.*

George Breitman, review of *American Hunger* in *International Socialist Review,* monthly supplement to *The Militant,* copyright © 1977 The Militant Publishing Association; reprinted by permission. Theophilus Lewis, review of *Native Son,* and E. A. R., review of *12 Million Black Voices,* reprinted by permission from *Interracial Review,* a publication of the Catholic Interracial Council of New York.

Jane A. B. Parker, "Richard Wright Explores a Nation in a Candid Report," reprinted by permission of the *Jackson Daily News*. Reviews of *The Outsider* and *Black Power,* reprinted by permission from *Jet Magazine,* copyright 1953 and 1954 by Johnson Publishing Company, Inc. L. D. Reddick, "Negro and Jew," in *The Jewish Survey,* reprinted by courtesy of the author. E. Bruce Thompson, review of *Black Boy,* reprinted by courtesy of *The Journal of Mississippi History*. John Lovell, Jr., "Negro-True," reprinted by permission of *The Journal of Negro Education*.

Jack Conroy, review of *American Hunger,* reprinted by permission of the *Kansas City Star*. Reviews of *The Color Curtain* and *White Man Listen!,* copyright 1957, The Kirkus Service, Inc., reprinted by permission.

William Hugh Jansen, "Pretentious Is the Term," reprinted by permission of the *Lexington Herald-Leader*. Ernestine Rose, review of *12 Million Black Voices* (November 15, 1941); Robert S. Taylor, review of *Black Power* (October 1, 1954); M. S. Byam, reviews of *Pagan Spain* (February 15, 1957) and *White Man, Listen!* (September 15, 1957); A. N. Barnett, review of *The Long Dream* (October 15, 1958); Louise Giles, review of *Lawd Today* (April 1, 1963); reprinted with permission from *Library Journal,* published by R. R. Bowker Co. (a Xerox Company), copyright © 1941, 1954, 1957, 1957, 1958, 1963 by Xerox Corporation. Samuel Whitman, review of *American Hunger,* reprinted by permission of *Long Beach Independent, Press-Telegram*. "Tragic Pictures of Far South Negro Life," copyright 1938, *Los Angeles Times,* reprinted by permission. Herbert Agar, review of *Uncle Tom's Children,* and Philip Harsham, review of *Black Power,* from *The (Louisville, Ky.) Courier-Journal,* reprinted with permission.

Malcolm Purcell, Jr., review of *Uncle Tom's Children,* reprinted by permission of the *Macon Telegraph*. William H. L. Tyus, review of *Uncle Tom's Children,* and anonymous review of *Black Boy,* reprinted by permission of *Memphis Commercial-Appeal*. Rabbi Herman Pollack, review of *Uncle Tom's Children,* reprinted by permission of *Memphis Hebrew Watchman*. Nixon Smiley, contributed commentary on *Uncle Tom's Children,* reprinted by permission of the *Miami Herald*. G. E. M., review of *Uncle Tom's Children,* reprinted by permission of *Michigan Chronicle*. Gloria Bramwell, "Articulated Nightmare," reprinted with permission of *Midstream*. Ellen Gibson, "Mr. Wright's Spain," and Frank Campenni, review of *American Hunger,* © the Milwaukee Journal; reprinted with permission. John Chapman, "Beware of the West, Negro Writer Warns Africans," reprinted with permission of the *Minneapolis Star*. J. K. S., "A Searing Picture of Childhood in the South," reprinted with permission from the *Minneapolis Tribune*.

Roy E. Perry, review of *American Hunger,* reprinted with permission of the *Nashville Banner*. L. M. Collins, review of *Black Power,* reprinted with permission of the *Nashville Tennessean*. Sterling Brown, "From the Inside"; Margaret Marshall, review of *Native Son;* Charles Curtis Munz, "The New Negro"; Lionel Trilling, "A Tragic Situation"; "Reverie of Frustration" (unsigned review of *The Outsider);* Joyce Cary, "Catching Up with History"; Guy Wint, "Impatience of the East"; Robert Hatch, "Either Weep or Laugh"; copyright © 1938, 1940, 1941, 1945, 1953, 1954, 1956, 1958 by *The Nation;* reprinted with permission. R. P. O., "Titillating Spain," reprinted with permission of *The National Review,* 150 East 35 Street, New York, N.Y. 10016. Reviews of *Black Boy* by Richard Bentley and F. K. Richter reprinted from *Negro Story—A Magazine for All Americans* by permission of Alice C. Browning. Bob Greenlee, review of *American Hunger,* reprinted by permission of *New Haven Register*. Reviews from *The New Leader:* Harvey Curtis Webster, "Richard Wright's Profound New Novel" (April 6, 1953); William S. Poster, "Black Man's Burden" (August 31, 1959); Saunders Redding, "Home Is Where the Heart Is" (December 11, 1961); copyright © The American Labor Conference on International Affairs; reprinted with permission. Reviews from *New Masses:* Granville Hicks, "Richard Wright's Prize Novel"; Samuel Sillen, review of *Native*

Son, "The Response to *Native Son,"* "The Meaning of Bigger Thomas," and "Richard Wright's Latest Book"; Isidor Schneider, "One Apart"; reviews from *Masses and Mainstream:* Lloyd L. Brown, "Outside and Low"; Charles Wisley, review of *The Color Curtain;* review from *Mainstream:* Philip Bonosky, "Man Without a People"; reprinted by permission of Prompt Press, 418 West 25 Street, New York, N.Y. 10001. Malcolm Cowley, "Long Black Song" and review of *Native Son;* Charles Shapiro, "A Slow Burn in the South"; Irving Howe, "Richard Wright: A Word of Farewell"; reprinted by permission of *The New Republic* © 1938, 1940, 1958, 1961. Reviews from the *New York Herald-Tribune* reprinted by permission of I. H. T. Corporation; reviews by Maxwell Geismar, Milton Rugoff, and Saunders Redding also by permission of authors. Herschell Brickell, review of *Uncle Tom's Children;* May Cameron, "Prizewinner Pens Novel"; Ted Poston, review of *Black Power* in "Travelers Report on India and Africa," "Wright's Terrible Reality," "Wright, He's Out of Touch," "Wright's Last Book"; and Granville Hicks, "Spain the Fossil"; reprinted by permission of the *New York Post* © 1938, 1940, 1953, 1954, 1958, 1961, 1957 New York Post Corporation. Robert Van Gelder, "Four Tragic Tales"; Charles Poore, review of *Uncle Tom's Children;* Peter Monro Jack, review of *Native Son;* Charles Poore, review of *Native Son;* William Shands Meacham, review of *12 Million Black Voices;* Ralph Thompson, review of *12 Million Black Voices;* R. L. Duffus, "Deep-South Memoirs"; Orville Prescott, review of *Black Boy;* Granville Hicks, "Portrait of a Man Searching"; "Orville Prescott, review of *The Outsider;* Michael Clark, "Struggle for Black Man Alone?"; Tillman Durdin, review of *The Color Curtain;* Herbert L. Matthews, "How It Seemed to Him"; Oscar Handlin, "Patterns of Prejudice"; Saunders Redding, "The Way It Was"; Richard Sullivan, "Lives of More Than Quiet Desperation"; © 1938, 1940, 1941, 1945, 1953, 1954, 1956, 1957, 1958, 1961 by The New York Times Company; reprinted by permission. Clifton Fadiman, "A Black 'American Tragedy' " © 1940, 1968 The New Yorker Magazine, Inc.; reprinted by permission of journal and author. "An Indictment of Western Colonialism," copyright 1954, Newsday, Inc.; reprinted by permission.

Jack Mason, "Sense of Outrage Dominates Outlook of Negro Novelist," reprinted by permission from the *Oakland Tribune.* Mrs. Zack Brandon, review of *Black Boy,* reprinted by permission of *Oklahoma City Star,* All-Church Press, Inc. Kent Ruth, "An Outsider Queries Why?" reprinted by courtesy of the *Daily Oklahoman—Oklahoma City Times.* Victor P. Hass, "20 Years of Misery," reprinted by permission of the author and the *Omaha World-Herald.* Reviews in *Opportunity* by Sterling Brown of *Uncle Tom's Children* and *Native Son,* and by Patsy Graves of *Black Boy,* reprinted with permission of the National Urban League.

James T. Farrell, "Lynch Patterns," copyright © by *Partisan Review,* reprinted by permission of journal and author. David Daiches, review of *Native Son* excerpted from "The American Scene," copyright © May 1940 by *Partisan Review,* reprinted by permission of journal and author. John Cournos, review of *Black Boy,* reprinted by permission of the *Philadelphia Evening and Sunday Bulletin.* Jerome W. Mondesire, review of *American Hunger,* the *Philadelphia Inquirer* June 12, 1977; reprinted by permission. N. T., "As the Twig Is Bent"; L. D. Reddick, "A New Richard Wright?"; Nick Aaron Ford, "Blunders and Failures of the White Man," "A Long Way from Home," survey of literature, and review of *Lawd Today,* copyright © 1945, 1953, 1958, 1958, 1961, 1964 by Atlanta University, publishers of *Phylon;* reprinted by permission. Horace Cayton, review of *12 Million Black Voices,* reprinted by permission of the *New Pittsburgh Courier.* John D. Paulus, review of *Black Boy,* reprinted by permission of the *Pittsburgh Press.* Excerpts from Lillian Smith, "Richard Wright Adds a Chapter to Our Bitter Chronicle," in *PM,* reprinted by permission of McIntosh and Otis, Inc., literary agents for the estate of Lillian Smith. Review of *Uncle Tom's Children,* reprinted by permission of the *Portland Oregonian.* Milton Mayer, "Richard Wright: Unbreakable Negro," and Paula Snelling, "Import of Bandung," and "Warning Voice" copyright © 1945, 1956, 1957 The Progressive, Inc.; reprinted by permission from *The Progressive,* 408 West Gorham Street, Madison, Wis. 53703. P. H., review of *Uncle Tom's Children;* James N. Rhea, review of *The Outsider* and review of *Black Power* from "Two Views of a Continent in Conflict"; Ted Holmberg, "Spain and Richard Wright"; reprinted by permission from the *Providence Journal-Bulletin.*

David Bradley, "Soul on Ice," QUEST/77 Copyright © 1977, Ambassador International Cultural Foundation, all rights reserved; reprinted from the July/August issue by special permission.

"Native Son in Africa," copyright 1954 by The Fortnightly Publishing Co., Inc.; reprinted from *The Reporter* by permission. Charles E. Moran, Jr., "Richard Wright Reports on Gold Coast Colonies"; Mary Ellen Stephenson, "Spain Gets Bitter Barbs from Visitor"; Jay Thiemeyer, review of *American Hunger;* reprinted by permission from the *Richmond News-Leader Book Page.* Gerard Tetley, "A History of Bitterness"; Sarah Patton Boyle, review of *The Outsider;* W. Archer Wright, Jr., "Emotional Undertones of Today's Spanish Life"; reprinted by permission from the *Richmond Times-Dispatch.* Amy H. Croughton, review of *Black Boy,* reprinted by permission from *Rochester (N.Y.) Times-Union.*

Doris Talbot Hetlage, "From the Negro Viewpoint" (April 3, 1938); Fred Gottlieb, "Candid Book by Negro Novelist" (February 28, 1945); Philip Harsham, "Richard Wright's Bitter Pen" (October 30, 1954); reprinted by permission of the *St. Louis Post-Dispatch.* "Pilgrims in Africa," reprinted by permission of the *San Antonio News.* Lewis Vogler, "Once Again Richard Wright Has Written Controversial Novel"; Richard S. Israel, "People of High Rain Forest"; William Hogan, "Gloomy Report on Spain"; R. J. G., review of *White Man, Listen!* © 1953, 1954, 1957 Chronicle Publishing Co.; reprinted by permission from *San Francisco Chronicle.* Zora Neale Hurston, "Stories of Conflict"; Jonathan Daniels, review of *Native Son;* Arna Bontemps, review of *The Outsider;* Granville Hicks, "The Power of Richard Wright" and "Dreiser to Farrell to Wright"; copyright by *The Saturday Review* 1938, 1940, 1953, 1958, 1963; reprinted by permission. Thomas Berry, review of *White Man, Listen!,* reprinted by permission from *The Sign* (February 1958), National Catholic Magazine, Union City, N.J. W. B. Hamilton, review of *Black Boy,* copyright 1945 by Duke University Press; reprinted from *South Atlantic Quarterly* by permission. Allen Maxwell, review of *Uncle Tom's Children;* Harry Estill Moore, "Racial Antagonisms"; copyright 1938, 1945 by Southern Methodist University; reprinted from *Southwest Review* by permission. Marshall Bragdon, review of *Black Boy,* reprinted by permission of *Springfield Sunday Union Republican.*

"White Fog" (review of *Uncle Tom's Children);* "Bad Nigger" (review of *Native Son);* "Black Boyhood" (review of *Black Boy);* "Native Doesn't Live Here Anymore" (review of *The Outsider);* "Tract in Black and White" (review of *The Long Dream);* "Native Sons" (review of *Lawd Today);* reprinted by permission from TIME, The Weekly Newsmagazine; copyright Time, Inc. Horace Cayton, "Frightened Children of Frightened Parents," reprinted from *Twice-a-Year* by permission of Dorothy Norman.

Review of *Uncle Tom's Children,* reprinted by permission of United Automobile Workers.

Wallace Stegner, excerpts from review concerning *Native Son,* copyright 1940 by *Virginia Quarterly Review* and renewed; reprinted by permission of journal and author.

Melvin Altschuler, "An Important But Exasperating Book"; Theodore Rosengarten, review of *American Hunger;* reprinted by permission of the *Washington Post.* Mary Carter Roberts, review of *Native Son* and review of *Black Boy;* anonymous review, "Spain Today"; Kenneth Walker, review of *American Hunger;* reprinted by permission of the *Washington Star.* Ray Thompson, "Chip in Africa," reprinted by permission of *Winston Salem Journal Sentinel.* Alan Calmer, review of *Uncle Tom's Children,* and Abner Berry, "Richard Wright's Report on Bandung" in *The Daily Worker;* Benjamin Davis, Jr., review of *Native Son,* and review of *12 Million Black Voices* in *The Sunday Worker;* reprinted by permission of *Daily World* (New York City), successor to *Daily Worker.*

Robert Littell, review of *Native Son;* Robert Kennedy, "A Dramatic Autobiography"; copyright Yale University; reprinted by permission from *The Yale Review.*

"The Preacher Ate the Chicken," reprinted by permission of the Boston Wesleyan Association, Publishers, *Zion's Herald.*

UNCLE TOM'S CHILDREN

FOUR NOVELLAS

BY

Richard Wright

HARPER & BROTHERS PUBLISHERS

New York and London

1938

Uncle Tom's Children

Herschel Brickell. *New York Evening Post,* March 25, 1938.

A bitter protest against racial injustice in the form of four short stories, Richard Wright's "Uncle Tom's Children" was awarded a $500 prize by Story Magazine for work submitted by any one connected with the WPA Federal Writers' Projects.

The judges were Lewis Gannett, Harry Scherman and Sinclair Lewis, and Mr. Wright, so we are told, won out over 500 competitors. He is a native of Mississippi now living in Harlem and a believer in Communism as a cure for the ills of the existing system.

But with the exception of "Fire and Cloud," the last story in the collection, his political and economic beliefs do not enter into his work, and in the one mentioned only incidentally. It is a plea for racial solidarity and mass action rather than for any adherence to a revolutionary party.

Of the three judges, I understand Messrs. Gannett and Scherman did the voting in Mr. Wright's favor. I like Mr. Gannett's comment on the stories, as it seems to me to sum up their peculiar quality perfectly. "They sing as well as sear." They have the bowel-wrenching impact of extremely well written and well acted short plays and are every one striking examples of blazing passion under the control of a notable degree of artistic skill.

The first is a lynching story, but it avoids the usual stereotypes. The second is a flood story which is almost too poignant and too terrible to bear. The third is the story of how a white man took advantage of a Negro's wife and of the revenge that followed. The fourth concerns a Negro community's efforts to protest against being allowed to starve to death for want of relief.

If I were asked of the truth of Mr. Wright's indictment of the South's attitude toward the Negro, I should have to say, regretfully, that he had made legitimate use of authentic material. It is not at all a whole or a just picture, but the artist has perforce to select and when his heart and mind are aflame he quite naturally chooses the most strikingly dramatic incidents at his disposal.

Just what useful purpose such revelations serve I have never been able to determine, but this is less the point than that Mr. Wright speaks for his own people in a voice which demands to be listened to, and it is more than likely that we shall hear from him further. His talent is individual and unmistakable.

Lewis Gannett. *New York Herald Tribune,* March 25, 1938, p. 17.

"Uncle Tom's dead," says a new and more upright-standing generation of colored folk. "Uncle Tom's Children" is the title Richard Wright, a dark-skinned son of Natchez, Miss., gives to his stinging stories of that fighting generation.

These "novellas" won the prize offered by "Story" magazine for the best manuscript submitted by any writer working on the Federal Writers Projects under the W.P.A. I was one of the judges; Harry Scherman, president of the Book-of-the-Month Club, and Sinclair Lewis were the others. And, though I have determined never again to attempt to judge a literary contest—so awkward is the usual dilemma of the judge called on to criticize his own award—this time, and this time alone, I felt unreservedly happy in the award. Richard Wright's work stood head and shoulders above the rest.

"Unreservedly happy?" Well, not quite. I'd like to have found prettier stories of equal merit. I wish there were a greater variety of strings to Richard Wright's instrument. The terror, the sheer horror that grips you as you read these swift-moving, inevitably doomed tales of black life in the Southland can leave no one unreservedly happy. But, of their power, of their brutal reality and also of the occasional high-singing note of black manhood in them no reader will have any doubt. This man can write. I can only hope that life may bring him happier experiences that will move him and his readers as profoundly.

One of these four tales is of a group of black boys who went swimming in a forbidden pool, and of what happened when they came out naked to roll in the white man's pasture. One is a powerful story of floodtime on the big river—I have never read a better or more ghastly flood story. In a third a white phonograph salesman comes to a black man's farmhouse when the husband has gone to town. The fourth, perhaps the finest story in the group, deals with the dilemma of a colored minister, called on by his own hungry people to lead them in a hunger march, and by the white Mayor to call his people off.

In all of these stories the black men, when provoked, stand their ground. "We just as well get killed fighting as to get killed doing nothing," says one of these children, or grandchildren, of cringing, black Uncle Tom.

These stories are more than American literature. Their spirit is a part of a new American history.

One brief ironic line might well have been quoted in the recent Senate debate on the anti-lynching bill. It is overheard by a black boy who, hiding in a clay kiln, has watched the lynching of his chum. The lynching is over; the watchers are going home. "I'll take some of you ladies home in my car," says one of the chivalrous lynchers to a group of watchers.

"Vigorous Stories Portray Tragedy of Southern Negro. Negro Writer's Painfully Authentic Sketches Carry Powerful Indignation at Oppression." *Dallas Morning News*, March 27, 1938, Section 3, P. 10.

There is no rollicking minstrelsy in "Uncle Tom's Children." The Negroes who are the central figures of the four long stories composing the book are tragic characters trapped and tormented in the white man's world by their own sensitiveness, their own sense of individual being, their self-consciousness which is ruthlessly invaded at will by men made lords of creation through lack of a certain pigmentation in the skin. For the black man's lot becomes tragic in proportion to his comprehension of his weakness and hopelessness in the world as it is. Richard Wright does not concern himself with the happy darkie singing in the cornfield, happy through ignorance, content through lack of desire. He turns rather to the man of color caught by his yearning for peace and self-respect, bewildered at being denied human rights.

The negro life pictured in "Uncle Tom's Children" is negro life in the South, which means that Richard Wright is tackling a mighty ticklish subject. But he wades right in. His bitter and poignant stories are all too painfully authentic sketches of the Negro in trouble. The first, "Big Boy Leaves Home," (which was originally published in the New American Caravan) is the only one which contains an orthodox lynching, complete with tar-and-feather ritual and souvenir-snatching orgy. Buck's crime had been his presence on the scene of the killing of a White man by a Negro, Big Boy (in self-defense, of course—Wright is no fool). The mob gets him. "Jack! Jack! Don leave me! Ah wanna see im." "They're bringin im over the hill, sweetheart." . . . "Les git souvineers!" "Look! he's gotta finger! . . . He's got one of his ears, see?"

"Down by the Riverside" is a calmly furious depiction of raging white wrath in time of raging flood. Here, too, a Negro has killed a White man after the White man had fired two shots at him and missed. Here martial law is substituted for lynch law. "Bullets hit his side, his back, his head. He fell, his face buried in the wet, blurred green. He heard the sound of pounding feet growing fainter and felt something hot bubbling in his throat; he coughed and then suddenly he could feel and hear no more . . . one black palm sprawled limply outward and upward, trailing in the brown current. . ."

"Long Black Song," rhapsodic and unhappy, has miscegenetic implications.

"Fire and Cloud," printed in the March issue of "Story Magazine," contains the "social message" of the book. In short, mass action is the solution to the Negro's problems. "Freedom belongs to the strong!"

Lewis Gannett, literary critic of the New York Herald-Tribune, has said that "Mississippi has as good title to be proud of Richard Wright as of William Faulkner." Certainly, Wright has the makings of a major writer. He is an excellent technician; his prose has the terseness and structural clarity of John Steinbeck's. He has Ambrose Bierce's ability to crystallize the awfulness of eternity in a second. But he is so occupied with racial indignation that he forgets to make his characters real people. Each of his colored heroes is merely a typical representative of his oppressed race, a black Everyman. In Wright's effort to make the racial issue clear-cut, he has resorted to the melodramatic device of the one-sided character. His protagonists are made a bit too blameless for belief. But much can be expected of Wright in the future; "Uncle Tom's Children" is his first book, and he is only 29. His race has already just cause to be proud of him. . . .

"Tragic Picture of Far South Negro Life." *Los Angeles Times*, March 27, 1938.

Here's fire that sears the south in four short novels in which the power is cumulative. We are not surprised to learn that these stories by Richard Wright won first prize in Story Magazine. Not surprised, because Wright himself burns with feeling; not with any "gem-like flame," but with furnace fury. Before he approaches his reader, however, all this has been covered over with a deftly woven screen.

Indeed he approaches with songs and laughter and beauty; then, before you know it, but well after your sympathies have been ineluctably engaged, the furious element is all over you.

Here, then, are the children and grandchildren of Uncle Tom, in a land where they are no longer the "property" of any man; where they are met on every hand by prejudice. In these stories (four novellas) the black folk draw near in song and dance; then, in all innocence, they attract the fury of white mobs, and terror descends.

It would be impossible to outline these stories. I may content myself by saying that they are told with the utmost simplicity and power. And the power is all the more effective, because of the simplicity and restraint of the style.

Mr. Wright is a young Negro writer who makes his living as a journalist. But his style has nothing of the journalist about it. His themes are terrible, but never deliberately sensational. In truth, as a southerner is compelled to testify, these stories bear the stamp of verihood. And they create those effects which, according to Aristotle, are the aim of tragedy.

"White Fog." *Time*, 31 (March 28, 1938), 63–64.

The U.S. has never had a first-rate Negro novelist. Last week the promise of one appeared. *Uncle Tom's Children*, the first book of a 29-year-old, Mississippi-born Negro, won a $500 prize from *Story Magazine* as the best creative work done by any of the 1,200 writers on the Federal Writers' Project.

Unlike most Negro writers, Wright is neither subjective nor sentimental. A few readers will find misleading resemblances to John Steinbeck. But a closer comparison is with Stephen Crane. Like Crane, who wrote his Civil War masterpiece, *The Red Badge of Courage*, without ever having seen a battle, Richard Wright has written the most powerful stories of lynch violence in U.S. literature without ever having seen a lynching. (He did, however, spend most of his first 17 years in Mississippi, which in all the U.S. has the worst record for lynchings: 591 out of 5,112 recorded since 1882.)

Crane's imaginative compass, which held his story to a psychological true North, was the conflict between his hero's blind instinct for self-preservation and an impersonal war machine. The core of Wright's stories is the conflict between the Negro's instinct for self-preservation and an impersonal, unpredictable lynch machine. The sadistic, melodramatic physical details of his lynchings occur with an almost off-stage irrelevance. Their reality is the "white fog" of lynch terror which hangs over the Negro community, impenetrable to the brightest Southern sunlight. It is this central psychological core of Negro life in the Deep South, communicated in clear, unemotional prose, which gives Wright's stories their intensity, and a kind of impersonal eloquence in voicing the tragedy of his people.

Harry Hansen. *New York World-Telegram,* March 28, 1938.

Richard Wright has power. Power to tell the tragedies of his own people—the Negroes who became victims of the ignorant, brutalized whites. Power to put it into prose, so that it gets to the libraries and reading tables of white folks.

Born in Natchez, Richard Wright did all sorts of odd jobs in his youth—picking up coal, selling papers, going on relief. Somewhere he learned to write dramatic prose. Now he lives in Harlem and writes for a newspaper. His collection of four long stories, published as "Uncle Tom's Children," won the prize of $500 offered by Story Magazine for the best manuscript submitted by anyone connected with the Federal Writers Project of the WPA. The judges were Harry Scherman, Lewis Gannett and Sinclair Lewis.

These four stories are part of the new campaign of emancipation, for it must be plain to anyone who can read that abuse of the underdogs must stop in the United States. Thus the first reaction to these stories is one of indignation and horror, because here the author portrays the terrible lot of the meek. Only after we have thought of the stories as social documents do we recognize the powerful impact of straight-shooting prose. The way Richard Wright builds up the catastrophe, pursuit, killing and escape in "Big Boy Leaves Home"; the way he handles the uprush of prejudice during the flood; the way he builds up the desperation and terror of the husband whose wife has been abused—this is dramatic writing, and unforgettable.

The title comes from the expression of the Negroes indicating that they are no longer "Uncle Toms," that is, cringing servants. They dream about equality before the law, but for those whose hard lives are bared in these stories there is neither equality nor justice. Most revealing is the anxiety and fear that grips innocent people the moment they hear that the whites are after them—fear that betrays a long history of previous reprisals. In Mr. Wright the race has won a powerful champion.

Herbert Agar. *Chicago Times* and *Louisville Courier-Journal,* March 29, 1938.

"Uncle Tom's Children," by Richard Wright, is a book that should give us something to worry about closer to home than the Danube or the Yangtze Rivers. Richard Wright is a Negro. "Uncle Tom's Children" tells four stories of conflict between blacks and whites in America. It should be read by all white men who are inclined to make Fourth of July speeches.

There is small variety of mood in these stories. In every case the end is despair and bitterness. But there is no thought of submission. These Negroes do not "know their place." They are bewildered but not broken in spirit. They can be murdered, but they cannot be made to acquiesce.

They do not resemble in any way the comforting white man's picture of the contented Negro who doesn't even notice that he has been denied his oft-promised citizenship.

These men and women have a capacity for enjoying life, but too few chances to indulge it. They do not expect the world to be just or men to be kind. But neither will they accept injustice and unkindness with a smile. They will take what is necessary; but they will not pretend to like it.

According to Richard Wright, "The post War Between the States household word among Negroes—'He's an Uncle Tom!'—denoted reluctant toleration for the cringing type who knew his place before white folk." If this book gives a fair picture, Uncle Tom's children are a very different type.

This book would be even more disturbing if it were more many-sided. The repeated tale of oppression and defeat begins to lose its power before the book is ended. The stories are all possible, and they all feel true. And they leave a white reader wounded in mind and spirit. But they would be even more afflicting if they showed more of the variety of life.

The cruelty of man is only tragic because man does not need to be cruel, because he also has kindness and imagination, and because under luckier stars these latter traits might have found expression. But the white men in this book are not so complicated. Their badness is a foretaste of the simple monotony of hell.

"Somehow," thinks one of Richard Wright's characters, "men, black men and white men, land and houses, green corn fields and gray skies, gladness and dreams, were all a part of that which made life good. Yes, somehow, they were linked, like the spokes in a spinning wagon wheel." But in this book the wheel has come undone, and the spokes are broken, and there is no chance for any end but woe.

I suppose Richard Wright would answer that this is the way he has seen it, and that if I see it with more variety that is because I have been lucky. He might answer in the words of the poet:

If wrath embitter the sweet mouth of song
And make the sunlight fire before these eyes
That would drink draughts of peace from the unsoiled skies—
The wrongdoing is not mine, but mine the wrong!

In spite of faults, this is a book which should make Americans uneasy. It might even lead us to take time out for reforming ourselves, instead of spending all our moral disapproval on those bad Germans and those deceitful Japs. We have had the Negro problem on our hands from the beginning. We have not solved it. We have not even faced it honestly.

If Negro authors go on writing books like this, they will at least make it impossible for the rest of us to hide from the problem. A few such books and there will be no more fairy tales about how the Negro really loves his lot.

Granville Hicks. "Richard Wright's Prize Novel." *New Masses*, 27 (March 29, 1938), p. 23.

You cannot read these four stories without realizing that the literature of the left has been immeasurably strengthened. Although Richard Wright is certainly not a new name to readers of NEW MASSES, and although the talents of this young Negro have not gone unrecognized, *Uncle Tom's Children* will not only make the name familiar to all literate Americans but also startle those whose expectations have been high. The truth is that the revolutionary movement has given birth to another first-rate writer.

It is Wright himself who gives the revolutionary movement credit. Born in Natchez, he wandered about the South with his parents until, at the age of fifteen, he went on his own. In Chicago, where he worked as a clerk, a waiter, and a street sweeper, he joined the John Reed Club. There, he says, he learned to understand the significance of his harsh boyhood. "I owe my literary development," he has said, "to the Communist Party and its influence, which has shaped my thoughts and creative growth. It gave me my first fullbodied vision of Negro life in America."

These are four tales of Negro life. . . .

They are bitter stories, cruel stories. Each one tells of the white man's discrimination against the Negro, of his stark, irrational, savage prejudice. In the first story it is not the barbaric, sadistic fury of the lynch mob that impresses the reader, but the white man who shoots first and asks questions afterward. In the second one notes the colonel who, just after a Negro's wife had died, turns to his soldiers and says, "Give this nigger some boots and a raincoat and ship him to the levee." The white man in "Long Black Song" not only combines seduction with salesmanship but also salesmanship with seduction.("I'm leaving that clock and gramophone. You can have it for forty instead of fifty. I'll be by early in the morning to see if your husband's in.") And it is instructive to see how easily the mayor's patronizing friendship for Reverend Taylor ("It's not every nigger I'd come to and talk this way") yields to the Chief of Police's brutality ("A nigger's a nigger! I was against coming here talking to this nigger like he was a white man in the first place. He needs his teeth kicked down his throat.")

Each story tells also of resentment deep beyond any reckoning. The carefree boys in "Big Boy Leaves Home" interpret the No Trespassing sign: "Mean ain no dogs n'niggers erllowed." The husband of the seduced Sarah says: "From sunup to sundown Ah works mah guts out t pay them white trash bastards whut Ah owes em, n then Ah comes n fins they been in mah house! Ah cant go into their houses, n yuh knows Goddam well Ah cant! They dont have no mercy on no black folks; wes just like dirt under their feet! For ten years Ah slaves like a dog t git mah farm free, gives ever penny Ah kin t em, n then Ah comes n fins they been in mah house." It is no wonder he and countless others feel that there is nothing better for them to do than die defiantly.

But there is something better, as Wright knows, and he is not content to leave his knowledge unexpressed. That is why, in the fourth story, he shows a Negro beginning to learn what he himself has learned so well. "Its the people!"

the minister tells his son. "Theys the ones what mus be real t us, Gawds wid the people! . . . Ah been wrong erbout a lotta things Ah told yuh, son. Ah tol yuh t work hard n climb t the top. Ah tol yuh folks would lissen t yuh then. But they wont, son! All the will, all the strength, all the power, all the numbahs is in the people. Yuh cant live by yoself!"

So Wright says what he wants to say, or, rather, lets his stories say it for him. He writes with an intensity that makes you clench your fist. Big Boy in the cave, watching the mutilation of his comrade; Mann, brought to his death by the woman he has rescued; Silas, calmly waiting for the cruel end of a barren life, glad to pay any price for revenge; Taylor, thinking his way out of confusion as the lash falls on his back: these are things one feels rather than reads about.

Wright's technique is simple: straightforward narrative and beautifully direct dialogue. But there is no lack of artistry. He is always reaching beyond the simple event to catch all the complexity of emotion that surrounds it. The horseplay of the first part of "Big Boy Leaves Home" adriotly leads up to and contrasts with the frenzied tragedy of the shooting and the lynching. Sarah's downfall is not a rape but a complicated emotional experience that she cannot understand, and Silas's response is no conventional indignation at a sexual affront but hopeless resentment of the ultimate invasion of his personal life. Taylor becomes the focal point of innumerable forces in his community: white fear, white hatred, white tyranny; black desperation, black timidity, black courage.

If there is any weakness that Wright reveals, it is in construction. Two of the stories move with magnificent speed and clarity. In "Down by the Riverside," however, the author has difficulty in handling the rapid sequence of events after Mann reaches the hospital. And in "Fire and Cloud," when the mayor, the two "Reds," and the deacons are all in Taylor's house, the situation, instead of seeming dramatic, has for a page or two the confusion of a bad movie. Apparently Wright is so eager to move ahead with the main action that he will not pay sufficient attention to subordinate details even when they are essential.

This is a defect that can be remedied without too much difficulty, and I am confident that Wright will remedy it in the novel on which he is reported to be working. Certainly, he has all the other gifts that go to make a novelist. *Story* magazine made no mistake when it selected *Uncle Tom's Children* from the five hundred manuscripts submitted by authors on Federal Writers' Projects. It is not only a fine piece of writing; it is the beginning of a distinguished career.

Charles Poore. *New York Times*, April 2, 1938, p. 13.

. . . Sinclair Lewis, Harry Scherman, and Lewis Gannett chose "Uncle Tom's Children," by Richard Wright, as the winner of the $500 Federal Writers Projects Prize offered by Story Magazine. In choosing Mr. Wright's book the three judges have discovered a new author who has an amazing ability to make you see searingly melodramatic episodes in a memorable way.

There are four long stories—*novellas*—in "Uncle Tom's Children." Each one presents—from the Negro's point of view, naturally, since Mr. Wright is a Negro—the tragedy of violence that race hatred turns loose. I cannot think of any writer who has used this material out of American life with such bitter, driving vehemence.

The stories begin quietly, gather momentum slowly, incident by incident, and mount to the predestined climax of violence. In the first story a cheerful lot of boys unwittingly frighten a white woman who happens to pass near a swimming hole, have a desperate fight with a man who wants to kill them—though they have done no harm nor intended it—and in no time at all are dead or facing the prospects of blazing deaths. In the second a man who wants only to get his wife to a hospital during a flood gets fatally enmeshed in racial conflict. In the third the cause of the conflict is a white man's attack. In the fourth it is a clergyman's attempt to get his people food.

Mr. Wright's descriptive power, particularly in the flood story, is uncommonly forceful. His stories suffer from one minor fault, which is a needless attempt to make his dialogue continuously phonetic. And one major one, which is that he has merely shifted a bad process by making nearly all the white characters villains. That heightens the drama and the melodrama. But it plays havoc with plausibility.

Zora Neale Hurston. "Stories of Conflict." *Saturday Review of Literature,* 17 (April 2, 1938), 32.

This is a book about hatreds. Mr. Wright serves notice by his title that he speaks of people in revolt, and his stories are so grim that the Dismal Swamp of race hatred must be where they live. Not one act of understanding and sympathy comes to pass in the entire work.

But some bright new lines to remember come flashing from the author's pen. Some of his sentences have the shocking-power of a forty-four. That means that he knows his way around among words. With his facility, one wonders what he would have done had he dealt with plots that touched the broader and more fundamental phases of Negro life instead of confining himself to the spectacular. For, though he has handled himself well, numerous Negro writers, published and unpublished, have written of this same kind of incident. It is the favorite Negro theme just as how the stenographer or some other poor girl won the boss or the boss's son is the favorite white theme. What is new in the four novelettes included in Mr. Wright's book is the wish-fulfillment theme. In each story the hero suffers but he gets his man.

In the first story, "Big Boy Leaves Home," the hero, Big Boy, takes the gun away from a white soldier after he has shot two of his chums and kills the white man. His chum is lynched, but Big Boy gets away. In the second story there is a flood on the Mississippi and in a fracas over a stolen rowboat, the hero gets the white owner of the boat and is later shot to death himself. He is a stupid, blundering character, but full of pathos. But then all the characters in this book are elemental and brutish. In the third story, the hero gets the white man most Negro men rail against—the white man who possesses a Negro woman. He gets several of them while he is about the business of choosing to die in a hurricane of bullets and fire because his woman has had a white man. There is lavish killing here, perhaps enough to satisfy all male black readers. In the fourth story neither the hero nor his adversary is killed, but the white foe bites the dust just the same. And in this story is summed up the conclusions that the other three stories have been moving towards.

In the other three stories the reader sees the picture of the South that the communists have been passing around of late. A dismal, hopeless section ruled by brutish hatred and nothing else. Mr. Wright's author's solution, is the solution of the PARTY—state responsibilty for everything and individual responsibility for nothing, not even feeding one's self. And march!

Since the author himself is a Negro, his dialect is a puzzling thing. One wonders how he arrived at it. Certainly he does not write by ear unless he is tone-deaf. But aside from the broken speech of his characters, the book contains some beautiful writing. One hopes that Mr. Wright will find in Negro life a vehicle for his talents.

G. E. G.
"Writer's Project Product." *Chattanooga Sunday Times,* April 3, 1938.

There is no more interesting development in any literature than the growth of American Negro writing from its early comic minstrelsy or imitation of the white to a serious presentation of the varying aspects of contemporary Negro life. As James Weldon Johnson has pointed out, there were more books published by Negroes in the single decade from 1920 to 1930 than had been published in all the preceding history of this country. This development is probably a consequence of the increase of literacy among the Negroes, providing an audience for the Negro writer who wished to discuss seriously the problems of his own group. Accompanying this, it may be as a consequence of it, has come a changed attitude toward Negro writing and artists by a portion, at least, of the white audience. The more intelligent and better informed of both groups realize that there must be mutual understanding and trust, but this can only be brought about by a more complete knowledge on the part of both of the problems with which each is faced. For the whites, there is no better way to secure such information than by a reading of the books which have been created by Negro writers out of the problems which are of importance to the writers and their fellows.

Those who have watched these developments will not be surprised when told that this book by a young Negro writer, born in Mississippi and largely self-educated, was chosen out of more than 500 submitted as the best manuscript by a writer connected with the WPA Federal Writers' project. Nor will they be surprised at the material which the author has chosen to present. These four stories are about blacks and whites in small rural communities in Mississippi. In each of them, violence plays a prominent part. That is not, however, the important thing about the book. This, to me, is the reflection of misunderstanding, distrust and fear—a consequence of the relations between the two races. A woman encounters a group of Negro boys in swimming. The circumstances should be a rather natural one in rural communities, but because of the fear each feels for the other and the situation there is a violent and unnatural outcoming. Who, caught in the peculiar group of circumstances with which Mann is confronted in the second story, would have acted differently—up to a certain point? Again, the tragic result is not due to inevitable circumstances but is a consequence of the fear and misunderstanding which lie so close under the surface of race relations. And the same is true, although in different ways, of the last two stories. In moments of excitement, each racial group believes the worst of the other, each abandons reason, and ignorance and violence have their bitter way.

Such is the lesson of this book. It is a lesson whose telling some will resent, but the fault rests not with the teller—it should be charged to the circumstances. If there be resentment, let it be directed at the ignorance and injustice out of which such violence grows. The book is written naturally and vividly, with a faithful reproduction of the rich and racy Negro speech. "Uncle Tom's Children" is one of the important contributions of the Negro group to contemporary literature.

Robert Van Gelder. "Four Tragic Tales." *New York Times Book Review*, April 3, 1938, pp. 7, 16.

Mr. Wright employs a talent in some respects comparable to that of Hemingway to rouse his fellow Negroes to unite and fight against the whites. His book is made up of four tragic tales, filled with violence and death and drama. The subject of all of them is the bitter war between the races in the deep South. The stories build on gall and wormwood to a climax of hope for the Negro through unified action.

When "Big Boy Leaves Home"—the title of the first story—he is the only survivor of a group of four adolescents who had the bad luck to frighten a white woman when she accidentally discovered them in a swimming hole. Two of his companions have been killed by rifle shot. The third has been mutilated and burned.

The second story, "Down by the Riverside," is an amazingly well written tragedy concerned with the plight of a Negro family caught by flooding river waters. A Negro who displays every admirable quality of heroism when he is trying to save others, fails through fright when he has a chance to save himself. An "Uncle Tom" at the crucial moment, he pays for his weakness with his life.

The third story is of a Negro who does fight, who kills to avenge an attack made by a white man upon his wife. He dies while trying to fight off a lynch mob.

Taylor, a Negro preacher, is the hero of the final story. Taylor, as a leader of his own people, has been able to win favors for them by representing their cause in parleys with the whites. When Communists try to organize a mass demonstration, Taylor discovers that his white patrons are irrevocably in the opposite camp. They have favored him as a "good nigger," but when their own interests are endangered by Red propagandizing they expect him to make return for the past by keeping his people obedient to them. A sound beating administered by the whites causes Taylor to make up his mind. He can expect nothing that is good through white patrons. They can only do harm. The blacks are engaged in war. Let them know it, and unite in strength, for there is no freedom without strength. "Freedom belongs to the strong."

Mr. Wright is far more than an ordinary radical propagandist. A Negro born in Natchez, Miss., and almost entirely self-educated, his writing has no least trace of the amateur in it. For all the load of bitterness and hate they carry, his stories come alive as art. Illustrative of the freedom that minorities enjoy in this country is the fact that this bitter book, so highly inflammatory, was a prize winner in a contest open only to persons associated with the WPA Federal Writers Projects. Freedom, despite Mr. Wright's evidence to the contrary, is not really dead in America. His own recent history as a writer must prove that.

Doris Talbot Hetlage. "From the Negro Viewpoint." *St. Louis Post-Dispatch,* April 3, 1938.

The four long stories which comprise this book form a moving and powerful plea for the case of the Negro in a "white man's civilization." The work of a young Negro newspaper man, they are of course written entirely from the Negro viewpoint, but the stories ring so true and show such thorough understanding of the barriers between the races that no intelligent white person will question their authenticity. They are not pleasant reading. All of them are violent and emotionally devastating. But their terse prose and great power make them memorable.

The first story, "Big Boy Leaves Home," is a cruel tale of torture and murder which grow out of a thoroughly innocent escapade of four adolescent Negro boys. The terror of bewildered "Big Boy," as he sees his schoolmate tarred and feathered and burned to death by an insane mob of "white folks," is something the reader will not easily forget. The second and third stories are concerned with the murders of white men by Negroes and the consequent inescapable retribution. The first murder is the result of the effort of a Negro to save his critically ill wife from their flood-surrounded shack in a boat stolen from a white man; the other is the result of miscegenation. Both are thoroughly justified—from the viewpoint of the character involved at least—but the Negro has no chance to justify himself. The last story is a slightly less violent one of a Negro minister whose congregation looks to him for help when their "relief" is cut off and who, in his simplicity is utterly confused between the threats of the town officials and the promises of the Reds. While the character of the minister, Dan, is excellently done, this last tale carries the only slightly false note of the entire book. . . .

Alan Calmer. *New York Daily Worker,* April 4, 1938, p. 7.

This book of four novelettes of Negro life has a clean, straightway and forceful pace; it never swerves or stalls or detours in its streamlined, non-stop movement ahead. People who complain about the torturous windings or blurred focus of many proletarian novels will have no loophole for complaint here. Dick Wright is one of those "natural" story-tellers, who not only has quick and clear ears and eyes, but who instinctively selects the right sort of events and puts them into the kinds of arrangement that hammerlocks your attention.

He gets this grip on the reader largely through action. Each story in this book is chockful of rousing episodes and violent clashes. "Big Boy Leaves Home" has three shootings and a lynching, in addition to several lesser struggles; "Down by the Riverside" is about a flood and two murders; "Long Black Song" has more killings; "Fire and Cloud" seethes with exciting incidents. But these are not pulp tales. Except possibly for the series of coincidences in the flood story, all the situations are handled with a steady sense of realism. The acts of violence rarely turn into melodrama; in the main they explode inevitably out of the pattern of events.

Moreover, the book is laid in the locale of lynching and serfdom, and it deals with characters who are not meek Uncle Toms but a courageous, fighting lot, as the introductory sentences of the book point out.

In each story, the new Negro doesn't take it lying down: the army officer who has just killed two of Big Boy's buddies has his own gun turned upon himself; the postmaster who shoots at Mann, the desperate Negro who is trying to get his pregnant wife to the hospital, is himself shot; Silas murders the white salesman who has seduced his wife; the Negro preacher who is beaten by the vigilantes leads his flock to the unemployed demonstration.

Nor is this social-moral lesson driven home in a stereotyped way; the stories are not formulas but are composed with imaginative cunning, and with a fidelity to particulars. For example, the lynching scene in "Big Boy Leaves Home"—and the whole build-up before it—shows genuine imagination, creativeness; it is real and true not as a social generalization but in the specific way of life itself—from which generalizations are made.

Finally, the book is successful because everything in it dovetails: the elemental action of the characters is in tune with the pace of the stories and the primitive level of life and emotion in the deep South; even the hard driving prose style—bare, supple, stripped for action—is perfectly suited to the characters, the subject matter and the narrative method.

Yet, in many ways the book attains a too-easy kind of success. As a matter of fact, the qualities which make the book successful—the action, the simplicity of movement, the rudimentary level—may in the long run be the severest handicaps to the author's progress. The method, it seems to me, is too simple and surfacy and narrow; its unilinear, one-dimensional nature is all right as far as it goes, but that isn't very far. This foot-on-the-gas, eye-on-the-road manner holds the interest of the reader—it makes him keep his eye on the road, too—but it does just that and no more; and, after a while, the reader gets tired of watching nothing but a passing ribbon of concrete.

What I mean is that, for one thing, this method doesn't dig down, excavating its material; and, because it doesn't it can never show the reader more than just the hazy outline of characters, as is the case in this book. For another, since it never tries to get off the ground—to soar—it rarely reaches upward toward an intensity of perception and imagery; sticking to the road, it relies for its excitement and interest upon a succession of scenes of action rather than upon heightened perception and description of ordinary happenings. Again—to plug our mechanical metaphor for all it's worth—this eye-on-the-road method never allows the reader to see the subject matter against the whole background of the countryside, to see the material in its whole social perspective and form.

It is difficult to define these three qualities in the space of a review; but there are a few samples in the book itself of what I mean; in a few places the book transcends its usual manner. For instance, the opening pages in "Long Black Song" make a good start in molding a deeper-than-surface picture of Sarah. Then there are a few sentences in "Down by the Riverside" ("He breathed hard, trying to build in his mind something familiar around the cold, wet, smooth pieces of wood. A series of pictures flashed through his mind, but none fitted. He groped higher, thinking with his fingers.") which clutch.

The third quality is shown in parts of "Fire and Cloud," where the more complex, higher social content often raises the story out of the general plane of the book. This is particularly so in the portrayal of the dilemma of the Negro preacher. Fearful of losing his respectability, but troubled by the suffering of his congregation, his mind is made up for him by the beating which the vigilantes administer. The manner in which the beating becomes the "word" from above, the "sign" telling him which way to go and which way to lead his children—the manner in which this "conversion" is worked out in familiar religious terms and symbols—is extremely ingenious and yet thoroughly convincing.

Another example of social perspective is to be found in one or two pages in each story; in these passages the reader gets a flashing glimpse—from the inside—of the fierce resentment of the Negro at his oppressed social position: they open your eyes to the lava-like fury of a persecuted people.

These highspots, I think, show the direction which the author must take if he is to grow. He has got to aim higher, wider and deeper. The going will be much tougher than before, but, judging from the promise of this book, he can make it.

Malcolm Cowley. "Long Black Song." *New Republic,* 194 (April 6, 1938), 280.

Story magazine offered $500 for the best book-length manuscript submitted by anyone connected with the Federal Writers' Project. The prize was awarded to Richard Wright, a young, serious, quiet-spoken Negro born in Natchez and haphazardly educated in Chicago. His book, published last week, consists of four long stories that the publishers insist on calling novellas. I found them both heartening, as evidence of a vigorous new talent, and terrifying as the expression of a racial hatred that has never ceased to grow and gets no chance to die.

The first story, "Big Boy Leaves Home," is my favorite. Four Negro boys play hookey from school and go swimming beside a no-trespass sign. When they come out to get their clothes, a white woman thinks they are trying to molest her. Her husband shoots two of the boys, a third is lynched for killing him, and only the fourth escapes on a northbound truck. The beginning of the story had been all horseplay and high spirits, yet even the jokes had revealed a consciousness of the never ending war between the races. "See tha sign over yonder?—Yeah.—Whut it say? 'NO TRESPASSIN,' read Lester.—Know whut tha mean?—'Mean ain no dogs n niggers erlowed,' said Buck." That sets the tone for the tragedy that follows.

"Down by the Riverside," the second

story, is a Mississippi nightmare of rising water. A Negro sets out with his sick wife in a stolen rowboat, but finds on reaching the hospital that she has died along the way. There is no time to rest or mourn. Everybody gives him orders—sending him now to the broken levee with sandbags, now to the roof with an axe, now downstream to rescue the wife of a white man he has killed in self-defense—while the water swirls higher and the poor Negro's only choice is between death by drowning and death by lynching. . . . The third story, "Long Black Song," is about a Negro woman seduced by a white salesman. I liked it less than the others, chiefly because Wright seems florid and bombastic when dealing with sex. It is only at the end of the story that he returns to his general theme of interracial hatred and recovers his usual power and simplicity.

These first three stories have dealt with essentially the same plot: a Negro is goaded beyond endurance, a white man is killed, a Negro is lynched. All three of them are headlong narratives, written without technical devices (except for a skillful use of Negro songs) and without psychological subtlety, but carried ahead by the rush of events and by a single fierce emotion that the author shares with his characters. It is best expressed by Silas, the wronged husband in "Long Black Song." "The white folks ain never gimme a chance! They ain never give no black man a chance! There ain nothin in yo whole life yuh kin keep from me! . . . Ahm gonna be hard like they is! So hep me Gawd, Ahm gonna be *hard!* When they come fer me Ahm gonna *be* here!" An hour later Silas dies in his burning cabin, after killing two of the white besiegers.

A fourth story, "Fire and Cloud," tries to show that a different ending is possible. In a small Southern city, there are plans for a big relief demonstration. Dan Taylor, a black preacher with a starving flock, refuses to join it, but he won't forbid it either, and therefore he is taken into the woods and whipped by white men acting for the chamber of commerce. The whipping makes him a rebel. He marches to the city hall with thousands of hungry people, black and white together, and the police don't shoot or club them and at last they are given food. "Black and white, unite and fight." It is the old Communist slogan that Wright is presenting in terms of action, and it is a good slogan too, even for those like myself who are more attached than the Communists to things as they are. If the black and white sharecroppers and miners and steel workers could make a defensive alliance, then the race conflict would be at least partially transformed into a class conflict. That would still be a dangerous situation, but at least our society has developed peaceful methods for dealing with class conflicts. For dealing with race conflicts, the common method is violence—and except in this one story. Wright makes us feel that the violence in the South will never end.

Marvel Cooke "Prize Novellas, Brave Stories." "*Uncle Tom's Children* by Richard Wright Seen as Poignant Cry Against Evils." *New York Amsterdam News,* April 9, 1938, p. 16.

Richard Wright's *Uncle Tom's Children* is quite the most exciting proletarian literature produced during the past twelve months.

The four "novellas" of life in the Deep South are a poignant cry for the immediate anti-lynching legislation and for Negro workers to unite with white workers for improvement of their conditions—for Uncle Tom is dead.

Mr. Wright, with his first book, carves for himself a place in the vanguard of American literature with these stories—startling, tragic stories that sear the soul as with a white hot torch—brave, strange stories that touch the sky and plunge straightway to the depths of despair.

No one before him, even Zora Neale Hurston, whose stories of the Southland have elicited high praise from the critics, has written such readable, realistic and authentic Negro dialect and few have his unusual mastery of underwriting. With a few brilliant strokes, Mr. Wright describes a lynching, a rape or a hunger march.

The first of the four long stories, "Big Boy Leaves Home," starting on a joyous note, ends in a barbaric lynching so dramatically told that the reader is left weak and inarticulate. Big Boy, hidden from a blood-thirsty mob in a kiln in the hills, is watching the lynching of his chum, Bobo.

"The flames leaped tall as the trees," writes the young author. "The scream came again. Big Boy trembled and looked. The mob was running down the slopes, leaving the fire clear. Then he saw a writhing white mass cradled in yellow flame and heard screams, one on top of the other, each shriller and shorter than the last. The mob was quiet now, standing still, looking up the slopes at the writhing mass gradually growing black, growing black in a cradle of yellow flame."

No words wasted there.

Nor in the thoughts crowding the mind of a conscientious Southern minister, who, seeking to lead his fold along the right path, finally leads them, together with white workers, to the city hall in a brave demonstration against hunger and exploitation.

"A baptism of clean joy swept over Taylor. He kept his eyes on the sea of black and white faces. The song swelled louder and vibrated through him. This is the way! he thought. Gawd ain no lie. He ain no lie! His eyes grew wet with tears, blurring his vision: the sky trembled; the buildings wavered as if about to topple, and the earth shook. . . He mumbled out loud, exultingly:

"Freedom belongs t the strong!"

The other stories that make up this brilliant volume are "Down by the Riverside," "Long Black Song" and "Fire and Cloud."

With *Uncle Tom's Children* Mr. Wright, who is only 29 years old, won a national contest which Story magazine offered for the best manuscript submitted by anyone connected with the WPA Federal Writers' Project. The judges in the contest were Harry Scherman, president of the Book-of-the-Month Club, Lewis Gannett and Sinclair Lewis.

Mrs. Eleanor Roosevelt commented favorably on Wright's excellent book in her column "My Day" last Thursday. And Macy sold over 500 copies on the same day.

P. H.
Providence Journal,
April 10, 1938.

"A naught's a naught and five's a figger, all fer the White Man and none fer the Nigger." So hummed Reverend Taylor as he went his suffering way. So chants every page of this painful book. There are four stories between its covers, all having to do with the brutal treatment of the Negro by the white man, all full of an aching bitterness which communicates itself poignantly to the most casual reader.

This is the first literary effort of the young Negro, Richard Wright. It won "Story's" $500 prize for the best novel submitted from the Federal Writers' Project. At least some white men have shown a dearth of hatred toward their darker brothers when "Story" awarded the prize to Mr. Wright and the Harper Company published the book! It is to be hoped that the race hatred that animates these tales will be softened somewhat in the author's future work.

Not that one feels that there is exaggeration in these pages. It is true indeed that community hysteria would bring about such loathsome cruelty as the beating of Reverend Taylor in "Fire and Cloud," the lynching of Bobo in "Big Boy Leaves Home," the shooting of Mann in "Down by the Riverside" and the burning of Silas's poor little shanty in "Long Black Song." But there are some white folk of balance and humanity and it would make Richard Wright's next stories of greater worth if he could introduce one note of sympathy into his next pages if only for virtue of contrast.

Malcolm Purcell, Jr.
Macon Telegraph,
April 15, 1938.

Regularly the South receives a slap in the face for its treatment of Negroes. This time the slapping is done by Richard Wright, a former Mississippi Negro, whose life in New York has not given him any better perspective of a difficult problem.

The book contains four novellas, each telling of harsh injustices to Negroes. Were the stories true pictures of Negro treatment in the South, then they would be a terrible accusation. But each relates occurrences so rare and scattered that the result cannot be fair.

Wright left the South at the age of fifteen after a nomadic life with little or no education. Since, he has worked over the United States "at every kind of a job from ditch-digging to clerking in a post office, and always reading everything that fell into my hands." He is now the head of the Harlem branch of a New York newspaper.

If, from his fifteen tender years in the South, Wright has retained a clear picture and understanding of the race problem, then he deserves rank above men of the highest intelligence who have been working on this problem for many years and are yet to find a true solution.

The literary style is blunt, clear and forceful. The descriptions are vivid; the dialogue has a force that is unfettered by the stiffness often attending the English language. The use of such literary instruments enables Wright to give his plots a swift-moving, powerful action.

The first novella concerns itself with murder as a consequence of the rash actions of four Negro boys. Two are shot; a third is lynched; and the last escapes to the North.

The second covers the hard life of a Mississippi Negro during the flood stages of the river. Driven to use a stolen boat at a time when boats are priceless, he carries his pregnant wife to a hospital, kills a white man in self-defense and is shot by soldiers.

Murder again appears in the third novella when a Negro farmer kills a white boy for seducing his wife, then is burned alive in his own home by a revengeful white mob.

A more modern note is injected into the last selection, which deals with the relief, in this case denied to the Negro population of a small city. Rebellious, they march through the streets and this show of force gains for them the food they seek.

Wright, with his vigorous, powerful style could present a clear picture of a great problem; instead, he covers only one side, and that side only partially. . . .

Sterling A. Brown. "From the Inside." *The Nation,* 146 (April 16, 1938), 448.

The distinction of Mr. Wright's prose was apparent in his contributions to the "New Caravan" in 1936 and to "American Stuff." His "Uncle Tom's Children," the winner of the prize awarded by *Story Magazine* for the best manuscript submitted by anyone connected with the Federal Writers' Project, fulfils the earlier promise. The four long stories which make up the book have power and originality, revealing a people whose struggles and essential dignity have too long been unexpressed.

Big Boy Leaves Home tells of one of the many twentieth-century fugitives from the South. Caught in a forbidden swimming hole, Big Boy's gang, certainly one of the best in fiction, run for their clothes; a white woman's scream brings a white man with a gun; two boys and the white man are killed in the fracas. The mob lays waste the Negro section, but after long, terrible hours in a kiln Big Boy gets away. Down by the Riverside effectively records a tragedy during a Mississippi flood. Mann makes use of a stolen boat to get his wife, in childbirth, to a hospital. Discovered in the stolen boat he shoots it out with the stranded owner, and it is the white man who topples into the high waters. Ironically, Mann is doomed by his heroic flood labors, for he saves the family of the man he has killed. In Long Black Song a young Negro farmer kills a white salesman who has attacked his wife, and is killed by the mob. Fire and Cloud deals with the dilemma of a Negro preacher who, unable to make up his mind in a depression crisis, has it made up for him by a gang of thugs who defend law and order by horsewhipping. The lashing strips away his faith that as the compromising trusty he can gain any important favors for his convicted people. He joins the protest march of poor whites and Negroes, believing that "Freedom belongs to the strong."

"Uncle Tom's Children" has its full share of violence and brutality; violent deaths occur in three stories and the mob goes to work in all four. Violence has long been an important element in fiction about Negroes, just as it is in their life. But where Julia Peterkin in her pastorals and Roark Bradford in his levee farces show violence to be the reaction of primitives unadjusted to modern civilization, Richard Wright shows it as the way in which civilization keeps the Negro in his place. And he knows what he is writing about.

Some of the tragedies may seem too coincidentally contrived, may seem to concentrate too much upon the victims, but the book has its great importance in spite of this. The essential quality of certain phases of Negro life in the South is handled here vigorously, authentically, and with flashes of genuine poetry. Here are characters seen from the inside: Big Boy, alert, full of animal spirits, suddenly turned into a hounded fugitive; the perplexed preacher with a stake in keeping quiet and orderly, and a bitter knowledge of what his people suffer; the farmer who has labored for a home that a white man casually disrupts. In these little shacks, overburdened with poverty, the first mention of trouble with the white folks brings paralyzed fear and a conniving that is pitifully feeble. The people show a wisdom brewed of suffering, not the artless philosophy endeared to Southern mythologists. And finally there are those who are not only aware of what is being done to them but determined to do something about it, resolutely muttering: "Ah'll go ef the nex' one goes!" and "Ah ain' got but *one* time t' die." The South that Mr. Wright renders so vividly is recognizable and true, and it has not often been within the covers of a book.

Richard Lanman. *Atlanta Journal*, April 17, 1938.

These are stories of the south, the negro's south, as seen through the eyes of a young negro writer who is dissatisfied with things as they are and would have them changed.

They are poignant, lusty tales of episodes removed from the lives of negroes, episodes caught and held up before a background of the south as it is today. They hold more of sorrow than joy, but more of hope than defeatism. And Richard Wright has mastered his medium and his metier so thoroughly that a great deal may be expected of him in the future.

Portland Oregonian, April 24, 1938.

Uncle Tom's Children, by Richard Wright, is a collection of four stories of the deep south by one who knows it from the bitter side. Richard Wright, Negro, was born in Natchez, Miss., at one time a very tough river town, but it has been a dreamy old place these many years.

Wright left home as a youngster. No chance for him in Natchez. He drifted to one job, then another. He knew how to read and write, so he read stray magazines and old newspapers. In Arkansas, where he worked for some time, he saw members of his race brutally treated. In time he wandered to New York.

He wrote of life as he knew and saw it, along the river, in the swamps, in cabins south of the Ohio. Four stories submitted to a WPA federal writers' project won first prize.

The first, including a striking line, "Yo mamma don' wear no drawers," is a picture of life of poor Negroes. The second, most striking of the four, is of death. Death in the south that hates Negroes who refuse still to be slaves.

The soldiers rolled the body over. No question, the boy was dead. The soldiers shoved the body along, it rolled along but stopped a foot from the water's edge. No one gave a damn whether it stopped or just slid on into the stream. As one reads, he wonders how it is that the blacks of the south don't really avenge the killing of so many of their people.

Two other stories are "Long Black Song" and "Fire and Cloud." If you want southern life as the Negroes experience it, "Uncle Tom's Children" will tell you.

Countee Cullen. *The African,* 2 (April 1938).

This is a significant book in many ways. The writing is significant; the viewpoint is significant; the author is an important and impressive addition to American writers.

In discussing *Uncle Tom's Children* with this reviewer, another Negro writer spoke, with no intended disparagement, of Richard Wright as an angry little man. The diminutive is probably non-descriptive, but angry he is, without a doubt. Anger, red-hot, soul-searching and uncontrollable is nothing new in Negro writers. If Mr. Wright were simply angry, that might win our respect but not necessarily our admiration for him as a writer. It is the restraint of his anger that moves us, the objectivity of it, the ability to do what the Negro author usually finds so difficult, to dissociate himself and his own hurts and bitternesses from the lives of his characters. Here is artistic detachment at its absolute.

Uncle Tom's Children are still cabin-bound in many ways, but they are not satisfied; they are not chips off the old block, and barely recognizable as the offspring of their famous, but hardly admirable forebear. These children are after what belongs to men; they want happiness, better homes, better economic conditions. They still find the getting hard, but (here the blood is different) they are willing to fight. These Negroes are different; there is in them something of what must have been in the first African slaves, something of the fine, healthy anger that saw in death a brighter destiny than slavery.

It is hard to say which of these four striking stories is the more arresting, although if pressed for a choice we should probably choose "Fire and Cloud" a breath-taking chronicle of the birth of a real leader of his people. We have seldom, however, read a story in which there was so much human happiness and terror commingled as in *Big Boy Leaves Home,* a story in which an innocent and natural gathering of a group of Negro boys leads to the shooting of two of them, the lynching of one, and the escape of another to live a life of nightmare remembrance. The beginning of that story was a delight, the ending more terrible because Mr. Wright had so purely depicted the happiness of those four rollicking Negro boys. Perhaps he will resurrect them in some other story. Those boys or their cousins germane could be the delight of countless other youngsters.

In spite of its anger, there is no bias in this book. All the black men are not brave nor all the black women virtuous, and there is much that can be laid at the door of human cussedness, both white and black. Yet those in high places have much to answer for. Let them not deplore the anger, the terror, the sickening horror of these stories. Let them remove the causes.

Allen Maxwell. *Southwest Review*, 23 (April 1938), 362–65.

The Negro race in the United States has contributed little of permanent value to literature. There have been the writings of a few gentle professors proud of their approximations to white culture, and there has been sprawling and crude folk material. But the transplanted black race, in every way centuries behind other races, has had to wait until now for a sturdy storyteller, an artist with integrated power over words, a sincere people-spokesman who can sear the agony of lynching and the misery of immemorial injustice into tolerant but hitherto complacent minds. Richard Wright need fear no Jim Crow law as he takes his seat among the most promising young writers in America today.

Uncle Tom's Children is made up of four long stories, each of which carries a bitter poignancy and a breathless, low-pitched anger. The members of his race whom Richard Wright has characterized unforgettably are honorable, well-meaning black men trapped by circumstance in the white man's world, where there is no mercy. In "Big Boy Leaves Home" four joyful Negro boys are swimming in a creek when a white woman walks on the scene and stands by their clothes, staring at them. When they advance toward her to retrieve their clothes, she screams, and her red-faced husband appears, rifle in hand. He shoots down two of the boys before Big Boy grabs the rifle and kills him in self-defense. Big Boy and the other boy, Buck, then flee; very shortly a mob is after them. Big Boy successfully hides and finally escapes to the North, but not before he has witnessed from his hiding place the lynching of the unfortunate Buck, tarred, feathered, then burned, a "writhing white mass gradually growing black, growing black in a cradle of yellow flame." Buck, screaming shrilly, is burned, but not before souvenir hunters have wielded their sharp knives: "Look! Hes gotta finger! . . . Hes got one of his ears, see?"

"Down by the Riverside" is a tale of floodtime on the Mississippi, of elemental wrath loosed by nature and man. A religious, self-respecting Negro uses a stolen boat to take his desperately ill wife to the hospital. On his way he stops to ask for help at a house. The householder recognizes the boat as his own and begins to shoot at the Negro, who fires back in self-defense and kills the white man, then rows on to the hospital. He finds that his wife is dead. He spends the rest of the night doing heroic rescue work, and saves the wife and the son of the man he killed. They recognize him and denounce him, and he is riddled with soldiers' bullets when he tries to escape.

An attractive Negress is seduced by a white peddler in "Long Black Song." Her husband, a proud, independent, thoughtful Negro, who owned all his land and owed nobody, finds out about it, throws his wife out, kills the peddler, and is in turn killed by a white posse.

"Fire and Cloud," which appeared in the March *Story,* is rather more optimistic than Wright's other stories. In it the black race is offered a solution for its problems: mass action. A kind, intelligent Negro pastor, who has always been proud of the high regard that the white authorities had for him, discovers that the whites have been using him to keep the Negroes from complaining of oppression. When his fellow Negroes are starving and can get no relief because of race prejudice, he is expected to keep them quiet. But he will not be quiet; he forsakes his white associates and stands with his race. He is threatened and finally flogged painfully by masked thugs; but he is not deterred from marching at the head of his people in a great demonstration in which the poor whites join. The mayor is forced to grant relief to the Negroes, and the pastor realizes that "freedom belongs to the strong."

Wright's style is in the favorite Steinbeck tradition of meaty terseness. There is copious and skillful use of dialogue, in marvelously natural dialect. A tendency toward the dramatic and the sensational is tempered by admirable unity of emotion and effective understatement. And not less telling than Steinbeck's is Wright's narrative technique. Progress of the stories from ominous sadness to white, restrained fury and finally to quiet pathos is in gradual, intensifying stages. The reader's sympathy is always invoked effortlessly at the very beginning. And at no time is there sacrifice of the dominant, tense impression for "message." . . .

Sterling A. Brown. *Opportunity,* 16 (April 1938), 120–21.

Richard Wright's life reads like one of his stories, combining the tragically familiar with the unexpected, the dramatic highlight; and jammed with troubles that were courageously faced. With his family often on the move, he got to know many southern towns and cities: Elaine, Arkansas; Jackson, Memphis; he saw sharecropping life, church life, life on the river. His own forced roving from job to job is recorded in "The Ethics of Living Jim Crow," one of the finest pieces in *American Stuff,* the anthology of creative writing by members of the Federal Writers' Project. The schools of his boyhood had little enough to give him, but he did not care even for that; he played hookey regularly in spite of the prediction of his elders that he would end on the gallows. But after years of bumming about he became as inveterate a reader as he had been a truant. His first volume reveals the closeness of his reading of books and American life. Mr. Wright has made full use of his none too numerous years.

Uncle Tom's Children, the prize winner in a contest conducted by *Story* Magazine for the best manuscript submitted by anyone connected with the Federal Writers' Project, comprises four long stories. The first of these, "Big Boy Leaves Home," appeared in *The New Caravan* in 1936 and its superior quality gave assurance that Mr. Wright's first book would be a literary event. "Big Boy Leaves Home" pictures with robust humor one of the most convincing gangs of boys in fiction. But they go swimming in a hole posted, "No Trespassing," which means "no dogs n niggers erllowed" and their lark ends in tragedy. With two of his mates killed, Big Boy gets the white man's gun in a tussle and shoots him. From the high-spirited playfulness of the boys, we are suddenly switched to the mute, dull fear of the Negro settlement. Graphically Mr. Wright shows the despair of the old ones, too well acquainted with the workings of the mob, helpless except for feeble subterfuges, wanting to help each other out and pitifully unable. Big Boy escapes by the greatest of good luck, but the mob gluts its vengeance on many of the innocent. "Big Boy Leaves Home" is a bitter transcript of reality, more powerful because of the poetic handling.

The reviewer was startled recently to read in an essay by a Mississippian that the Negro, being a creature of mirth and inertia, did not find the Mississippi in flood to be a tragic event: he knew that while highwater lasted there would be no work and his boss-man would look out for him. "Down By the Riverside" is too important a work to be used for demolishing such a flimsy bit of Americana, of course, but the essay came back to mind while reading this tragedy of the black waters. It is worth remarking that for all of the vivid descriptions of the Old Man on the rampage, no previous story has so driven home the ugly facts of forced labor, of Negro heroism casually regarded as the expected thing, and of the abuses of prejudice made more acute by catastrophe. A wife in childbirth, a boat stolen to get her to the hospital, trouble with the stranded boat owner, an exchange of shots, and a white man falls into the turbulent waters—such things prepare the tragic end, which for all of his courage and service, Mann cannot avert. The pictures of the hospital, of the refugee camps, of the callous soldiers and the gangs at back-breaking labor on the levees, are well done. In one of the finest narrative sections, two Negroes drive a motorboat on a long search over the waste of waters for marooned survivors, who have had little in the past for their rescuers except a blow and a curse. In spite of all the near-escapes from death and the tragic losses, the older, fiercer excitement rages when Mann is captured in the camp: "They caughta coon!"

To the reviewer "Long Black Song" is the least of these stories both in characterization and structure, but there is no gainsaying its vigorous drive. The heroine and her husband remain incompletely realized, sketched instead of rounded out. "Fire and Cloud," however, strikes a new note in Negro fiction. Starvation is threatening the crowded huts of the Negro section of a southern town. Reverend Taylor, far more convincing than most of his brother preachers in fiction, is torn between desire to help his flock and fear of jeopardizing his family, church, and standing with the wealthy and powerful whites who occasionally have doled him out favors for his people. He cannot make up his mind. Certain whites who believe in direct action where Negroes are concerned, take Reverend Taylor out and horsewhip him to teach him a lesson. But the lesson he learns is that "Freedom belongs to the Strong," and, done with compromising and blind faith, he leads a protest march of Negroes and poor whites, side by side, singing.

With the foreshortening to be found in this sort of fiction, Mr. Wright makes too great use of coincidences. His characters are often like the "Time's Laughingstocks" of Thomas Hardy; but the ills heaped upon their heads do not come from Fate, but from a man-made, poorly ordered world. Mr. Wright wished to show the melodrama and tragedy of southern Negro life, and a critic would have to be bold and blind to deny that such melodrama and tragedy abound. Many white readers, disliking the book, will state that Mr. Wright has lost his perspective because of his northern sojourn. But perspective is just what this author has. Some Negroes may condemn the book as "propaganda;" fiction not showing Harlem to be a round of cabarets and parties or the South to be a sunny pastoral is considered propaganda and therefore is not to be taken seriously. But not since Toomer's *Cane* has there been such a fictional rendition of the southern scene by a Negro author, and in many respects these stories go beyond *Cane*. Erskine Caldwell, William Faulkner, T. S. Stribling and Paul Green have contributed valuable panels to the understanding of the South. The reviewer does not wish to compare Mr. Wright with these; they are the authors of many books, and this is Mr. Wright's first. But it is worth pointing out that certain of their qualities appear in Mr. Wright's work; like them he speaks of the South with authority and persuasiveness and a surprising skill.

James Saxon Childers. "This Kind of Book Does Little Good and Much Harm." *Birmingham New Age–Herald*, May 1, 1938.

If only there had been an occasional light in all the darkness, if only Richard Wright, author of "Uncle Tom's Children," hadn't been so completely bitter, he could have written a better book, a more honest book, a more artistic, a more useful, a more valuable book. But, no! Into the old trap he went and, denying all progress, denying all efforts of enlightened whites and blacks to come together in the South, he screams so loudly that we can't distinguish his words: their meaning is lost. That is unfortunate, because Mr. Wright has something of importance to say to the South.

In these four stories two Negroes are burned alive, one is shot to death, several are beaten almost to a pulp by white men. Such brutalities have happened in the South. But their end is not achieved by cursing all white men, by lashing out against the South as a whole. There are honorable white men in the South trying every day to block out the wretched conditions of which these race killings are surface indications. But Mr. Wright has no place for such men in his book. He had rather tell a fierce story than, with more patience, honesty, artistry, seek the truth and present it in its myriad conflicting sides.

The stories are written with a vividness that is at times startling. They are dramatic, cruel, full of misery and misunderstanding. They depict, without benefit of mercy or full truth, the life of the Negro in a white man's civilization.

In each story the Negro is innocent of wrong doing. He is forced into the crime of defending himself against white persecutors; for this defense he pays with his life. Such stories, written in venom and for the dramatics of the moment, make permanent betterment, for which honorable white men and honorable black men are steadily working throughout the South, so much more difficult to bring about.

Fred T. Marsh. "Hope, Despair and Terror." *New York Herald Tribune Books*, May 8, 1938, p. 3.

I suppose it should be mentioned that these four dramatic narratives of Negro life by a young Negro author won a prize—the $500 prize offered by "Story Magazine" "for the best manuscript submitted by any one connected with the W. P. A. Federal Writers' Projects."

The judges were Harry Scherman, Lewis Gannett and Sinclair Lewis. It won the prize from more than five hundred entries.

But never mind all that. This book would be published by any publisher at any time; and it would make its way in the world as fiction of distinction in any year. Wright calls the four tales novellas, and the title refers to the two phrases so commonly heard in educated Negro circles—"He's an Uncle Tom" and "Uncle Tom is dead." The sentimentalized "good nigger" of proprietary Southerners and tutelary Northerners is not to be found here. These are one-act plays, poetic dramas, translated into a narrative prose that is nothing short of magnificent. The novellas are compounded of music and passion; and three of them (I except "Down by the Riverside") are as fine long short stories as any of modern times.

The three are "Big Boy Leaves Home," "Long Black Song" and "Fire and Cloud." You might bear these titles in mind. You'll hear about them again—and again—for some years to come. I am writing about them from around the edges—for how would you discuss and explain "The Cherry Orchard," for example (which has no remote connection with them except that, like them, it is intangible)? Nor, in a brief review, do I want to discuss the "Negro problem" or Wright's social slant—which is present. That seems to be, in brief, that "our people" must find their way together, taking what they can get from those who offer them help, but never allowing themselves to be blindly misled for ulterior purposes, hoping eventually to become a part, pulling their proportionate weight, of the body social and politic.

The opening pages of "Big Boy Leaves Home" could be turned (by Wright himself) into as lovely an idyll of country boyhood, poor boys but for the moment free and happy and animal, as was ever written. No sloppiness or sentimentality here; only sheer poetry. But the boys get into trouble. And being Negro boys in the South, that trouble is serious, terrible in its seriousness and ghastly in its consequences. "Long Black Song" is, I thought, the most nearly perfect of the collection. "Flesh and blood is weak and frail, susceptible to nervous shock," and that sort of thing happens all the time in all kinds and classes of men and women. But when Sarah, weak and melting, surrenders to the white man who comes around selling junk on the installment plan to ignorant, beauty-loving black people, tragedy comes of it. The tragedy is the eternal one of jealousy and revenge. But the Negro is not even allowed to spend his passions in dignity.

"Fire and Cloud" is the story of a Negro preacher who stood by his people in the face of white officials' flattery and maneuvers. He had influence, respected by black and white alike, but when he stepped out of line he was just another "nigger" and suffered the consequences. But there is triumph in this tale. And there are passages of hope, despair and terror that make you rock in your seat. This is a story—I don't care when, why or by whom written or with what intention.

I suspect that there was only one choice for this prize. That verdict might well win another—the Pulitzer Prize.

Rabbi Herman Pollack. *Memphis Hebrew Watchman*, May 26, 1938.

Richard Wright springs from the ranks of obscurity, the segregated and despised. He writes about his own flesh and blood who suffer and perish because of prejudice. In four sketches. . . he portrays their existence in a manner more gruesome and horrifying than a mystery tale by Poe.

UNCLE TOM'S CHILDREN shows that in order for art to attain fulfillment, life must be portrayed as it is, not as it is wished for. Wright touches upon experiences that in polite circles are usually hushed and when mentioned publicly have thrown into confusion for weeks gatherings such as Congress. . . .

As is implied in the title, Wright deals with the life of the contemporary Negro, but departs from the usual presentation of the colored people in that he does not picture them as hopelessly indifferent to their plight but becoming increasingly concerned in their welfare and that of their fellow-men. Thus he explains that the Uncle Tom of a generation ago "which denoted the cringing type has been supplanted by a new word from another generation which says: 'Uncle Tom is dead'."

The background of Richard Wright has enabled him to present a phase of human experience that concerns all minority groups and those persecuted and oppressed. Born of Negro parentage in Mississippi, he lived as the ordinary youth of his race—tasting poverty and want, and receiving a meager education. Later in life he educated himself, he tells, "by always reading everything that fell into my hands."

The first three sketches depict the ruthless terror, bestiality, and animal passion unleashed by prejudice. Angry mobs lynch innocent people, families find themselves dispossessed, their homes burned to the ground. There is no rest and peace for God's children, is the plaintive cry of the victims who, in each case, face death heroically. Big Boy, hunted by the mob for defending his rights, hides in a black kiln at the foot of a hill and though he escapes, his friend, Bobo, is caught and lynched. Mann meets with death during a flood in his attempt to carry his dying wife to a hospital. Silas is burned in his home for defending the honor of his wife.

The fourth account describes Reverend Taylor leading the people of his community to the City Hall to ask for food for the needy. Although previously intimidated and beaten, he does not abandon his mission. He finds reality by identifying himself with the lot of the masses. When the Mayor announces that "they can get food," Taylor experiences the joy of achievement. " 'This is the way!' he thought. 'Gawd ain no lie!' His eyes grew wet with tears, blurring his vision. He mumbled out loud, exultingly: 'Freedom belongs to the strong.' "

Every expression of race prejudice breeds Fascism. Regardless of one's personal views, the book has a message our people, in particular, should heed. As it has been said: "The Jew owes the Negro of America very much, for if the reactionaries were not lynching Negroes they would be lynching Jews."

J. F.
"Literary Achievement by Young Negro Brings Picture of Race's Plight." *San Diego Sun*, May 29, 1938.

"Freedom," the Rev. Daniel Taylor mumbled, waving a gnarled black hand before a thousand black men, "freedom belongs to the strong."

It had taken this Negro minister all his life to learn this one phrase, and now that he knew it, it was all he could do to say it. For it was the summation of "Uncle Tom's Children's" philosophy of living, voiced dynamically by young Negro author Richard Wright in his prize-winning book by that name.

Richard Wright, Mississippi-born, dust trail-bred, has given us probably the greatest literary achievement from the Negro race—at least the most authentic picture of the modern American Negro's plight at the hands of men who first stole the black man from his native land.

Here are four stories, stark, searing, sensitive. They are stories of Big Boy, the carefree Negro youth hunted and sought for the self-defense killing of a white man who had slain two of his companions; of Mann and the river flood; of the fickle Sarah and her devoted Silas, and of old "Revrun Taylor and de Lawd."

Written in the dialogue of the Southern Negroes, "Uncle Tom's Children" is as readable as Hemingway, as powerful as Steinbeck. . . .

Mixed with the potency of Wright's first book, is a style as typically musical as the Negro race itself. You will find yourself humming as you read this fine book, just as you will feel your hands clench in some of the passages from this young writer's stories.

James T. Farrell. "Lynch Patterns." *Partisan Review,* 4 (May 1938), 57–58.

Richard Wright's *Uncle Tom's Children* will serve as an excellent refutation for those who are now writing such fancy nonsense about fables and allegories. These four novelettes are written in a direct and realistic manner, and their impact is most powerful. I submit that they are worth more as literature than whole anthologies full of tortured allegories.

Uncle Tom's Children was submitted to a contest conducted by *Story* magazine, which offered $500 for a work written by an employee of the WPA Federal Writers' Project. This book was selected as the prize winner from among five hundred manuscripts. I think there is no question that it was an excellent choice.

Each of Mr. Wright's four novelettes is different, yet all have a common background. In consequence, they fit together to make a genuinely integrated book. What Richard Wright does here is to recount the bitter experience of the Negro in a white man's world, and the bitter meaning of his experience. His stories are full of the violence, the brutal injustice, the terror, the utter misery that arise from economic exploitation and the rule of lynch law. In each of the stories, the tragedy, the brutality, and the misery seem to result from some accidental occurrence, some unfortunate coincidence. For example: in "Big Boy Leaves Home" a carefree group of boys are swimming in a forbidden pond. Their actions are harmless. But just when they come out of the water, a white woman appears. They are all naked, and the white woman stands in the path they must take to reach their clothes. Two of the boys are shot dead on the spot. One is burned by a mob. Big Boy shoots the white woman's escort in self defense, hides out from the mob, and manages to escape to the north next morning. There is real pertinency in Wright's use of accident and coincidence. He is not contriving. By using such devices as hinges for his narrative, he is able to present vividly and concretely a sense of the social effects of the patterns of lynch law. And the moment the reader realizes what is being done, the stories acquire intensified meanings for him. A tension runs through them that contributes greatly to their impact. The atmosphere is constantly explosive, and anything that happens can result in the calling of a mob. I know of no more effective presentation of the pernicious effects of the lynch pattern than these stories of Richard Wright's. We see the consequence concretely in terms of human destinies. The white men are always inclined to shoot first and then ask questions as to why they shot. Nerves pop. Trigger fingers are given deadly exercise. Ropes are brought out. With great courage and passionate protest Richard Wright has told the story of his own people. He minces no words. And there is no questioning the authenticity of his work.

Especially remarkable is the handling of dialogue. Richard Wright uses simple speech as a means of carrying on his narrative, as a medium for poetic and lyrical effects, and as an instrument of characterization. Through the dialect of his people he is able to generalize their feelings about life, their fate, the social situation in which they live and suffer and are oppressed. Here is demonstration—which many writers might study—of the possibilities of the vernacular.

However, it should be remarked that Wright is addicted to certain mannerisms which are unnecessary and which detract from the development of his stories. He is inclined to spread capital letters all over his pages in order to gain emphasis, when such sensationalism is absolutely needless. He shows a tendency to overwrite when he speaks auctorially and when he wants to describe complicated emotions and poetic backgrounds. Then he has bare feet whisper too much in the dark, and there is too much ebb and surge in the blood of his characters. And at times he gets lost in complicated or swift moving narrative. In part, at least, these are mannerisms which can easily be dropped with a little more work and some self-conscious reflection on writing as a technique. Such criticisms notwithstanding, *Uncle Tom's Children* remains as a true and powerful work by a new American writer. It is a book of bitter truths and bitter tragedies written by an able and sensitive talent. It is not merely a book of promise. It is a genuine literary achievement.

Agnes M. Reeve. "Far Cry from Uncle Tom." *Dayton Journal*, June 12, 1938.

If you have a strong stomach, one that relishes murder, lust, rape—and more murder, then "Uncle Tom's Children" is for you. This collection of four long short stories won the prize for the best literary work done under the Federal Writers' Project and if it is a sample of what we may expect few readers will consider the public funds allocated to this project well spent. It is a far cry from Uncle Tom of Civil War days to "Uncle Tom's Children of today"—a far cry from the kindly relations between the faithful Negro and his "white folks" to the Negro Communists and their ilk.

The author of "Uncle Tom's Children" is a Negro and he can write—unquestionably he can write. His portrayal of race conflict is not one likely to be relished by either race, for Negro and white man of these stories are equally cruel, lustful and bloodthirsty.

Mr. Wright's style is terse, but with marked economy of words he builds emotional and dramatic situations which make his climaxes, tragic though they are, seem inevitable. The few brief descriptive passages are colorful and vivid, especially those depicting the Mississippi flood in "Down By the Riverside." When Mr. Wright develops to the point where he can see truth and beauty as clearly as he sees cruelty and tragedy we may have something memorable from his pen. "Uncle Tom's Children" has literary merit, but it is not reading for a pleasant summer day.

Eugene C. Holmes. "New Stories of the Negro People." *American Teacher,* 22 (May-June, 1938), 34.

In these four prize winning novellas, which were awarded the Harper Story Magazine prize for the best manuscript submitted by a WPA writer, the author achieves new heights and establishes an unforgettable landmark in American fiction. For their drive, their burning message and their style, these stories will echo through our times as splendid examples of the artist who is so much in accord with his environment that he can write about it with such painstaking reality. Wright tells of the Negro people, a people he knows and loves, who are learning now that "freedom belongs to the strong." These stories will so tear your heart and carve themselves into your marrow that there will arise a determination to do something about a hell that enslaves millions of human beings. If the essence of high writing displays the ability to translate and to transmute the living that men do, then Richard Wright has won for himself a deserved niche in American literature.

The Modern Monthly, 10 (June 1938), 14.

Negro literature was tops in the late twenties. Countee Cullen, Eric Walrond, Walter White, Rudolph Fisher, Gwendolyn Bennett, Jesse Fauset, Claude McKay, and many others were names to conjure with those days. In the thirties, however, Negro literature, so-called, experienced a premature death. Few of the Negro writers have continued to function. Claude McKay has written an autobiography recently, a good but not significant book, and rumor has it that Walter White is working on another novel. But that is all. The only Negroes of those days who continue to do good work are Langston Hughes, Sterling Brown, and George Schuyler. Since then three other Negro writers have sprung into prominence: Zora Neale Hurston for her novels *Mules and Men* and *Their Eyes Are Watching God,* M. B. Tolson for his *Portraits in Harlem,* and now Richard Wright for his volume of short stories *Uncle Tom's Children.*

Uncle Tom's Children is a remarkable book. The author has managed to catch more of Negro psychology within a relatively few pages than most authors have in many volumes. His first story "Big Boy Leaves Home" is a little masterpiece. It is genuine stuff, rooted in the soil and people of which it is part.

Marion Hendry. "Prize Stories." *Florida Times Union*, July 3, 1938.

These stories are written in the negro's own dialect, but it is easily read and understood. The tragedy of the negro in a civilization of white people, a great number of whom do not understand the negro nor know how to deal with him, is made real by the author. Here we have many incidents, which we either know from personal experience or about which we have read in the newspapers, presented from the black man's point of view. In one of the stories four adolescent colored boys found themselves in a tragic situation which resulted from innocent fun in which any white boy may have participated. The colored boys, innocent though they were, had not a chance against a hateful white man who did not like "niggers," and treated them more ruthlessly than he would deal with the lowest form of animal life. Of the four boys, one escaped the punishment which all "niggers" receive from a seething mob, led by some rough, common white man who knows no discipline nor way of getting along with the negro except with the use of whips, guns and lynching mobs.

Another story deals with a poor, honest, conscientious negro preacher with a large congregation of faithful "brothahs and sistahs." The Reverend's influence was widespread among the colored people, and it had always been for good. He was the one to whom the white officials went when there was any question which arose concerning the whites and blacks. At the time of the story, however, the colored people were at the point of desperation. They had been denied land to work for their living; they were hungry; the Relief Agency had told them in no uncertain terms that they could not have anything. All his people looked to old Taylor, their preacher and friend. The cruel treatment he received at the hands of heartless white men will make one's blood boil.

These accounts of negro life sing with a plaintive melody, haunting our souls, in telling of the few simple things necessary for the happiness of the negro; they shout the protests of the black man against the misunderstandings and mistreatment by brutes who have no code of discipline save the lash; they plead for sympathetic understanding and a chance to be left alone.

"Uncle Tom's Children" is a challenge to every honest, sensitive, humane white person in America. It is written with the simplicity of truth, and it is powerful in that simplicity.

United Automobile Workers, August 13, 1938.

No white man can read "Uncle Tom's Children" without a feeling of horror and shame. No union man will read it without feeling a sense of joy that he has taken the first step to form a brotherhood between white and black workers.

"Uncle Tom's Children" is a product of the WPA Writers' Project. It won the $500 prize offered by Story Magazine for the best manuscript submitted by anyone connected with the project. Richard Wright, the author, is a young Negro who has had many and varied experiences. He has strong passion, keen dramatic sense, and the power to tell a stirring tale in simple language. He puts all this to use in the four stories that make up "Uncle Tom's Children." These are stories of frustration, of a race that is exploited, battered and bruised. The first tale, "Big Boy Leaves Home," left me trembling, almost afraid to finish the book, yet impelled to read on. It is tragedy, but tragedy with a purpose.

"Down by the Riverside" is the story of a flood and a heroic black man. Here, too, is the same underlying theme. Misunderstanding, prejudice. "Long Black Song" tells about Silas and his struggle to rise and again he is beaten by the white man. The last story in the book, "Fire and Cloud" is the only one that gives us hope. It brings together the workers, white and black. The theme is hunger—which both races can understand. That is a thrilling march they make, poor whites and Negroes, marching together and singing and the last dramatic sentence, "Freedom belongs to the strong."

Yes, "Uncle Tom's Children" is a great book. A book that should be read by every auto worker in this union where white worker and black worker stand side by side in a fight for human rights.

Nixon Smiley. *Miami Herald*, December 25, 1938.

. . . If any member of his race ever won the right of a hearing it is Richard Wright, 30-year-old negro author whose amazingly realistic use of negro folk dialect in "Fire and Cloud," one of four stories in "Uncle Tom's Children," itself a prize-winning book, won second award in the recent O. Henry Memorial Award short story contest.

Actually a short novel, "Fire and Cloud" is one of the really great stories of our generation. It already has been rated as a negro classic. The author has won the distinction of having his works studied by Columbia University students after Columbia's professors became interested in his phonetic developments.

This best of four fine stories is about a liberal but cautious negro preacher, Reverend Taylor, who is driven by hunger and want of his people into a defiance of all authority. The people of his village are without work and Taylor is faced with the task of obtaining relief for them. The officials treat him civilly but can give him no assistance. Dejected and full of earnest doubt he returns to learn that patience has just about come to an end and that the more radical members of his race are planning a demonstration to demand relief. . . .

All the demonstration lacks for success is Taylor's participation, the lack of which would cause many to hold back. If only a few marched they would be driven back by armed whites and police but if everybody marched the whites would not bother them and there would be no bloodshed. Triumphantly Taylor takes the lead, the marchers file out and are joined by the white workers. At city hall the mayor, seeing the great numbers, comes out to meet the peaceful demonstrators, anxious to see that they obtain their needed relief.

Whatever the Southern reader's objection to any of the facts of this story, he cannot help becoming absorbed in the presentation of the negro dialect. The characters actually live and ring unbelievably true to life. Reverend Taylor's prayer at the beginning is presented so realistically that you can almost imagine yourself hearing the words instead of reading them. The dialect contains no apostrophe. The author said his seeking for shortcuts in punctuation after working all day at turf-digging finally led to elimination of the apostrophe altogether.

Wright, who is working on a full length novel, was born in the South but lives in New York. Success was won, he says, after many years of hard earnest study and creative endeavor.

John Lovell, Jr. "Negro-True." *Journal of Negro Education,* 8 (January 1939), 71–73.

Literary critics, professional and amateur, find the trueness-to-life of books an ever-present, knotty and dismaying topic. "We know that Mr. Cornstalk knows Cornville," they will sometimes say, "but why doesn't he tell the truth about it? Who is paying him and promising him fame to twist the facts, and for what species of propaganda is this book being published?" The common reader, archest of literary critics, thinking himself perfectly hand-in-glove with "life," is always shaking his head over the infidelity of some promising genius to his *tranche de vie*.

The common reader, and even the professional critic, sometimes forgets that the romantic and the fanciful play as big a part in the deep meanings of life as hard experience. The psychologist must explore dreams, half-thoughts, and hallucinations, along with lucid moments; the sociologist finds grotesque and antic fairylands in the slums; the laywer conjures up a wonderland, stranger than Alice's, in the mind of his client who committed murder while "away." No one can escape the romantic; it is useless to try. It does not often supply our substance, but it does supply our color and glow and thrill, our mental vitamins.

But the habit that people and critics have of putting temporary phases of the romantic in a mold and labeling the thing permanent, avoiding the close and constant scrutiny of natural phenomena, is not justifiable, and is not romantic. It is sentimental. The American Negroes, in a so-called plantation tradition—which Sterling Brown and others are still debunking—were portrayed as sinfully meek, sinfully religious, sinfully devoted to men whose rough boots were always in their faces, perpetually merry, unmoral and sweet-singing. Now, after many decades, every Negro in the movies, on the radio, in books, in hill houses, in employment agencies, on the street, or emerging not empty-handedly from the chicken-house, is expected to conform to the exact pattern. In the eyes of most Americans, he is still carrying log cabins and cotton patches on his back, and razors, pork chops, rabbit's feet and watermelon seeds in his pockets.

It is bad enough when white writers continue the cruel joke, merely because they are lazy or malicious or fearful of contamination. But since the beginning of our present era, these white writers have been ably assisted by a corps of Negro writers, who, in exchange for the glory of having their least expressions writ in the water of flashly publication, have given the whole proceedings a new coating of authenticity. They have shown the Negro population, from Harlem to Florida, unchanged from Uncle Tom except for more gaudy exteriors. They have refused to smash the mold to bits, and show its absurdity and impossibility in the face of environmental and evolutionary change. They have preferred to "get published" rather than to tell the truth, both hard and soft. We appreciate their temptation but deplore its outcome.

That is why we are so genuinely refreshed at the dawn of Richard Wright. He was aware of the temptation. He knew the hundred-headed dog at the gates of publication *a la* Negro. He knew that only the greatest coordination and skill, only the keenest refinement of principles would admit him to speech where all the others had had to bow the knee to Baal or remain silent. He accepted that challenge and his work shows the effect of the brutal demands of art—like Beethoven's or Michelangelo's—putting to shame the writers on the Negro of all races and degrees of radicality, with one or two exceptions. For have not the artists on the Negro been presenting us, under the guise of genius, poems and stories which were seen, felt and all written down in from ten minutes to a few hours!

Wright wrote five long stories, four of which, "Big Boy Leaves Home," "Down by the Riverside," "Long Black Song," and "Fire and Cloud" are published as *Uncle Tom's Children*. They are all stories of the Negro in the deep South, centering in benighted Mississippi, where Wright was born and reared, and did his slow, careful and accurate observing and reconstructing of Negroes. He paints the same Negro that a dozen Negro and white literary "geniuses" have painted for at least fifteen years. But instead of pretending that romantic qualities alone can produce character, as his predecessors did, he uses as his basis the suppressed, hard thoughts of Negro workers and serfs, and their children, their deliberate actions squeezed out by these thoughts. He uses romantic attachments as they should be used, for decoration, for embellishment, for somber or brilliant coloring. In other words, he gives us who know Southern Negro life the very substance which in previous stories we have felt the omission of, and had to supply as we read along.

We wonder, however, if Wright by giving all his attention to the Negro who is lynched and beaten is saying that this is the only Negro who possesses a literary problem. Or is he saying that this is the only Negro worth writing about? We recognize the sheer tragedy in the story of a Negro hunted animal who hides under a rock and witnesses his buddy's lynching and in the story of a wife who watches from afar the destruction of her husband after he has killed the white salesman who ravished her. We confess to a suspense so great as to be called helpless. But we wonder if the real, and most deeply dramatic, fight is not in the lives of those thousands who live and trade and sing and fear day by day in the country so vociferously called the white man's, and protected with so much flamboyance. In other words, the essential tragedy of the Negro is in the *threat* under which he lives, not in the fulfillment of it. His essential drama is in his maneuvers to circumvent this threat.

The timid ought to be warned that Wright's solution to the Negro problem is so revolutionary that the chief of circulation in the New York Public Library, for one, has refused to buy the book except for the Harlem branch. His fifth story in this series was refused for the present book and published in a "radical" magazine. He really means his "Uncle Tom is dead!" And yet, it is a purely artistic solution. One may read vicious propaganda into these stories if he so desires, or if he can't help it; but Wright's plots are so constructed and his idealisms so directed that his revolutionary answer is inevitable, after the fashion of all high art. In considering this answer, though, the careful reader will remember that the Negro's position in America is unorthodox for the same reason it is predominantly romantic; and if unorthodox, why not, honorably, revolutionary?

When we stop to weigh what we have written here about Wright, we are frightened at these few simple facts. Has it actually taken so long for America to develop a fiction writer who is "Negro-true?" Isn't he likely to be lonely for a long time yet? Must he be set so far apart from all these students of Negro life, these grandiose penmen and philosophers drenched in African and Aframerican and Afro-Harlem and Afro-Florida and Afro-Charleston tradition, and similar flailers of the air? Indeed he must, and for the same reason that a Cather stands above a Hurst, or a Dutch master above a sign painter. The latter paints to overtake the fancy or to please the eye or to display the prevailing catchy style; the former to make the mind hot with ideas and eventually calm with understanding of the truth.

And there is no better reason for my belief that this book should be read and reread by every person who can get a copy than the consummate art with which this truth is accomplished. If there is any education in literature at all, it is in the way literature suggests how life, with all its vast complexity of things which will and will not mix, can be made to have simple, definite meanings through the chemistry of hard thinking and deep feeling. When that chemistry succeeds, you have literary art; and you have it in Richard Wright without any question. He has no superior in America today as a storyteller. But beyond that, he can take these story facts and construct meanings and ideals which convince and inspire, and inspire even when they do not convince. When he can take a Negro preacher, known for his diplomacy with gouging whites and vacillating Negroes: send him through a mill of trouble which breaks his individual spirit but hardens his social will; and have him, at the end, to mumble out loud, exultingly, "Freedom belongs to the strong!" Richard Wright is on his way toward great art.

William H. L. Tyus. *Memphis Commercial Appeal.*

Unquestionably grossly fictionalized, but made all the more interesting because of it, the four novels included in this volume emphasize the sad plight of the negro when his path crosses that of his white masters. And though the incidents so ably described are without doubt pure imagination of the author, they are so close to the truth that they give a searing insight into the fact that the cards inevitably are stacked against the black man.

Written by a negro, as might be imagined, the book still does not rankle in the mind of the white reader. On the other hand, it provokes only his sympathy. And this is saving grace for a Southerner. There are certain factions in the North who would deliberately seize upon the book and hail its statements and implications just as did the Yankee in the day of Harriet Beecher Stowe's "Uncle Tom's Cabin," a book many believe helped to inflame the North against the South before the War Between the States.

From a solely literary viewpoint, the book is fast moving and exciting. Its staccato dialogue makes for speedy reading with no lulls.

For two reasons, the volume is not for juveniles: (1) It is written in negro dialect readily understandable only to one familiar with negroes, and (2) It makes no effort to avoid obscene language and it makes no bones of sexual tendencies. . . .

This reviewer approached "Uncle Tom's Children" out of pure curiosity. He began reading it with his mind made up that he was not going to enjoy the book. But he became so interested in the story itself and so enthralled at the author's unique style that he completed the entire 317 pages at a single sitting. It is a volume well worth reading.

G. E. M.
(Detroit) *Michigan Chronicle.*

Using several lines from the popular song of a few seasons ago, "Is It True What They Say About Dixie," as introduction for his book, Richard Wright shows in four well-written stories that what they say about Dixie is definitely not true for the Negro. . . .

The stories are set in the South, but not the South of magnolias, honeysuckle vines and happy, singing Negroes. It is the South where oppression and indignities of every sort are the Negro's lot. No horror to which he is subjected has been omitted from these grim stories; lynchings, seduction, beatings, humiliations of every kind are here. It is our hope, probably a vain one, that this book might be read by those who defend, tacitly or otherwise, the treatment the Negro receives in the South.

The title indicates the type of character Mr. Wright has chosen to present. These men are not the servile Uncle Toms of a generation ago, but are willing to face the white man bravely even if death is the result. In each of the stories the principal character defies one or more white men. . . .

In this first book, Richard Wright shows himself an able writer. His prose is swift-moving, vivid and realistic. He has chosen to describe moments of crisis in the lives of four men, omitting any account of what happened before or after. This technique makes for greater dramatic force and intensity. The subject matter of the four stories is fundamentally the same, and the total impression is one of tragedy and horror. Mr. Wright writes simply with no exaggeration for effect, and the reader is constantly aware of his deep sympathy for his characters.

"Uncle Tom's Children" deserves attention not only for the excellent way in which it is written but also for its presentation of certain aspects of Negro life in the South. However, Mr. Wright has not given the total picture. Reading the book straight through as I did, I felt as though I had been given an overdose of tragedy. I believe that the introduction of a few pleasant details, granting that they are rare, might have added to the effectiveness of the book.

Checklist of Additional Reviews

Charlotte News and Courier, March 27, 1938.

Aubrey L. Thomas. *Philadelphia Evening Public Ledger,* March 29, 1938.

Helen B. Parker. *Nashville Banner,* April 2, 1938.

Carl Roberts. *Dayton News,* April 3, 1938.

Harvey Curtis Webster. *Louisville Courier-Journal,* April 3, 1938.

Jack Conroy. *New York Sunday Worker,* April 9, 1938, pp. 6-9.

Arthur Bernon Tourtellot. *Boston Evening Transcript*, April 9, 1938, Book Section, p. 1.

Lexington Herald-Leader, April 10, 1938.

Joseph Henry Jackson. *San Francisco Chronicle,* April 19, 1938.

Work [Workers Alliance of America, Wash. D.C.], 1 (April 23, 1938).

Jackson Daily News, April 26, 1938.

Lewis Gannett. *Book Union Bulletin,* (April 1938), 2-3.

Booklist, 34 (May 1, 1938), 318.

M. L. *Workers Age* [Independent Labor League of America, N.Y.], 7 (May 7, 1938).

Henry Seidel Canby. *Book-of-the-Month-Club News* (May 1938).

Philip Jewett. *Philadelphia Inquirer,* June 18, 1938.

National Educational Outlook Among Negroes, 2 (June 1938).

Worcester Sun-Telegram, July 17, 1938.

Esquire, 10 (August 1938).

Alain Locke. *Opportunity,* 17 (January 1939), 8.

Durham Herald-Sun, October 27, 1940.

August Derleth. *East Side News* (Madison, Wis.), November 7, 1940.

E. B. Garside. *Boston Evening Transcript,* November 9, 1940.

Baltimore Afro-American, November 16, 1940.

B. Mifflin. *Austin Tribune,* November 21, 1940.

Frederic R. Gunsky. *San Francisco Chronicle,* December 2, 1940.

Charles C. Walcutt. *Daily Oklahoman* (Oklahoma City), December 21, 1940.

Notes

NATIVE SON

BY

Richard Wright

Author of

UNCLE TOM'S CHILDREN

Even today is my complaint rebellious,
My stroke is heavier than my groaning.
—Job

HARPER & BROTHERS PUBLISHERS

New York and London

1940

Native Son

Henry Seidel Canby. *Book-of-the-Month-Club News*, February 1940, pp. 2–3.

This powerful and sensational novel is very difficult to describe so as to convey its real purpose and its real strength. But it is important to describe it accurately, because it is certainly the finest novel as yet written by an American Negro—not that it was chosen by the Book-of-the-Month Club just because it was written by a Negro. It would have been chosen for its deep excitement and intense interest whether written by white, yellow, or black. Yet, nevertheless, this is a novel which only a Negro could have written; whose theme is the mind of the Negro we see every day; whose emotion is the emotion of that native born American under the stress of a social situation difficult in the extreme; whose point and purpose are not race war or propaganda of any kind, but to show how a "bad nigger" is made from human material that might have become something very different.

Superficially, *Native Son* is a crime story, adventurous, exciting, often terrible—with two murders, a chase and a gun fight over the roofs of Chicago, a trial, and what might have been, but was not, a rape. It is the old story of a man hunted down by society. But the reader will get through only a few chapters before he realizes that there is something different in this story. Bigger—and we all know Bigger—is no persecuted black saint. His family is a good family, as tenement families go; but he is a bad actor from the first. He is mean; he is a coward; he is on occasion liar, thief, and bully. There is no sentimentalism in the writer who created Bigger and made him chauffeur in the family of a wealthy philanthropist who spent some of the money wrung from Negro tenements on benefits for the race. Bigger is headed toward jail from the first chapter. When Mary Dalton, the flighty daughter of the philanthropist, asks Bigger to help along her intrigue with her Communist lover (also a negrophile), he has no compunctions. But he did not mean to kill her, he did not want to kill her, though he hated patronizing whites. Had her blind mother not come in at the fatal moment, the girl would have slept off her drunkenness, and Bigger would never have got beyond petty crime. With a skill which any master of the detective story might envy, Mr. Wright builds his book on the inevitable and terrifying results of an unpremeditated killing; the burning of the body; the false accusations; the murder of Bigger's Negro girl friend, lest she implicate him; the capture; the trial in which Mr. Max, the defending lawyer, pleads unsuccessfully the cause of a race driven toward crime, against a district attorney needing notoriety for his next election. And finally comes Bigger's confession—not of the murder which was not a murder, and of the rape which was not a rape, but of the obscure inarticulate causes which made him hate, and made him try to make up for his sense of inferiority by aggressive acts against the society in which he lived.

All this highly complicated story is handled with competence by Mr. Wright in a swift narrative style proceeding by staccato dialogue and with rapidly mounting suspense. The characters, too, are fully realized. There is a deadly satire in the portraits of the young radicals. Mary who is killed, and Jan, the Communist, who chooses Bigger to work on, not realizing that this kind of political pity is more offensive to a Negro than color prejudice. And the mob itself is a character, stirred up by sensational newspapers, getting bloodthirsty, wanting to lynch—the mob whose threatening roar is always in the background of the book and of the Negro's mind. Yet even in its characters this is not a vindictive book. Bigger dies without hate for anything, except the obscure circumstances which compelled him to be what he was. Max, his lawyer, with the ancient wisdom of the Jews, pleads for him on the broad basis of an America in grave danger from a conflict of races which only a deeper-going justice can ameliorate. Even the Negro evangelist who tries to bring back Bigger to the emotional religion which has helped so many men and women of his race, is presented with sympathy and pathos.

Indeed, two statements may be made with safety by the most conservative critic about this remarkable novel. No reader, however harrowed by its frank brutalities, will be able to stop in its engrossing story, which coils and mounts until a tale of crude violence broadens into a human tragedy. And no white man—and, I suspect, few Negroes—will finish this narrative without an enlargement of imagination toward the psychological problems of the Negroes in our society—and an appreciable extension of sympathy. This will hold, I prophesy, for South as well as North. Indeed, I suspect that this book and its probings will be less of a surprise to, and more readily understood by, Southerners than by Northerners. Mr. Wright himself was born and educated in Mississippi, and has lived his later life in the North. It is not the ex-slave of the South, or the almost-like-a-white-man Negro of the North, but the essential Negro-in-America of both, that he gets into Bigger and his book.

Let me repeat, this novel is no tract or defense plea. Like *Grapes of Wrath,* it is a fully realized story of unfortunates, uncompromisingly realistic, and quite as human as it is Negro. To the growing list of artistic achievements of a high quality, by a race which is, perhaps, singularly gifted in art, *Native Son* must surely be added, with a star for notable success.

Lewis Gannett. *New York Herald Tribune,* March 1, 1940, p. 17.

Bigger Thomas was a "black ape," a "bad Nigger," a killer. He was a coward, a thief, a bully, a murderer. His crimes were acts of instinctive passion rather than planned villainies, but he regretted none of them; in them he found his only realization of life. And Richard Wright, who tells Bigger's story in "Native son," neither sentimentalizes nor excuses Bigger, though he explains him.

The result is something new in American fiction, and something terrifying; it is not strange that the publishers, a little alarmed at what they had caught in their net, should have invited Dorothy Canfield to write an introduction preparing the reader for the impact of the novel, or that in her foreword she should say that "this novel plumbs blacker depths of human experience than American literature has yet had, comparable only to Dostoievski's revelation of human misery in wrongdoing." What is surprising is that the Book-of-the-Month Club dares to send this powerful book to its hundred thousand members. It may have been influenced toward that courage by memory of its hesitation when, a year ago, it had a chance at John Steinbeck's "Grapes of Wrath"; the public, time proved, had a stronger literary digestion than the club's judges had foreseen.

Two years ago, Harry Scherman, president of the Book-of-the-Month Club; Sinclair Lewis and I served as judges in a contest for the best stories written by a worker on the Federal Writers' Project. We were a bit alarmed by the violence of emotion evident in some of the stories assembled in Richard Wright's "Uncle Tom's Children," but we could not help giving it the prize. I met Mr. Wright afterward; I think I remember telling him sappily that I hoped his next book would be less harrowing. I think he replied vaguely that he would not be sure what would come out next. Well, here is his next book, demonstrating a long wind, a depth and subtlety, a talent for organizing a full-length novel, which were not evident in "Uncle Tom's Children"; and it is a far more harrowing story. "Grapes of Wrath" is gentle by comparison.

This is, I suppose, the story of the boy Richard Wright just missed becoming. Like Bigger Thomas, he was born in Mississippi and never got far in school. His mother was stricken with paralysis during the World War, and Wright was sent to an uncle in Greenwood, Miss. There he so distinguished himself by fighting, lying, stealing and cutting school that he was sent back to a grandfather who predicted that the boy would end on the gallows. Another uncle tried to influence Richard by forcing him into a Seventh Day Adventist school. That, too, failed. Richard Wright, at fifteen, packed his cardboard suitcase and started North.

He learned discipline on a job in Memphis, and drifted on to Chicago. Somewhere he picked up H.L. Mencken's "Book of Prefaces"; reading Mencken made him a potential writer. What made him a real writer is one of those mysteries of genius which no geneticist and no social historian can explain. But somewhere in that shift from truant to creative writer there is another—and a less harrowing—story which I still hope Richard Wright will set down on paper. It is no less, and no more, true a part of the story of the Negro in America than is the story of Bigger Thomas.

Bigger's story begins with a rat fighting for his life in the filthy Chicago tenement where Bigger, his mother, his brother and his sister camp. Bigger fights, all through his life, much like that trapped rat. He lived in a hostile world. He was afraid of it; he suspected deception in any hint of friendship; he was ready to knife his own pal. He had no sense of belonging anywhere. He had done a little robbing when the story opened, and in his heart he had done a little killing. If he had not done more, it was only because he had been too afraid. And the only way he knew to assert his manhood was by conquering that fear.

To Bigger all white folks were enemies. "They got things and we ain't. They do things and we can't." He felt them all the time "right down here in my stomach." They weren't really people; "they were a sort of great natural force, like a stormy sky looming overhead or like a deep swirling river stretching suddenly at one's feet in the dark."

So Bigger couldn't understand white folks who tried to be "friends of the colored people." He got a job with a man who had given millions of dollars to enterprises in behalf of colored people. But Bigger had no understanding of that man's mind; he distrusted him all the more because of his friendliness. Still less could he understand that man's "parlor pink" daughter, Mary, and Mary's Communist friend, Jan. Jan bade Bigger shake hands with him; "don't say 'sir' to me," he said; "I'll call you 'Bigger' and you'll call me 'Jan'." Mary smiled and said: "It's all right, Bigger. Jan means it." Bigger, puzzled, was angry. "Damn her soul to hell," he said to himself. "Was she laughing at him? Were they making fun of him? What was it that they wanted? Why couldn't they leave him alone? He wasn't bothering them. Yes, anything could happen with people like these."

Anything did happen. Bigger was shaken by terror, and he acted as men act, under the influence of terror—primitively, cruelly, violently. He killed. He was a rat against a wall. In killing, for the first time in his life, he became important; in crime he acquired his first sense of a kind of freedom. A mob howled for his blood; the atmosphere of the crowd in the courtroom taught Bigger that he was not alone; his death was to be used as a bloody symbol of fear to be waved before the eyes of the black world. In his prison cell and in the courtroom, touched for the first time by a lawyer who appears as a sort of Jewish Clarence Darrow, Bigger grew into humanity. He began to understand the springs of hate, in others as well as himself.

Dorothy Canfield says that there is no finer effect in Dostoievski than the last page of "Native Son." Henry Seidel Canby says that "Native Son" is "certainly the finest novel as yet written by an American Negro." It is more than that. It is a super-shocker; it is also a deeply compassionate and understanding novel. As nearly as anything can be, it is the "Grapes of Wrath" of 1940.

May Cameron. "Prize-Winner Pens Novel." "Richard Wright Tells a Fury Packed Story." *New York Post*. March 1, 1940, p. 19.

An intense and powerful novel not only of American Negro life but of life in America appears today in "Native Son" by Richard Wright, whose first book, "Uncle Tom's Children," won first prize in a contest sponsored by Story magazine a couple of years ago. A March selection of the Book-of-the-Month Club, "Native Son" moves for the most part with tremendous force and speed in telling us the tale of the last few weeks on earth of Bigger Thomas, a twenty-year old Chicago Negro.

Superficially, Bigger was a mean, shiftless, unscrupulous youth. Fundamentally he was that tragic misfit, a rebellious, unenlightened, inarticulate black man in a white man's world. He had no patience with the hymn-singing, church-going colored folk who find in religion some sort of recompense for the long hours of underpaid drudgery doled out by the whites. He knew the truth, and the futility, of his sweetheart Bessie's plaint: "All I do is work, work like a dog! From morning till night. I ain't got no happiness. . . . I just work! I ain't had no happiness, no nothing. I just work. I'm black and I work and don't bother nobody. . . ."

There had been things Bigger thought he might like to do. Once he wanted to join the army. But "Hell, it's a Jim Crow army," he said. "All they want a black man for is to dig ditches. And in the navy, all I can do is wash dishes and scrub floors."

Whether there may or may not be a trace of self-pitying defeatism in this thinking, Bigger's fear and hatred of the white man's world increased. He became a petty thief and a bully. At home, he lived on relief with his mother, brother and sister until the relief bureau offered him a job and the alternative of taking it or starving with his family. Cursing the narrowness of the choice, Bigger took the job.

He became chauffeur to the Daltons, a white family consisting of a wealthy philanthropist, his blind wife and a dilletante-Communist daughter. (Mr. Dalton owned apartment houses in the Black Belt, rented rat-ridden rooms at eight dollars per week each, and contributed heavily to Negro charities; the first time young Mary Dalton saw Bigger she asked him whether he belonged to a union and if not, why?)

With mounting suspense, Mr. Wright spins his plot. Bigger's first task turned out to be that of driving Mary to a rendezvous with her Communist sweetheart, Jan. Eager to show their lack of prejudice, the two whites forced themselves upon the terrified Negro boy, sat with him in the front seat, made him eat with them in a Negro restaurant, made him swig rum with them from the same bottle. When Bigger at last drove Mary home, she was in a drunken stupor. He had to carry her to her room. There, accidentally, and yet in a sense inevitably, her murder occurred.

Then, in a sense of sheer but uncontrolled horror, came the disposal of her body, detection, flight, the murder of Bessie, to whom Bigger had betrayed himself, a man-hunt through empty buildings and across the snowy rooftops of Chicago, capture, trial and sentence while troops held back a howling mob outside the courtroom windows.

Why did Bigger commit these murders? He himself fumbled for an answer: "For a little while I was free. I was doing something. . . . I killed 'em because I was scared and mad. But I been scared and mad all my life and after I killed the first woman, I wasn't scared no more for a little while." Then, finally: "I didn't know I was really alive in this world until I felt things hard enough to kill for em. . . ."

With consummate psychological skill Mr. Wright analyses the dim compulsion of this spiritually sick young man. And he shows us how, on Bigger's last living day, he found some sort of answer to the life that was no longer his.

Charles Poore. *New York Times*, March 1, 1940, p. 19.

Richard Wright's "Native Son," an enormously stirring novel of crime and punishment, is published this morning. It is a story to trouble midnight and the noon's repose, as Mr. Eliot once said about another matter, and to haunt the imagination many days.

It was widely praised long before publication. Indeed, few other recent novels have been preceded by more advance critical acclamation, or lived up to the expectations they aroused so well. Mr. Wright is a Negro. His novel concerns a young Negro, Bigger Thomas, who twice commits murder before your eyes, and the whole dark background of his crimes. It is an extrordinarily difficult task he has undertaken—on the Dostoievskian scale—and the praise is soundly based on his accomplishment as a novelist.

Edward Weeks, editor of The Atlantic Monthly, calls "Native Son" "a performance of great talent—powerful, disturbing, unquestionably authentic." We'll question the authenticity of Bigger Thomas's ability to discuss the wider implications of his tragic destiny so expertly. But that is another matter. Henry Seidel Canby calls it "the finest novel yet written by an American Negro"—which it is, without a doubt. It would be a fine novel no matter who wrote it: though, to perpetrate an Irish bull in all sincerity, only a Negro could have written "Native Son." In a special introduction Dorothy Canfield Fisher makes the parallel with Dostoievsky, observes that this novel "can be guaranteed to harrow up any human heart capable of compassion or honest self-questioning," and shows how the story of Bigger Thomas bears out the studies in racial barriers carried out by the American Youth Commission under the chairmanship of Owen D. Young.

The praise has been cumulative. It gathered while "Native Son" awaited publication after it had been chosen (with Conrad Richter's "The Trees". . .) by the Book-of-the-Month Club for March. Finally, we are told that the Guggenheim awards committee read "Native Son" in manuscript, and, on the strength of its strength, gave Mr. Wright—whose earlier book of stories, "Uncle Tom's Children," was also a prizewinner—one of its fellowships.

Mr. Wright drives his story forward at a furious yet skillfully controlled pace. The full drama is unfolded in just about two weeks. There is first of all the prophetic killing of a rat in the room where Bigger, his mother, his sister and his brother live in quarreling, desperate squalor. Then Bigger, who has a bad name as a braggart living by shady devices, goes out to meet the poolroom gang environment provides. He plans a hold-up he is afraid to carry out. To hide his cowardice he terrorizes one of his friends.

You see his character. That is the point. Mr. Wright is champion of a race, not defender of an individual wrongdoer. Bigger gets a job as chauffeur in the house of Mr. Dalton, who is a philanthropist toward Negroes and owner of many Negro tenements. Mary Dalton, the daughter of the house, and her friend Jan, a supernally noble radical, make him drink with them. Through an accident, Bigger kills Mary Dalton. That is the first murder.

There is a gruesome dismemberment to hide the crime. Bigger thinks of demanding money, and makes his girl, Bessie, help him. His crime is discovered. After that there is the flight, the second murder, deliberate and brutal, the manhunt spreading terror over the whole South Side, then the spectacular capture and the day of reckoning in court for all concerned.

It is a long time since we've read a new novelist who had such command of the technique and resources of the novel. Mr. Wright's method is generally Dreiserian; but he has written his American tragedy in a notably firm prose. He knows how to tell a story. He knows how to develop a character, how to show influences playing on a man or a situation. Reflection blends into action. Accents and intonations are caught. Ideas are dramatized with concrete and inescapble images. And dialogue goes crackling down the page.

Bigger is a symbol. But, as we have suggested, he is able to express what he symbolizes more fluently than seems natural, considering how clearly Mr. Wright has made us see his life. There is a constant, probing inquiry into the state of the world that creates people like Bigger Thomas. We do not doubt it. We cannot. But we can and do doubt that it could flow so coherently through Bigger's mind. It's better left to the lawyer's summation in the court-room scene.

"Native Son" is, in truth, one of those compelling books to which people pay the uneasy tribute of saying their picture is impressive but overdrawn. That places Richard Wright in very good company—from Charles Dickens to John Steinbeck. After all, we do not lack stories of quaint Negro life.

Apart from the ideas that give it volume, force and scope, "Native Son" has some magnificently realized scenes: in the early part, where Bigger, a stranger and afraid, as Houseman said, in a world he never made, gropes for freedom from the walls that hold him; in the flight across the roofs and the stand high over the world, in the jail where processions of people come to see him, at the inquest and in the howling mob outside the court. The measure in which it shakes a community is the measure of its effectiveness.

Howard Mumford Jones. "Uneven Effect." *Boston Evening Transcript*, March 2, 1940, book section, p. 1.

"Native Son" enters the publishing world with such a fanfare of trumpets and beating of drums as somewhat to abash quiet folk who are looking for a good book to read. It is a Book of the Month Club selection. The dust jacket is occupied by a long quote from Henry Seidel Canby, and Henry certainly do let himself go: "highly complicated story," "handled with competence," "swift narrative style proceeding by staccato dialogue," "rapidly mounting suspense," "the characters, too, are fully realized." Mr. Edward A. Weeks, not unknown in these parts, is Mr. Canby's fellow traveler on the book jacket. He announces: "It has us all by the ears." A throwaway from Harper and Brothers declares that the author's life is as interesting as one of his own novels, and speaks darkly of the purchase of a razor at one stage of his development. Then there is a preface by Dorothy Canfield Fisher. I usually admire Mrs. Fisher, but she has constructed the worst written sentence of the year: "The other point I would like to make is that the author shows genuine literary skill in the construction of his novel in giving so few pages to show us in concrete detail the exact ways in which American society constantly stimulates the powerful full-blooded human organism to action, which is as constantly forbidden to him by our mores." I shall come back to that sentence presently.

The first impact of the novel on me was one of great power. In retrospect, however, I find that this sense of power fades, and, a week after having read it, I cannot remember the name of a single character except that of the hero-villain, and I have only a vague memory of anybody's personality except his.

I am compelled, contrary to rule, to reveal the plot in order to discuss the novel. It concerns a colored boy named Bigger. The novel opens admirably in a single room in the morning. In that room a colored family gets up, kills rats, dresses, and has breakfast. It is soon evident that Bigger is a bad nigger—I use the term without offence in its technical sense. He drifts down to a poolroom, almost kills a friend with a razor and almost commits a robbery. He is then engaged as a chauffeur for a white family known for its sympathy for Negroes. The daughter of the house is a "radical." She insists on being driven with a male Communist friend by Bigger to a Negro restaurant, where she and the Communist get more or less tight. The Communist leaves, Bigger takes the girl home, helps her to her room and there, fearful lest the family discover him, he smothers her. He then burns the body in the furnance. Native wit and white stupidity for a time fend off suspicion, but his refusal to shake the ashes arouses the interest of some newspaper reporters, and his guilt is surmised. He flees with his Negro sweetheart, whom he kills, is trapped on a roof, pleads guilty, is defended by a lawyer of vaguely radical tendencies, and is eventually electrocuted.

There are three tests for a tale of this sort. Is its plot well constructed and does it maintain interest? Are the characters credible? Does the story spring out of, or illustrate, any thesis?

Well, all murder stories are exciting, and when a black man kills a white girl, most of us, to put it mildly, are stirred. When in addition he threatens to carve his friend and bashes in the head of his sweetheart with a brick, a pleasant titillation of horror is felt along the spine. The pursuit-and-capture motive is sure-fire stuff. In melodrama, moreover, we expect villainy to be punished. Bigger is punished.

But what is "highly complicated" about this? The simplest of narrative techniques is employed—straight-line narrative as in "Robinson Crusoe." We begin with Bigger in an excellent domestic scene, and we follow him to the hour of his death. The story is about as complicated as "Three Blind Mice." It is evident to experienced readers from the beginning that retribution is bound to overtake Bigger, and the only question is how long the author can keep him from capture. If this be "rapidly mounting suspense," it is rapidly mounting suspense bought in the oldest of literary markets. As for the "staccato dialogue," it is often excellent, but the conversation bears about the same relation to the narrative in "Native Son" that it bears to the narrative in "The Three Musketeers."

What about the characters? There are none except Bigger, and Bigger wavers between being a poor colored boy and being a monster of amorality. Most of the time he is a monster of amorality whose proceedings we contemplate with horror, and we are startled in the last quarter of the tale to discover that all this time the author has been thinking of him as a misunderstood colored boy. The other characters exist either (a) to be knocked down or (b) to be set up in order to illustrate something.

What do they illustrate? A thesis. Mrs. Fisher's infractious sentence darkly hints that Bigger's character is the result of American society arousing desires in the "powerful fullblooded human organism" which it does not satisfy. Mrs. Fisher of course does not mean that American society incites the "powerful full-blooded human organism" to murder and then disobligingly gives it no opportunity to kill. She has in mind the wrongs done by the white race to the colored man, and she thinks (and the author thinks) that Bigger's criminal career is traceable to this cause.

But the essential wrong done the colored race is not that it drives Negroes to murder, but that it does not drive them even to work. They are unemployed and stifled. Bigger, however, gets a job.

At this point the author drives him to murder. But the murder does not follow from this thesis, but from another thesis—the same thesis that Dreiser set forth in "The Hand of the Potter" and "The American Tragedy." It is determinism. Men do what they are born to do. Bigger happens to be a colored man. But if he had been of any other race, he would still have acted as his nature compelled him to act. He did not murder the white girl to avenge the black race; he murdered both girls because he was born that way. His sociological background does not "explain" the murder in terms of race-relationships, though his inheritance may "explain" his character. To say that American society incited this "powerful full-blooded human organism to action" is to confuse humanitarianism with determinism.

The novel seems to me imperfect and uneven. If it were all like its opening scenes, it would be a moving study of Negro life. If it were simply melodrama, it would, being shortened, have great emotional punch. If it were all like its last quarter, it would be dull propaganda. As it is, one is sympathetic with Bigger, then one shudders at him, and, lastly, one is glad when he is dead just as one is glad when the villains in Victor Hugo are dead. At times Mr. Wright shows a Dostoievsky-like insight; at other times he writes like a ten-twent-and-thirt melodrama.

Harry Hansen. *New York World-Telegram,* March 2, 1940.

Richard Wright's novel, *Native Son,* is the big book news of the moment—a story that packs a tremendous punch, smashing like a big fist through the windows of our complacent lives. A story so horrible that it makes readers shudder, it also carries so much truth and justice in the telling that we read it to the end with the rapt attention that we gave Theordore Dreiser's *An American Tragedy* over 15 years ago.

A wide hearing is gained for the book on publication because the editors of the Book-of-the-Month Club wisely chose it as one of two books for March distribution to its members. This act will do more than put a new and powerful novelist before the national public; it will start people wondering what Wright's chief character Bigger Thomas might have become if white society had not warped and stunted him.

Native Son is not solely the story of a Negro who does wrong. It is a story of a bewildered lad who had small chance and incentive to fight.

Bigger Thomas is partly a lad of tangled emotions, partly a fellow who thinks. Perhaps the novelist is a bit confused about him; at least in places Bigger seems to understand more than he should. He grows up in a household so poor that one room, infested with rats, suffices for him, his mother, sister and brother. The white folks have everything, go everywhere; the aviator in the sky is white. "They don't let us do nothing," is the conclusion of the black boys. Bigger is ready to break the law, but his associates are moved by fear. And even Bigger "was divided and pulled against himself."

Through circumstances he takes a job as chauffeur for the Dalton family, after Mr. Dalton has assured himself that Bigger won't steal. Then Bigger meets their daughter, Mary, and through Mary he meets her boy friend, Jan. These two are playing at being Communists, and they promptly make a pal out of Bigger, taking him to dinner with them. Here Wright has built up a terrible picture of the provocation the white race gives to black boys to misbehave. But the point is that Bigger doesn't misbehave, despite the chumminess of Mary and Jan, even when Mary gets drunk. Bigger takes her home, and the ensuing tragedy, when he inadvertently suffocates her in order to keep her from betraying her condition to her mother, grows out of the situation.

Here Mr. Wright does his best for Bigger and incidentally drives home the white man's immense responsibility. Afterward Bigger reacts to the crime and its results because of his early conditioning. He tries to exploit the crime by writing an extortion note; he drags his mistress down with him; he feels himself pursued and acts as does a man "when he feels he must defend himself against, or adapt himself to, the total natural world in which he lives." The author has put into the mouth of Bigger's lawyer the more formal arguments on behalf of the blacks who are stripped of opportunity and devoid of hope, asserting that the hate and fear that lead a lad like Bigger to commit crimes are "woven by our civilization into the very structure of his consciousness."

Maybe Bigger's experience doesn't completely illuminate the arguments that are in the author's mind. But Mr. Wright has said enough, and with such force that many will see in this more than the narrative of a criminal career. It is a story of brutal deeds, but I have read many stories that seemed much more brutal because the story teller was completely unconcerned. Richard Wright has his heart in this tale. That is patent from the quotation from the Book of Job that he puts on the title page: "Even today is my complaint rebellious, my stroke is heavier than my groaning." We have had other examples of his smashing writing—in his long story *Uncle Tom's Children,* which won the WPA contest conducted by Story in 1938, and in the story titled "Fire and Cloud" which won one of the O. Henry Memorial prizes in the same year. . . .

Clifton Fadiman. *New Yorker,* 16 (March 2, 1940), 52–53.

Richard Wright's *Native Son* is the most powerful American novel to appear since *The Grapes of Wrath*. It has numerous defects as a work of art, but it is only in retrospect that they emerge, so overwhelming is its central drive, so gripping its mounting intensity. No one, I think, except the most unconvertible Bourbons, the completely callous, or the mentally deficient, can read it without an enlarged and painful sense of what it means to be a Negro in the United States of America seventy-seven years after the Emancipation Proclamation. *Native Son* does for the Negro what Theodore Dreiser in *An American Tragedy* did a decade and a half ago for the bewildered, inarticulate American white. The two books are similar in theme, in technique, in their almost paralyzing effect on the reader, and in the large, brooding humanity, quite remote from special pleading, that informs them both. *Native Son,* as Henry Seidel Canby says in his illuminating comment printed on the jacket, "is certainly the finest novel as yet written by an American Negro." True enough, and it is a remarkable novel no matter how much or how little melanin its author happens to have in his skin.

Bigger Thomas is a twenty-year-old black boy, living with his mother and sister in one room in a Chicago tenement. Bigger is, when the story opens, already a "bad nigger" with a reform school past. Dimly he knows why he is bad, morose, a thief, a bully. It is because the pressure of his environment makes it difficult for him to be anything else. Were his temperment more malleable, he might become totally passive, like his mother and sister. Were he endowed with shrewdness, or talent, he might rise in the social scale, as a small and brilliant percentage of his race is doing. But something in him demands an outlet other than mechanical, reflex living, other than the simple pieties of a consolatory religion. As Dorothy Canfield Fisher makes clear in her fine introduction, society holds out to him a picture of what the American citizen should be—independent, decent, courageous—and then prevents him from doing anything toward the realization of these ideals. The result of this frustration is a neurosis. The result of Bigger's neurosis is, as so often happens, the most horrible violence. Dimly, Bigger feels all this. "He knew that the moment he allowed what his life meant to enter fully into his consciousness, he would either kill himself or somebody else."

This surly, half-maddened, groping Negro is given a chauffeur's job in the home of the Negrophile Daltons, Chicago millionaires, "liberals," nice people. Within twenty-four hours he has unpremeditatedly murdered young Mary Dalton, stuffed her corpse into the furnance, and is ready to understand the real meaning of his life. This Bigger is a stupid fool; he does everything calculated to get himself caught; he murders again, this time his woman, Bessie. But his stupidities are not only the effect of his rudimentary intelligence; they are the almost inevitable blind reactions of the neurotic rat, a rat cornered by a society it fears and cannot understand. "To Bigger and his kind white people were not really people; they were a sort of great natural force, like a stormy sky looming overhead, or like a deep swirling river stretching suddenly at one's feet in the dark."

Caught after a breathtaking fight and chase over the rooftops of a block of Chicago tenements, Bigger is imprisoned and brought to trial. He is defended by Max, a labor lawyer, through whose compassionate eyes we are made to see, very slowly, the larger implications of Bigger's monstrous deeds. There is a long scene in the prison in which he tries to explain to Max why he did what he did, and an even more extraordinary one in which Max traces before the court the jungle tangle of motives that have made Bigger the murderer he unquestionably is. There is no hope for Bigger. He is sentenced to death. With the electric chair but a few days away, Bigger thinks out his life, a life which has not yet begun, which has not been permitted to begin. "I hurt folks 'cause I felt I had to; that's all. They was crowding me too close: they wouldn't give me no room. . . . I didn't know I was really alive in this world until I felt things hard enough to kill for 'em." That last sentence, quite terrible, one feels, is not an "excuse" for Bigger, but it is an indictment of a society, itself fearful, blind, and groping, which has not yet learned how not to produce Biggers, whether white or black. Max, no sentimentalist, no Negrophile, sums it up in court when he says, "He has murdered many times, but there are no corpses. . . This Negro boy's entire attitude toward life is a *crime!*"

Mr. Wright is too explicit. He says many things over and over again. His characterizations of upper-class whites are paper-thin and confess unfamiliarity. I think he overdoes his melodrama from time to time. He is not a finished writer. But the two absolute necessities of the first-rate novelist—passion and intelligence—are in him. That he received the most rudimentary schooling, that for most of his life he has been an aimless itinerant worker are interesting facts but of no great moment in judging his book.

Native Son is no whining plea for "generosity," nor is it a bellicose proletarian tract. Mr. Wright has obviously been deeply affected by the labor movement, but he does not base the argument of his horrifying story upon any facile thesis of economic determinism. He goes deeper than that, often into layers of consciousness where only Dostoevski and a few others have penetrated, into the recess of "a human soul in hell because it is sick with a deadly spiritual sickness," if I may quote Mrs. Fisher once more.

The comparison with *An American Tragedy* comes to my mind again for the two books are hewn out of the same block and indeed tell almost the same story, with a half-accidental murder as the central episode in both cases. Dreiser's book is greater, more monumental, more controlled, more knowledgeable, but *Native Son* is apt to have much the same effect on any reader who is not afraid to go through its dark and bloody pages. I say "afraid" advisedly, for this is strong meat. It is not merely a book but a deep experience.

Jonathan Daniels. *Saturday Review of Literature*, 21 (March 2, 1940), 5.

For terror in narrative, utter and compelling, there are few pages in modern American literature which will compare with this story of the few little days which carried Bigger Thomas, Negro from Mississippi in Chicago, from bullying cowardice through murder to the position of black fiend against the hating world hunted across rooftops in the snow. It is authentic, powerful writing, about a young Negro driven by his cramped destiny to crime, but only flung up by accident and anger as quarry for roaring fury. But I doubt that Bigger Thomas proves any more about the Negro than he does about the world. Man's inhumanity to man did not begin in Mississippi. It did not end with Bigger Thomas in Chicago. What Mr. Wright has written again and wonderfully well, in terms of a member of his own race, is the very ancient story of all criminals who have advanced through the cruel caprices of environment into the frenzy of unequal enmity against a continually imperfect world. Undoubtedly, however, with the wise choice of an unpopular symbol Mr. Wright has pointed in the case of the Negro the place where with deepest unreason we shape the criminal we kill.

The story of Bigger Thomas is the story of a rat. He may be, as Dorothy Canfield Fisher suggests in a brief introduction to the stirring story, the blocked and frenzied rat in the psychopathic laboratory of the world. He is also what a good many of us call a rat when we speak of the Bigger Thomases who recur in our civilization. In his story of Bigger's crimes and flight Mr. Wright does not make him anything else. Indeed, to begin with, he emphasizes the boy's furtive and ugly cowardice better in his attack on a Negro member of his petty poolroom gang than in any act against the surrounding and constricting white world.

Nevertheless Mr. Wright skillfully delivers our sympathies to Bigger. We feel the constricting white world around him. We share his sullen timidity as he enters the rich white world as chauffeur. We resent with him the insensitive fraternizing of the communist Jan Erlone and the rich radical Mary Dalton, for whose accidental murder after an evening of drinking he died. We stand in terror with him across the slow questioning hours beyond Mary's disappearance. And we run with him when the remnants of Mary Dalton's bones are found in the ashes of the furnace where he burned her. Our fear is even on his side when he follows accidental murder with a deliberate attempt to extort money by a kidnapping note to the rich and conventionally kind parents of the girl he killed—as it is when he kills his own colored sweetheart in the frenzy of flight. The cowardice as well as the sympathy which is in us all runs with the rat. We are all caught; the holes we might flee into are stopped. And the police and the mob which come in roaring search behind sirens and shouting represent the wild fury of our own world.

In the almost aching narrative which carries Bigger to his capture, Mr. Wright has written his story with an objectivity which is irresistible. He is the story-teller and the story-teller alone, though one who shocks our minds and squeezes our hearts. And beyond that flight Bigger's story goes on with power in the ordered violence of the law's processes. But even though skillfully written, the preaching comes, the tract emerges. In the satire both of the brutally ambitious district attorney and of the brutally sensational journalism, as well as in the almost mystical plea for Bigger's life by the wise radical Jewish lawyer who would identify Bigger's crime with the guilt of us all, there is a slowing of pace toward solemnity and almost—not quite—to sentimentality.

As a Southerner I may be suspect, but I think this book is better as a headlong, hard-boiled narrative than as any preaching about race relations in America, North or South. Certainly no sensible Southerner will deny the authenticity of Mr. Wright's picture of the plight of his race. But not only Negro boys in pool rooms and slums in Chicago feel caught and find a distorted manhood in violence. The rules of an insensitive world may be more binding, more hope-denying among them. But every order creates its rats and rebels and every civilization—so far in existence—deserves them. Bigger Thomas, for Vermont, for Mississippi, for Chicago, is a symbol of man's failure and, in his fear of contemplating it, the object of his frenzy, his cruelty, and his hate. He is not pretty. But he is the child of our living in this land.

Milton Rugoff. "Feverish Dramatic Intensity." *New York Herald Tribune Books,* March 3, 1940, p. 5.

It is difficult to write temperately of a book which abounds in such excitement, in so much that is harrowing, and in so profound an understanding of human frailty. The first extraordinary aspect of *Native Son* is that it approaches the tragedy of a race not through an "average" member but through a criminal who commits such atrocities as are dealt with only in the most sensational tabloids. Addressing a world which will not perhaps be affected by anything less, this book speaks with a voice of horror calculated to pierce even the thickest skin.

As a story it is above all unflaggingly exciting. For almost from the moment we meet him there hovers around Bigger Thomas an air of suppressed violence and emotional tension of the most ominous sort. Whether in the rat-infested tenement where he lives with his mother, brother and sister or among his pals in the pool parlor, he is like a vessel that keeps boiling over, and promises, some day when clamped too tight, to explode. Bigger Thomas is 250 years of Negro frustration incarnate. He is filled with fear and uncertainty for himself, and with hate for the white men around him. Instinctively he learns that the one thing that can give him confidence and a sense of power is the act of transgression. The bolder it is, the more adequate.

But this states in static terms what *Native Son* presents with a dramatic intensity that is almost feverish. When Bigger boils over at first he merely snarls at his nagging long-suffering mother, or abuses a crony. When he explodes, when all the pent-up fear and hate of his own dark life and all his racial memory erupts, he commits the most heinous deed that an American black can commit. The explosion comes the first night that he goes as chauffeur to the Daltons. Once he has struck out successfully at his white enemies, Bigger undergoes every emotional extreme from exultation and catharsis to quaking dread.

What follows is sensational in the extreme. Whirled in a maelstrom of warring instincts, Bigger burns the body, frantically tries sending a ransom note, and then flees when the girl's bones are discovered. His visit to his sweetheart—violence now is the only way he can stave off terror—and his mad flight through abandoned tenements and over snow-covered roof tops with the whole inflamed city howling at his heels is not meant for queasy stomachs.

There is much here that may be simply the excitement of violence or the fascination of the morbid, but in the end each act is traced to a significant reflex, and all these, finally, to the social set-up that conditioned it. Like a diver locked with an octopus, Wright wrestles on and on with the chaos that is Bigger's reaction to life, until he has laid bare every fibre and nerve and, at the last, its very heart. Although from the first page we are kept vividly aware of Bigger as the inevitable product of his environment, it is in the last third of the book, in the events that follow his capture—the lurid trial and his defense by a radical attorney—that *Native Son* graduates from one individual's pathology to the whole tragedy of the Negro spirit in a white world.

The aftermath of Bigger's superhuman exertions is apathy; he spurns even religion because he knows it as something meant to lull his people into submission. The one who finally reaches him is the Jewish lawyer who comes to his aid. Against the travesty which is the state's case, the lawyer's defense is an attempt to show how society made Bigger what he is. Through his tongue, *Native Son* strikes with all its strength. It does not beg; it indicts. It hits even those like the Daltons who give millions to Negroes; for even they sanction discrimination. It bends no knees, it asks no pity; it seeks to scourge.

Part of Wright's triumph is that we know without being told that fathoms beneath Bigger's terrifying public personality lies a core of trembling flesh within which rots the seed of the man who might have been. Once, in a quite wonderful scene, this comes to the surface—facing the chair and surprised out of himself by the lawyer's plea for him, Bigger breaks through the great wall of his mute pain and reaches out to his defender in the most moving of human gestures. Elsewhere one may feel that a novel which relies too heavily on frantic excitement and abnormal situations cannot reach the largest emotions, that high tragedy cannot be wrought from horror and hate alone. However, in such a scene—and there are several almost as good—the impact is overwhelming.

The faults of the book should be recognized; it is more than once guilty of melodrama, adding artificial excitement to a sufficiency of the natural kind; it heaps up complications beyond the reader's powers of assimilation; occasionally the plot skates on thin ice; and several times Bigger's confusion seems to baffle even his creator—but in the end these all seem easy to overlook, negligible imperfections on the surface of an extraordinary story movingly told. If the tests of a memorable novel are that it engage the reader completely, move him profoundly and constitute a revelatory intellectual experience, then *Native Son* will not soon be forgotten.

Peter Monro Jack. "A Tragic Novel of Negro Life in America." *New York Times Book Review*, March 3, 1940, pp. 2, 20.

A ready way to show the importance of this novel is to call it the Negro "American Tragedy" and to compare it roughly with Dreiser's masterpiece. Both deal seriously and powerfully with the problem of social maladjustment, with environment and individual behavior, and subsequently with crime and punishment. Both are tragedies and Dreiser's white boy and Wright's black boy are equally killed in the electric chair not for being criminals—since the crime in each case was unpremeditated—but for being social misfits. The pattern in both books is similar: the family, the adolescent, the lure of money and sex, fortuitous events, murder, trial and death. The conclusion in both is that society is to blame, that the environment into which each was born forced upon them their crimes, that they were the particular victims of a general injustice.

The startling difference in Mr. Wright's "Native Son" is that the injustice is a racial, not merely a social, one. Dreiser's Clyde Griffiths represents a social "complex" that could be reasonably taken care of. Mr. Wright's Bigger Thomas is far beyond and outside of helpful social agencies. He represents an *impasse* rather than a complex, and his tragedy is to be born into a black and immutable minority race, literally, in his own words, "Whipped before you born." Mr. Wright allows Bigger a brief moment of illumination into his hopeless condition before he is finally whipped out of the world.

It will be obvious, then, that Mr. Wright has the simpler and more melodramatic story. Where Dreiser broods slowly and patiently over the intricate social scene, Mr. Wright leaps at the glaring injustice of the racial code, takes it by the throat and spills blood in every direction. His story is direct, lurid and alarming; in effect it is the bloodiest and most brutal story of the year; it makes the reader realize and respond to, as he has probably never done before, the actual, dangerous status of the Negro in America.

The narrative of Bigger's life begins with a symbolic incident worth remarking on. He is 20 years old living in a one-room tenement apartment in Chicago's South Side Black Belt, with his mother, his young sister Vera and a younger brother Buddy; they pay $8 rent a week; they are on relief. Bigger's first job when he wakes on the morning of his story is to kill a huge black rat that has got into the room. His intent destruction of the rat is a characteristic act. Later in the day we see him in a poolroom savagely attacking one of his gang as they are planning a holdup. Fear of the consequences drives him into this assertive brutality. It makes him feel easier to hit something. His obscure fears are replaced for the moment by the exhilaration of mere physical power. But so far this might be the story of any moral coward, black or white, who tries to turn himself into a tough braggart, an ordinary and rather contemptible item in any social worker's casebook.

It is later in the day when Bigger turns up to the job where the relief people have sent him, as chauffeur to one of Chicago's big executive types of the benevolent kind. This Mr. Dalton has given millions for social welfare, earmarked particularly for the Negro cause, for the National Association for the Advancement of Colored People, although most of it has dribbled into ping-pong tables in exemplary social clubs and the like. Bigger knows nothing about this, nor does he know that a good part of Mr. Dalton's money for charity comes from the exorbitant rents Dalton charges the Negroes to live in the overcrowded, rat-infested tenements that he owns in the Black Belt—in part, from the very room Bigger had left that morning. Bigger gets the job easily, and all the more easily because his record includes an early sentence for thievery to reform school. The Daltons plan to reform him still more. Before her marriage Mrs. Dalton had been a school mistress.

On the night of the first day Bigger is to drive the daughter Mary to a university lecture. . . . How Bigger inadvertently murdered Mary that same night can be told only in the words that Mr. Wright uses. The necessary point is that he found he had killed her out of fear, out of his certain knowledge that he would be suspected (unjustly) of having raped the girl. . . .

This is the beginning and end of Bigger's fatal history. The body he burns in the furnace, the head cut off with a hatchet because he cannot force it in, the exhaust fan switched on to clear the air of the basement of the smell of burning flesh. Bigger's mind reaches a rapid solution. As a Negro he will be the first suspect, but Jan, the Communist, he considers, is almost an equal object of mob hatred. He has been told by the politicians that the Reds are the dirtiest kind of criminals; he can only throw the blame on Jan by asserting that Jan also went home with the girl, he can even collect kidnapping money on the pretense that Mary is still alive. This, one might say, is a typically criminal mind, but it is Mr. Wright's purpose to show it as a typical kind of social and racial conditioning. Bigger's crime is discovered. He commits another crime (this time merely the murder of his Negro mistress) to cover his tracks, but it is now only a matter of time between his flight and his fate. A Jewish Communist lawyer makes a brilliant speech in his defense, but there is nothing to be done save an attempt at explanation.

What Mr. Wright has done with this sensational criminal story is extremely interesting. Dorothy Canfield Fisher, who writes a preface for the book, explains Bigger partly in terms of the neuroses and psychopathic upsets in animals that we have read about in the research-psychology journals. Bigger, then, in a sense is scarcely more percipient than the rat he had killed at the beginning of the story. Mrs. Fisher continues with an excerpt from Owen D. Young's National Youth Commission's report, couched in the usual maze of language: "conclusive evidence that large percentages of Negro youth by virtue of their combined handicap of racial barriers and low social position subtly reflect in their own personality-traits minor or major distortions or deficiencies which compound their problem of personality adjustment in American society." What Mr. Wright has done is to turn this dry phraseology into the living language of today, into a person, not a personality adjustment, into a scene, a drama, a memorable experience.

It will be argued, and I think with truth, that his character, Bigger, is made far too articulate, that he explains much too glibly in the latter part of the story how he came to meet his fate: "seems sort of natural-like, me being here facing that death chair. Now I come to think of it, it seems like something like this just had to be." Later he has romanticized and rationalized himself into the declaration that "What I killed for must've been good! . . . It must have been good! When a man kills, it's for something . . . I didn't know I was really alive in this world until I felt things hard enough to kill for 'em." This, I believe, is so much romantic nonsense. Dreiser was wiser in allowing the reader to think out Clyde Griffiths in his own realistic terms; he did not interfere too much in the interpretation of his character. Mr. Wright does spoil his story at the end by insisting on Bigger's fate as representative of the whole Negro race and making Bigger himself say so. But this is a minor fault in a good cause. The story is a strong and powerful one and it alone will force the Negro issue into our attention. Certainly "Native Son" declares Richard Wright's importance, not merely as the best Negro writer, but as an American author as distinctive as any of those now writing.

Mary-Carter Roberts. *Washington Star*, March 3, 1940, Section 5, p. F-6.

This novel, just selected by the Book-of-the-Month Club, is by that same Richard Wright who won Story Magazine's contest with his "Uncle Tom's Children" some seasons ago. He is a Negro and he writes of Negroes. In "Uncle Tom's Children" he gave us a series of tales in which virtuous colored men and women were brutally wronged by vicious white men and women. He wrote with a perceptible power, but his formula was unchanging. The injuries of his race apparently had filled his mind to the exclusion of any other artistic preoccupation.

Now, with his first novel, he continues on the subject of the Negro wrongs, but shows a disposition to qualify his previous position. His present novel tells of the railroading to the electric chair of a Negro boy by a vote-seeking district attorney, but it contains certain elements which, on the basis of past work, one would not have expected to find. For he allows his boy to be guilty and he makes it plain from the beginning that the youth, introduced at the age of 20, has by that time grown incurably into the pattern of the petty criminal. This is a distinct innovation, Mr. Wright's heroes in the past having been virtual saints. Furthermore, the scene of this book is not in the lynch-belt or in the South at all, but in Chicago.

The story tells how the boy, Bigger Thomas, after having enjoyed a career of petty thievery and a term in the reform school, is offered a job as chauffeur in the home of a wealthy philanthropist whose chief interest is in uplifting the Negro race. (Subsequently we are told that this same philanthropist has made his millions by renting wretched tenements to colored people, but we do not know this until the story has developed considerably. Nor, as far as the reader can tell, does the boy know it.) He is received kindly by his employer and promised a chance to educate himself if he wishes to do so. He has been shown to be a bully, a coward and a sneak by this time and he reacts to his new good fortune simply by sullen suspicion.

Before he has a chance to arrive at any clearer understanding, fate takes a hand and makes him the unintentional killer of his employer's dim-witted daughter. The girl is a parlor red and fancies herself a Negrophile. On the first evening of Bigger's employment, she has him drive her to a rendezvous with her Communist sweetheart, where the pair inspiredly insist that the servant join them in getting drunk, all in the name, as they assure him, of liberty, equality and fraternity. The accidental killing results and Bigger, from that moment, is an outlaw. He burns the girl's body in the furnace of her father's house and writes a kidnap note demanding $10,000 ransom.

There then follows as exciting a manhunt as you will want to read. In the course of it Bigger kills again, this time deliberately, doing to death his Negro sweetheart because he fears she knows too much about his crime. When he is taken the Communists rally 'round to protect him from "race prejudice." A famous lawyer volunteers to take his case and the district attorney makes the most of the "Red" implications. The conclusion is foregone—Bigger is condemned to die.

Those are the bare outlines of the story. The reviewer, however, cannot for the life of her tell you what Mr. Wright means by it. He seems objective enough in his portrayal of Bigger as a bad lot, but he also interrupts his story from time to time to assure us that the boy is, after all, a victim. He has had no opportunity, says Mr. Wright, and every influence of society has acted to make his crime inevitable. Similar sentiments are put into the mouth of the lawyer at the trial: his plea is that prejudice, and not the individual, is responsible for the crimes.

If this is what Mr. Wright wants us to believe, it would seem that he might be a bit plainer about it. We are told almost nothing about any wholesome desires which the boy may have had before he became a criminal. We are only assured that he once wanted to be an airplane pilot, but found that Negroes could not enter the training schools. Whether he had aptitude as a pilot, we do not know. His desire seems to be only the vague day-dreaming of an adolescent and is mentioned just twice. Yet it is the only hint that we get as to Bigger's supposedly crushed better nature. When his employer offers him a chance to go to school, we are told that he mentally rejects it. So just why he is a victim—just what are the conditions of his victimization—is not clear. But there can be no doubt that Mr. Wright considers this boy typical of the vast Negro population. He puts into the lawyer's mouth a solemn warning to white society as to what it may expect if it continues to brutalize Negro youth in the manner in which Bigger has been brutalized.

Yet, while the issue of justice is not clearly defined, the story as a story is splendid. Horrible as it is, it has a fascination which cannot be denied. A reader simply has to know what is going to happen next. Perhaps Mr. Wright meant to leave us vague about the true nature of the business—perhaps he meant that, in life, nobody ever gets the whole truth about anything.

"Bad Nigger." *Time*, 35 (March 4, 1940), 72.

Richard Wright is a 31-year-old Mississippi-born Negro who two years ago won a $500 prize competition with a collection of short stories titled *Uncle Tom's Children*. Among them were the most powerful lynching stories in U.S. fiction.

This week he dwarfed his first performance with a full-length novel, *Native Son*. Laid in Chicago, only a Negro could have written it; but until now no Negro has possessed either the talent or the daring to write it.

Native Son tells the story of a "bad nigger," coal-black, 20-year-old Bigger Thomas, who lives with his pious mother, a mild sister and brother in a one-bedroom tenement apartment on Chicago's South Side. In a flawlessly keyed first scene Bigger smashes a rat with a skillet, frightening his sister into a faint. Sullen and sassy through breakfast, he begs the last quarter in the house, joins his poolroom pals to plan a delicatessen stick-up. Instead, getting cold feet, he picks a fight with them. Bigger and his pals play a game of mimic called "white," speculate on whites' lives, particularly as portrayed in movies of the rich. Rarely has literature afforded such ruthlessly intimate glimpses into anti-white thoughts.

That afternoon Bigger is hired as chauffeur by Philanthropist Dalton, who makes his money in Negro tenements. It is a good job except for the philanthropist's radical daughter Mary. His first instructions are to drive her that evening to a lecture. She redirects him to a rendezvous with her Communist lover. What follows, as baffled and suspicious Bigger is accepted as a comrade, is one of the most devastating accounts yet printed of that tragi-comic, Negrophilous bohemianism which passes among Communists as a solution of the Negro Problem.

About four that morning Bigger murders Mary in her bedroom, carries her downstairs in a trunk, burns her body in the furnace, conceives an alibi to implicate her Communist lover. Bigger's explanation to himself is that the murder was an accident, would not have happened if she had not passed out on rum. Shortly before he is caught in a roof-top chase, he murders his girl Bessie with a brick, throws her down an airshaft.

But for all its murder-mystery suspense, *Native Son* is no more simply a crime story than was *Crime and Punishment.* Bigger's murders only pull the trigger of Author Wright's bigger story—the murderous potentialities of the whole U.S. Negro problem.

Samuel Sillen. *New Masses,* 34 (March 5, 1940), 24–25.

The tremendous power of *Native Son* has its ultimate source in a revolutionary vision of life. It is, in the most profound sense, a philosophical novel, a creative affirmation of the will to live and to transform life. Wright has often said that the discovery of *meaning* in the suffering of an oppressed group dooms the social order that is responsible for the suffering. His novel is a dramatization of the tortured search for values by which Bigger Thomas is to struggle, live, and die. Every arrangement of a class society conspires to maim Bigger for refusing to submit without challenge. The overbearing environment which engenders his suffering mutilates the forms of his protest and aspiration. But if the process of discovery is tragic, it is also, in the end, emancipatory; and if Bigger is condemned to die at the moment he has learned to live, our own minds have been flooded with meaning. A bold conception of human dignity gives this novel its stature. The episodes of violence, the sensitive notations of life in a segregated community, and the subtle documentation of a social machine which grinds down human personality, are important only in so far as they materialize this conception.

Only a courageous novelist would have attempted so difficult a theme. Only a supremely gifted one could have executed it so perfectly. For Bigger Thomas, externally, is the stereotyped monster of a lynch-inciting press. So far as the police record is concerned, he is the murderer of Mary Dalton, the daughter of his wealthy white "benefactor." He is a "brutish sex-slayer." His Negro mistress is the victim of his "primitive blood-lust." His trial for murder is the subject for horrified editorials in the Jackson (Miss.) *Daily Star* and gory news columns in the Chicago *Tribune.* This is explosive material. And it does explode—in the faces of the stereotype makers. The police record is here turned into its opposite, an indictment not of an individual but of a brutal and discriminatory order.

Bigger Thomas is not a "sex-slayer" at all. He is a fear-ridden boy whose attitude of iron reserve is a wall between himself and a world which will not allow him to live and grow. A deepening sense of hysteria has accompanied the blocking of his normal impulses. "Playing white" with his friends on a Chicago street corner is a grim substitute for living white, for living in a world, that is, where one may presumably be an aviator, or a President or a millionaire or whatever one wants to be. Bigger acts tough toward his poverty-stricken family, sensing that if he allows the shame and misery of their lives to invade his consciousness his own fear and despair will become intolerable. The victim of movie-inspired fantasies, he cannot find a possible order or meaning in his relations to other people. He does not know, at the beginning of the novel, that his crushed existence is part of a much larger pattern which includes Negroes *and* whites.

The events which lead to Bigger's unintentional smothering of Mary, his burning of the body, his flight from the police, and his murder of his mistress, Bessie, who he fears will betray him, create a sense of dramatic excitement that catches us up in the tensions and rhythms of Bigger's life. Though he did not plan Mary's murder, Bigger accepts it as his own act. Like Dmitry Karamazov, who felt guilty because in his heart he had wished his father's death, Bigger feels that he has killed many times before, "only on those other times there had been no handy victim or circumstance to make visible or dramatic his will to kill." The murders give him a sense of *creation*. He feels that they have given a focus to the chaotic circumstances of his existence. The acceptance of moral guilt makes Bigger feel free for the first time.

But such a commitment to life was doomed to disillusion. After his capture, Bigger realizes that he is as defenseless in the face of death as he had been in the face of life: "a new pride and a new humility would have to be born in him, a humility springing from a new identification with some part of the world in which he lived, and this identification forming the basis for a new hope that would function in him as pride and dignity." Having renounced fear and flight, he must possess a conception of man's fate which will enable him to die. He cannot respect the submissive path of religion which his mother and Reverend Hammond urge him to follow. He must have an affirmative idea. And he discovers its spirit in the Labor Defender lawyer, Mr. Max, and the young Communist, Jan Erlone.

In an essay published two years ago, Richard Wright declared that "If the sensory vehicle of imaginative writing is required to carry too great a load of didactic material, the artistic sense is submerged." He might have added that when the artistic sense is submerged, the didactic material becomes ineffective. In *Native Son,* as in the stories of *Uncle Tom's Children,* he has skillfully avoided the danger. Idea and image are remarkably integrated. Only a critic whose esthetic senses are blunted or whose social prejudices are unalterable will attempt to shout this novel down with the old cry of "propaganda." And yet, like *The Grapes of Wrath,* it will jar men and women out of their routine ways of looking at life and sweep them toward a new conception of the way things are and the way they ought to be.

But an effort will undoubtedly be made by some people to distort the plain meaning of the book in order to bolster their own bigotry. The reader must be warned against the blurb by Henry Seidel Canby which appears on the jacket of the book, and I hope that the publishers will be persuaded to withdraw it as a gross and vicious misrepresentation. Canby describes Jan Erlone, the Communist, as a "negrophile"! He suspects that the book will be "less of a surprise to, and more readily understood by, Southerners than by Northerners." He relishes the "deadly satire in the portraits of the young radicals—Mary who is killed, and Jan, the Communist, who chooses Bigger to work on, not realizing that this kind of political pity is more offensive to a Negro than color prejudice."

This is the most blatant stuff I have ever read. It angles the novel away from itself to the very stereotype which the novel demolishes. For the plain fact is that the radicals, Mr. Max and Jan Erlone, are the only ones who make Bigger aware of his dignity as a human being. To be sure, this does not happen overnight. To be sure, Jan makes an initial blunder in treating Bigger as a comrade before Bigger has learned to believe in the very existence of comradeship. But if one reads the novel in its full sweep one cannot mistake the overwhelming significance of Bigger's final remark: "Tell . . . Tell Mister . . . Tell Jan hello." It is, at last, a dropping of the Mister, an affirmation of that solidarity with other human beings in which only Jan and Max have taught him to believe.

It is difficult to think of an American novel that provides a more brilliant analysis of the interplay of social and psychological factors in experience. Wright has fused the valid elements in the naturalistic and psychological traditions, and the result is something quite new. For lack of a better phrase, "dramatic realism" will do. Structurally, the novel is divided into three sections corresponding to the three acts of a play. The action is not chopped up into chapters; it moves in a long sweep toward three climaxes. The tonal unity and psychological tension which we associate with an intense drama can be sustained only with great difficulty in fiction. As a sheer achievement in structural craftsmanship, *Native Son* is worth careful study. There is nothing wayward, either in detail or in mood. It is the work of a writer who feels his material deeply and authentically at the same time that he can view it from an ideological perspective.

What this perspective is, Wright has explained elsewhere. The Marxist analysis of society, he holds, "creates a picture which, when placed before the eyes of the writer, should unify his personality, buttress him with a tense and obdurate will to change the world. And, in turn, this changed world will dialectically change the writer. Hence, it is through a Marxist conception of reality and society that the maximum degree of freedom in thought and feeling can be gained for the Negro writer. Further, this dramatic Marxist vision, when consciously grasped, endows the writer with a sense of dignity which no other vision can give. Ultimately, it restores to the writer his lost heritage, that is, his role as a creator of the world in which he lives, and as a creator of himself." *Native Son* is his first full-length embodiment of his conception in the warm and living terms of fiction. It is a first novel, but it places Richard Wright, incontrovertibly, in the first ranks of American literature in our time. There is no writer in America of whom one can say more confidently: He is the creator of our better world and our greater art.

Margaret Wallace. "A Powerful Novel About a Boy from Chicago's Black Belt." *New York Sun*, March 5, 1940, p. 3.

Some novels—and not, by any means, only great novels—have a kind of life of their own, a peculiar vitality which amounts almost to independent being. They add something to the reader's mind which was not there before, and which cannot be lost or taken away. Usually they father other books in turn and may end by coloring the thinking of a generation which has scarcely heard of them. "Native Son," by Richard Wright, at a fair venture, is such a novel. Richard Wright's cruel and absorbing story of a Negro boy from Chicago's Black Belt leaves one with the feeling that never before, in fiction, has anything honest or important been written about the American Negro.

You may like this book or you may

hate it. You may like it for its sheer excitement. It is a murder story and nothing on the list of current crime fiction is half so engrossing. You may hate it because, in spots, it is ugly and brutal enough to give you bad dreams at night. If you have a conscience sensitive to questions of social injustice it may remain to trouble you long after you thought you were through with it. In no case will you be able to put it aside and ignore it. It has a factual quality as hard and real as a paving stone.

Mr. Wright might have chosen for his protagonist—but by some grace of artistic insight did not choose—a "good Negro." Bigger Thomas at 20 is a big, surly, dangerous black boy. He had already served a term in reform school for stealing automobile tires. He and his mother and a younger brother and sister are living, on relief, in one ill-ventilated, rat-infested room for which they pay $8 a week. Bigger spends his time at movies, or hanging around a pool room planning petty crimes, always against members of his own race. He and his pals understood that the police did not search very diligently for thieves who preyed upon Negroes. It was really criminal, and therefore dangerous, to tamper with white property.

Always present, whether they mentioned it or not, was this cleavage between black and white. . . . If you were black they didn't even want you in the army, except to dig ditches.

"I know I oughtn't to think about it," Bigger said, "but I can't help it. . . . We black and they white. They got things and we ain't. They do things and we can't. It's just like living in jail. Half the time I feel like I'm on the outside of the world peeping in through a knot hole in the fence."

This is the hard core of fear and hatred central to Bigger's character. . . . The murder was accidental. Not so much a murder, really as a natural reaction to the interpretation Bigger knew would be placed on his presence in a white girl's bedroom. . . . Bigger's reaction to the murder—he accepts it as such, without bothering about extenuating circumstances—is not accidental. It is rooted in the past which has conditioned him. For the first time in his short life he has done something even the white world would regard as significant, and for the first time he is not afraid. This recognition is the great psychological triumph of the novel. Everything else follows inexorably. . . .

"Native Son" comes through heaped-up horror to an emotion not far removed from those Aristotle described as pity and terror. For abnormal as the events seem, a regular tabloid sensation in cheap melodrama, Richard Wright forces us to understand Bigger. We accept without question the convention which makes him, at least in thought, more articulate than he possibly could have been. We concede that, given this train of circumstances, he could have done nothing else. It is harder, though still not impossible, to accept him as representative of his race. The defense plea arranged by his Jewish lawyer . . . is an indictment of society already sufficiently indicted by the story as it stands.

Beyond question, "Native Son" is the finest novel yet written by an American Negro. It is an amazingly expert performance for a man so new to his trade, and we are informed that Richard Wright was awarded a Guggenheim fellowship to complete it. In all probability we shall hear more of him in the future. If by chance we should not, it would still be hard, on this showing alone, to deny him recognition as an important novelist.

Edward Skillin, Jr. *Commonweal,* 31 (March 8, 1940), 438.

It is nearly twenty years since Theodore Dreiser published his bulky *American Tragedy,* an indictment of America's heartless worship of money and business success. Environment was meant to be the real villain in his rough-hewn tale of crime and inevitable punishment. However he produced a rather different effect. His hero Clyde Griffith's sense of guilt was developed so painstakingly and he seemed so normal an individual that the reader came to identify himself individually with Clyde and feel personally guilty of the crime.

Richard Wright has followed a strikingly similar pattern in *Native Son.* In this case it is more difficult for the reader to identify himself with young Bigger Thomas, who, by the time the story opens, is in a highly pathological state. Besides, the environment of South Side Chicago's Negro district is far more vicious, more potent for evil, than Clyde Griffiths' smaller mid-western factory town. Finally, Mr. Wright handles the problems of style with far greater ease than Mr. Dreiser. Except for the defense attorney's long speech toward the end of the book—a wholly unnecessary pointing of the moral—*Native Son* fairly races along both in narrative and dialogue. So Mr. Wright really does succeed in making environment the principal villain in this new American Tragedy.

Even compared with Dreiser this volume is strong meat. From the moment a giant black rat steals into the Thomas family's one-room flat, on the opening pages, till Bigger in his death cell bids his attorney farewell on page 359, *Native Son* is a "shocker." It is brutal, frank, sordid. It is no book for adolescents or for squeamish adults. But this brutality is skillfully subordinated to a wider purpose.

To be sure most Americans are no longer ignorant that the Negro over here is a victim of the most unjust discrimination. Many have heard, for instance, that in some parts of Harlem people sleep in three shifts in order to meet the high rents. Negroes have to pay the piper since they are barred from other sections of Manhattan. Lynching in the South and border states and the mental-emotional outlook that violence manifests are also widely known. But from most of us these situations are as far removed as a Chinese flood or the inhumanities of a French penal colony in the Guianas. Yet the problem is at our very doors.

Mr. Wright makes it real by reducing it to very simple human terms. When young Bigger Thomas goes to work for a wealthy family which might eventually have helped him, he already is a problem case. He is a member of a poolroom gang that has not yet pulled off a major crime but might well do so any day. He regularly has illicit relations with a young waitress. And deep in his breast rankles a burning resentment against the white race which seems to thwart his ambitions at every turn and keeps his family in abject misery. He cannot bear to face his true situation squarely.

What makes *Native Son* doubly tragic is that Bigger's first victim is a white girl who is sincerely trying to be his friend, to treat him as a fellow human being. Mary's sweetheart is a communist who also tries to befriend Bigger to the very end. Her mother, who is blind, loves to encourage Negroes to study and get ahead. The only poetic justice is that Mary's father was one of the landlords whose exorbitant rents cause such widespread misery in Chicago, New York and in all the other cities where Negroes are so harshly segregated.

The very first night of his new job Bigger finds that he has accidentally killed Mary Dalton. The story then rushes through a series of other crimes to Bigger's arrest and conviction with a sort of grim inevitability. Again it is highly reminiscent of the even more acute sense of impending doom that comes upon Dreiser's Clyde Griffiths, who knows and makes the readers of the *American Tragedy* painfully aware that nothing will save him from the chair.

Here and there Richard Wright gives hints as to the way out of the tragic situation he has epitomized so stirringly in Bigger Thomas. Boys' clubs and ping pong tables he holds in contempt; palliatives such as settlement houses do not provide the answer either for the injustices to his race. Religion appears in his pages as well-meaning but futile. Some new social system—not necessarily the Marxist one—is implicitly his prescription. As is so often the case in real life, only the communists in this novel succeed in convincing the Negro that they sincerely believe and act on the principle of the brotherhood of man.

There is one final reason that this startling book provides such a challenge to all Americans. Bigger knew that he, like many innocent lynch victims, would be presumed guilty as a matter of course if he was apprehended under suspicious circumstances. To be looked upon as ignorant, lazy, shiftless, vicious, subhuman by a white master race was what enraged him most. His deepest satisfaction is to know at the very end something that might have saved him six months earlier, that one white man really accepts him on equal terms as a man. Is that an impossible prescription for a starter?

Chicago Defender, March 16, 1940, p. 22.

Another Alexandre Dumas has risen in the New World. Not the Dumas of the *Three Musketeers* and the *Count of Monte Cristo,* important and popular though he be, but the younger Dumas whose *Lady of the Camelias* shook the whole structure of the French society. Just as he, through the pages of a vibrant, realistic novel, had exposed to full view the shocking aberrations and unmitigated strictures of the social organism of his time, so has Richard Wright in his *Native Son* paraded before the eyes of an indolent, indifferent public the organic weaknesses of the American social order.

Though Dumas's novels, as literary critics are fond of saying, are classed in the category of sociological theses, shocking as they are to the senses of polite society, they nevertheless must be considered in the light of the romantic striving of an artist whose sole aim is the faithful reproduction upon the canvas of the spasms of a world in agony. The result is a picture, well painted, beautifully executed, revealing the delicate touch of an artist with consummate skill; drawing sympathy, exciting admiration but conveying no definitive compelling message.

In *Native Son,* Richard Wright has done more than painting a distressful, lurid picture of contemporary America. He has subjected to microscopic examination the panorama of the social, economic and political disparities that deter the cultural integration of the black minority into American society. With the deftness and precision of the experienced surgeon whose scalpel cuts through dead tissues in order better to excise a malignant tumor, Mr. Wright has gone into the very matrix of our social organization.

The demented university student, in *Native Son,* expresses much of the plight of the Race when he says that he will tell the President of the United States that

> you make us live in such crowded conditions on the South side that one out of every ten of us is insane! I'll tell 'im that you dump all the stale foods into the Black Belt and sell them for more than you can get anywhere else! I'll tell 'im you tax us, but you won't build hospitals! I'll tell 'im the schools are so crowded that they breed perverts! I'll tell 'im you hire us last and fire us first!

Though uttered by a disordered mind, these lines reflect some of the basic issues which confront us not only in Chicago but all over America—issues that are verbalized often more violently by the sane among us. Their presence may well be responsible for the chronic neurosis which manifests itself in uncontrolled emotional reactions.

As Dorothy Canfield Fisher, who wrote a preface for the book, explained:

> Our American society creates around all youth a continual pressure of suggestion to try to live up to the accepted ideals of the country—such ordinary, traditional, taken-for-granted American ideals as to fight injustice fearlessly; to cringe to no man; to choose one's own life work; to resist with stout-hearted self-respect affronts to decent human dignity, whether one's own or others'; to drive ahead toward honestly earned success, all sails spread to the old American wind blowing from the Declaration of Independence. But our society puts Negro youth in the situation of the animal in the psychological laboratory in which a neurosis is to be caused by making it impossible for him to try to live up to those never-to-be-questioned national ideals as other young Americans do.
>
> *Native Son* is the first report in fiction we have had from those who succumb to these distracting cross-currents of contradictory nerve-impulses, from those whose behavior-patterns give evidence of the same bewildered, senseless tangle of abnormal nerve-reactions studied in animals by psychologists in laboratory experiments. It is not surprising that this novel plumbs blacker depths of human experience than American literature has yet had, comparable only to Dostoievski's revelation of human misery in wrongdoing.

Dostoievski's *Crime and Punishment* deals with the universally unchanging and unchangeable human instinct; Dreiser's *American Tragedy* is the representation of a social complex that has not disturbed greatly the conscience of our present generation. But Wright's *Native Son* is neither an experimental nor a philosophic novel. It is a penetrating, realistic, clinical examination of a raw, open wound which is yet bleeding.

While the critics are in unanimity in proclaiming Richard Wright a novelist of the first magnitude, we, who belong to the world of social proscription, of frustrated hopes, of organized discrimination out of which came Bigger Thomas—the main character of the book—fervently hope that *Native Son* shall not only focus attention upon the evils which are visited upon us, but that it shall, by the very urgency of its message, transform a rotten social, economic system into a living democracy for all.

Margaret Marshall. *The Nation,* 150 (March 16, 1940), 367–68.

The Negro in America is confronted by two attitudes. He is treated either as an inferior and an outcast or as the member of an oppressed race who is therefore owed special consideration by "enlightened" whites. These opposite attitudes are in fact the two sides of the same coin of race prejudice, since both deny to the man who happens to be colored his standing as a human being—to be accepted or rejected as such in his relations with other human beings. This is the real tragedy of the black man in America, and this is the basic theme of *Native Son* by Richard Wright.

With a boldness entirely justified by the result Mr. Wright has chosen for his "hero," not a sophisticated Negro who at least understands his predicament and can adapt himself to it, but a "bad nigger," a "black ape," who is only dimly aware of his extra-human status and therefore completely at the mercy of the impulses it generates. Bigger Thomas, a twenty-year-old colored boy, lives with his family—a meek, religious mother and sister, and a younger brother who worships him—in a grisly tenement room on the South Side of Chicago. Bigger hangs out at pool halls with a gang of friends who go in for petty robbery and spend their idle hours planning "jobs" and talking about white folks, about cars and airplanes and all the symbols of power in free America which are forever flaunted yet pretty consistently forbidden to 11,000,000 of its "native sons."

In the first part of the book one gets a picture of a dark world inclosed by a living white wall to which the black inhabitants react according to their natures. Bigger's mother and sister are humble; Bigger and his friends are resentful; all feel powerless and afraid of the white world, which exploits, condescends to, and in turn fears the race it has segregated. Against this psychological and social backdrop, which hangs over the reader like an overcast sky, the terrible story of Bigger unrolls. He is removed from the WPA to be given a job as chauffeur and handyman in the establishment of a rich white real-estate operator who owns the tenement in which the Thomas family lives but who has contributed millions to Negro philanthropies. Bigger's first task is to drive Mary, the daughter of the house, to a lecture. Instead she orders him to take her to a rendezvous, with her lover, Jan, a Communist, whose views she shares after the romantic fashion of the college revolutionist. In their "proletarian" exuberance Mary and Jan insist that Bigger eat and drink with them. Bigger, who is terrified of "reds" and regards the strange friendliness of Jan and Mary as only another expression of white scorn, sullenly complies. At the end, drunk and confused and frightened, he carries the girl, who cannot walk, to her room; and out of fear, when her blind mother enters, he smothers her to prevent an outcry and his own discovery. From there on the sands run out fast. Faced with the evidence of his unpremeditated murder he burns Mary's body. Then, driven by an inexplicable sense of power and release which his crime has given him, he evolves a stupid scheme for extracting ransom money, forcing his girl Bessie to act as his accomplice. When suspicion falls upon him, he kills Bessie in order to protect himself. After a police hunt during which race feeling rises and innocent Negroes are persecuted for his crime, Bigger is caught and tried while troops guard him from the anger of the mob. A Communist lawyer, Max, takes up his defense but pleads in vain, and Bigger is condemned to death.

The tale is sheer melodrama, but it is no Grand Guignol in black and white. For Mr. Wright has laid bare, with a ruthlessness that spares neither race, the lower depths of the human and social relationship of blacks and whites; and his ruthlessness so clearly springs not from a vindictive desire to shock but from a passionate—and compassionate—concern with a problem obviously lying at the core of his own personal reality that while the reader may recoil he cannot escape from the conviction that this problem is part of his reality as well. It is not pleasant to feel at the end that one is an accessory to the crimes of Bigger Thomas; but that feeling is impressive evidence of the power of Mr. Wright's indictment with its cutting and accurate title of *Native Son*.

As narrative, the story of Bigger Thomas carries its own dreadful fascination. Bigger's world is made real and terrifying; the theme is developed with such passion and honesty—Mr. Wright plays so directly upon the sense of guilt that is inevitably part of the white American's attitude toward his black fellow-citizens—that the critical faculties tend to be held in abeyance while one reads his book. Only afterward does one take stock of its defects as a work of art. And here, too, it is Mr. Wright who forces one's hand, for he would be the first to scorn indulgence.

The defects have to do with characterization and style. Aside from Bigger, the characters are too lightly sketched. Bigger's friends are real; the girl and her father are not; the Communist lawyer, Max, is only a voice, though a stirring one. In the case of Bigger Mr. Wright has not solved the admittedly difficult problem of projecting in terms of an ignorant and confused, though intelligent, Negro boy the forces that motivate his actions. As a result the author often ascribes to Bigger thoughts of which he is plainly incapable. The situation is saved because Bigger's behavior is authentic and because Mr. Wright's analysis of the roots of that behavior is so patently true.

Mr. Wright's style often reminds one of a stream "riled" by a heavy storm. Its element of Biblical rhetoric is not out of place since it is part of the colloquial heritage of the Negro in America, but there is in addition a bookish quality, often encountered in the self-educated writer, which should be weeded out. Mr. Wright's boldness in choosing to develop his theme through the story of a "bad nigger" is all to the good, but his flair for the melodramatic could bear curbing.

These defects cannot be described as minor, but they are extenuated by the wealth of evidence in *Native Son* that they can be overcome by a writer whose talent and seriousness are apparent on every page, who displays a maturity of thought and feeling beside which the eloquence of *The Grapes of Wrath* grows pale. And Mr. Wright's youth demonstrates once more that maturity is not necessarily a matter of years.

Malcolm Cowley. *New Republic*, 102 (March 18, 1940), 382–83.

Native Son is the most impressive American novel I have read since *The Grapes of Wrath*. In some ways the two books resemble each other: both deal with the dispossessed and both grew out of the radical movement of the 1930's. There is, however, a distinction to be drawn between the motives of the two authors. Steinbeck, more privileged than the characters in his novel, wrote out of deep pity for them, and the fault he had to avoid was sentimentality. Richard Wright, a Negro, was moved by wrongs he had suffered in his own person, and what he had to fear was a blind anger that might destroy the pity in him, making him hate any character whose skin was whiter than his own. His first book, *Uncle Tom's Children*, had not completely avoided that fault. It was a collection of stories all but one of which had the same pattern: a Negro was goaded into killing one or more white men and was killed in turn, without feeling regret for himself or his victims. Some of the stories I found physically painful to read, even though I admired them. So deep was the author's sense of the indignities heaped on his race that one felt he was revenging himself by a whole series of symbolic murders. In *Native Son* the pattern is the same, but the author's sympathies have broadened and his resentment, though quite as deep, is less painful and personal.

The hero, Bigger Thomas, is a Negro boy of twenty, a poolroom loafer, a bully, a liar and a petty thief. "Bigger, sometimes I wonder why I birthed you," his pious mother tells him. "Honest, you the most no-countest man I ever seen in all my life." A Chicago philanthropist tries to help the family by hiring him as chauffeur. That same night Bigger kills the philanthropist's daughter—out of fear of being discovered in her room—and stuffs her body into the furnace. This half-accidental crime leads to others. Bigger tries to cast the blame for the girl's disappearance on her lover, a Communist; he tries to collect a ransom from her parents; after the body is found he murders his Negro mistress to keep her from betraying him to the police. The next day he is captured on the snow-covered roof of a South Side tenement, while a mob howls in the street below.

In the last part of the book, which is also the best, we learn that the case of Bigger Thomas is not the author's deepest concern. Behind it is another, more complicated story he is trying hard to explain, though the words come painfully at first, and later come in a flood that almost sweeps him away. "Listen, you white folks," he seems to be saying over and over. "I want to tell you about all the Negroes in America. I want to tell you how they live and how they feel. I want you to change your minds about them before it is too late to prevent a worse disaster than any we have known. I speak for my own people, but I speak for America too." And because he does speak for and to the nation, without ceasing to be a Negro, his book has more force than any other American novel by a member of his race.

Bigger, he explains, had been trained from the beginning to be a bad citizen. He had been taught American ideals of life, in the schools, in the magazines, in the cheap movie houses, but had been denied any means of achieving them. Everything he wanted to have or do was reserved for the whites. "I just can't get used to it," he tells one of his poolroom buddies. "I swear to God I can't. . . . Every time I think about it I feel like somebody's poking a red-hot iron down my throat."

At the trial, his white-haired Jewish lawyer makes a final plea to the judge for mercy. "What Bigger Thomas did early that Sunday morning in the Dalton home and what he did that Sunday night in the empty building was but a tiny aspect of what he had been doing all his life long. He was *living,* only as he knew how, and as we have forced him to live. . . . The hate and fear which we have inspired in him, woven by our civilization into the very structure of his consciousness, into his blood and bones, into the hourly functioning of his personality, have become the justification of his existence. . . . Every thought he thinks is potential murder."

This long courtroom speech, which sums up the argument of the novel, is at once its strongest and its weakest point. It is strongest when Mr. Max is making a plea for the American Negroes in general. "They are not simply twelve million people; in reality they constitute a separate nation, stunted, stripped and held captive *within* this nation." Many of them—and many white people too—are full of "balked longing for some kind of fulfilment and exultation"; and their existence is "what makes our future seem a looming image of violence." In this context, Mr. Max's talk of another civil war seems not so much a threat as an agonized warning. But his speech is weakest as a plea for the individual life of Bigger Thomas. It did not convince the judge, and I doubt that it will convince many readers.

It is not that I think Bigger "deserved" the death sentence for his two murders. Most certainly his guilt was shared by the society that condemned him. But when he killed Mary Dalton he was performing the first free action in his whole fear-tortured life; he was accepting his first moral responsibility. That is what he tried so hard to explain to his lawyer. "I ain't worried none about them women I killed. . . . I killed 'em 'cause I was scared and mad. But I been scared and mad all my life and after I killed that first woman, I wasn't scared no more for a little while." And when his lawyer asks him if he ever thought he would face the electric chair, "Now I come to think of it," he answers, "it seems like something like this just had to be." If Mr. Max had managed to win a life sentence for Bigger Thomas, he would have robbed him of his only claim to human courage and dignity. But that Richard Wright makes us feel this, while setting out to prove something else—that he makes Bigger Thomas a human rather than a racial symbol—shows that he wrote an even better novel than he had planned.

Ben Davis, Jr. (New York) *Sunday Worker,* April 14, 1940, Section 2, pp. 4, 6.

Native Son has, overnight, become a literary work of national interest and discussion in which varied opinions are expressed by people in all walks of life. That the reactions to the book have differed, even among Communists, is not surprising. My own conclusions, set forth in this review, were arrived at only after lengthy consideration, based upon reading and re-reading the book.

It is clear, however, that *Native Son* is

the most powerful and important novel of 1940. It deals with the life of the Negro people. The fact that it projects the role of the Communist Party, even though in a confused manner and in a distorted form, gives it great political as well as literary consequence. It is an achievement in the world of letters and, despite its shortcomings, is a document of positive social significance.

With *Native Son,* Richard Wright, the Negro author, already known and recognized for his literary talent by his earlier writings, notably *Uncle Tom's Children,* has leaped forward into the front rank of American novelists. Bourgeois critics are compelled to compare the book with such a modern classic as John Steinbeck's *The Grapes of Wrath* and with such a generally accepted work as Theodore Dreiser's *An American Tragedy.* The very literary excellence of the book once more attests the deep cultural genius of the Negro people, expressing their ability to produce artists who can articulate their most bitter oppression and their burning aspirations.

Through slum-bred Bigger Thomas, the author has taken an unemployed Negro youth with frustrated desires for opportunity, traced him through the labyrinth of horrible crimes into which he is forced and entrapped by his white capitalist oppressors, and shows to this youth and to the world that the Communist Party is the only organization profoundly interested in relieving the terrible plight of the Negro people.

Wright runs into many difficulties—serious and sometimes unconquered difficulties—in trying to achieve his objective, but the objective is nonetheless there. He wants to show the most degrading oppression of the Negro—what capitalism can do to a human being, and he tries to show the road that leads to victory. The first he accomplishes through the most superlative and realistic craftsmanship. The latter he does not fully achieve but even here he reflects the fact that the Communist Party is the only organization which can give the ray of light to penetrate the swamp of degradation into which the Negro people have been hurled.

Native Son has a value, first, in that it brings relentlessly to the fore in the form of a realistic novel, the existence of special oppression of the Negro people as a nation. Even in the "best" of novels, the oppression and aspirations of the Negro people are either understressed, distorted or wholly glossed over. But Wright has made use of the art of fiction to burn this problem and responsibility for it deep into the conscience of the American people.

The book is a terrific indictment of capitalist America, which deliberately robs vast Negro communities and holds them in subjection in "Southsides" and "Harlems," under appalling conditions of misery and discrimination, of childhood and adulthood without opportunity; of blockings of the main social highway and of forced detours to criminal by-ways. Bigger Thomas is the product of this special and bitter national oppression and, again and again, he finds himself caught in its web. The very beginning of the book—a picture of Bigger and his whole family battling a giant slum rat—is symbolic of the capitalist monster which devours the Negro people with peculiar relish. Wright does this picture with a marvelous bit of stark writing.

Bigger, Gus, and their pals, like millions of unemployed youths today, find themselves in a dead end, imprisoned by a social system which attempts to hold open only one door to them—the door to crime. But in the process capitalism is digging its own grave, and it tries to keep barred another door which the

Communist Party alone hails the Negro people and white workers to enter. That door leads to struggle against capitalism. *Native Son*, at least, cracks that door.

A wall of discrimination exists around the aviation school which Bigger wants to attend; the disruptive factor of poverty and want reaches into Bigger's own family life to impair and strain relations which should be normally warm, human and sympathetic. The almost inconceivable wretchedness of the poor Negro—worse than even the squalor of the poor white—is drawn by Wright in all its rawness. Many of those who are shocked by the crimes into which Bigger is driven by an anti-Negro social system, are too often unshocked by the unendurable conditions under which Negroes are compelled to live.

The pious mask of the white, richman "benefactor" of the Negroes, is abruptly torn off. In Mr. Dalton, the millionaire philanthropist—who typically came into his money through his heiress wife—we have what the bourgeoisie prides itself upon, the "well-disposed, upright and kindly friend" of all the Negroes.

One cannot fail to see that this very Mr. Dalton is a part of that white ruling class whose subjection of the Negro it tries to "atone" for with unctuous and ineffectual gifts. He, the donor of philanthropic sums and ping-pong tables to Negro institutions; he, the "Christian-hearted" employer of the wayward Negro boy, is exposed as the wealthy landlord of the slum houses in which these derelict boys and their crowded families are compelled to live—at rentals considerably in excess of what is mulcted even from poor whites.

Mr. Dalton virtually burglarizes Negro tenants because it is the "custom," and he cannot reduce the rents on the overcrowded Chicago Southside because that would be "unethical" toward his fellow landlords. Bigger himself is the victim of this widespread "ethical custom" of the realty owners. As Max, Bigger's lawyer, says to Mr. Dalton at the coroner's inquest in one of the most penetrating passages in the book:

"So, the profits you take from the Thomas family in rents, you give back to them to ease the pain of their gouged lives and to salve the ache of your own conscience?"

Mr. Dalton tries to explain away the forced Jim-Crow ghettos by saying the Negroes are "happier together," only to be ripped to pieces in cross-examination by Bigger's counsel, who points out the ghetto is "more profitable." Mr. Dalton has to admit that he gives no jobs to any of the Negroes his philanthropy and ping-pong tables "help to educate." In baring the false tissue of white ruling class philanthropy and the hideous double-bookkeeping of capitalism, Wright makes one of the best contributions of the book. There's scarcely a Negro in America who cannot see in Mr. Dalton, the class of hypocritical Carnegies, Fords and Rockefellers, who are the very causes of the unemployment, poverty and misery among the Negro people, which their million-dollar gifts are falsely alleged to cure.

Exposed too—and with magnificent writing—are the mechanics of the state machinery that sets in motion, in collaboration with the press, the mob violence which accompanies Bigger's trial. However, this is not a typical case, for like Scottsboro, the typical lynch trial is where the Negro is completely and wholly innocent. Neither do I.L.D. attorneys in life, plead their clients guilty. Nevertheless, the mob scene in the book does show how the state apparatus seizes upon individual cases to terrorize entire Negro communities, to whip up hysteria for persecution of the Communist Party and labor unions.

This mob hysteria is still a technique of the capitalist class, as just witnessed in the brutal lynch hysteria against the Negroes on the Maryland Eastern Shore in Show Hill. But more and more, as a result of the courageous fight of the Communist Party and the I.L.D. in Scottsboro and in other cases—and as a result of the great CIO recruiting drives particularly in the South—the state machinery finds it more difficult to whip up its "democratic citizens" mobs, even in the South. It is these courageous activities which made Wright see the light.

Now the tendency is for lynchings to be perpetrated by local officials through underground and dead of night gangs, as in the recent Atlanta floggings. These Klan bands very seldom choose to face the wrath of the community. Twenty unreported lynchings in Mississippi last year mark the new technique which must be taken into account in the up-to-date treatment of the lynching evil. The strong and still developing labor and progressive movement in Chicago would make it difficult indeed for such a mob to take over as in *Native Son*.

In his characterization it is clear that Wright deliberately chose Bigger Thomas, and developed him into a dangerous criminal, to make his indictment of capitalism airtight. He certainly did not pick the average unemployed Negro youth, who does not become a rapist, a murderer, and fall into the pitfall of crime, as Bigger did despite the intense pressure on the average youth exerted by his white ruling class oppressors. In fact one of the serious weaknesses of the book, particularly in the third part, is that the author overwrites Bigger into a symbol of the whole Negro people, a native son to the Negro people.

The bourbon enemies of the Negro people will try to seize upon this weakness to further their slanders against the whole Negro people despite the fact that the book as a whole says the contrary. It is, of course, inevitable that where they do not see the light some of the Negroes are forced to take the path of the anti-social criminal but the overwhelming majority are responding to the changed attitude of large sections of white labor as a consequence of Communist and other progressive struggles. One does not find this latter Negro majority in the book in more than a suggestive form.

It is nevertheless a source of dramatic power to the book that Wright chooses a Bigger instead of a more moderate, and less spectacular average Negro as protagonist. The average white person has been taught through the press and radio, through lying history books and whatnot, that the Bigger Thomases are typical of the Negroes. As Jim, one of Bigger's pals says after Bigger is found out:

"We's all dogs in they sight! Youh gotta stan' up 'n' fight these folks . . . We's all murderers t'them . . ."

And the book has sought to take that very bourbon conception of the Negro to use it as a boomerang against the same capitalist bourbons.

Thus does Wright speak to America in terms of the kind of Negro which they have been taught exists. America must listen because Wright talks to them in their own personal medium, and on their own grounds. A picture of the hundreds of thousands of Negroes who are swelling progressive ranks accepting at last the proffered hand of white workers for their freedom, might not reach this America so poignantly, for capitalist propaganda has taught that these Negroes are unreal, "not typical" or, at best, "an exception." Wright has not permitted this excuse to be used.

It cannot be contended successfully

that Bigger is a natural killer, a born monster whose criminal bent is inherent. Bigger begins with the same aspirations as any other American youth. He says repeatedly that this "white world" has "everything" and he and his people nothing. When he and his pals "play white" that symbolizes the inaccessibility of the good things of life to them as Negroes. They are driven into petty thievery for money that jobs, not available to them, would provide.

Bigger had ambitions, as he told Max, his lawyer:

"I wanted to be an aviator once. But they wouldn't let me go to the school where I was suppose' to learn it. They built a big school and then drew a line around it and said that nobody could go to it but those who lived within the line. That kept all the colored boys out.

". . . I wanted to be in the army once . . . Hell, it's a Jim-Crow army. All they want a black man for is to dig ditches. And in the navy, all I can do is wash dishes and scrub floors."

Battered down in his every desire and wanting to fight instead of submit, is there any wonder that Bigger views with admiration Japan's bloody "conquering" of China, or the necessity of a "Hitler" to save the Negro people with fire and sword? Did he not get his slanderous impression of Communists from the movies? Is this not life itself for a crushed member of an oppressed people who sees no one to whom he can turn? Does Bigger not express a natural distrust of those reactionary Negro leaders who have so often betrayed their people to the white ruling class, when he tells Max:

"Aw, hell Mr. Max. They (Negro leaders) wouldn't listen to me. They rich, even though the white folks treat them almost like they do me. They almost like white people, when it comes to guys like me. They say guys like me make it hard for them to get along with white folks."

Even in the introspection of Bigger—which is sometimes baffling and mystical—he is brought face to face with this "hostile white world" which he is trying to defeat and which is constantly trying to strangle his very existence. Here is no "dumb brute" as the capitalist class tries to make of the most undeveloped Negro, but a living, thinking being, trying to reason out his way to freedom, equality and opportunity, and who becomes lost before he finds the way. It is true that Wright's explanation of Bigger's murders as "creation" is somewhat mystical, but it is even more true that Bigger's desire for creation symbolizes the desire of an oppressed nation to live its own life, to express its own creation, in art, culture, and in its full nationhood.

The contrast of splendor, opulence and power in the white ruling class (which Bigger erroneously attributed to the undifferentiated "white world"), especially in a city like Chicago, as compared to the bleak misery of the Negro hovels, is a contradiction which would naturally whet Bigger's creative impulses even more. The urge to "be somebody" and measure shoulders with this "white world" pushes Bigger desperately onward.

Throughout his hair-raising plot, Wright definitely brings each crisis in Bigger's short life, each major event back to its cause in the capitalist social structure. That is the essential unity and strength of the plot and weaves through the entire book. Bigger accidentally kills Mary Dalton because he finds himself in a circumstance in which discovery means sure death, probably lynching for him. The life of any Negro found in such an ambiguous situation under capitalist society with a white woman, though the question of intimacy were never involved, wouldn't be worth a dime. Bigger knew this, and in trying to save himself, accidentally killed.

It seems, however, that it would not have injured Wright's general purpose and structural unity if the victim had not been Mary, but some other person entirely disconnected with the labor and progressive movement. There is a touch of unreality here, in that it permits of the impression that had it not been for Bigger's contact with Communists, however untypical these Communists were, he would not have been forced to kill.

The particularly brutal murder and rape of Bessie, Bigger's sweetheart, is traceable to a certain callousness Bigger acquired in his effort to free himself of the capitalist "justice" closing in on him. He feared revelation of the ransom plot. To divert suspicion he implicates the Communists in the ransom note. Bessie too—who cannot be regarded as typical of Negro women servants—is dragged by Bigger into the maelstrom of the anti-Negro "white world," because Bigger needs her in his plan to defeat this hostile white capitalist state. But every single Negro character, including Bigger's own family, is pretty much beaten and desperate—utterly devoid of a smattering of the progressive developments among the Negro people, and in a city like Chicago where the Negroes are so politically articulate. That situation is rather unconvincing, and strains the realism of the artistic medium.

This is where the book falls into one of its most serious errors. Bigger is exaggerated into a symbol of the whole Negro people. It is true that Bigger symbolizes the plight of the Negro, but he does not symbolize the attitude of the entire Negro people toward that plight. Therefore, because no other character in the book portrays the Negro masses, the tendency becomes that the reader sees Bigger and no distinction whatever between him and the masses who are finding the correct way out despite capitalism.

The book could have, for example, made of Bigger's mother a strong woman typical of Negro womanhood of today. And it seems only natural that through some of Bigger's pals or in some other way the progressiveness and the constructive power of the Negro masses could have been brought forward more distinctly.

There is little that directly shows the power of the Negro people, although the book as a whole assumes the existence of the Negro mass as a background. Yet that power is historically present and is evident today in political struggle. It is shown in cultural achievement and in the developing alliance between the Negro people and white workers in the advancing Negro liberation movement. The white masses also are left out, except in the mob scene, which gives an incomplete and untruthful picture by omitting trends among white workers and progressives in the fight for Negro rights. John L. Lewis typified this in his recent address in Washington for the right of the Negroes and poor whites to vote in the South. The problem of including the mass psychology is a difficult literary one, it must be admitted, since a novel must deal with individual characters, but this is bound to be hammered out in the development of fiction of social consciousness. In this case the failure of the book to bring forward clearly the psychology of the Negro mass will find the capitalist enemies of the Negro trying to attribute Bigger's attitude to the whole Negro people.

Since it is clear that Bigger is a product of brutal national oppression, it is correct to defend him, and to hold guilty the capitalist oppressors who drove him to crime. It is very easy to defend a class conscious white worker or Negro. But to give up Bigger, to abandon him, is to condone the system which crushed his social aspirations and enmeshed him in crime. To give him up—the most oppressed—is to give up the thousands of dead-end white youths who are driven to crime daily.

The role of the Communists is projected by the book through characters who are not typical and who reflect distorted ideas which are far from adequately expressing the policies of the Communist Party. But our Party shares the condemnation of such attitudes and such dilettante types even though ruling class enemies will seize upon Jan and Mary and present them as typical of all Communists and Party sympathizers. The Communist Party, in life, ruthlessly burns out such chauvinist ideas. The patronizing attitude of Jan and Mary led Bigger to include them in his "hostile white world."

But notwithstanding these shortcomings, the book portrays the Communist Party as the main and only force having an understanding of the difficulties of the Negro people and of the relation of these difficulties to the rest of society. The book would have been immeasurably strengthened with a Communist character more typical of the Communist Party. But even as it is, the Party is that force which comes to the defense of Bigger, and tries to instill into him the self-confidence and understanding of the way out.

Certain passages in Max's speech show an understanding of the responsibility of capitalism for Bigger's plight, even though Max's otherwise distorted defense brief must be categorically rejected as an example of the working class defense policies of the Communist Party or the I.L.D. Max well says in his speech to the jury:

> The hunt for Bigger Thomas served as an excuse to terrorize the entire Negro population, to arrest hundreds of Communists, to raid labor union headquarters and workers organizations. Indeed, the tone of the press, the silence of the church, the attitude of the prosecution and the stimulated temper of the people are of such a nature as to indicate that more than revenge is being sought upon a man who has committed a crime.
>
> What is the cause of all this high feeling and excitement? . . . Were labor unions and workers halls raided solely because a Negro committed a crime? . . . Your Honor, you know that this is not the case! Negroes, workers and labor unions were hated as much yesterday as they are today. Crimes of even greater brutality and horror have been committed in this city. Gangsters have killed and have gone free to kill again. But none of that brought forth an indignation to equal this. Your Honor, that mob did not come here of its own accord! It was incited! Who then fanned this latent hate into fury?
>
> The State Attorney knows, for he promised the Loop bankers that if he were re-elected demonstrations for relief would be stopped! The Governor of the State knows, for he has pledged the Manufacturers Association that he would use troops against workers who went out on strike! The Mayor knows, for he told the merchants of the city that the budget would be cut down, that no new taxes would be imposed to satisfy the clamor of the masses of the needy.
>
> There is guilt in the rage that demands that this man's life be snuffed

out quickly! There is fear in the heat and impatience which impels the actions of the mob congregated upon the streets beyond that window! All of them—the mob and the mobsters: the wire-pullers and the frightened; the leaders and the pet vassals—know and feel that their lives are built upon a historical deed of wrong against many people, people from whose lives they have bled their leisure and their luxury!

But Max represents the type of so-called legal defense which the Communist Party and the I.L.D. have been fighting, dating from Scottsboro. Some of his speech is mystical, unconvincing, and expresses the point of view held not by the Communists but by those reformist betrayers who are being displaced by the Communists. He accepts the idea that Negroes have a criminal psychology as the book erroneously tends to symbolize in Bigger. He does not challenge the false charge of rape against Bigger, though Bigger did not rape Mary, and though this is the eternal bourbon slander flung against Negroes. He does not deal with the heinous murder of Bessie, tending to accept the bourbon policy that crimes of Negroes against each other don't matter and are not cut from the same capitalist cloth.

Worst of all, he pleads Bigger guilty to both rape and murder of Mary, though it was plain that the killing of Mary was accidental. He argues that Bigger, and by implication the whole Negro mass, should be held in jail to protect "white daughters" though capitalism is plainly the guilty criminal which threatens poor white womanhood as well as Negro. He states that Bigger's existence is a "crime against the state," when really the capitalist state is a crime against Bigger. Max should have argued for Bigger's acquittal in the case, and should have helped stir the political pressure of the Negro and white masses to get that acquittal. From Max's whole conduct the first business of the Communist Party or of the I.L.D. would have been to chuck him out of the case.

The difficulty is that the book tries to answer the powerful actions of misguided Bigger, with words instead of with powerful counteractions drawn from life. The defense of the Biggers, of the slum-oppressed Negro people, is primarily the work of the Communist Party among the masses, fighting for decent housing, for jobs, for the organization of the Negro workers into unions, against lynch justice, and for the day to day needs of the Negroes. A Communist is not seen in action in the book—the Communists in life would have been fighting for better conditions for Bigger families, against Dalton's high rentals.

The main center of Communist activity is not in the courts—as indispensably important as that is—but in the communities among the people. The Communists appear to have come into the plot accidentally, and not out of community struggles, as in life. And in presenting only white Communists, the book omits the great role which the Negroes play in the Party—from top to bottom—as the best instrument to fight for the full liberation of their people. What political party in the United States has a Negro leadership? None other save the Communist. To omit this great historic fact, is to permit the misconception that the Communist Party is something "foreign" to the Negro people.

However, in seeking to save Bigger, whom the State prosecutor refers to as a "black thing," the Communist Party in the book was attempting to defend a people all of whom are "black things" to the vicious white ruling class. It is through the taking of his defense by the Communist Party, that Bigger finally gets a ray of understanding, not quite of the Communist Party, but of the fact that his allies include whites as well as blacks who will fight with him against the common capitalist enemy. This is perhaps the meaning of Bigger's last goodbye to Max:

"Tell . . . Tell Mister . . . Tell Jan hello . . ."

Wright has done a brilliant and courageous job, with bold initiative. He, himself, is part of that great progressive Negro mass which is barely suggested in the book. He is an example of the creative genius of the Negro, the ability of an oppressed people to overcome all obstacles. Our Party joins with the Negro people in rejoicing over his magnificent artistry, as a native son of his people and of America. Wright is young, and *Native Son* projects for him a potential future rich in development, and historic in achievement.

James W. Ivy. *The Crisis*, 47 (April 1940), 122.

On the surface, this is merely another sensational crime story, but at bottom is much more than that; it is a profound and searching analysis of the mind of the American Negro and a penetrating study of the tragic position of the Negro in American life. *Native Son* is Dostoevskian in its sweep and significance and tugs at the very guts of the reader. No one can read this story and continue to be complacent about the position of the Negro in American society. It churns up the emotions and performs the cleansing effects of the catharsis of Greek tragedy. Bigger Thomas is a creation worthy to rank with Raskolnikov or one of the Brothers Karamazov.

The center of the story is Bigger Thomas, the twenty-year-old black boy who is killed ostensibly for killing a white girl, but really because he is a social misfit. Bigger is the victim of social injustice and that deeper malignity of race prejudice. He is no saint and the author does not sentimentalize him, but he is just as much a victim of his environment as was Clyde Griffith. He is the perfect "bad nigger" of Chicago's South Side living in a mouldy and decaying one-room tenement with his sister, his brother, and his pious mother. His instincts are bad and he snarls all through breakfast. The author paints this in an almost artistically perfect first scene where Bigger kills a rat with a skillet. Begging a quarter from his mother Bigger joins his pals in a shady poolroom to plan the holdup of a delicatessen. But Bigger is a coward and picks a fight with one of his pals to hide his blue funk. He is furious because he knows that Gus knows that he (Bigger) is afraid. Gus is afraid too; but Bigger is equally as afraid.

That same afternoon he goes to take a job as a chauffeur with Mr. Dalton of Drexel Boulevard, where the relief people have sent him. Mr. Dalton is a philanthropist who has made some of his millions out of rotting South Side tenements, but he returns part of his tainted gains to Negroes in charity contributions. Mrs. Dalton likes to send her Negro chauffeurs to night school, and the daughter, Mary, is a radical flirting with Communism. At eight o'clock Bigger is supposed to drive Mary to the university to a lecture, but Mary directs him to a rendezvous with her Communist lover Jan. Then they direct Bigger to a South Side Negro restaurant, and later they order him to drive around the park while Mary and Jan drink and make love on the back seat. It is a very drunk Mary that Biggers returns to her bedroom at two that morning, but before he can get out, the blind Mrs. Dalton comes in to see her daughter and Bigger smothers Mary in a pillow to keep her from speaking of his presence. If Mrs. Dalton had known that he was there, she would have suspected him of rape, and Bigger knows this. He has unwittingly killed the girl; so he puts her body in a trunk, takes it down to the basement, and burns it. But her head won't fit in the furnace and he has to chop it off with a hatchet. He now turns on the exhaust fan to clear the basement of the odor of burning flesh.

The next morning Mary is missing, but since she had planned to go to Detroit no one thinks her absence unusual. But in the meantime, Bigger knows that with the first suspicion of foul play he is going to be the suspect; therefore, he plans to pin the crime on Jan. He also figures that he can collect kidnap money on the pretense that Mary is alive, and takes his girl Bessie into the plot. Mary's bones are discovered in the ashes of the furnace and Bigger flees.

He takes Bessie along because he can't afford to leave her behind. But when he finds that she is a burden, he batters her head in with a brick and tosses her body down the airshaft of an empty building. After a brief roof-top chase, he is soon caught and brought to trial. He is tried in an atmosphere of mob hysteria and race hate. Though defended by the able Jewish lawyer, Max, he is found guilty and condemned to the chair.

In a part of his last confession Bigger admits that he has never "felt a sense of wholeness" in his entire life, and this is the tragedy of his life as it is of the members of his race caught in the hot desert of the white man's prejudice. There are many Bigger Thomases in actual life; one of their snarls is, "I'll go to hell for a white man any day." Almost every American Negro is frustrated, but he escapes from reality through socially more acceptable means: excessive religiousness, Uncle Tomism, jazz, back-to-Africa movements, Father Divineism, "research," and various other futile doings. Most of the personality-traits of the American Negro are to be explained through the deep frustrations which he suffers in American life. His often strange illogic, intense emotionalism, and sudden and fretful switches from Pollyannaism to cynical fatalism are explicable on these grounds. Anything to escape from consciousness of the galling realities surrounding his position in America.

Native Son is undoubtedly the greatest novel written by an American Negro. In fact, it is one of the best American novels, and Mr. Wright is one of the great novelists of this generation.

Samuel Sillen. "The Response to *Native Son*." *New Masses*, 35 (April 23, 1940), 25–27.

In a critical essay published three years ago Richard Wright complained that too many Negro novels, poems, and plays in the past were like "prim and decorous ambassadors who went a-begging to white America." They entered the Court of Public Opinion, he wrote, "dressed in the knee-pants of servility, curtsying to show that the Negro was not inferior, that he was human, and that he had a life comparable to that of other people." As a reward for their docility, most of these artistic ambassadors were condescendingly received "as though they were French poodles who do clever tricks."

Challenging the validity of this direction, Wright urged his fellow authors to explore the meaning of their own lives with a view to creating a bolder and more affirmative literature. Negro writing must lose its defensive character. It must cease to be acquiescent. It must dig to the roots of Negro existence in a capitalist society and it must mold the lives and consciousness of the Negro masses toward new goals. The Negro writer "must learn to view the life of a Negro living in New York's Harlem or Chicago's South Side with the consciousness that one-sixth of the earth's surface belongs to the working class." His perspective must not be the palliation of an evil, but the total and unequivocal emancipation of a people and a class.

The intensely charged nerves of *Native Son* originate in this glowing center of revolutionary feeling. Every one of its hundreds of thousands of readers experienced its shock in some degree. This book does not curtsy before the orthodox canons of literary opinion. It is a decisive challenge to our moral and economic order, and readers throughout the country have recognized it as such. Like *The Grapes of Wrath,* says a typical review in the Washington, D. C., *News,* "it is another superb novel to stagger the conscience of the nation." Little more than a month after its publication the book has been bought by a quarter of a million Americans. According to Cass Canfield of Harper, *Native Son* has started off faster than any novel the firm has issued in twenty years. Everywhere one goes, one hears: "What do *you* think of *Native Son?"* And the question is being asked with an insistence that reflects a shattering experience. Only a novel that raised some of the deepest and most troublesome issues of our time could evoke such a disturbed response.

To give a simple answer to the many questions that are raised about the book is to do an injustice to its complexity and subtlety. Before giving my own further reflections on the novel in a second article, I think that it will be useful to examine the response of the nation's press to the book. For it is clear that many questions which people ask have reference to the larger social effects of the book. Has this novel by a Negro been used by the press to reinforce anti-Negro prejudice? Has this novel by a Communist been used against the Communists? Are there any variations in the sectional approach to the novel? What has been the response of the Negro press? Such questions are inevitably raised by a novel which deals with vital social materials. In order to answer them as objectively as possible, I have examined over two hundred press clippings, evaluated their tendencies, and sorted out representative expressions for citation in this article.

The general response of the Negro press to *Native Son* is summarized in a leading editorial appearing in the Chicago *Defender* of March 23. The reaction of the *Defender* is particularly interesting, since this influential paper is published in the city where Bigger Thomas was condemned to die. Wright is praised for showing "an indolent, indifferent public the organic weaknesses of the American social order":

> While the critics are in unanimity in proclaiming Richard Wright a novelist of the first magnitude, we,

> who belong to the world of social proscription, of frustrated hopes, of organized discrimination out of which came Bigger Thomas—the main character of the book—fervently hope that *Native Son* shall not only focus attention upon the evils which are visited upon us, but that it shall, by the very urgency of its message, transform a rotten social, economic system into a living democracy for all.

An editorial in the April issue of *Opportunity* points out that "Richard Wright unquestionably has the touch of genius. He belongs to the Negro, but in a larger sense he belongs to America and the world of art and literature." Reviewing the novel for *Crisis,* James W. Ivy says that "it is a profound and searching analysis of the mind of the American Negro and a penetrating study of the tragic position of the Negro in American life." Mr. Ivy believes that "No one can read this story and continue to be complacent about the position of the Negro in American society." Many Negro papers throughout the country carried the Associated Negro Press review by Frank Marshall Davis.

> It's going to be interesting [wrote Mr. Davis], to watch the reaction of both black and white America to this masterpiece. Many of our pale brothers, blind to life among Negroes, will want to deny the cruelty of the nation's color attitude; still others, angered at the truth, will try to condemn the book in self-defense.

One extremely interesting statement by a Negro woman writer appeared as a leading feature article, "Native Daughter," in the Catholic weekly *Commonweal* for April 12. Ellen Tarry wrote:

> As a Negro, I have been greatly pleased to note the haste with which the literary world has acclaimed Richard Wright . . . as the greatest writer of his race. . . . However, it is not Richard Wright's laurels that concern me so greatly. It is rather that in Catholic circles many have lamented the fact that the Negro writer who has arisen as the spokesman for his race should be a Communist. . . . Yet as an American Mr. Wright is entitled to his own political and religious beliefs. And we must accept, even if regretfully, the fact that Richard Wright, acclaimed America's most powerful Negro writer, is a Communist. . . . There may be Catholics who will not read *Native Son* because its author is a Communist. But did you ever stop to think that Catholics may be among those who are responsible for some of the conditions that have led Richard Wright into the ranks of the Reds? The time has come for Christian America to shed its coat of hypocrisy and admit its sin.

Reviewing the book for the same publication Edward Skillin, Jr., notes: "As is so often the case in real life, only the Communists succeed in convincing the Negro that they sincerely believe and act on the principle of the brotherhood of man."

The response of the Southern press was far from uniform. The reviews from the border states were most sympathetic. Texas and Louisiana writers appear to have been the most hostile. One of the most outspoken adverse reviews appeared in the New Orleans *Times-Picayune.* It declared that,

> while it is a striking and, in spots, beautifully written story, its implications fail to impress us, despite the

> apparently sincere flavor of the author's psychology. . . . Most Southern readers will find this material irritating, if not outright revolting; if we thought that *Native Son* were significant enough as a novel to warrant the advice, we would recommend that they shove aside their biases and read it in any case. But somehow we do not have that feeling about the book.

On the other hand, the Kansas City *Star* commented:

> In a year when the ideals of democracy are once more under challenge and when all Americans are deeply concerned for the plight of Europe's racial minorities, *Native Son* will serve as a reminder that the United States has a race problem that has yet to be solved.

The reviewer for the Louisville, Ky., *Courier-Journal* was encouraged by the fact

> that there are those today who are daring to tell us the truth, however unpleasant it may be. One cannot but think of Hugo, Zola, Tolstoy, Dostoevsky, and Gorky, and the name of Richard Wright must be added to the list of those who through the medium of the novel have cried out against injustice and oppression.

The Louisville *Times* carried an editorial suggesting that the issuance of this book by a Negro who got his education by using a white man's card to get his books from the Memphis Library, "constitutes the best publicity in behalf of better educational opportunities for Negroes."

Several reviewers attempt to give the impression that this is an anti-Communist novel. *Time* magazine, discussing the scene in which Mary Dalton and Jan Erlone behave with blindness toward Bigger, speaks of the "tragi-comic Negrophilous bohemianism which passes among the Communists as a solution of the Negro problem." The lady reviewer for the Houston, Tex., *Chronicle* declares that "at this point the reader damns the stupidity of such idiotic, idealistic Communists and wishes them all in Siberia." (She adds that the novel "defeats its purpose by virtue of sheer universality of appeal—the plea of the 'have-nots' against oppression by the 'haves.' ") The Dallas *News* also uses the review to point out that the whole trouble with Bigger is to be traced to the "patronizing" whites of the North. And the Memphis *Commerical Appeal* plays up the impression that the killings in the book are caused by the radicals. The Cleveland *Plain Dealer* and the San Francisco *Chronicle* similarly stress the Jan-Mary-Bigger episode in order indict the radical movement.

But just as many reviews, particularly in the North, object to the book for quite opposite reasons. They criticize the book for being belligerently *pro*-Communist. The St. Louis *Globe-Democrat* says that it is "a distinctive story despite a suspicion of special pleading on behalf of Communism and the Jewish question." The New Bedford *Standard Times* attacks Wright's "warped ideology" and asserts that the major fault of the book is that "its course is twisted by an attempt to make the Communist Party seem the friend of the Negro." The Des Moines *Register* finds that "the injection of Communism and radical theorizing weakens both the plot and the author's plea." The Worcester *Telegram* says that "As a novel, it is hindered by too much analysis, too much talk, too much propaganda, if we may use the term, for the cause of the Negro and of labor unions."

Some reviewers, like Fanny Butcher of the Chicago *Tribune,* completely ignore the social problem and convey the impression that the novel is a psychological thriller. "The story as a story is splendid," writes the literary critic of the Washington, D. C., *Star,* but "the reviewer cannot for the life of her tell you what Mr. Wright means by it." Prof. Howard Mumford Jones of Harvard, writing for the Boston *Transcript,* would sympathize with the lady from the *Star,* though he could at least plead that he didn't like the story to begin with. After all, he reasons, Bigger Thomas did get a job, so what's all the kicking about? By contrast, the opinions of the New York reviewers were on the whole intelligent and fair. Most dismal of all the reviews, next to that of Professor Jones, was the one by Jonathan Daniels in the *Saturday Review of Literature.*

In a detailed and stimulating analysis appearing in the *Sunday Worker* of April 14, Ben Davis, Jr., reports that reactions to the book have differed among Communists. His own conclusion is that, despite certain shortcomings, Wright's novel is a "brilliant and courageous job . . . the most powerful and important novel of 1940." The Communist Party, writes Davis, "joins with the Negro people in rejoicing over his magnificent artistry, as a native son of his people and of America." Stressing the fact that the novel is "a terrific indictment of capitalist America," Davis nevertheless feels that the book errs in giving the impression that Bigger Thomas is a symbol of the whole Negro people. He points out that a distorted impression of the Communist position is given by the actions of Jan Erlone and certain portions of Mr. Max's defense speech. He regrets the absence of characters who would balance the picture by showing Negroes whose rebellion against oppression is expressed in constructive mass action rather than in individual violence. Enthusiasm for the book has also been expressed in a warm comment by Mike Gold, who says:

> After ten years of fumbling and experiment, of great visions, and uneven fulfillments, our American social realism, our American proletarian literature, or whatever critics wish to name it, has finally culminated in two sure classics—Steinbeck's *Grapes of Wrath* and Richard Wright's *Native Son.*

Gold remarks that critics like Henry Seidel Canby would squeeze an anti-Communist moral "out of even a non-partisan turnip." Finally, the reaction of the militant working class press is indicated by Ben Burns' review in the San Francisco *People's World,* which declares that:

> [into] the life of white Americans who could never begin to realize what being black meant has come a searing, scorching novel written like a wild, blazing prairie fire, burning indelibly an impression that becomes to every reader a vital experience of a lifetime.

What is one to conclude from all these reactions? There is fairly universal agreement that Richard Wright, who was virtually unheard of a year or two ago, is one of the leading American novelists. Most readers and critics are agreed that *Native Son* is a novel of tremendous dramatic impact. On the social meaning of the novel there is a division of opinion. The Negro press regards *Native Son* as a smashing challenge to inequality. A section of the nation's press uses the book as a confirmation of anti-Communist prejudice. Another treats it as a propaganda tract for Communism. The press reaction indicates that there is a correlation between the degree of a reviewer's progressivism and the degree of his enthusiasm for the book.

And yet there are some people whose questions about the book derive from their uncertainty that its total effect will be progressive—an uncertainty which, incidentally, is not shared by the Birmingham, Ala., librarians who banned the book. There is obviously a problem here which goes to the heart of esthetic and social theory. Was Sterling North of the Chicago *News* right in saying that if the novel is read with the sensitive perception with which it was written, it will be a powerful force for progress; but that if it is read unsympathetically by a reader whose social prejudices are deeply entrenched it may have a contrary effect? Of what subtle elements must a novel be compounded to produce such contradictory possibilities? Could Wright have mastered his problem more skillfully? Are there elements in the book which need more emphasis than they have so far received? . . .

The Christian Century, 57 (April 24, 1940), 546.

There is eminent critical authority for the judgment that this is the finest novel ever written by an American Negro. It is one of the most terrible ever written by a novelist of any color—revolting in many of its details, fascinating in the suspense and intricacy of its plot, completely convincing in the stark reality of its people, and profoundly disturbing to those unaccustomed to look beneath the respectable surface of city life except perhaps for a glimpse and a sniff at its crooked politics. This is too good a novel to be a tract on any subject, but it might easily be used as collateral reading in a study of crime and correction, or one in the psychology and sociology of the urban Negro in the lower cultural and moral brackets. The story is that of a young Negro in Chicago, a roughneck from the start, who commits an unpremeditated murder. From that act consequences radiate in all directions. The author is not concerned to vindicate Bigger and throw the blame on "society." But in painting this ruffian and his associates and the white people with whom he comes in contact, the communists and the anti-communists, the police and the district attorney and the reporters, he gives a devastating delineation of a complex of forces and motives which leave little more chance for Bigger than if an immutable decree had foreordained him to wrath. Mr. Wright makes his central character a Negro for the same reason that Dostoievsky made his characters Russians, and with no more intention of dealing merely with racial material. The meaning of the novel goes far beyond the color line.

Samuel Sillen. "The Meaning of Bigger Thomas." *New Masses,* 35 (April 30, 1940), 26–28.

It is my impression that most reviews of *Native Son,* whether favorable or hostile, suffer from two closely related faults. The first is a tendency to consider events and character apart from their context and development. The second is a failure to analyze the organic relation between the esthetic and social effects of the book. These faults reflect two essential characteristics of undialectical thinking: atomism, or the chopping up of reality into disjointed bits; and dualism, or the application of a double standard of life and literature.

Criticism must overcome the error of thinking in compartments before it can hope to register sound judgments of artistic work. For the creative process is a dialectical process. It is characterized, in other words, by a sense of organic change and development; it does not differentiate mechanically between content and form; it sets up a reciprocal influence between the parts and the whole; it strives toward the resolution of conflict on progressively higher levels of consciousness. If we are properly to understand and evaluate the product of such a process, we must ourselves think dynamically. This is certainly our first responsibility to a novel like *Native Son*. It is not an impulsive or haphazard creation. To discover its deepest meaning, to appraise its weakness and its strength, we must grasp the novel as a carefully planned accumulation, rather than as a broken sequence, of events, characters, moods, and ideas.

By isolating various aspects of the book from its total meaning, most commentators of both the right and the left have apparently missed the real significance of the central character, Bigger Thomas. At one pole Bigger has been treated as a mean, contemptible, ignorant, and brutish killer; the subterfuge of quotation marks around the expression "bad nigger" has again and again been used to convey this impression. At the opposite pole Bigger has been treated as a poor victim of circumstance, a helpless creature whose human dignity has been stamped out by an oppressive society; according to this view he is to be pitied, not hated. Neither approach, I believe, gets us close enough to the truth.

The first approach is a flat distortion of the novel. The horrible external details of Bigger's actions are maliciously ripped out of their human and social context with a view to creating hostility toward the Negro people. This is precisely the impression that State's Attorney Buckley and the lynch-inciting press seek to create *within the book itself.* Indeed, Wright deliberately portrayed a conflict of interpretation over Bigger's actions as an integral part of his dramatic structure. In this conflict, the class forces of our society are revealed; the esthetic effect of this clash is identical with its political effect. Through the behavior of the prosecution at the coroner's inquest and at the trial, Wright exposes the bigoted, deceitful, and hypocritical impulses of the anti-Negro forces in America. Buckley, the machine politician, has to get Bigger, at whatever cost to decency, in order to ensure his reelection. The press raises the lynch cry of "sex-killer" in order to still the South Side demand for better housing. It is not Bigger who is obscene, vicious, cruel; it is the men who convict him. The intelligent reader must shudder at the thought of any past or future identification between himself and the powers that a Buckley represents.

The approach to Bigger as a creature of circumstance is more sympathetic, but it misses an essential point. I would emphasize most firmly that the analogy to Dreiser has been overdone. For Bigger Thomas is not, like Clyde Griffiths in *An American Tragedy,* a weakling who tends merely to reflect the pressures of his environment. The difference between Wright's dramatic realism and Dreiser's naturalism is connected with a difference in their conception of the role of personality in fiction. In *Native Son* the social pressures meet the resistance of a positive and creative individual. There is a revolutionary potential in Bigger, however frustrated or perverted it may be by the discriminatory order in which he lives. Too much attention has been paid to the unfortunate ways in which society has forced him to express himself, and not enough to the dynamic emotional force which drives him toward an assertion of his will to create a different world for himself. It is only partly true to say that capitalism makes him what he is; it is even more important to insist that capitalism *unmakes* what he is, a sensitive, imaginative, and creative personality.

Bigger is a rebel whose every word and gesture is a challenge to those who have attempted to curb and crush his talents. "Why they make us live in one corner of the city?" he cries. "Why don't they let us fly planes and run ships. . . ." His mother and the Reverend Hammond urge him to accept the consolations of religion. His friend Gus advises him not to think so much or he will go mad. His girl Bessie, weary and worn from her work in other people's kitchens, offers to snatch salvation out of forgetfulness in sensual pleasures. But Bigger cannot forget, he refuses to forget that he is being elbowed out of life.

And Bigger is tender and warm beneath his hardboiled exterior. Everybody comments on the opening scene, where Bigger is mean and tough toward his sister Vera and his mother. One should balance that with the jail scene near the end of the book when his family comes to visit him. "How you l-l-like them sewing classes at the Y, Vera?" he asks the sister whom he had once scared to tears. And when he learns that she has had to leave the Y because she is now ashamed before the other girls, he realizes that his family is a part of him in spirit as well as in blood. Three times he tells his mother: "Forget me, Ma," though he knows, with a new and mature insight, that she will never forget. Similarly, Bigger's attitude toward Jan Erlone undergoes a profound change which reveals his unfolding attitude toward other people. At first, Bigger had attempted to implicate Jan in the death of Mary Dalton, knowing that the authorities would jump at the chance to punish a Communist. But after he has been captured, and after the sincerity of Jan's friendship has been proved, Bigger refuses to allow the court to blame his actions on the Communists. "He didn't have nothing to do with it," he says. "There wasn't nobody but me. I don't care what happens to me, but you can't make me say things about other people."

Indeed, the whole meaning of Jan in this story has been widely misinterpreted. Jan has been described by reactionary critics as a horrible example of how Communists treat Negroes; here again such an interpretation is portrayed and refuted in the novel itself through the Red-baiting, anti-Semitic tactics of the press and prosecution.

Some Communists, on the other hand, are disturbed by the portrayal of Jan because, as they rightly point out, certain of his actions are not representative of the behavior of Communists and therefore open to reactionary propaganda against Wright's own party, the only party which has fought consistently and courageously on behalf of the Negro people.

It is quite true that Jan's behavior in the opening section of the book is not that of a mature Communist. Indeed, it is Jan himself who later on admits his blunders. His good will toward Bigger Thomas outruns his understanding of Bigger. By overwhelming Bigger with his impetuous kindness, by over-reaching himself in his quite sincere demonstration of friendship, Jan manages to increase the bewilderment of the man whom he would enlighten. I believe that Wright was driving home the point that mere good will may turn into its opposite unless it is coupled with a rich understanding of human personality. This is not a new conception. It is certainly a Marxist conception. As I have already suggested, Jan himself grows up toward his idea, which he must always have had in theory, as a result of bitter practice. "I was kind of blind," he tells Bigger. And the real stature of Jan's new understanding is revealed in the scene in which he pleads with Bigger to let him help, despite the fact that the girl he loved had been accidentally killed by Bigger, and despite the fact that Bigger has tried to pin the murder on him. Later on, at the coroner's inquest, the prosecution attacks Jan—for shaking hands with Bigger, for eating with him, for urging him to drop the Mister! As a result of such a cross-examination, I for one feel the strength and humanity of Jan. His character, like Bigger's, emerges from the novel as a whole, rather than from one scene. Both men *grow*. And in the end, both men have made a bridge over the great gulf which originally separated them.

There is, however, an element of validity in the criticism of Jan as a character. I think it is this: that the first Jan scene, coming as it does at a moment of high tension, burns itself deeper into the reader's mind than the second, which comes immediately after the tension of the murder and the flight has been snapped. There is a difference in the dramatic impact of the two scenes. The second is unfortunately less fully developed than the one before the death of Mary. Moreover, too long an interval has elapsed between the restaurant and the jail scenes, so that readers tend to have a first impression of Jan which no later explanation will quite succeed in modifying. On the other hand, too many readers have evidently ignored what is actually in the book.

Another aspect of the book that has caused much comment is the trial scene. My own feeling is that Mr. Max's defense speech is weak in two respects. For one thing, it is a lengthy rhetorical restatement of the issues which the novel has already stated in powerful dramatic terms. It is a set speech which makes one feel that Wright, a little uncertain that his meaning has been communicated, interpolated what amounts to a summary draft of the story. Because of his concern with explicit statement, Wright does not take advantage of the scene's potential dramatic values. This artistic weakness is linked with an even more important fault: the absence of clarity in the appeal. Whatever judgment legal experts may pass upon the correctness of the procedure adopted by the defense, the plea itself leans too heavily on an involved psychological approach that gives a confusing picture of the political issues in the case. Mr. Max's over-studied phrases in the courtroom suffer by contrast with his simple and effective talk outside.

The absence of Negro characters who have identified themselves with the labor movement has been noted as a defect of the book. It is pointed out that Bigger is projected as a symbol of the Negro people, and that that is unfortunate because such a symbol does not suggest the socially constructive reactions of masses of Negroes to their oppression under capitalism. I believe that we must move cautiously here. It is true, of course, that *Native Son* is not an all-inclusive picture of Negro life. It is equally true that American fiction has so far failed to give an adequate picture of Negro men and women in the trade union and progressive political movements. In this respect, novelists are lagging behind reality. I think that Wright might have given more explicit indication that there is a quite different side of Negro life from that which he has dealt with here—several indirect suggestions do appear—but I also believe that to have developed this side to the extent which it deserves would have meant the writing of another novel. This is *Bigger's* story. It had to be told; and I rejoice that it has been told so well. If Bigger must be interpreted symbolically, it is only to the extent that he represents the deep urge to live and create which no exploitative society can permanently subdue. Properly directed, the positive aspects of Bigger's nature to which I have referred are loaded with a significance and hope for the future toward which we aspire. On the title page of the novel, Wright has quoted a verse from Job which pointedly expresses the meaning of Bigger Thomas: "Even today is my complaint rebellious. My stroke is heavier than my groaning." It is a meaning that will not easily be forgotten.

Theophilus Lewis. *Interracial Review*, 13 (April 1940), 64–65.

A dozen times a year, more or less, the police are confronted with an astoundingly ghoulish murder, the motive for which eludes sane comprehension. While the authorities search for clues the city editors have a field day. The papers publish horrendous details of the crime, and describe the movements of the police as they follow the trail of the fiend, lose it, pick it up again, and finally corner the quarry, regaling the public with the excitement of a vicarious man hunt.

In *Native Son*, the thrill of the newspaper crime story is stepped up to high voltage and the point of view reversed. Instead of following the maneuvers of the police as they close in on the criminal, the reader is made privy to the mental and emotional processes of the murderer as he skulks and dodges to escape the tentacles of the law. It is an experience that will not be quickly forgotten.

The technique of the novel follows the journalistic pattern so closely that its plot might be the literal transcription of any one of half a hundred horror stories recently played up in the newspapers. Bigger Thomas has a subnormal mentality that cannot adjust itself to the inequalities of life. He feels that race prejudice bars him from all the larger activities of society, shuts him up in a dark and cramping corner, from which he can see the glory and gaiety of the world but cannot participate in them. As a consequence he harbors an ingrowing hate and suspicion of white people. The author does not explain that if Bigger had been white he would have fear just as bitter toward some other inequality, and we have no right to ask him to. It is the author's privilege to select the materials that serve his purpose best. He has given us a plausible, no, convincing reason for Bigger's conduct and that is all we can fairly demand of him.

The narrative opens when Bigger, a Chicago reliefer, is on the eve of getting a job, his first after a long period of idleness. His employer is a real-estate magnate who, with his blind wife, is benevolently interested in Negro welfare; so interested, indeed, that he has contributed several millions of dollars for eleemosynary work among Negroes. Their daughter is a Red sympathizer, and her sweetheart is an active Communist. All of them are bent on helping Bigger reach a normal and active adjustment to society, although the younger people have more specific and radical ideas in mind. But Bigger, whose mind has been conditioned to hate and distrust the white world, is perplexed and alarmed by the attitude of these friendly white people, and he suspects their motives. He is like an animal caught in a snare, as dangerous to a man who wants to release it as it is to one who intends its destruction.

When Bigger finds himself in a perilous situation, he murders his employer's daughter, hacks off her head and shoves head and torso into the furnace. The reader who likes thrills in his fiction will find plenty here, for the narrative omits none of the grisly details. There are as many shivers in these pages as one will find in half a score of vampire mysteries. And more are to follow.

The effect of his crime on Bigger, after the first shock of fright, is to cause a tremendous expansion of his rage. He is no longer a puny victim of the white world, he is its enemy. The white world cannot ignore him now. It must exert its wits and strength to discover and punish him, while he stands at bay guarding his secret. As his feeling of self importance mounts, he concludes that while outwitting the white world he can lay it under tribute. Forthwith he decides to make his employers believe their daughter has been kidnaped and pay ransom for her return. As he needs a confederate in that venture, Bigger confides his scheme to his girl friend who reluctantly consents to join in the plot.

But the murder is discovered at an embarrassing moment, and Bigger's thoughts turn from ransom to escape. Aware that his girl friend knows he is implicated in the crime, he fears that she may betray him. To forestall that danger, he kills her—by the comparatively humane method of braining her with a brick and pitching her out of a fourth-floor window into an areaway, where she freezes to death in the snow. But the murder is out now. The police are on his trail and the hue and cry rises to crescendo.

In the depiction of Bigger's chase and capture the reader discovers the peak passages of the book. With delectable irony, the author describes a town gone wild. Instead of sending out two or three detectives to arrest Bigger—a force ample for the job—the police make a show of his pursuit. They deploy riot squads, get out their gas bombs, deputize swarms of special officers and conscript the aid of the fire department. The States Attorney, ham actor that he is, steps into the floodlight to announce that he will make Bigger's swift punishment a warning to other potential murderers. While the law is making an ass of itself, the newspapers go to town plastering the community with inflammatory headlines that incite public clamor and boost circulation. As the crime is too atrocious to be exaggerated, the papers enhance its horror by embroidering it with superstitions culled from the folklore of race prejudice. The mature reader will find grim humor here. That an underprivileged boy who is none too bright should commit a senseless crime is not astonishing. That his crime could throw a huge civilized city off balance into tumultuous hysteria, making its officials and editors act the part of clowns and procurers. . . . That decreases one's respect for the "superior" race.

As Bigger is rushed to inevitable doom, his defense is undertaken by a humanitarian lawyer, a sort of fictional Clarence Darrow or Samuel Deibowitz, who pleads that the crime is a psychological end product of race prejudice. The plea does not impress the court, nor is it likely to impress the reader who has advanced beyond the belief that race friction is a comparatively simple problem. Indeed, even the naive reader is likely to remember the gruesome murders and the exciting chase long after he has forgotten the evils of race prejudice to which the author attributes the crime, while those who believe Negro character is essentially primitive or bestial will feel that the book confirms their opinion.

To that serious weakness one might add several minor technical flaws. Nevertheless, in point of style and general craftsmanship it is one of the strongest novels written by a Negro author.

Burton Rascoe. *American Mercury*, 50 (May 1940), 113–16.

Concerning no novel in recent times, with the possible exception of *The Grapes of Wrath,* have the reviewers in general displayed a more utterly juvenile confusion of values than they have shown in their ecstatic appraisal of Richard Wright's *Native Son*. The only way I can account for the cataclysmic impact this novel made upon their brains is by deducing that they have kept themselves virginally aloof from the sort of reading which daily gives millions of us the stimulation and catharsis of pity and terror in the tabloids and in the magazine fiction professionally described as the "pulps." To this may be added the further deduction that, so hysterical have the strains of the times made many of us, these good people, the reviewers, go easily haywire about anything which looks to them like a social document exposing "conditions."

Sanely considered, it is impossible for me to conceive of a novel's being worse, in the most important respects, than *Native Son*. It has many technical excellences. They are such as any Street & Smith editor would applaud, or as Walter B. Pitkin, in his writing classes at Columbia, would grade as A-1. But the editors for Street & Smith, and Mr. Pitkin, would probably say very sensibly that there are faults in this novel which even a tyro in fiction should not be guilty of. Let me enumerate some of them:

(1) If there is a moral message to be emphasized, that message should be made implicit in the consistent action

and dialogue of the novel. It should not be in the form of a running commentary by the author, particularly not when the author is very confused about what he wants to prove.

(2) If a character is conceived as being inarticulate and dumb about the economic and social forces which have (in your mind) been responsible for his social and moral delinquency, it is an artistic error to portray that character, at times, as being fully conscious of the "conditions" which have mentally and emotionally crippled him. It is an elementary principle not only of art but of moral law, of legal principle, and of common sense, that, if you are aware of yourself and of the factors under which you live, you are, *yourself,* responsible for what you do and you must accept that responsibility. Mr. Wright has Bigger Thomas, the hero of his story, commit two murders on the appalling theory that he is justified in so doing because, as ecstatic reviewers assure us, "he knows religion as something meant to lull people into submission" and because Bigger feels "powerless and afraid of the white world, which exploits, condescends to, and in turn fears the race it has segregated." (The quotes are, respectively, from Milton Rugoff in the New York *Herald Tribune* and Margaret Marshall in the *Nation*.)

(3) It is a violation of a fundamental esthetic principle—sanctioned from Aristotle on down—to portray a character in speech, thought or action in a way not consistent with what you, the writer, might conceivably do in similar circumstances and in similar conditions.

Recently I witnessed a *reductio ad absurdum* of Mr. Wright's fundamental thesis in *Native Son*. Mr. Wright was a luncheon guest, in New York, of a club whose membership comprises men who have achieved a degree of importance in the creative arts—writers, musicians, painters, illustrators, engineers, editors, etc. Mr. Wright was introduced eulogistically by Mr. William Chenery, editor of *Collier's*, who dwelt upon the young novelist's accomplishment as a writer who had achieved best-sellerdom. There was no reference, condescending or otherwise, to the guest's color.

Mr. Wright had been told that, as the club's guest, he need not make any speech unless he felt like doing so. He is a handsome young man; his face is fine, kind and intelligent. It was a spontaneous tribute to him and to the success he had attained that the club gave him an ovation such as it has rarely given to anyone but artists like Pablo Casals and Jascha Heifetz. Mr. Wright was, on this occasion (though he may not have realized it), an embodied refutation of his theme in *Native Son*. He was the only black man there, surrounded by white people. Yet they were all rejoicing in his success, eager to do him honor—even if there were many, of course, who had not read his book.

They were not, even unconsciously, trying to make things so difficult for Mr. Wright that he would have artistic or any other justification if he should choose to murder the first two debutantes he met after leaving the luncheon. Mr. Wright must have had some intimations of this anomaly—this contrast between himself and his fictional hero—when he arose to speak. In response to the spontaneous acclaim, he got up to say a few words. He was doubtless confused and embarrassed. Good writers, and Mr. Wright in his best vein is decidedly good, are rarely good speakers. He faltered, as most of us do who have not been trained to speak in public, and in his confusion he said, with the nicest air of camaraderie—as if to say "Come up and see me some time": "I hope you will all have a chance to meet Bigger Thomas."

I don't know what others who had read *Native Son* felt about the author's hope, but I for one shuddered. Bigger Thomas, in the novel, is a murderer because (so his creator tells us) he resents the white race. Bigger murders a rich white girl who is sentimentally interested in "the Negro problem" and whose family has contributed millions to alleviate conditions among the poor in the Negro quarters of Chicago. Bigger also murders his Negro mistress. He indulges in this slaughter not because of anything these poor, misguided women, white and black, have done to him, since they haven't harmed him at all, but because (Mr. Wright argues) all of us who happen to have white skins instead of black have made Bigger what he is.

In the midst of the hurrahing I rise to assert that I think the moral in *Native Son* is utterly loathsome and utterly insupportable as a "message." When I carefully examine all the evidence Mr. Wright offers to prove that Bigger Thomas should have become a murderer and that the guilt lies on our own heads, I remain emphatically unconvinced. I can't see that Bigger Thomas had anything more to contend with, in childhood and youth, than I had or than dozens of my friends had. Their lives and mine have not been velvety but we do not want to kill people because of this. And I have known fine priests, fine rabbis, fine Protestant ministers (black and white) whose "conditional environment" was even worse than this "conditional environment" which Mr. Wright would have us believe makes murderers out of Negro men.

Mr. Wright is as much an American as you are or I am. We Americans are constitutionally for the underdog, so long as it does not seriously interfere with the business at hand of getting along. It is quite the thing now, among our intellectuals, to contend that whites have given the Negroes a dirty deal, forgetting that whites have given themselves a dirty deal also. These intellectuals deplore Hitler, Stalin and Mussolini on psychopathic grounds, but they are unable to see that by their own logic Bigger Thomas is just a small-scale Negro Hitler. Or a Negro Stalin or Mussolini. The partiality of these dictators for bloodletting also can be traced to conditional environment. If I am supposed to start grieving over what I have done to Hitler and Stalin in their hard early life, I won't take any.

And the same applies to Bigger. This is also to serve notice that despite all the eloquence Bigger's lawyer and Wright's reviewers bring to Bigger's defense, if I were on the jury I would vote to hang Bigger. Bigger, I have been amply convinced, wouldn't hesitate two minutes to shoot me or his lawyer or his author, even if we were going about business and paying him no mind. I don't like the idea of being shot, even fictionally, just because my color is not like Bigger's. I wouldn't like it even if I knew that all the Bigger Thomases think I am somehow responsible because life hasn't been cushy for them. I'm just unreasonable in these matters of murder, where I'm the murderee.

Mr. Wright, one may note, is doing very well. A lot of white writers with talent doubtless are wishing they were making as much money as he is making. But they are not envious of him, nor do they begrudge his success in the least. They hope he prospers. For myself, I hope that now he has got *Native Son* out of his system, he will use his talents to more sensible ends. He is one of the two writers, white or black, who have ever had the ear to catch and transliterate Negro speech correctly. The other writer is Louis Paul, who is white.

David L. Cohn. *Atlantic Monthly*, 165 (May 1940), 659–61.

Richard Wright, a Mississippi-born Negro, has written a blinding and corrosive study in hate. It is a novel entitled *Native Son*. The race hatred of his hero, Bigger Thomas, is directed with equal malevolence and demoniac intensity toward *all* whites, whether they are Mary Dalton, the moony Negrophile whom he murdered, or the vague white men who seemed to bar his youthful ambition to become an aviator or join the navy. This book has far-reaching qualities of significance above and beyond its considerable virtues as a novel, because Mr. Wright elects to portray his hero not as an individual merely but as a symbol of twelve million American Negroes.

Bigger is very young. His exact age is not stated, but we are told he is too young to vote, and he is therefore under twenty-one. Although his life has hardly begun, his career and hopes for the future have been blasted by the Negro-hating whites of Chicago. On page 14 of *Native Son*, Bigger and his friend Gus are watching an airplane above the city. 'I *could* fly a plane if I had a chance,' Bigger says. 'If you wasn't black and if you had some money and if they'd let you go to that aviation school, you *could* fly a plane,' Gus answers. And time after time, throughout the length of this book, Bigger bitterly complains that he is denied access to the broad, glittering world which the whites monopolize for themselves to the exclusion of Negroes. Toward the end of the novel (p. 302), Bigger, in jail for murdering a white girl and his Negro mistress, says: 'I ain't asking nobody to be sorry for me . . . I'm black. *They don't give black people a chance*' (my italics). Bigger's crimes and his fate in the electric chair, the author makes clear to us, are consequently to be laid at the door of white society.

In the speech of Bigger's lawyer at his trial, one finds the fullest summation of Mr. Wright's point of view toward the Negro question in America, and the most explicit statement of his use of Bigger as a symbol of the oppressed Negro. 'This boy,' says lawyer Max, 'represents but a tiny aspect of the problem whose reality sprawls over a third of a nation. . . . Multiply Bigger Thomas twelve million times, allowing for environmental and temperamental variations . . . and you have the psychology of the Negro people. . . . Taken collectively, they are not simply twelve million; in reality they constitute a separate nation, stunted, stripped, and held captive *within* this nation, devoid of political, social, economic and property rights.'

Mr. Wright might have made a more manly and certainly more convincing case for his people if he had stuck to fact. In all of the non-Southern states, Negroes have complete political rights, including the suffrage, and even in the South Negro suffrage is constantly being extended. So powerful, indeed, is the Negro vote, and so solidly is it cast en bloc in Negro-populous Eastern and Midwestern states, that in closely contested Presidential elections the Negro vote may decide who shall become President of the United States. Hence the scramble of both parties for the Negro vote. Nowhere in America save in the most benighted sections of the South, or in times of passion arising from the committing of atrocious crime, is the Negro denied the equal protection of the laws. If he is sometimes put in jail for no reason at all in Memphis, so too are whites put in jail for no reason at all in Pittsburgh. This is the unjust fate, not of the Negro alone, but of the poor, the obscure, and the inarticulate everywhere, regardless of pigmentation. The ownership, also, of more than a billion dollars' worth of property by Negroes in the South alone, and the presence of prosperous Negro business concerns throughout the country, are some refutation of the sweeping statement that Negroes are denied property rights in this country.

Through the mouth of Bigger's lawyer we are told in unmistakable terms that the damming up of the Negro's aspirations, and the denial to him of unrestricted entry into the whole environment of the society in which he is cast, may lead Negroes, in conjunction with others, toward a new civil war in America. Mr. Wright seems to have completely forgotten the unparalleled phenomenon—unique in the world's history—of the *first* American Civil War, in which millions of white men fought and killed one another over the issue of the black slave. If it be granted that the original enslavement of Negroes was a crime against justice, then it must also be granted that its bloody expiation was filled with enough death and destruction to satisfy even the most hate-consumed Negro. But it doesn't seem to satisfy Mr. Wright. A second civil war must begin where the first one left off in order to bring about the eventual freeing of the Negro minority, even if it means the destruction of the society of the majority. Justice and understanding are to come through the persuasive snouts of machine guns.

Bigger's lawyer is a Jew. As a member of a race which has known something of oppression,—not for three centuries, the length of the Negro's residence in America, but for more than twenty centuries in nearly every country of the world,—he pleads extenuation for his client both on broad grounds of justice and on the ground that white society drove Bigger to crime by repressing him. If repression of the members of a minority drives them to slay members of the majority, it would follow that the principal occupation of Jews in Tsarist Russia, Poland, Rumania, and other bitterly anti-Semitic countries would have been to use their oppressors as clay pigeons. Jewish revolutionists there have been, indeed, but over the whole sweep of two thousand years of dark Jewish history the mass of these people, enduring greater oppression than Negroes knew here even in slavery, created within the walls of their ghettos an intense family and communal life and constructed inexhaustible wells of spiritual resource. They used their talents and energies as best they could, serene in the belief either that a Messiah would ultimately come and deliver them out of bondage into the Promised Land or that justice would ultimately triumph. Mr. Wright uses a Jewish lawyer as his mouthpiece, but he has learned nothing from Jewish history, nor gleaned anything of the spirit of that group whom Tacitus called 'a stubborn people.'

It is beyond doubt that Negroes labor under grave difficulties in America; that economic and social discrimination is practised against them; that opportunities open to whites are closed to blacks. It is also beyond doubt that the position, if not the status, of the Negro is constantly improving in the United States. The evidence on this point is overwhelming. But there is one hard and inescapable fact which must be courageously faced. The social structure of America, despite many racial admixtures, is Anglo-Saxon. And nowhere on earth—save in isolated instances—do whites and Negroes in Anglo-Saxon communities intermingle socially or intermarry. And so long as this is a fact, neither the Negro—and this is what completely escapes Mr. Wright—*nor the white man* will function as a full-fledged personality. It could easily be demonstrated that Southern whites living in the presence of masses of Negroes, and maintaining at least tolerable racial relations through the exercise of exquisite, intuitive tact on both sides, suffer aberrations and distortions of the spirit only slightly less severe than those suffered by Negroes.

It is no fault of the Negro or of the present generation of whites that the Negro is here. But the preaching of Negro hatred of whites by Mr. Wright is on a par with the preaching of white hatred of Negroes by the Ku Klux Klan. The position, moreover, of a minority struggling toward the sun must be gauged at any given time by its relative rather than its absolute state, and in accordance with this postulate it is clear that the Negro's lot in America is constantly being ameliorated.

It is highly significant of the whole hate-headlong point of view of Mr. Wright that he has chosen to make his hero so hopelessly despairing of making a good life for himself because of white repressions, that he drives him to crime and execution when his adult life has hardly begun. Contrast this with the experience of the Jews in England, who were first granted full civil rights only after five centuries of living in the country.

Mr. Wright obviously does not have the long view of history. He wants not only complete political rights for his people, but also social equality, and he wants them now. Justice demands that every right granted to others shall be granted to Negroes, but men are not gods. A hard-headed people will be conscious of the Pauline law of expediency: 'All things are lawful unto me, but all things are not expedient.'

Justice or no justice, the whites of America simply will not grant to Negroes at this time those things that Mr. Wright demands. The Negro problem in America is actually insoluble; all profound, complex social problems are insoluble, and only a politically naïve people will believe otherwise. In the meanwhile, recognition by both sides that the question is insoluble, followed by tempered, sincere efforts to make the best of the situation within its frame of reference, will produce the most equitable results for both. Hatred, and the preaching of hatred, and incitement to violence can only make a tolerable relationship intolerable.

Even Abraham Lincoln did not envisage a time when the Negro question would be solved upon Mr. Wright's terms. In 1862 he said to a Negro delegation who called on him:

> You and we are different races. . . . But even when you cease to be slaves you are yet far from being placed on an equality with the white race. . . . The aspiration of men is to enjoy equality with the best when free, but on this continent not a single man of your race is made the equal of a single man of ours. . . . Go where you are treated best, and the ban is still upon you.

And Mr. Wright's hero kills and dies in Mr. Lincoln's state of Illinois.

The Reverend Joseph McSorley. *Catholic World,* 151 (May 1940), 243–44.

This Book-of-the-Month Club story—wholly fictitious—describes the criminal career of a psychopathic Negro youth who has been stunted mentally and morally by the environment in which White America forces the members of his race to live; and most of the book is taken up with the thoughts and impulses provoked in Bigger Thomas by endless repression and frustration. He is bestial, treacherous, utterly unlovable, with no redeeming trait—a typical product of the policy which wealthy, cultured, liberty-loving America has consistently pursued in dealing with the Blacks. Barring obscurities and exaggerations, the author's work has been well done to this extent that he gives us a striking and, indeed, a profoundly moving picture. What purpose he had in mind, however, the reader will find it difficult to surmise.

The story will impress reasonable people with an acute sense of our common responsibility for the present condition of the Negro in America. But that impression might much better have been produced by some other means. In so far as this tale may be taken to represent actual conditions, it will have the effect of spreading and deepening distrust of the Negro. Granted that our society is criminally responsible for having taken an attitude toward the black man which tends to turn him into a savage moron, brooding on his wrongs, merely waiting his chance to rape and kill—and there is at least some truth in this assumption—what is the logical deduction? First of all of course that we should acknowledge our guilt and then undertake to co-operate intelligently with the Negro in his attempt to rise to a higher level. But meanwhile, what? Why if Mr. Wright's description is true to life, then every healthy young Negro male must be regarded with justifiable suspicion and carefully barred from the opportunities of crime which are open to the average American citizen. In a word, the argument has been carried far too far.

It was easy to see that this book would be a best seller. Immediately its transcendental merits were proclaimed by that chorus of critics who in respect of faultless timing and perfect unison are superior even to a symphony orchestra. Nevertheless, discriminating people will regard the book as a wordy presentation of a familiar, irrefutable thesis. Wordy because something like 360 pages lie between the prospective reader and the last line of the book. And not capable of refutation, because our treatment of the Negro has been obviously as unintelligent as it has been brutal and the futile throwing of crumbs from the tables of well-meaning white people easily produces new misery and new crime. Incidentally, the wholly admirable character in Mr. Wright's cast is the Communist lawyer Max, and the sole hope of lasting improvement for the Negro is contained in Mr. Max's program.

David Daiches. *Partisan Review,* 7 (May-June 1940), 245.

. . . Mr. Wright's novel has already been widely discussed in the press, and hailed as a powerful study of a certain type of Negro mind, a type of mind, as the book makes clear, which has been produced by the treatment of the colored people by the whites through the generations. The sullen helplessness of an oppressed race living in the midst of its oppressors, yet cut off from them, is well portrayed, and the conclusion—that under these circumstances a man will find the only freedom he has ever known in accepting full responsibility for a crime which was unpremeditated and unintentional, and that we can only understand this by understanding the psychology produced by his environment—is convincingly pushed home. There is a real honesty in the book, a patent desire to understand thoroughly, and to make the reader understand, what the story of Bigger Thomas *means*. The story is deliberately organised so as to bring to light the psychological and sociological factors underlying the action. The events are unimportant; the author is concerned to point out that this *kind* of thing is produced by this kind of attitude, and the responsibility lies not with those who adopt it but with the community in general. It is a pity, therefore, that the actual crime of Bigger Thomas should have been made so violent and unusual. To hack off the head of an accidentally smothered girl with a hatchet so as to be able to stick her body more conveniently into the furnace is not the kind of action to which the Bigger Thomases of America are likely to be driven, and consequently Mr. Wright's novel, as interpretation, suffers. True, the author is at pains to insist that the actual crime is unimportant, that it is the attitude that lay behind it that matters. But why, then, does he introduce such a violent and fortuitous piece of action? The whole point about a novel of this kind, which is trying to probe behind action to an explanation of the nature and origin of the typical situation the action represents, lies in its general applicability, and the action therefore should be conceived as illustrative fable. The fable would have been more powerful had it been made up of events of less melodramatic quality, showing the murder of personality by environment and the death-in-life that follows by suggesting the cumulative effect of petty crimes and petty frustrations. Mr. Wright is trying to prove a normal thesis by an abnormal case, and though the case he chooses is one proof of his thesis it is not the most convincing. Yet in spite of this fault, this is an important and a persuasive work. The gap between the fable and the moral may weaken the book as a novel, but the separate parts are well done. . . .

Sterling A. Brown. *Opportunity*, 18 (June 1940), 185–86.

A Book-of-the-Month Club selection, its first edition sold out within three hours, a quarter million copies called for within six weeks, Richard Wright's *Native Son* is a literary phenomenon. Magazines have run articles about it after the first reviews. It is discussed by literary critics, scholars, social workers, journalists, writers to the editor, preachers, students, and the man in the street. It seems important to the reviewer that debates on *Native Son* may be heard in grills and "juke-joints" as well as at "literary" parties, in the deep South as well as in Chicago, among people who have not bothered much to read novels since Ivanhoe was assigned in high school English.

One commentator writes that the

book "has torn the surface veneer from a condition which is awakening the conscience of the entire nation." Only the future can decide whether the revelations in *Native Son* awaken the conscience of the nation; according to history that conscience is not easily aroused. But, if such a great and difficult task could be achieved by a single book, *Native Son* is that book.

Richard Wright is, of course, not the first Negro to compound bitterness and wisdom eloquently, nor the first to see the terrible effects of frustration. He is the first, however, to give a psychological probing of the consciousness of the outcast, the disinherited, the generation lost in the slum jungles of American civilization. Mr. Wright has urged that novelists should have perspective and an integrated vision of their material. In *Native Son* he gives such a philosophical novel. With a narrative skill all of his own, with what he has elsewhere called "the potential cunning to steal into the inmost recesses of the human heart," with a surprising mastery of the techniques of fiction, tested in the past as well as the present, Mr. Wright has struck with tremendous impact. Earlier writers have likewise struck out; sometimes their blows were powerful; sometimes they were scattered, or glanced off, or missed altogether.

In one of Mr. Wright's short stories, Big Boy left "home"—a community in the deep South where white violence erupted spasmodically and where Negroes lived in a slow paralysis of fear. In Chicago Bigger meets with forces as destructive, but unlike Big Boy, he cannot leave his home. Daily, as with so many of his fellows on the Southside, or in Harlem, or in Philadelphia, Washington, Atlanta, Birmingham—wherever you choose by insult, indignity, and injury, now petty, now gross, always constant—the iron is driven into Bigger's soul. The first scene, where Bigger and Buddy corner a rat and smash it with a skillet, sets the tone for the grim sequence. *Native Son* would be distinguished if for no other reason than the social realism with which Chicago's Southside is presented. Here are the rickety "kitchenette" flats, which produce such exorbitant returns for the realtors' little investment that the human wastage does not count. Here are the dives, the poolrooms, the ineffectual boys' clubs where crimes are planned. The crushed products of this environment—although slightly sketched, for Bigger gets the lion's share—are quite convincing: Bigger's gang of Jack, G. H., and Gus; Buddy the brother (the last two are brilliantly characterized); the tragic kid Vera, sensitive to the quick, gentle-hearted and doomed; Mrs. Thomas who seeks escape through religion but cannot find it there; and Bigger's sweetheart Bessie: "She worked long hours, hard and hot hours seven days a week, with only Sunday afternoons off; and when she did get off she wanted fun, hard and fast fun, something to make her feel that she was making up for the starved life she led."

The narrative drive of this novel from the killing of the rat, through the two murders, the flight, to the capture on the tenement roof is amazing. In contrast, the last section slows down. This is to be expected, but there is likewise some repetitiousness. *Native Son* is naturally compared to Dreiser's *An American Tragedy,* but there are great differences, and one of these involves technique. A naturalist, Dreiser piles detail upon detail to gain verisimilitude; but Wright, seeking truth to a reality beyond naturalism, makes use of the devices of the symbolic novel, as do such writers as Steinbeck, Faulkner, Caldwell and Dos Passos. He compresses a great deal in small space and time; for instance, a philanthropist interested in Negro education, a politician riding to power on Negro baiting, representatives of a sensational press, the overzealous young Communist Jan, and Mary, the victim of the accidental murder; the older, more understanding Communist lawyer, Max, a Negro preacher; these and other symbolic personages cross Bigger's tragic path. With so much compression, verisimilitude is sometimes sacrificed. The hiding of the girl's body, the delay in discovering the crime, the ease with which the kidnapping note is delivered are details not completely convincing. From melodrama (even though of such a high order) some losses are as inevitable as the sure gains.

But Mr. Wright's greatest achievement is not his description of a setting, as revelatory as that is, nor his conduct of narrative, as thrilling as that is, but his characterization of Bigger Thomas. It took courage to select as hero, a wastrel, a sneak thief, a double-killer. Most writers of minority groups select as heroes those who disprove stereotypes. Here is the "bad nigger" set down without squeamishness, doing all that the "bad nigger" is supposed to do. But that is merely the start. Mr. Wright sees all around this "bad nigger" and through him, and we get the interpretative realism that shows how inevitable it was that he should get that way. Here in brief compass we see a youngster who could have been, should have been, so much more, stunted and twisted into a psychopathic hater, feeling free and important only after a murder, exercising his new power in concocting a kidnapping plot absurdly fashioned after the movies which, with the poolrooms, were his chief educators. Mr. Wright uses more than once the symbol of the rat, now cornered, now dashing into a hole, and Bigger's concept of the meeting ground between whites and Negroes as a No Man's Land. "What can I do? They got me," he asked. He knew that they had had him for a long time.

The lawyer, Max, in a profound speech (less a courtroom plea for life imprisonment than a philosophical statement of the tragic race problem) says: "Multiply Bigger Thomas twelve million times, allowing for environmental and temperamental variations, and for those Negroes who are completely under the influence of the church, and you have the psychology of the Negro people." Max's statement is considered to be Richard Wright's. If this point is debated one should give full weight to the words: "allowing for environmental and temperamental variations." David Cohn in the current *Atlantic Monthly* considers *Native Son* "a blinding and corrosive study in hate," and lectures the author, reminding him of the Civil War "in which millions of white men fought and killed one another over the issue of the black slaves." This seems to miss the point of the novel, especially the fine closing. Other critics disagree with Mr. Cohn; Henry Seidel Canby in the Book-of-the-Month Club News, for instance, says that "this is not a vindictive book." Among so much else, Mr. Wright has established authentically and powerfully that hatred exists among the kicked around, the dispossessed. It is a further indication of the Negro's position in America that this inevitable fact, known so well by Negroes, recorded often by social scientists but never before so forcefully by our creative writers, has caused such perturbation. *Native Son* should silence many of the self-appointed white "interpreters" of the Negro, who, writing from a vantage (?) point above and outside of the race, reveal the Negro as one peculiarly endowed to bear the burdens and suffer the shame without rancor, without bitterness, and without essential humanity.

Wallace Stegner. *Virginia Quarterly Review,* 16 (Summer 1940), 462.

. . . A breathless melodrama by Richard Wright, "Native Son" has invited comparison with "An American Tragedy." The fate of Bigger Thomas is the fate of a social outcast. But I fail to be quite convinced of Bigger's representativeness, and the plea of Bigger's lawyer is a plea for such broad and uncritical pardon for personal weakness or viciousness that it sinks the behaviorist boat. Bigger has been wronged, but he wrongs, too. A pitiable and warped figure, he is hardly tragic. . . .

Robert Littell. *Yale Review,* 29 (Summer 1940), x.

. . . A best-seller, and a powerful one (as we reviewers say of a book when we find it strong but ugly), but a novel that would be better if the blueprint weren't so clear, is *Native Son,* by a Negro, Richard Wright. The story of two peculiarly brutal murders, it is a strange one for a man to be telling about a member of his own race. Mr. Wright apparently deliberately shuns the possibilities of surprise and suspense which the situation offers him. He slogs ahead with an effective but bludgeoning realism. We lose interest in the victim because of the ease with which his creator forces him to be caught. At the end, there is a curious attempt to explain the inevitability of the crime, and even to excuse it as the outcome of race oppression. But by this time, one is a little too numbed by the tank-like march of events to listen very carefully. Perhaps the book's success can be explained by the existence of a great many people who like to see a triphammer in action, even when they know well before-hand what the hammer is going to squash and when and how. . . .

Checklist of Additional Reviews

Allen Maxwell. *Dallas Morning News,* March 3, 1940, section 3, p. 14.

Des Moines Register, March 3, 1940, p. 9.

New Bedford Standard Times, March 3, 1940, p. 19.

New Orleans Times-Picayune, March 3, 1940, section 2, p. 9.

Fanny Butcher. *Chicago Tribune,* March 6, 1940, p. 19.

James E. Daugherty. *St. Louis Globe-Democrat,* March 9, 1940, p. 13.

Wilbur Needham. *Los Angeles Times,* March 10, 1940, section 3, p. 7.

Louisville Courier-Journal Sunday Magazine, March 10, 1940, p. 7.

Jack Lockhart. *Memphis Commercial-Appeal,* March 10, 1940, section 4, p. 10.

Springfield Republican, March 10, 1940, p. 7e.

Joseph Henry Jackson. *San Francisco Chronicle,* March 11, 1940, p. 15.

Mike Gold (New York) *Sunday Worker,* March 31, 1940, section 2, p. 7.

Booklist, 36 (April 1, 1940), 307.

Ben Burns. *San Francisco People's World,* April 2, 1940, p. 5.

J. D. Jerome. *Journal of Negro History,* 25 (April 1940), 251-52.

Ralph Ellison. *TAC* (Theatre Arts Committee), April 1940.

Cleveland Open Shelf (May 1940), 12.

"Readers' Replies (to Sillen reviews)." *New Masses,* 35 (May 21, 1940), 23-26.

J. R. Johnson. *The New International,* 6 (May 1940), 92-93.

Wisconsin Library Bulletin, 36 (May 1940), 101.

Equality [N.Y.], 2 (June 1940).

Joseph H. Jenkins, Jr. *Phylon,* 2 (Second Quarter 1940), 195-97.

Pratt [Institute Quarterly Library Booklist] (Autumn 1940), p. 24.

Don Stanford. *The Southern Review*, 6 (Winter 1940), 619.

12 Million Black Voices

A FOLK HISTORY OF THE NEGRO IN THE UNITED STATES

TEXT BY

RICHARD WRIGHT

PHOTO-DIRECTION BY

EDWIN ROSSKAM

THE VIKING PRESS

NEW YORK · 1941

12 Million Black Voices

"Richard Wright's Powerful Narrative Beautifully Illustrated in New Book." (New York) *Sunday Worker*, November 9, 1941, p. 22.

The combination of Richard Wright's devastating pen and the vivid, skillfully selected pictures of Mr. Rosskam hits the reader with terrific impact.

The net effect is a brief but sweeping picture of the Negro in America, from the first boat-load of slaves to reach Jamestown in 1619 to the present moment when the sons of Uncle Tom wend their way in unison with the white worker into the mills and factories of America. The raw unposed photographs merge into the tragic but fearless text which Wright has woven around them.

It is perhaps the first realistic, class-conscious narrative of the Negro people in the United States ever to be gotten together. Written in a popular, picturesque fashion, it telescopes the Negro's history and strivings in terms of the clash between him and his class and national oppressors.

When it talks about the Negro steel worker, the Negro sharecropper, the Negro domestic woman, the Negro slum life, the Negro's fate at the hands of the Ku Klux mob, the Negro's evictions and discriminations—there are strikingly appropriate pictures to illustrate the point. And the pictures are placed in such proximity to the relevant text as to be of maximum reader convenience and so as to achieve the added poignancy which skillful integration affords.

Who are the Negro people? The outlines of the Negro people as a nation are deftly drawn by Wright's words: "the steady impact of the plantation system upon our lives created new types of behavior and new patterns of psychological reaction, welding us together into a separate unity with common characteristics of our own." And who is the enemy? Wright answers, the "Lords of the Land"—the slaveowners and now the plantation lords—and the "Bosses of the Buildings."

Centering his fire upon these two collaborating oppressors, the author weaves the full pattern of bitterness which the system of private profit has poured into the days of the Negro people. He tells of the heartless jettisoning of human cargoes by the captains of the slave-bearing ships. He tells of the merciless inhumanity of slavery of the tread mill sharecropping system with its feudal policies still going today, of the studied efforts of the Lords of the Buildings to keep their divide-and-rule system going at top speed against Negro and white unity in the industrial centers.

It is all told with Wright's undying words and burning feeling and acid satire, which tears saintly mask from the capitalist who dares to speak of "brotherly love." Wright tries to see the predicament of his people through the eyes of the lowliest Negro worker or peasant—who form the backbone and the great majority of the Negro people. He emphasizes this by writing in the first person, giving the work an intensely personal aspect and dramatically emphasizing his identity with the sufferings and aspirations of his people. The compelling word pictures he paints are illustrated by this comment on how the slaves adapted the forms of their new life on the plantation to their own purpose:

"We stole the words from the grudging lips of the Lords of the Land, who did not want us to know too many of them or their meaning. And we charged this meager horde of stolen sounds with all the emotions and longings we had; we proceeded to build our language in inflections of voice, through tonal variety, by hurried speech, in honeyed drawls, by rolling our eyes, by flourishing our hands, by assigning to common, simple words new meanings, meaning which enabled us to speak of revolt in the secret language, extended our understanding of what slavery meant and gave us the freedom to speak to our brothers in captivity; we polished our new words, caressed them, gave them new shape and color, a new order and tempo, until though they were the words of the Lords of the Land, they became our words, our language."

The book is divided into four parts—first, Our strange Birth; secondly, Inheritors of Slavery; thirdly, Death on the City Pavements; and fourthly, Men in the Making. Together they make a scathing indictment of the tortuous plight of the Negro people, and must impress into the consciousness of all who read that all Americans who wish a better land must make common cause with the Negro. Necessarily, Wright has not gone into detail nor attempted to give an all inclusive portrait.

Perhaps the key to the author's approach is best hinted in the opening paragraph:

"Each day when you see us black folk upon the dusty land of the farms or upon the hard pavement of the city streets, you usually take us for granted and think you know us, but our history is far stranger than you suspect, and we are not what we seem."

And the book goes on from there to explain just what goes on in the mind of the Negro as a result of his environment. The result is a winding story of detective-story suspense and thrills, claiming the minds of the Negro who has been most immersed in the story as actor and victim, as well as the rapt attention of the white public which has already begun to shed much of its bourbon-inspired misinformation with regard to Negro Americans.

We play and we laugh says Wright, but even our songs tell of our yearnings and they serve as cultural reservoirs for the pain of our breaking backs. Moreover, says Wright, it is the custom of the oppressors to speak of the victims as great players and frolickers to siphon off their own class guilt. But this ruling class practice has erected a studied system of caricaturing the Negroes while carefully avoiding all mention of the Negro's heroic struggles. . . .

Most interesting is Wright's handling of "Cotton" whose sex he changes from "King" to "Queen" and who holds a stranglehold on Negro life; his dealing with the Negro women as "triply" oppressed, the latter being strikingly demonstrated with two pictures, one showing how the Negro domestic must tend an infant heiress while her baby must rest in a roach-infested kitchenette.

One could wish, however, that the picture would have been a bit more balanced. Interwoven in the desperate heart-rending trials and tribulations of the Negro have been great achievements both individual and of a mass character. There were slave revolts, Denmark Veseys, Nat Turners, Douglasses and Harriet Tubmans. There were Emancipation Proclamations in which the Negro people fought back, bled and died that they and America might be free. There were 20th Century Dred Scott cases—Scottsboro and Herndon—which under the leadership of the Communist Party raised the whole status of the Negro liberation struggles and set America's conscience aflame. There is a distinctly new South growing up today, where great bodies of poor and liberal whites are rejecting the Ku Klux fascism of a Talmadge.

This is not to say, however, that the book does not contain these things. . . . The Negro people—especially their strong young sons and daughters of today—must have heroic qualities and must be following the vision of a better world to survive the demoralizing misery which Wright has so brilliantly etched. But one does not feel the same creative scope and power in the heroism of the Negroes as is so realistically depicted in the devastations wrought by class oppression upon Negro life.

There is the emergence of a Negro proletariat which is fighting its way into the leadership of the Negro liberation movement and taking its place beside the white workers for the equality and freedom of all from exploitation. To be sure, an indication of the bright future is described in the book's final chapter, Men in the Making. But it would have been considerably stronger if the richness and vividness of the previous chapters had been included here too.

In the foreword, Wright pointed out that his narrative would not touch upon the Negro higher income and upper class groups. This statement is recognition of the fact that in any study of the Negro and his plight, the upper classes, who are not in terms of treatment, too far removed from the basic proletariat, belong in the plan. The struggle for the complete liberation of the Negro people is a people's struggle, that is, one of a nation, in which all classes have a stake in striking down the fetters of the Lords of the Land and the Bosses of the Buildings. More, too, might have been said of the common interests of the Negroes with other immigrant minority groups who are but one rung higher than the Negroes on the economic ladder.

Written before the character of the war had changed and before America's national existence was placed in such dire peril, the book does not touch upon the stake of the Negroes in battle to crush Hitler. Not only are all the vital gains that the Negro people have made in America in danger, but the right to continue the fight against the terrible evils which Wright so eloquently describes are now being fought out before Moscow, Rostov and Chungking.

America would be stronger today, Wright tells us, if its black citizens were freed from the cancerous racial discrimination which divides and weakens the land. He says with deadly, unanswerable accuracy:

"We black folk, our history and our present being, are a mirror of all the manifold experiences of America. What we want, what we represent, what we endure is what America is. If we black folk perish, America will perish."

"The March of the Negro." *New York World-Telegram,* November 11, 1941.

Another book that ought to be pondered by American citizens is a book of photographs with a running text called *12 Million Black Voices*. The pictures have been chosen by Edwin Rosskam; the text is by Richard Wright. Both deal with the condition of the submerged Negro in the United States and much of what they reveal is not pleasant for us white folks who have airy offices in which to work, well-equipped homes to go to at night and a fine board at which to dine.

The message is a serious one, and the text is far from commonplace. Indeed, the name of Richard Wright guarantees sincerity, earnestness and a degree of power. He has written as if he were interpreting the experiences of the race, thus holding to a definite point of view. He reminds us how the Negro welcomed freedom and then made the best of the competitive world into which he was projected, the women faring better than the men. He speaks of the white belief that the Negro would perish outside of slavery, but by migration, adaptation and accepting the landlord's terms on the field the Negro has survived. The laws of King Cotton became dictatorial. The harsh conditions under which the field hand worked bore down upon his spirit. . . .

Life north and south, in the city and the town, shows that not all Negroes are poor, not all are field hands. As Richard Wright records that 300-year pilgrimage of the black people in America, the Negroes say: "We ask you to grant us nothing. We are winning our heritage, though our toll in suffering is great. . . . We are with the new tide."

Mr. Wright purposely omits "the talented tenth" for the sake of simplification. As always, his lines ring with vitality. He writes powerfully. If you read Erskine Caldwell's *You Have Seen Their Faces* you will want this.

Horace R. Cayton. "Wright's New Book More than a Study of Social Status." *Pittsburgh Courier,* November 15, 1941.

Although this column usually concerns itself with labor and economic questions, this week I'm taking time out for a book review. Some of you may wonder what book is important enough to divert my attention from the industrial scene when things are happening with such rapidity. The answer is the new book "12 Million Black Voices" by Richard Wright and Edwin Rosskam.

In the first place, it is my opinion that Richard Wright is a great writer, not a great Negro writer, but the real McCoy. Probably one reason why I think this is because he is writing about a social scene with which I am very familiar. With my associates in Sociology and Social Anthropology I studied the social, economic, and psychological background which produced Bigger Thomas of "Native Son." For every adjective which Wright used we have a label, for every move that Bigger took, we have a map; for every personality type he encountered we have a life history. What I am trying to get over is the fact that in general a large research project which was carried on in Chicago's Black Belt for a period of four years substantiated the entire thesis of "Native Son." We produced the material, we know the theory, but we could not state it in the power or form it needed. We could also write a book about Chicago, but it won't sell three hundred thousand copies nor reach one per cent of that number of readers nor have the social impact of Wright's book. That's why I think Wright is a great writer—and by now I guess you have gathered that it is going to be a "rave" notice.

This new book is magnificent in its simplicity, directness and force. It is the obverse side of "Native Son," for it is a study of the habitat, the mileu, the social matrix from which warped social personalities such as Bigger Thomas arise and will continue to arise until there is some fundamental change in the position and status of the American Negro.

But "12 Million Black Voices" is more than just description; it is a philosophy of the history of the Negro in America and a frame of reference for the study of Negro-white relations in this country. It seems hard for me to see just how any intelligent social observer can disagree with Wright. The experience of the Negro through slavery to the "Shadows of the Plantation" during the mass migration are described in the first two sections. It was the chapter on the city, however, that intrigued my imagination. For those of you who have worked on the problems which confront urban Negroes—who are, for example, interested in housing—the force and power of these passages are thrilling. . . .

It's not a pretty picture that Wright paints but he has two answers for that possible criticism. He states in the preface that he is not writing about the "talented tenth," that group of largely mulattoes who, because of fortuitous circumstances, blood relationship with whites or historical accident, were able to escape from the black masses and achieve positions of security, cultural advantage and comfort. Many persons will not like the book. They will say that it shows the worst side of Negro life, that white people should not be told about all of these things. To them Wright says:

"As our jobs begin to fail in another depression, our lives and the lives of our children grow so frightful that even some of our educated black leaders are afraid to make known to the nation how we exist. They become ashamed of us and tell us to hide our wounds."

This review, or no review of the book, would not be complete without some mention of the marvelous photographs which illustrate the text. The pictures were taken by the Photographic Section of the Farm Security Administration and edited by Edwin Rosskam. Recently I had an opportunity of looking over the entire 1500 shots which were taken in Chicago alone. When I had finished, my reply to Rosskam was that I, who had helped to pick out the scenes and had worked with him in Chicago, could not believe what I had seen. Unrelieved by riding through better neighborhoods on the way for other shots, to turn over these 1,500 pictures, one after another, with the drabness, squalor, horror and poverty was too much for me to longer put credence in my own senses. The society about which Wright wrote and which Rosskam illustrated just couldn't exist in America . . . but it does, and for years my associates and I have tried to describe it by figures, maps and graphs. Now, Wright and Rosskam have told the story as it has never been told before.

Ernestine Rose. *Library Journal,* 66 (November 15, 1941), 999.

This is much more a documentary film than a history. The simple language and terse, forceful narrative heighten this effect, which is also emphasized by the striking photographs, selected by Edwin Rosskam from the files of the United States Farm Security Administration. The book is a passionate indictment of the unjust and cruel social condition of the Negro masses, and describes their slow struggle to free themselves. Mr. Wright concerns himself with this submerged group alone, calling his story a folk history. Within these limits, it is fair, honest, and very moving.

Ralph Thompson. *New York Times,* November 18, 1941, p. 29.

The enormous collection of documentary photographs in the Farm Security Administration files (now numbering 65,000, more or less) has again been drawn upon to illustrate a striking book, this time a report on the plight of the Negro in the United States: "12 Million Black Voices," by the author of "Native Son," Richard Wright.

A more eloquent and belligerent statement of its kind could hardly have been devised. Mr. Wright's text is neither "impartial" nor does it attempt to show "all sides"; it is a stinging indictment of American attitudes toward the Negro over a period of 300 years. The photographs, selected and arranged by Edwin Rosskam, reinforce the text and bear it out: here a ramshackle hut in a cotton field, there a dirty cold-water flat in Harlem; here black women and children in burlap or rags, there a black man, riddled with bullets hanging from a tree.

Mr. Wright speaks as a rebel; his people, he declares, have no choice but to be either victims or rebels. "Our years pass," he cries, "within the web of a system we cannot beat." First came slavery with its horrors, then "abrupt" emancipation, then "migration, disillusionment, bewilderment, joblessness and insecurity." What, he asks bitterly, is to come next, and how much longer are we expected to wait?

It will probably be argued that Mr. Wright ought to have shown "all sides," or at least have tried to balance the equation somewhat by pointing out what has been done for the Negro in recent years and, above all, what the Negro has succeeded in doing for himself. But books of protest are never written in the spirit of a grocer weighing out sugar or flour, and there is no reason to expect that they should be or ever will be. "Look at us and know us," Mr. Wright says, "and you will know yourselves, for *we* are *you,* looking back at you from the dark mirror of our lives."

The photographs are reproduced in gravure. Of the eighty or ninety included, all but a half dozen are from the FSA files. The photographers most often represented are Jack Delano, Marion Post, Arthur Rothstein and Russell Lee.

William Shands Meacham. "The Bitter Saga of the Negro." "The Drama of Centuries Compressed into a Short Book Written in Astringent Prose." *New York Times Book Review,* November 23, 1941, p. 11.

Since democracy is now engaged in a desperate struggle to prove its right to survive before the world, there could hardly be a better time for the retelling of the story of that portion of the American population which came to our shores during another "nightmare interval" of history. This was a long nightmare, as long as the macabre history of the slave trade and the traffic in men. The saga of the black folk in America is more than three centuries old, and *nobody knows the trouble they've seen,* if the title of their folksong may be slightly paraphrased.

All this story has been factually told at encyclopedic length in the histories and the learned journals of the social sciences, but it has needed a more poignant recital in the voice of the folk themselves. Richard Wright has become this voice, respecting the historians, the economists and the sociologists, but out of his own consciousness as a Negro telling the story from the wings of the stage across which he sees his people move in a plot that has been made of a strange "paradoxical amalgam of love and cruelty." The narrator speaks in flawless prose that takes on at times the quality of a folksong—a bitter folksong, not at all in the tone of resignation with which those on the stage sing their songs.

To compress all this drama of centuries into a book of less than 200 pages, the prose must be astringent: "The opinion of the nation divided into two opposing constellations—a world of machines and a world of slaves." Thus we are told that the irrepressible conflict between the cotton kingdom of the South and the industrial North is approaching. Mr. Wright sees the Civil war as a struggle between the lords of the land and the bosses of the buildings. The "gnawing of some obscure sense of guilt" that was in part responsible for the freeing of the slaves did not, in the end, we are told, bring about the real emancipation of the black folk.

Of all the Negroes in the United States more than one-half are tillers of the soil, says the narrator, and "three-fourths of us who till the soil are sharecroppers and day laborers." When it is settlement time at the plantation commissary, says this voice of the twelve million, "we lower our eyes, shake our heads and mutter:

A naught's a naught,
Five's a figger;
All for the white man,
None for the nigger.

As cotton sapped the fertility of the soil of the South, the scene did undergo a change, and there was a migration of Negroes from the farms to the cities. In 1890 there were only 1,500,000 black folk in the cities, but in 1920 there were 3,500,000 in the urban centers of the nation. "In Chicago our endless trek inflated the Black Belt population by more than 125,000 from 1920 to 1930," says Mr. Wright. In the cities the hapless pilgrims met the Bosses of the

Buildings, who crowded them into little "kitchenette" apartments, that brought high profits to the owners but condemned to death the children of the tenants, as contagious diseases spread like fire. The Bosses of the Buildings used the confused black men as strike-breakers, but they could not take hold of the tools of the trades, for the Lords of the Land in the South had not provided schools. "What we mean, of course," says Richard Wright, "is that we know nothing but manual labor. Hence, while the Croat, the Welshman, the Frenchman, the Spaniard, to whom opportunities are open, merge with the river of American life, we black folk remain out of touch with the quickening fluids of American hope."

The author writes of the mass of the Negro folk of America, and not of the "talented tenth" of his race. He ends his book on a note of hopefulness and courage, but the shadow over his people has been more greatly lightened than he cares to admit. His people have heard vague talk of a government in Washington that desires the welfare of all. The homes which the United States Housing Authority is helping to build all over America for the Negro folk who lived in the "kitchenette" apartments in the North and in the tumbledown shacks in the South, are tangible with concrete foundations. Yet, they are made for the humblest. The Roosevelt Administration has done more to further the second emancipation of the Negro than any since the Civil War. It has, indeed, done more for the South, and all its people, than any administration since the issue of slavery was settled in the United States. This is not the story Mr. Wright started out to tell, yet almost all the excellent photographs selected for his book by Edwin Rosskam came from the files of the Farm Security Administration. That far-away government at Washington has seen the faces of Mr. Wright's folk.

Samuel Sillen. "Richard Wright's Latest Book . . . Is the Tearless Narrative of the Negro People's Life in America: A Magnificent Literary and Pictorial Study." *New Masses*, 41 (November 25, 1941) 22–24.

While reading this magnificent book I kept thinking of a remark made by Richard Wright shortly after the publication of *Native Son*. I remember the occasion vividly. Wright had given a talk at Columbia University that evening on "How Bigger Was Born." In the discussion which followed, a member of the audience complained, in all good faith, that the author had gone too far in *Native Son*. The speaker felt that the experience had been too devastating, that Wright had failed to provide some kind of emotional release. It was in answer to this criticism that Wright made a comment which has great significance for any interpretation of his work. He pointed out that some readers of his earlier volume of stories, *Uncle Tom's Children,* had praised the book because it made them weep. And Wright had made up his mind that in his future work he was not going to provide, so far as he could help it, "the consolation of tears." He was not interested in that kind of emotional release.

The remark may have seemed hardboiled and even cruel to some listeners. Actually it was nothing of the sort. What Wright was getting at, I believe, was his deep and passionate conviction that any approach to Negro life in terms of "the pathetic" falsifies reality. We have had enough tears. We have had enough of those who feel badly about Negro oppression and who comfort themselves with the thought that they are sufficiently sensitive to feel badly. Something deeper than sympathy is required. Nothing less than the transformation of human consciousness is needed. The meaning of Negro life as an organic part of American life must be burned into our minds. At the core of that meaning there is "an uneasily tied knot of pain and hope whose snarled strands converge from many points of time and space." And the writer, if he is to be in truth an engineer of human souls, must disentangle these historical threads and chart the future in which, by our common effort, they will be bound together again in a greater and more purposeful unity.

History, then, to begin with. Of course, Wright has not attempted a formal and detailed chronicle of the 300-year experience of the Negro people in America. He has depicted the basic patterns of that complex experience in its movement from the debased forms of feudalism toward the industrial and urban society of the twentieth century. The past 300 years, crowded as Wright says with suffering and abrupt transitions, have been equivalent to 2,000 years in the history of whites. In a very short space, Wright has brilliantly done the nearly impossible through the magic of his prose. By the use of powerful symbols and richly suggestive overtones he has recreated a historical drama. We see the African torn from his native soil, brutally wrenched from his family, uprooted from his own highly developed cultural milieu. The horrors of the slave ships are portrayed in a few paragraphs; but every word is aflame with imagery and understanding. And then the years of degradation under slavery, years of incredible torment and noble revolt; the new slavery of the sharecropping system; the terrifying problems of urbanization following the world war. The vast panorama unfolds. The scales fall from our eyes.

If the story has such a tremendous impact, it is not merely because a superbly gifted master of living speech has told it. "Each day," the text begins, "when you see us black folk upon the dusty land of the farms or upon the hard pavement of the city streets, you usually take us for granted and think you know us, but our history is far stranger than you suspect, and we are not who we seem." It is *we* who tell the story and the story is *ourselves*. The voice is that of 12,000,000 Negroes whose manifold individual experiences has a basic identity. And the choral form of expression is not a literary mannerism or device. It is the inevitable form for this material. The result is far from that chaotic and noisy cacophony which some writers have falsely assumed to be the only "realistic" expression of mass experience. On the contrary, the prose is harmonious, resonant, eloquent. A *nation* is speaking, with dignity and passion and pride.

There is no pretense here, no disposition to forget or hide the truth, however ugly or brutal. The life of the Negro people is interpreted in the only light that can make it intelligible: in the light, that is to say, of historical materialism. Wright makes it clear that at the bottom of the various shifts and wrenches in the Negro experience there are shifts and wrenches in the productive relations of society. The Negro has been an object of exploitation by a ruling class, whether under feudalism or capitalism. The forms of his exploitation have changed; the fundamental fact remains. One need only look at the photos in this volume to see at a glance that life in a twentieth century city tenement can be as grim as life on the plantation; that the uniformed policeman in a factory town can be just as tough as any constable in the rural South. In every area of American contemporary life, in school and church, politics and industry, Jim Crow rules in whatever disguise.

But the economic and class factors underlying Negro history do not constitute the whole story. What Wright succeeds in doing is to show the influence of these factors on the ideas and emotions of people. He communicates the fears and desires, the agony and hope of real human beings. He suggests the profound differences between the folk culture of a pre-industrial environment and the new consciousness emerging in the new environment of the North. For the irony is that the new forms of exploitation enabled millions of Negroes to come in contact for the first time with the essential processes of modern life and they created the conditions for understanding between more and more Negroes and whites. Until the moment, now reached, when the Lords of the Land say, "We will not grant this!"—only to be answered, "We ask you to grant us nothing. We are winning our heritage, though our toll in suffering is great!" The moment when the Bosses of the Buildings say, as they always have said: "Your problem is beyond solution"—only to be answered, "Our problem is being solved. We are crossing the line you dared us to cross, though we pay in the coin of death."

This book is a shattering answer to the glib newspaper talk about a "crime wave" in Harlem. The crime goes far deeper than newspaper editors and real estate executives are prepared to admit. The crime is in the ghetto institution itself, bitter symbol of repression and discrimination and greed. The owners are shrewd. They prosper on suffering. Why not take a seven-room apartment that rents for fifty dollars a month to whites, cut it up into seven tiny apartments, rent these "kitchenettes" to Negroes for the "reasonable" sum of twenty-four dollars a month? The fifty-dollar apartment is now worth about $170. There is no competition; Harlem residents have to take what they get. And:

"The kitchenette is our prison, our death sentence without a trial, the new form of mob violence that assaults not only the lone individual, but all of us, in its ceaseless attacks.

"The kitchenette, with its filth and foul air, with its one toilet for thirty or more tenants, kills our black babies so fast that in many cities twice as many of them die as white babies. . . .

"The kitchenette blights the personalities of our growing children, disorganizes them, blinds them to hope, creates problems whose effects can be traced in the characters of its child victims for years afterward. . . .

"The kitchenette is the funnel through which our pulverized lives flow to ruin and death on the city pavement, at a price. . . ." These are the headlines of a crime which does not come in "waves" but in the steady undertow of exploitation. Not the accused but the accuser is the criminal.

We are moving, says Wright at the end of the book, "into the sphere of conscious history." History, that is, which is understood, mastered, and directed by men for human purposes. "Voices are speaking. Men are moving! And we shall be with them. . . ." It is this hopeful determination which is the triumphant note of a narrative that unflinchingly records a thousand and one moments of defeat, humiliation, despair. In the last few pages there is a strengthening of purpose; there is a prophecy of fulfillment.

The photographs accompanying the text . . . have been skillfully arranged by Edwin Rosskam so that there is a steady interplay of word and visual image. Most of the pictures were selected from the files of the Farm Security Administration. They show the Negro in both his rural and urban environment, at work, at play, in the home and school and church, on the picket-line. I was disappointed that so few photos were included in the section on "Men in the Making," the last in the book. Both text and pictures might very well have been elaborated here, particularly with regard to Negro industrial workers.

In *12 Million Black Voices* Richard Wright has applied his brilliant talents as a novelist to a great historical theme. In heightening our understanding of the Negro people he has clarified our understanding of American life. For, as he says: "We black folk, our history and our present being are a mirror of all the manifold experiences of America. What we want, what we represent, what we endorse America *is*. If we black folk perish, America will perish. . . . The differences between black folk and white folk are not blood or color, and the ties that bind us are deeper than those that separate us. The common road of hope which we all have traveled has brought us into a stronger kinship than any words, laws, or legal claims. Look at us and know us and you will know yourselves, for *we* are *you,* looking back at you from the dark mirror of our lives." And, in holding up this clear and meaningful mirror to America Richard Wright has demonstrated again and with new intensity that he is one of the great, one of the truly great American artists of our time.

George Streator. *Commonweal*, 25 (November 28, 1941), 147–48.

Mr. Richard Wright has written a strictly Marxian text to Mr. Edwin Rosskam's photographs, but the book belongs in the library of every student of American life. There is no need to say that this book is propaganda, for it is. But what is not? And why should we not have a good propaganda, after four centuries of vicious propaganda to make life easy for white folk who have bled and exploited black folk?

So far as this Marxian angle is concerned, I think the worst part comes in the foreword, where Mr. Wright speaks words that seem to me, related to Toussaint L'Ouverture and the black slaughter of whites and mulattoes in Haiti that marked the first sharp break between the New World and the Old. I am sensitive about mulattoes, although I am not a mulatto: just a plain light-skinned Negro of legally married light-skinned Negro parentage. My sensitivity grows out of the conviction that the communists and many other forces that want to use black shock troops in the future, the not too distant future, are inclined to separate if possible, blacks from near whites, in the US just as in the West Indies.

Inasmuch as Mr. Wright "intentionally does not include in its considerations those areas of Negro life which comprise the so-called 'talented tenth,' or the islands of mulatto leadership which are still to be found in many parts of the South," the business groups, etc., which he styles a "liaison corps" between whites and blacks, I am moved to join once more the ranks of Mr. Wright's critics.

Hence, I am thrown into the laps of the intelligent Catholics who believe that it is just as stupid to preach separatism among the heterogeneous peoples who comprise the American Negro as it is to preach separatism among the Americans, generally. I hope that this booknote makes my own propaganda clear; that those forces which tend to over-emphasize the *color* of the colored people from our backward rural South are missing the bus as completely as any Chamberlain in world history.

That leads me to formulate a "line" for all our radical social scientists. (1) Work to liberate the oppressed, regardless of color. (2) Help black people feel that they, too, are children of the Creator without turning them against the two-thirds of the colored population who are not exactly black. Since their not being black is scarcely the result of a plot on their part, we must fight efforts of Mr. Wright and his followers to make American "Eurasians" out of us.

Other than this, we have a good book to hand to our policy formers. If nothing more, these photographs give us the fruits of human ignorance and disease—things that are not solved by political action alone.

Charles Curtis Munz. "The New Negro." *The Nation,* 153 (December 13, 1941), 620.

If a book is to be judged by what it claims to be, this book is disappointing. It is described in the subtitle as a folk history of the Negro of the United States, but beyond a little doggerel verse from a few Negro folk songs and an occasional sharp interpretation of the Negro's mind at work, it is not a folk history at all. Little or nothing will be found here that is not already known to the moderately keen observer, and certainly this book does not contain half as much information about the Negro as other writers already have presented. What history the book does contain is only a cursory survey of the better-known facts about the Negro: how he was brutally snatched from Africa and pounded down into slavery; how the question of his continued bondage helped to provoke the Civil War; how after that war the Negro discovered his new freedom was essentially empty; how he migrated from the cotton fields of the South to the cities of the North, and found his freedom there rather empty, too. Even this cursory survey is not always sound. For example, Mr. Wright sees the Civil War as mainly a struggle between two groups of leaders, "the Bosses of the Buildings and the Lords of the Land." This is an extreme simplification of what was actually a complicated struggle.

No, there is not much here in the way of history, either folk or political. This book is really something quite different. It is sometimes an appeal, sometimes a defense, and again a defiance, a demand, and a promise—and possibly even a threat—and as all of these it often rings with a bitter and stinging eloquence. It might, in still another sense, be taken as a manifesto that Uncle Tom is finally dead and buried, and that the New Negro, or the Embattled Negro, has arrived, and stands now at his Lexington Green or at his Concord Bridge. What Mr. Wright has to say here is the defiant promise that the Negro, despite all the burdens and humiliations that have been laid upon him, is determined to take what he regards as his proper place in the American scene. Mr. Wright declares: "We are with the new tide. . . . Voices are speaking. Men are moving! And we shall be with them! . . . We are crossing the line you dared us to cross, though we pay in the coin of death!" Some people may object that the promise is too defiant, too much like a threat, the tone too clamorous, to be effective. But it will doubtless be useful for the Negro to acquire a reputation for being clamorous, and even noisy; he has been humble and docile too long; to be noisy is quite probably the only way to be heard.

The numerous photographs, with the exception of half a dozen from other sources, were selected by Mr. Rosskam from the already famous collection of the Farm Security Administration, which of course is the same thing as saying that they are excellent.

E. A. R. *Interracial Review,* 15 (January 1942), 17.

I began with prejudice and ended with pride as I read through the latest book of Richard Wright, *12 Million Black Voices.*

My prejudice was aroused by the title of the book, for at once I noted that two million Negro voices were left out. And the reason the author gave was not satisfying: "intentionally (the book) does not include in its consideration . . . the so-called 'talented tenth' . . . or the growing and influential Negro middle-class professional and business men of the North . . . who have formed a sort of liaison corps between the whites and the blacks." This sounds too much like the "divide and rule" formula which even Wright complains about when he says, "The Lords of the land proceeded to neutralize the strength of us blacks and the growing restlessness of the poor whites by dividing and ruling us, by inciting us against one another."

He has dug deep down into the past and brought to light the trials and tribulations of a minority group doomed to begin life in slavery in a new country. But with pen and picture, in collaboration with Edwin Rosskam, whose pictures are well suited to the text, Richard Wright unfolds a tragic though inspiring story of a people whose bodies were bent and burned, but whose spirit cannot be crushed.

Unlike *Native Son* wherein he employed a white lawyer to defend the brute "Bigger Thomas," in his *12 Million Black Voices* Richard Wright elects to be the spokesman. The story is told in the first person, and as he tells it, he stands in the midst of those "12 Million Black Voices" like a Paul Robeson singing the solo part of "Deep River" to the accompaniment of 11,999,999 voices taking up the refrain. There is no more beautiful passage in the book than that which it takes five pages to say with pen and picture: "Our lives are walled with cotton. We plant and plow cotton. We chop cotton. We pick cotton. When Queen Cotton dies . . . how many of us will die with her?"

The author compresses a story of three hundred years into a book of not over 150 pages. The pictures in the book are like the "song without words," for they speak eloquently: "We have never been allowed to become an organic part of this civilization." He likens these 300 years of progress to the 2000 years of progress of the white race. He says, "we have tramped down a road 300 years long" and "weary but still eager, we stand ready to accept more change." Then he cautions, "If we black folk perish, America will perish."

12 Million Black Voices is satisfying but not all-inclusive. If and when Richard Wright includes the story of the two million silent voices, we shall then have the story of fourteen million voices which will include his own.

L. D. Reddick. "Negro and Jew." *The Jewish Survey*, 2 (January 1942), 25.

It is, perhaps, unnecessary to point out to readers of THE JEWISH SURVEY that there are significant parallels between the experience of the Jewish and Negro peoples. Historically, their periods of slavery, oppression and "emancipation" as well as their responses to them reveal strikingly similar patterns. In the modern world this is inescapably true. Black folk from Georgia appreciate the Jim Crow of German Jews.

And yet, there has not been a widespread or high consciousness of their common dangers among either Jews or Negroes. Unfortunately, so many members of these, as of other "minorities," have been content to fight their own battle with only a glance toward a potential ally.

This mutual apathy is underscored when the pages of Negro and Jewish publications are thumbed in search for discussions of the other's problems and triumphs. On the lowest level may be found those Jews who would classify themselves as "white" and join in the exploitation of the Negro, and those mostly urban Negroes who would classify themselves as "Gentile" and give free rein to anti-Semitism.

To be sure, these anti-Semitic Negroes and anti-Negro Jews have, in recent years, received much more publicity than their numbers deserve. Too, the large ignorance and deep passivity mentioned above seem to be withering away before the doorstep threat of Hitlerism.

A great aid to this solidarity would be a steady stream of books, articles and other materials which would project vital experience in universal symbols—not narrowly racial or by exclusion, indirectly chauvinistic. One such work is *12 Million Black Voices*. Here, within the space of 152 pages, is the statement of the "Negro Question"—historically and currently—in terms understandable to all.

This is a picture book of the Bourke-White type. The 147 photographs are themselves eloquent testimonials. Comment is often unnecessary. We see the faces and hands and homes of share-croppers and stevedores, waiters and dancers, old men and youths, shouting sisters and street urchins, miners and pickets—"and lots more."

Richard Wright's text, though not an historian's summary, is the most poetic prose statement of the folk history of the Negro in this land yet published. Its poetry, as to be expected, is not of the moonlight and magnolia romancing; rather, it is the brilliant, flint-like spark of language which is stark, finely imaginative and yet restrained. The whole suggests America's Epic.

John Field Mulholland. "Negroes in Pictures and Text." *Christian Century,* 59 (February 18, 1942), 219.

In an era of pictorial magazines, books which are primarily pictorial are to be expected, so only a book of exceptional photographic excellence needs mention. The various agencies of the federal government have made an exceptional record of our modern life. The making of motion pictures like "The River" and "The Plow that Broke the Plains" are only part of this photographic record.

From the files of the Federal Security Administration Edward Rosskam has culled an incomparable series of photographs relating to the life of the American Negro. Richard Wright, with the magnificent prose which distinguished *Native Son,* has written a commentary on the pictures. Pictures and text are so interwoven as to make a book of unusual appeal.

Consider the following accusation in Wright's prose: "We black men and women of America, as we look upon scenes of rapine, sacrifice and death, seem to be children of a devilish abberration, descendants of an interval of nightmare in history, fledglings of a period of amnesia on the part of men who once dreamed a great dream and then forgot."

When an accusation of such force is followed by a picture wherein the haunting eyes of a frustrated Negro youth add silent accusation, the book achieves an integration of photograph and text which is rare in books. The text escapes from being merely captions for pictures, and the pictures are far more than mere illustration. At times the book escapes from being the publisher's filler-in that it was probably designed to be and becomes a promise of a new literary form. As it is, *12 Million Black Voices* is a photographic study of the finest and a distinct contribution to the sociology of the American Negro.

Checklist of Additional Reviews

D.I. *PM*, November 2, 1941, p. 56.

New Yorker, 17 (November 15, 1941), 110.

Louisville Courier-Journal, November 18, 1941.

Richard F. Crandell. *New York Herald Tribune Books,* November 23, 1941, p. 8.

U.S. Week, December 20, 1941.

Booklist, 38 (January 1, 1942), 152.

New Republic, 106 (January 5, 1942), 29.

The New Sign, February 5, 1942.

W. E. B. DuBois. *United States, 1865-1900* (Hayes Memorial Foundation of Ohio) (September 1941-August 1942), 26.

Black Boy

A Record of

Childhood and Youth

by

RICHARD WRIGHT

Harper & Brothers Publishers

New York and London

Black Boy

John D. Paulus. *Pittsburgh Press*, February 18, 1945.

Let me acclaim Richard Wright's autobiography, "Black Boy," as one of the best books in its class that you are ever likely to read.

With that fervid encomium we begin consideration of this unusual, unforgettable, fascinating and moving human story which tells of the first 19 years in the life of a sensitive Negro writer who admittedly ranks high among the people, white or black, in his craft.

Setting down intimately and freely the story of his childhood and youth, Richard Wright has here given us a document that could easily take its place alongside the Autobiography of Benjamin Franklin and the Education of Edward Bok. For it is a typically American product—it could never have happened anywhere else in the world.

"Black Boy" tells of a very sensitive child who is manhandled from the cradle. Faced with brutal poverty, the social and economic unbalance of the South, and by his own family, the boy lived a horrid and shameful 19 years—and those in a nation where one of the guiding principles of human relations is the concept that "all men are born free and equal."

At four he sets fire to his own home in play and is burned alive. He is beaten for this childish error until he is delirious and nearly dies.

He strangles a kitten because it keeps his father awake. In punishment, his mother fills his imagination "with a horde of invisible demons bent on exacting vengeance on me for what I had done." She then sends the boy into the dark night to bury the kitten while he recites his guilt.

His miserable family is forced to move, time and time again. On one of these frequent changes, the boy is forced to sleep on a bed in which another boy has died. This terror, quintupled by the imagination of every little boy, keeps him sleepless for many nights.

His father deserts the family—and the boy comes face to face with the sordid conflict between parents who are themselves the victims of a cruel system, cruel neighbors, and a cruel fate. In saloons, whisky is forced upon the little boy so often that he admits, "I became a confirmed drunkard in my sixth year."

Accompanying these maladjustments, these everyday horrors of life, is always hunger, "bitter hunger," as Richard Wright calls it. And hunger, as the world should well know by now, is not only an unforgivable sin in this, the middle of the Twentieth Century, but an economic absurdity in the face of great human and technological advances.

But such is the stature of Richard Wright that he tells his story with a dignity and restraint that characterizes a great artist and a great man. Too many others would have injured a narrative such as this by writing with less self-possession and thus the intense feeling, told here in self-controlled statements of fact, would have been lost in a maze of hot words.

This story is a rich and manysided tale. As a story of child-life among Negroes in the South, it has sheer narrative power that sweeps you from one chapter to another. The people whom Richard Wright presents are not literary shadows—they are real people, they behave like real people.

Picturesque folk-lore, hidden Negro fears and aspirations, colorful superstitions—they abound in this excellent volume. The book's emotional tautness never slackens, despite some light passages. Here is a greatly gifted human being, the reader decides, who is stubbornly resisting the pressure on him to deny and renounce the best in his nature.

The book is a serious indictment of our South—not in any direct accusations by Mr. Wright, but by the strength of his narrative, the power of the facts that he has set down.

Read the book and see for yourself. If you can watch this desperate, trapped, beaten, and hopeless fellow human without a tug in your heart—you need salvation. Richard Wright, despite the first 19 years of his life, doesn't.

"20 Years of Misery." *Omaha World-Herald*, February 25, 1945.

A few days ago a girl student at the College of William and Mary at Williamsburg, Va. created a bitter stir when she suggested in the school's paper that the time should come when Negroes should join our clubs, be our roommates and marry among us.

Almost as a man, the college board expressed "thorough disapproval and condemnation" of the girl editorialist's sentiments. Publication of the paper was suspended. Southern papers sounded clarion cries of indignation.

Even Richard Wright, I suspect, would not indorse all the suggestions proposed by the girl student. For his people this brilliant Negro asks only the right to live with dignity as human beings. Clubs, roommates, intermarriage probably do not interest him at all. His story, told in the pages of this bitter, blunt, forceful indictment of race prejudice is one of the most powerful appeals for understanding ever penned in America.

Mr. Wright covers 20 years in his autobiography—the 20 years between the time he was born on a plantation near Natchez, Miss., to the day when he struck out for Chicago in a bewildered attempt to get away from the prejudice that was wrecking his life. There, as his novel "Native Son" proves, he found something of tolerance, certainly less of cruelty.

It would be useless, I think, to review here the frequently sordid, sometimes sadistic, almost universally unfair treatment Richard Wright suffered not only in his home town but in a half-dozen Southern cities before he turned to the North to seek the right to live. The ignorance and superstition of some of his own people is only short of frightening and this coupled with the ignorance and bigotry of many of the white people he encountered makes for bitter, thought-provoking reading.

His story is a stinging indictment of race prejudice and a ringing challenge to democracy. Because it is told in tolerant vein, it invites tolerant reading and understanding. He has laid bare the foul sores of America's greatest inner conflict. Those sores must be healed if America is to be worthy of itself.

Here, it seems to me, is a book that no thinking person—black or white—can afford to miss. Almost as an afterthought, I might add that "Black Boy" is something very close to being literature.

Lewis Gannett. *New York Herald Tribune,* February 28, 1945, p. 17.

"Man, you reckon these white folks is ever gonna change?" one black boy asked in West Helena, Ark., about 1921, when Richard Wright was nearing twelve years old.

"Hell, no! They just born that way," said another.

"Shucks, man. I'm going North when I get grown," announced a third, meaning that up North both black and white men dared change.

Richard Wright, at seventeen, went North, and changed. But the story he tells in "Black Boy" is not of the change in the North that, ten years later, made it possible for him to write "Uncle Tom's Children" and "Native Son"; it is of the Southern soil from which he sprang: of the mush-and-lard-gravy poverty, the hunger and fear and loneliness that were his home, of the swinging doors of saloons, the cindered railroad tracks, the ribald street gangs that were his escape; and of the "strange and separate road" which, even in that fear-chained childhood world, he somehow could not help traveling.

It is an unforgettable book, and one which leaves you at the end questioning and wondering, as good books do. Why should this boy, alone in the darkness of his bitter, beaten boyhood, have caught the sense of freedom, felt the warmth from an unseen light, and developed the power to seize and express it? What was the miracle that made him want to write, and able to write? Mr. Wright never quite explains that; but then, no one has ever quite explained the miracle that was Mozart. Genius defies explanation. This autobiography, if it does not quite explain Richard Wright, at least explains what made Richard Wright write "Native Son."

His was a terror-haunted childhood. He hated his father when the father stumbled home from his night job and complained of the children's noise. Annoyed at a kitten's mewing, the father cried "Kill that damn kitten," and the boy killed it, and was punished for that grim obedience. Richard's father left home for another woman; Richard's mother worked out in white folks' kitchens, and the five-year-old boy, left alone, crept under the swinging doors of saloons, was set up on the bar and taught to drink. He ran away from an orphan asylum. He was beaten at home for using the filthy words he had heard in the streets. In the race tension that followed the first world war one of his uncles was lynched, another escaped from town by night. When his pious grandmother found him reading a story, she snatched the magazine from him; to her any non-Bible story was a "lie."

By all the odds of nature, this boy should have turned out like his own Bigger Thomas. It was, of course, because he had grown up so dangerously close to Bigger's ratlike childhood that he would one day write so memorably of Bigger. But what made Richard different?

Some innate sense of human dignity made him refuse all the easy acceptances. Instinctively he understood that his grandmother's religion was only "the hunger of the human heart for that which is not and never can be"; it could be no solace to him. In his angry small boy's way, he fought back against his family, against his schoolteachers, against companions who tried to teach him the only way for a black boy to live in the South. "Boy, do you steal?" his first employer asked him. Richard kept his face closed, and got the job, but he left it that night. He kept still when another employer assured him a dog bite couldn't hurt a nigger.

He read mostly trash. Even his grandmother's Bible could not compete with the condensed action of the pulp stories that were his introduction to literature. Somehow, by the time he was twelve he was an instinctive rebel, a question asker, a wonderer, a boy who was always in his own mind putting words together and amazed at the result. At fourteen he had a story published in a colored newspaper; his schoolmates hardly believed that he had really written it, and wondered why he had done so, if he had.

School was only a small part of his schooling. At sixteen, a friendly Irishman made it possible for Richard to obtain books from the library. He had to keep those books hidden in a newspaper, lest he appear dangerously uppity. Mencken, his first eye-opener, taught him how effectively words could be weapons. The books Mencken's comments led him to read gave him a sense of worlds beyond his horizon. But something born in Richard Wright before he ever saw a book must have given him the strength to reach out and make that light his own.

"Black Boy" may be one of the great American autobiographies. This, too, is America: both the mud and scum in which Richard Wright grew up, and the something that sang within him, that ever since has been singing with an ever clearer, painfully sweeter, voice.

Orville Prescott. *New York Times*, February 28, 1945, p. 21.

Richard Wright is a famous writer now, the author of one of the most widely read and hotly debated novels of recent years, "Native Son," an acknowledged leader of his race. But the way was long, and the road was rocky. Not very many years ago he was just "a black boy in Mississippi," which means few men in the world have begun life under a burden of graver handicaps or faced more difficult obstacles. That he has gone so far, accomplished so much, entitles Mr. Wright to an honored rank among that traditionally American select group, the "self-made men." His success story does him great credit. The troubles he knew in his childhood and youth were terrible, the wounds he received deep. He carries indelible scars and still burns with bitter fury. The life he knew as a child is not over. It has not changed. Hundreds of thousands of other little black boys are enduring it today. Such a life is usually completely outside the comprehension of white Americans, either Southern or Northern. But those who care to can now share it in Mr. Wright's "Black Boy: A Record of Childhood and Youth."

This is a story from America's own lower depths. No nostalgic memories of childhood are these, no sentimental yearnings for innocent years when the hills were so much higher. Mr. Wright's childhood was an obscene and monstrous nightmare, a malign inferno that might well have destroyed him utterly. He survived, but not unscathed. "Black Boy" is not the work of an objective artist or of an open mind. It could not have been. The neuroses, the overemphasis, the lack of balance and the emotion recollected in turmoil are the bitter fruit of an old injustice.

Mr. Wright in this explosive autobiography does not suggest any constructive means for improving the lot of the Negro in this country. Like Lillian Smith, he can only display suffering and cruelty with harsh dramatic power, he can only arouse anger and sympathy. If enough such books are written, if enough millions of people read them, maybe, some day, in the fullness of time, there will be a greater understanding and a more true democracy.

Richard Wright grew up in the slums of Memphis and in the rural slums of Arkansas and of Mississippi near Jackson. His father deserted his mother, so the poverty he knew was double the usual lot. The two dominant influences of his childhood were hunger and fear, a gnawing hunger that kept him weak and half-starved and a fear that grew and multiplied and filled his entire life. He feared his mother's anger, the whippings of his uncles and aunts, the abuse of other children, ghosts, white men with their inexplicable and capricious cruelties, fear itself. Terror was his companion night and day, violence the norm of all experience. Foul language and foul habits, ignorance and superstition, primitive religious fanaticism surrounded him on all sides. The proud, sensitive, intelligent child looked up from below at a grotesque, outrageous world.

Some of the evils he knew were caused by poverty and ignorance alone and would not have been much different in Ireland or Iran. But even these evils were intensified by the shibboleth of color and many others were caused by race alone. Mr. Wright's uncle was murdered by a white man and no one dared even to protest. A boyhood acquaintance was lynched. He learned to be servile and obsequious, to say "sir" to drunken and contemptible white men, to conceal his thoughts and emotions beneath a mask of humble good humor and deference. Not to do so, to forget the "sir" or the "mister," to aspire to learn a skilled trade, to show resentment of sneers, condescension and abuse, was to invite "trouble." And trouble could mean death.

"Black Boy" only takes Mr. Wright into his late teens when he escaped to Chicago. His experiences there and in radical politics will doubtless be material for another book. It could conceivably be an intellectually more interesting book, one more concerned with thought and ideas. But it could hardly be a more emotionally dreadful one. Part of the raw shock of "Black Boy" is caused by Mr. Wright's excessive determination to omit nothing, to emphasize mere filth. This springs from a lack of artistic discrimination and selectivity. He has not added to the bleak tragedy of his story; he has only distorted it and confused it with such material.

It is also obvious in reading "Black Boy," and Mr. Wright admits it, that his is not a typical story. He felt isolated from Negroes as well as from whites; other Negroes resented their lot but did not feel at all so acutely as he did. Perhaps with the hindsight of the years in which he has brooded and with a natural literary instinct to capitalize and dramatize his emotions Mr. Wright has exaggerated his sufferings. It would be only human if he had.

"Black Boy" has little subtlety, little light and shade, no restraint. It is written in a continuously strained and feverish manner. It is over-written. But it is powerful, moving and horrifying. It is certain to be extravagantly praised and roundly condemned. It will be widely read.

Fred Gottlieb. "Candid Book by Negro Novelist Tells of Growing Up in South." *St. Louis Post-Dispatch,* February 28, 1945.

Richard Wright's story of his childhood and youth is as tensely written and almost as grim in atmosphere as "Native Son," his best-selling novel of 1940. Indeed, there is so great a resemblance in the spirit of the two books as to demonstrate that many of the author's early experiences and impressions went into the creation of Bigger Thomas, central figure of the tragic novel.

Wright, born in 1908, grew up in the Deep South, at Jackson, Miss., and Memphis. The theme of his biography is the blighting frustration imposed upon the Negro by the rigid racial taboos of the region. Wright knew what his "place" was supposed to be under the prevailing social pattern; he could sometimes force himself to go through the required forms, but he never inwardly accepted them. So he felt the discriminations and injustices keenly, and his book is a powerful protest against them.

The book is also a candid self-portrait, a fact that lessens its impact as a plea for inter-racial fair play. Many of the author's torments and conflicts, as he unsparingly relates them, had no direct connection with the color line. There were fierce family clashes, rebellion against his parents, violent quarrels with uncles and aunts, revolt against teachers, brutal fights with other boys, beginning in the early years when the child knew nothing of racial distinctions. In relations with his own people as well as with whites, the sensitive, stubborn boy was, to put it mildly, difficult.

This refractory personality aside, the book still is a case history that offers abundant substance for thought. How much, the reader will ask himself through the pages, is white society responsible for this human being's maladjustments and tortures? Poverty and ignorance and lack of proper early care are in the picture. So are poor schooling, supersitition, exploitation, fear of lynch law. There is much in the vivid episodes about all these to stir deeply the conscience of the racial majority.

Wright, gifted and ambitious, rose above his sordid surroundings. He studied and read, determined to become a writer, struggled desperately to hold a job long enough to pay his way to the North. The volume ends with his departure, at 19, for Chicago, where he hoped to find economic opportunity.

He did become a writer, an honest, forceful writer, whose success does not make him forgetful of a bitterly unhappy youth or of the system that is at least partly responsible for the Bigger Thomases and drags them to their doom.

Joseph Gollomb. *Book-of-the-Month-Club News,* (February 1945), 8–9.

Compare the child in Richard Wright's autobiography, *Black Boy,* with the man today, and either they are two other fellows or psychologists should modify their stress on how easily violence may mar a sensitive youngster for life.

For in *Black Boy* a very sensitive child is manhandled from the cradle by brutal poverty, by some Southern whites, and by the boy's own family who mean well, but beat him unmercifully. At four he sets fire to his home in play, is almost burned alive, then is lashed for it till he is delirious and nearly dies. He strangles a kitten because it keeps his father awake, and, in punishment, his mother fills his imagination "with a horde of invisible demons bent on exacting vengeance on me for what I had done." Then she sends the shuddering boy into the night to bury the kitten while he recites his guilt. In one of his many changes of home he has to use the bed in which a boy has died, and stays sleepless so many nights that he comes to the verge of collpase. His father deserts the family, and the boy gets the full brunt of the sordid conflict between the parents. In saloons, whiskey is forced on the little boy so often that "I was a drunkard in my sixth year." To protect himself against beatings at home he takes to kitchen knives and razors, but when whites almost kill him he dares not raise even his eyes in protest.

These are only a few of the assaults on the everlastingly harrowed child and adolescent, and accompanying them always is hunger, "bitter hunger." This keeps up till his nineteenth year, where *Black Boy* ends with Wright leaving the South for Chicago, "bearing scars visible and invisible."

Even when he was free of the South and at liberty for the first time in his life to read, speak, and write as he pleased—for in Chicago he began to try to write—life was still hard and often violent. He worked long hours as errand boy, porter, dishwasher, and street cleaner. He saw Negro families evicted, and shivering on the sidewalks with cold and hunger. When some of them in desperation tried to get back into their former homes, police shot them. These things might just as well have happened to Wright, such was their impact on him.

When he met Socialists and Communists who interpreted such things for him he listened. At the Communist-led John Reed Club he met writers who encouraged him to express himself, and after a laborer's hard day he would try to put into words all that was churning within him. He got a clerkship in a post office, but just as life was taking on a bit of stability the depression of 1929 set in and he lost his job. One morning he got a letter. He had passed a civil service examination with an almost perfect score, and a post office job at $2100 a year was his if he wanted it. The depression was deepening and the government was offering him security at a higher pay than he had ever earned. But Wright tore the letter in two, then tore it again to back up his decision to hitchhike to New York and take his chances on living as a writer.

In New York, Wright delivered telephone books and did other odd jobs, then he got on the Federal Writers' Project. A short story won the *Story Magazine* Prize and led to the publication of his first book, *Uncle Tom's Children*. He got a Guggenheim Fellowship. Then *Native Son* as a novel (it was a choice of the Book-of-the-Month Club judges) established him.

Psychologists who emphasize the fateful importance of early impacts would say that six years of relative ease in a man's later life cannot heal the hurts of such years as *Black Boy* depicts. If so, it is hard to detect in the Richard Wright of today just how those years have harmed him. Well built, poised, objective, he is already mellow in his middle thirties.

As deep a hunger as any in *Black Boy* was the boy's need to feel that he was like other boys, that he belonged to his community. But he was a Negro in a white-dominated South, and his own grandmother isolated him even from the other Negro boys. She was a Seventh Day Adventist and made the boy observe the Sabbath on Saturdays instead of Sundays, as the others did. She sent him to a church school instead of public school where the other boys went, and pork was taboo for him in a community that relished it.

In Chicago, Wright found fraternity at last, the Communist Party. The word, comrade, moved him profoundly. Yet the moment he found that the Party wanted to regiment his thoughts and feelings, he left it. He feels that he belongs to his race in every way. Yet a ruthless objectivity makes him say such things as, "I used to mull over the strange absence of real kindness in Negroes." He explains this readiness to risk losing precious friendships. "Something more is involved than politics or race. I am as collectivist and proletarian in my outlook as when I belonged to the Communist Party, and the Negroes are my people. But there is the need to think and feel honestly, and that comes first."

He does not depend on intuition alone to guide his thinking and feeling. He is trying to understand human nature also by way of voracious reading of economics, sociology, anthropology, psychoanalysis, art, philosophy, travel, newspapers, magazines, and whatever else reports on it. He goes to Negro churches often, and as often visits criminal courts.

When he talks of Dostoievsky and Joseph Conrad there is more than a hint of awe in his voice. Dreiser tops American novelists for him. He defends Gertrude Stein against those who laugh at her. "For instance, I had heard my grandmother speak ever since I can remember, so that I was not conscious of anything particularly distinctive in her speech. Then I read a sketch of Negro life by Gertrude Stein, and suddenly it was as if I were listening to my grandmother for the first time, so fresh was the feeling it gave me."

Currently Wright is interested in juvenile delinquency in Harlem, and he spends days in court, with psychiatrists, on Welfare Island. He piles up notes on everything he sees and reads on the subject. Some of his material suddenly sends him off on a writing streak, unplanned, thousands of words in the form of fiction, at other times in scenes which he describes as "documentary," borrowing the term from the movies.

He works on several projects at the same time, writing till the impulse and interest in one temporarily runs down—then he turns to another that had been resting. He writes on occasion in long hand, at other times on the typewriter, or talks into an Ediphone he has, and which he exhibits affectionately. "I love gadgets."

When he speaks of himself it is with comparative inattention, even avoidance of the subject. Yet you feel that he is not edging away from remembered or even buried pain, but rather that he is interested in any individual ego only when it is part of some sizable perspective.

Edward A. Laycock. "Richard Wright Records Rebellion, Horror and Despair of His Youth." *Boston Morning Globe*, March 1, 1945, p. 15.

It's to America's credit that this book has been written and will be given wide circulation. Nowhere except in America could it have been written. Nowhere except in America could such a rebel thrive. But what made him a rebel should be on America's conscience.

This reviewer started to read this book with misgivings. After the violence of "Native Son," he expected a violently written autobiography. There is violence and turbulence in the book, but the writing is remarkably restrained and quietly beautiful. There is sordidness, more than the average boy experiences but not as much as you would expect.

Richard Wright was born near Natchez, Miss. His early life and schooling were complicated by a constant shifting of the family from one Southern town to another, mostly in his native state, the least progressive at that time in the Union. . . .

Richard's home life was a mixture of ignorance, poverty and superstition, with constant bickering culminating in violence toward the rebellious boy who could cope with it only by returning the violence.

But Richard finally fled all that and went to Chicago. He was a superior and sensitive youth and many of his difficulties were of his own making. He knows that. Richard Wright could not conform to what fear and ignorance dictated. And the South may yet learn to be grateful to him for that.

Richard Wright's story is a sad story but not a tragic one. There is more psychology in it than in many a psychological novel. He gives you an insight to a boy's—black or white—mental processes. This reviewer wouldn't have missed this book for anything, and you shouldn't miss it.

Charles Lee. "Black Hunger." *Philadelphia Record*, March 1, 1945.

Richard Wright's autobiography, "Black Boy" may very possibly go down as one of the most memorable books of our time, a kind of 20th century "Uncle Tom's Cabin."

Though it may not cause the immediate sensation stirred up by the author's lurid best-seller, "Native Son," it is in our judgment much the better book, more potent, more dramatic if less theatrical, more accurate in its aim, more telling in impact. Indeed it is the raw material out of which that unforgettable novel was forged.

Subtitled "a record of childhood and youth," Wright's new work is quiveringly animate. Life breathes in its pages with a reality and an intensity given only to the great recorders of the human scene. The result is that "Black Boy" is as intimate a personal-story as you have ever read, fearlessly candid, a revelation of the clockwork beneath the ticking of one man's heart. But it is not an exhibitionist exposure, not self-exploitation, neither is it the product of masochism; it is, instead, a laying open of personality, at obviously great pain, in the interest of a cause, a cause greater than self and worthy of the sacrifice of soul's peace and privacy, the cause of human dignity, in this particular case the cause of the American Negro.

Wright is today recognized as both an outstanding member of his race and a distinguished artist, and could easily coast along on the esteem and riches which his talent has won him. But he is no coaster. He is a crusader. He does not only dirge, he is hotly angry, he points, he speaks out, he challenges. And on his feet, not his knees.

"Black Boy" is no Hollywood serving of magnolia and julep; it is a piece of immediate Danteian reality made in the U. S. A., a candid-camera recording of the virulent Fascist tumor that exists in our democratic body. The cure? Democracy itself. Not the promulgation of ideals, but their acceptance; the practice of all those attitudes which make for a decent respect between men, regardless of race, color and creed.

As Wright unfolds the bleak story of his incredibly underprivileged life from Mississippi odd-jobs man to Chicago writer—nor in the telling of it does he spare the sins of his people or minimize his own faults—it reduces itself to a series of gnawing hungers, hunger for food, for friendship, for love, for normality, for security, for the things of the spirit and mind, in the end, in near-madness and dreams, for a totally different existence.

Living in one squalid house after another, starved for even subsistence sustenance, set upon by gangs, let to wander the streets (he was a drunkard at six), clutching his rags, threatened with hell by religious fanatics, poorly schooled, never medicated, brutally beaten by his own family, nearly killed by whites and living in constant terror of their sadistic whimsies and coded arrogance, Wright's miracle is that he did not end up as either the degraded, grinning "non-man" caricature of humanity resignedly accepted by his fellows as the typical Negro's lot, or a murderer. Yet more wonderful is that out of this day-and-nightmare of a life he arose a commanding artist in realism (he details his artistic and intellectual beginnings, crediting most to his mother and H. L. Mencken), a man not softened but ennobled by suffering and dedicated, in the belief that it can and must be won, to the battle for those educative, economic and, fundamentally, spiritual conditions which are necessary to the democratization of Negro life.

Robert Malloy. "The Author of *Native Son* Tells of His Childhood." *New York Sun*, March 2, 1945, p. 22.

Add to the literature of protest Richard Wright's story of his childhood and early youth, "Black Boy" in which the gifted Negro author of "Native Son" portrays the background of his life.

Bitterness is the keynote of Mr. Wright's book. He has long refused to accept the status conventionally accorded to a Negro in our society. He began to rebel at an early age. In "Black Boy" he traces, often with considerable objectivity, the sources of that early rebellion.

Richard Wright was born thirty-six years ago on a plantation near Natchez, Mississippi. When he was a very small boy his father deserted his family. A sickly mother, too ill to be sympathetic or even kind; a fanatically religious grandmother, ignorant and harsh, and other relatives whose twisted lives and difficulties were reflected in their treatment of young Richard, were his earliest experiences.

He tells us that he was a drunkard at 6. But he was a bright student, and he obviously made the best of his sporadic schooling. His encounter with the white man's world, he says, came too late for him to learn how to get along in it Southern fashion: "I could not make subservience an automatic part of my behavior. I had to feel and think out each tiny item of racial experience in the light of the whole race problem, and to each item I brought the whole of my life. While standing before a white man I had to figure out how to perform each act and how to say each word."

His story is one that men of good will cannot read without indignation. Perhaps his experiences were harsher than those of others similarly situated; more likely, he was far more sensitive than most people. This book has none of the compromising attitude we find in Booker T. Washington's autobiography, or in the life of Dr. George W. Carver as told by Rackham Holt. Yet it raises the same sense of wonder in the reader. How did these men, and others like them, find the incentive to distinguish themselves? Richard Wright grew up in the midst of ignorance, and of squalor that as he describes it is revolting. (Some of the details should have been omitted.) He became one of the most promising writers of his generation, possibly because of a background the cost of which, in human misery, is too appalling to be estimated.

As writing, the style of "Black Boy" lacks much of the power and brilliance of the novel, "Native Son," but the book is a tremendous document. Mr. Wright really makes you realize how it felt to be a Negro in the South.

Ben Burns. *Chicago Defender*, March 3, 1945, p. 11.

When Richard Wright writes, he commands perhaps the widest white audience of any Negro author today. He is without doubt one of America's top literary men, regardless of color.

His searing prose, his blockbuster stories strip bare the thin veneer of democracy in our land, expose the festering sore of racial hate, and rip apart the caste system that sets apart every tenth American to live a hunted, animal-like, psychopathic existence in the terrifying jungle that is Dixie.

His "Native Son" was a horror story, a frightful nightmare of terror and desperation for one Negro who went berserk in Chicago's "black ghetto." But in many ways, "Native Son" was mild, soft, diluted stuff compared to Wright's new "Black Boy," which will wield a haymaker wallop to Wright's readers.

"Black Boy" is a study in sadism. It is Wright's own story, a startling, shocking and sometimes weird series of autobiographical episodes that picture with incisive, sharp strokes his early years of life in the South. It is a portrait of fear and frustration, of viciousness and violence.

But in his new book, Wright has done more than spotlight the misery of the Negro. He has bared his own self, opened his embittered heart to public view. For Wright's own life, his childhood was a fugitive existence, full of hunger, pain and grief. He never knew what normal family life meant, his father abandoning him, his brother and mother at an early age. Home was a constant series of whippings with a switch, beginning at the age of four when his mother came close to beating him to death. Religion for him became a terrible prison, its rigid restrictions actually keeping him from food and learning. He was constantly fleeing, constantly hunted, constantly fearing.

Adding to this the full impact of racial exclusion in Dixie, Wright became a self-centered, anti-social rebel. He is that unto today, uncomfortable with people, living to himself, almost suffering from a persecution complex. And despite his common suffering with his people from racial oppression, actually he is without feeling of solidarity with the Negro people. He is a lone wolf, wily and wise to the ways of the white man, yet still so suspicious and wary of his own that he cannot bring himself into common struggle with them.

It is this inner, subconscious distrust of all men, an emotion that constantly crops up in the pages of "Black Boy," that perhaps explains his failure to find any genuine identity with the Communists, that gives point to his sorry slander of Negroes generally when he talks in his book about "the strange absence of real kindness in Negroes, how unstable was our tenderness, how lacking in genuine passion we were, how void of great hope, how timid our joy, how bare our traditions, how hollow our memories." Actually Wright is thinking of himself in these terms.

What else could he believe? He became a drunkard at the age of six, peeked into brothels not long afterward. He mocked Jews with other children, not knowing the poison of prejudice was hitting him, stole money at an early age. He felt the sting of caste when he went to work in an optical shop and was beaten because he wanted to learn a skilled trade. He knew shame when white prostitutes paraded nude before Negro bellboys, considering them less than men. He fought to learn, smuggling books out of a Memphis library with a white man's card.

Wright never knew love—not even for or from his mother. He was never loved by anyone. He never knew what it meant to love someone. The one person that tried to comfort him, a Mrs. Moss in Memphis who rented him a room, he repulsed with coldness. She immediately saw through him and told him: "You just ain't never had no home life. I'm sorry for you."

And that summation must stand too with those who would criticize Wright because he has seen fit to picture Negroes generally as sombre, barren, listless, bitter, helpless. "The essential bleakness of black life" of which he speaks is more an accurate chronicle of his own life rather than symbolic of Negroes generally.

In "Black Boy" he is again erring as he did in "Native Son" in his emphasis on the hopelessness of the Negro's lot, in his total failure to see that the clock of history is moving ahead, not backward. As he himself states it, he is "running more away from something, than toward something." In his dread of life, he has lost the zest of living.

Reading his autobiography, one cannot condemn his lack of lust for life. It is to be marveled that he has recovered from his youthful wounds so remarkably. "Black Boy" makes his motives, his strange behavior more easily understood.

Despite its faults, the fiery pages of "Black Boy" that blast racial hate with the effect of a flame-thrower will scorch America's conscience.

John Cournos. *Philadelphia Bulletin*, March 3, 1945.

To have been born in the slums, with the additional handicap of being black and the scene of your struggle south of the Mason and Dixon Line, is a story told with great power and vividness by the Negro novelist, Richard Wright, in "Black Boy".

"Black Boy" is not a novel. It is a straightforward piece of autobiography, and it wrings the heart and stirs indignation. It is not only a human document of great value at this moment, when the question of race threatens to become an issue; it is also the challenge of a thinking, sensitive Negro to his fellow human beings, the white men.

The sensitiveness of the author speaks for what a Negro is capable when he has the chance. His chance in this instance happens to owe nothing to the white man. And the plea that the Negro be given a chance is implicit in the eloquent narrative, which contains some pages not intended for the squeamish.

Mr. Wright makes no bones about the shortcomings of his race. Looking back over his childhood, he reflects rather sadly "over the strange absence of real kindness in Negroes, how unstable was our tenderness, how lacking in genuine passion we were, how void of great hope, how timid our joy, how bare our traditions, how hollow our memories, how lacking we were in those intangible sentiments that bind man to man, and how shallow was even our despair."

While admitting all this to be true, Mr. Wright seems to pose the questions: Is this a natural condition for the Negro? Is the Negro incapable of being better, of doing as the white man is doing? Or is the Negro's condition a consequence of his treatment by the white man? He applies his strictures, of course, particularly to the South. And he answers these questions in a revealing paragraph:

"Whenever I thought of the essential bleakness of black life in America, I knew that Negroes have never been allowed to catch the full spirit of Western civilization, that they lived somehow in it but not of it. And when I brooded upon the cultural barrenness of black life, I wondered if clean, positive tenderness, love, honor, loyalty, and the capacity to remember were native with man. I asked myself if these human qualities were not fostered, won, struggled and suffered for, preserved in ritual from one generation to another."

The author did not arrive at his conclusions in the shelter of a study. They are definitely the hard-earned result of his childhood life described in this book, a life of hardship, of hunger, of intense suffering.

So far we have the story of the first seventeen years, at the end of which the author had struggled out of his environment and started North to seek a better life, for he had heard that it was to be had there. It is to be hoped he will in the near future give us the benefit of his further experiences.

The chronicle teems with a host of native types, rendered alive for us by the writer's competent pen. There was Granny, who came of Irish, Scotch and French stock, "in which Negro blood had somewhere and somehow been infused." There was his father, a shiftless, irresponsible man, who had Indian, white and Negro blood. This mixture was no help. "They'll call you a colored man when you grow up," his mother warned him. He was to find out in good time—he didn't have to wait to grow up—what it meant.

Incredible misfortune dogged the footsteps of the family. First the father abandoned it. Then the mother had a paralytic stroke. The boy had to shift from one relative to another for food and shelter. Here a bigoted aunt tried to force her own narrow religion on him, a religion mostly superstition. There an uncle gave him a savage whipping. The sensitive boy was in a constant state of revolt.

He went hungry most of the time. When he found himself at Uncle Hoskins' he could not believe his eyes. There was so much food here, yet he was apprehensive lest there be no bread for next day. So he stole from the table and stuffed his pockets with biscuits; so great was his fear that he did this repeatedly.

Above all there was, in these early years, the intangible yet growing fear of what the whites might do to him. As a boy, he already had a foretaste of his lot in each succeeding job with the white folks. His experiences as an employee are particularly illuminating; for here we learn of the deliberate race baiting that goes on in the South among men who ought to know better. Their sadistic impulses seem to find an outlet in tormenting helpless colored boys.

It is impossible not to believe Mr. Wright. There is in his writing the simple ring of truth. Now and again it is pure Dostoevsky without the trimmings.

Amy H. Croughton. *Rochester Times-Union*, March 3, 1945.

"Black Boy," the autobiographical story by Richard Wright, is an epochal book. It is the story of a Negro boy, from infancy to the 'teen age in which he took his way North in the belief that greater opportunities awaited him there. But it is also the story of an egoistic, anti-social personality who would have been unhappy no matter what the color of his skin.

Wright spares no word to picture the loneliness of soul, the neurotic fears and reactions, and the antagonisms of the "black boy" who haunted saloons and dives and was a baby alcoholic at six, who killed his kitten to spite his father who had ordered him to give the animal away; and who seemed to dislike, and even hate, his mother and other relatives as completely as he did the "white people" with whom he had little contact, but whose shadow seemed to hover over him.

Reading the book, one's heartstrings are so wrung that one hopes the novelist and playwright has allowed his imagination and dramatic flair to color what is presented as straight autobiography. Even so, there is plenty in the book to make white readers think, and be ashamed that any human being, of any race or creed, could be made to feel as Wright must have felt at some time of his life in order to be able to write this hard, bitter, arraignment.

"Black Boy" is a book that will bruise many white readers. It will make some of them angry, others sorrowful and determined to right injustices and clear away the thoughtless indifference that caused such an indictment to be written.

For many who have admired the Negro and his achievement in the arts and professions, and who have never felt toward him anything but friendship, "Black Boy" will come as a slap in the face. Yet it is, perhaps, just these people who need to realize what lies on the other side of the shield.

There is little in the picture of the

child and youth of "Black Boy" to make understandable the present-day author of "Native Son," except for the compelling power that lies in the boy's feeling of inferiority—or, rather, of being looked upon as inferior—to urge a keen, self-centered personality on the road to success. The book cries out for a sequel in which Wright's experiences in trying out philosophies and theories and finding himself, will be told. . . .

J. K. S. "A Searing Picture of Childhood in the South." *Minneapolis Tribune*, March 4, 1945.

For those who can take it, Richard Wright's "Black Boy" will prove a searing and unforgettable reading experience. It will force attention on unpleasant aspects of American life that none of us cares to think about if we can find a way out.

Wright doesn't leave you a way out, for once launched in his story of a bleak and tragic childhood you can't stray away into more congenial literary paths. You enter a fear-filled world—the Negro's world in the South—and you know, finally, what it must mean to be born black in that part of the United States.

Wright pens no propaganda tract. Essentially an artist, he writes only of what happened to him in Mississippi and Tennessee in the early years of his life. Bitterness is there, but it is implicit in the writing, in the story he tells, rather than being used as a weapon in a bill of complaints.

Wright frankly admits surprise at the recurring reference to "bitterness" in his writing. "I'm really not conscious of the bitterness imputed to me," he remarked when I talked to him recently in New York.

"And as for 'Black Boy'," he went on, "I'm merely using a familiar literary form to unload many of the memories that have piled up in me, and now are coming out."

Certainly you don't get the impression of bitterness when talking to the author of "Native Son," for he is a good-natured, moon-faced man who is quick to laugh and to seize upon the point of a joke. What he went through as a boy and young man in the South apparently hasn't warped him, or even made him a professional uplifter of his race. He is deeply interested, naturally, in all the movements and ideas which look toward a better deal for the Negro.

"The southern Negro," he says, "has never really been understood. I'm confident that if the Negro problem down there were settled, and along with it the white problem that is linked to it, our whole American civilization would be improved."

Those problems look fairly insoluable, as viewed in Wright's "Black Boy." The South probably hasn't changed too much since the period covered in his book, and in this grim chronicle of suppression and poverty, it looks like one of Herr Goebbels' nightmares.

Race prejudice is automatic, a reflex action. A Negro who doesn't know his place, who doesn't say "Sir" when addressing a white man and say it fast, is under suspicion. The South "understands" the Negro and knows what is good for him. Any ambitions that strike outside the subservient role he is supposed to fill are quickly beaten out of him.

It is a wonder that Wright, under the terrific handicap of squalid environment and hatred and oppression, reared in ignorance and weaned on the brutalities and meannesses which were his daily sustenance, could have developed the gifts he has, kept alive the sensitivity and vision of the good to which this book so eloquently testifies.

W. E. Burghardt Du Bois. "Richard Wright Looks Back." *New York Herald Tribune Weekly Book Review,* March 4, 1945, p. 2.

This book tells a harsh and forbidding story and makes one wonder just exactly what its relation to truth is. The title, "A Record of Childhood and Youth," makes one at first think that the story is autobiographical. It probably is, at least in part. But mainly it is probably intended to be fiction or fictionalized biography. At any rate the reader must regard it as creative writing rather than simply a record of life.

The hero whom Wright draws, and may be it is himself, is in his childhood a loathsome brat, foul-mouthed and "a drunkard." The family which he paints is a distressing aggregation. Even toward his mother he never expresses love or affection. Sometimes he comes almost to sympathy. He wonders why this poor woman, deserted by her husband, toiling and baffled, broken by paralysis and disappointment, should suffer as she does. But his wonder is intellectual inability to explain the suffering. It doesn't seem for a moment to be personal sorrow at this poor, bowed figure of pain and ignorance.

The father is painted as gross and bestial, with little of human sensibility. The grandmother is a religious fanatic, apparently sincere but brutal. The boy fights with his aunt. And here again the artist in Richard Wright seems to fail. He repeats an incident of fighting his aunt with a knife to keep her from beating him. He tells the tale of his grandfather, a disappointed veteran of the Civil War, but tells it without sympathy. The Negroes whom he paints have almost no redeeming qualities. Some work hard, some are sly, many are resentful; but there is none who is ambitious, successful or really intelligent.

After this sordid, shadowy picture we gradually come upon the solution. The hero is interested in himself, is self-centered to the exclusion of everybody and everything else. The suffering of others is put down simply as a measure of his own suffering and resentment. There is scarcely a ray of light in his childhood: he is hungry, he is beaten, he is cold and unsheltered. Above all, a naturally shy and introverted personality is forced back upon itself until he becomes almost pathological. The world is himself and his suffering. He hates and distrusts it. He says "I was rapidly learning to distrust everything and everybody."

He writes of a mother who wanted him to marry her daughter. "The main value in their lives was simple, clean, good living, and when they thought they had found those same qualities in one of their race they instinctively embraced him, liked him and asked no questions. But such simple unaffected trust flabbergasted me. It was impossible!"

He tells of his own pitiful confusion, when as an imaginative, eager child he could not speak his thought: "I knew how to write as well as any pupil in the classroom, and no doubt I could read better than any of them, and I could talk fluently and expressively when I was sure of myself. Then why did strange faces make me freeze? I sat with my ears and neck burning, hearing the pupils whisper about me, hating myself, hating them."

Then here and there for a moment he forgets his role as artist and becomes commentator and prophet. Born on a plantation, living in Elaine, Ark., and the slums of Memphis, he knows the whole Negro race! "After I had outlived the shocks of childhood, after the habit of reflection had been born in me, I used to mull over the strange absence of real kindness in Negroes, how unstable was our tenderness, how lacking in genuine passion we were, how void of great hope, how timid our joy, how bare our traditions, how hollow our memories, how lacking we were in those intangible sentiments that bind man to man, and how shallow was even our despair."

Not only is there this misjudgment of black folk and the difficult repulsive characters among them that he is thrown with, but the same thing takes place with white folk. There is not a single broad-minded, open-hearted white person in his book. One or two start out seemingly willing to be decent, but as he says of one white family for whom he worked, "They cursed each other in an amazingly offhand manner and nobody seemed to mind. As they hurled invectives they barely looked at each other. I was tense each moment, trying to anticipate their wishes and avoid a curse, and I did not suspect that the tension I had begun to feel that morning would lift itself into the passion of my life."

From the world of whites and the world of blacks he grows up curiously segregated. "I knew of no Negroes who read the books I liked, and I wondered if any Negroes ever thought of them. I knew that there were Negro doctors, lawyers, newspaper men, but I never saw any of them."

One rises from the reading of such a book with mixed thoughts. Richard Wright uses vigorous and straightforward English; often there is real beauty in his words even when they are mingled with sadism: "There was the disdain that filled me as I tortured a delicate, blue-pink crawfish that huddled fearfully in the mudsill of a rusty tin can. There was the aching glory in masses of clouds burning gold and purple from an invisible sun. There was the liquid alarm I saw in the blood-red glare of the sun's afterglow mirrored in the squared planes of whitewashed frame houses. There was the languor I felt when I heard green leaves rustling with a rainlike sound."

Yet at the result one is baffled. Evidently if this is an actual record, bad as the world is, such concentrated meanness, filth and despair never completely filled it or any particular part of it. But if the book is meant to be a creative picture and a warning, even then, it misses its possible effectiveness because it is as a work of art so patently and terribly overdrawn.

Nothing that Richard Wright says is in itself unbelievable or impossible; it is the total picture that is not convincing.

R. L. Duffus. "Deep-South Memoir." *New York Times Book Review*, March 4, 1945, p. 3.

In this poignant and disturbing book one of the most gifted of America's younger writers turns from fiction to tell the story of his own life during the nineteen years he lived in the South. The book is poignant because Richard Wright as a child and adolescent was a highly sensitive individual subjected to a series of cruel and almost unbearable shocks. It is disturbing because one wonders how many similarly sensitive individuals have been crushed by the circumstances which did not crush Richard Wright. He escaped intellectually by reading H. L. Mencken, Theodore Dreiser and Sinclair Lewis. He escaped physically by going to Chicago. But escape in these terms has not been possible for all gifted Negroes; and New York, Detroit and Chicago have not answered satisfactorily the questions they asked when they went there.

The wonder is that Richard Wright, poor, perennially hungry, limited on his native soil to menial jobs, harassed and baffled by the failure of his own family to understand him, abandoned by his father, unable to find refuge in the religion which eases the strain of so many human hearts of all races, did not end in some wild and futile revolt. He had in him a strain of violence. Once he killed —lynched might be the apter word —a kitten whose mewing had disturbed his father. When boys waylaid him on the way to the grocery and took away his money he learned, with his mother's grim backing, to take a club and fight them back. He attempted to use a knife on his Aunt Addie when she had driven him to desperation by repeated injustice. He stood off his abusive Uncle Tom by threatening him with a razor in each hand. Against his will he allowed his white employer in Memphis to egg him into a mad fist fight with another Negro boy with whom he had no quarrel. He "could not grin" when white folks were around, though this was the accepted way of keeping out of trouble. Yet somehow he did keep out of trouble. Somehow he learned to control himself. The violence that was in his soul was subdued and sublimated to appear in another form—that is to say, in the written word.

It is not easy for those who have had happier childhoods, with little restraint or fear in them, to face up to the truth of this childhood of Richard Wright. One doesn't like to think that the world in which he lived was an American world. How many Negroes saw that world in the same way, to what extent Richard Wright's experience was exceptional, one doesn't know. The experience may have been uncommon in its family aspects. The Negro child in Natchez saw his father as many white children have done—an alien with whom and for whom he could have no sympathy. His mother was doomed by paralysis to long years of invalidism and suffering—and that, too, might have happened to a white boy. He fought against accepting the family religion—and white boys have done this and suffered for it.

Indeed, Mr. Wright does not idealize either his relatives or his race. The reader will come to understand that the family troubles and dissensions were intensified by the fact of race and racial discrimination, but Mr. Wright does not make a thesis of this point. They were what they were. This was one way of getting on—not the bravest way but the easiest. Mr. Wright does not even believe in the passionate quality sometimes attributed to Negroes in America, the depth of feeling behind the mask. He came to think that "what had been taken for our emotional strength was our negative confusions, our flights, our fears, our frenzy under pressure."

Mr. Wright does not, in fact, speak for all Southern Negroes. Some of them, intellectual, highly educated and of unimpaired dignity, have managed to survive in the Southern environment. But this Mr. Wright, conditioned as he was by the circumstances in which he found himself, could not do. He did not feel himself inferior, yet in order to survive, he had to act the part of an inferior. A human sense of dignity—not a black or white sense—was born in him. It may seem simple for a Negro to remember that it is an insult to a white man to speak of him by his name without prefixing a "Mr." or to speak to him without affixing a "Sir," to laugh when he is not amused. Perhaps it is simple for some individuals. It was not simple for Richard Wright. Nor was it easy for him to understand that there was supposed to be a point at which he must stop learning the optical glass trade, or any other trade, or any knowledge.

So Richard Wright escaped—from Southern ways, from the South which had formed him, even against his will, from a brown girl named Bess in a home on Beale Street, Memphis, but not altogether from himself. In leaving, as he says, he was "taking a part of the South to transplant in alien soil, to see if it could grow differently, if it could drink of new and cool rains, bend in strange winds, respond to the warmth of other suns, and, perhaps, to bloom." The words reflect a magic in his style. He could have been a poet and possibly, in his realistic way, is one. The question as to what extent his grim childhood and youth developed his creative power, or to what extent it twisted it, must remain unanswered. Certainly it did not kill it, for the power remains. But what would Richard Wright have been in a more genial social climate? In France, perhaps?

The Negro has his real as well as his merely self-acclaimed friends in the South. There is a movement there, not against segregation but against privileges for one race that are denied to the other. There are Southerners who are not afraid to preach the human dignity of the Negro, knowing that the abasement of any individual degrades in some degree all others. To such Southerners, Richard Wright's book will be a challenge and an occasion for searching of hearts.

Lillian Smith. "Richard Wright Adds a Chapter to Our Bitter Chronicle." *PM*, March 4, 1945, p. m15.

The story is being told. Little by little, it grows clear in our minds, this tragic, painful life of shame which white folks and black folks have lived together in America.

In turning the leaves of his life, Richard Wright has turned many a bitter page of America's chronicle. We read again of that ugly blend of poverty and ignorance, of fanatical religious zeal and fanatical sex fear, of the white man's desperate, regressive concern with skin color and of the Negro's terrible loneliness. We know that black and white are caught in the web, strangers stripped of human dignity, hating and fearing each other, yet pushed into shameful intimacy by that web's tightly interwoven strands.

As a white Southerner, I find few surprises in this book. It is an old, familiar thing of pain and guilt to us who were born there: this story of a black boy whose culture refused him the right to be human and forced him to crawl through dark, underground, evil, slimy ways into the sunlight of faraway places—whose culture tells every black child, born in the South, that not for one day can he feel at home there.

The wonder is that the creative potentials of his personality developed so consistently. The wonder is that Richard Wright today is a sane, creative, highly intelligent artist and man, bringing presents back to the very culture that spat him out when he was a child.

How did it happen? What early experiences of warmth and tenderness and human worth did he have that convinced him of his own dignity, that tied him to reality and kept him from totally rejecting the good with the bad? We should know. Yet his book does not tell us.

His childhood is still, in large part, a closed door to him. He has not yet found the key that will unlock old memories and bring back deeply buried childhood feelings. He tells little incidents, little, heartbreaking, pitiful and sometimes amusing anecdotes. But they are told with a strange lack-of-feeling tone, with little of that quality of imagination that interprets even as it narrates, and gives focus and perspective even as it conveys a sense of nearness.

When he writes of his boyhood, Richard Wright becomes the artist. He makes us experience with him that restless, striving period of growth when manhood was something he craved more than food, when he found, and fell in love with the world of ideas and books.

He shows us again here the power of prose, the warm, urgent use of word and phrase that made us recognize his great talent in *Native Son*. . . .

Marshall Bragdon. *Springfield* (Mass.) *Sunday Union-Republican*, March 4, 1945, p. 4d.

Richard Wright's "Black Boy, A Record of Childhood and Youth," is a shocking unforgettable book. It will be widely read, furiously discussed, praised beyond its considerable merits by some and condemned as extravagantly by others. On the whole its wide circulation will be of public service. If that tag makes it sound like "duty reading," let us add that few readers will stop halfway through.

The wonder is that Richard Wright ever survived to write the best-selling novel, "Native Son." The mark of the ordeal, however, is on everything he writes. To the average American the most shocking fact about "Black Boy" is that he has none of the pleasant memories of childhood which warm most of us. He was a black boy in Mississippi, Arkansas and Tennessee. The poverty and ignorance of those years was bad enough. Add to it "white supremacy" as seen and felt in Darktown, and the resulting scars upon a sensitive spirit were ugly and lasting.

"Black Boy" makes all too palpable the terror that surrounded him then. It was in the air. Only at long intervals were there overt, violent reminders of the invisible boundaries—but enough to "keep him in his place." When he was a youth an acquaintance was lynched. His uncle was killed by a white man, with impunity. And later he was "persuaded" not to master a skilled trade; such jobs were for whites only in

Mississippi and even in Memphis.

To get the books he hungered for at a public library he had to pretend he was fetching them for his white boss. And always he had to cultivate the masklike face, to remember his "sirs," to choke every angry impulse in the fact of contempt and maltreatment. At last, in his late 'teens, he escaped to Chicago. And none too soon, he was getting known as a "fresh nigger"; that is, a Negro who thought himself a human being.

Later books will tell of Wright's literary beginning, his experience with the Communists, and so on. On them, we are sure will be the continued distorting effect of his youth. That grim heritage is an indictment of part of American society, of course. But it must be said, for clarity's sake, that Wright's was not a "typical" childhood. Certain universal injustices scarred him more deeply than most because he was not typical. His own family was difficult to live with. To them and to white supremacy alike he reacted hypersensitively. Even now he is not a happy man because there is so much he can't forget. As a seasoned writer, if this were another's life being portrayed he would have presented it with more effective restraint and artistic selection.

Yet these are minor qualifications of our general praise. Perhaps even the exaggeration beyond the typical is necessary to wake up white America. . . .

M. C. R.
Washington Star,
March 4, 1945.

For an author of comparatively limited output, Richard Wright has won remarkable fame. His first volume, a short collection of stories *Uncle Tom's Children,* brought him wide attention and a Guggenheim Fellowship. His novel *Native Son* won the Harper prize and was made into a successful play. Yet, for all the acclaim which has attended him his stock of ideas so far has been one, a message of racial issues. In this new book he leaves the field of fiction and goes into autobiography. He tells us the story of his boyhood and youth in Mississippi, and he produces the most convincing thing yet to come from him.

It is a story of horror worse than those with which Mr. Wright loads his Negro fictional heroes and yet, writing of himself, he does a thing which he has not done for the characters of his creation—he displays a sense of life apart from race issues. He lived his early years in a solely Negro environment; indeed, he says, he was not aware of white attitudes until he was in his teens. But long before that he was in rebellion.

He found Negro conventions, superstitions, and social mores intolerable before he came into conflict with white prejudice. He was well innured to brutality before he learned that the source of Negro misery was white oppression. The picture of life in grandmother's home, where he suffered the most wanton cruelty from his pious and conforming elders, is not a picture of race wrongs. It is the old picture of the incipient artist baited by the Philistines in all societies. Except that it was carried out on a level of ignorance and poverty which compels some extenuation, the process could be the history of a hundred young white artists of a dozen nationalities.

But when he went from home into the working world of the South, Mr. Wright did meet race oppression in all its ugliness, and from the experience he drew, as he says, his "life's passion." He was by then obsessed with a sense of being wronged and race prejudice was the great overall cause. He made it his target. The mere fact, however, that he can now present Negro society objectively indicates that his work is becoming free of his bitter personal emotions. If the present book is an indication, he is moving toward a breadth which in the past he has conspicuously lacked.

"Black Boyhood." *Time,* 45 (March 5, 1945), 94, 96, 98.

Richard Wright, 36, is generally accounted the most gifted living American Negro writer. His new book makes it clearer than ever that he has one of the most notable gifts in U.S. writing, black or white: a narrative style that is simple, direct, almost completely without pretense or decoration, yet never flat. In *Black Boy,* that narrative tells the story of his first 18 years, in Natchez and Jackson, Miss., Elaine, Ark., and on Beale Street in Memphis. The story is a brilliant account of how it feels to be a sensitive Negro growing up in the U.S. South.

Author Wright's early books *(Uncle Tom's Children, Native Son)* won high critical praise. Violent and unsparing, they contained passages (as does this book) too strong for most readers' stomachs. His fellow Communists first praised Wright to the skies, then turned savagely against him when he broke with the party. More honest than most Communists, he has never tried to sweeten up his down-trodden Negroes. His typical story is of some accidental clash between Negroes and whites springing from the fear and misunderstanding of both people, suddenly flaring into a lynching, a riot, a murder. Brilliant and melodramatic though these are, they seem to flash by like a scene of violence caught in the spotlight of a passing automobile, clear, vivid, frightening, but without relation to the life around it. *Black Boy* helps to explain that lack of relation. It is the story of a man set apart from his own race by sensitivity and intellect, yet barred forever from the white race by the color of his skin.

At four, Richard Wright tried to burn down the house in which his grandmother lay ill. Restless at being kept indoors, he built up a fire with broomstraws, touched off the window curtains, hid under the house when the fire got out of control. His frantic parents thought he was inside, were so relieved and angry when they found him unhurt that they whipped him until he lost consciousness.

The shock was lasting. "For a long time I was chastened whenever I remembered that my mother had come close to killing me." Throughout his childhood, at moments of extreme tension, he would become immobile, in full possession of his mental faculties but without the power to make his hands or his voice obey his will. He was nervous and imaginative in a world where only the strong-willed and easy-going get along. When his mother got a job as a cook, he ran wild in the streets of Jackson, sneaked into saloons and begged drinks from customers, who taught him obscenities and laughed at his drunken staggers. He was then six years old.

Richard's uncles and aunts were solid, successful people: schoolteachers, carpenters, mail carriers. When his mother fell ill, they impoverished themselves to pay for her operations and care. She was in bed for ten years. "My mother's suffering grew into a symbol in my mind, gathering to itself all the poverty, the ignorance, the helplessness; the painful, baffling, hunger-ridden days and hours. . . . A somberness of spirit that I was never to lose settled over me during the slow years of my mother's unrelieved suffering, a somberness that was to make me stand apart and look upon excessive joy with suspicion, that was to make me self-conscious, that was to make me keep forever on the move, as though to escape a nameless fate seeking to overtake me."

Richard sold papers, worked in a drugstore, a credit clothing store, a brickyard, an optical factory. He was hopeless at each job. He could not cover up his feelings. He forgot to say "Sir," or said it too slowly. He did not know how to get out of white people's way. One of his bosses said, "Why don't you laugh and talk like other niggers?" The other Negroes privately talked a venomous, unrelieved hatred of the whites, but joked and laughed in their presence. Richard could not. Moreover, in crises—as when a white man hit him in the mouth with a whiskey bottle—his old immobility came back and left him paralyzed.

He did better as a bellboy. The naked white prostitutes paid no attention to him when he delivered bootleg whiskey to their rooms, though their customers sometimes objected. Because he had never been in jail, he was picked by racketeers as front for a movie-ticket racket. He made $50 the first week. But he knew he was headed for the chain gang. He saved his money, stole everything he could lay hands on, pawned it, and fled to Memphis. There he began to read Mencken and Sinclair Lewis, and to see the white men around him in a different light.

His reading also gave him a profound awareness of his people's plight. "I used to mull over the strange absence of real kindness in Negroes, how unstable was our tenderness, how lacking in genuine passion we were, how void of great hope, how timid our joy, how bare our traditions, how hollow our memories, how lacking we were in those intangible sentiments that bind man to man, and how shallow was even our despair. . . . Whenever I thought of the essential bleakness of black life in America, I knew that Negroes had never been allowed to catch the full spirit of Western civilization. . . ."

W. I.
St. Louis Star-Times,
March 8, 1945.

"Black Boy" is the partial autobiography of Richard Wright, author of the remarkable and sensational novel, "Native Son," a best seller of 1940 which later found its way to Broadway in play form. The new book covers his boyhood in the South until, at 17, he had saved enough money to flee from the terror which he found behind the everyday existence of Negroes below the Mason-Dixon.

That one word, terror, describes the motivating power and force of the entire book. It was terror of two things, white people and hunger, which Wright, like any sensitive and intelligent Negro youth, felt personally and deeply. Poorer even than most of his colored brothers, he long remained ignorant of the intricacies of racial prejudice. When eventually they were impressed upon him, he had met severe personal injuries several times and suffered near death. When he became old enough to rationalize his situation, it appeared to him that, in the relations between whites and blacks, the latter could thrive only by dishonesty and, incongruously enough, their lack of independence.

He describes some terrorizing scenes: That of a Negro woman being beaten by the proprietors of a store for nonpayment of her bill while a policeman stood by and watched; his own experience (which illustrates the economic insecurity behind most of the Jim Crow laws) of being fired from a job because another worker was afraid for him to be taught the trade.

Being a man of unusual integrity and resourcefulness, Wright was able to rise above the limitations and restrictions which he found in his early environment. When he moved to Chicago, he was able to develop his talents, and to win a name for himself in American letters. Yet he has not forgotten that others of his race do not possess his assets, and whereas more and more Negroes are finding their individual independence in the South . . . and North, the situation is still a tough one for most.

Again, the book is a terrorizing one, and many readers will be quick to say that it is full of exaggerations. This is an easy and comfortable attitude to take but may or may not be a sound one. After all, no one can say for certain unless he has lived as a Negro in the South. Few people would be willing to do so.

L. A. S. "One Negro's Life Story." *Christian Science Monitor,* March 9, 1945, p. 14.

Richard Wright's BLACK BOY is a moving human record and an important social document. This story of a Negro's childhood and youth in the South should remove the last touch of complacency in American thinking on the racial problem. It should also help toward a solution by awakening a sense of responsibility.

It is not a pleasant story. It contains much that is shocking, from the time when the boy of four years was beaten nearly fatally by his mother to the day when, in his late 'teens, he left Memphis for the North. The record of the years between is strewn with brutality, filth, and terror, and the language employed matches the scenes described.

Whether Mr. Wright's story is typical is open to question. His own early life was a long battle to escape from the tyranny of white men who looked on a Negro as a natural inferior and who demanded not only that he "keep his place" but that he pretend to enjoy keeping it; who enforced their rule by economic pressure, by blows, and by cold-blooded killing.

Undoubtedly, there are Southern whites who behave in this way, through economic or political fear, or vanity, or mere sadism. But it is equally certain that there are liberal, freedom-loving Southerners who have done and are doing a great deal, to promote justice to the Negro, to help him win decent living conditions, education, and a solid position in society.

Then, too, Mr. Wright was an exceptional child, and the victim of what probably were exceptionally difficult circumstances. The poverty into which he was born and in which he grew up was very likely much worse than the average. His father deserted the family. His mother was well-meaning but in her ignorance and indigence and illness she was unable to give him a normal up-bringing. His grandmother was fanatical in her religious belief and harsh on unbelievers.

Richard was bewildered and miserable. But as he grew, he decided that he was unwilling to accept the role he saw played so readily by other Negro boys. He did not feel inferior, and it was difficult for him to act as if he did. He was mentally alert, and he had intellectual curiosity and the hankering to write. He felt that he must escape from his environment.

The means he took were the only ones he could find. He bootlegged liquor and he stole, to get the money to flee to Memphis. But Memphis did not bring freedom. Although there was less violence than in Mississippi, there was much the same opposition to his progress. He could get books from the public library only by subterfuge. His opportunities for employment were limited. His race were still regarded by many whites as lower animals, and fights between Negroes were promoted for white entertainment, just as they were between cocks or dogs.

In spite of discouragements, Richard finally succeeded in breaking open the world of intellectual life and in saving money enough to go to Chicago. There he made himself known to his fellow countrymen by producing the short stories collected under the title of "Uncle Tom's Children," and the novel, "Native Son."

And this is the most extraordinary fact in his history: that there was within him a spark that enabled him to rise in a few years from the lowest social depths, a member of a race despised and oppressed, to a position of eminence in the literary world.

What of the Negroes who have not that spark, or in whom it is less well developed? Is it not for the intelligent and liberal-minded of both races to help to give them at last the full rights of freemen? Richard Wright's book should contribute to this end.

Frank McCallister. "Rejection, Rebellion, Aggression." *Atlanta Journal*, March 11, 1945.

> "The white South said that it knew 'niggers,' and I was what the white South called a 'nigger.' Well, the white South had never known me—never known what I thought, what I felt. The white South said that I had a 'place' in life. Well, I had never felt my 'place,' or rather, my deepest instincts had made me reject the 'place' to which the white South had assigned me. . . ."

Thus speaks Richard Wright, 37 year-old Negro author, in "Black Boy," a part of his autobiography which deals with a record of his youth and childhood spent on the Mississippi delta amidst grinding poverty, religious and racial prejudices, fear and terror.

The whites, who live in the South and the North and think they know the Negro will do well to read this vividly told story and then ponder whether or not they really know what is going on in the minds of Negroes. Do they understand what Negroes think about their relegation to second-class citizenship, their unfavorable economic status, discriminations suffered not only in the South but in all parts of the nation? This volume, written with great force and drama, will give part of the answer.

Of course, Richard Wright's own experience is atypical. He was able to free himself from the deadening effects of his early environment and exercise a talent for writing which has brought him fame and fortune.

This book helps to explain Bigger Thomas, central character in Mr. Wright's earlier "Native Son." Bigger Thomas, as a Negro brute, living on almost an animal plane, was no more popular with Negro intellectuals than was Nonnie Anderson in "Strange Fruit," who, although a graduate of Spelman College, worked as a nurse to a demented white child. Both, however, depict in an unforgetable manner the predicament of the Negro.

It is truly a wonder that Richard Wright survived to exercise his masterful talents of writing.

When he was only four his mother beat him nearly to death for setting their house afire in Natchez, Miss. . . . After his father left home with another woman, Richard and his younger brother were put in an orphanage. His most vivid memories about youth are the gnawing pangs of hunger which never seemed to leave him.

His mother finally took him to Arkansas to live with an aunt and uncle but the uncle was slain by white men who wanted his flourishing saloon and they had to move back to Mississippi.

Plotting to escape the region became an obsession with the author. He finally accumulated enough money to get to Memphis. Some of the most vivid scenes in the book describe the sadistic pleasure some white men indulge by having "fun" at the expense of the Negro and trying to fix him in a dilemma from which he cannot escape without paying obeisance to "white supremacy."

The book is written with stark realism and bitterness. The reader is spared few details of the miserable existence the author suffered under. This bitterness is likely to prevent the gifted writer from attaining the full stature unless he outgrows it.

To those who feel "I know the Southern Negro," I say, get this book and find out if you do.

W. T. Winston. *Best Sellers*, 5 (March 15, 1945), 219–20.

The author of *Big Boy Leaves Home, Uncle Tom's Children* and *Native Son* here tells the story of his own first nineteen years. Now in his middle thirties, Richard Wright looks back at his childhood and youth in Mississippi, Arkansas and Tennessee, and sets down his memories of one Negro boy's experience with hunger and raggedness, harshness from relatives at home and brutalities from blacks and whites abroad; of his own reactions to the bleak, bitter life around him; and above all, of his growing awareness of racial tension, his overmastering sense of unreasoning hate and capricious tyranny on the part of the dominant whites. . . .

Mr. Wright has performed a remarkable feat in so vividly recapturing the moods and reactions of his early years. Perhaps he has succeeded too well in this, for *Black Boy,* well written as it is, bears marks of moral and mental immaturity. This accounts for its author's naive egoism; his disregard of the historical background which, without justifying, accounts for—and in a measure excuses—anti-Negro prejudice; and his fondness for needlessly dragging verbal vulgarities and obscenities into his story.

The last-mentioned characteristic bars Mr. Wright's book from recommendation to any but mature and scholarly readers. Which is a pity, for, were it written with better observance of the reticences of decent speech, *Black Boy* could play a useful part in making the general public realize to what degree white discourtesy and injustice poison the intelligent Negro's soul. And it is the intelligent Negroes, not the traditional "Uncle Toms" and "Aunt Jemimas," who today mould Negro thought and in a not over-distant tomorrow will lead Negro action.

Newark Evening News, March 17, 1945.

Undoubtedly there are people, both whites and blacks, who can parallel some of the horrible experiences that Wright chronicles in this record of his childhood and youth. But not many others have had the extremely keen sensitivity to suffering, injustice, pain and oppression that Wright displays; nature in pity gave them more of a protective integument of callousness.

Yet in one sense pain has not been without its compensation for Wright, since in his case hyperaesthesia has been accompanied by remarkable gifts of artistic expression, so that some pages of his book approach greatness.

Of course, "Black Boy" will be read chiefly as a study in race prejudice, and yet it has some curious limitations as such. The book is really the most ferocious exercise in misanthropy since Jonathan Swift. Wright does not merely hate whites; he seems to hate all human beings, including Negroes. Some of the most nauseating passages in his book relate episodes in which members of his own family figure. Apparently a tract directed against race prejudice, "Black Boy" is itself far from free from that evil trait. It is a book that apparently seeks to prove the truth of Swift's despairing remark about men—"the most pernicious race of little odious vermin that nature ever suffered to crawl upon the face of the earth."

Bruce Haddon. "A Fight Against Fear." *Erie Dispatch-Herald*, March 18, 1945.

Writers can portray their realism in several different ways. The most common is the most sensational. With a flare for the dramatic, the author describes in minute detail the individual, the setting, or the event he wants to convey to his readers. If this means lurid description of vulgarity and cruelty, he writes that description. Whatever the literary merit of the product of this kind of writing, in the last two decades it has flooded our American homes. Small wonder that now a moral reaction against it has set in.

There is, however, a form of realism that only a polished artist can produce. That is the restrained writing which in a word or a sentence can not only picture a full drama but also its emotional impact.

This is the realism of Richard Wright. It is the realism with which he tells the story of his boyhood.

"Black Boy" might be the history of

any young Negro, born and reared in the deep South except that this boy was by nature shaped into the kind of individual who cannot accept his environment, and in rejecting it creating a burning passion within himself to become the kind of person he wants to be in the kind of world which he knows must exist somewhere. . . .

It is in his mature years that Wright tells this story of his youth. But even as a refugee from the Blackman's South, he did not carry bitterness with him. "With ever watchful eyes and bearing scars visible and invisible, I headed North, full of a hazy notion that life could be lived with dignity, the personalities of others should not be violated, that men should be able to confront other men without fear or shame, and that if men were lucky in their living on earth they might win some redeeming meaning for their having struggled and suffered here beneath the stars."

That is a high note on which the book ends. But it is not an afterthought meant to soften the harshness of the incidents of the story. It is the logical culmination of the theme of the youth's driving inner force, and as such it helps make the book the masterpiece of modern prose that it is.

For, when all is said and done, when the social message of the story is transcended, this autobiography remains a brilliant literary achievement, one that is in the mainstream of great English literature.

George Streator. *Commonweal*, 46 (March 23, 1945), 568–69.

Richard Wright is not yet a unanimous choice among Negroes who are reading his books, mainly because they do not accept the thesis he seemed to expound a few years back, that equal poverty forces one to wade through equal filth. It was felt, too, that Mr. Wright was being led around by the communists in those days. It was felt that he rejected all the education gained in this world except that arrived at by trial and error, the sort of training an ignorant bell-hop in a fifth-rate Southern hostelry would receive from his guests.

There was also grave fear that Mr. Wright was an *ersatz* artist to tell the appropriate shocking story, just shocking enough to hasten the revolution then deemed to be lurking just around the corner. Since that time, however, the Negro has experienced Lillian Smith, with much more to come. It is good to have Richard Wright's autobiography, for he has a strong story to tell. If middle-class Negroes do not "get" this story we should know by now that the Negro is made up of all classes, albeit the proportions are quite different from those arrived at in describing white people in America.

A lot of white people have been feigning radicalism in this country for political and other reasons for the past twenty years. But if a Jewish radical does not know something of the part his people have played in the exploitation of the Southern Negro peasant for the past forty years, he will be unable to understand Negro anti-Semitism which Mr. Wright describes but does not adequately account for in this book. That God's Chosen People (Negroes still believe that) could stoop to exploit Negroes is unbelievable!

Again, if Irish Catholics turn up their noses at this story of the black underdog and begin to relate the number of priests in every family in the old country, they forget the origins of many Southern police, deputy sheriffs, and labor-union officials whom the *black boy* has been struggling against. Obviously, an understanding of this book requires sound, critical judgment. It is not always safe to predict what the general conclusions of the average reader might be.

Does a Negro steal? The people who give a starvation job to the *black boy* ask this question. Wright chuckled when he heard this. But it is still being asked. The white man does not steal. He deals with bigger words. He misappropriates, mislays, misdirects, unwisely invests, often diverts funds from their lawful owners. But steal? Do not make me laugh.

Richard Wright had a very hard childhood. His was an active mind that did not have enough guidance. A lot of us cannot understand how he could have thirsted so for learning without getting a trolley out to LeMoyne College where some Congregationalist would have given him all the books he wanted to read—but after all, we did not have Wright's immediate surroundings. His awakening came after he had lived about seventeen years. Besides, there are several tens of thousands of Negroes in Memphis today who do not go out to LeMoyne College. And he was thrown in among the most backward of these.

The *black boy* was drinking whiskey in a saloon when he was six years old. The temperance movement will jump for that. But I have seen white children given liquor at an early age to break them of any longing for it in later years. Last year I saw a white man in Connecticut give whiskey to his boy, a child of three.

This book is another milestone in the road to emancipation. At least one Negro has admitted in print that his early life was a humdinger, but he got over it in spite of the white and Negro blood-letters around him as a child. If the white readers just do not take this book as definitive, or any other book on Negroes as definitive, with a great human problem to deal with! Let's get down to our chores and do as much as possible to get money for Southern schools, for black and white. Let's train the *black boy* to do something with his hands, and train the white boy to do something with his hands. If they want to write and go to college later, it will not hurt them. I say this because I have proof.

The Austinite (Chicago), March 28, 1945.

It is hard to believe that the dismal, maltreated colored lad who is the central character of "Black Boy" could grow up to become the author of this powerful, disquieting volume. That Richard Wright, the child, evolved into Richard Wright, the man, is the only happy implication in the whole sad, wretched account of negro childhood in the south.

Mr. Wright has used the story of his own youth in Mississippi and Tennessee as the pivot for this book which he has written as an angry indictment of an America which tolerates such conditions as he describes. The tone of the book is an unrelieved mud-color. There is no light of happiness or kindness in the past; no ray of hope for the future. . . .

It is inconceivable that any human being could grow up without finally having some happy experience, meeting at least one person of character and kindness. But if Richard Wright had anything of the sort in his early life, he does not mention it in "Black Boy."

Whether or not the reader is inclined to question the complete veracity of Mr. Wright, he cannot deny that the author has assembled a book which is disturbing and terrible. It was obviously Wright's intention to shock his audience into action; time alone will tell whether or not he has succeeded.

Edward Weeks. "The Atlantic Bookshelf." *Atlantic Monthly,* 17 (March 1945), 131.

. . . To write the record of rough justice, a Negro must pull himself out of the slough of ignorance and rise above the prejudices of his own people and the mortifications of white supremacy. Even today few have come through the ordeal, and those few carry with them an accumulated bitterness. *Black Boy* by Richard Wright is, as Dorothy Canfield Fisher truly says, "an honest, dreadful, heart-breaking story of a Negro childhood and youth." It is also a modern story, for the childhood began on the shores of the Mississippi in the year 1909. Richard's father was a shiftless farmhand, a slave in mind if not in body, with no vestige of loyalty towards his wife or family. His mother was struck down by paralysis shortly after her husband had deserted her, and Richard's boyhood was passed in the crowded homes of his relatives, where he lived on charity. He was usually hungry, often strapped and browbeaten by his elders, held back by the most illiterate prejudices, and—because he was a strong boy whose will would not be subdued—mortified again and again by white animosity.

Good schooling was out of reach. There was no one to befriend him. What he learned about human nature, he learned in the barrooms, as a water boy, in the hotel lobbies where he worked as a bellhop, in the doing of odd jobs which kept his head just above water. He was goaded by curiosity and by the unshakable belief that some day, somewhere, he would be free to speak his mind. But that meant he had first to escape from his family in the South. And to escape he had to earn the hundred dollars which would take him North.

How far Mr. Wright has traveled since those early days in Memphis stands clearly revealed in the telling and terrifying passages of this book. Mr. Wright is not the first Negro to write of his emancipation with power and beauty. *Father Henson's Story,* for which Mrs. Stowe wrote the Introduction in 1858, is a Negro classic of the underground of that day and of the physical tyranny an American Negro could overcome if he had the mind and will. Like Father Henson, Richard Wright traveled a painful road, though his torture was more mental, before he could come into the clear.

Indeed, Mr. Wright has come so far from his beginning that I am not sure that I always trust his hindsight. I find it hard to believe that a boy of four would so calmly and surely set fire to his family's cabin, and that a boy of nine would have heard no word about the First World War then being fought. In his concentration on the poverty, the foulness, and the terror in which he was brought up, the author almost completely ignores those tentacles of natural affection which must have held him and his mother together in their misery. There is a curious detachment in this book, as if the author had so covered up his affection that it can no longer be revealed. "During the day," he writes of one painful episode, "I overreacted to each event, my banked emotions spilling around it. I refused to talk to anyone about my affairs, because I knew that I would only hear a justification of the ways of the white folks and I did not want to hear it. I lived carrying a huge wound, tender, festering, and I shrank when I came near anything that I thought would touch it." Readers should remember that such wounds have made this man indignant and tight-lipped. They should accept this book with all its imperfections as a stark, powerful proclamation that black ignorance is being dispelled in our time. What is white America doing to help? . . .

Fort Worth Star Telegram, April 1, 1945.

In challenge to the average Southerner's conviction that the South best "understands" the Negro and his "place in life," one of America's most outstanding Negro writers, Richard Wright, tells the story of his boyhood in the deep South.

In "Black Boy," Wright's autobiography, the author simply and movingly paints a portrait of Negro life in the years 1915 to 1925. His childhood was darkened by the total lack of any economic security, by a constant hunger that "greens and corn mush" could not satisfy.

Although the early 20s was an unfortunate period of intensified racial strife in the South, Wright says that he actually saw little of it. However, he adds, although he never knew a man who was lynched, a youthful terror of white people was instilled in him by his own race.

A few white people were particularly kind to him, but none crossed the racial line to try to understand the boy as a human being.

His schooling was sporadic. After his father's desertion of his family and his mother's early paralysis, Richard and his young brother were passed from relative to relative, with a short stay in an orphanage as well. He worked before and after school to help support his family and to buy a few school books. After the ninth grade he had to leave school.

The one motivating dream of his boyhood life was to go to the North, not to be able to mingle socially with white people, as many Southerners suspect, but rather to be able to maintain his self-respect. Conditioned by his childhood, Wright could never forget the cultural schism of the South.

No comparison is valuable between Wright's autobiography and his famous "Native Son." The latter deals with an adult Negro in the North, and the former, a Negro boy in the South. The same angry prose and clarity of style, however, are evident. "Black Boy" does show a kinship with Wright's first book, a short story collection titled "Uncle Tom's Children." Both actualize in print the atmosphere of terror and shame that Wright claims is the heritage of the Southern Negro of his generation.

Paul Flowers. "No Solution in *Black Boy*." *Memphis Commercial-Appeal,* April 1, 1945.

For an ideal, detached, and objective evaluation of this autobiography, it would be necessary to find a reader who lacks all vestiges of emotional feeling toward the problems of minority groups in the United States. Since, in all probability, no such person exists, it is necessary for some one who has a fair share of prejudices to strive for objectivity and strict justice.

"Black Boy" is the unvarnished story of a negro boy's struggle against his environment in the South, within the past three decades. The author, with considerable effectiveness, has delineated the difficulties he overcame in his rise from obscurity. Obviously the hardships and handicaps he met made a far greater impression on him than the fewer morsels of encouragement that came his way, but he admits, on almost every page, that he possessed a rebellious spirit, not only against a broad and deeply intrenched social system, but also against the mores and habits of his own people, even his own family.

His story of poverty, ignorance, the cruelty of his own father toward him, the inertia of his own people, the absence of strong family ties, and the frictions between his people and the dominant group, is an old one, a story told and retold many times. It relies on violence and scatology for melodramatic effect, and the author appears to be overwhelmed by his own sincerity. The trouble is that he leaves some of the story untold, as an advocate of any cause is prone to do when seeking an indictment or conviction. The greatest weakness of "Black Boy" seems to be its obvious tendentiousness, its extremism in seeking to make out a case. The author could have painted his picture with graduated tones, and possibly made it more effective. However, he made it an out and out propaganda document, when he might have accomplished more with deftness.

"Black Boy" has stirred considerable comment in all sections of the United States, as most "social problem" documents do. Those readers whose emotions are attuned to the author's views have hailed it as a classic, those at the other extreme have denounced it categorically. To the detached observer, if there is such a creature, it appears neither an earthrocking document as claimed by its enthusiasts, nor as an entirely evil mass of untruths, as charged by its severest critics. It is merely the melodramatic retelling of a story which most Americans know, or should know, by this time.

And the critical reader may wonder if a touch of fiction has crept in, for example, as when the author confides that he commenced reading Harper's, the Atlantic Monthly, and the American Mercury soon after he had finished the ninth grade. If the author, with such educational preparation, had an appetite for such literature, he was an exceptional youth indeed.

Admitting that a book of this sort must contain heroic doses of melodrama in order to attract attention, the reader may wonder why this or some other author does not eschew the familiar, the routine formulas which inevitably characterize such documents, and dwell for a moment on realistic approaches to a solution. . . .

Isidor Schneider. "One Apart." *New Masses,* 54 (April 3, 1945), 23–24.

As autobiography *Black Boy* has all the faults of that riskiest form of writing; as a picture of the Negro people it is a distortion; but as a document of the psychological patterns of race tension it is unique, powerful and of considerable importance.

The fatal risk of autobiography is that the determination to tell the truth is frustrated by the accompanying impulse for self-preservation. The mind, fearful of its vulnerability in the nude, at once covers itself with justifications. That is why the heroes of autobiographies and of autobiographical fiction are generally nullities, cancelled out in the process of confession and simultaneous self-justification.

But Wright's form of self-justification also prevents him from realizing character in any other of his figures. They are all cast in active or passive phases of antagonism to him; all are obstacles to his self-fulfilment. By their antagonism he justifies his alienation. Their role is to serve the ego purpose of autobiography: "See what I have surmounted!"

What Mr. Wright reveals in *Black Boy* helps to explain his characteristics as a writer, his choice of material, his attitude toward people. The tension of conflict leaves its mark in the obsession with violence.

By the evidence in *Black Boy* these characteristics took form from some early childhood wound or maladjustment traceable only by a psychiatrist. We see them operating already in the child of four, as Wright recollects him, who sets fire to his house in retaliation for adult prohibitions. They are on view in the book in an almost unbroken record of hostility, cruelty, alienation, guilt sense, and violence.

The obsession with violence is particularly marked in Wright's early reading memories. This is how he recalls the story read to him by a friendly young woman boarder in his grandmother's house:

> She told how Bluebeard had duped and married his seven wives, how he had loved and slain them, how he had hanged them up by their hair in a dark closet. As she spoke reality changed, the look of things altered and the world became peopled with magical presences. My sense of life deepened and the feel of things was different somehow. Enchanted and enthralled, I stopped her constantly to ask for details. My imagination blazed. *The sensations the story aroused in me were never to leave me.* (My emphasis, I.S.)

In a similar vein he recalls a pulp serial in a newspaper that he sold in order to be able to read it:

> I was absorbed in the tale of a renowned scientist who had rigged up a mystery room made of metal in the basement of his palatial home. Prompted by some obscure motive, he would lure his victims into this room and then throw an electric switch. Slowly, with heart-wracking agony, the air would be sucked from the metal room and his victims would die, turning red, blue, then black.

The chief significance in these passages lies not in Wright's enjoyment of such stories but in the place they have in his memory. They are the only early reading experiences recorded in detail and commented upon for their hold on his imagination. Indeed, as Wright notes, they never left his mind. In various forms the closet of crime, the torture chamber, the images of locked-in guilt, recur in Wright's fiction along with other fantasies of hostility and violence. What it fed on gives us the quality of Wright's imagination.

Hostility and alienation has not only kept Wright from intimate understanding and rounded presentation of individuals but also from sympathy with his people. There are derogatory epithets and allusions all through the book . . . "peasant," "wall-eyed yokels," "bleak pool of black life," etc. They are summed up in these parenthetical paragraphs printed early in the book:

> I used to mull over the strange absence of real kindness in Negroes, how unstable was our tenderness, how lacking in genuine passion we were, how void of great hope, how timid our joy, how bare our tradition, how hollow our memories, how lacking we were in those intangible sentiments that bind man to man, and how shallow was even our despair. After I had learned other ways of life I used to brood upon the unconscious irony of those who felt that Negroes led so passional an existence! I saw that what had been taken for our emotional strength was our negative confusions, our flights, our fears, our frenzy under pressure. Whenever I thought of the essential bleakness of black life in America, I knew that Negroes had never been allowed to catch the full spirit of Western civilization, that they lived somehow in it but not of it. And when I brooded upon the cultural barrenness of black life, I wondered if clean positive tenderness, love, honor, loyalty, and the capacity to remember were native with man. I asked myself if these human qualities were not fostered, won, struggled and suffered for, preserved in ritual form from one generation to another.

Following out the implications of the last sentences one would have to assume doubts, on Wright's part, of Negro capacity for culture. Its existence could certainly not be proved from any testimony in the book. No reader would learn from it that there were any Negro cultural institutions or influences; or that Negro culture, even at the folk level, had made major contributions to American culture; or that a Douglass, a Carver, a Robeson had ever existed and stirred the Negro people; or that Negro struggle and protest was a proud strand in the American chronicle. It is, perhaps, no accident that Wright's own grandfather, who fought for Negro freedom as a Union soldier in the Civil War, is reduced to a ridiculous figure, bilked of his pension and presented, in possibly conscious symbolism, as somebody so impotent as not even to be of use to scare children into obedience.

Yet Wright's picture of bleak and shallow life is self-contradicted by episodes that the record compels him to set down. It would be difficult for any racial group to offer a finer example of deep feeling, of family solidarity and responsibility than his own far-scattered family who came in, some from Northern and Western towns, to assume the burdens brought by his mother's physical collapse. And it is contradicted in Wright's own book, written when he was a Communist, *Twelve Million Black Voices*.

Wright attempted to break out of the isolation that *Black Boy* defends by activities in the Communist Party. As published the book does not go into those years but it throws light on the chapters of recantation, published elsewhere, with which Wright brought that phase of his career to a squalid close. *Black Boy* renders any farther speculation on the causes unnecessary, as it renders his own self-justifications more specious and contradictory than was apparent at the time.

The causes which keep *Black Boy* from attaining stature as a work of art are the same which distort it as a picture of the Negro people. Yet its very concentration on the negative, the hostile, the violent, leads into explorations not attempted before. His innate interests heightened by a conscious interest in psycho-pathology, Wright makes keen observations of the neurotic behavior patterns and thought patterns produced by the race tensions in America. They form the major part of the second, and, by far, the most objective and successful part of the book. Set down with a sort of cold passion, they are powerfully and vividly realized. It is these contributions that give the book importance and a substantial compensating value.

Mrs. Zack Brandon. *Oklahoma City Star*, April 6, 1945.

Quite frequently a book is published that should be on the "must" list for every avid reader. The March selection of the Book-of-the-Month Club is just such a book.

"Black Boy" is an autobiography which, without a doubt, was written with a great innerpassion—such a one that burns and wells up in the heart of a man until finally it must come forth.

The gifted and talented Mr. Wright has depicted his youth and childhood days in the South with such sincerity and reality that it captures your heart and keeps you intensely interested until you have read the last word.

To every person that has the feeling that the door of opportunity should not swing open for the colored race, but should be subjected and squelched in everything they do: this book should be given so that they might read the thoughts expressed by a colored man on the subject. He relates the things that affected his life, the drama, the superstitions, the religious meetings, the relatives, along with the inner-turmoil of being continually suppressed by the white race. In his own words he states, "The safety of my life in the South depended on how well I concealed from all whites what I felt."

Mr. Wright ends his book with the thought that "Men should be able to confront other men without fear or shame, and that if men were lucky in their living on earth, they might win some redeeming meaning for their having struggled and suffered here beneath the stars."

Lionel Trilling. "A Tragic Situation." *The Nation*, 160 (April 7, 1945), 391–92.

Richard Wright's "Black Boy" is a remarkably fine book. Perhaps a Negro's autobiography must always first appear under the aspect of sociology—a fact that is in itself a sociological comment—and "Black Boy" has its importance as a "document," a precise and no doubt largely typical account of Negro life in Mississippi. That it is the account of a tragic situation goes without saying. Here is the Negro poverty in all its sordidness; here is the calculated spiritual imprisonment of one racial group by another; here, above all, is the personal humiliation of Negro by white, the complex cruelty of the dominant race practiced as a kind of personal, spiritual necessity, sometimes direct and brutal, sometimes sophisticated with a sensual, guilty, horrible kindness.

But if "Black Boy" were no more than a document of misery and oppression, it would not have the distinction which in fact it does have. Our literature is full of autobiographical or reportorial or fictional accounts of misery and oppression. I am sure that these books serve a good purpose; yet I find that I feel a little coolness toward the emotions they generate, for it seems to me that too often they serve the liberal reader as a means of "escape." With honest kinds of "escape" there can be no quarrel—to find a moment's rest in dreams of heroic or erotic fulfilment is as justifiable as sleeping. But the moral "escape" that can be offered by accounts of suffering and injustice is quite another thing. To sit in one's armchair and be harrowed can all too easily pass for a moral or political action. We vicariously suffer in slippers and become virtuous: it is pleasant to exercise moral indignation at small cost; or to fill up emotional vacancy with good strong feeling at a safe distance; or to feel consciously superior to the brutal oppressor; or to be morally entertained by poverty, seeing it as a new and painful kind of primitivism which tenderly fosters virtue, or, if not virtue, then at least "reality"; or to indulge in self-pity by projecting it—very pleasant, very flattering, a little corrupting. Mr. Wright's autobiography, so far as it is an account of misery and oppression, does not tempt its readers to such pleasures. This is the mark of the dignity and integrity of the book.

In other words, the sociological aspect of "Black Boy" is the field—I will not say *merely* the field—for a notable exercise of the author's moral and intellectual power. It is difficult to describe that power except, as I have tried to do, by speaking of its effect, by remarking that it does not lead us into easy and inexpensive emotions, although the emotions into which it does lead us are durable. If I try further to understand this, I can only surmise that it comes about because the author does not wholly identify himself with his painful experience, does not, therefore, make himself a mere object of the reader's consciousness, does not make himself that different kind of human being, a "sufferer." He is not an object, he is a subject; he is the same kind of person as his reader, as complex, as free.

"Black Boy" is an angry book, as it ought to be. I would be surprised and unhappy if it were not. But the amount of anger that Mr. Wright feels is in proportion only to the social situation he is dealing with; it is also in proportion to the author's desire to live a reasonable and effective life. For what a Negro suffers in the South—what, indeed, he might suffer in the North—calls for illimitable anger. But the full amount of anger that would be appropriate to the social situation alone would surely have the effect of quite destroying the person who felt it. And Mr. Wright, almost from infancy, seems to have refused to be destroyed. For example, by what, as he describes it, seems to have been a kind of blessed unawareness, even a benign stupidity, he simply could not understand the difference between black people and white. That his grandmother was so white as to be almost white may have had something to do with it. In any case, the young Richard had to be taught the difference, and it seems to have been at best a learned thing. This, to be sure, could scarcely have protected him from all psychic wounds and scars. But although he suffered, he seems never to have been passive. He seems thus to have been saved from the terrible ambivalences of the oppressed, from the self-indulgence, the self-pity, the ripe luxuriousness of sensitivity; and he does not, as the oppressed so often do, give himself or his oppressors a false glamour.

Mr. Wright's autobiography does not go beyond the time when he left the South at the age of nineteen. To me this is a disappointment, for Mr. Wright's life after his departure from the South is a great theme—the entrance of an aspiring and relatively ignorant young man into the full stream of national life is always a subject of the richest social and moral interest, and Mr. Wright's race makes that interest the richer. The chapters which appeared in the *Atlantic Monthly* under the title "I Tried to Be a Communist" are not included in "Black Boy"; they are not so interesting as they might be, although they have their point, but they suggest the kind of cultural and social experience I should like to see Mr. Wright explore. He has the directness and honesty to do it well. He has the objectivity which comes from refusing to be an object.

It is this objectivity that allows Mr. Wright to believe that oppression has done something more than merely segregate his people. He dares, that is, to take the oppression seriously, to believe that it really does oppress, that its tendency is not as much to exempt the oppressed from the moral flaws of the dominant culture from which they are excluded as it is to give them other flaws of feeling and action. He himself suffered from the fierce puritanical religiosity of his own family. He can speak tenderly of the love that his mother gave him, but he can speak with sorrow and bitterness of the emotional bleakness in which he was reared. . . .

I suppose that it is for saying this, or other things of a similar objectivity, that Mr. Wright has, as I have heard, come under the fire of his own people. And that, perhaps, is understandable. But if, like Mr. Wright, we believe that oppression is real, we must sadly praise his courage in seeing that it does not merely affect the body but also the soul. It is only a grim and ironic justice that the deterioration is as great in the oppressor as in the oppressed.

Milton Mayer. "Richard Wright: Unbreakable Negro." *The Progressive*, 9 (April 9, 1945).

This is not a great book. It couldn't have been; the author, without the surpassing genius of a Proust, is writing about his own passion. But my fellow-reviewers are right when they say it is a terribly important book.

You ought to read it, if for no other reason than that its author is a great man and a great novelist. This is the story, as well as he can tell it, of the man who wrote *Native Son*, and *Native Son* is a great novel.

What is great about *Native Son* is exactly what isn't great about *Black Boy*. The novel is the story of the Negro; of the Negro held by the throat by a mad racist culture; of the Negro born hopeless, reared wretchedly, schooled in the lowest varieties of escapism, and, finally, gone completely bad in his behavior and completely blind in his outlook. *Native Son* is the story of what white men, collectively, do to black men, collectively, in America.

Black Boy is the story of Richard Wright, who was born with a silver spoon (though without any bread) in his mouth. He had as fearless and ingenious a mother as he was a son. *Black Boy* approaches being literature—it never reaches it—in the delineation of Richard's mother's life. Black boys and white boys do not always have such mothers. Richard's really loved him, and he really loved her, and all that they suffered was not enough to convert one more black boy into one more Bigger Thomas (of *Native Son*).

Black Boy is not, as many reviewers and even many readers may think, the story of a black boy in the South. It is the story of *this* black boy in the South. *This* black boy was born proud, talented, and unbreakable, and into a family which, though it starved, never dreamed of stealing. True, the story tells us this. But the fact remains that it is not the story of *a* black boy. *Native Son* is.

Compared with *Native Son,* the autobiography is actually naive. Mr. Wright tells us at every point *how* and why he felt, and we are a little embarrassed, almost giggly, at the commonness and superficiality of expression. (Only in the 3 paragraphs beginning at the bottom of Page 88—read them yourself—is the penetration real and mature at this level.) *Native Son*—except in the last third, the weakest part of the book—tells us what happened and what was said, and moves us ourselves, as great work does, to figure out how the persons involved felt, and why. Mr. Wright does not move us to horror and anger; he feels them for us. What *Native Son* doesn't *try* to do, it does better than *Black Boy* trying.

Black Boy is meant to be a polemic, and it should be. As a true polemic, it is, I am afraid, unsuccessful. It is neither poetry (like *Native Son*) nor science (like the Reeves' commission's statistics on Negro educational opportunity). It is history; it is an account of singular events, befalling a given person at a given time and in a given place. The white man, North or South, who either actively or passively mistreats Negroes, reads this book and says: "*I'm* not in that book. *I* never ran into a nigger like that. All the niggers *I* ever ran into were lazy, stupid, and crooked. If *I'd* ever run into a nigger like that, you can bet your life I'd have treated him well." And the polemical impact is lost.

But the book is important, away beyond its merit, and away beyond its authorship, because it points the finger to the race problem, the problem on which our civilization, what is left of it, is likeliest to break. It points the finger to the urgency of the problem, to its desperateness. It does not figure it out. It displays the scabs, but it leaves us poor white lepers still afflicted. Mr. Wright —and I hope he is at work on a novel about a white man—might well answer me with: "What do you want in our time—Holy Writ?"

Theophilus Lewis. "Survival Through Flight." *America,* 73 (April 14, 1945), 39.

Autobiography is usually considered a field of literature reserved for the mature author who has reasons for believing his life has made an important impression on his time. It is difficult to understand why several contemporary Negro writers have turned to autobiography while still in their creative youth. Why should the author of *Black Boy,* for instance, assume that his life has been important enough to make present and future readers curious about his rather uneventful childhood and youth?

As the story of a life, *Black Boy* is as unexciting as the classified advertisements in your newspaper. In his youth the author lived in the shadow of destitution. So have many other black boys—and white boys, too. If he encountered any unique experiences that millions of poor boys have not encountered, he does not mention them. And his craftsmanship is not of the best, for there are places in the book where at least one fairly careful reader cannot tell at what age the author had the experience being described in the narrative.

One instance is a conversation he had with a youngster trying to persuade him to become a member of the church. The youth attempts to convert him with the naive clichés which have long been standardized in the evangelical sects, while the author's evasions are those one would expect of a sophisticated man of the world. At the time, the narrative indicates, the author was about thirteen years old. It is true that a precocious youngster of thirteen might have talked as the author says he talked. It is also true that the author was precocious. But precocity does not feed on thin air. When and where did he associate with the people or get hold of the books from which his absorbent mind acquired comparatively mature ideas? If he had ever met intelligent people or read enlightening books, why doesn't he mention the experience? It would certainly make more interesting reading than his meticulous record of the cuffs and scoldings he received at the hands of the elder members of his family.

As autobiography, *Black Boy* is neither interesting reading nor a competent writing job. The volume, however, has considerable value as a tract on race prejudice. In the middle and later chapters the author describes his early efforts at earning a living in the Deep South. The picture is a bit overdrawn, perhaps, for the author paints almost exclusively in vivid colors. There seem to be no soft tints or neutral shades on his palette. Nevertheless, his picture of conditions in the South is essentially true.

Those conditions are unjust and frequently cruel, but thousands of black boys have achieved success in spite of them, and a few have carved out enviable careers for themselves. Obviously some temperaments, like the author's, are unable to make an adjustment to the Southern pattern; and their only hope for survival is in flight. That is the crowning evil of race prejudice—that it compels an individual to spend in evasion or escape the energy that should be used in developing his personality. As a factual description of the evil, *Black Boy* is a valuable book to place in the hands of those who are unconvinced or only half convinced of the injustice of color prejudice.

In the early chapters there are indelicacies which veer perilously close to the margin of decency. One cannot casually recommend the book to minors or immature adults.

Layle Lane. *The Call* (Workmen's Circle), April 1945.

To be both poor and black is a crime for which materialistic America exacts a heavy price. Since poverty is the constant companion of the majority of colored people in America, the story of Richard Wright in "Black Boy" is the story of millions of Negro children. The only variants are those of individual personality and of locale. The price of poverty and of dark skin is both physical and spiritual hunger . . . frustration . . . meek submission or misdirected energy.

A few of the strong are able to escape from the "southern swamp of despair and violence." Wright is one of these. He is also one who can write of this swamp and interpret it for others with insight and power.

His story is honestly told with the same compelling descriptions of physical sensations and mental questionings as were found in "Native Son." The relations of whites and Negroes are marked with the daily injustices and humiliations which Negroes endure. For these reasons "Black Boy" is a far more terrible and just indictment of white America than "Native Son."

In Wright's home life he experienced all too frequently a blow or a whipping resulting from the strained nerves of a mother and grandmother trying to eke out an existence relieved by faith in the Lord.

There was also the all-too common occurrence in Negro homes of the father's desertion and indifference to the welfare of his children. This hangover from the slave system which broke down, in every way possible, parental and home ties in order to make the sale of human beings easier, has placed a double duty on the Negro mother. It explains the high rate of juvenile delinquency among Negroes as well as much of the violence Wright experienced.

It explains, too, Richard Wright's constant, childhood hunger, which he describes so vividly. . . .

Twenty five years later, when next he saw his father "a sharecropper, clad in ragged overalls, holding a muddy hoe in his gnarled veined hands," he "forgave and pitied him." "I was overwhelmed," Wright explains poignantly,

> to realize that he could never understand me or the scalding experiences that had swept me beyond his life and into an area of living that he could never know. . . . From the white landowners above him there had not been handed to him a chance to learn the meaning of loyalty, of sentiment, of tradition . . . my father was a black peasant who had gone to the city seeking life . . . a black peasant whose life had been hopelessly snarled in the city.

Therein is the tragedy of many Negroes in our city Ghettos.

Just as bitter as his attitude toward his father was his attitude toward whites. Inwardly he rebelled at their dominance, and those who came in contact with him sensed this rebellion. . . . Shorty, the Negro elevator operator in the building where Wright worked for a while, showed just how race prejudice and poverty debased a man. For a quarter, he would forget his indignation about the wrongs of his people and resort to the most degrading clowning. . . . "Quarters is scarce," was his explanation.

Providing an economy in which quarters are plentiful for all who work will make possible the dream of Black Boy heading North . . . "that life can be lived with dignity."

Ray Gibbons. *Advance* (April 1945), 33.

The story of the struggles of a black boy to escape the coils of prejudice and become a free, creative spirit is told with exquisite taste and fine insight by the author of *Native Son,* Richard Wright. Since it is the story of his own life he uses retrospection and introspection to good effect, but even the story of such a turbulent childhood as his would have sagged in the hands of a less skillful artist. Beneath the bombardment of his words and the flares of his speech one beholds the strongest attack upon the citadels of prejudice, repression and superstition that has been waged by any author of recent date.

The book begins with a house a-fire, set by the author at the tender age of four. It proceeds through his intermittent schooling to the ninth grade, through his humiliating job rejections, his rebuffs by his playmates, cruelty by his family, and the repression of "white supremacy" until at last he escapes to the North. . . .

All the time he was building up in himself "a dream which the entire educational system of the South had been rigged to stifle." He had an insatiable lust for life, to learn about people. "I could endure the hunger. I had learned to live with hate. But to feel that there were feelings denied me, that the very breath of life was beyond my reach, that more than anything else hurt, wounded me. I had a new hunger." Nothing could make him doubt the "worth of my own humanity," not even the effort of the South to keep him in the "place" to which it assigned "niggers." "True I had lied. I had stolen. I had struggled to contain my seething anger. I had fought. And it was perhaps a mere accident that I had never killed . . . But in what other ways had the South allowed me to be natural, to be real, to be myself, except in rejection, rebellion and aggression?" Yet he holds out hope since he himself has emerged from that culture. "I was taking a part of the South to transplant in alien soil, to see if it could grow differently, if it could drink of new and cool rains, bend in strange winds, respond to the warmth of other suns, and, perhaps, to bloom . . . And if that miracle ever happened, then I would know that there was yet hope in that southern swamp of despair and violence, that light could emerge even out of the blackness of the southern night."

Lillian Smith's novel "Strange Fruit" dealt with a form of underground southern behavior, the running sore of illicit sex relations between whites and blacks. Richard Wright's "Black Boy" reveals the cancer as it attacks child life. The one reveals the passion of "eros"; the other shows how the passion for "ego" can be thwarted, mauled but remain unbroken. That the ego was not killed in such a spirited child as Richard Wright is the hero-saga of this tale. Little Eva needled the North into violent hatred of slavery. Perhaps Richard can stab the South broad awake.

S. W. Garlington. "An Ugly, Yet Factual Portrait." *The African*, 5 (April 1945), 19–20.

Richard Wright has written another best-seller—namely, *Black Boy: A Record of Childhood and Youth*. Before the manuscript was transformed into book-form, The Book-of-the-Month Club made it its March selection. Before critics could get around to having their say—and all of them were laudatory—the book was in its second printing with nearly 200,000 in circulation via the first run. All of this is good because Wright's latest work is a masterpiece of romanced facts—telling a story that the world should read . . . especially the American white man.

BLACK BOY, contrary to the misconception of many, is not an autobiography. Instead it is at best a sort-of-autobiography or pseudo-autobiography, recounting not only the life of the author but of thousands of blacks. Nevertheless it is a valuable addition to anyone's library.

"This book tells a harsh and forbidding story and makes one wonder just exactly what its relation to truth is," declared reviewer W. E. Burghardt Du Bois, reputed Dean of African-American scholars and author of *Black Reconstruction*. "Nothing that Richard Wright says is in itself unbelievable or impossible," he concluded, "it is the total picture that is not convincing."

Dr. Du Bois undoubtedly did not know that the author himself admits that his BLACK BOY is not supposed to be an autobiography. Instead, he "tried to give my tongue to the voiceless 'Negro' youth of the South." This Wright does with both ease and effectiveness. He tells a story of a definite type of African-American childhood and youth which is just as natural and American as hot dogs and baseball.

In this light, even though the book is a sort-of-autobiography, it is nevertheless autobiographical and should not be confused with either fiction or fictionalized biography. Nor should one merely regard it as creative writing because BLACK BOY *is* a record of life—even if the facts are romanced (which makes it easy to read, gets the message across better, and expresses the real mastery of the author in handling the King's English).

Many African-Americans know parts of the record found in Wright's book—especially those acquainted with the South. Nevertheless it is still MUST READING for African-Americans as well as others because the volume, without preaching, or Marxist interpretations, tells a story of American life that we should not forget until the causes are no longer present. In short, as Dorothy Norman of the *N. Y. Post* put it: "BLACK BOY is a declaration of independence of every sensitive human being who strikes out against tyranny, ignorance, and cruelty."

BLACK BOY, although not intended as such, is an enlightening sociological study—and a needed one, too. It does not offer a solution to the problem it treats. Neither does Sociology. But BLACK BOY is even more—it is literature—portraying harsh, forbidding memories of African-American childhood and youth. In brief, BLACK BOY is a MUST BOOK.

James W. Ivy. "American Hunger." *The Crisis*, 52 (April 1945), 117–18.

This book is one of the frankest autobiographies ever written by an American. I can think of no other American life story in which the author lays bare his soul and mind with such fierce directness. He tells unpalatable truths about himself, his family, his race, and the white South. I was about to say his friends, but friends, it seems, he never had. He does not play up nor glorify Negro virtues, and he is thoroughly unabashed in recounting our vices and shortcomings. Or specifically, the integrity and the failings of those he knew. These individuals, however, are seldom from the upper group.

"I knew of no Negroes who read the books I liked and I wondered," he mused, "if any Negroes ever thought of them. I knew that there were Negro doctors, lawyers, newspapermen, but I never saw any of them. . . . Well-to-do Negroes lived in a world that was almost as alien to me as the world inhabited by whites."

But to argue, as some have done, that the Negroes sketched by Mr. Wright are not typical of even the illiterate and ignorant southern peon is mere speciousness and a dodging of the issue posed by the sort of segregated living described. Even if we grant that his Negroes are not typical, we must admit that their sullen rebelliousness and bitterness as articulated in Mr. Wright is. Negro professional and business men in the South are happily, or luckily, insulated by their very economic status from the raw winds of white hatred that buffet the masses. . . .

But his life was not all bleakness, bitterness, and torment. Even his Seventh-Day Adventist relatives with their narrow and often mean orthodoxy could not prevent him from reveling in the magic possibilities of folk superstitions, the cool sensuality of the dew on his cheeks, "the tantalizing melancholy in the tingling scent of burning hickory wood," the blue-pink crawfishes, "the aching glory in masses of clouds burning gold and purple from an invisible sun," the serials of Zane Grey, and the books he borrowed from the public library.

"In me," he writes, "was shaping a yearning for a kind of consciousness, a mode of being that the way of life about me had said could not be. . . ." Introduction to this world came through the works of H. L. Mencken. After he had happened upon a denunciation of Mencken, he figured that anyone the white South denounced must be all right. So with the library card loaned by a white man (Negroes were not allowed to borrow books from the Memphis public library) he borrowed and began to devour the books of Mencken. A new and magic world now opened before his eyes. "I had once tried to write, had once reveled in feeling, had let my crude imagination roam, but the impulse to dream had slowly been beaten out of me by experiences. Now it surged up again and I hungered for books, new ways of looking and seeing. It was not a matter of believing or disbelieving what I read, but of feeling something new, of being affected by something that made the look of the world different."

Soon after this discovery of the great world of books, we find our black boy born of the Mississippi plantation, now nineteen, packing up his bags for new worlds and horizons in the North. The rest of the story is well-known.

Beatrice M. Murphy. *Pulse,* 3 (April 1945), 32–33.

"What," said a great writer once, "if I have no sword? I have a pen!" Richard Wright has demonstrated anew the power of the pen. He has used it as a sword to stab his own race in the back. For this story of his life which is being hailed by white critics as "A true story of life in America," "the moving and terrible story of how a Negro boy grew up in the South," is, rather, a story of how a terrible Negro boy grew up. There is a vast difference. The first presupposes that all Negro children experience such tragedies, the second points out that this particular child was an exception, not the rule.

Richard Wright had a good mother; a decent, respectable, hard-working mother whose "religious disposition dominated the household." Sometimes she beat him. There is no excuse for that. But certainly there was reason. Her son, Richard, gave her plenty of provocation. I wonder what the average mother would have done if her child first maliciously burned the house down and then while a whole family distractedly and frantically searched for him among the ruins, was found to be hiding safely under a building to escape punishment. Evidently even being beaten into unconsciousness had no effect on this child, because as he says: "She beat me, then she prayed and wept over me, imploring me to be good, telling me she had to work, all of which carried no weight to my wayward mind." I wonder what the average mother would do with a conniving child who killed a helpless kitten to get back at his father—in defiance of the latter's authority!

Richard Wright pictures himself as a boy who respected nothing or no one, who on his first day at school spent his lunch hour listening to "a long funny piece of doggerel, replete with filth, and memorized it word for word after having heard it but once. Yet despite my retentive memory, I found it impossible to recite when I went back into the classroom," a child who displays throughout the book no moving sympathy or affection for his crippled, broken mother who carried the family burden alone, by "cooking in white folk's kitchens," yet who "taught me to read, told me stories. On Sundays I would read the newspapers, with my mother guiding me and spelling out the words." "I told my mother I wanted to read and she encouraged me." He pictures himself as a bully who drew a knife or razor on older people to prevent beatings; who boasts that he was a "drunkard" at six; that his mother appealed to every decent instinct he might possess and could not get his cooperation in her struggle for existence.

Up to his 19th year, Mr. Wright spent 4 years in school. We find none of the burning ambition of a Lincoln, who read by the light of a fire, or a Mary McLeod Bethune, who walked five miles to school every day.

Let it be remembered that all of these things had nothing to do with the pressure of white society upon his childhood. Any white child under the same conditions, if he wanted, could have reacted the same way. Any child—Negro or White—living in the slums of a northern city could have done so. But there are thousands of slum children who do not—or, if they have such experiences and thoughts they obey the Bible injunction and "When I became a man I put away childish things."

Two important questions need to be answered:

1. Why write such a book? What good purpose will it serve? Even admitting that a modicum of responsibility for a turbulent childhood has made the White race search its soul and its conscience, does not seem sufficient reason for the writing of the book. A finger pointed straight is better than one pointed around a shady corner. The White race can always say, and is saying, that most of the responsibility rests elsewhere. The Negro race will probably reciprocate by heaping upon Mr. Wright the same contempt and misunderstanding which he has heaped upon it. The Negro race will retaliate to his charge of "the strange absence of real kindness in Negroes, how unstable was our tenderness, how lacking in genuine passion we were, how void of great hope, how timid our joy, how bare our traditions, how hollow our memories, how lacking we were in those intangible sentiments that bind man to man, and how shallow was even our despair," with a charge of "no loyalty, pride in self or race, no respect."

The second serious question concerns discrepancies. One of the first pieces to flow from Mr. Wright's pen was an autobiographical sketch, "The Ethics of Living Jim Crow." Not too long ago, Mr. Edwin Embree, borrowing heavily from Mr. Wright's own words as well as from his writings, included the author in his "13 Against the Odds." Although I am sure no one will dispute the fact that the past is static; that if the Japs struck at Pearl Harbor in December, 1941, that five years later the date will still be 1941, Mr. Wright's accounts of events in his own life do not agree. A letter to his publisher (and Mr. Wright) sent two weeks ago, has at this writing elicited no response or defense of these discrepancies. I only repeat them here and ask the reader to believe what he will:

On pages 72-73 of "Black Boy," Mr. Wright describes a fight between himself and a group of white boys in which he was cut behind the ear, and "when my mother came from work I was forced to tell her that I was hurt, for I needed medical attention. She rushed me to a doctor, who stitched my scalp; but when she took me home she beat me, telling me that I must never fight white boys again."

In his "Ethics of Living Jim Crow," Mr. Wright says "a kind neighbor saw me and rushed me to a doctor, who took three stitches in my neck" . . . and that his mother "grabbed a barrel stave, dragged me home, stripped me naked and beat me until I had a fever of one hundred and two." "Ethics of Living Jim Crow," as you will probably remember, is the autobiographical sketch of Mr. Wright's life which originally appeared in the WPA publication and was later reprinted by Harper & Bros. in "Uncle Tom's Children."

In "Black Boy" and also "Ethics of Living Jim Crow," Mr. Wright describes his mother as "a cook in white folks' kitchens," but Mr. Edwin Embree (who borrows heavily—with permission, of course—from Mr. Wright's own accounts in his "13 Against the Odds") says that "his mother, light brown, good looking, possessed of a few years of book learning, got jobs a few months as a teacher at $25.00 a month."

Embree continues: "His darker father, who had never been inside a school, tilled the soil on shares on a big plantation . . . There was not much in that kind of life to hold a family together. The father drifted off. The mother . . . took little Dick . . . to live with her parents in Natchez." But Mr. Wright says his father was with them in their tenement in Memphis and "worked as a night porter in a Beale

Street drug store." He tells us that his father left the family in Memphis for another woman—not because he couldn't make a living as a sharecropper.

Again I note from the jacket of "Black Boy" that "At fifteen he went to Memphis and struck out on his own, earning in two years enough money to go to Chicago."

Mr. Wright says on page 182, "I arrived in Memphis on a cold November Sunday morning in 1925." If, as all accounts agree, Mr. Wright was born in September, 1908, was he not 17 when he arrived in Memphis?

I say Mr. Wright put a sword in the back of his race for the very reason that he has genius. His book will reach a wider reading audience and receive more acclaim from certain elements than, for example, the story of George Washington Carver, who was born a slave and became one of the world's greatest scientists or Mary McLeod Bethune, who was raised in the heart of the South, and today commands the respect of all races.

One can understand why Mr. Wright writes the stories he does. He wants, as he says, to shock people; to write stories that can't be wept over. Certainly this writer had no inclination to weep over such an obnoxious child. If any weeping were to be done let it be over the years our race has spent building a heritage and the damage this off-color stone will do to the building.

J. C. W.
Social Progress (Presbyterian Church in the U.S.A.), (April 1945).

The story is incredible. But it is true, because it is the author's own experience. It would scarcely seem possible that any child could grow up under such conditions as Richard Wright describes, and become anything other than an antisocial being. To have known almost constant hunger, to have lived nineteen years practically without experiencing love, and to have spent much of this time in fear that he might be killed for any little mistaken reaction—these together would be enough to warp any normal personality. But, like a certain type of steel that becomes more useful and a better grade of material when it is pounded relentlessly, so this boy would not be beaten, scared, or starved out of his humanity. When he was graduated from high school he stood at the head of his class. Today he is a talented author.

The book is vivid realism, written in a gripping style. Its message disturbs the complacency of any sincere reader. The truth is a terrible indictment of some American practices. The triumph of this man's soul is a glowing tribute to other conditions in America. There are persons in the North and in the South, "morally responsible Americans," as Dorothy Canfield Fisher terms them, who are giving thoughtful and intelligent consideration to such social conditions as beat upon the sensitive soul of this Negro boy. That such dreadful things should happen to any child in America as a planned part of our way of life is almost inconceivable. That such things should continue to go on unchallenged would mean that America had lost its soul.

"The Preacher Ate the Chicken." *Zion's Herald* (Boston), May 16, 1945.

Richard Wright's most recent book, "Black Boy," has in it one of the most amazing diagnoses of the Negro's personal problem that this editor has ever read. The story is not a pleasant one, and probably will be shunned by many people because of its frank discussion. (Some southern cities have already banned the book.)

The little boy has his whole outlook on life warped and distorted by an unfortunate kind of religion. His first estimate of the idea of God was thrown out of balance because of the preacher! "The preacher had finished his soup and had asked that the platter of chicken be passed to him. It galled me. He smiled, cocked his head this way and that, picking out choice pieces. . . . There were already bare chicken bones on his plate, and he was already reaching for more. . . . 'That preacher's going to eat *all* the chicken!,' I bawled. . . . The preacher tossed back his head and roared with laughter, but my mother was angry and told me that I was to have no dinner because of my bad manners. . . ."

Richard Wright discusses this incident and others that influenced his thinking. Forced conversions—fear of the devil—and a host of other poorly managed religious experiences, all combined to build a stoical sort of resentment in the boy's spirit. It is a timely book, for it deals with a constant danger in organized religion. Whenever we get a situation where religion is *staged,* or becomes bound to traditional practices, the spirit of Christ cannot get through. Religious education that becomes routine; prayer that becomes perfunctory; methods of worship that become ends in themselves—these are dangerous things!

Our world needs the source of power that comes from a personal relation to a loving God. People everywhere are tired of the fringes of the truth—they must now get down to the more fundamental task of translating the spirit of Christ into every phrase of living. (Even preachers who tend to eat all of the chicken—and parents who take away food!)

Augusta J. Strong. *Congress View* (National Negro Congress), 2 (May 1945), 8.

Richard Wright has again written a book that is a moving and effective record of a Negro life in America. Gentle souls will find it brutal, violent, and a trifle filthy. Undoubtedly, it will cause many staunch Southerners to rage at the uncomplimentary picture they find of themselves. Those of a humane turn of mind will be tempted to take refuge in the thought that the story is certainly exaggerated. For it is difficult to believe that the Mississippi and Tennessee described here are present day America and that children are still growing up in the same misery, terror, and frustration.

Black Boy makes unpleasant reading, but it carries the weight of absolute truth. It is autobiographical, relating the childhood and early youth of the author up to the time when, at the age of 19, he left the South and headed for a different life in Chicago.

Richard Wright's father deserts the mother while her two sons are still too young to go to school, and the mother is forced to go to work as a cook while her children roam the streets from morning to evening. From that time on, the boy's life becomes a series of shiftings from one home to another, from one city to another, always under the burdens of poverty and hunger. Often his clothing is too ragged for him to attend school. Except for two or three years of public schooling, his education comes from the gangs in the streets, from whispered tales of beatings and lynchings of Negroes, from jobs where he earns from twenty-five cents to a dollar a week.

Skilfully the author builds up his picture of Negro reaction to Southern life. There is fear mixed with a resentment. There is suppressed anger which has to hide itself behind laughing antics because the white world demands this reaction. There is always tension and fear that even one's expression may not be humble enough to satisfy the boss. There is always the desire to flee the situation which the individual can find no way to solve—as Wright determined he had to do even before he left his childhood. Finally, there is the envy that those who cannot leave (either because they do not have the money or the initiative) feel for those who can escape to the North and freedom.

No other writer of fiction has written so realistically of average Southern Negro life in the city slums, from its psychological as well as its physical aspects. Even in the progressive schools of fiction far too little is understood of the Negro in the Southern scene and too little has been told of the ceaseless day to day struggles that the average black man encounters there.

One criticism has been made that Richard Wright's life story is not a typical experience, and therefore cannot be taken too seriously as an indication of handicaps in Negro life. Unfortunately, it is too typical. The author himself is exceptional, and is so now in manhood as he was in boyhood. Many of his experiences that left indelible impressions upon him as a sensitive child, with unusual intelligence and maturity, would still affect the less impressionable child who might never grow up to be an author equipped to tell the world about his life.

It is true, however, that Wright seems to regard himself as an exception among his own people. His account of his childhood is filled with a sense of personal bitterness against men and women, mostly his relatives, who were caught in the same hopeless trap as himself. He has scarcely a kind word for any of the households in which he lived, admittedly as a problem child, during the years of his dependent youth. Frequently he accuses the Negro people in part and as a whole with lack of kindness, lack of hope, shallowness of sentiment. This should be strange for him to believe, when every word he writes of his own life tells of powerful feelings while daily oppression forced him to conceal and give no expression.

Wright's clarity about his own plight and constant blind spot to the fact that in greater or less degree all the Negroes surrounding him were victims of the same frustrations is perhaps caused by a common human quality—his intense preoccupation with himself. No other character of any importance appears in the book. There are other people, but they are names without souls or thoughts that Wright discerns. His attitude toward others reveals more contempt than pity. He leaves the belief that he alone feels the onus of discrimination. As he puts it:

"Often, when perplexed, I longed to be like the smiling, lazy, forgetful black boys in the noisy hotel locker rooms, with no torrential conflicts to resolve. Many times I grew weary of the secret burden I carried and longed to cast it down, either in action or in resignation. But I was not made to be a resigned man and I had only a limited choice of actions, and I was afraid of all of them."

This self-absorption has a way of becoming a bit tiresome, but perhaps that is the prerogative of the artist. Perhaps many people who need to know the world *Black Boy* describes will be far more impressed by this first hand account of actual experiences than they would by a broader, sociological novel. Richard Wright has certainly demonstrated that he has the technique for such a novel. His earlier short stories, "Native Son," and this present work give ample proof to the most critical that he has command of his instrument. *Black Boy* is a good book, not the best that can come from Richard Wright's talent, but further proof that he is our best Negro writer to date, for whom the future holds much promise.

Daisy M. Kuhnes
Educational Forum, 9 (May 1945), 481–82.

Above everything else *Black Boy* is an honest book. As honest and revealing as "a patient etherized upon a table." Not often has the soul of man, either black or white, been laid bare to the extent that the very sensitivity of his being is made to penetrate the consciousness of the reader, a consciousness which becomes a most understanding one as the boy's life unfolds.

The book covers the first nineteen years of the author's existence. These years are crammed with episodes the accumulation of which gradually and finally fixate in this sensitive organism a dread of the southern white man's cruelty. Early in the book he says:

> Tension would set in at the mere mention of whites and a vast complex of emotions, involving the whole of my personality, would be aroused. It was as though I was continuously reacting to the threat of some natural force whose hostile behavior could not be predicted.

His home life offered no surcease from this Nemesis. Economic instability pervaded this home which he apparently took for granted. Forces of circumstance—mother desperately ill, fanatically religious Granny, uncongenial and carping relatives, from one city to another, from one squalid hovel to another—did not deaden his sense of wonder and awe in the face of the drama of human feeling which is hidden by the external drama of life. But the answers to his questions concerning "these two sets of people who lived side by side and never touched except in violence" were brusquely evaded or answered by his gang associates. From them he learned rapidly how to watch white people, how to observe every move and fleeting expression, how to interpret what was said and what was left unsaid. To his retentive memory came much racy and daring knowledge.

By the time he had reached his fifteenth year his reactions to the current of his environment had fused into a dream. A dream to go somewhere and to do something that would redeem his being alive, to prove the worth of his own humanity. Came now a realization that living in a culture and living in a civilization is not synonymous. Vicariously he began to understand through books and to become identified with life. H. L. Mencken and Theodore Dreiser were the first to convince him that he had overlooked an important aspect of life which was not a matter of believing or disbelieving but of a new feeling. Their naturalism and realism were the culmination of his own Jim Crow station in life, and now through his very sensitivity he began to realize the possibility of being a part of that civilization which had become known to him through Mr. Mencken and Mr. Dreiser along with other writers whom he met through the public library by means of a forged library card. This new hunger hurt more than knowing what being a Negro meant, knowing the meaning of hatred, knowing the hostile, cruel white. Hurt because the distance between his newly created world and his own mean existence posed an imponderable gap. Now the dream became heart-sickening with terror, tension and anxiety.

Finally on a northward-bound train we bid him hail and farewell! We are impressed by this strong and sincere individual who did not permit the South to deprive him of his honesty and self respect; who had sufficient confidence in his own integrity to struggle with destiny in order to gain and to keep that comprehension and realization of that same world which he feels must exist for him as well as for the white man.

The writing in *Black Boy* indicates that Mr. Wright is finding that for which he seeks, for in this book is more than desire and feeling. He is not cynical concerning his native southland for a cynic is a disillusioned idealist. He says:

> I was taking a part of the South to transplant in alien soil, to see if it could grow differently, if it could drink of new and cool rains, bend in strange winds, respond to the warmth of other suns, and, perhaps, to bloom. . . . And if that miracle ever happened, then I would know that there was yet hope in that southern swamp of despair and violence, that light could emerge even out of the blackest of the southern night. I would know that the South too could overcome its fear, its hate, its cowardice, its heritage of guilt and blood, its burden of anxiety and compulsive cruelty.

On alien soil a stranger needs hospitality and an emigré needs a chance. The tragic spirit of the South he saw, transplanted to other climes, may indeed thrive on hospitality and a chance and so give to life a dignity and a meaning through having struggled and suffered here beneath the stars.

Sinclair Lewis. "Gentlemen, This Is Revolution." *Esquire*, 23 (June 1945), 76.

Black Boy, the story of his own youth in the South by Richard Wright, the enormously talented young Negro who also wrote *Native Son*, has been greeted by several placidly busy white reviewers and by a couple of agitated Negro reviewers as betraying too much "emotion," too much "bitterness."

Now this is the story of a colored boy who, just yesterday, found in his native community not merely that he was penalized for having the same qualities that in a white boy would have warmed his neighbors to universal praise—the qualities of courage, energy, curiosity, refusal to be subservient, the impulse to record life in words—but that he was in danger of disapproval, then of beatings, then of being killed, for these qualities, for being "uppity." Not bitterness but fear charges the book, and how this young crusader can be expected to look back only a few years to the quiet torture with anything except hatred is beyond me.

When we have a successful comedy by an ex-prisoner about the kindness and humor of the warders in a German concentration camp, then I shall expect Mr. Wright to mellow and to speak amiably of the teachers who flattened him, his colored neighbors and relatives who denounced him, the merchants who cheated him, the white fellow-mechanics who threatened him for wanting to learn their skills, and the librarian who suspected him—quite rightly—of reading that militant and bewhiskered Bolshevik, that polluter of temples and Chambers of Commerce, Comrade H. L. Mencken. . . .

N. T.
"As the Twig Is Bent." *Phylon*, 6 (Second Quarter, 1945), 185–86.

The first twenty years of Richard Wright's life comprise a physical and mental odyssey that the author frankly reveals in his recent autobiography, *Black Boy*. Except for his last journey, the physical distance that he travels is not great; but his mental wanderings are long and tortuous and range from the privy-cluttered section of the Negro district of lethargic Jackson, Mississippi, to the dream-world of the masters of fiction.

The life-story begins in Mississippi, where Wright was born and spent his early years, largely with his mother, for his irresponsible father deserted the family while the boy was very young. In the declining years of the father, Wright visited him; and the central thought that ran through his mind was the vast gulf that lay between them, the begetter and the begotten. Thrown upon relatives, who themselves were usually marginal people, the mother and two sons in their search for bread move from Mississippi to Arkansas and back again, finally settling with the author's grandmother, who was steeped in the prohibitions and traditions of her religious sect. The sensitive youth is baffled at home and turns to an "unintelligible world" that had treated him none too kindly in his earlier years. And here he experiences for the first time the mental and physical oppression that all Negro boys in America eventually know. In Memphis, where he spends several years struggling to save enough money to take the family to Chicago, he meets a kindly but dangerously ignorant mother whose interest in her daughter almost draws him from his path. Finally, by fair means and foul, he secures enough money for the Chicago trip, but not for the whole family—and the story ends as he leaves in search of a "brave new world."

Some will complain that Wright emphasizes too much the bitterness of his life, the unfriendliness of whites, and the lack of understanding in his elders. But the story bears the mark of authenticity. Most of it could not only be duplicated in the Jackson of twenty years ago, but it can also be matched today in the thousands of villages, towns and cities of America. In a country where freedom is set up as the highest good, Negroes are denied all the basic privileges of citizenship. This paradox confuses both black and white youth alike. Such is the harvest we reap.

Black Boy would serve as an excellent case study in psychology or sociology, for it shows how the two greatest influences in the life of any Negro "shaped him into the thing he is." It is the clearest exposition that has been written of the feelings of a sensitive Negro boy as he grows up under the domination of family ignorance and bigotry and the terror inspired by the practices of white supremacy. And, in showing this, it reveals for the most part the reaction of the majority of Negro boys and girls. But it is much more than this. It is such an artistic presentation of the facts of Negro life that the book will disturb the South and help to awaken America generally to the immensity of its crime against humanity in its treatment of Negroes or in its neglect of the most fundamental problem in our democracy. It is the voice of one of the most articulate Negroes in the world—one of the finest writers of prose in our day. Coming at a time when the world is growing conscious of the sacredness of human personality, it can not but be heard.

Richard Bentley (Alice C. Browning). *Negro Story,* 1 (May-June 1945), 91–92.

Only a Negro can appreciate the life of Richard Wright, whether absolutely true or whether part fiction and part truth. However, this point is irrelevant because every Negro has had to endure some of the experiences which Wright so clearly puts in story form. The individual Negro may belong to the so-called "talented tenth" or the vast ranks of the lower middle class, he may be privileged to have an intelligent cultural home environment but unless he has spent his life "passing," to some degree he has felt the terrific impact of Negro-white relationships. A Negro awakening to his plight frequently finds himself becoming revengeful. A white man cannot understand. When anyone states that the poor of any race suffer the same indignities as the Negro he doesn't realize the truth.

There is hardly a Negro who has not been close to the wrath and injustice of the "superior" race, who has not seen the brutality and cunning and utter callousness of some white Americans. He has seen it spread to foreigners here and abroad. He has seen the sneer and the deceit and the repugnance, heard the cry of "nigger," felt the bitterness, heard the insinuations, felt the insincere attempt to cover up prejudice, the intolerance, the unexpected slight; he has been a Negro. Can a white man ever really know what this means?

Richard Wright, sensitive to his environment, may have felt a little more keenly insults which most of us learn to ignore and to laugh at. All of us would like to tell a story. Wright tells his. He screams. He shocks. He beats realistically at the shackles. He is brutal in his condemnation of Negro and white, but he shows a reason for his Negro's ignorance, stupidity and viciousness. How can the Negro be different? Why is he jealous, petty, unusually uncooperative, prone to tear down his own people, spiteful, passionless in his passion, loud and wrong and hollow in his joy—and *he is*—let's not deny it. Sometime it's comedy expressed in tragedy—sometimes tragedy in comedy.

He has conflicts and complexes which are inherent in him. Why is he like this? Because of his environment, because of his position in America, because of forces that build up his psychological entity.

The Negro *is* musical, understanding, intuitive, humorous, gay, warm, jazzy and spontaneous. His qualities are innate, can never be taken away from him. However, he has been forced to have a psychological complex. America has made him the way he is.

Richard Wright perhaps really feels that he succeeded by his own efforts, overcame all obstacles because of something within him. This happens once in a life time. Only rarely does one individual's genius so flow in spite of his opportunity. He gives credit to his mother for satisfying his intellectual craving to some extent and for giving him love despite her lacks. He inherited some characteristics of greatness that impelled him to go forward, a courage, a stubbornness, a gift of self expression. *Black Boy* is a chance to fight back, to stir, to accuse, to cry out in chanticleer fashion. What a lot of fun he must have had; what a relief it must have been to rid himself of these pent up feelings! Even *Native Son* could only partially empty him. The author I would venture to say is a new man after bringing forth these books. He will be able to see even more objectively. He has rid himself of a great burden. He lives a retired life most likely so that he *can* write, so that he can think, so that he will not be wrapped up in the meaningless, the hollow sham of most circles which would lionize him and in time would kill his talents. He will continue to *create* until all of his accumulated passion has reached a climax. The next half of his life should unfold an even more important story—not quite so bitter in some ways perhaps, and then probably just as bitter in others. Wright has his limitations. Some of his critics have said neither of his books will live. That fact only years can tell; they approach the sensation in our time that *Uncle Tom* did in his. They will certainly go down in literary history because they muckrake democracy. But if they do only live for ten years, they will live so poignantly, so vivid a life as to change most who read them. Only the greatest of masters, the universal live forever. We know one thing; there will be those who still go about being afraid to hire Negroes, degrading Negroes and seeing only one side of the picture. Why worry? They would think that way no matter what happened. Only a stick of dynamite could uproot their prejudices, shame, their intolerance.

Black Boy tells a much needed story and tells it in poetic prose, in meaningful word pictures. It digs to the depths and reflects as a mirror our short-comings and our ignorance. If we fail to see the implications for America and Americans that this book portrays, we are indeed blind, as blind as the old women in *Native Son,* so blind that only great tragedy like an internal revolution could cure us. The war hasn't cured us. We are still some of us either holding on to our pet prejudices or merely shelving them temporarily. We think only of our skin. The fact that Negro boys are fighting for America in spite of America's brutality to them means nothing. That is as it should be. That's different. When they return, then that is the time to start in again to show them their places. We need them now. But that, fellow Americans, is another Black Boy Story, and who will delineate this picture and tell this story as *Black Boy* has done?

F. K. Richter. *Negro Story,* 1 (May-June 1945), 93–94.

Richard Wright's new book, a non-fictional work, presents to us the records of his childhood and youth. Born into a very poor Southern family, he spent his childhood and school years at Natchez and Jackson, Mississippi, Elaine, Arkansas, and a few other places, until he moved back to his grandmother's home in Jackson, Miss., because of his mother's poor health. He was usually under the supervision of women, as his father had left the family when Richard was about 4 years of age. At eighteen he decided to escape the family's domination and went to Memphis, Tenn., where he worked for a few dollars a week, until he had enough money to send for his invalid mother. Like him, she could not bear the domineering character of "Granny", whose strict Adventism had a disturbing effect right down to the dishes she prepared. The book ends with Wright's exit from the South, Chicago-bound.

The author records all these first experiences, which nearly every boy shares with him: revolt against the father, meeting death and being told about it, facing older and stronger boys, quarrelling and fighting with them, seeing prisoners for the first time, hearing about murder by lynching, getting curious about sex through the lowest channels possible, seeing his mother suffer, being rejected, refused, maltreated.

Wright does not contribute anything decisively new to bring the race problem nearer to a solution; but placing his experiences before the nation, and Richard Wright will be heard by the nation, is of tremendous value. His continuous pointing out and hammering into our ears how America's largest racial minority is being treated in an ante-bellum fashion may finally awake the conscience of larger groups and maybe, even of the South. He succeeded very well in depicting the whole Southern situation without any signs of vengeful hatred. He shows the Southerners' unbelievable hypocrisy, as they actually think (if they think at all), that they are doing the most good to the colored people. He also depicts very well the acceptance of this situation by the suppressed; how they carry that mask, how they bow in a Jim Crow manner, despising themselves for doing so. It speaks for the greatness of Richard, the eighteen year old boy, that he was too sincere and too good to carry that mask any longer and so left the South.

Of course, the cruel experiences which happened to Richard during his boyhood did not happen to him only as a black boy. They may happen to many other poor boys of any minority group. I could tell many a story of white friends who went through similarly tragic childhoods, who were shuffled around by others, mistreated and rejected. In those cases another excuse was found—another label was tagged on to them, like "Dago", "Hun", or "Jew". Richard Wright's book, speaks therefore, for any minority group of our nation, and its value and importance grows through this new aspect.

A word should be said about the beautiful prose in which these "records of a youth" are presented. There are lyrical passages that praise the Southern landscape and show the deep love of the Southern Negro for his soil. There also is stored a treasure of old-time proverbs, and lovers of Southern folklore will find a new source for their research. And there are beautiful and obviously new similes which ought to become a part of our daily speech.

The only disturbing fact, however, is that the reader gets an unreal feeling that Richard always succeeded by his own efforts. He himself overcame all obstacles. His mother helped first a little, but then, after all, it was he who dragged himself out of that mess. Wright does not show us any friendly guidance he received from others. There are, of course, Mr. Crane and Mr. Falk, but they have no decisive influence upon his development. The author demonstrates, perhaps without knowing or wanting it, Aristotle's entelechy, which teaches that the man-to-be is already in the child, just as the tree is already in a little seed—it only has to develop and to grow. But (and here is my point of objection), in order to develop, does it not need friendly light and warmth and fertile earth?

Wright reports about the seed but tells little or nothing about indispensable factors that made it grow. In omitting these facts, the book loses some of its value as auto-biography and non-fiction and takes on, however slightly, a quality of fiction.

United States Quarterly Book List, 1 (June 1945), 15–16.

The subject of this autobiography is a well known Negro writer, who has here set down the record of his first nineteen years. This powerfully written, violent story of cruelty and frustration takes shape within the pattern of contemporary (1909-28) race-relations in southern small towns of Mississippi and Tennessee, and illumines the subject with an angry intelligence. More profoundly, it is the particular history of the effect of this pattern on a highly sensitive, original personality conditioned from infancy by extreme poverty and brutality. He is so conditioned that even his recollections of intimate family life show no warmth of affection, or understanding. Along his way he meets no sympathetic spirit, nor finds consolation in any typical racial "outlets," such as religious gatherings, laughter, or song; yet his imagination is continually fired by the possibilities of a different life, and the drive and integrity of his literary ambition. Thus while it is social history it is particularly the "portrait of the artist as a young man."

Unlike the historic biographies of Booker T. Washington, or Frederick Douglass, largely because it holds no vision of a "happy ending," it is also better written and more frank than other recent Negro biographies. Richard Wright's work continues the standard set by his novels. His psychological penetration is deeper, his style is sharper. *Black Boy* is an unrelieved story which perhaps had to be written once by an American.

Theatre Arts, 29 (June 1945), 382.

It is still impossible to predict which field of literary endeavor will eventually give Richard Wright the greatest opportunity and the greatest rewards. So far he has tried his hand at short-stories, a novel and a play, each with a large degree of success. But this much is clear: wherever his talents lead him, he will bring along the capacity to shape his stories in terms of dramatic conflict—of the impact of man on man at moments of heightened tension—that makes them natural theatre material.

It is for this reason that his latest offering, *Black Boy,* should be of special interest to readers of THEATRE ARTS. The first part of an autobiography, it carries the author from boyhood in Mississippi to the elated moment when he headed North to Chicago at the age of seventeen. 'In Chicago', says the blurb on the cover, 'he dug ditches, ran errands, washed dishes, sold insurance, and was a clerk in the United States Post Office. Always an omnivorous reader, he began to write.' But that saga remains to be told in Volume 2 of Richard Wright's autobiography. Meanwhile the reader must look to volume 1, not only for its own innate literary merits, and they are many, but for what it reveals of the creative impulse in man, which somehow presses through the severest confines of bitter frustration and the most alien of environments.

Richard Wright is not representative of his people, any more than any leader is 'representative' of his group (though he sometimes appears to be trying to generalize racial characteristics from his own uncommon and often abnormal experiences). To read *Black Boy,* however, cannot help but sharpen the perceptions that the reader turns back upon the problems of race, as well as on the tortures of the artist who struggles through darkness into light.

> "They meet with darkness in the daytime
> And they grope at noonday as in the night . . . .'
>
> JOB

This is the quotation that Richard Wright chooses to print on the title page of *Black Boy.*

Patsy Graves. *Opportunity,* 23 (July 1945), 158–59.

In light of the tremendous strides made in the field of psychiatry, a piece of popular writing has been long overdue that showed the psychic wounds inflicted upon Negroes by the contradictions in our society. The short biography of Richard Wright included in last year's volume devoted to thirteen successful Negroes commented upon Wright's respectable knowledge of psychology. *Black Boy,* purportedly a record of his childhood and youth, does reveal that Wright's avowed desire to "find out some day" has carried him deep into the study of behavior. In this story of his growing up experience, he has applied the psycho-analytic technique to a study of his familial relations, and has come out with a bitter commentary upon family life as he knew it and an even more bitter indictment of the position of the Negro in American life.

In this record of a Negro child trapped between the Scylla of a hateful family and the Charybdis of a hostile world, we may find the story of any child, white or black, rich or poor. Growing up in the world may be a painful process at best. Even with the buffer of a sympathetic family, the first brushes with cold reality are likely to be hurting. Psychiatry teaches that the wounds—or trauma—inflicted in childhood and adolescence may scar the personality forever, and inhibit the full, free development of a child into happy, adjusted adulthood. A simple example: Due to economic circumstances, the Wright family moved no less than a dozen times in the space of a few years. Wright tells us that as a result he has never been able to abide any one place for long at a time. Of course, the opposite could have happened and the desire been born in him for a permanent home from which he would only emerge due to the direst exigency. Psychiatry, however, has not yet explained why any individual makes his own peculiar reactions to a situation or set of circumstances.

Add to this more or less natural phenomenon of growing up with its inevitable hurts, a child like Richard Wright who (to use the psychiatric lingo of which he is so fond) was never able to establish a satisfactory object world relationship to anything or anybody in his environment and we may get the stuff of which criminals are made. Once in a great while, luckily for society, we get a Wright, whose evolution can only be explained by the God in Whom the adolescent Richard Wright struggled to believe.

The constant moving and reshuffling, the never ending necessity to adjust to new people and situations, and above all, the ceaseless hunger and deprivation left this boy unanchored and afraid, both physically and emotionally. He was never able to love anything, or to experience a really strong sustaining relationship between himself and anything outside of himself. Locked in his own egocentric struggles, Wright did not permit himself (or was afraid to permit himself) to be touched by the few rays of positive feeling that sometimes came his way. There was Ella who secretly taught him something about books, but somehow he could not cling to her. Rather, he reveled in his misery, being happiest in unhappiness. It was not even love for Betsey, the little dog, that kept him from selling her. Nor was it the difference between the ninety-seven cents he was offered and the dollar that he demanded. It was his hate for the white woman who wanted Betsey, his taste of the ego satisfaction accruing when he found something in his possession wanted by someone else—something he had the power to withhold.

There are moving passages of fine writing in *Black Boy* that surge and exalt. There is in this story of one boy a portion of every boy's story, irrespective of race: the fear of the unknown, the growing pains, the bout with religion and the struggle to "feel something," the desire to please one's elders, but the pressing necessity to please oneself, the wish for the esteem of his peers and associates. But the simple law of averages would prevent any one boy from getting into as many situations as we have related in this story, and one senses, with regret, that it is hard to know where biography leaves off and fiction begins. This serves to weaken the whole structure of the book, and to make it unconvincing in its entirety.

Laying aside the fact that all this probably did not happen to one boy, the fact remains that such things can happen, do happen. Is the conditioning imposed upon Negroes by the South as brutal as this? Ask this reviewer who spent more years in the deep, deep South than she cares to remember. The answer is yes. Do mothers, grandmothers, aunts, uncles, reject children as completely as this boy was rejected? Ask any family case worker, visit the children's court and watch the naked, unadulterated hate that can exist between parent and child. The answer is yes. Do schoolteachers like Aunt Addie wreck their sex-starved, frustrated repressions upon helpless childhood? Ask any objective observer of an average public school system. Again the answer is yes.

Too, there are some blatant assertions, some bland generalizations in *Black Boy* that are themselves denied in the unfolding of the story. Wright speaks of the "strange absence of real kindness in Negroes," but upon the occasion of his mother's first paralytic stroke he relates how the neighbors came in and nursed her, fed the children, cleaned the house, washed the clothes, gave freely of what was their's to give. Well, what is kindness anyway?

In spite of any and all weaknesses, either as a literary achievement or as a record in race relations, this book is required reading. There is grim warning in these pages that the absence of wholesome family life in which the members are bound together in a spirit of love and mutual helpfulness is one of the main factors producing hostile, antisocial members of the community. Here is your proof that the absence of an ego-ideal to which youth may aspire and emulate either in a parent or parent substitute can turn upon the world a generation of moral degenerates. But the real power and strength of *Black Boy* lies in the question it poses that society will be hard put to answer: How long will you go on inflicting these psychic wounds upon all youth, upon Negro youth particularly, that fester and grow and finally burst with all the fury of a hurt and cornered animal upon you, its creator? Richard Wright is a miracle, one in a million, or in several millions. Not many who have all their lives been torn from hate to hate stumble accidentally upon the world of books, there to find surcease from anguish in the written word. Those millions of others in all races who have been and are being hurt as Wright was hurt are not so fortunate as to be able to write hostility out of their systems. They get it out in bloodier, uglier ways, ways that are inimical to themselves and to society. Will you, can you, be warned by this boy's story?

E. Bruce Thompson. *The Journal of Mississippi History*, 7 (July 1945), 178–80.

Black Boy comes as a welcome and convincing refutation of the claims of those southern whites who boast that they understand the "nigger" and who naively rationalize that "niggers" are the happiest and most contented people in the world. It comes as an urgent challenge to that increasingly large number of southern whites who are willing, even in the face of a violently hostile public opinion, to proclaim the gospel of the dignity of all men. It *should* come to *all* southern whites as a disturbing indictment of that inherited social structure which, in a reputedly democratic society, relegates a large percentage of the population to the status of pariahs and serfs.

Dealing as it does with the futile attempts of a sensitive and ambitious Negro youth to adjust himself to a color-conscious society, *Black Boy* is both a psychological and sociological case study. Richard Wright's nineteen years in the South—mostly spent in Jackson, Mississippi—were one continuous nightmare of terror, anxiety, and humiliation. Hunger, fear, and despair constantly stalked him. In order to survive both the intra- and inter-racial conflict, he had to lie, to cheat, and even to steal. Confronted on all sides by racial injustices and indignities, he became increasingly—and bitterly—aware of the insuperable gulf between the white and black worlds. Every time the door of opportunity opened, color rudely slammed it in his face. He had literary ambitions, but he soon found that he was experiencing feelings which the state of Mississippi had spent "millions of dollars" to stifle. He wanted to learn an optical trade, but he soon discovered that the skilled jobs were a white monopoly. With every discrimination his hatred of the white man grew increasingly intense—a hatred which he found almost universal among the Negroes, though most of them, for the sake of self-preservation, had learned to conceal their bitterness behind poker faces or servile flattery. More philosophical than most boys of his age—either white or black—young Richard concluded that "the meaning of living came only when one was struggling to wring a meaning out of meaningless suffering." Though unquestionably overdrawn (surely the author must have met at least one decent southern white person within nineteen years), *Black Boy* should leave the reader—be he white or black—sobered and abashed.

While intended primarily as a scathing indictment of the white man, the book is equally damning to Wright's own race. The author makes no attempt to gloss over the weaknesses of either himself or his people. He portrays blacks in roles as despicable as those of the whites with whom he came in contact. Wright's worthless father abandoned him, his mother lashed him to the point of death, and his nearest relatives tormented him cruelly. Nor was his fate exceptional among the colored children whom he knew. In fact, the author found few admirable qualities among the people of his own color. To him they seemed docile, debauched, frenzied with fear, barren of human tenderness, lacking in pride, and devoid of a sense of loyalty. While he made no thesis of it—though one suspects he intended to do so by indirection—the author might have contended, with considerable justification, that such racial traits stemmed from years of white oppression.

Unable to adjust himself to an environment which refused to recognize his human dignity, Richard Wright found escape in flight to the North. His mother's religion, which he found superstitious and hypocritical, gave him no comfort; outright rebellion, which he seriously considered many times, seemed futile; sex and alcohol as means of release seemed repugnant; and fighting his own kind—the manner in which many Negroes gave vent to their hatred of whites—seemed utterly heartless. The only remaining alternative was flight to the land of promise—Chicago (one wonders how Chicago received him). But while Richard Wright found escape in physical flight, thousands of equally gifted Negro youths have been economically, physically, or morally unable to do so. The real tragedy of *Black Boy,* however, lies not in the inability of Negroes to escape but in the fact that their native environment denies them the opportunity to develop their latent potentialities and refuses to recognize their basic human dignity.

W. B. Hamilton. *The South Atlantic Quarterly*, 44 (July 1945), 329–30.

This story of an American to his eighteenth year is the case history of a sensitive Negro growing up in Jackson and Memphis, beset with fears and tensions engendered by unhappy family relationships and repressive race relations. In spite of the use of dialogue and in spite of the rigid selection of data by the artist, the book possesses a documentary character. Unfortunately, the situations are not unusual; fortunately, they were experienced by a sentient and articulate master of the craft of writing. It is psychological autobiography, devoted with single-mindedness to that which affected the author. No clear picture emerges of either his times or his environment.

To the more usual traumatic experiences of childhood were added such scarring ones as desertion of his family by the father, a miserable stay in an orphanage, insensate corruption by tipplers in Memphis saloons, the paralytic invalidism of his mother, residence with religiously fanatical Grandma and Aunt Addie. The boy was often physically, and always emotionally, hungry. On top of these factors were piled the fear and frustration of white and black antagonism, which denied him not only opportunity, but even peace.

He was too quick, too impatient, and too individual to please either family or whites with good-natured conformity. Granting the currency of Freudian postulates, Wright sketches his formative period with meaning and (as contemporary literature goes) even a sort of delicacy. His racial experiences being what they were, he is restrained and almost objective in that vital part of his story which deals with his relations with the whites. He gives the impression of a boy sincerely struggling to understand why he could not get along with the dominant race, and deciding that it was because his contacts with it did not begin until he was too old to grow into the subtle etiquette required of this complicated relationship. This thought, of course, is only a small part of the truth; but it illustrates why this book is not a tract, a diatribe, or a caricature—it is, rather, genuine and particular. It does not recite the clichés of the race struggle; nor, although written by a former member of the Communist party, does it dull the narrative with the undiscriminating opiate of Marxian terminology.

How, one asks, did the boy escape either frustration or surrender? How acquire the will to escape? How develop the ability to handle the English language with rare economy and dexterity? Wright gives us the answer: through books. With the aid of the tool of reading (practically self-taught), a few brief years in the Jackson Public School system, and a precious library card used through the connivance of a friendly white man, he entered the magic and democratic world of the printed page. This simple explanation offers as eloquent an argument for education in the South as could be penned.

This moral is not driven home by the author; in fact, he draws none. The reader cannot escape doing so.

Harry Salpeter. *Congress Weekly*, 12 (August 17, 1945), 12.

This is a frightening book. The wonder is that the author lived to write it and those other books, such as *Native Son,* by which already he has made his reputation. As a man, he enjoyed a double blessing, which, for a Negro in the South, became a double curse. The integrity by whose command he became the artist led him into dangers which he could have avoided only by living the life or enacting the role of "a good nigger"—a life and a role based upon such a series of white man's taboos that, for a black man endowed with an innate sense of human dignity, they constituted an exchange of physical life for moral death.

From his earliest boyhood until his 17th year, when he succeeded in escaping from the South, by train from Memphis to Chicago, his life was shadowed by the threat of violence. An uncle in Mississippi was shot dead for refusing to abandon a prosperous saloon; a friend's brother was lynched. In the earlier part of his record he writes: "I had never in my life been abused by whites, but I had already become as conditioned to their existence as though I had been the victim of a thousand lynchings."

The rest of the book gives the lie to both statements, for is it not to be abused to be goaded by lies and terror into fighting another black boy—as Wright did in Memphis—for the sadistic delight of white men? And had he been sufficiently conditioned to the white man's existence he would not have had to live in a constant state of dread that those ever-smoldering embers of race hatred which he saw in the white man's eyes would flare up and consume him in the flame.

After having been summarily dismissed by a white employer for not having the "right attitude," the boy Wright seeks out a friend who has the gift of adjustment to the white world. The friend asks:

> "Do you want to get killed?"
> "Hell, no!"
> "Then, for God's sake, learn how to live in the South! . . . You act around white people as if you didn't know they were white, and they see it!"

Black Boy is the record not only of the failure of a black boy to adjust to the white South on terms which would have destroyed him as a potential artist; it is also the record of an unceasing and remorseless guerrilla warfare with members of his own family who sought to dominate and tyrannize over him because they may have sensed that in his attitude there lay the seeds of menace to their, as well as his own, survival. They beat him with terror in their own hearts. They feared and distrusted the character and quality of his ambition, principally because it was a violation of taboo, and struggled desperately to force him into a mould which would make him a tractable and surviving Negro in a white man's South. The beatings which seem regularly to have been inflicted upon him and the worse punishments which he narrowly avoided by the threat of knife seem fantastically unmotivated and disproportioned to the offense, until we see these actions within the frame of the South's race relationships.

For the Jew all over the world who knows at what cost of blood and tears the remnants of his decimated people have re-emerged into the clearing of at least legal egalitarianism, this record of one black youth's life in the South is full of significant accents and overtones; this autobiography describes directly and indirectly the moral climate of a large section of this country which is at least potentially hostile to the free functioning of minorities. This may sound like a highfalutin phrase, but you will realize what it means when you ponder upon the subtle, devious, and dangerous strategy which the boy Wright had to employ in order to borrow from a public library, with the conspiratorial aid of a sympathetic white man, the first books he had ever read. Yet it is strange to read here of the ways in which the black boys of the mean little Mississippi town in which Wright was brought up tormented the Jewish family who ran the corner grocery store. Having been brought up in the legend that Jews were "Christ killers," the black children chanted the traditional jingles of anti-Semitism. "To hold an attitude of antagonism or distrust toward Jews was bred in us from childhood; it was not merely racial prejudice, it was a part of our cultural heritage."

Richard Wright's account of "the culture from which I sprang, . . . the terror from which I fled," is horrible testimony of the terms on which ten million black people live in the South. For them and for their progeny, the South, for its own health's sake, must devise a solution other than flight to Chicago, or Detroit, which can be only a fractional solution, at best. Our internal peace is involved.

Bernard A. Tonnar, S.J. *The Catholic Mirror* (August 1945), 45–46.

The emaciated and trembling fingers of hunger and fear sketch a story that hurries the reader from episode to episode in the life of a Negro boy born and reared in Dixie. It is a story that breaks the heart, awakens the emotions, fires the human faculties. It lingers on in the thoughts like a bitter experience.

Richard Wright is a masterful writer to produce so many reactions in his reader. He tells the story of his youth. To him it is the ordinary life of an ordinary southern Negro pinned down by Jim Crowism, white supremacy and hate. The Negro according to the author lives a Jekyll-Hyde life—a smiling front covering resentment, distrust, bitterness and an eagerness to escape to the North.

This reviewer, who never lived far from the setting of Mr. Wright's story, becomes suspicious at times. He feels the reader will question some of the author's impressions and statements. Mr. Wright leads his reader to such conclusions that all whites dislike the Negroes and wish to keep them in a state of servitude. Many southern white people are more anxious to help their Negro neighbor than whites in other sections of America. Never to meet this type of Southerner was Mr. Wright's misfortune. In fairness to Mr. Wright, he does mention one Southerner who helped him greatly. It happened to be an Irish Catholic. But the reader feels as if the Black Boy never really showed his appreciation for the service he received. It was a small service, lending him a library card, yet that trifle opened the eyes of the boy to the world of literary achievement in which world Mr. Wright would later hold an eminent position.

To make his Black Boy a powerful story, Mr. Wright has exaggerated. He has over emphasized white domination and Negro discontent. He gradually builds up a theory that the North is the only place where the Negro can live a full life. When he finally escapes to Chicago, he leaves the reader wondering if this theory is true. If his escape was an escape after all. To clinch his argument, Mr. Wright could have added a chapter or two about his bright new world in the Windy City.

Although Black Boy gives some faulty impressions, it is still a moving and interesting story charmingly written. It is full of drama, skillfully depicted characters, delightful folklore and amusing superstitions.

Because of several rather realistic passages, Black Boy cannot be a book for youth.

J. M. Braude. *Chicago Jewish Forum*, 3 (Summer 1945), 287–89.

Whether entirely autobiographical or partly fictional, Richard Wright in *Black Boy* has given us all something about which to think. Published at a time when millions of young men are engaged in a conflict to stabilize human values and to put real meaning into the word "democracy," it throws a challenge at all who have the power to think and reflect. With thousands of young men laying down their lives so that those who continue to live may live on a more common and decent basis, it hurls a challenge at those who would call themselves superior because of race or creed.

Delving deep into his childhood days, he tells of the gnawing pangs of hunger which he suffered constantly because there was little more than a loaf of bread and a pot of tea for him and his brother as his mother went off to work for white people who had more than they needed. Watching white people eat, he tells us, would make his empty stomach churn as he would ask himself why could he not eat when he was hungry—why did some people have enough food when others did not.

He bares his heart and lays it open to public exposure—he gives us an insight into the thinking and actions of Negroes which explains to many of us much about their actions and reactions at which heretofore we might only have guessed. He tells us of the unconscious irony of those who have held that Negroes lead so passional an existence, and informs us that what has been taken for their emotional strength was really their negative confusion, their flight, their fears, and their frenzy when under pressure.

One is touched by a feeling of guilt as he reads the indictment which Wright hurls at the Whites. He charges that the essential bleakness of black life in America is due to the fact that Negroes have never been allowed to catch the full spirit of Western Civilization and tells us that they are left somehow in it, but not of it. His frankness is at times both refreshing and depressing. At the age of 10, he tells us, the touchstone of fraternity among his associates was his feeling toward white people and of the hostility he held toward them—what degree of value and honor he assigned to race. None of this, he tells us, was premeditated but sprang spontaneously out of the talk of black boys whom he met at the crossroads and, while still comparatively a child, a dread of white people came to live permanently in his feelings and imagination.

While all of his experiences, as related in the book, have taken place in the South and his bitterness is directed chiefly against Southerners, there is still much for those above the Mason-Dixon line to learn about the brotherhood of man and the spirit of democratic institutions. Richard Wright has given us all food for thought. As for myself, I have personally found the answer in the book to many of the questions which I have been asking myself these past ten years. My own observations through ten years of court work are born out by the statistical records which indicate that proportionately we find more Negro boys in conflict with the law than white boys. Some of the reasons for the situation have been known to all of us—inadequate housing facilities and unequal educational and employment opportunities have long been known to be important factors in this respect, but Wright gives one reason for so much stealing among especially Southern Negroes which is rather new and intriguing. He tells us that Southern Whites would rather have had Negroes who stole work for them than Negroes who knew, however dimly, the worth of their own humanity. He concludes that Whites place a premium on Black deceit and encourage their irresponsibility; and their rewards were bestowed upon the Blacks in the degree that they could make the Whites feel safe and superior. He tells us that the very nature of Black and White relations in the South has bred thievery. For the Negroes to have organized and petitioned their white employers for higher wages would be impossible and would have resulted in quick retaliation, and with swift brutality, and so he tells us that pretending to conform to the laws of the Whites, the Negroes let their fingers stick to what they could touch, and that the Whites seemed to like it because it helped them maintain their elevated positions.

Mr. Wright terminates his story just as he leaves the South to take up his home in the North. I am sure that all who read *Black Boy* will look forward to the day when a companion volume entitled *Black Man* issues from the pen of this forceful writer which will take up the story where it is now left off.

Harry Estill Moore. "Racial Antagonisms." *Southwest Review*, 30 (Summer 1945), 387–88.

Self-revelation is an exceedingly difficult thing to accomplish, even when one is writing or talking to oneself only; it is almost too much to expect when one is writing, consciously, for a wide audience composed in large part of those conceived as one's enemies.

Whether or not Richard Wright has succeeded in his task of describing accurately the facts and factors which made him into the youth he became is something known only to him. But that he has given an accurate description of the forces playing on a developing, sensitive Negro child in the South is apparent to those who have achieved even a slight insight into the souls of black folk.

This is no mean accomplishment, in itself. But Mr. Wright has done more. He has written with a sincerity that is so apparent as almost to carry conviction that what he says is true. At least, this reader found himself compelled to believe that what was written was truth as the writer saw it. The result is a work of art which illumines and makes understandable a phenomenon puzzling to most of us on the white side of the color line.

Although *Black Boy* is the autobiography of a Negro born and growing up in the South, it is also, in sociological jargon, the history of the development of a racial attitude; and an excellent case study of a Negro family, displaying the manner in which this fundamental unit is organized and operates among this particular group.

Although the story itself is entertaining and enlightening, it was these more generalized aspects of the book which attracted and held the attention of this reader. Particularly interesting is the development of racial attitudes of intense antagonism.

Many of us have been prone to believe that such attitudes are a direct outgrowth of personal conflict between Negro and Caucasian. *Black Boy* demonstrates what social scientists have argued for decades: that attitudes of all sorts are taken over mostly from other members of the groups to which we belong and then are intensified or moderated by personal experiences.

Richard Wright learned to hate white folk before he had anything more than casual and unimportant relations with them. This hate he acquired from his own family only in small part; mostly it came from other Negro children. As a consequence, when he did come into personal contact with whites, he saw them as types of the enemy, not at all as other human beings. That is, he saw what he had been taught he would see, not what was before his eyes. As a Negro child he learned to see white people in very much the same way that white children learn to see Negroes. In both cases the developing person has his vision circumscribed by blinders and clouded by colored glasses, the tinting of which may vary only slightly from person to person. The implication of such a situation for those who would change the present system of race relations is too obvious for discussion.

Black Boy carries the author only through his childhood and early youth, up until the time he fled from the South he hated to the promised land of Chicago. What happened there—whether he found the land of milk and honey he expected or whether he found himself still frustrated—remains to be told. His article in *Atlantic Monthly* telling of his attempts to make himself a Communist indicate that his flight from the South was not as successful as he had hoped and that he became increasingly militant. But that is only one chapter from the latter portion of his Odyssey yet to be published. It is to be hoped that Mr. Wright will bring us up to date on his struggles.

Just as Richard Wright left the South in his efforts to solve his personal problems, so has the "race problem" moved out of the South and become a matter of national concern. Just as the story of Richard Wright's childhood in the South is a most excellent portrayal of what may happen to a sensitive Negro child in this region, his completed story gives promise of illuminating a still less known area of Negro life through telling us what happens to an intellectual and discriminating person in the large cities of the Midwest and the Northeast when that person happens to be a member of a minority and subordinate group.

Raymond Kennedy. "A Dramatic Autobiography." *Yale Review*, 39 (Summer 1945), 762–64.

This book has tremendous power. Its intensity of feeling, sustained drama, and sheer eloquence make reading it an unforgettable experience. This is because it is the product of a remarkable combination: an author of superb talent, a life story of pathos and tragedy, and a human theme of monumental significance.

The story of Wright's own life in the South during his childhood and youth is a true document of race relations in America, for, although as autobiography it is highly personalized, the author's eyes and ears and emotions were vibrantly sensitive, so that he missed as little of what went on around him as what went on inside him. Man and *milieu*, as described by Wright, demonstrate certain truths about the South, and about Negroes in the South, which seldom strike the consciousness of the American public—certainly not with the impact of this book.

"Black Boy" has been criticised by some reviewers for painting an unrelieved picture of misery, terror, and degradation among the masses of Negroes in the Southern States. Yet this is, in my judgment, the reality, as anyone who has come to know the situation intimately can testify. Of course, Negroes do adjust to their unhappy circumstances, but in doing so they become abnormal, pathological. They must yield self-respect, dignity, and personal honor; and, as Wright shows in his portraits of his fellow Negroes, this causes such a warping of personality that various forms of erratic behavior result. Some Negroes react to the constant succession of psychological shocks by subsiding into a kind of torpor, and live their lives in a spiritual and mental coma. Others seek escape in a fantastic dream world of grotesque religious beliefs and practices. Still others, in frenzied frustration, vent their desperation on the only permissible objects of aggression, their fellow Negroes. ("I had seen many Negroes solve the problem of being black by transferring their hatred of themselves to others with a black skin and fighting them.") Wright himself experienced savage physical and emotional brutality from his own family and other Negroes. And the whole dark-skinned group is exposed to any cruelties the white dominators may wish to inflict.

Not only are Negroes as individuals and a group rendered abnormal by their status and treatment; their relations with whites, as defined in the unwritten code of the South, are abnormal too, for the normal balance of rights and duties in human relationships does not exist in inter-racial matters. The Negroes may never strike back, may never stand and defend themselves, no matter what injustice or mistreatment they suffer from the whites; this, in my opinion, is the single worst feature of the Southern Caste system, and Wright reveals it in all of its revolting ugliness. ("There existed men against whom I was powerless, men who could violate my life at will.")

The Southern myth of Negro happiness has been shattered by the disclosures of Dollard, Powdermaker, and other researchers. Wright documents this exposure by showing exactly what degree of happiness is possible for a Negro in the South. He experienced joy in sudden bursts ("there was the aching glory in masses of clouds burning gold and purple from an invisible sun, . . . there was the excitement of fishing in muddy country creeks, . . . there was the greedy joy in the tangy taste of wild hickory nuts"), but it was quickly snuffed out by an overwhelming resurgence of pain or fright or sorrow. Every slight flowering of delight, every small thrill of elation was crushed almost as soon as it was felt, and the black boy slipped back into the dull mood of misery and despair which possessed him almost all of the time. ("My days and nights were one long, quiet, continuously contained dream of terror, tension, and anxiety.")

Southern whites cherish the illusion that they know Negroes well, but they never hear the secret discussions of Negroes, in which almost invariably race relations form the main topic. Wright reports many of these clandestine conversations, and what he tells will be a startling revelation to Southern readers. ("At noon . . . I would join the rest of the Negroes in a little room. . . . Here . . . we munched our lunches and discussed the ways of the white folks towards Negroes. When two or more of us were talking, it was impossible for this subject not to come up. Each of us hated and feared the whites. . . . The lunch hour would pass and we would go back to work, but there would be in our faces not one whit of the sentiment we had felt during the hour of discussion.")

Probably the most common criticism of this book by reviewers is that there are no half-tones in the author's picture of Negro life in the South, that the scene is sketched entirely in stark black and white. Here again, in my opinion, the accusation of overdrawing is little justified. This, with few exceptions, is precisely how race relations are in the Southern States: clean-cut black and white. The Negroes must either surrender and allow themselves to be spiritually stunted and deformed, or they must get out of the South. To a sensitive and high-spirited Negro like Wright, surrender was impossible. ("I was not made to be a resigned man. . . . I could submit and live the life of a genial slave, but that was impossible.")

And so Wright left the South. His book ends at the moment of flight, and in a magnificent passage he delivers his valedictory beginning with these lines: "I was not leaving the South to forget the South, but so that some day I might understand it, might come to know what its rigors had done to me, to its children."

Horace Cayton. "Frightened Children of Frightened Parents." *Twice-a-Year*, 12–13 (Spring-Summer/Fall-Winter 1945), 262–69.

Richard Wright has had but one story to tell. That story is how it feels to be a Negro in the United States. He has told it in many ways. He has employed many tools: concepts gathered from religion, science, and politics. He has used every literary device from stark realism to fantasy. But always he has had the single story to tell. In *Black Boy* he has retold it with even greater insight—with sharper tools he has dug out a deeper meaning.

The story Wright has had to tell has always been more important to him than the form, or the concepts employed to arrive at the reality he is trying to describe. Concepts, frames of reference, literary styles are but instruments which Wright uses, discarding some and blending elements of others, to communicate the tissue and texture of the Negro's experience in America. In his early works, like the stories "Big Boy Leaves Home" and "Down by the Riverside," he employed simple poetic realism. In "Long Black Song" he borrowed concepts from Sherwood Anderson and Lewis Mumford. "Fire and Cloud" and "Bright and Morning Star" were a mixture of ideas obtained from both Marxism and Christianity. In *Native Son* he employed sociological and psychoanalytic concepts within the frame of a political and economic analysis.

Just how completely and consciously he has utilized the tools of science is evident in his book, *Twelve Million Black Voices*. It is a volume of prose-poetry written out of a sense of complete identification with the debased masses of the Negro people. Beneath its impassioned exterior, however, Wright exploits the most sophisticated concepts of both sociology and anthropology. In spite of its emotional overtones, this work is basically a study of the impact of urbanism on folk people and a description of their living in two contrasting types of society. He introduces the device of "Lords of the Land," which is a personalization of the primitive social forces controlling the destiny of Negroes in the rural South. This he contrasts with the "Bosses of the Buildings," the impersonal anonymity of the urban North which the migrant Negro is pitted against. Thus he has translated into literary form the polar types of social organization: the anthropological concepts of Robert Redfield—culture and civilization—and the sociological concepts of Louis Wirth—sacred and secular societies.

The eclecticism of Wright arises naturally out of his conception of literature and of his role as an artist. In a recent statement he said:

> I have always taken the writing of literature very seriously, and I've looked upon fiction and writing in general as a means of revealing the truth of life and experience rather than purely as a means of entertaining people. In other words, I feel that literature ought to be a sharp instrument to reveal something important about mankind, about living, about life whether among whites or blacks. That is why my work hews so close

> to facts, and yet why I try to float these facts on a sea of emotion, to drive them home with some degree of artistic power, as much as is humanly possible, to the level of seriousness which characterizes science. I want people to enjoy my books but I also want them to be moved and conditioned by them.

In *Black Boy* Wright has chosen himself as the subject matter and has brought to bear on that material all the tools which would give it a deeper meaning. Although he relies mainly on the psychoanalytic frame of reference in selecting incidents of his life, he has brought to play on this material all the insight he has derived from sociology, anthropology, and literature. Indeed, all these instruments were necessary to achieve an objectivity which would allow him to tear himself out of the context of his every day environment and describe the life of Negro people through his own personality.

The literary form which Wright chose was autobiography. It might seem strange that a young man of thirty-six should write his autobiography. But this is not an autobiography in the popular American sense; it is rather written out of a more European tradition. On the whole Americans write autobiographies when they are about to die. It could be said that Europeans do so more often when they are compelled by a driving necessity to express something so personal, so emotional, that it can only be done by portraying the life through which the idea-emotion was conceived and nurtured—through revealing the idea-emotion by completely revealing themselves. *Black Boy* is such an autobiography.

Other great writers in the European tradition have written similarly at an early age. James Joyce's "Portrait of the Artist as a Young Man" and George Moore's "Portrait of a Young Man" are cases in point. None of these artists, including the present one, write his autobiography to tell other people how many famous men he had met and knew and what exciting things he had done, but rather from a driving desire to communicate imbedded emotions and deep convictions about life and living.

The central theme of *Black Boy* can be summed up in the fear-hate-fear complex of Negroes. The fears and insecurities and above all the feeling of guilt and the fear of punishment for that guilt, which all men have to some extent, according to the psychoanalysts, is different for the Negro. In the white man this feeling can often be shown to be false, a figment of his imagination, a holdover from early childhood experiences. It can more easily be resolved by treatment by the psychiatrist or even by rational cogitation.

But the Negro living in our society cannot so easily be convinced of the irrational nature of his feelings of fear and guilt. For him, punishment in the actual environment is ever present; violent, psychological and physical, leaps out at him from every side. The Negro's personality is brutalized by an unfriendly environment. This reinforces the normal insecurities he feels as a person living in this highly complex society. Such attacks on his personality lead to resentment and hatred of the white man. However, the certain knowledge that he will be punished if his emotions are discovered produces feelings of guilt for having such emotions. Fear leads to hate; but the personality recoils with an intensified and compounded fear. This is his reaction to his own brutalization, subordination and hurt. It is this vicious cycle in which the American Negro is caught and in which his personality is pulverized by an ever mounting, self-propelling rocket of emotional conflict. The Negro has been hurt: he knows it. He wants to strike back, but he knows that he must not—there is evidence everywhere that to do so would lead to his destruction.

This complex of emotion is the heritage of the race. Wright states in *Native Son*:

> If only ten or twenty Negroes had been put into slavery we could call it injustice, but there were hundreds of thousands of them throughout the country. If this state of affairs had lasted for two years, we could say that it was injustice; but it lasted for more than two hundred years. Injustice which lasts for three long centuries and which exists among millions of people over thousands of square miles of territory, is injustice no longer; it is an accomplished fact of life. . . . What is happening here today is not injustice, but oppression. . . .

The closest analogy which one can find to the quality of the Negro's living in America is that of a soldier under battle conditions.

Wright has pointed out again and again the similarity between these two experiences in living:

In *Native Son*:

> Do men regret when they kill in war . . . ? No! You kill to keep from being killed! And after a victorious war you return to a free country, just as this boy, with his hands stained with the blood of Mary Dalton, felt that he was free for the first time in his life.

In *Twelve Million Black Voices*:

> Again we find, of the North as of the South, that life for us is daily warfare and that we live hard, like soldiers. We are set apart from the civilian population; our kitchenettes comprise our barracks; the color of our skins constitutes our uniforms; the streets of our cities our trenches; a job is a pill-box to be captured and held; and the unions of white workers for a long time have formed the first line of resistance which we encounter. . . . We are always in battle, but the tidings of victory are few.

In *Still Time to Die,* Jack Belden describes the quality which distinguishes a battle from any other sphere of human activity. That quality is the uncertainty arising out of fear:

> Feel your emotions overwhelming your intellectual conviction and know that your tact and judgment no longer have the power to penetrate through the clouds of uncertainty, or to pick out of all the contradictory welter of alternatives the proper course; and even while your soul draws back from action crying: "I cannot do it!" then come to a decision.
>
> It is too hard. You cannot imagine this uncertainty if you have never been there.

This uncertainty of when, how, and where the white enemy environment will strike—this uncertainty as to what the black boy should do when it does strike—the intensified uncertainty which arises out of the fear-hate-fear complex has been the essential quality of Wright's life. It is, further, Wright believes, the nature of the experience of the Negro in America. For some it has been more intense, more tragic, more poignantly real than for others. But no Negro could have been nurtured in America and not have been possessed by it.

It is curious that one finds little exposition of this thesis in either scientific or literary writings. To the writer's knowledge the only other statement comes from a psychoanalyst, Dr. Helen V. McLean, who has said:

> Fear is probably the predominating feeling of any persecuted minority toward the strong dominating group. In the winter of 1943, Richard Wright, creator of "Bigger," the hero of *Native Son*, gave us at the *Institute for Psychoanalysis* a tragically beautiful analysis of how this fear, with its concomitant reactive hostility, affects the entire life of the Negro. The final character of the Negro may be a protesting, fighting Bigger or a passive, submissive figure like Bigger's mother, but at the core of the personality with either extreme of character reaction lies fear and hatred of the white man who has humiliated and frustated him.

Undoubtedly there is a connection between the discovery of this point of view by the psychoanalysts and the fact that Wright chose the autobiographical form to tell his story of Negro oppression. Wright wanted to show the nature of Negro personality—that fear and hatred go to its core. He tried in *Native Son*. But many people said that the story was overdrawn, fictional, not typical. But Wright said, "I feel it—it's here within me. I'll write about myself; then people must know." Like the psychoanalyst who discovers fear and hate in his Negro patient and must reckon with it, cannot dismiss it, so Wright performs this painful surgery on himself. He is saying in *Black Boy*, "You see, you can't dismiss this as a literary device. It isn't a dreamed up Bigger Thomas—it's me."

A note about bitterness. Bitterness is a sustained hate grown cold and hard until it has become an organic part of the personality. America puts a great value on not being bitter, especially if the person who might be bitter is the one who is oppressed. That a Negro should be bitter about his treatment in America shocks white Americans to their moral depth. Wright's characters—Wright himself—are not without bitterness. For Wright, to deny that Negroes fear and hate and that that fear-hate turns to bitterness is to deny their essential humanity. This is an unpleasant point of view for white Americans, who in spite of their racial practices and deep-seated emotional attachment to racism love to cling to the myth that Negroes are treated fairly. Sixty per cent of white Americans voted this in a recent poll. They are unwilling to face even the fact that the Negro is brutalized and still less willing to entertain the notion that he is bitter about his treatment. America is a moral nation and wants to feel that it is good, decent, and fair. To be confronted with the fact that a group of people hate, even though these people have been outraged, creates a feeling of guilt and force on the American conscience the necessity of making a moral judgment of itself.

If there is hatred and bitterness in the Negro's heart, as Wright describes in *Native Son*, there might be a sudden and violent rent in the veil behind which the Negro is living, like the "rent which allowed his [Bigger's] feelings of resentment and estrangement to leap forth and find objective and concrete form." Dr. McLean has described the tragic implications of this guilt-fear with which white America is possessed:

> The intense and ever-increasing rebellion of the Negro is now creating a very real fear in white men. Such incidents as the Detroit riots remind us that the white man may someday be the victim of the old talion law of "an eye for an eye and a tooth for a tooth." I wonder if the attack at Pearl Harbor by men of pigmented skin did not stir up our latent fear of a punishment that might be meted out to us by other men of color who live in the same country? An external danger often reactivates internal guilt and fear of punishment in an individual. Perhaps the external attack by the Japanese stimulated our dormant guilt toward, and fear of, minority groups in our internal body politic.

I have said that Wright's characters are bitter. This cannot be denied. But a distinction should be made between his characters, the material with which he works, and his writing. His characters are bitter because that is a social reality, because to deny their bitterness is to deny their humanity. His writing is not bitter. He writes with the detachment of a surgeon, the objectivity of a scientist. It is not his responsibility that his subject matter—even when it is himself—has bitterness inherent in it. His style is tense, terse, and dramatic. He loves vividness of presentation. But he would use that same technique regardless of subject. This is simply saying that Wright is an American Negro with all the bitterness which American Negroes embody (whether they know it is or not) but that he is also a great artist. One should be distinguished from the other.

Wright's bitterness—the material which he presents in *Black Boy*—he nursed from his frightened mother, who beat him to make him conform so he could survive. That bitterness is the fear-hate-fear complex grown hard. He is bitter because he is a man who is taunted by being told that he is a man but not allowed to act like one. This is not hard to account for psychologically. What is difficult is to explain how an educated son of a sharecropper could find the strength and genius to wrench himself out of the context of Negro life, to recognize his emotions, to be able to study them as a scientist, and to write about them with such great artistry.

R. A.
Charm
(September 1945), 208.

. . . There were no reservations in our liking for Richard Wright, whose autobiography, *Black Boy*, is a powerful indictment of racial prejudice in the United States. Not that this brilliant Negro writer is vehement or preachy; he merely tells the tale of his childhood and youth, and the facts speak for themselves. However, his enthusiasm for living is undaunted by vicissitudes; this, and his will to succeed against odds, make the book vivid reading. . . .

William Harrison. *Boston Chronicle,* December 8, 1945.

So powerful is Mr. Wright's mastery of the craft of writing that his books always perform the service of shocking their readers into the much needed recognition of the gravity of the Negro question in the United States. As the most distinguished Negro novelist Mr. Wright's approach is necessarily imaginative, but his fiction (to adapt an epigram of Oscar Wilde's) is indeed stranger than truth, of which it is compounded. This autobiography often strains the reader's credulity on account of the vividness in detail with which Mr. Wright recounts experiences reaching back to the period (the age of four) generally hazy and dim in the memories of most of us. Perhaps his stenographic account of conversations verbatim, with the appropriate emotional responses in tone and action, from the very fact that it is so real, evokes disbelief in the critical reader who forgets that Mr. Wright appears to have been always an introvert, aloof and detached and sensitively observant.

Despite the extremely personal character of Mr. Wright's incidents, since it is the story of his own life that he is relating, their representative features are also made obvious on reflection. For although he dwells on the meanest side of a mean society, such as that in Mississippi, where he was born and where the maximum oppression of the Negro people through exploitation and terrorism occurs, he dignifies and elevates it by eliciting its intrinsic meaning for others to understand. The awful horror of insecurity, fear, and frustration induced by inescapable poverty cannot fail to shape itself before our minds as we follow the course of Mr. Wright's career through childhood and adolescence—a career which had as its North Star the hope of eventual escape. . . .

Checklist of Additional Reviews

Kirkus Reviews, 13 (January 1, 1945), 9.

L. D. Reddick. *Library Journal*, 70 (February 15, 1945), 163–64.

Joseph Henry Jackson. *San Francisco Chronicle,* February 25, 1945.

George F. Minot. *Boston Herald,* February 28, 1945.

David Appel. *Chicago Daily News,* February 28, 1945.

Dorothy Canfield. *Book-of-the-Month-Club News* (February 1945), 2–3.

Harry Hansen. *Survey Graphic*, 34 (February 1945), 68–69.

Dorothy Canfield. *Elizabeth City Daily Advance,* March 2, 1945.

Frank Marshall Davis. Associated Negro Press: *Tampa Bulletin; Detroit Tribune,* March 2, 1945.

Constance H. Curtis. *Amsterdam News,* March 3, 1945.

Gertrude Scott Martin. *Michigan Chronicle* (Detroit), March 3, 1945.

Howard Mumford Jones. *Saturday Review of Literature,* 28 (March 3, 1945), 9–10.

Horace Cayton. *Chicago Sun Book Week,* March 4, 1945, p. 3.

Tarleton Collier. *Louisville Courier-Journal,* March 4, 1945.

Paul Engle. *Chicago Tribune,* March 4, 1945.

O. O. *Boston Post,* March 4, 1945.

Philadelphia Inquirer, March 4, 1945.

Jessie Rehder. John V. Blalock.

Durham Herald-Sun, March 4, 1945.

W. T. Scott. *Providence Journal,* March 4, 1945, pp. 4–6.

Paul L. Wiley. *Milwaukee Journal,* March 4, 1945.

Newsweek, 25 (March 5, 1945), 93.

Beulah Rector. *Watertown Times,* March 7, 1945.

Samuel Sillen. *New York Daily Worker,* March 9, 1945, p. 11.

Bill Strawn. *Charlotte News,* March 9, 1945.

Hamilton Basso, *New Yorker,* 21 (March 10, 1945), 86–89.

Horace Cayton. *Pittsburgh Courier,* March 10, 1945, p. 7.

La Vere Anderson. *Tulsa Daily World,* March 11, 1945.

George Mayberry. *New Republic,* 112 (March 12, 1945), 364–65.

Blanche Hixson Smith. *Meridian Record,* March 14, 1945.

Columbia Record, March 15, 1945.

Justice, March 15, 1945.

Army and Navy Review, March 16, 1945.

Philip Levine. *Philadelphia Jewish Times,* March 18, 1945.

Ide Gruber. *Parkchester Press* (Bronx, N.Y.), March 22, 1945.

James Neill North. *Terra Bella News* (California), March 23, 1945.

Mary Thomas Woods. *San Francisco Argonaut,* March 23, 1945.

Alice Frost Lord. *Lewiston Evening Journal,* March 31, 1945.

Nyman W. Newlin *Northwest Life* (Minneapolis), March 1945.

Charles C. Renshaw, Jr. *Townsfolk* (Chicago), March 1945.

Homer A. Jack. *Unity,* March 1945.

Booklist, 41 (April 1, 1945), 224.

Ora G. Morrow. *Chicago Bee,* April 8, 1945.

Mrs. Paul Robeson. *Hartford Courant,* April 8, 1945.

Galveston News-Tribune, April 8, 1945.

Nancy Barr Movity. *Oakland Tribune,* April 8, 1945.

Gertrude B. Murphy. *San Jose Mercury Herald,* April 9, 1945.

Elizabeth B. Knight. *Dallas Times-Herald,* April 15, 1945.

Eastern Kansas Register, April 20, 1945.

American Mercury, 60 (April 1945), 389.

Michael McLaughlin. *Catholic World,* 161 (April 1945), 85–86.

Patterson McLean Frederick. *Cresset,* 8 (April 1945), 44–46.

Headlines, April 1945.

Mademoiselle, 10 (April 1945).

E.G.P. *More Books* (Boston Public Library), 20 (April 1945).

Ione Rider, *Now* (American Council of Race Relations (April 1945).

Mildred Barish. *Opinion* (Orange, Conn.) (April 1945), 29–30.

Augustine Patrick McCarthy. *The Sign,* 23 (April 1945), 499–500.

Wisconsin Library Bulletin, 41 (April 1945), 47.

Pulse, 3 (May 1945), 20–23. [Comments by E. Franklin Frazier, Frank Marshall Davis, Ira De A. Reid, Paul Hanley Furfey, Dutton Ferguson, Church Terrell, Sherman Briscoe, Henry Putzel, Jr.]

Mary McCarthy. *The New Leader,* 28 (June 23, 1945), 10.

Jack English. *The Catholic Worker,* June 1945, p. 6.

Lewis Roy Sprietsma. *Chicago Daily Law Bulletin,* June 1945.

George W. Crockett, Jr. *National Bar Journal,* 2 (June 1945).

Negro College Quarterly, 3 (June 1945).

Max Nomad. *338 News* (New York), (June 1945).

M. B. *Fraternal Outlook* (International Workers Order, N.Y.) 7 (June-July 1945).

Richard Beale Davis. *The Southern Literary Messenger*, 3 (July 8, 1945).

Common Ground, 5 (Summer 1945).

Ralph Ellison. *The Antioch Review*, 5 (Summer 1945), 198–211.

Elizabeth Hardwick. *Partisan Review*, 12 (Summer 1945), 406–7.

Stanton A. Coblentz. *Different*, 1 (September 10, 1945).

Companion (October 1945).

Irving Brodkin. *New Mexico Quarterly Review*, 15 (Fall 1945), 369–71.

Everett McManus. *View*, 5 (January 1946).

The Outsider

by Richard Wright

Harper & Brothers Publishers, New York

The Outsider

Orville Prescott. *New York Times*, March 18, 1953, p. 29.

It is thirteen years since the publication of Richard Wright's famous novel, "Native Son," and eight since that of his even more celebrated autobiography, "Black Boy." Both those books were bitterly angry, fiercely eloquent denunciations of the racial discriminations and social and economic pressures that condition the lives of Negroes. And both were so powerfully written that they established Mr. Wright as the leading American Negro writer of his generation. His new novel, his first book since "Black Boy," is published today.

"The Outsider" marks a complete reversal in the direction of Mr. Wright's literary career. It is just as preoccupied with violence as the earlier books, just as harshly effective in its melodrama and its narrative impact. But the first two books were concentrated on the plight of the Negro and they interpreted it in terms of the sins of society, emphasizing the dominant power of environment in the tradition of literary naturalism. "The Outsider" has a Negro for its hero; but it is not primarily his plight as a Negro, but as a thinking, questioning man in the perplexing twentieth century that concerns Mr. Wright. And instead of a realistic sociological document he has written a philosophical novel, its ideas dramatized by improbable coincidences and symbolical characters. "The Outsider" has the plot interest of a rousing murder story, and its characters are as unreal as they are in most murder stories. And because of their unreality "The Outsider" seems artificial and lacks the persuasive impact that only fully individualized characters can give to fiction. But this partial fictional failure is compensated for to some extent by the interest of Mr. Wright's ideas.

This is the story of Cross Damon, a Negro mail sorter on the night shift in a South Chicago post office. Cross was consumed with despair, guilt, shame and self-loathing, trying to anesthetize his overpowering sense of dread with whisky. He was in debt. His mistress was pregnant and his wife, from whom he was separated, was threatening legal steps. So when Cross had a chance to let another man's body be mistaken for his in a subway wreck he never hesitated. He fled from all personal responsibility, feeling no obligations to his wife or children or mistress. And to make good his escape, he impulsively murdered his best friend.

It is one of the unbelievable things in "The Outsider" that Cross should act so suddenly and violently when he is presented as meditative, introspective, addicted to self-analysis and philosophical speculation. But Cross did not stop with one murder. In New York he murdered three more people!

Cross' murders and his battle of wits with the District Attorney in his efforts to conceal his guilt make lively if incredible reading. But there are other factors in "The Outsider" that are of considerably more interest.

One of these is Cross' relations with several leaders of the Communist party and Cross' (for Mr. Wright's) analysis of the driving force behind communism as nothing except a lust for naked power. If power over the nation is a remote ambition, power over lesser members of the party is a present and delicious satisfaction. Idealistic talk about crusading for the working class is just hypocritical cant, which the Communist leaders don't believe themselves, Cross realized. Believing in no faith or ideals or ethical restraints, the Communists just want to reorganize the world, with themselves in positions of power on top.

And Cross felt that he understood the Communists because he, too, believed in nothing. An outsider in American society because of his black skin, he was much more of an outsider because of his conviction that existence was senseless, that society had no moral claims upon him, that there were no divine or traditional or logical laws that applied to him. Cross believed that life was an incomprehensible disaster and human beings were "nothing in particular." So, if no ideas were necessary to justify his acts, he could kill impulsively to satisfy a passing whim or for his own convenience.

Cross had reached these nihilistic depths only after reading widely, particularly in several existentialist writers. He was a highly intelligent and widely informed man, but he used his intelligence and his information only to destroy himself and others. He despised the Communists for their cruelty and duplicity; but he could not see that if he despised such sins he ought logically to love kindness and honesty. He saw the confusion and suffering and fear of the modern world and the only step he could find to take was abdication from human responsibilities, failing to see that in times of change and crisis there is more need than ever for loyalty to responsibilities.

Toward the end of "The Outsider" Richard Wright has devoted a dozen pages to a speech in which Cross outlines his philosophy of negation and despair. It is a fair assumption, I think, that Mr. Wright deplores Cross' moral weakness and irrational behavior, but that he finds much cogency in Cross' philosophy. That men as brilliant as Richard Wright feel this way is one of the symptoms of the intellectual and moral crisis of our times.

Ralph De Toledano. *Classic Features,* March 22, 1953.

Richard Wright is the author of two tremendously successful books, "Black Boy" and "Native Son." The impact of these books, bound up as they were in subjective experience, was solid, whatever technical lacks they demonstrated. In "The Outsider," Wright has moved partly out of himself to deal more directly and objectively with the relation of man to society. He has, moreover, attempted to weld together the novel of violence and the novel of ideas—a project which requires a sure touch and the ability to make the implausible convincing.

If Wright fails in this exacting assignment, he succeeds in depicting one man's alienation from the world of action and the world of ideas. As a study in morbid nihilism, "The Outsider" is a work of compelling force. For, where the external violence is contrived, the internal violence of his central character is real and terrifying.

The novel, then, is its protagonist, Cross Damon. A young, self-educated Negro, working at a routine job in the Chicago Post Office, Damon is beset by a shrewish wife, a pregnant underage mistress who seeks to destroy him, and the bottle. It takes a "deus ex machina" and a quick murder to rescue him from this existential pit. Fleeing to New York where he establishes a new identity, Damon evolves a new philosophy of life, above law and morality—an insulation against the appeals and pressures of the world. The insulation, interestingly enough, makes him self-alien in both the White and Negro communities. It is Damon's vision and determination to remove himself from all things which impinge on his inner consciousness.

But Damon must move about in the external world, must eat and sleep and make love. The mechanics of living enmesh him in the life he would negate. He is involved by the Communist Party, with incredible abruptness, in the creation of an incident against a racist landlord, cynically staged by the party to set off a "cause célèbre." And this involvement leads to situations where, with godlike wrath and detachment, he commits three more murders. Hating the party and the revolutionary platitudes it mouths to gloss over a ruthless power-urge, he sees himself as the avenger.

He has, in effect, made his appointment in Samarra—for Damon is now faced with new conflicts: the police who eventually discover his guilt but cannot prove it, the Communists who also suspect but kill him without proof, and the flesh which is mortal and makes continual demands. He is dead before the Communists kill him—a suicide of the spirit, because he is neither Man nor God, but a man linked by his soul to other men. He cannot shut them out without shutting himself out.

This is a concept which Damon cannot grasp as an individual and Richard Wright cannot handle as a novelist. Damon's apocalyptic vision of a degenerate and decaying world—shorn of God, shorn of sight, and left only with a technology which negates an outworn social structure—is only partially expressed in "The Outsider." Perhaps Wright is aware of this. He stops the action to allow Damon to engage in a 34-page Socratic dialogue with his Communist tormentors. It is a beautifully expressed essay on man, but in a novel it is an intrusion and a concession of defeat.

"The Outsider," however, is successful because it poses the figure of the Nihilist, the symbol of contemporary revolt, in a confused and ironic world—and does so with a passion and a drive seldom encountered in contemporary novels. It is no exaggeration to say that the book is gripping from first to last. This despite the fact that, like Dreiser, Wright lacks topflight technical mastery. His prose is unlimber, his touch often heavy. But, unlike Dreiser, his rough perceptions are full and overpowering.

He can build around the protagonist, but most of his other characters are just that—figures extracted from the tragic literature of ex-Communist confession and testimony, commonplace in that region of human extraterritoriality but somehow strange and strained in "The Outsider." Like the tapestry in "Hamlet," however, they play an important role.

This is, perhaps, over-exacting criticism. It does not take into account the trauma of Wright's break with Communism—at a time when the American literati considered such a break treason—and of his expatriation to Paris. It does not take into account the maturity of his approach, the good taste which encompasses a sordid cast. But "The Outsider," because it is head and shoulder above most of the current output, cannot be measured by the standards of the book merchants. Precisely because of its virtues it must be judged by a more stringent set of criteria. "The Outsider" is a book to be read seriously and discussed seriously—as Wright is a novelist to be nurtured—but its blessings are not unmixed.

Milton Rugoff. *New York Herald Tribune Book Review*, March 22, 1953, p. 4.

One would have thought that in "Native Son" Richard Wright had gone about as far as he could go in making the enormity of a Negro's crimes an index to the oppression he had suffered. A few even felt he had gone too far, had been guilty of sensationalism and a perverse defense of the indefensible. But, next to Wright's latest protagonist, Cross Damon, Bigger Thomas of "Native Son" seems merely a pathetic victim of circumstance, a creature who was never given half a chance. Damon is, to put it briefly, a monomaniac. He is described as having a decent job and an education and having had a more or less stable childhood; in making him a supercriminal, one who believes himself outside all law, Wright goes beyond horror to something like fantasy.

If only Wright had prepared us for Damon by indicating at the outset that the character is a monster, or has the makings of one, we might make shift to accept him as a study in abnormal psychology. But Damon is presented as relatively normal up to the time the novel opens, his twenty-sixth year. He has been to college and has worked in the Chicago postoffice long enough to have several cronies there; he has a respectable wife, three children and a very proper mother. True, he is separated from his wife and children, is involved with a sixteen-year-old girl who is bearing a child by him, and he is deep in debt. But nothing convinces us that such circumstances can overnight make a man a "killer." Because both his pregnant mistress and his estranged wife threaten him, he turns from an average young man in a jam into a psychopath who can express his theories of society only in murder.

The first of the incredible accidents that makes his career in extermination possible is a subway wreck. He walks away uninjured but is listed among the dead and immediately sees a perfect opportunity to start a new life. Before leaving Chicago, however, and while tarrying with a white prostitute he runs into an old friend, who, since he recognizes Damon, must be killed off. On the train to New York he talks freely to a sympathetic white man (who turns out to be the District

Attorney of New York), and even describes a Negro who, finding himself treated as though not quite human, decides to become a true "outlaw," a god unto himself.

In New York he ingeniously constructs a new identity for himself and then allows himself to be adopted as a pet Negro by a leading white Communist, Gil Blount. Invited to live with the Blounts in their Greenwich Village apartment (as a test of a "Fascist" landlord), he immediately falls in love with Blount's naive wife Eva, comes on Blount in a deadly struggle with the landlord, and since he actually despises the Communist who would use him as much as the Fascist who would abuse him, he brutally kills both. When another Communist leader stumbles on the truth, Damon does for him, too. In jig time Eva, who has gone to live with him in Harlem, glimpses the true Damon and commits suicide. Although the D.A. has now also divined the truth, he hasn't, it develops, the evidence to convict Damon and must set him free. But the Communists, recognizing in Damon a rival who is, like them, beyond the law, deal with him in the style to which he has become accustomed.

If such an outline makes "The Outsider" seem like sheer melodrama, a compost of sex and crime, the fault is not altogether in the outline. Although the action is interlarded with Damon's self-analyses and with his disquisitions on society and morality (one of them runs to fifteen pages), these interrupt the action without making it seem much less lurid. If the narrative does have a fascination, it is chiefly morbid—the hypnotic power of a bad dream. To this quality the Communists contribute as much as Damon. But where there is perhaps some excuse for Damon's fiendishness—he at least is discriminated against and his crimes are more or less impulsive—the Communists are apparently ruthless on principle. Sketchy as Wright's portraits of Comrades Blount, Hilton, Blimin and Menti are, they are none the less hair-raising. He does them like a man settling an old score.

A comparison between this book and Wright's earlier fiction makes clear the fatal weakness of "The Outsider." Where "Uncle Tom's Children," the collection of stories that established Wright's reputation, concentrated simply and powerfully on character and incident, letting the implications fall where they might, almost every episode in "The Outsider" seems designed to demonstrate a social theorem. Even in "Native Son," where the message sometimes threatens to take over the narrative, the story is finally that of a youth named Bigger Thomas. In the figure of Cross Damon, Wright is no doubt asserting that what was true of an illiterate Negro is no less true of an intellectual, but not by the force of fiction and the logic of drama.

Even the writing in "The Outsider" is sometimes strained and fumbling, as though the author were groping for effects he did not quite believe in. When occasionally he does have complete control of his materials, we get moments of such naked intensity and unbearable frustration—as of caged animals flinging themselves against the bars until they die—as made his earlier books unforgettable. This power will, one hopes, stand him in good stead later.

Granville Hicks. "The Portrait of a Man Searching." *New York Times Book Review,* March 22, 1953, pp. 1, 35.

It was in 1938 that Richard Wright, then 30 years old, published his first book, a collection of four tendentious stories called "Uncle Tom's Children." In the Forties he published only two books; only two books, but each of them with a heavy impact upon its readers. The first, in 1940, was "Native Son," that turbulent, baffling, unforgettable story of the violent life of a young Negro. Then, five years later, Wright described the misery, humiliation, violence and resentment of his own early life in the South in a fragment of autobiography, "Black Boy." The three books not only made it clear that Mr. Wright was the most eloquent spokesman for the Negro people in his generation; they suggested that this was one of the important literary talents of our time. How important it is, and how little limited to a particular group of people, is demonstrated by his fourth book and second novel, "The Outsider."

Readers of "Native Son" will remember that its climax comes just before the execution of Bigger Thomas for a double murder. Mr. Max, Bigger's lawyer, delivers a long plea in which he tries to demonstrate that Bigger's crime is the result of a form of civilization that is based on discrimination and exploitation. So far as the judge is concerned, Mr. Max fails, but he does succeed in giving Bigger a conviction that his life has meaning.

"The Outsider" also is concerned with the quest for meaning; not, however, in terms of racial discrimination nor in any sociological terms whatever, but in purely philosophical terms. The leading character is, to be sure, a Negro, but his principal problems have nothing to do with his race. They are pre-eminently the problems of the human being as such, for this is, so far as I can recall, one of the first consciously existentialist novels to be written by an American.

It begins, deceptively, in a realistic vein, with a description of a group of Negroes as they are coming home from their work in a Chicago post office. One of these men, Cross Damon, is in trouble—bad trouble but believable. As the result of an early and unfortuante marriage, he is supporting a wife, with whom he does not live, and three children. Since he has a mistress and the mistress is pregnant, it is not hard to understand why he is drinking heavily.

But Cross' real troubles are not of that order at all. He is one of those people who are "fated, like Job, to live a never-ending debate between themselves and their sense of what they believed life should be." What is happening to him comes to seem more and more like the progress of a dream, and we can therefore accept the accident, implausible enough in itself, that wipes out his practical problems by wiping out his identity. After he has supposedly been killed in a subway accident, Cross no longer has to worry about women and money; he is free to face the fundamental issues. "It was a great challenge," he thinks, "that went straight to the heart of life. What was he to do with himself?"

What Mr. Wright is up to becomes clear as he describes Cross' trip to New York. In the dining car Cross has a talk with a hunchback named Ely Houston, who turns out to be not only New York's District Attorney but also a man whose attitude toward life resembles his own. Houston says, "Negroes, as they enter our culture, are going to inherit the problems we have, but with a difference. They are outsiders, and they are going to know that they have these problems. They are going to be self-conscious; they are going to be gifted with a double vision, for, being Negroes, they are going to be both *inside* and *outside* of our culture at the same time."

Given Mr. Wright's own political experience, one is ready to predict at this point that he will confront his outsider with communism, and so he promptly does. In almost no time Cross is living in the apartment of a party leader, Gilbert Blount, and his painter wife, Eva. Cross, it appears, is attracted to the party, but in a curiously perverse way.

"It was not the objective reality of the revolutionary movement that was pulling so magnetically at Cross; it was something that movement had and did not know it had that was seducing his interest. It was its believing that it *knew* life; its conviction that it had mastered the art of living; its will that it could define the ends of existence that fascinated him against his volition. Nowhere else save in these realms had he encountered that brand of organized audacity directed toward secular goals. He loathed their knowledge, their manners, their ends, but he was almost persuaded that they had in a wrong manner moved in a right direction for revealing the content of human life on earth."

It must be observed that the Communist party Cross encounters is not the party that I knew in the late Thirties, and it resembles only in a general way the party about which Mr. Wright wrote in his essay in "The God That Failed." The difference is not in what the party leaders do but in their awareness of why they do it. The leaders in "The Outsider" not only have no other aim but power; they are so acutely conscious of it that Mr. Wright can speak again and again of "this systematization of the sensuality of power." They have none of the weaknesses that have made actual party leaders ludicrous as well as sinister; they are beyond good and evil; they are supermen.

Within the context of the novel, however, these men have their reality, both because they are, in existentialist terms, a legitimate projection of the spirit of communism and because the speed and violence of the narrative demand figures of such stature. The pace becomes faster and faster, as Cross murders two Communists and a Fascist, but the true climax of the novel is in the realm of ideas, not that of violent deeds. Questioned about his attitude toward communism by a party leader after the murders, Cross sets forth his philosophy of history in a long speech that is comparable, as an expression of Mr. Wright's thinking, to Mr. Max's speech, already mentioned, in "Native Son." But Cross' chief antagonist is really not the party but District Attorney Ely Houston, whom he has encountered at various times in the course of his crimes. In the end Houston is convinced of Cross' guilt, but lets him go, saying, "You are your own law, so you'll be your own judge." The communists, however, decide differently.

Cross' speech to the party leader and Houston's speech to Cross are the ideological high points of the novel.

The former is impressive, though not always perfectly logical. The latter is bewildering. He really understood Cross, the D.A. says, when he saw a list of the books he had been reading: "Your Nietzsche, your Hegel, your Jaspers, your Heidegger, your Husserl, your Kierkegaard, and your Dostoevsky were the clues." But Houston, whose behavior is not anti-social is himself a good deal of an existentialist, and so obviously is Mr. Wright. Both would agree with Jean-Paul Sartre, who gave existentialism its present vogue, that "man is nothing else but what he thinks of himself." Both could say with William Dilthey, "man does not have a nature but only a history."

In just what sense, then, is the blame for Cross' crimes to be attributed to his existentialist reading? Some kind of answer can be suggested, but only vaguely. Like Whittaker Chambers in "Witness," Mr. Wright feels that communism is a logical outcome of the whole development of rationalism in the Western World, but, unlike Chambers, he cannot accept a religious view of the universe. Cross' principal objection to communism is its denial of subjectivity, and this reminds us of things Mr. Wright has said in "The God That Failed."

Yet Cross' subjectivity, operating in the existentialist context, has impelled him along a road that he can only describe, at the end of it, as horrible. There is, Mr. Wright seems to be saying, an alternative to religion, to communism, to willful crime. Man, Cross intimates in his deathbed stammerings, may yet learn to live decently in the world as it is, and his own horrible futile life may be, in the Nietzschean sense, a bridge.

"The Outsider" is both melodrama and novel of ideas, attempting to render Mr. Wright's "sense of our contemporary living" in both emotional and inellectual terms. If the ideas are sometimes incoherent, that does not detract from the substance and power of the book. It is in the description of action, especially violent action, that Mr. Wright excels, not merely because he can make the reader see but because he compels him to participate. There is not a murder in the book that the reader, at the moment of reading about it, does not feel that he would have committed under the same circumstances. Nor is the sense of participation limited to the dramatic scenes; the expression of ideas, even in the long and more or less incoherent speeches, becomes a form of action in which one is swept along. And Mr. Wright achieves all this in spite of a persisting clumsiness of style.

He has always been a demonic writer, and in the earliest of his stories one felt that he was saying more than he knew, that he was, in a remarkable degree, an unconscious artist. He has grown in awareness since then, and in "The Outsider" has made his most valiant and his most successful effort to come to terms with his feelings about the human condition. But there are still unrecognized compulsions and one suspects that they have a great deal to do with the power of the book. No one who has read "Black Boy" can be surprised that Mr. Wright is preoccupied with violence, but almost certainly the causes of this preoccupation lie even deeper than the experiences he has described. The preoccupation would be less significant if this were a less violent world.

It must be clear that "The Outsider"—like "Invisible Man," which it resembles in several ways—is only incidentally a book about Negroes. Being a Negro helps Cross Damon to understand that he is an outsider, as it helps Ralph Ellison's hero to understand that he is an invisible man, but there are many invisible men and many outsiders. "The Outsider" is, as it was intended to be, a book about modern man, and, because of Mr. Wright's irresistible driving force, it challenges the modern mind as it has rarely been challenged in fiction. It is easy to disagree with, impossible to disregard.

James N. Rhea. *Providence Sunday Journal,* March 22, 1953.

For some time I have defended the writings of Richard Wright against the sneering criticism of several of my friends.

Well, at last Wright has delivered himself of a novel for which I have no defense. "The Outsider" is the worst novel I have ever read. But, paradoxically, it is interesting.

In a letter to his publishers Wright said that his hero, Cross Damon, probably would be "bewilderingly offensive" to 999 out of every 1000 American Negroes.

Damon is not bewilderingly offensive. He is pathetically insane, despite Wright's efforts to give him great intellectual powers.

The novel traces the murderous career of a Negro postal clerk from Chicago's South Side through the intricate maze of communism in New York.

Our hero permits his relatives and friends to believe he has been killed in a subway accident, goes name-hunting in a cemetery, fakes the identity of an unlamented Newark Negro, reads Nietzsche as proof of his intellect, and expresses all sorts of morbid opinions on the nature and destiny of mankind.

His general aim seems to be to depopulate the city of New York. In one scene intended to symbolize something or other he catches a Communist and a Fascist locked in mortal combat, seethes with disgust, and bashes in the skulls of both with a table leg.

This book was written in France. I don't know what goes on in literary circles over there, but if this sort of writing is the French vogue, I figure we could use a literary McCarran Act with some special French provisions.

Wright ought to catch up on race relations in America. They are bad enough, of course; but if there are white public officials in Newark, N.J., who openly ridicule Negroes as do two in this story, somebody ought to inform Newark Negroes about them.

The novel is filled with improbable incident and coincident. The unrealistic passages are at odds with the realistic framework.

Running through the book is an involved theory about the dark days ahead for mankind. This is probably sound—yet in projecting it Wright has hit an intellectual level miles above my head. It will be either over the head or beyond the immediate interest of the average reader, I fear.

However, the swift pace, clear style, weird action and mounting suspense make this awful novel a readable one. Without the intellectual and symbolic trappings, it might have been a corking good Mickey Spillane sort of thriller.

Sarah Patton Boyle. *Richmond Times-Dispatch,* March 22, 1953.

After eight years of comparative silence, Richard Wright, author of "Native Son," "Black Boy" and others, has written another book which is as well done and as depressing as these.

It concerns a young Negro who launches forth upon life possessed of a brilliant and cultivated mind but having neither emotional moorings nor spiritual goals. With all the power of his sensitive and tremendous longings, through one agonizing bewilderment after another, he strains to lift himself by the bootstraps of ratiocination onto a plateau of meaningful living. His final and hopeless failure is inevitable from the first.

Wright says that his hero could have been of any race. Yet into this melancholy story he has woven the moving theme that American Negroes, having been made "outsiders" in our nation, are forced by the very nature of their position to view life with a soul-shattering detachment. They share this fate, Wright shows, with the physically deformed, the crippled and all others who are set apart.

Wright himself points to the chief weakness of the book as though it were a strength. The story was, he says, "projected out of a heart preoccupied with no ideological burden. . . ." His characters are well drawn, the theme is gripping, and his style is firm and fresh. But has "a heart with no ideological burden" anything important to say to other hearts in an age when we have grown weary of mere negation for negation's sake? No matter how skillfully executed it may be, a novel without a central philosophy is like a picture without a center of interest.

Ted Poston. "Wright's Terrible 'Reality' Shocks in a Violent, Explosive New Novel." *New York Post,* March 22, 1953.

In his first novel in 13 years, Richard Wright has written an explosive story even more violent and disturbing than the "Native Son" which established him as one of the most gifted American writers of his time.

For Cross Damon, the hero of "The Outsider," is no uncomplicated, slum-shocked Bigger Thomas. He is a highly literate, well-read product of our civilization who becomes a cold-blooded killer because he rejects the very civilization which created him.

Damon, like Bigger Thomas, is a Negro, but as Wright points out repeatedly, he could have been of any race. And although the author rather belabors this point, the frightening thing about Damon is the thought that he may exist in any group, in any community.

You meet him as a seemingly innocuous Chicago postal clerk beset by more than his share of domestic difficulties, with a vindictive wife, an over-religious mother and a pregnant, teen-age mistress. But you find later that these are the least of his problems.

For, through his exhaustive reading of Nietzsche, Hegel, Kierkegaard and Dostoevsky, Cross Damon has come to reject humanity and civilization as we know it.

"Maybe the whole effort of man on earth to build a civilization is simply man's frantic attempt to hide himself from himself," he remarks at one point. "There is a part of man that man wants to reject. Man wants to keep from knowing what he is. . . . Maybe man is nothing in particular. 'Maybe' that's the terror of it."

The Communists, Damon believes, the real dedicated Communists recognize this instinctively. And so do all real totalitarians. And that is why they strive for power, real power. As Damon sees it:

> To hold absolute power over others, to define what they should love or fear, to decide if they were to live or die and thereby to ravage the whole of their beings—that was a sensuality that made sexual passion look pale by comparison. It was a noneconomic conception of existence.

So rejecting ALL beliefs, Damon goes his violent way, killing cold-bloodedly and in a manner that a Bigger Thomas could never envision. . . .

But "The Outsider" is no mere philosophical treatise. It is a fast-moving murder story which exploits all of the elements of the chase. And the characters are sharply drawn as only Wright could picture them.

There are Blount and Hilton, the dedicated Communists who chose him as a victim only to become victims themselves. There is Eva, the white girl who loves him and whom he destroys as surely he killed others who hated him.

Wright says that his novel is an attempt "to depict my sense of our contemporary living as I see it and feel it." He writes that "The Outsider" was "projected out of a heart preoccupied with no ideological burden save that of rendering an account of reality as it strikes my sensibilities and imagination."

Whether or not the reader agrees with his conception of reality, he will be engrossed by what will probably be one of the most controversial novels of the year.

Melvin Altshuler. "An Important, but Exasperating Book." *Washington Post*, March 22, 1953.

This much must be said—and at the outset—of Richard Wright's new book: That it is not at all a good novel, that it exasperates and abrades—but that it may be for its reader nearly as important a book as it was for its author.

It may be that Wright's greatest error in "The Outsider" was to start off with 65 pages worthy of any man, then—in an attempt to put across a rather unique set of contentions—to strain and torture his plot. Neither the plot nor his readers ever gets over those first 65 pages. . . .

Now as any musing reader of any newspaper knows, life has its little soap operas, its twists and turns of fate and plot. But to have so many as Wright has forced into what is basically a novel of ideas, is too much. If Mickey Spillane were to rewrite "The Outsider," even he—with his formula that nothing succeeds so well as excess—would not tax credulity as much as Wright has.

But "The Outsider" is a novel of ideas. So supposing that to match these divagations of plot there were a set of philosophical ideas—some worthy, but too many of them brummagem stuff? Well, we have this, too. Concepts so crass and gross that they could only have been uttered by the sophomore majoring in philosophy that Cross Damon is. Concepts ranging from, "Maybe man is nothing in particular . . ." to "Man is all we've got."

The result is not one book, but many of them—none complete and none really good: a pastiche, a potpourri, a mishmash. What Wright has tried to do cannot be done in the way Wright has chosen. It is as if a man were to buy a live horse, kill it, stuff it, mount three tires on it, and expect it to run on gasoline.

Then why is this book important?

First and preeminently, because as a pioneer and perhaps the finest Negro writer, Wright has produced a novel in which the least important thing about his main character is that he is a Negro.

Second, because of his concept of the "outsider." To be "Outside," in Wright's definition, is to be apart from the normal lives of men. To be the "outsider." To be "outside," in of difference as a vantage point to observe men and to know what and who they are. Cross Damon is an outsider because of his race. The hunchback District Attorney is an outsider because of his deformity. It is no new concept; Wright has merely explained it forthrightly, directly, almost formally. The pity is that his exposition gets lost in the welter.

Third, because Wright, once an active Communist, has written as good an analysis of the Communist's rite of power as can be found in any book.

Fourth, because despite its wanderings and waste, "The Outsider" is well written and well constructed. This merely adds to the exasperation.

In "Native Son," which still is Wright's best novel, Wright showed a complete understanding of and compassion for his race-ridden Bigger. That book was great. In "The Outsider," Wright has the D.A. call Damon "abandoned, fearful, without a form or discipline for living." And, although Wright could not have been expected to show compassion toward his cool quadruple slayer, he fails to make him understandable: his passionless slayer bears no relation to the Cross Damon of the first 65 pages. We can identify with the first Cross Damon, but not the later one. Wright goes out of his way to make this identification impossible.

But from "Native Son" to "The Outsider" is a gigantic step in the development of any writer of any race. Wright permits his publisher to say that, having cast out the "set of Marxist assumptions" which once guided his life and writings, he has conducted—and still conducts—an "uneasy search" for a "new attitude" to replace them.

When Wright has settled on this "new attitude"—perhaps he already has—he may well realize the immense potentialities he displayed in "Native Son" and which are still apparent, but distorted, in "The Outsider." There's a great book a-coming!

Roi Ottley. "Wright Adds a New Monster to the Gallery of the Dispossessed." *Chicago Sunday Tribune Magazine of Books*, March 22, 1953, p. 3.

The racially ubiquitous Richard Wright has created one more monster to add to his gallery of dispossessed people in his brutally explosive book. This time the main character is an intellectual Bigger Thomas, so to speak, who has read and absorbed the gloomy thoughts of Nietzsche, Hegel, Jaspers, Kierkegaard and Dostoevsky and concludes the world offers him little in the way of self-expression and self-fulfillment and proceeds to run amuck on a rampage involving betrayals, deceptions, lying, and murder.

The story, done in rapidly changing scenes, involves Cross Damon, a Negro postal clerk of Chicago's south side, who finds himself inextricably snarled in the rat race of domestic responsibilities. A freak subway accident, in which he is supposedly killed, offers him the opportunity to emancipate himself. He deserts his wife, two children, and destitute mother, and abandons a trusting girl. A friend who stumbles into a brothel where he is hiding discovers his secret and is tossed out the sixth floor window.

This, I presume, is merely the background to the real story Wright is telling. His hero escapes to Harlem, where he meets several Negro and white Communists. He gets involved in their machinations, and, in the process, betrays a Negro comrade, murders two party functionaries, a "white fascist," and drives to suicide a white girl who loves him.

The enormity of his crimes, which ordinary folk can't grasp, enables him to escape the law's detection. But the Communist party exacts its pound of flesh. As he dies, he murmurs, "I wanted to be free . . . to feel what I was worth . . . what living meant to me . . . I loved life too . . . much. And when asked, "And what did you find?" He answers, "Nothing."

I suspect Wright is mocking us with a ghastly joke. His main character, Cross Damon, was driven by no discernible motives—racial, political, or religious—even though the author would have us believe he is a rational person. Actually, he is not a Negro, but what Wright describes as the "psychological man."

Kent Ruth. "An Outsider Queries Why?" *Daily Oklahoman* (Oklahoma City), March 26, 1953.

This new novel by Negro Richard Wright—his first since "Native Son," published in 1940, and his first book of any kind since his autobiographical "Black Boy" appeared in 1945—is not easy to review. Nor, we'll wager, was it easy to write, for Outsider Cross Damon is, in many ways, a dramatic projection of Novelist Wright.

"Cross," one of his friends asks him on page 6, "you ain't never said how come you was reading all them books." "I was looking for something," he answered. "What?" the friend asked. "I don't know," Cross confessed. "Did you find it?" "No." A week or so later, on page 347—after he has abandoned his mother, his wife and three children, his pregnant mistress and a white call girl who had befriended him, calmly killed a fellow Chicago postal clerk to protect a secret, fled to New York and assumed a new identity, flirted with the Communist party and casually killed again—he admits to himself that the fault lay in the fact he "had had no party, no myths, no tradition, no race, no soil, no culture, and no ideas. . . ."

One day and 57 pages later, having lost everything, he mumbles: "I wish I had some way to give the meaning of my life to others . . . Tell them not to come down this road." His has been a brief, dazzling, tragic, fruitless career. Even when repelled by what he does, the reader is largely sympathetic with what it is . . . an outsider struggling blindly and tragically to find a purpose in life.

Psychologically Novelist Wright's case has not been too dissimilar. An outsider, even a one-time Chicago postal clerk, he joined the Communist party during the depression, left it ("The God that Failed") in 1944 to search for "a new attitude to replace the set of Marxist assumptions" that had guided his writing for ten years. And today he admits (as Cross Damon admitted to the end): "That uneasy search is still under way."

"The Outsider" is a powerful, if somewhat negative, picture of man struggling with, and in the end being destroyed by, life. The Negro-white communist-capitalist struggles, as Wright himself admits, are but secondary.

Jet Magazine, (March 26, 1953), 42.

A new novel by Richard Wright is a major literary event. It has been 13 years since his *Native Son* burst forth with searing power onto the book scene and overnight made the former WPA writer a top name in U. S. literature. Since then Wright has been silent in the field of fiction, although his autobiographical *Black Boy* was a big success in 1945. Living in France since 1946, Wright finally decided to write a long-delayed second novel. Called *The Outsider*, it will be one of the most-discussed books of our time.

The Outsider almost reads like a revised version of *Native Son*. Basically the plot is exactly the same. A Negro youth, unable to adjust to his Jim Crow environment, goes berserk and winds up a killer. Instead of Bigger Thomas, there is Cross Damon, who Wright attempts to portray as a kind of mixed-up intellectual. Instead of two murders, there are four that Damon commits. Perhaps the only basic difference in the two novels is that instead of making the Communist Party the hero of his book, the reds are now the villains.

Damon tangles with the party after some contrived melodrama that involves him in a spat with his wife and a Chicago subway wreck in which someone else's body is mistaken for his. Heading for Harlem with a new name, Cross becomes embroiled in some Communist shenanigans that finally lead to his downfall.

In *The Outsider* Wright still displays his terrific gift for writing brilliantly. But his almost psychopathic lust for violence gets the better of him in this second novel and his story becomes as completely phony and unreal as a cheap drugstore whodunit.

Arna Bontemps. *Saturday Review*, 36 (March 28, 1953), 15–16.

Richard Wright's boisterous new novel, "The Outsider" arrives like a band of brigands from the hills with horses snorting, guns blazing, bent on shooting up the town. It will be difficult to sleep through this new assault on our nerves. . . . Mr. Wright's novel reopens the intriguing and often disputed question of the Negro's place in contemporary American fiction.

In the past, of course, the central problem has been the stereotype, and perhaps it is wrong to place too much blame on the creative writer for the more or less standard portrayals of Negroes. We now know that there are minds that need such stereotypes for their comfort, that the root of the matter is a national attitude and that the recurrence of these over-simplified types cannot be honestly accounted for without reference to the sociological environment in which they exist.

In these terms it is possible to trace a sort of evolution of stereotypes. One recalls the shiftless, improvident, and musical predecessors of the slum-shocked Depression folk. New phantoms glide in as the older ones glide out, and the otherwise serious reader is consoled without being convinced. Thus it was, no doubt, that the latest racial stereotype of the Negro as problem emerged.

This was the prevailing attitude when Ralph Ellison's "Invisible Man" appeared last year. It is the dominant one this year as Wright's first novel since "Native Son" . . . comes up for attention.

When "Native Son" was published in 1940, Richard Wright was given the acclaim usually reserved for writers of major importance. Thousands of readers were shocked speechless by it, and most of them had not completely recovered five years later when "Black Boy" was published. By this time Wright's position in the ranks of American writers seemed clear. That this was the most impressive literary talent yet produced by Negro America was only rarely disputed. Interest in him as a personality was widespread.

The fact that he was largely self-educated and that he sprang from the sharecropping element in Mississippi served to point up the sharpness of his insights, the restlessness of his mind. While much of his strength was in his narrative power, much more was in the freshness of his vision, his daring exploration of a more or less taboo subject matter. Readers detected a correlation between his own odyssey and the world of fiction and semi-fiction which he created.

His first book, for example, "Uncle Tom's Children," reflected his discovery of Communism and his application of this dogma to the struggles of a sensitive migrant boy newly arrived in Chicago's black belt. "Native Son" came next, and again the writer's frame of reference was Communism; but equally apparent here was his preoccupation with another discipline quite new to him, sociology. "Black Boy" was written while Wright was learning about psychoanalysis and reflects an awakened interest in the subconscious roots of personality.

"The Outsider," his first book in eight years, and his first novel in thirteen, has now appeared, and almost the first observation one can make of it is that the black boy from Mississippi is still exploring. He has had a roll in the hay with the existentialism of Sartre, and apparently he liked it. Wright went to France with his family in 1948. This would have been true to form for almost any American writer, ready to enjoy the fruits of two best sellers in a row. For the boy who had not been allowed to draw books from the main public library in Memphis, it was more than understandable.

But what would it do to him as a writer, some asked. Certainly the works on which his reputation was based had been sparked by anger, anger at indignities and racial discrimination. Would Wright be able to write at all away from the conditions that riled him? Months and years passed with no word from Wright. Nelson Algren charged him with powdering-out on his old stamping grounds, and Wright admitted to someone that he had café-itis. He was sitting and enjoying himself. He was reading and thinking. If he was writing, he was not telling anyone about it. And if this was the whole story, who could blame him?

Oddly enough, however, Richard Wright has gone back to the Chicago of his earlier books for the people and the situations of the novel he was writing meanwhile. Cross Damon is a postal clerk with a college education. Nervous, disturbed, drinking too much—even in the opinion of his hearty, non-critical buddies—he carries on his mind a problem which he cannot share. It is this problem which Wright, the good storyteller, sets out to unravel, and knowing Wright, one soon suspects that he knows where it is going. But one is mistaken.

Cross Damon's problem has nothing to do with color. This may surprise those who have been led to believe that all Negroes on the south side of Chicago eat, sleep, and breathe racial thoughts. Cross's difficulty is much older and even more puzzling. Its name is woman.

A more hag-ridden young man than the fretting and sweating hero of "The Outsider" is hard to imagine. His wife, mother, and sweetheart are closing in on him as the story opens. While refusing to divorce him, the wife from whom he is separated increases her demands beyond all conscience. The mother pounds at him for his drinking and wenching and his neglect of her. The sweetheart, whom he has gotten in trouble, reveals that she is two years younger than he had known and that makes him guilty of statutory rape in Illinois; she can send him to prison. Hopelessly trapped, Cross yields to his wife's blackmail and borrows $800 against his salary. He has boarded the subway with the cash in his pocket when his deliverance comes: a hideous wreck.

When he drags himself out of the mess of glass and steel and makes his way to the platform, nurses, doctors, and crowds of people are waiting. But Cross is all right. He can walk to the ambulance. The attention of the bystanders shifts back to the broken bodies still being rescued, and Cross remembers that he has left his overcoat in the wreckage. Well, never mind. And never mind about that ambulance. The attention of the bystanders shifts back to the broken stretcher on which a hopelessly mangled body is carried, he doesn't bother. He heads for a restaurant. He is at a table waiting for his order when the radio bulletins begin to come over the air. Soon the announcer is naming victims. Cross hears his own name called. That gives him the notion that is crucial to Wright's story. He will play dead. He will run away, take a new name, make a new life.

The second-half of the novel is the author's account of this strange flight by a man whose furies are many. Almost immediately Cross starts killing through fear, and a string of murders dot his trail thereafter. He meets a Communist and decides to join the Party as a means of giving himself some sort of identity, though he has no interest in its aims. He finds love as he rushes feverishly, but by then the end is clear. He can neither escape from himself nor from the society in which he lives.

Richard Wright's mind has always run to melodrama, and in "The Outsider" it does just that, but with him melodrama is a device rather than an end. His real concern is with such matters as his hero's awareness of "his body as an alien and despised object over which he had no power, a burden that was always cheating him of the fruits of this thoughts," with his version of the time-honored debate between body and soul, with "woman as body of woman," with guilt, with fear, and with the havoc that can follow them. Cross's dilemma in his story is that "each act of his consciousness sought to drag him back to what he wanted to flee." As Wright tells it, "The Outsider" makes gripping reading. . . .

"Native Doesn't Live Here." *Time*, 61 (March 30, 1953), 90–92.

When Novelist Richard Wright was a teen-ager in the South, he once forged a note and handed it to the local librarian: "Please let this nigger boy have the following books." Among the books he wanted was Dostoevsky's *Poor People*. From his own bitter experience of life, young Wright already knew just about all there was to know about poor people; he was looking for other kinds of enlightenment—eye-openers for young writers. In Dostoevsky he found his eye-opener, and in world Communism his herald. Less than 20 years later, Moscow's critics were comparing Mississippi's Richard Wright to his Russian model.

It was *Native Son* that prompted the comparison, a powerful, brutal reminder of black resentment and confusion in a white man's capitalistic world. It made Wright at 31 a world-famed author and the literary darling of the Communists. His new novel, *The Outsider,* will hardly add to his reputation on either front.

The Outsider of the novel is Cross Damon, a Chicago Negro mail carrier (Wright was once a post-office clerk in Chicago). Cross, a discontented man with a vast appetite for sex and drink, is married, but separated from his wife Gladys and their three children. His newest sweetheart is pregnant, under the age of consent, and threatening him with jail if he doesn't divorce his wife and marry her. His wife Gladys feels well rid of Cross but won't divorce him. His dilemma is solved by a subway accident. Cross heads for New York.

In Harlem, Cross gets tangled up with the Communist Party, but sees through it almost at once. In quick succession he kills two top Communists as well as his landlord. The wife of one of the Communists, a white woman, becomes his mistress, but commits suicide when Cross is exposed as a murderer.

Novelist Wright, now disillusioned with his Communist friends, writes from the thesis that Cross Damon, weakling and murderer, is the victim of a world bereft of values and decency, haunted by fear and peopled by despairing creatures who have quit on life. Damon, he says, could be any man, black or white, not just a pushed-around Negro. Moreover, Wright argues, the whole world, including the U.S., is getting worse and is in for a totalitarian age. The Soviet Union, though he now rejects it, is not much worse than any place else. As a novelist, Wright has resorted to so much ludicrous coincidence, unlikely conversation and soapbox bombast that his story becomes a bore.

While Wright sits out the threat of totalitarianism in Paris, an abler U.S. Negro novelist sees the problem of his race differently. Says Ralph (*Invisible Man*) Ellison: "After all, my people have been here for a long time. . . . It is a big, wonderful country, and you can't just turn away from it because some people decide it isn't your country."

M. D. Reagan. "Violent Search for Freedom." *America*, 89 (April 4, 1953), 20.

The person who is *in*, but not *of*, a given culture is in a uniquely advantageous position to understand the problems of that culture. But such a man is often also cursed with a clear realization of society's evils, of the fear and brutality hidden from most men by their emotional dependence on the society in which they live.

Such freedom from the dominant myths and involvements of society may cause a man to seek within himself a solution to the problem of human existence, or he may succumb to fear and, being alienated from society, become a tool of any organization which promises to give his life a purpose larger than self-gratification. In our time, the breakdown of the Judeo-Christian tradition has left vast masses of people of the West without a society in which they can believe. Fascism and communism have resulted.

Most men accept uncomplainingly a burdensome web of social obligations tieing them to the existing social organization, no matter how unsatisfactory it may be. But others possess a "sharp sense of freedom" that somehow escapes "being dulled by intimidating conditions." Cross Damon, the protagonist of Richard Wright's first novel since *Native Son* (1940), is one of the latter type, an "outsider" who bolts his self-burdened life in Negro Chicago, becomes entangled with the Communist Party in New York but revolts against it with direct violence, and dies while attempting escape to a freedom that will not be found.

As elements of surprise and suspense are basic to Mr. Wright's plot, it would be unfair to author or reader to disclose its pattern. There need be no doubt, though, of the story's interest. It is a raw, violent and lightning paced novel. A little too raw sexually, but otherwise a craftsmanlike job and tremendously exciting as a tale of modern adventure and suspense.

The greater importance of *The Outsider* lies in its thoughtful portrayal of a man searching vainly for personal freedom in our society. The dominant characteristic of man today, says Wright, "is an enormous propensity toward fear." Science and industrialization have uprooted man and de-personalized his life. "There is no modern industrial nation on earth today that makes decisions based upon anything remotely resembling the injunctions of the Old or New Testaments . . . God no longer really concerns us." As we don't know what else to live by, fascism and communism enter the scene as religion-substitutes, and multitudes of anxious men are used by the leaders of these false social organizations in their quest of naked power.

There are many who want to fight this power by force of arms, but that won't work because "communism and fascism are but the political expressions of the twentieth century's atheistic way of life." War can't smash atheism. But because modern society fears to admit that it is atheistic, it brands as a criminal any man who cannot in conscience live by the godless society's rules. Lacking the courage to be free, we enslave ourselves in a rotting civilization. The man who would be free finds himself an outsider.

This is the message of a perceptive ex-Communist who happens to be an American Negro. The Christian will endorse its protest while regretting the author's characterization of Christianity as a myth contributing to man's blindness toward the "real world." *The Outsider* is a bold and significant book—for the sophisticated reader with a strong stomach.

Lewis Vogler. "Once Again Richard Wright Has Written a Controversial Novel." *San Francisco Chronicle,* April 5, 1953, p. 19.

The dread which undermines a world grown in power, the guilt and anxiety in which man's search for values has bogged down, above all, man's fear of himself and his bewildering universe—these are obsessive themes in modern writing.

Richard Wright's first book in several years is a striking attempt to examine man's spiritual quandary. Strongly Existentialist in tone, "The Outsider" is a violent, troubled novel—not for the squeamish, still less for those who are disinclined to admit the psychological realities of industrial civilization.

The story of Cross Damon, a young Negro caught in dangerous political currents, is one Mr. Wright is particularly suited to tell. Readers of "Native Son" and his autobiographical "Black

Boy" will recall how powerfully he writes of the problems of his race. His rejection of the Communist Party in 1944, after ten years of active membership, suggests that he is in an excellent position to know of its attractions as well as its real motives and practices.

Although Cross Damon is an outsider by race, it is more important that he is alienated by intellect. Sensitive, weak-willed, humiliated by the terms of all human existence, he has read and thought his way through most of the illusions which surround men's activities, has become "convinced that bad faith of some degree was an indigenous part of living." He is, when the reader first meets him, a post office employee in Chicago. He is caught in a pattern of self-loathing, and hatred (as well as sympathy) for the three women through whom he believes he has allowed his life to get out of control: His mother, whose Christian moral strictures had aroused in him the very desires they were meant to stifle; his wife, Gladys, whom he has tortured into releasing him from family life and the care of their three children; and Dot, his 16-year-old mistress whose unborn child threatens his hope for decent behavior still further.

At this crisis in his affairs, a terrifying subway crash offers him a way out, a chance to change his desperate identity. As Cross, who has escaped stunned but almost uninjured reads of his death and this awareness grows in him, so does the complexity of beginning again. He is uncertain that he wants so uneasy a freedom until it is accidentally threatened and he finds he has killed an innocent friend to preserve it.

Fleeing to New York, a nameless Orestes, suspicious of the world of strangers, uncertain how to plan a life on his own assumptions, he is witness to an unpleasant incident on the train—an accident which is to seal his destiny. It involves him with Ely Houston, a celebrated District Attorney—also an outsider—who is to become a strange kind of spiritual father as well as Grand Inquisitor. It draws him, in still another direction, into an orbit of Communist activity.

Assuming a dead man's name, he is taken by Gil Blount, a member of the Central Committee, to live in his apartment as an open affront to Gil's Fascistic landlord, Herndon. Emotionally attracted to Communism, feeling greater affinities with its turbulent spirit than with its professed aims, believing almost religiously that it was "the one thing that could transform his sense of dread," Cross is soon shocked by Party ruthlessness and cynicism, by a bad faith greater than he had dreamed could exist.

He is soon aware that the Party is using him—as they are also using Gil's wife, Eva, a painter who later becomes Cross' mistress. Cross is rapidly drawn into a nightmare of violence: in sickeningly brutal scenes he kills again—not once, but three times more.

Guilt-fevered, he confesses only to the unbelieving Eva Blount. Realizing slowly that it will be difficult to prove him guilty, that he is suspected only because of his unknown past, he submits cooly to relentless questioning by Blimin, a Party leader, and later by Ely Houston. It is at this point, as Cross is being brought to a rough kind of justice outside the law, that Mr. Wright's novel widens into a full-scale ideological melodrama which allows him to elaborate his views of the human condition and the Twentieth Century's totalitarian drift.

What the reader did not learn of Wright's renunciation of Communism in "The God That Failed" is given here in dramatic detail. Since the author is equally critical of other power systems and sees only worse absolutes to come, his book may here occasionally arouse the ubiquitous Herndons. (When Cross Damon explained to the landlord that he was anti-Communist, Herndon shrieked: "I don't care what kind of Communist you are!"—the nearest thing to humor in the book.)

The revolutionary Communists Wright sees as super-cynical intellectuals seeking naked power by exploiting men's fears while pretending reason: "These jealous rebels are sustained by a sense of the total meaning—or lack of meaning—of human life on this earth."

It is significant that Mr. Wright's—or at least Cross Damon's—interpretation of modern life lies now almost entirely in individual and subjective terms. Fear, he believes, may well be the most important part of it.

As industrial man's science has shorn him of the myths which used to placate his dread, and of his faith in his religion, he has been left with nothing but fear of himself and hatred of his world. Both Communism and Fascism are only expressions of man's atheism, systems of power which exploit this fear. The individual who can no longer accept myths, even the new totalitarian ones, may become as dehumanized as Cross Damon. He may be driven by fear and the nameless guilt he cannot expiate to an objectification of it in violence.

This is the man the author has sought to portray, the tortured nihilist, a man who kills not quite in the motiveless "acte gratuit" of Andre Gide, for example, but because his sense of life is outraged, because he is confronted by reality. A dangerous man, both effect and cause of dangerous times.

As Mr. Wright sees him, Cross Damon is symbolic of all mankind whose sense of life needs correcting. If Cross Damon's reading has been Nietzsche, Hegel, Jaspers, Heidegger, Husserl, Kierkegaard and Dostoevsky, it is fairly obvious that Ely Houston's has also included Ortega y Gassett for he observes that Damon has acted "individually just as modern man lives in the mass every day."

"The Outsider" has faults as a novel, but it is never dull. While it may seem over-plotted and while Cross Damon, whatever his psychological or symbolic validity, does not always emerge as a convincing human being, it is a tribute to Mr. Wright's power as a writer that he has given even the ideological portions of his book a strong sense of urgency. He has also left them open to controversy. It is not precisely news that man's fears make him dangerous, but it is a profound truth all the same.

The author indicates that he is still searching for a "new attitude to replace the Marxist assumptions which in the past more or less guided the direction of my writings." "The Outsider" indicates that he is currently having an uneasy time of it in the Existentialist part of the maze. One suspects that the act of searching, even though it leads through all these alleys of dread, is better than attempting to ignore the labyrinth.

Harvey Curtis Webster. "Richard Wright's Profound New Novel." *The New Leader*, 36 (April 6, 1953), 17–18.

The first thing I must say about Richard Wright's *The Outsider* is that I have spent the greater part of four days reading and rereading it, thinking and writing about it. I do not say this to prove my conscientiousness, but to show the degree of my interest, the extent of my confusion, and the extent of the novel's complexity. *The Outsider* is an exasperating, exciting, profound, careless and (perhaps) great novel. Beside it, Ralph Ellison's *Invisible Man* seems almost simple; beside it, all the other novels written by Negroes seem almost inconsequential. I do not say this to depreciate Ralph Ellison's excellent book or to depreciate the very good fiction other Negroes have written. I say it to indicate that I think Richard Wright has a legitimate claim to rank with Hemingway, Mann, Gide and Faulkner as one of the possibly great novelists of our time.

The good but not great writer is distinguished often by the horizontal line of his development. Like Maugham or Edith Wharton or Sherwood Anderson, he seizes a significance and exploits it in a series of books that are inferior or superior to each other largely because they less or more adequately convey an insight that does not change fundamentally. The graph of a great writer's career looks like jagged ups and downs that go more up than down.

Faulkner descended to *Sanctuary,* ascended to *Light in August,* rose to *Intruder in the Dust* (that uneven great book), went down to *Knight's Gambit,* possibly went up to *Requiem for a Nun,* which I have not read. Hemingway's insight and craft progressed from *In Our Time* to *Farewell to Arms,* regressed or digressed until *For Whom the Bell Tolls,* fell sharply in *Across the River and Into the Trees,* rose sharply in *The Old Man and the Sea.* Similar chartings could be made for probably great novelists as ancient as Fielding, as modern as Robert Penn Warren. The writer who may last is always obsessed by the search for answers and sometimes fumbles because he tries to encompass so much. The good writer rarely overreaches himself; sometimes he descends in craft, but his insight never changes basically. He does not grow, he persists.

Anyone who read *Uncle Tom's Children* realized that Richard Wright was a writer of great talent wedded to dogmas of dangerous simplicity. The power of "Big Boy Leaves Home" and "Bright and Morning Star" is indubitable. A unifying faith in the blackness of white oppressors and the whiteness of exploited Negroes is matched by a craft that selects always enough, never too much.

Native Son was more imperfect, more ambitious, and better. Bigger Thomas's problems were magnificently realized and so were his emotionally inevitable acts; the talk that was supposed to lead toward a solution of Everyman's problems read more like a handbook of Marxism than what the characters would have said naturally.

Black Boy was a moving, exaggerated account of one Negro's experience with the South; most of its pages were memorable; few of them displayed the insight into America's dilemma—its feeling of guilt about both white and black prejudice—one might expect from as intelligent a writer as Wright.

In these, his first three books, Wright showed an ascending and descending grasp of himself and the world he did not make. In none of them was there the faltering brilliance one finds in the novel he has written after eight years of thoughtful and probably tortured silence, *The Outsider*.

The plot is as violent and implausible as that of *Hamlet*. Cross Damon—in his spare time a student of philosophy at the University of Chicago, in his working time an employee of the Post Office—marries Gladys because he desires to desire her, falls out of love with her because his commitment to marriage keeps him from realizing himself as the free, existential man. Desire for desire makes him fall in love with Dot, a young Negro girl who inhibits his hope for freedom when she becomes pregnant and wants to force divorce and marriage upon him. A convenient accident enables him to let Gladys, Dot and his oppressively religious mother (who made him think of God as the great No he must negate) believe he is dead, and permits him to start a new life in which he thinks he will be unencumbered. When he is discovered by an old friend, he kills to preserve his freedom and goes to New York to assume a new identity.

Once he has escaped, presumably, the cramping circumstances he compulsively willed to be his past, he tries to put into practice his belief that he can make himself. But it is not long before he allies his outsideness with that of the Communists. Tentatively, he joins forces with Gil Blount and Jack Hilton—members of the Central Committee of the Communist party—and fights against the fascist Herndon, who heads a group that wants to preserve apartments for "pure" Anglo-Saxons. Cross's hatred of these three who conspire to become the little god he himself would like to be leads him to kill Blount, Hilton and Herndon as well as to compel the suicide of Eva Blount, the one woman he nearly succeeds in loving; and it ultimately leads him to be liquidated by the party he hates because it denies his freedom to become a little god himself.

Most of this action might, but probably would not, have happened. It is doubtful that the most atheistic existentialist would have harried his mother, his wife and his mistresses as Cross Damon did. It is improbable that he would have killed the friend who could have proven him alive and vulnerable to responsibility, that he would have assumed godship in killing Herndon, Blount and Hilton. These events, nevertheless, are made plausible by the eloquent force of Wright's prose, and, even if esthetic implausibility enters in, as when Cross out-talks at great uninterrupted length a top Communist functionary, one is excited by what is said even as one disbelieves that it ever was said. It is also extremely unlikely that Houston, the New York district attorney and the most interesting talker in the book, would say, after discovering Cross's murders, that he will let him be his own judge and executioner, but Houston's decision seems esthetically and morally right. In other words, implausibilities, artistic and inartistic—as unlikely as the ghost of Hamlet's father, the killing of Polonius, and the callous treatment of

Ophelia—are essential parts of this novel, which is as true a lie as Kafka's *The Castle* and as moving an unlikelihood as *Crime and Punishment.*

The center of *The Outsider* is the thought-obsessed inability to feel of Cross Damon, who exaggerates but does not distort the potentialities of the modern intellectual. Cross is an outsider more because he is an intellectual than because he is a Negro. An atheist who cannot find a focus outside himself, he thinks he must create values peculiar to himself. Divorced by both knowledge and race from his own culture, which he nevertheless lives inside of and understands, Cross becomes an ethical criminal, "one of the millions of men who lived in the tiny crevices of industrial society completely cut off from humanity, the multitudes of little gods who ruled their own private worlds and acknowledged no outside authority."

His chief problem is "the relationship of himself to himself," how to callous [sic] the fear that is universal, how to become reconciled to the terms of existence he believes every sensitive man must accept and wish to reject. Cross's is not the humiliation of Bigger Thomas; ignorance does not enter in at all, race only as it makes him an outsider who knows better than the complacent and accepts with anguish what the insider easily accepts. Significantly, most of his ideas are shared by the hunchback district attorney, Houston, and it is implied that any intellectual alienated from the grosser stupidities of his culture and compelled to seek an idiosyncratic faith is, like Cross, an outsider. Like Ivan Karamazov and Hamlet, Cross is driven into a horrible objectivity that is based upon the dreadful subjectivity of the intellectual who knows or thinks he knows what he must accept and hate.

In summarizing the complicated and often confusing (if not confused) meaning of *The Outsider,* I oversimplify and amputate. Wright's novel is also about how men who live without God may be destined to live without hope and in perpetual fear and anxiety, about how the liberals who sustained the values of Christianity without believing in its sanctions have inevitably tended toward a position that could produce George Orwell's *1984.* It is arguable that *The Outsider* strives with the imperfection of genius to demonstrate both the emotional and humane undesirability of existentialism and its rational possibility. When Cross is dying after his execution by the Communists, which Wright has described with the plausible improbability one has come to expect in the books by the most wounded of ex-Communists, he tells Houston, his counterpart in everything but action, that he in his lonely, anarchic search for meaning found "Nothing." "Never alone. . . . Alone a man is nothing. Man is a promise that he must never break."

If one can take this to be the deepest meaning of a novel that proliferates other importances on almost every page—and I so take it—then Wright has come a long way from his naive and justified resentment of white folks, a long way beyond and above Communism and existentialism, a long way toward a theory of man in our universe that may enable him to write novels better than he has yet written and as good as those that have been written by the best outsiders of our century. Whatever and however, *The Outsider* is one of the most tantalizingly imperfect novels of the past two decades. In its great imperfection, it belongs with those other novels that enbale us to understand the cursed condition of humanity, which is born to one law and to another bound.

Marjorie Crow Hughes. "Anguish." *Commonweal,* 58 (April 10, 1953), 29–31.

Mr. Wright's new book is a novel of ideas which examines life in the light of modern philosophies. It struck this reviewer as a sort of morality play with ideologies acting the vices—and the virtues left out.

The hero of *The Outsider,* named with rather fuzzy symbolism, Cross Damon, represents twentieth century man in frenzied pursuit of freedom. Cross is an intellectual Negro, the product of a culture which rejects him. He is further alienated by his "habit of incessant reflection," his feeling that the experiences and actions of his life have so far taken place without his free assent, and a profound conviction that there must be more to life, some meaning and justification which have hitherto eluded him.

When Cross is introduced in the first pages of the novel he is drinking too much, partly in an effort to forget his problems (of which he has many) but mostly to deaden the pain caused by his urgent and frustrated sense of life. There is an accident in which he is reported dead and so he sets out to create his own identity, control his own destiny, and thus, he hopes, to discover truth.

This search for the absolute compels him to four murders and ends in his despair and violent death. En route, he encounters totalitarianism in its most-likely-to-succeed form, Communism. Though he agrees with these other "outsiders" that power is the central reality of society and that "man is nothing in particular," he is outraged by their acceptance and cynical exploitation of these "facts." "That's not enough," he screams before he kills a Communist who has just told him that there is no more to life. And in the same conversation he asks, "What's suffering?"

Having rejected religion, the past and present organization of society, the proposed totalitarian alternative and the kindred uncontrollable violence of his own behavior as a "free" man, Cross abandons ideas and pins his last hope on love. But his mistress commits suicide when she sees him as he is.

There follows a fascinating chapter in which the law, personified by a hunchbacked district attorney who understands Damon Cross, convicts him of crime and condemns him, but is powerless to give his life significance by punishment. After this, Cross is murdered and dies murmuring, "It was horrible."

In spite of the analytical clarity with which the roots of the modern dilemma are exposed, this is a confusing and unconvincing book intellectually. Rationalism is evil, it seems to say, a road leading nowhere traveled by a monstrous superman; but around the very next bend truth may perhaps be found and superman will then be free and good—perhaps.

Mr. Wright, or at least Mr. Wright's hero, is so hypnotized by what the evil man does individually and socially that he is aware of little else. None of the chief characters is consistently believable as a human being, though this is perhaps inevitable in a novel of ideas. The writing is marred, particularly in the first chapters, by clinical shortcuts, little paragraphs describing character in psychoanalytic terms.

Nevertheless, *The Outsider* is a work of tremendous emotional power. It elicits the *feel* of the chaotic twentieth century—frustration, confusion, anxiety, violence, conflict in action and paralysis in thought, all the terrible panic of man in a shaken world—with a breadth and accuracy that are almost overwhelming. And the interior life of proud Cross Damon, with its dark descent through doubt and fear to anguish, despair and emptiness, has a harrowing reality which could be achieved only by an artist of exceptional sincerity and unusual perception.

"Reverie of Frustration." *The Nation,* 176 (April 18, 1953), 331–32.

Richard Wright and Henry Miller are among the few writers of stature who emerged from the transitional period of the 1940's, when the older generation went sour. For that reason, the failure of Wright's new novel is deplorable; it betrays our hopes as well as his. The story, despite some excellent scenes of realism in Wright's old manner, is symbolistic in structure. Quite like Ralph Ellison's "Invisible Man," it presents the predicament of the Negro intellectual, separated from his race, disenchanted with communism and perhaps all political salvations, attempting to evaluate the meaning of an existence that is completely in the void.

There are remarkable passages in the narrative. The analysis of the "sensuality of power" in the Communist mentality is devastating. Rejecting Ellison's meliorism, Wright's "hungry mind" explores the farthest extremes of desperation and surveys almost every unpleasant aspect of the Negro's social status, or lack of status. But these intellectual sorties—a kind of incessant, compulsive reverie of frustration—gain their brilliance at the expense of the narrative itself, during which the hero becomes an abstract monster, and even murder is only the occasion for another bout of introspection. Perhaps Wright can profit from the career of Jack London, who traversed much the same literary path from illegitimacy to paranoia. In any case the book is bad, but only as a work of genuine talent can be bad, and nevertheless full of interest.

Roland Sawyer. "About a Monomaniac." *Christian Science Monitor,* April 30, 1953, p. 11.

On the ground floor of the Library of Congress there is a shelf where cast-off books can be purchased for 10 cents each. You will find odd items on these shelves, manuals on how to operate shucking machines, social registers, pamphlets proclaiming to be divine revelations of life. No publisher would touch these latter monographs whose authors have printed their own copies by this inexpensive device. Few readers understand what these particular authors are trying to say and, indeed, they represent a sort of lunatic fringe.

This book by Richard Wright, his fourth, might not be out of place on the Library of Congress's cast-off shelf. It cerainly represents a fringe of thinking comparable to certain of these mimeographed treatises, although it is incomparably better written.

These are harsh words to say about a work of a writer of the technical caliber of Richard Wright and I suppose they represent an intensely personal reaction. But this is a sordid, sensual, sanguinary, story of a not very enterprising young man who had a reasonably decent start in life yet, because of his own exceptional psychological mentality, became steeped in alcoholic and animal lusts. These take him across 400 pages of rapid, violent destruction to himself and six other people.

Why should such a book be published? Because Mr. Wright is the leading Negro author of the United States today—though living in Paris—who has written three books of standing—"Native Son," the novel which made his reputation in 1940; "Black Boy," his autobiography up to the point of his leaving the South, which was an impressive social document of 1945; and more recently [sic], a collection of short stories, "Uncle Tom's Children." All three of these books spoke out in behalf of the Negro people in the United States. Mr. Wright has an audience and deserves serious consideration.

"The Outsider" marks, let us hope, only a dip in Mr. Wright's literary journey. His competence as a wordsmith is still with him, but a writer must be more than that. He must be a designer, an architect, as well as a carpenter.

There are, to be sure, humans such as Cross Damon, the Chicago "outsider" and Negro who was a monomaniac. But what does a theme of a man's self-destruction, told detail by detail, contribute when it primarily illustrates the weaknesses of humans, as the fault, rather than some injustice of society?

Literature is the stuff of centuries and it is hard enough for any of us to read, within a lifetime, "the best that has been said and thought in the world." Only a few have time for books such as "The Outsider"—or those obscure monographs of fringe thinking to be found on that shelf in the Library of Congress.

Lorraine Hansberry. *Freedom,* 14 (April 1953), 7.

Remembering Richard Wright's *Black Boy* and *Native Son*, certain sharp literary experiences yet hang in our minds. Experiences etched hard and true by the skill of the young Negro writer from the South. We remember, that whatever his weaknesses as a writer—he had power. He had the ability to scoop out the filth and sickness of white supermacy and present it to his readers with a stark and terrible realism. And we still remember how that power almost realized itself once when a strong hint of its mighty potential escaped in a short story called *Bright and Morning Star*.

It is 18 years since Richard Wright wrote that powerful little glimpse of the promise of dignity achieved through human struggle. And now Richard Wright has written *The Outsider.*

The Outsider is a story of sheer violence, death and disgusting spectacle, written by a man who has seemingly come to despise humanity. The hero is Cross Damon, a twenty-six year old Negro postal clerk on Chicago's Southside. For 45 pages Wright describes Damon's deterioration into a drunkard who leaves his wife and children, has an affair with a fifteen year old girl, murders one of his best friends, fakes a new identity and murders three other people and finally winds up being shot in the street by some grotesque characters who are supposed to be agents of the Communist Party. And that is the story.

Cross Damon is someone you will never meet on the Southside of Chicago or in Harlem. For if he is anything at all, he is the symbol of Wright's new philosophy—the glorification of—nothingness.

Richard Wright has been away from home for a long time. He has forgotten which of the streets of the Southside lie south of others, an insignificant error, except that it points up how much he has forgotten other things. In one passage he describes in great detail the contents of a garbage can. And a stark, real description it is. But nowhere in his four hundred pages can he bring himself to describe—say, the beauty or strength in the eyes of the working people of the Southside. It seems that he has forgotten.

As a propaganda piece for the enemies of the Negro people, of working people and of peace, *The Outsider* has already been saluted with a full page spread of praise by the *New York Times Sunday Book Supplement* (3-22-53). On the other hand it has been appointed to the trash category by the Negro newsweekly, *Jet* (3-20-53) which summed the book up simply and accurately, ". . . his almost psychopathic lust for violence gets the better of him in this second novel and his story becomes as completely phony and unreal as a cheap drugstore whodunit."

Such is the pronouncement on Negro America's onetime most promising writer. Richard Wright is correct in one thing: he is an outsider, he is outcast from his own people. He exalts brutality and nothingness; he negates the reality of our struggle for freedom and yet works energetically in behalf of our oppressors; he has lost his own dignity and destroyed his talent. He has lost the bright and morning star—but the Negro people have not.

R. F. Grady, S.J.
Best Sellers, 13 (May 1, 1953), 24–25.

A novel of violence that is also honest, a novel portraying some of the pagan depravity possible among men and women in modern cities which yet preserves a decent reticence, a novel concerned with racial and political strife which yet maintains an objectivity of observation and emotion, deserves commendation to readers adult and mature enough to know that living is not all sunshine and sweetness and that human beings are capable of monstrous crimes and hideously pathetic confusion. Such a novel is Richard Wright's *The Outsider.* It is a second novel and, in my opinion, much superior to his first novel, *Native Son,* published more than a decade ago. Mr. Wright has a superior talent and a superior intelligence. He should be recognized, too, as one of the few American writers who is interested in why people do what they do; not merely what they do.

Cross Damon, the central figure of this novel, one of "the outsiders" by reason of his race, his turbulence of spirit, his quest for some answer to what appears to him the futility of being, and also by reason of his crimes, is no hero of gallantry and chivalry. He is, however, very much like any of hundreds or thousands of urban dwellers, white or black or yellow, American, European, Asiatic. In spite of his mother's prayerful devotion and entreaties, in spite of his indiscriminating reading and his interrupted collegiate studies, in spite of a mind that is curious and able to probe for causes, he has no guiding philosophy, no spiritual anchors. Actually, his being a Negro is not the reason for his being "outside" at all; his color is only one factor and by no means the major factor. What makes Cross Damon an outsider is common to men of all colors and nationalities.

Cross Damon had had to give up his studies in psychology when he married. His marriage is far from happy and he has sought solace in other women, particularly with a young wanton whose possessive insistence began finally to bore and frighten him. He has a good job in the Chicago Post office, but his drinking and his marital disputes threaten to take that from him. In a subway accident, that is more dramatic than probable, Cross Damon escapes only to realize that someone else's body has been identified as his. His identity wiped out with his apparent death, he goes to New York and becomes involved with a group of Communists, headed by Gilbert Blount.

Thinking to use Damon as a party "weapon" to win publicity for the Party's boast of championing the black against the white, Blount invites the fugitive to share his apartment, knowing that the landlord will object furiously. In the inevitable fight that develops between Blount and the landlord, Damon intervenes only to kill both; thinking, thus, to free Blount's wife, Eva, from the tyranny of her husband. Eva falls in love with Cross and then commits suicide when Cross is arrested on suspicion of murdering Blount's superior, Hilton, as well as Herndon and Gilbert. His nemesis proves to be a shrewdly loquacious lawyer, Ely Houston, whom he had met on the train from Chicago to New York and who is not only New York District Attorney but strangely sympathetic and understanding of Damon's outlook on life.

Taken by itself, the story line of this novel may well strike a reader as melodramatic; and there are coincidences at which many a reviewer and reader may raise an eyebrow. But the story line is made probable enough by the writing and by the character of Cross Damon as Mr. Wright portrays him. And Mr. Wright is using his fictional character to thrash out some of his own perplexities and to present his scornful hatred of the unscrupulous perfidy of the Communist Party and its zealots. Something of the cynical disillusionment and desperate idealism of the existentialist philosophy seems to be all that Cross Damon or D. A. Houston can salvage from the morass of machine-age urban life. Deliberately, even defiantly—or, perhaps more precisely in despair and disillusionment—both reject religion, because the only manifestation they know of religion is one of emotions, a kind of hysterical faith. What is left them to base their philosophy on is only the chimaera of humanism, a philosophy of man for man which carries with it its own disillusionment and despair. They reject religion because it seems to them unable to *do* anything; to offer only an irrational escape, blind flight from reality.

For those who are willing to think about some of the basic problems that confront the confused millions who acknowledge no faith, and who do not expect every novel to be both a compendium of dogmatic theology and an edifying moral tract, this would seem to me to be an honest and, in many ways, compelling novel. The average reader is warned that this is rare meat, somewhat tough to digest and likely to revolt appetites used only to bland fare and meringues.

In spite of many shortcomings—and every writer has many—Mr. Wright seems to me to deserve a sincere salute. He has come a long way since *Native Son,* and my guess is that he will go much further.

Max Eastman. "Man as a Promise." *The Freeman,* 3 (May 4, 1953), 567–68.

Richard Wright seems in his momentous new novel, *The Outsider*, to be wrestling more earnestly with problems torturing his own mind in passing from the Communist conspiracy to the Existentialist racket than with those confronting his hero in a sufficiently perplexing life. That is all right with me—I like thesis novels—but it does detract somewhat from the verisimilitude of the story. The hero is a rather incredible character to begin with, a prodigious highbrow, a man possessing both intellect and intelligence (in itself a hard combination, these days, to believe in), and yet not possessed of enough sense to refrain from murdering people just because they get in his way, or because he doesn't like what they stand for. From the standpoint of the thesis this is correct, for the hero represents individualism as against Communism. He represents individualism going to the same extremes of criminal immoralism that the Marxist party does—setting up the same claim, that is, to be or to replace God. But from the standpoint of effective storytelling it is not so good. It lowers the intensity of the reader's participation in what were otherwise a breathlessly exciting, and is anyway a magnificently contrived and constructed, plot.

Mr. Wright knows how to wind a man up in a combination of matrimonial and extra-matrimonial, parental and nonparental and trying-not-to-be-parental love, law, and money predicaments, in comparison to which a barbed-wire entanglement is a pleasant invitation to come through and have some fun. He knows how to get him out of it too, the only way—but I am not going to expose that secret. Suffice it to say that Richard Wright can concoct a story with the best of his colleagues in the murder mystery business, and season it with a rich, if somewhat confused, comment on many of the vital problems of life.

The main problem he wrestles with seems a little unreal, or at least unnecessary, to me. It must be real enough for those whom he describes as feeling "insulted at being alive, humiliated at the terms of existence." This affliction, elsewhere described as a feeling that something has been promised and the promise not kept, gave his hero, Cross Damon (named by his mother after the cross of Christ), "a sense of loss that made life intolerable." It led him into a life that was indeed intolerable. But it does not seem to me a sane feeling, or a good starting point for the journey toward a philosophy of life. "Existence was not perpetrated in malice or benevolence, but simply is, and the end of our thinking is that here we are and what can we make of it." This remark, with which I concluded a book when I was about Cross Damon's age, kept coming into my mind as I traveled with him through his fear-and-gloom-ridden career. It would have undercut a lot of his agonized lucubrations, and might have saved him a few murders, and quite a number of false starts and involved blunderings. It would certainly have spoiled this story!

Also I think it would have immunized Cross Damon, or his creator, against the blandishments of the Existentialists, for it contains about all there is that is valid, and valuable, in their philosophizings. When I called Existentialism a racket, that was too extreme. I meant only that it is a product of the purely literary mind, a mind interested in having ideational experiences and making art works or commodities out of them, rather than in ascertaining facts and using ideas for guidance among them. A solemn toy that Existentialists have unctuous fun with is the question: *What is man?* It obviously has no answer except either in the experience of any one man, which cannot be generalized, or in the generalizations of anthropological science. But it can yield some wonderful intellectual playcastles, if you pose it in a realm called "philosophical anthropology," suspending for the purpose your sense of fact and of humor.

Cross Damon asks this question and seems to be spending his short life hunting for the answer. This is what makes him an "outsider"—not his being a Negro. Race troubled him very little. His trouble was that "he knew he was alone and that his problem was one of the relation of himself to himself." That I take to be the beginning of the main thread of Existentialist philosophy that runs through this book. If the reader is puzzled as to just how a self can relate to itself, he will find the matter clarified, I am sure, in these more explanatory lines which I quote from Kierkegaard, the father of Existentialism:

> Man is spirit. But what is spirit? Spirit is the self. But what is the self? The Self is a relation which relates itself to its own self or it is that (which accounts for it) that the relation relates itself to its own self; the self is not the relation but (consists in the fact) that the relation relates itself to its own self.

Notwithstanding that he is bogged down, for the time being, in this literary swamp, Richard Wright has wise and profound things to say about many challenging problems in this book. He gives you, along with some tense and terrible excitement, an experience of the nature and behavior of the factotums of the central committee of a Communist Party in feeling out the qualifications of a proposed new member—and disposing of him when they find he knows too much—that is unforgettable. The fifteen-page speech with which Cross Damon stalls and baffles them when they get him in a corner, and seem on the point of exterminating him, is a masterpiece of learned reflection. As an essay in the *Freeman* it would provoke arguments to fill the magazine for a year. And what an ingenious way to compel a lazy-minded nation to read an essay!

I must add, too—I hope without taking back everything I've said—that the answer Wright finally arrives at to that question, *What is man?*, when Cross murmurs it with a faint last summons of breath on his deathbed, is as great and memorable an aphorism as modern literature contains: "Man is a promise that he must never break."

Harold Monroe. "*The Outsider* Not Up to Par." *Fort Worth Star Telegram*, May 10, 1953.

Richard Wright was deservedly praised as among America's greatest writers when he turned out "Native Son"; he was in his stride five years later when his autobiography, "Black Boy," appeared. With this, his first novel in 12 years, the unanimity of opinion will not stand up. For, although there are passages showing the old fire, and some that are greater, there are also long, involved discussions that almost get lost. And there is a degree of violence and disregard for human values that does not mesh with the central character to whom it is attributed.

The concept of a man who places his own thinking above that of all mankind and, indeed, of all mankind's gods, is perhaps a thought that can be realized. Indeed, such men have lived. But such a character, no matter how ruthless (often, in fact, by virtue of ruthlessness), becomes a leader of men and not a cringing, self-doubting individualist.

But aside from this basic inconsistency, the novel has other faults. It moves too slowly at first and too rapidly later. The original buildup is neither convincing nor even interesting; the later development moves too rapidly and makes a plea for understanding which is not backed by a sufficient insight into the character we are asked to understand.

Admittedly, Wright's task is difficult because his central character is burdened both with the stigma of a minority race and with the author's own flirtation with, and later rejection of communism. The character's rejection of the Communists, however, is one built upon his own personal analysis of the party and its motives, rather than upon the larger base of its sham and its menace.

Edmund Fuller. *Episcopal Church News* (Richmond, Va.), May 17, 1953.

This book epitomizes some of the most destructive thoughts and emotions current today. It is an ugly, tragic document, objectively as well as internally. Since Wright is an articulate ex-Communist, and since he has written eloquently on the experience of being a Negro (*Black Boy*) it's worth noting what he is now doing and saying.

Mr. Wright has lived in Paris since 1946. In his own words, these years have been: ". . . a period during which I found it urgently necessary to search for a new attitude to replace the set of Marxist assumptions which had in the past more or less guided the direction of my writings. That uneasy search is still under way.

"*The Outsider* is the first literary effort of mine projected out of a heart preoccupied with no ideological burden save that of rendering an account of reality as it strikes my sensibilities and imagination."

Unhappily, the new attitude with which he has replaced his set of Marxist assumptions appears to be the existentialism of Jean-Paul Sartre. Ironically, it appears to have isolated Mr. Wright from existence.

The book is a pseudo-Dostoyevskyan tale of cold violence too complex to review in the space we have for it. His protagonist is the man who stands outside, with no discernible pattern of loyalties, beliefs, motives or commitments. He is beyond good and evil. In the ultimate meaning of the word, he is antisocial . . . alone. He does not kill "the enemy," for to him, no facet of the world is any more the enemy than any other. This man, Cross Damon, has no significance except as a symptom of mortal sickness of the soul and mind. If this, to repeat Mr. Wright's words, is "reality as it strikes my sensibilities and imagination"—then in all compassion, God help him.

Donald Urban. *Cincinnati Enquirer.* c. May 18, 1953.

Richard Wright once again has chosen to hang the theme of his novel on the peg of the racial problem. Though, in "The Outsider," he is not so much concerned with the problem's discriminatory aspects—as in his two previous works, "Black Boy" and "Native Son"—but rather with the psychological problems encountered by any minority group. . . .

As a novel, "The Outsider" suffers from the lack of a creditable plot for Mr. Wright has had to "rig" his to conform to Cross' purposeless life. As a "think piece," the book cannot be regarded lightly, for the author obviously has a keen grasp of the central character's problem which is set forth in a long speech by Cross to a party leader.

Whether or not "The Outsider" is a true picture of a Communist party that will appeal to the Negro is a question I cannot answer.

J. Saunders Redding. *Baltimore Afro-American,* May 19, 1953.

Richard Wright's first novel in nearly a decade, *The Outsider*, is a disappointment. In it he attempts a realistic projection, nay, an embodiment of existentialism. And even if one assumes the intellectual and moral validity of the existentialist philosophy—which Wright does not—one must face squarely the fact that philosophy is after all a species of abstraction; and that the personification of abstractions, being a trick, a device for the representation of truth, leads away from rather than toward reality. The fabulist is something different from the novelist. The first is not committed to creating an illusion of reality; the second is committed to this exactly, for it is this illusion of reality that produces truth. The fabulist begins where the novelist ends.

Nor does the use of the paraphernalia of the realistic method—dialogue that more or less exactly reproduces speech, detailed description, probable or even credible events—assure this illusion of reality.

If the mere employment of these means did create it, then *The Outsider* would be altogether a success, for Richard Wright employs them with no diminishment of the skill that he has shown in *Native Son*.

But only Book One of *The Outsider* is successful. The remaining 300 pages are like a furnace fire that gets no draft from below. Beneath the glowing surface coals lies a bed of choking ashes.

Which is to say that after the first book, the realization of the man Cross Damon, the principal character, slips away from his creator. Damon becomes an idea, an abstraction, an evilly tormented apotheosis of soul-stuff and mind-stuff that has no true relation to the concrete circumstances the author invents for him.

Part of this lack of relationship is due to the elaborate dogma of philosophical existentialism which declares, among other things, for man's awareness of himself as primally free and for his complete responsibility for what he is. Wright symbolizes Cross Damon's freedom in the episode of a subway wreck in which a body mangled beyond recognition is certified as Damon's.

Now he can start again without the ties—his wife and children, his pregnant mistress, his debts—that bound him to a life he had come to hate. He is free.

The fundamental weakness of the philosophy of existentialism is in its definition of freedom. It seems to suppose that every man is "an island entire," a being unto himself.

The existentialist is strictly introspective, finding entirely within himself the justification for life. His philosophy has been set up in gross opposition to the grossest dogma of another extremist philosophy, communism in which man finds the justification for life in the State.

Caught in a morass of celebration that must of necessity feed upon the experiences he has known—experiences of things and people, of events and acts and ideas—and knowing that by token of these very things he is not free, Damon sweats and groans and suffers exquisitely to attain what no man living can ever attain.

By this time—halfway through Book Two—Damon has been reduced to an idea made vocal, an idea made animate. The only freedom is death.

But Damon refuses to recognize this. Without for a moment giving him our full credence, we follow him along an impossible trail of violence and blood. He goes to elaborate pains to acquire another name. After two days he comes smack up against his philosophical opposite number, a Communist named Blount, whose person, character and ideas are meant to quicken the reader's sympathy for an identification with Damon.

But this does not happen. The reader simply realizes that the most extreme evils in the world—man as god and man as beast—are vis-a-vis.

Within 24 hours Damon (man as beast) has killed Blount (man as god) and the fascist Herndon (man as superman) and another. But he has also come upon Eva Blount, betrayed, innocent and lovely, who seemed to him "the cure of his nameless malady."

She represented what he had to live for. She was the justification for life. She was humanity's essence. But in another forty-eight hours she too is dead, prompted to self-murder by the guilty knowledge of his evil, senseless crimes.

And in the same span of time, Cross Damon, brought to his deathbed by communist thugs, realizes that the life he had lived was full of horror because only beasts can be truly innocent and free.

The Outsider is often labored, frequently naive, and generally incredible. Some of its faults are technical, not structural. The time element, for instance, is mishandled, and there are many inconsistencies there. Certain critical episodes are made to depend completely on fortuity—the first evening in the company of the communists; the finding of Eva's diaries; and certain critical characters, including Damon himself, and Houston, Blount and Eva, are too frequently seen to move by strings held in the author's hands.

Yet *The Outsider* will be read—there is enough of the old Wright shock and skill to assure that; and it will be discussed, for there is enough of a foreshadowing of a "new" Wright to make guesses interesting.

Phoebe Adams. "The Wrong Road." *Atlantic Monthly,* 191 (May 1953), 77–78.

Richard Wright's new novel, *The Outsider*, is his first since *Native Son*, published thirteen years ago, and his first book of any kind since his autobiography came out in 1945. If anyone wonders how a writer manages to keep out of print for eight years, the answer is clear in *The Outsider*. Mr. Wright has been meditating, or rather brooding, on mankind and Western civilization. He doesn't see much hope for either of them.

Mr. Wright's conclusions on the nature of humanity and the future of society run piecemeal through his novel, involving a good deal of repetition and ramification. In simplified terms, he holds that science and industrial society, by destroying the restraining power of traditional religion, give men of sufficient courage the opportunity to feel, and act, as gods—that is to say, with complete moral irresponsibility. Since Mr. Wright also holds that man is a chronically terrified animal, and the condition of self-elected divinity is fearlessness, he does not foresee a world full of acting gods. The number of men capable of facing life entirely out of spiritual context will always be small and Mr. Wright believes that their activities will be directed either to the control of a totalitarian rank and file, well doped with noble-sounding slogans, or to the gratification of random impulse.

Understandably alarmed by his own reflections, Mr. Wright has undertaken in *The Outsider* to display what might be called ultimate twentieth-century man in action. Cross Damon is an outsider in every sense of the word. As a Negro he is outside the majority pattern of American life; as a shrewd, self-centered cynic, he is outside the claims of family and friendship; as a casual atheist, he is outside the morality demanded, if not enforced, by religion. When a subway crash gives him the chance to be officially dead, he takes it, and gets outside even his own identity. There are no strings on Cross. Without being aware of his own state of mind, he descends on New York like a tiger on a new stretch of jungle.

There he becomes entangled with the other type of outsider, the men whose absolute freedom of conscience has focused on power over other men. They are, naturally, Communists, and the party has a hard time with Cross, suffering anxiety and the loss of several valuable members before getting the upper hand.

Cross is no gallant crusader against Communism. He refuses to accept systems, and Communism happens to be the system in his way at the moment. If Cross is a better man than his Communist victims, it is in a very slight degree. He comes to realize that godhood is uncomfortable and impractical. "Tell them not to come down this road" is his final comment on his career of impersonation, arson, and murder. Since the only other road Mr. Wright acknowledges is that of totalitarian politics, *The Outsider* may be fairly described as a pessimistic novel.

It is also a very disappointing novel, for the qualities of sympathy, directness, effective detail, and mordant humor which distinguished Mr. Wright's earlier, more personal books seem to operate at cross-purposes in *The Outsider*. The best sections of the book are dominated by one or another of these elements, but they are so little integrated with its theme that Mr. Wright is obliged to let Cross state his case in a fourteen-page monologue of no plausibility whatever. Remove the monologue and Cross's conversations with a district attorney who seems to have been borrowed from Dostoevski, and *The Outsider* becomes blood-and-thunder adventure, Cross an opportunistic thug with some intelligence, and the Communists mere caricatures.

Whether Mr. Wright nailed his grim thesis to a plot already in his mind, or concocted his plot, which is full of coincidence, accident, and blind luck, to fit his thesis, the book shows a hiatus between means and ends. It's a pity that the two halves of *The Outsider* never fused, for the novel Mr. Wright saw in his own mind must have been far better than the one he has actually written.

John Patrick O'Connell. "Confusion and Despair of a 20th Century Man." *Books on Trial,* 11 (May 1953), 294–95.

Cross Damon was a young Negro who had some college training. Things could have been better, but he had a few weaknesses. He liked wine and women, but he didn't like whites. He had a destitute mother, an unhappy wife and family, and a pregnant girl friend. His job was in jeopardy.

Fortuitously—a subway crash—mistaken identity—Cross is listed as dead. He plans to live anonymously. A friend discovers him. He kills that friend and heads for New York City. There he changes his name and commits a dual murder. He gets involved in a Greenwich Village love affair, with the Communists, in another murder, in many psychological discussions of the essence of communism and its techniques, in the Party harassment, and finally in his own murder; all in a month's time.

This is quite a story. Richard Wright, who has been living in Paris since 1946 and who has also authored *Native Son* and *Black Boy,* is familiar with the workings of the Communist Party. But like a gourmet who's lost in his condiments, Wright's ideas on things racial and intellectual are often too highly seasoned to be digestible.

The Outsider seems to be an apologia for the author's contact with communism as well as a brief for his new thesis of futile godlessness. Enroute to the core of truth he arbitrarily disposes of what he describes as the myths of organized religions, although willing to admit the pragmatic value of religion to society. Upon arrival at the core he discovers, "All of the vast dramas which man once thought took place in the skies now transpire in our hearts and we quake and are moved compulsively to do what we know not. . . ." "It's the strong at the top who represent modern man. Beyond themselves, their dreams, their hopes, their plans, they know that there is nothing. . . ." Thus he must mean that man is All; the law, the judgment, the reason and the end.

The author declares, "In *The Outsider* I have tried to depict my sense of our contemporary living as I see it and feel it." The following are his depictions:

> We twentieth-century Westerners have outlived the faith of our fathers. . . . The degree and quality of man's fears can be gauged by the scope and density of his myths. . . . The ancient nations today we call great are the ones who left behind them those towering monuments of fear in the forms of so-called cultures! . . . The ravaging scourge that tore away the veil of myth worlds was science and industry; science slowly painting another world, the real one. . . . Most men today are atheists even though they don't know it or won't admit it. . . . Since God as a functioning reality in men's minds and hearts has gone— . . . Every event of the modern world feeds the growing movement toward the total and the absolute. . . .

Despair is heartbreaking to witness.

Gilbert Highet. "Mind-forged Manacles." *Harper's Magazine,* 206 (May 1953), 97–98.

If a Dostoevski should appear in American literature, he would come from one of those spiritual and social half-worlds which appear between widely different levels of society—Madame Terentyev's fourth-floor apartment in *The Idiot*, the inn at Mokroe in *Karamazov*—and he would describe those agonies of doubt and despair which fall on men and women when their routine life has ceased to have significance, when all the standards they have known crumble and dissolve, when nothing survives but an individual surrounded by vague acquaintances and ill-perceived enemies, uncertain even of his own continuous existence, and confused by memories of a set of creeds which have become meaningless and yet retain some emotional power.

This doubt and this despair are the subject of Richard Wright's new book, *The Outsider,* which is something very close to a Dostoevskian novel. Lonely, puzzled but constantly brooding, warm-hearted but impelled into savage hostilities, his hero lives and dies as a rebel against traditional morality, against social distinctions and divisions, against friendship and love, against organized law and organized rebellion, and against religion. His aim is to be free. He becomes an anarchic individualist. To all who love him and many who hate him he brings suffering and death; he dies alone, yet still not free, tormented by solitude and remorse. It is a moving story, for the most part expertly told. America (particularly colored America) is full of these lonesome wanderers, sad and dangerous men. Faulkner created another of them, the hero of *Light in August*; and we remember the book that opens "Call me Ishmael."

Still, the novel has one major defect. After the rebel, Cross Damon, has been running wildly into darkness for some time, the Communists attempt to recruit him. Right away he understands nearly all their tricks. He actually outfaces a CP organizer, lecturing him for a dozen pages on the perversion of human ideals implicit in all totalitarian systems; and we see him recalling the heavy reading he has done in philosophy—Nietzsche, Heidegger, Jaspers, Husserl. At this point Mr. Wright is showing us the career and beliefs of a man who became a moral anarchist on profound intellectual grounds, after reading and meditating for many long years. But the story he tells us is different. His hero (when we meet him first) is a distracted, debt-ridden, heavy-drinking, lustful postal clerk, desperate to escape from the disasters his own lack of self-control has brought upon him. When the opportunity of escape is created by a terrible accident, he seizes it with astonishment and relief and goes on his way, killing and dodging like a rat caught in a henroost. We watch his agonies with understanding and even with sympathy, wishing he would sober up and straighten out; but when—only a week or two later—he emerges as a cool philosopher with his head full of Nietzsche and the answers to Lenin, we find the transition impossible to believe. It looks, in fact, as though Mr. Wright had written two different tales and then tried to blend them: one, the story of a poor incontinent man haunted by drink and desire until he would welcome any disaster as a relief; the other, an account of the adventures of a dispassionate intellectual who was educated into violence by the brutality and treachery of the Communist party until he revolted against it and became an existentialist. Both men are solitary and rebellious; the same man could have led both lives; but not in the same short space of time. Such violent developments take many years.

Lloyd L. Brown. "Outside and Low." *Masses and Mainstream*, 6 (May, 1953), 62–64.

Discussing *The Outsider* in the *Saturday Review*, Arna Bontemps says that Richard Wright "has had a roll in the hay with the existentialism of Sartre, and apparently he liked it." But hay never smelled like this.

The commercial reviewers find the odor exhilarating, of course, even while wrinkling their noses at the mere literary flaws they find in this book. ("Improbable coincidences . . . unreal characters . . . unbelievable . . . incredible reading . . . incoherent."— Granville Hicks and Orville Prescott in the New York *Times*.)

It seems that the author's "fictional failure is compensated for to some extent by the interest of Mr. Wright's ideas."

Mr. Wright's ideas or "angles," as they are known in the trade, are simple and salable: homicide and anti-Communism. His hero, a sensitive, tortured soul, begins by deserting his wife and children and his pregnant mistress, then struggles through the book killing other people, confounding the Communists who threaten his spiritual integrity, and spouting great gobs of the author's deep philosophy in soul-to-soul conversations with New York's District Attorney.

Hay nonny nonny! For the contemplative we have here a "book about modern man"; for lovers of action we advertise "a novel of violence." (Wright's hero commits four murders: one skull is cracked with a whiskey bottle; two skulls are battered with a table leg; the fourth victim is put away with philosophical detachment—he is shot.)

Renegade Hicks, who is deeply stirred by it all, compared Renegade Wright's anti-Communism pitch with that of Renegade Chambers: "Like Whittaker Chambers in *Witness*, Mr. Wright feels that communism is a logical outcome of the whole development of rationalism in the Western World. . . ."

So what? Even the incredible reviewers of incredible books must suspect that reason and its results cannot be bludgeoned out of existence no matter how many skulls are crushed in the season's best-sellers.

Irrationality, irresponsibility and homicidal hatred of mankind may be glorified on the front pages of the Sunday literary supplements, but a better day is coming and its tokens get the daily headlines: Peace Offensive!

"Stupid," said Richard Wright of Jean-Paul Sartre who climbed out of the barnyard pile and went to the Vienna Peace Congress. "That was a stupid move."

Yes, it's truly wonderful how many people there are who are too stupid to believe that "life is an incomprehensible disaster." And one of these fools here recalls an old time song of his people, whom Richard Wright has long since deserted:

You better mind how you lie,
You better mind what you're lying about,
'Cause you got to give an account in the Judg-a-ment,
You better mind!

L. D. Reddick. "A New Richard Wright?" *Phylon,* 14 (Second Quarter, 1953), 213–14.

Richard Wright is no longer a mere novelist. At the least, he is no longer a story-teller, interested in a tale for what it is worth. As a matter of strict accuracy, Wright was always something more than that; in *The Outsider* he comes forth as a full-fledged philosopher—a Thinker, who uses the novel as a vehicle for ventilating his views of the complicated process of living.

Some time soon somebody ought to look at Wright's own experience against the profile of his writings. This inquiry would follow this son of a Mississippi sharecropper up to the slums of Chicago, to New York where he became rich and famous, and then to Paris, where he has tried to remold his own existence, to reshape it "nearer to his heart's desire."

What is Wright after? What is he trying to say? What answers to the great questions of life in our time does he seek? How successful has he been in his long, painful search that on one level took him from Mississippi to Europe and on another level has taken him from *Uncle Tom's Children* to *The Outsider*?

It should be said quite quickly that this short review is not that patient inquiry suggested above. Just now, no more is attempted than a few comments on the first product of Wright's retreat to the Continent, the alien brother, shall we say, to *Native Son* (1940) and *Black Boy* (1945).

The Outsider is the story of a Chicago mail clerk, who, through a freak accident, got a chance to do his own life over again, to emerge in New York City as a "new," "free" man, without a past and with his own future in his own hands. This Negro intellectual tries to analyze objectively the struggle for power in the modern world and to relate himself subjectively to it; that is, to make his own life whole in the mad sweep of the social and psychological forces about him. Because he is a Negro in America, he has a special perspective on life; he is, of course, living within the culture, but being a Negro he is *outside* of the dominant myths of the time and society. He, above all others, should see life "as it really is." He has less excuse for being naive. In the truest sense, he should be a sophisticated and modern man.

Externally, this is another novel of violence. As usual in Wright's writing, there is more cruelty than tenderness or anguish. Most of the characters are horrible and horribly brutal in their relations with each other. The left-wing politicans, as Wright draws them, are fantastic. They are party hacks, denuded of ideals; they have no faith, no inner loyalty voluntarily given to a great cause. Cynically, they exploit the idealism of lesser men and manipulate human emotions to further their own drive for power. This portrait is fashionable today.

Cross, the leading character, is, of course, the spokesman for Wright himself; otherwise, only Eva is attractive. She is beautiful and incorruptible, and finally, she is deluded by her own good faith and by those about her who grasp, struggle, lie and kill.

At times the first part of the novel bogs down a bit. This seems to happen whenever the essayist, the philosopher, intrudes upon the narrator. Wright has a definite talent for narration, amounting to a genius. When he is free and unhindered, he can tell a story with an unrivalled deftness and conviction. It is a pity that "the scholar" throws his weight upon the raconteur, from time to time. At these moments there is too much *explaining* of the character and the situations; too many "big" words. For example, the editor might have asked the author to simplify such phrases that appear in a sample paragraph from page 53: "simulated surprise he could convincingly sustain," "pretended incredulity," "keep her judgment torturingly uncertain." Any reader with a good Webster's Dictionary, of course, could keep up, but all this slows the pace.

Wright's other forte, his sensitiveness to human motivation, comes into play in the later stages of the book, giving it the articulation and force of the best passages of *Native Son*.

Much more could be said, but in a word this is a very interesting book. Readers may quarrel over its message; highly conscious men may reject its final implications as unjustified; but sooner or later we all will have to face the issues that are raised so eloquently in *The Outsider*. (P.S. Those who enjoy a "good" murder story will like this one almost as much as they did *Native Son*).

Jack Mason. "Sense of Outrage Dominates Outlook of Negro Novelist." *Oakland Tribune*, June 14, 1953.

Richard Wright until 1944 was a communist. He quit the party in disgust and has since, apparently, been having a rather desperate time of it, trying to resolve his life into a wholesome pattern.

Since 1946 he has been living in France where, like many another disillusioned communist intellectual, he has fallen under the spell of nihilism—or existentialism, if you prefer.

It is very much, of course, like falling out of the frying pan into the fire. As a communist, he was outraged over the injustices of a capitalistic society; as a nihilist, he is still outraged, although the incentives to resentment are vaguer in his mind.

Outrage No. 1 produced a telling novel, "Native Son," the story of a Negro who became a killer as the result of the Chicago slum housing evil.

Outrage No. 2 has produced a less effective novel, if a more brutal one. The reason seems to be that Wright has tried to make literary capital of his moral indignation. In this story he is interested not so much in creating a hero of flesh and blood and heart, as in getting across a social message. The hero is a means to an end.

Naturally, the Cross Damon of this book is no match for the Bigger Thomas of the other.

Damon is a Chicago postal worker, father of three, estranged from his wife, with a mistress who is driving him to the bottle. He escapes from his predicament during a subway accident; he is presumed to be one of the dead.

Old trouble spawns new, however; in the following weeks he murders a pal, meets and abandons a new woman friend, and finally, inevitably, drifts into the company of communists who offer him a ready solution to all of his problems.

The solution is made up in equal parts of blood and rue. Three more murders ensue. The district attorney, who knows a bad hombre when he sees one, catches up with Damon, but unable to pin anything on him, lets him go. Ironically, the communists who had befriended him take care of him with a bullet.

One feels that Damon has died, as he lived, still seeking the meaning of life, still at odds with the demoniac forces that drive a man to distraction if he does not come to sober terms with them.

"Were we really that much alone in this life?" he asks himself. "Were all human hearts encased in this irredeemable isolation?"

We are all of us alone, all of our lives in one sense; but there are ties of love and selflessness that help us bridge the river of despair. To Cross Damon this simple truth seems never to have occurred. One begins to wonder if it has occurred to the author.

The United States Quarterly Book Review, 9 (June 1953), 166–67.

His second novel, *The Ousider,* is even more violent than Richard Wright's first, and considerably less credible. In fact, the narrative generally is so melodramatic and full of coincidence as to alienate the reader almost from the start and to impede his sympathetic attention to the very real importance of the ideas which the work contains.

This is a nihilistic chronicle of modern man, not just Negro man, and the violence is part of the stage setting, like the glow above Yucca Flats in Nevada. Cross Damon, the protagonist, is a lineal descendant of Dostoevsky's Raskolnikov. Damon, having sought and failed to find meanings in life, believes in nothing; he has cut himself off from all the sustaining or confining codes that are the heritage of mankind. Thus, his principle is violence, of a particularly gratuitous sort. He is a Jealous Rebel, a modern Lucifer, who properly enough inherits the hell within him and, untouched by the law, must live out his days in painful isolation within himself. This measure of the modern man helps to define the nature of the Communist, whose characteristics are the concern of most of the novel. Cross Damon, after his flight to New York, is sought out by the Party, which would like to use him. Because of his complete dissociation from codes of morality he alone is able to understand the Party leaders for what they are, seekers of naked and unrestrained power. He in turn is shot down by a Party zealot, since what the Party can neither harness nor understand it must destroy. Here, then, is a parable about a major aspect of contemporary experience; it must be read and meditated in its main outlines. Although Mr. Wright has not grown as a novelist, and it remains to be seen whether he has acquired depth as a thinker, his turbulent and disquieting novel cannot be disregarded.

Henry F. Winslow. "Forces of Fear." *The Crisis*, 60 (June-July 1953), 381–83.

It is today a matter of serious concern in high academic circles that from the creative literature of our times has come no full-sized, tragic hero. Cross Damon, the foremost of at least a dozen "outsiders" in Richard Wright's new novel, is a protagonist who fits the prescription. Deeply realized, in great measure Byronic, in greater measure symbolic of the prime force of contemporary civilization: fear, we meet him for what he first means on page 2:

> "Crossy, how come you're drinking so much these days?" Booker asked in a tone free of moral objections.
>
> "My soul needs it," Cross mumbled.
>
> "Makes you feel better, hunh?" Booker asked.
>
> "No. Makes me feel *less*." Cross corrected him.

True, Cross, who has come into his name and psychological heritage by reason of his mother's fierce devotion to an invisible and forbidding God, is an extension of the pattern of murder motivated by fear as formulated in *Native Son*. But he is so much more Bigger that one is led to read that his reactions gather a dignity, however proud, apart from their supposed origin. Moreover, Cross loves as profoundly as he hates, and thinks as deeply as he feels.

A proud man laying about him with the sword of terror, he cannot kill the thing he loves—Eva; an intelligent man with a probing mind, he has thought his way "through the many veils of illusion," and thus "stripped himself of the hopes and consolations of the mass of mankind"; a psychological creation which is "Negro" man, he is endowed with a "double vision" which gives him the peculiar perspective of standing at once *inside* and *outside* of our culture: hence, "Every emotional and cultural convulsion that ever shook the heart and soul of Western man" shakes him, and he wonders why some people are "fated, like Job, to live a never ending debate between themselves and their sense of what they believed life should be?" A man, he is naturally moved by the desire for "the body of woman as woman," often too intensively given over to the given moment. Such is Cross Damon the character.

The novel structure in which he moves and realizes his being is an ingeniously woven tale of two cities. Action packed, *The Outsider* leads us from the dawn of South Side Chicago to the darkness of Manhattan's Central Park. Cross enters as a postal clerk living physically and/or spiritually outside his family and friends, and trapped between the threats of an enraged wife set on revenge and an impregnated child-sweetheart set on marrying him—or else. How he manages to rid himself of his wife and then of his terrible situation is a feat of intuitive insight and narrative cunning worthy of a Homer. With weird curiosity he finds a hiding place from which he observes his funeral and a few days later is headed for New York City. On the train he meets Bob, another "outsider" with whom he shares a "defensive solidarity" in response to "latent white hostility," but also district attorney Ely Houston (yet another "outsider"), between whom and Cross there is fought out upon the darkling plain of psychological spirits a Dostoevskian battle of intuitive wills.

Once Cross is settled in New York the Communists begin to make provisions for his indoctrination. The result of his decision to feign cooperation with their plans for him is the most shattering evidence against Communism yet recorded—if not the most devastating possible. Moreover, this story is all the more significant for the reason that there was great need for someone of political, intellectual and artistic integrity to tell it. Nevertheless, it will afford no measure of comfort for the Byrnes's and the Bilbo's who are hardly less real and ruthless as ideological cancers festering in the body politic of the Free World. For if Gil, Hilton, and Menti are representative of an obsessing "*life* strategy using political methods as its tools," so is Herndon the epitome of a system of social tyranny equally evil and thorough in its capacity to warp the minds of men into instruments of hell. And it is with this story, in the telling of which Cross meets Eva, that *The Outsider* cuts its sure way into classic greatness as a work of art. Here Damon becomes multi-dimensional, a credibly coherent part of all he has met as modern man. In this respect, the "irrational compulsion" which spells murder to those for whom he has contempt and fear becomes less arguable, since he is also man as nation.

The supporting cast in *The Outsider* reveals as never before that Wright knows woman with all the penetrating thoroughness of a Strindberg. Cross' mother, whom her son knew too well, had returned to teaching in the South after pursuing in vain the man who betrayed her love. But she was ever to relive her sad story and transfer both the passion and the blame for it from father to son. Gladys, his wife, whom he knew as well, had turned to mercenary vindictiveness after losing him on the terms by which she had won him. From Dot, whose craving for security expressed itself through deception, he learned that "A woman's business is emotion and her trade is carried on in cash of tears. . . ." Cross was not to experience a true love until Eva came to him out of the trap which the Party had sprung on her. And when at last it came, the shadow of Cross' violent past was to snuff its light.

It is quite likely that the little men with big words will beat upon Wright's creation, for they who stand upon the principles of the Pharisee at the temple and thank *their* God that they are not like the others (and certainly not quite like the others) will reject this book. They are too much like the fish who could not conceive of water. They live by the fear which is the novel's basic theme and moral:

> "White folks in America, France, and Italy are the scaredest folks that ever lived on this earth. They're scareda Reds, Chinese, Indians, Africans, *everybody*."
>
> "But how come you reckon they so scared?" an elderly man asked.
>
> "Cause they're guilty," the tall man explained. "And guilty folks are *scared* folks!. . . "

Nevertheless, what is here rendered is a true account of our times in humble and facile prose, an eloquently articulate reading of the handwriting on the iron walls of contemporary civilization. It puts before us as only a truly gifted artist can, a character (among characters), a novel, and a question in dimensions hardly equaled by any other American novelist who ever lived. Indeed, this, above all, is the artist's responsibility. "As they see or fail to see, understand, act or fail to act, so may the warm sun continue to shine upon living men or the cold moon rise upon an empty earth."

Checklist of Additional Reviews

*Kirkus Reviews,*21 (January 15, 1953), 54.

Booklist, 49 (March 1, 1953), 213; (March 15, 1953), 238.

Richard O'Connor. *Los Angeles Herald-Express,* March 6, 1953.

John Barkham. Saturday Review Service, March 21, 1953.

Marie Moore. *Houston Chronicle,* March 22, 1953.

Van Allen Bradley. *Chicago Daily News,* March 25, 1953.

New Yorker, 29 (March 28, 1953), 115-16.

W. G. R. *Omaha World-Herald,* March 29, 1953.

Luther P. Jackson. *Newark News,* April 5, 1953.

Richmond News Leader, April 13, 1953.

M. S. Byam. *Library Journal,* 78 (April 15, 1953), 732.

John Henry Raleigh. *New Republic,* 128 (May 4, 1953), 19.

James J. Foree. *Philadelphia Tribune,* May 9, 1953.

Abner Berry. *New York Daily Worker,* May 10, 1953, pp. 8,14.

Riley Hughes. *Catholic World,* 177 (May 1953), 154-55.

L. S. Munn. *Springfield Republican,* June 14, 1953, p. 9c.

V. A. B. *Trenton Sunday Times,* June 14, 1953, p. 12.

Arkansas Gazette, June 21, 1953, p. 6F.

Frank Meyer, *American Mercury,* 76 (June 1953), p. 143.

H. I. Fontellio-Nanton. *Sepia,* 2 (July 1953).

David Wieck. *Resistance,* 11 (August 1953), 15.

Paul Pickrel. *Yale Review,* 42 (Summer 1953), x.

Elvin Byrom. *Daily News Digest* (Beckley, W. Va.), September 18, 1953.

Nick Aaron Ford. *College English,* 15 (November 1953), 87-94.

Steven Marcus. *Commentary,* 16 (November 1953), 456-63.

William Shands Meacham. *Virginia Quarterly Review,* 30 (Winter 1954), 137-39.

Henry Popkin. *Chicago Jewish Forum,* 13 (Spring 1954), 192.

SAVAGE HOLIDAY

RICHARD WRIGHT

Complete and Unabridged

AVON PUBLICATIONS, INC.
575 Madison Avenue
New York 22, N.Y.

Savage Holiday
(no reviews)

BLACK POWER

A Record of Reactions
in a Land of Pathos

by
RICHARD WRIGHT

HARPER & BROTHERS, NEW YORK

Black Power

"An Indictment of Western Colonialism." *Newsday*, September 25, 1954.

Richard Wright visited Northwest Africa's Gold Coast as a stranger, but returned angry and with a feeling of kinship for the nationalists of that colony. Only recently have they been granted self-government in partnership with the British, who retain control over such "minor" agencies as the Army, Treasury and Foreign Affairs.

Since 1471, this 100-mile coastal strip has experienced the rummagings of Portuguese, Dutch, Danes, and Britons for slaves and a wealth of minerals. Today, Wright views the wreckage and indicts western colonialism for failing to advance popular and technical education, shaming tribal people into hiding their religion, and shattering their culture.

Although Wright deals only with a small percentage of Africa's 200 million people, he sees here a typical relationship which can cost the West a vast human and economic reservoir which it may need in the future. To balance that relationship, Africans must obtain complete national freedom to convert from tribalism to capitalism and from manpower to machine-power.

Wright points out that there is no turning back the clock to primitivism nor can evolution, a slow "teasing torture," be acceptable. He suggests a rigid economic and social regimentation of African life designed to do in one generation what the West has done over a period of centuries. Whether such revolutionary methods could sweep away age-imbedded beliefs and habits, or as much as lay the groundwork for a mechanized society, is sheer conjecture.

One thing, however, is certain. Richard Wright, best remembered for his novel **Native Son,** writes with emotional persuasiveness and power, relentlessly probing men, motives, myths and history for a terrifying glimpse of a continent in turmoil.

Walter White. *New York Herald Tribune Book Review*, September 26, 1954, p. 1.

"Why don't you go to Africa?" Dorothy Padmore, wife of George Padmore, West Indian journalist and associate of Prime Minister Kwame Nkrumah, asked Richard Wright, breaking the silence as the Wrights and Padmores sat in Paris after an excellent Easter Sunday luncheon. Going to Africa was very far from Wright's plans, although he shared the interest of thoughtful people in the exciting transition from colonialism to self-government which is taking place in Africa's Gold Coast. But his compliance with the suggestion of Mrs.

Padmore, in which her husband and Richard Wright's wife vigorously concurred, has resulted in the most important, informative and infuriating first-hand account of what is happening in today's Africa of the scores of books which have come from that troubled continent during the past few years.

Richard Wright was given a cordially reserved "To Whom It May Concern" letter by Prime Minister Nkrumah, entertained and invited to accompany him on an electioneering campaign and then allowed to roam wherever Wright wished throughout the Gold Coast. Seldom has such freedom to learn been used more effectively. Wright makes his readers sweat and smell the fetid odors of open latrines in the hot lowlands and shiver in the uplands. With total frankness he pictures the pettiness, fear and greed of the native chiefs, the British-educated intellectuals and the British exploiters of the people and natural resources of the Gold Coast—all three opposing the self-government which Nkrumah and his associates are carving out against incredible odds. The story he tells of how young Africans are battling and defeating the "squalor, vitality and fantastic disorder" which the Gold Coast represents today is close to being the most exciting saga of a bloodless revolution taking place anywhere in the modern world.

It is doubtful whether any person in the Gold Coast—Nkrumah, tribal chiefs, intellectuals, missionaries, British business men and administrators, or followers of *juju*—will approve "Black Power" in its entirety. Certainly the Negrophobe Daniel Malan of the Union of South Africa and the frightened British in Kenya will hate its revelation of how native Africans whom they have looked down upon and exploited are succeeding in disproving their longheld notions of African inferiority. But for the rest of us, "Black Power" is the most up-to-date, hopeful and valuable picture yet written of the most important experiment in democratic living which is taking place in Africa or anywhere else in the world.

The white western world would be well advised to study and learn what a lot of Africans (as well as Asians and Latin Americans) are thinking as revealed by a young Gold Coast man quoted by Mr. Wright: "Russia's a gadfly! I'm not for her, but I'm not against her! Let her stay where she is and harass the West! Why are the British treating us a little better? They're scared of our going over to the Russians, that's all. If Russia were defeated tomorrow, a tide of reaction would set in in all the colonies. But, with the cold war raging, even an Englishman, when he passes you on deck is willing to say 'good morning!' "

In that sapiently cynical remark Richard Wright epitomizes the importance of the so-called democratic world sloughing off its old notions about "inferior peoples" and waking up to the grim truth that unless freedom is shared by the haves with the have-nots, it may be lost by all.

And now let me get rid of a couple of criticisms, though they do not detract from my sincere admiration for the objective-subjective job of superlative reporting Wright has done on what is almost the sole hopeful development which may save Africa from the ghastly evils of Mau Mauism or communism. Wright admits with frankness that he had been a Communist from 1932 to 1944. He makes equally clear his total disillusion with communism as a hope for Africans or any one else—a disillusion he had demonstrated previously in his brilliant essay in "The God That Failed."

But in "Black Power" Wright illustrates how the vestigial remains of the evangelical essence of communism continue to influence those who once have believed even though they have rejected it. Wright attributes Nkrumah's skill and success in organizing and directing Gold Coast aspirations to the lessons Nkrumah learned from British Communists (elsewhere in "Black Power" he gives credit to the ruthless example of British traders in West Africa). Nowhere does he give recognition to what Nkrumah learned in the United States when the Gold Coast Premier was a student here. This reviewer knows that influence to be considerable as is evidenced as recently as June, 1954 in a letter from Nkrumah regarding the Supreme Court decision outlawing educational segregation. According to Wright the only impact of America on Africans is the color bar; he says nothing of the effect of the continuing struggle, the tactics of democracy and the victories against race prejudice which have influenced and aided men like Nkrumah in the Gold Coast and Nnamdi Azikiwe who has just become Prime Minister of Nigeria.

My second criticism is of Wright's tendency toward the end of the book to write about African psychology and practices, although he has visited only the Gold Coast, as though all Africans react and think identically. This simply isn't so. Save for their continent-wide hostility to white colonialism, there is as wide diversity among African cultures, political systems, economies and religious beliefs as would be found among other peoples of like pastoral, agricultural and communal backgrounds.

Enough of criticism. For the magnificent contributions "Black Power" makes toward understanding what used to be called "the dark and unknown continent," this reviewer urges you to read it as one of the most important books written in recent years. For upon the success—or failure—of Africans like Nkrumah hangs the decision as to whether Africa explodes in violence, succumbs to communism, or finds an answer to the undeniable demand for freedom by Africans and other colonial peoples all over the earth.

Michael Clark. "A Struggle for the Black Man Alone?" *New York Times Book Review,* September 26, 1954, p. 3.

In "Black Power," Richard Wright, the American Negro author of "Native Son," and "The Outsider," reports on a recent visit to the Gold Coast. The Gold Coast has just become the first self-governing territory in British West Africa and now stands on the threshold of independence and dominion status. Put Mr. Wright and the Gold Coast together and what happens? The answer—to be found in "Black Power"—cannot fail to startle anyone interested in Africa and the race problem.

Mr. Wright's reaction to the Gold Coast is soon found to be so passionate and subjective that his book emerges more as a tract than as a considered study. The reader of "Black Power" will be grateful, no doubt, for many fascinating, and even illuminating, glimpses of primitive tribal life in a country marked out for precocious political development. But he will also get a mighty dose of Mr. Wright's own emotional processes.

Mr. Wright was convinced of many

things before he ever set out on his African journey—convinced that colonialism was wholly evil, convinced that the redemption of the African could be achieved only through the development of the black state and of black nationalism as a "secular religion." It does not appear to have occurred to him that the two races, black and white, might be able to go it together in Africa, to work out a common destiny on a continent they both have helped to shape. A partnership of this kind is in fact beginning to grow in French territory next door, but Mr. Wright did not go there, and he never so much as alludes to the concept of assimilation, which many hold to offer the best, if not the only hope for true racial equality and peaceful "co-existence."

On the contrary, Mr. Wright contends that the Gold Coast must be freed both from its own fetish-ridden past and from the shackles of colonialism by the black man alone. He calls on Prime Minister Kwame Nkrumah of the Gold Coast to catapult his primitive country into the twentieth century even if a generation of black people has to be sacrificed in the process (shades of the Marxist doctrine Mr. Wright has renounced!).

But the white man must go. To Nkrumah he says, "You can pour a libation to the nameless powers that there are no white settlers to be driven out." One wonders to what extent Mr. Wright has projected into the Gold Coast situation his own hidden or sublimated desires for racial revenge. For despite his claim that there is no "race" in his thinking, Mr. Wright did not hesitate to describe himself to an African political meeting as "one of the lost sons of Africa who has come back to look upon the land of his forefathers," and he added: "In terms of a common heritage of suffering and hunger for freedom, your heart and my heart beat as one."

From his first day on African soil Mr. Wright was able to find some virtue in everything black but none in anything white. His caricature of British colonialism is drawn, not from life, but from the dreary old arsenal of Marxist slogans. Africa, he says, has been "murdered" by colonialism, which he presents as a sordid, mercantile operation based on plunder and rapine. He observes that "no matter how jaunty the European pretends to be, he cannot rid himself of the idea that what he and his kind are doing is stealing." He explains that the "white man's power is being used to strip him (the African) slowly of his wealth, of his dignity, of his traditions, and of his life." At one point Mr. Wright asserts that if the Africans failed to follow the course advocated by him, the "British would continue to suck their blood and wax fat."

Mr. Wright does not want the British to stay in the Gold Coast, but gives them no credit for going because in his view their motives are necessarily base. Still less does he concede that the British have any claim to the gratitude of the inhabitants for building the Gold Coast into one of the best administered and most prosperous countries in Africa. His specific for the ills of the Gold Coast is the expulsion of the white man and the establishment, under Nkrumah, of a ruthless dictatorship. African life, he says, must be regimented for the "long pull."

Nothing could be as grossly unfair as his strictures on the subject of Christian missionary endeavor. He accuses the missionaries of conditioning the African psychologically for colonial bondage. He describes them as neurotics bent on warping the African mind while pursuing their own perverse personal salvation. Anyone at all familiar with the educational and medical work of the missionaries in the Gold Coast will know in what contempt this judgment must be held. Mr. Wright speaks nostalgically of "pre-Christian Africa." Apparently he is unaware that West Africa is being swept not by Christianity but by Mohammedanism.

Mr. Wright lectures the West on fidelity to its own ideals of democracy and freedom and on its duty to Africa, but his voice does not carry the authority that a more balanced appraisal of the situation in the Gold Coast would have given it.

"Pilgrims in Africa." *San Antonio News*, September 26, 1954.

This week sees the publication of two books—possibly the first of their kind—reporting the experiences of American Negro writers who recently visited Africa to study the lives and problems of their distant relatives.

The books are BLACK POWER, by Richard Wright, the novelist, who made a fairly intensive though short study of the semi-independent Gold Coast, and AFRICA, LAND OF MY FATHERS, by Era Bell Thompson, a staff writer for the Negro magazine, Ebony, who traveled over a large part of the continent in about 10 weeks.

The two books are similar in many ways, although Wright's is better written, more analytical, and strikes deeper. Both travelers learned in short order that they had more in common with European and American civilization than with the tribal traditions of Africa. In the countries where Negroes have a measure of self-government, they found little race-consciousness among the blacks, and the visitors were regarded as Americans, or even "Europeans," their skin-color eliciting only a mild curiosity. In South Africa, Rhodesia and Kenya, however, where the color bar still stands, their African cousins greeted them either with warm sympathy or fearful aloofness.

Both books show Africa as a tragic continent, but there is more hope in West Africa and the Congo than in the South and East, where a small minority of whites is struggling to retain its lordship over the cowed but restless African majority. From these and all other accounts, it is hard to think of any peaceable solution short of a miracle.

R. T. Horchler. *Best Sellers*, 14 (October 1, 1954), 97.

Black Power is Richard Wright's nonfiction report on the African Gold Coast. It is an ambitious project, involving the analysis and interpretation of complex political, economic, ethnological and religious factors. Moreover, as is indicated by the subtitle, "A Record of Reactions in a Land of Pathos," and as Wright notes in his introductory remarks, this is "a first-person, subjective narrative" of experiences and meditations during a several month tour of the Gold Coast. This highly personal, narrative quality is at once a strength and a weakness in the book.

Like any traveler to a distant, unknown land, Wright was overwhelmed and bewildered by the profusion of strange sights, sounds and customs. The record of his day-to-day discoveries, impulsive responses, gropings toward understanding of an alien culture makes compelling and provocative reading, but is ultimately of doubtful help in forming conclusions about the real nature of things in the Gold Coast.

The reliability of Wright's study of African conditions is further damaged by the inadequacy of his knowledge of many areas of the question (Christianity, or religion at large, for instance) and by the seething bitterness which pervades his book. The materialistic bias of Wright's mind makes him sincerely incapable, it seems, of comprehending non-materialistic considerations, and his deep emotional involvement in any racial struggle makes him impatient with qualification and complexity, even in regard to justice and truth. Wright's conviction is that every action of the white West in relation to Africa (past, present and future) must necessarily be motivated by greed, hatred and fear. And in the indictment of the Christian missionaries which runs through the book, Wright maintains that they were and are simply agents—conscious or unwitting—in the systematic looting of a continent; this is the whole of his understanding. The Christian missionaries are to Wright—and apparently to many Gold Coast leaders—the principal villains in the exploitation of a people and the shattering of a culture, because, among other reasons, religion became the opium of the people: it weakened their will to resist and instilled an "unrealistic" set of values.

But despite all this, *Black Power* is a moving and valuable reading experience. For one thing, it illuminates the mind and heart of Richard Wright, American Negro, man of good will, but lost, hurt and angry. It offers a wealth of revealing detail and incident about the Gold Coast, with flashes of poignant insight into the dilemma of the African today. And it draws the face of the West, not as it is, I pray, but as it looks to millions of people in the world: this is a deeply disturbing and depressing vision, but one good for us to know.

The dangers and trials which lie before Africa today, and before us in relation to Africa, call for calmness, trust, charity. Unhappily, as Richard Wright indicates in this book, we are not likely—any of us—to find these qualities when the naked "black power" of Africa erupts.

Robert S. Taylor. *Library Journal,* 79 (October 1, 1954), 1831.

Whether one agrees with author's use of Marxist interpretation or not, this is a most important book about a most important subject—African self-government. Obviously writing in a hurry, novelist Richard Wright nevertheless portrays with artistic insight and personal passion a situation of many compounds: western ideals and black slavery, industrialization and *juju* magic, white materialism and black power, European individualism and African family-tribal kinship. Often unable to break down the innermost wall of personality—"I was black and they were black, but my blackness did not help me,"—Mr. Wright, through perseverance, sensitivity and research nevertheless is able to gather the many threads into a fascinating and significant book. Highly recommended for all libraries as the best recent study of this complex new phenomenon of African nationalism.

John Chapman. "Beware of the West, Negro Writer Warns Africans." *Minneapolis Star*, October 1, 1954.

For three months last year Richard Wright, an American Negro author ("Native Son" and "Black Boy") and ex-Communist party member (1932 to 1944) who now makes his home in Paris, visited Africa's Gold Coast because he "felt that it was time for someone to subject a slice of African life to close scrutiny in terms of concepts that one would use in observing life anywhere."

That Wright achieved a remarkably close scrutiny in so short time is at once evident in his newly published report "Black Power."

But the sum effect of Wright's book is no more than "a slice of African life"—a very small slice, considering all that Wright did not see, and an often perplexing one in terms of his reactions to the clash of black nationalist and colonial forces.

It is wholly proper, of course, that a man of African descent should be as deeply disturbed as Wright is over the African's plight. "In terms of a common heritage of suffering and hunger for freedom," Wright told natives at a political rally, "your heart and my heart beat as one."

But there are two sides to the Gold Coast's struggle for independence, and in three months Wright apparently allowed himself too little time for the colonial side to form a truly balanced judgment. The impression is that Wright only wanted to see one side, that he went to Africa bearing an anti-colonial, anti-British chip on his shoulder.

Wright advises Kwame Nkrumah, the Gold Coast's prime minister, to "have no illusions" regarding westerners. "If until today Africa was static, it was because Europeans deliberately wanted to keep her that way," he writes. "They do not even treat the question of Africa's redemption seriously; to them it is a source of amusement. . . ."

Wright calls the Gold Coast "a captive nation," accuses the British of leading the natives astray, paints colonials as plunderers and thieves.

The trouble with this picture is that it overlooks the Gold Coast's position with respect to other African countries. The Gold Coast, since Nkrumah's rapid rise, has been a proving ground for African democracy and self-government. In no other British colony in the Dark Continent have steps toward self rule been so swift.

Besides an African prime minister, the country has an all-African legislature and cabinet. Complete independence and dominion status are predicted within a year. Nor does the Gold Coast have a color bar—the source of so much trouble elsewhere in Africa.

Wright's conclusions seem to rule out the possibility that the white man's presence in Africa for about 300 years has resulted in some benefit to the black population. More than a few observers of the African scene feel that whatever the colonial system's faults, it has opened the way for political and economic progress in areas plagued for centuries by utter stagnation.

Wright does not recommend a black and white partnership, which, incidentally, he would have seen working to good advantage had he visited the nearby Belgian Congo or French West

Africa. Instead he wants an all-black Africa, and the sooner the better.

"Our people," he tells Nkrumah, "must be made to walk, forced draft, into the twentieth century." To do this, Nkrumah must militarize his people and push them forward even if a whole generation must be sacrificed. "Russia will not help you," declares Wright, "unless you accept becoming an appendage of Moscow; and why should you change one set of white masters for another. . . ?"

But Wright's report on fetish-ridden tribalism is so vivid and so convincing that one cannot see how the mental cobwebs can be swept aside rapidly enough to achieve large scale black sovereignty in a generation.

It is unfortunate, perhaps, that this gifted Negro writer chose the Gold Coast for his first contact with Africa. Some of the things he saw there might well call for improvement, but certainly the Gold Coast—prosperous, self-governed and within reach of freedom—is the best that Africa has to offer.

James R. Randall. *Greensboro Daily News*, October 3, 1954.

This first person, subjective narrative of Richard Wright's visit to the Gold Coast of Africa is reading as profitable as it is exciting. Wright, a voluntary exile from America since 1946, is still haunted by his desire for individual freedom and still articulate in conveying the texture of his restless mind. This time, however, his backdrop is a land alien to him and an exploited people with whom he has sympathy but little cultural familiarity. Yet, by dint of a friendly persistence, an alert mind, some research and a willingness to adventure, his evaluation becomes something that is intellectually stimulating and qualified.

His writing technique involves a heavy reliance on the present tense in order that the reader may share the journey. Almost the moment he steps off the ship at Takoradi, we are made aware of the squalor, the brooding and the sudden, unexplained laughter of the people of this lush country in which tribalism and the 20th century are so incongruously wedded. We are soon also made aware of the importance of this strange world and of the necessity for realizing a just solution of the country's problem. Necessity on moral grounds has long existed; now the West and, more specifically, England is rapidly being faced with a practical necessity. Nationalistic movements are gaining strength and peoples of other countries are waiting to see if England will redeem her promises. To default might prove to be more than just a show of bad taste.

The man who most interests Wright is Kwame Nkrumah, an American educated (Lincoln University) native who holds considerable political power. In only five years this man has brought about an unforeseen unity in his people by answering their most pressing questions and organizing mass rallies that incorporate politics and tribal customs. Wright looks to him for hope, and he does seem justified. Even while Wright is in the country, Nkrumah wins a working majority of the Parliament.

Wright is no sociologist; he is too impassioned for that. However, where a sociologist would give us statistical "knowledge by acquaintance," Wright through his charged prose and his background as a novelist gives us almost a "knowledge by experience." We are led to tribal funerals and other ceremonies and made to see them as the participants themselves see them. We accompany Wright on a journey by taxi along jungle roads in an oppressively soggy heat. We become acquainted with tribal chiefs and their traditional ways and modern African sociologists such as Dr. Busia and their sophisticated views. And we become aware of the capacities of a land in which huge snakes can and occasionally do aimlessly slither into the most modern of living rooms.

Some readers will find Wright too frank and too liberal in his views, for he is never coy. Unlike Whittaker Chambers and others, Wright when he left Communism did not look for another authoritarian position to adhere to, but only retrenched to a less radical position. Readers who object on this matter can still profit from this blend of the travelogue and the socio-political analysis. All of us, however, should see the lesson that is becoming more obvious by the day, and that is—in the words of Marianne Moore—"We must learn to love one another or die."

Ted Poston. "Travelers Report on India, Africa." *New York Post*, October 3, 1954.

Two of America's most talented writers have been moving around recently. Saunders Redding went to India in 1952 at the invitation of the State Dept. to lecture on American life. Richard Wright went to the Gold Coast in Africa last year at the suggestion of friends.

The result is the publication of two highly informative but deeply disturbing additions to the rapidly growing literature of color and the world today. Both writers, incidentally, are Negroes.

And the books are as different as the personalities of the authors. Redding, a sensitive poet, novelist and college professor, displays the same insight and sophistication revealed in his "On Being Negro in America." Wright who could hardly produce a bad book if he tried, wields the same humorless bludgeon he used in his autobiography.

Redding accepted his State Dept. assignment with a certain amount of skepticism. He was through with carrying the black man's burden and "would not be tricked into taking up again some emotional baggage I had but recently jettisoned."

He planned to tell the clinical truth about America, because "I had no spiritual investment in it. The national unit called America meant nothing to me now."

But even before he crossed Europe, he found out it wasn't so simple. In Geneva, he was rejected for being an American. "It had not occurred to me that being an American here could give the same offense as being Negro in some parts of the U.S.," he observed wryly.

And he was totally unprepared for what he encountered in India. There he was denounced as an American, accepted—sometimes patronizingly—as a Negro, and then denounced again because he could not embrace a color consciousness so intense that all white people must be regarded as implacable foes.

From the Communists and pro-Communists, he expected it, of course. But there was both frustration and indignation when the anti-Communist Indian intellectuals were as critical—and often as misinformed—in their deep-seated feeling against the U.S.

And even more painful was the fact that there was enough truth in many of their charges to make many misconceptions perfectly acceptable to the Indians.

"We were not sensitive enough to the very high sensitivity of the Indian people," he said. "We were seeking to 'uplift' them. If jealousy played a part in their natural resentment of this, so also did cultural pride."

Unlike Redding, who thought he was through with race, Wright left his expatriate Paris to seek his own racial roots on Africa's Gold Coast.

With the exception of Prime Minister Kwame Nkrumah and his associates—probably the most significant native group on the African continent right now—Wright scorned and needled the intellectuals with whom he had necessary contact.

With real personal courage, he probably went further into the Gold Coast wilderness than any similar traveler. And although he is too prone to generalizations and as distrustful of most natives as they were of him, Wright does give a graphic picture of what British exploitation and tribal exploitation has meant to the people of the Gold Coast.

Through fleeting vignettes of Nkrumah and his native movement which has fused the tribal mores into an effective political machine, he offers some hope for the future. But Wright is impatient of that hope.

He urges Nkrumah to reject both the Communist East and the white West and to wrest Africa from all invaders, even at the price of limitless bloodshed and deliberate exploitation of his own people.

Redding, who thought he was all over it, came back home more in love with America for having had to defend it.

Wright, who long ago rejected the Communist doctrine of his youth, left Africa with the conviction that "Our people must be made to walk, forced draft, into the 20th century." And, as a parting shot, he suggests that another revolution was more successful than any Communist triumph.

"Your fight has been won before," he tells the Gold Coast leaders. "I am an American and my country, too, was once a colony of England."

James N. Rhea. "Two Views of a Continent in Conflict." *Providence Journal*, October 3, 1954.

Africa is a land of 175 million black people ruled directly by about five million whites. For some colonial powers, Africa is the last stronghold, and their tenure there is uncertain. The natives want the whites to get out. The rulers are Westerners in cold war with Russia and China and other Red-tinged nations. In this lies the significance of Africa today.

Into this land of intense racial conflict went Richard Wright, the most famous American Negro author, and Era Bell Thompson, a first-rate Negro journalist, to write books about how things looked to them here where their ancestors were taken slaves. Both visited the Gold Coast and talked with Africa's first black prime minister, Kwame Nkrumah. They came away believing that Nkrumah's Convention People's Party, fusing the best of tribal culture with the best of Western political organization, holds the key to Africa's future.

But neither Miss Bell nor Mr. Wright felt more at home in Africa than any other Westerner, regardless of color, would feel. To most Africans whom they met, they were outsiders, strangers, black white people. They sympathize with the struggling Africans as few white persons can do, however.

Of Richard Wright, a friend of mine likes to say "sometimes Wright write right, and sometimes Wright write wrong." No other Wright book is more worthy of this judgment than the one at hand. This is not to belittle Wright's genius. It is to regret the uncontrolled subjectivity and cynicism that mar Wright's evaluations, especially in recent years. He promises us he will not judge the African by Western standards; and yet, because he is first, last, and always a champion of the underdog he heaps scorn and abuse on the African chiefs and their elite, even though he understands the cultural factors that have produced them.

Always Wright is the prober, the searcher, the victim of an admirable, though doubtless painful, compulsion to get right down to the bottom of things. This drive serves productively when it exposes the African's ancestor-worshipping religion as one cause of backwardness and dreaminess. But it also brings Wright to the foolhardiness of speculating on the frequency of urination among the Africans, as if anyone really cares.

The former Communist says at the outset that much of his interpretations are Marxist. He does not tell us that much are Freudian, to use a general term for mind-probing. The latter approach has led Wright into a good deal of nonsense. . . .

Wright is on wonderfully sure and familiar ground when he describes how the British and other imperialists destroyed the African tribal civilization, kept the African out of their own Western civilization and left him dangling somewhere between the two systems, a confused, impoverished nobody. Well, the African cannot return to pure tribalism, Wright argues. He must go into the twentieth century, preferably in one generation. He urges Nkrumah to "militarize" the Gold Coast. By militarization, he merely means a strict social regimentation.

This advice may be good, but in giving it to Nkrumah I think Wright "write right wrong." After such a short time on the Gold Coast, he should think twice before advising the prime minister and his party. Nkrumah is an intelligent and a dedicated man, with far more political experience in Africa, which he left only to attend school in London and America. (I knew him when he was a student here.)

But this is a book every Westerner could read with profit, because: "Make no mistake, the West is being judged by events that transpire in Africa."

In some respects, Miss Bell Thompson's book is more interesting than Wright's, but it does not have the same weighty significance. Miss Thompson was not trying to be significant. Recognizing her limitations, she did not write a book about Africa, but about her experiences there. Whereas Wright visited only one country, she toured the continent from Liberia to Egypt. She did not tour South Africa. Although she had a visa to enter the country, she was kept out by her color. . . .

For Miss Thompson, the African tour was largely a frustrating, heartbreaking journey. Her American citizenship could not protect her from the cruelties of Africa's white rulers at all times—but it was a powerful deterrent to the imperialists. . . .

B. B.
Jet Magazine,
(October 7, 1954).

A gnawing hunger for racial freedom has driven author Richard Wright to a constant, unrelenting search for some racial utopia during much of his adult life. When he lived in the South, Chicago looked like mecca and he set out for the Windy City. There, he was quickly disillusioned and turned to communism as a new hope. But he learned Marxism was more mess than mecca and he departed for Paris to search in France for the promised land. There, he found fleeting freedom for himself personally but not for others of his race.

When the African Gold Coast shook off its colonial shackles and Kwame Nkrumah became the first native prime minister of a British colony, Wright saw another flicker of hope. He set off once again on his never-ending search. In *Black Power* Wright reports what he found during a six-months stay. Like many another U. S. Negro with high hopes, the brilliant writer came away from Africa with bitter disappointment after seeing how far behind the Western world Africans still are. While he condemns "the stagnancy of tribalism," his book is basically a blistering indictment of the Western powers, an expression of his "consternation at what Europe had done to Africa." With his trained eye and ear for detail, Wright has written a splendid report on the Gold Coast's new revolution.

But still the impatient, impulsive radical, Wright winds up his report with an impassioned letter of advice to Nkrumah which insists that the only way Africans can catch up with modern nations is through dictatorship. "African life must be militarized," he asserts. Strange words indeed for a man seeking freedom.

Fred R. Conkling.
"Wright Sees West Africa in Turmoil."
Fort Wayne News Sentinel,
October 9, 1954.

The dedication of Mr. Wright's "Black Power" is made to "The unknown African, who, because of his primal and poetic humanity was regarded by white men as a 'thing' to be bought, sold, and used as an instrument of production; and who, alone in the forests of West Africa, created a vision of life so simple as to be terrifying, yet a vision that was irreducibly human. . . ."

"Black Power" is a curious mixture of history, biographical sketches, exposition of social customs and political chicanery, and blistering jabs at British management of governmental affairs among the natives of the "gold coast," a section of Africa between Liberia and Nigeria. The significance of the present dynamite-packed situation is not clearly defined. To be sure the author points to the constant and rhythmic beat of the somewhat frightening chant of "Free-doom," "Free-doom." Is the accidental mis-accented second syllable prophetic? But just what do tribal dances about the empty coffin of a dead relative, questionable housing projects, open solicitation of men by courtesans, or the awful inferno of damp heat—what do these imply about black power?

The author slaps the British and looks obliquely at the efforts of Christian missionaries with their question-mark converts. He points to evidence of dissatisfaction and unrest among some few (?). What IS this black power?

David E. Apter. "A Negro's Dim View of Africa's Gold Coast." *Chicago Sunday Tribune Magazine of Books*, October 10, 1954, p. 6.

Richard Wright has written a strange and disturbing book. In his anxiety to find some mystical bond between himself and the Africans of the Gold Coast, Wright alienated both the nationalist African government and the people themselves.

With a burning dislike of British imperialism, he tried to find evidences of its evil in every aspect of African social and political life. It is little wonder that Nkrumah, the African prime minister, who welcomed him to the Gold Coast, soon recognized that Wright was not seeking to find out about Gold Coast life and problems, but was searching for his own soul. After two days of official hospitality, Wright was given the cold shoulder. He received few answers and was left to roam around the country in a taxi.

Wright demonstrates little understanding of the difficulties of social transformation, and indeed shows shockingly little respect for the people of the Gold Coast and their way of life. He feels so strongly that social life there is governed by magic, by the irrational, that he does not credit the accomplishments of the Africans themselves. He plays into the hands of the very people he dislikes by reinforcing their prejudices with his own.

Wright ignores the real problems of social change and development, many of which arise not out of malice, necessarily, but because of the collision of different ways of life. He shows little sympathy with the form in which change in the Gold Coast is actually taking place. As a matter of fact, Africans are in real control over the decisions of the country. The Gold Coast will be the first African colony to receive independence.

For all this Wright shows little concern. Rather he demands that Africans become Europeanized, and tells them to be quick about it. It is little wonder that the Africans treated him as a European—with caution and distrust. His book is far more revealing of Richard Wright than of the Gold Coast.

"Black Power" is by a person of great artistry and deep moral purpose. We cannot question his sincerity and emotion, but can only conclude that the people of Africa deserve more sober understanding.

Richard Mourey. "Gold Coast Turmoil." *Hartford Courant*, October 10, 1954.

A revolution of immeasurable energy is building strength rapidly in Africa's Gold Coast. Richard Wright, a top rank writer of this generation, has visited this country, which he calls "the land of my African ancestors" and has written a simultaneously fascinating and yet a disappointing work.

A former Communist who has fought long and hard for the improvement of the Negro's place in human relations, Wright has undoubtedly produced a book that cannot be ignored by those who make the world their study hall. In the Gold Coast a primitive population is trying to claw its way out of the mire of colonialism, illiteracy and paganism to place itself among the free and independent nations of the world.

The author feels the future of the Gold Coast and its fight for freedom is tied tightly to the mysterious thought of Nkrumah, the Prime Minister. If he fails, the fight will fail, for the Prime Minister is the only man now capable of demanding the fanatic devotion the people of the Gold Coast must have for a leader.

"Black Power" is a moving, deep probing examination of the black man's mind and life. It asks many questions but answers only a few, because only a few are now answerable. The author has brought vividly to the reader the many strange contradictions of African life. On the Gold Coast, Wright found an urgent desire for freedom among the countless illiterate tribesmen. But, conversely, he discovered an ingrained opposition to independence among the educated leaders in the cities.

The author has not a single kind word to say for British rule on the Gold Coast, nor has he a good word for the work of the missionaries among the "heathens." Religious teaching in Africa, he observes, has shattered old tribal customs and left a vacuum which the missionaries were unable to fill with Christian belief. He feels a religious fanaticism pervades African politics, manifesting itself in an almost pious devotion to political leaders, particularly Nkrumah.

The rise of the drive for freedom has been abrupt. If Nkrumah can maintain his Godlike control over the masses the revolution may be a success. If he loses control, disaster and chaos may result and plunge the country more deeply into the mire of illiteracy and paganism than ever before.

As a Negro, Wright seems to have succumbed to the very attitude he has dedicated himself to battle. He appears to have approached the African Negro with the same mental reservations the white man still entertains toward the American Negro.

If this is true, and it would appear so, Wright's product must be read carefully with a weather eye cocked for subtle misunderstanding.

Joyce Cary. "Catching Up with History." *The Nation*, 179 (October 16, 1954), 332–33.

This is the report of a British colony in West Africa, the Gold Coast, where Britain has lately appointed a Negro Prime Minister, Nkrumah, with large powers. As reporting, it is a first-class job and gives the best picture I've seen of an extraordinary situation.

The culture of Negro Africa is Stone Age. Nine-tenths of the people belong in mind at least five thousand years back. And the mind, the education of a people, is what finally you have to reckon with in politics. This culture, this mind, has now been pitched into the twentieth century by no fault of Africa, or of Britain. It is the consequence simply of the speed-up of history by two great wars and the enormous technical and scientific progress of the last thirty years. Wireless alone, apart from modern economics, makes it impossible to isolate any culture from external shock, from new exciting ideas, and from the demagogue. In a series of brilliant scenes Wright shows the effects, social and political, of this violent clash.

He describes traders, black and white, each as naive as the other, and as confused by a situation which is completely new and dangerous but inevitable: juju chiefs and their households, bound still by the magic rites of the blood in service and in sacrifice; funerals where the corpse is represented in the coffin only by a cutting from nails and hair, to deceive envious spirits, the actual body being hidden in some secret place.

He describes political meetings where each family head brings his dependents, who at word of command cheer, clap, and shout for freedom. He can tell a story against himself. At a great meeting summoned by Nkrumah, he addresses the crowd on the responsibility of the Gold Coast Africans as pioneers in the fight for African freedom. The local reporters ask him for the text of his speech. He submits it to Nkrumah for approval. The Prime Minister glances over it and then stuffs it into Wright's coat pocket. The speech is censored.

Wright not only reports against himself; he writes so honestly, so directly as he feels, that he gives the material for another book contradicting his own arguments. He tells us that the chiefs are all scoundrels but also that there is more genuine religion in tribal paganism than in the bourgeois Christian church; that Africa is in desperate need of education but Britain has been wrong in educating Africans too well. We read that Britain has shattered tribal culture and also that tribal life is breaking up because the people find it a bore and rush to the towns.

This latter is, of course, the significant fact. Tribal life is inconceivably narrow and boring—a combination of totalitarian government and authoritarian church in their most oppressive forms, a system that has succeeded with the help of the climate in preventing almost all progress. But humanity cannot stand boredom. Its imagination revolts instinctively and incessantly against the blimp. It may worship and tremble, but give it the smallest chance to escape and it will fly. So the tribes break up as soon as any paramount power establishes peace, stops slave raiding, and gives protection to the individual. The consequence is an immense growth in the towns—especially any town with industry, cinemas, shops—and enormous slums, more difficult to control even than the Negro districts of Chicago or New York. I say slums, but they are slums only to the European mind; to the African escaped from the tribe they are dwelling places full of delights, above all of freedom.

Governments in Africa, whatever they are, have the choice between seeing the tribes break, the slums grow, or bringing in legislation to control the movements of the people. And repression in Africa, especially in Africa's present explosive mood, can very easily produce shooting, which means more repression. How are you going to maintain the tribe by police action? How are you going to convey tribesmen with a Stone Age mind through developments that in Europe took thousands of years, fast enough to catch up with history?

When I joined the African service forty years ago, I was instructed that our aim was to prepare Africans for self-government by the development of their own native institutions—that is, we were to attempt to give Africa the social history of all civilized nations but to speed up the process as much as possible, without destroying our means. This limitation was highly practical. I found my local judge taking bribes. But

I did not sack him. I had been instructed that almost all African judges took presents, the question was whether he gave fair judgments. Also whether I could find a better judge, for men of the necessary education were very scarce.

So too among primitive pagans chiefs were kept in power but given councilors who spoke for various sections of the people—the first step toward popular representation.

This plan for West Africa brought about smooth and rapid progress: that is to say, it gave the primitive administration we found as much development in forty years as primitive Europe accomplished in a couple of centuries. Of course we had the advantage over the Dark Ages of modern techniques, a trained staff, and the telegraph.

But then there was the war, immense economic disturbance, slumps—the same political turmoil that fell upon the whole world, India, China, South America.

Nkrumah, on the Gold Coast, demands, of course, complete independence, but he has no other choice. As a nationalist and a demagogue he is obliged to do so or some other demagogue would overbid him.

Democracy, of course, is impossible in any state where 90 per cent of the people are illiterate. It exists only in literate and industrialized nations with a powerful middle class and organized unions capable of standing up to central government. All other states are dictatorships more or less disguised. Nkrumah will have to be a dictator whether he likes it or not, and the question is whether he has the kind of genius which Ataturk brought to a much less difficult problem in Turkey, with a far greater educated class to help him.

Wright himself vividly pictures this difficulty, as he does all the others which face an African national government—except one, the rising population. Yet this by itself can smash all efforts, however well organized, to raise standards of living and education.

Population in Africa is increasing fast, and the country as a whole is poor in soil, difficult in climate, full of deserts. The battle for land is already acute. Mau Mau is one consequence, and the elements of Mau Mau are present everywhere, in the breaking tribe, and in the shape of the primitive mind. For the mind is still the mind of the tribal mass and will be so long after the tribal sanctions which controlled its repressed passions and neurotic panics are no more.

Wright's own answers to these political conundrums are offered to Nkrumah in an open letter. He urges him to sacrifice a generation, and not to be afraid of *militarism* or *regimentation.*

The author has rejected the party, but his political thinking still belongs to communism. He imagines that violence, cruelty, injustice, and some clever lying can achieve a new civilization. But this is false. They can only produce new forms of oppression, new totalitarian states, which, because they are founded on oppression, face exactly the same difficulties as the ones they replace. If they do not educate, if they prevent the entrance of new ideas, new techniques, they stagnate and are finally destroyed by some outer force. If they educate, organize, develop, they generate large classes of rebels, more or less secret, who sooner or later will destroy them from within. Russia in the years since 1917 has had four or five internal revolutions, executed dozens of rebel leaders, purged thousands of their followers. And it is probably more unstable now, as a regime, than at any time before.

There are no easy answers in politics, especially nowadays. We are still groping our way, and need, above all, the facts of the new situation, facts all the harder to get because of universal propaganda, the practice, learned from Communist and Fascist alike, of the big lie. That is why books like this of Wright's are so valuable—so far, that is, as they give facts, and so far as the facts can be distinguished from the bias. Wright is so honest a reporter, so vivid a writer, that this is easily done in the course of reading.

It would be a public service if he could give us a similar report on Liberia, where a Negro government has been in full independent power for more than a century.

L. M. Collins. *Nashville Tennessean*, October 17, 1954.

Richard Wright and Africa are a combination to conjure up more than a passing specter.

The medicine man is still mysteriously powerful, but there are challenges in today's awakening Africa; there are representation, education, and a fervent desire for spiritual and economic emancipation. The old "ghosts" born of fear and ignorance and called forth by the mumbo-jumbo of painted priests are weakening their hold on the African mind.

Especially is this true of the Gold Coast, according to Richard Wright. Here the most sinister creature, the most potently harmful and malevolent, is the specter of communism to be averted, not by magical rites, but by a sane, unselfish, educated leadership; here the Convention Peoples' party, led by Kwame Nkhrumah, is to show the way to political and social emancipation and self-government. Here is black power.

Richard Wright knows the real worth of democratic living, having been born poor in Mississippi, having experienced certain misadventures of a black boy seeking manhood among those determined to deny it, and having turned to communism in desperation. He wrote of these events in "Black Boy," "Native Son," and in a powerful denunciation of communism, "The God that Failed."

On a six-months' tour of the African Gold Coast, from which the ancestors of many American Negroes came, Wright examined all aspects of life, and now he has reviewed that tour and set down his findings and impressions in "Black Power," a portrait of the Gold Coast African.

This is that African: He believes straightforwardly, lacking artful sophistication but also lacking "the inner strength to stand aloof from himself." The tribal mind is "sensuous: loving images, not concepts; personalities, not abstractions; movement, not form; dreams, not reality," the tribal African being caught between greater and lesser powers, some harmful, others helpful. His religion is law. His gods number 400. "Jesus Christ? God number 401." He lives a "family life," speaking a poetic language, satisfied with the errors of a system of native communism in the "single largest dollar-earning area in all of Africa." And as he reveals himself as carefree or naive, fearless or progressive, Wright is sometimes confused and angry but more often fascinated and entertained.

Gerard Tetley. "A History of Bitterness." *Richmond Times-Dispatch,* October 17, 1954.

Of the many books of recent publication seeking to interpret Africa—and North Africa particularly—during these fluid days of nationalism this may be branded perhaps as the most brilliant. It is written by an American Negro who went to the Gold Coast and studied that country—to find that the currents there towards freedom and self-government are the same as those now being watched in other territories by the suzerain powers.

Wright pens history in bitterness and he paints a backdrop of racial martyrdom which goes back to the slave trade days. He portrays the extraordinary clash and confusion of ideals, with officialdom westernized and anglicized, but with tribal magic and unashamed nudity rubbing elbows with modernism.

The author is a self-confessed former Communist. He belonged to that political wing in this country for 12 years until he suddenly realized that while he worked for the unfettering of his race, Communism held some 80,000,000 people enslaved. So he rejected Communism, but admits that he is not very happy in the free world camp, because he finds that there remains a form of colonialism which is bound to make freedom for the Negro difficult.

He also sounds a warning indicating that Africa will eventually go the way of China unless the free world concerns itself with the aspirations of the colored people in Africa towards freedom from the inferiority stigmata.

A lot of people may not like the tone of this book. They may think that it is cynical, but of the volumes written about Africa, this comes from the pen of a man who himself admits that his ancestors were torn forcibly from their roots to be carried into slavery and who exposes the bleeding heart of the Negroid race in no uncertain phrases.

Saunders Redding. *Baltimore Afro-American,* October 23, 1954.

Richard Wright accepted the personal challenge that the Gold Coast offered him in the same way one might issue a challenge to duel in the defense of the honor of his ladylove—that is to say, with more passion than thought. *Black Power* is a visceral book.

He begins calmly enough by setting the frame of reference in the struggle against colonialism. Being primarily a writer of fiction, the author chose to do this by the method of presenting a portrait—a telling and substantial portrait, let it be said—of one of the victims of colonialism whose story makes clear the inference that colonialism is the fatal disease of the western world.

But the trouble with the portrait of Justice Thomas is that it is too good. It lures the reader into expectations that Richard Wright fails to fulfill.

Within too short a time one is plunged into the dark complexity, not of the Gold Coast of Africa, but of Wright's involvement with his own socio-political orientation and his own philosophical ambivalence.

One cannot see the forest for the trees.

What one does see clearly is that Wright, having long since repudiated communism and having recently abjured existentialism, is adrift between the unfulfilled promises of Marxist politics and the unfulfilled principles of democratic dogma.

It is partly for this reason that *Black Power* is so confused a book.

The author is himself confused.

He says so time and again: he is "bewildered," "stunned," "thunderstruck" and "dumbfounded" by phenomena—African dancing, African heat, funeral ceremonies, social backwardness—phenomena that, even allowing for his writer's sensitivity, should not have phased him.

His concern with these things, never quite wedded to what is avowedly his chief concern—the socio-political struggle against colonialism—seems irrelevant.

And his method is another thing that makes for confusion. Without the least warning, Wright jumps back and forth from past tense narration to present transcription of his notes.

On the level of his principal concern, Wright finds the eager political consciousness of the Gold Coast amenable to Marxist analysis, and it is this that makes possible his insights into Africa's political possibilities and her social hazards.

He sees Kwame Nkrumah, Prime Minister of the Gold Coast, as a brilliant and conscientious leader, but he does not fail to see the dangers in the veneration the people accord him.

He makes short shrift of the once powerful tribal chiefs, colonialism's henchmen, because he is impatient with their ignorance and their old-fashioned political "morality," which refused to embrace the concept of freedom.

Wright believes that "Africa must be militarized for production," and for the sake of strengthening her social and political discipline and accomplishing her cultural independence of both western democracies and communism.

But all in all, *Black Power* is almost as tortured and tortuous as *The Outsider,* and one can only hope that this is a final purging of confusion, and that from now on Richard Wright can devote himself to the kind of writing that earned him his early reputation for brilliance.

Margot Jackson. "Black Power Is Strong Work." *Akron Beacon Journal,* October 24, 1954.

What would a black man think if he visited Africa? Just because his ancestors came from the Gold Coast region, 300 years ago in the days of slave-trading, would he understand better than the white man what the people here strive for?

Richard Wright is a black man, descendant of slaves sold by their own tribes. He is also an educated man, a believer in freedom. He was a member of the Communist Party until 1944 when he realized it was removing more freedom than it was establishing. He is a writer with sympathetic understanding and powerful passion. "Native Son" and "Black Boy" are his best known books.

Two years ago Wright went to the Gold Coast of Africa, a British colony, to look and learn. "Black Power" tells what he saw and felt as he poked and pried.

The Gold Coast is so rich in bauxite that it could keep the aluminum world supplied for 200 years. Diamonds, gold, timber are come by easily. But machinery rusts out in days, so steaming is the climate. His clothes were mildewed in a week.

The Gold Coast has more than four million people, but it has no cattle because the tsetse fly ravages them. Milk and butter must be shipped in, tinned. It is a one-crop country: the cacao bean.

Almost all these four million persons are black: 90% of them cannot read or write. Yet they have won suffrage from England; they have elected their own prime minister, Kwame Nkrumah. Wright stood at a political meeting and watched libations poured to the ancestors, then an oath taken personally to Nkrumah to "resist imperialist attempts to disrupt our ranks."

Missionaries oppose this rise of nationalism, Wright says. It can, in their eyes, become a force more powerful than Christianity. But he has scorn for the missionaries. They have made the word "Christian" a kind of social status; they have belittled the graceful wood carving since the figures portrayed were usually the tribal gods.

The Gold Coast has the most modern hospital in the tropics. Within yards of it is a stinking, fetid lagoon. Once a tribe was saved by the good gods living in these waters, and so it must not be drained.

Two states the size of Ohio would almost equal the area of the Gold Coast. But the natives rarely move from one part to another; they must die where their ancestors did so they may rejoin them. Funerals outrival a circus parade. Caskets whirl over the mourners' heads as the soul is sent triumphantly to another world.

In 1947, the Gold Coast won the right to vote and to choose its own representatives. Civil disobedience, somewhat similar to that used by Gandhi's followers in India, was the weapon. Now Nkrumah's party wants complete freedom from Britain, which still appoints a governor-general to the colony.

Wright saw enough to believe these people should have freedom. But he believes they must have confidence in themselves first. They must pull themselves up and out, without outsiders functioning as bungling statesmen, or money-mad businessmen, or neurotic do-gooders. They have been kept insecure, he claims, by a kind of teasing torture of false kindnesses.

"Black Power" is a powerful book. It is bitter and philosophical, funny and frank, rich in descriptions and interpretations. It's a good book to read now when Africa is churning toward freedom.

Philip Harsham. "Richard Wright's Bitter Pen." *Louisville Courier-Journal,* October 24, 1954. *St. Louis Post-Dispatch,* October 30, 1954, p. 4A.

The chip on Richard Wright's shoulder has at last found the opportunity to assume the proportions of a baobab tree.

Mr. Wright, the American Negro best known for "Native Son" and "Black Boy," and known also for his renunciation of Communism described in "The God That Failed," has been impelled by some mysterious inner force, it seems, to visit the land of his heritage, the Gold Coast.

And that chip on his shoulder apparently started growing even before he approached Africa's shores.

"Black Power," his report on life in British West Africa's first self-governing territory, is one of the most subjective, most one-sided, and most emotional pieces of writing to be labeled non-fiction in many a moon.

The Gold Coast, a self-governing British territory sweltering in equatorial heat, has made tremendous strides toward dominion status despite its climate, its illiteracy and its tight clutch on paganism.

It has been helped along by its British colonial status, and like all colonies it has been hindered in some respects by that status. A majority of those Gold Coast citizens who have been given the fundamentals of education have been given them by white missionaries—missionaries, admittedly, in search of converts.

Mr. Wright, however, found only white mercantilists intent upon robbing the Gold Coasters blind and missionaries intent upon satisfying their own "neurotic" desire for a place in the hereafter. Both, Mr. Wright found, pursued their selfish courses with no regard for the black African upon whose land they trespassed.

The author implores Kwame Nkrumah, Britain's first Negro colonial Prime Minister, to throw them all out, to rush his fetish-worshiping people into the twentieth century regardless of the toll, both psychological and physical, such a plunge might take.

Nkrumah must be militant, Mr. Wright insists, and he apparently would have the popular Prime Minister take up the tactics of an out-and-out dictator. Gold Coast people must be regimented. They must shake themselves loose from their tribal moorings, and most important they must shed the "shackles of slavery" white colonialists have fastened upon them.

"Black Power" contains a few bits of objective reporting and they reveal Mr. Wright as the very able writer he can be. Those pertain to tribal customs and life in Accra and they are vivid and readable.

They are sufficient to make the reader feel that the Gold Coast is indeed an enchanting place, populated by charming and likable natives, and it is regrettable that the country and its people are so often hidden behind that baobab tree on Mr. Wright's shoulder.

" 'Native Son' in Africa." *The Reporter*, 11 (November 4, 1954), 48.

Books on Africa have been cascading from the press in such flow recently that it seems little more can be said. Richard Wright's new book on Africa proves the contrary. *Black Power* is the story of a three-month visit to the Gold Coast by a distinguished American author. Saved by the color of his skin from the kindly condescension or the superior detachment of most western writers, yet steeped in the tradition and education of American life, Wright has been able to contribute something unique to the literature of the troubled continent.

It is not the passages of political analysis which give the book its power. These, fortunately few, are often both pompous and shallow. What makes the book live is the colorful, almost photographic portraiture of villages and market places drowsy in the sun, of savages drugged with heat and superstition, of dripping jungles, of the cities of black people. Wright is at his best in his reproduction of conversations. In letting the Africans talk to him, as they will talk only to a man of colored skin, he opens hitherto locked thoughts and emotions. As he lets sad houseboys, native chiefs, rich merchants, dedicated officials, and half-Europeanized leaders talk, he also lets the reader share the pity, hate, contempt, or admiration they arouse in him.

The composite of individual Africans that Mr. Wright presents, split among themselves, seeking self-expression in everything from juju to politics, illuminates the problem of Black Africa and of the Gold Coast in particular. Stripped of their own culture and pride by the European invasion, lost, uneducated, superstitious, and turbulent—how can these people be drawn together to manage their own freedom? For, without freedom, they must remain as they are; yet as they are today, they cannot manage a really effective democratic government. For this reason, Wright sees a necessity in Kwame Nkrumah's Convention People's Party, for all its bizarre flamboyance. Its cult of personal leadership, its tribal customs and blood oaths, and its demagogy, he feels, are indispensable to weld these people together long enough to learn how to manage modern life. Certainly many will quarrel with Wright's shrieking conclusion "AFRICAN LIFE MUST BE MILITARIZED!" (capitals his). But right or wrong, it is an honest expression of opinion, and, at the end of the book, the reader understands why Wright feels he must give it as parting advice to Kwame Nkrumah, however presumptuous it may sound coming from an American.

Most Americans will find equal interest in a relatively minor thread of the book's pattern. This is Wright's fascination, as an American Negro, with the land of his origins, his perplexity as he studies faces, gestures, and mannerisms seeking a clue to his own past. The anger and bitterness with which he explores each historic and shabby relic of the slave trade explains better than any treatise the weight of humiliation and sorrow that historic crime still presses on the descendants of its victims.

William Hugh Jansen. "Pretentious Is the Term." *Lexington Herald Leader*, November 7, 1954.

Richard Wright's "Black Power" is disturbingly uneven and sometimes a very verbose book. Its author never decides whether he is writing a picturesque travelog or whether he is carrying on a weighty sociological and political analysis of the Gold Coast and of its meaning to the rest of the world. When he is engaged in the former, he presents the reader with a series of brilliantly written sketches portraying his own encounters with the people, the towns, and the landscape of the Gold Coast. When he labors at the latter, he is frequently—but emphatically not always—pretentious, dull, or even ignorant.

Of late, it has been the fashion to dismiss Richard Wright as a fuzzy-minded Communist, despite his own open retraction—a retraction which he proudly points out was the result of his own private convictions and not the product of either police pressure or personal fears.

This assertion, I think, can be taken at face value, since Wright is an expatriate living in France.

In "Black Power," Wright, realizing that his personal political history is bound to influence interpretations and evaluations of the work, makes several interesting assertions in connection with his politics and the present opus: 1. He is writing from the point of a Marxist, not that of a Communist. 2. (Naturally in a different section of the work), the problems he is studying do not avail themselves to a Marxist interpretation, because of the absence of certain elements basic to Marxist interpretation. 3. Wherever he uses secondary materials, they are invariably bourgeois sources (are there any nonbourgeois accounts of the Gold Coast?), etc.

It is from this acute consciousness of his own political and political-philosophic points of view that much of the interest and value of "Black Power" derive. And most of this value is, I'm sure, quite unintentional.

But the book should serve now and in the future as a fine example to sociologists and social psychologists of the uneasy point of view which it does manifestly represent. The point of view is complicated, of course, by the fact of Mr. Wright's race, a point which he hammers at all day. His most interesting observation, but scarcely unique with him, is the constantly reiterated astonishment with which he discovers that being members of the same race does not mean that two people necessarily, therefore, have any more in common than the color of their skin. Over and over he discovered that he had no real sympathy for or understanding of the Africans, and they had none for him. Pathos there is galore, and mutual indignation at injustices and exploitation, but the other qualities—sympathy and understanding—cannot exist where there is no sharing of culture or no understanding of cultural differences.

Pretentious I have already labeled the book. I think "Black Power" has many faults. Yet I recommend its reading to anyone who is concerned with the problems of this one-world in which we all must live.

Mr. Wright reveals, sometimes despite himself, the overwhelming difficulties of what is merely one of the many African nations that pose a great threat to the world's equanimity. Mr. Wright points out that there are only two roads for the future, but he refuses to admit that they cannot take either road as tribal nations.

Finally, Mr. Wright is still the artist, and when he keeps his eye on his pen it is still the powerful tool it always has been. And he's honest. He states his own point of view and his own perplexity. He does not make it impossible for the reader to arrive at conclusions different from those set forth in the book.

Luther P. Jackson. "Wright in Africa." *Newark News*, November 14, 1954.

In "Black Power" the American Negro novelist, Richard Wright, issues this challenge to Kwame Nkrumah, native Prime Minister of West Africa's British Gold Coast.

"Africa must be militarized!. . . not for war, but for peace; not for destruction, but for service; not aggression, but for production; not for despotism, but to free minds from mumbo-jumbo."

By militarization Wright means "a temporary discipline that will unite the nation, sweep out the tribal cobwebs, and place the feet of the masses upon a basis of reality." Wright calls for this monumental accomplishment within a generation.

This challenge is culled from a valedictory statement made after a visit to the Gold Coast, where the British have relaxed their imperialistic grip in face of rising demands for "free- - -dooom." But Wright's plea for nationalism is singularly uninspired, not only for its vagueness but primarily because it follows a cold, contemptuous appraisal of the culture of the Ashanti people whose ancestral worship dominates every facet of their existence.

The author, however, is even more contemptuous of Christianity and the West and urges the black man to seek his own salvation. Meanwhile, he asks the native to cast away those customs which have been passed down from parent to child for untold centuries. He suggests nothing in their stead.

Further, the message falls flat because it is based on the presumption that Wright qualifies as a social analyst of the Gold Coast after spending only a few months there. As a novelist, Wright's passion for social significance is often a stumbling block, but with his great dramatic sense he usually picks himself up and leaves this reader, for one, completely absorbed by the circumstances that shape and twist the personality of Bigger Thomas, Cross Damon or the author himself in "Black Boy."

"Black Power" is something else again. The Wright of Paris, Chicago or Mississippi is as alien as the moon to his black cousins in the "bushes" of Africa.

There are ties that bind Negroes everywhere. Racial discrimination against them is one and racial resentment is its concomitant. Evidence of both is expressed by Wright through a young African boy who wants to borrow money from the author so that he can take an American correspondence course and learn how to be a detective. He would find out how the British "took our land, our gold and our diamonds."

"I would throw them in jail, sar," he says.

Wright could have served this boy and "Free- - -dooom" better if he had simply reported the facts of African life in terms of universal longings and strivings which make brotherhood more than a dream.

Doris T. Reed. "Richard Wright Uses Lash in Writing of West in Africa." *Dayton Journal Herald*, November 20, 1954.

There are various ways of rousing a man to a sense of his responsibilities; to a realization that his past misdeeds will provoke disastrous consequences unless corrected. One way is the lash. The result can only breed resentment. Seldom does it produce recognition of error and reversal of policy. Yet, Richard Wright looks at Africa and applies the lash.

His bitter, unmitigated indictment of British imperialism and the "neurotic flutterings" of the missionary effort as he reads the results in that slice of Africa, called the Gold Coast, stirs profound resentment in the reader. One needs to read and reread the author's introduction, remember that he has declared his viewpoint, "his frame of reference," be reconvinced of his sincerity in order to retain a balanced judgment.

Richard Wright, having tried communism, now rejects it, but admits his concern about human freedom makes him an uneasy member of the Western world. He declares that Africa challenges the West as it has never been challenged. That here in Africa the West must separate conviction from pretension and determine if it dares to practice the ideals of justice and freedom it has so persistently instilled into the hearts of men.

He warns that the greatest incentive to the growth of communism in Africa today would be the attempt on the part of the West to throttle the rise of African nations. With this declaration he presents facts he knows to be "unwelcome" so that we may see ourselves as others see and judge us.

Signs reading "proceed at your own risk" seldom deter the determined traveler. Such signs Mr. Wright has plainly posted when he says, "I am not a fair man," and when he admits that he is "areligious."

Mr. Wright had hoped to find some sense of kinship in his common ancestry with the African people but found himself mystified by many of their ways. Still unanswered is his question: "Why are they dancing?"

The hope of the masses, he believes to lie in their native leaders. That they, too, might not prove to be all-wise and incorruptible seems not to have occurred to their protagonist. Nkrumah's program for self-government is the answer to their aroused nationalism. No compromise must be tolerated. What Nkrumah has done in the Gold Coast other Nkrumahs can do elsewhere. None but Africans can accomplish Africa's "redemption."

Richard S. Israel. "The People of the High Rain Forest." *San Francisco Chronicle,* November 21, 1954, p. 26.

"I was black and they were black, but my blackness did not help me."

Heretofore, the author has been noted for the emotional impact of his novels upon the reader. This time the tables are reversed. The story Richard Wright has chosen to tell has had a visible personal impact upon the author himself. This is so, because told here is the true story of the black people of the Gold Coast of Africa. It is a history of the one-time slave trade center told with a human touch that only a great novelist such as Wright, himself a descendant of a slave, could possess.

Simply stated, more than 300 pages are devoted to a plain narrative of Wright's several month's wanderings through the Gold Coast. This is no academic treatise; no effort is made to give a logical pattern to the material presented. Rather these are just a multitude of impressions. . . .

But more than the exposition of his own philosophical orientation, the author has also used his keen sense of realism to make distinct human beings of the masses of people he has seen. The man in the street, the store clerk, the old tribal king, the nationalist leader, N. Krumah, the respected conservative, the British overseer—each is given a distinct personality; each is drawn so that we, the readers, can meet these people and know of their mores, their strange mixture of tribalism and Christianity, of capitalism and socialism, and of the forces that motivate their lives.

In 1954, Africa still is more unknown than known. But the years are few until these people from the "high rain forest with its stifling heat and lush vegetation" will become major factors in the fate of western civilization.

Before it is too late, we would do well to read carefully and critically what Richard Wright has written. We need to read other books about the people and land of Africa and to talk to people who have been there. Once we remove the shroud of mystery from the mysterious people of a mysterious continent, much of what the future holds for the West will begin to unfold.

Charles E. Moran, Jr. *Richmond News-Leader,* November 26, 1954.

The author of "Native Son," "Black Boy" and "The God That Failed" has broken a new field in his newest book. In "Black Power" Richard Wright is not attempting to set forth the personality-blighting effect of American racial attitudes or to proclaim the bankruptcy of communism as an instrument of human liberation. Rather he undertakes a straight reporting job on the current picture in the British colony of the Gold Coast.

Attracted to the land of his forefathers more by a curiosity to see paganism as it is practiced today than to examine Christian influences in Africa, Wright reached Accra just before Nkrumah's recent challenge to the British crown. With letters of introduction to personages, including a general letter from the Prime Minister of the colony, he found doors opened to him in all parts of the country.

Wright's reaction to what he saw is a rather odd combination of anger and whimsical amusement, of doctrinaire Marxism and equally doctrinaire capitalism. Underlying all of his observations is a smoldering resentment of the treatment accorded throughout history by whites to non-whites. Yet in spite of its biases, the book is a genuinely valuable document, giving as it does, a deeply sincere and articulate evaluation of the chances of the West to gain and hold the allegiance of uncommitted Africa.

Bob Senser. "Africa, as It Appears to a Negro Intellectual." *Books on Trial,* 13 (November 1954), 66.

"Free—dooom! Free—dooom!" The chant rang frequently on Richard Wright's ears during his three-month stay in Africa's Gold Coast, which may soon become the first Negro-run country in the British commonwealth of nations. In *Black Power* he reports favorably on Prime Minister Kwame Nkrumah's struggle to bring the Gold Coast freedom from British colonialism.

Unlike most tourists, Wright was interested not in sight-seeing but in seeing and talking with people. As a result he is able to describe situation after situation as fascinating as any he ever narrated in his novels. There is, for instance, the encounter with the young African who wants Wright to help him enroll in a correspondence course in detective work. The lad had seen Hollywood detectives in action on the screen and wanted to be able to catch criminals—meaning "the English who came here and fought us, took our land, our gold, and our diamonds."

Many natives, high and low, were close-mouthed, suspicious of outsiders, even one with a skin coloring as dark as theirs. But Wright found enough to give him an insight into how learned Africans are thinking. . . .

It is with deep feeling that Wright tells of his personal reaction to the poverty, the illiteracy, the superstition, and the other conditions in the primitive colony. He is at his best when he sticks to such narration, but he mixes in large doses of his own history, political science and atheism.

Angrily, he links Christianity with European imperialism, and blames both for past and present exploitations in Africa. He has no lack of specific evidence against the colonialists, from the slave days on down to the present, but his charges against the missionaries seem generalized and freely garnished with his own anti-religious prejudices.

James Aswell. "Famed Negro Novelist Takes Look at Africa." *Houston Chronicle*, December 26, 1954.

Richard Wright is the Negro novelist who wrote the excellent "Black Boy," a dirge etched in tears and poignantly human. It gained deserved celebration a good many years ago.

Afterwards [sic] he joined the Communists and made racist indignation his profession. His product suffered. He became, like all dupes, a bore. But Negroes are notably resistant to the Marxist Hadacol over the long pull and Wright in time rebelled and seceded.

Now he has gone to Africa to look into the chaos roaring in the land of his fathers. Out of his trip he has produced this book. It is a strange book, a novelist's book, and his earnest socio-economic observations and diagnoses are far less interesting and cogent than his boundless human curiosity.

He feels peculiar, a little shy, to be standing, in his tailor-made suit and $20 shoes among his brothers, the semi-savages of the great continent. He is a European man of the world, feted in the continental salons and he stares at the uncouth tribesmen and women with scar-pattern decorations with both aversion and compassionate fellowship.

He blames the whites for most of the troubles of Africa today and of course he is right, but it does not occur to him that he is the symbol of an ironic paradox. He would not be the famous writer, equipped with the tools of Western culture, literature, relatively secure in civilized splendor, if some slave-dealer had not bought an ancestor of his from a black chief.

He would be like the others, possibly with a bone in his nose, barefoot and headed for the ritual of human sacrifice this evening. Is he better off? Maybe not, but I doubt that he would switch.

But the interest of this book lies in Wright's intense and passionate gaze on human patterns wherever he goes.

Here is one example of his far-ranging, novelist's curiosity:

"And why do most of the people spit all the time? Young and old, men and women, people of high and low stations in life, spit. I observed a young girl of about 12 for about five minutes and she spat six times. And this spitting is not just ordinary spitting. It's done in a special manner. First, taut lips are drawn back over clenched teeth and from out through the clenched teeth comes a jet of saliva, straight, clean, strong, like a bullet from a gun, never touching the lips. . . I tried, before my mirror in my hotel room with the door locked, to spit like that and I succeeded only in soiling the front of my shirt."

Henry F. Winslow. "Beyond the Seas—An Uneasy World." *The Crisis*, 62 (February 1955), 78–80.

. . . Mr. Wright's journey was initiated when the suggestion of author-journalist George Padmore's wife was seconded by that of his own. The net result is such a report as only a Wright could give, and one which bears the indelible mark of a provocative but profoundly honest temperament. Welcomed and aided by Prime Minister Kwame Nkrumah (who is likewise the leader of his country's powerful Convention People's Party), Mr. Wright found on the Gold Coast three standard Western types: the business man, bent on fattening from its resources—it is the world's foremost producer of cocoa; the soldier, seeking an enemy to kill; and the missionary, yearning "to remake *his* own image" in order to save himself rather than the African. He charges that Westerners have wrapped up and disguised their naked lust for gold in Christian morality and in so doing have destroyed the mental habits and former vision of native Africans, whom he faithfully and vividly pictures as diseased and distrustful, but suffering most of all from "the psychological shackles of foreign misrule."

He therefore attributes the success of Nkrumah to the fact that this popular leader has on the one hand grasped an economic vision and on the other tapped "the abandoned reservoir that Christian religion had no use for." Hence Wright advises his friend Nkrumah to regiment the daily lives of his people to the end of "giving form, organization, direction, meaning and a sense of justification" to them. Here, therefore, is a large order and a heavy indictment—the latter more so because in this book Wright has forged Freud into a chisel and Marx into a mallet and begun to pound upon Western culture (or modern civilization) as he observes it operating in (or on) Africa. Actually, what Mr. Wright says is a re-statement in terms of Gold Coast problems of the fundamental argument in *The Outsider:* that the confusion and terror which stalk the world are in very fact a mirror reflecting the basically bestial motive in Western culture.

Black Power concentrates this view on the English in the Gold Coast and points it by presenting a most telling scene drawn from Wright's visit to Samreboi, where ten years ago the United African Company built the world's largest plywood and timber mill. At a party given by the company's general manager, and attended by company officials and their wives, Wright witnessed such a feast on contemptuous humor directed at Gold Coast natives as curdled his emotions.

As to the Africans, Mr. Wright's "over-all impression was that the black human beings had so completely merged with the dirt that one could scarce tell where humanity ended and the earth began. . . ." And his report on their lives is no help to those who insist that the key to what Negroes *really are* is imbedded somewhere in some lost sense of origin or some unfound tradition: ". . . I knew that I'd never feel an identification with Africans on a 'racial' basis."

He learned from Mrs. Hannah Cudjoe, an official in the Convention People's Party, that the tribal status of the African woman holds her the chattel of her husband; he reasoned as he talked with one of the Christian chiefs that this group puts its own "hereditary rights," perpetuated by magical authority, above the educational and health needs of the native population. Thus the African chiefs stand with the Christian missionaries in opposition to the Convention People's Party.

In *Black Power* Mr. Wright's mind displays much of the forceful imagination, if little of the objectivity, of the true scientist. Although his emotional involvement poses a temperamental handicap, it is largely offset by his disarming ingenuousness. Probably no other contemporary writer of American origin lays himself so bare as does Wright, and certainly no other can match the fiercely independent, Miltonic pride which saturates his essentially tragic outlook on life as he has come to know it. . . .

Bonnie Wulkan. *Boston Chronicle,* March 19, 1955.

Black Power is Richard Wright's "record of reactions in a land of pathos," the African Gold Coast. The book is written in a frank, familiar, easy-going style and deals with one of our most pressing current problems.

Mr. Wright's book is not written in the spirit of someone who is trying to prove a point, or by someone who is extremely biased. Rather, the author tries to give a fair picture of his findings when dealing with such topics as the present government of Kwame Nkrumah and the difficulties and failures of the British in their attempts to convert Africa to Western ways. Mr. Wright discusses the many paradoxes which have arisen in Africa with the introduction of Western culture. He describes the conflict of medicine men working alongside doctors, of tribal chiefs with politicians, juju magic with missionary teachings, and Christian services with ancestor worship.

He raises many pertinent questions. . . . Some of the questions he answers, some remain for history to answer.

Mr. Wright believes the future is with Nkrumah's independence program, but he stresses that Africa's future is in the hands of the Africans themselves and not in the hands of the outside Western Powers.

The main significance of *Black Power* is not as an historical document about the African Gold Coast, but that it aids us in obtaining a deeper understanding and insight into the current African revolution.

Roy Thompson. "Chip in Africa." *Winston-Salem Journal Sentinel,* April 3, 1955.

Today, while most of the world watches nervously the trouble brewing off Formosa, a second potential troublespot is getting little of the attention it deserves.

A growing wave of nationalism is sweeping over Africa. But, while world statesmen look elsewhere, it is noted mainly in the writings and lectures of professional travelers.

The latest of these is Richard Wright, American author of *Native Son* and *Black Boy* who has seen fit to move to France.

Mr. Wright has visited the Gold Coast to report on the growing demand for local sovereignty. . . .

One who forces himself through this book will come inevitably to the conclusion that it might better have been named *Black Power Unharnessed* or, perhaps, *Black Power Divided*.

Mr. Wright, who left his native land because he was unable to meet the challenge offered by racial segregation, finds the Gold Coast equally depressing.

He is opposed to British rule and, apparently, to all the many factions of Negro leaders who propose to end it.

He admits that his book is based on knowledge gained during a brief visit to the Gold Coast, but before the book is half completed, the author is making noises like a lifetime resident.

Mr. Wright is a writer of considerable ability: he has proved that in *Native Son*.

Unfortunately, he is a writer with a chip on his shoulder, and the chip has now grown so large that he is apparently unable to see anything else.

What little value this book has lies in his observations of the details of life on the Gold Coast.

When he becomes an expert on its problems, he loses his perspective.

Fabian Udekwu. *Catholic Interracialist*, 12 (July-August 1955), 7.

This powerful book comes from a man who needs no introduction to the American public. Richard Wright is a self-made man and a socialist with definite Marxist leanings. The reader should keep this in mind while reading *Black Power*.

Most of the book is spent on the author's interpretation of the political movements in Africa. He followed his leads with the adroit pursuit of a trained journalist. The facts recorded are disturbing but true.

Leadership of the people requires a welding of Christianity, tribalism, paganism, and socialism, but definitely not in the way that Wright shows. His general thesis is the age old European interpretation of African nationalism.

On the question of customs he is misled by the thought that the African is a mere slab of stone upon which the Colonial power can carve whatever effigies he might wish.

I personally believe that the African has his own ideas on politics and behavior which are not the same as the ones of the West. The book's analysis of various types of people and their political leanings is far from the African concept of government and society.

In spite of what Mr. Wright thinks, Pliny's statement that something new always comes out of Africa is still true. The author fails to understand the renaissance sweeping Africa today, overcoming dividing elements like colonialism and religions.

This is a fundamental error of the Western world. Though well-meaning, Westerners believe the African to be a child, and are convinced that without their protection and guidance he could not live. Mr. Wright characteristically suggests the creation of a totalitarian state as a solution. He also rationalizes the failings of the African as the result of the European influence.

I am quite sure that most African students of the native political system are agreed that imitating rugged individualism under the name of democracy will not succeed. On the other hand, the African is too religious to ever subject himself to the materialism of Marxist communism. But Mr. Wright and his followers are in one camp, and the bleeding hearts of the West in the other camp of rugged individualism. They do not present much of a choice for Africa.

Jeanne d'Ucel. *Books Abroad* (Norman, Oklahoma), 29 (Summer 1955).

The author of *Black Boy* and *Native Son* looks at the Gold Coast in ferment for emancipation. A shrewd observer, he notes the baffling complexities and paradoxes of the situation. His psychological probings are searching and stimulating. But he blames colonization and the whites for *all* the evils and shortcomings—which is a bit excessive and an oversimplification of very deep and tenacious problems. As he himself acknowledges, in the matter of the slave traffic alone, for instance, the black slaves were victims of their fellow blacks as well as of the whites. Conditions in nearby Liberia are also revealing. Alas! the eighteenth century's dream of the "noble savage" has been rather thoroughly shattered. This book, however, is an important item for our day and its problems.

Checklist of Additional Reviews

Kirkus Reviews, 22 (August 1, 1954), 511.

Cleveland News, September 22, 1954.

Lewis Gannett. *New York Herald Tribune,* September 23, 1954.

Fletcher Martin. *Chicago Sun & Times,* September 26, 1954.

Don Murray. *Boston Herald,* September 26, 1954, Section 11, p. 15.

Dayton Daily News, September 26, 1954.

Norfolk Pilot, September 26, 1954.

Anna C. Hunter. *Savannah Morning News,* September 26, 1954, p. 56.

John Allan May. *Christian Science Monitor,* September 30, 1954, p. 11.

Booklist, 51 (October 1, 1954), 2.

Richard P. Hafner, Jr. *Oakland Tribune,* October 3, 1954.

Walter L. Scratch. *Hollywood Citizen News,* October 4, 1954.

New Yorker, 30 (October 9, 1954), 167.

Shirley Ruth Tove. *Raleigh News Observer,* October 10, 1954.

Saunders Redding. *Saturday Review,* 37 (October 23, 1954), 19-20.

Ann Hansen. *Columbus Dispatch,* October 24, 1954.

Josephine Maury Worde. *Chattanooga Times,* October 30, 1954.

Detroit News, October 31, 1954.

Bookmark, 14 (October 1954), 6.

V. O. R. *Charlotte News,* November 20, 1954.

Roger O'Mara. *Arizona Daily Star,* November 28, 1954.

H. M. *Fort Worth Star Telegram,* November 28, 1954.

Sarah S. Hooper. *Birmingham News,* November 28, 1954.

College English, 16 (December 1954), 202-3.

Homer A. Jack. *The Progressive,* 18 (December 1954), 41-42.

The United States Quarterly Book Review, 10 (December 1954), 559-60.

Leonard B. Archer, Jr. *Rutland Daily Herald,* January 4, 1955.

C. Hartley Grattan. *The New Leader,* 38 (February 7, 1955).

Thompson Peter Omari. *Journal of Human Relations,* 3 (Spring 1955), 102-3.

The Calvin Forum (June-July 1955), 235.

THE COLOR CURTAIN

A REPORT ON THE BANDUNG CONFERENCE

BY RICHARD WRIGHT

FOREWORD BY GUNNAR MYRDAL

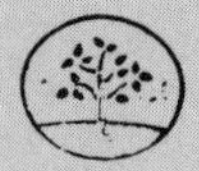

THE WORLD PUBLISHING COMPANY

CLEVELAND AND NEW YORK

The Color Curtain

Kirkus Reviews, 24 (January 15, 1956), 64.

Subtitled—*A Report on the Bandung Conference*—this is a more important book than this would seem to indicate. Perhaps because the Bandung Conference, the first meeting of the 29 free and independent nations of Asia and Africa, received less attention in the Western Press than it rated, a book on the impressions received by Richard Wright in attending this conference might also be slighted. Actually, Wright sees this as "the last call of westernized Asians to the moral conscience of the West". One feels the reason for his conclusion in reading this analysis of the *mood* of the participants; one recognizes the challenge in his realization that if the West does not meet the demand, Communist China alone has the desire and the experience to accept the challenge. The opening speeches were inflammatory, without exception, reflected the antagonism towards the erstwhile colonial powers. But the Bandung communique was extraordinarily moderate in its tone, stressing economic cooperation, with all its sacrifice on the part of the West; calling for a revitalizing of Asian and African cultures and religions; endorsing the principles of human rights and self-determination; asking for an end to surviving colonialism; requesting greater participation in the Security Council of the United Nations. Wright thinks the chances of implementing the contents of the communique are good—but that the problems are vastly greater than indicated. But is there TIME? How shall 65% of the human race be organized? The Communists of China know the magnitude of the problem. Will the West take the means, techniques and time? Religion and Race impressed Wright as the controlling factors. A personal approach—this; but a book that needs to be pondered.

Tillman Durdin. *New York Times Book Review,* March 18, 1956, p. 1.

The 1955 Bandung Conference on the Island of Java was probably the most unusual and exciting international gathering of recent times. It brought together for the first time representatives of a billion and a half people of Asia and Africa for a meeting at which delegates of the Western peoples were excluded. It was a coming-out party for the People's Republic of China and the Democratic Republic of Vietnam (North Vietnam) and marked the first time that emissaries of Asia's two Communist states had met with a general assemblage of Africans and other Asians.

It was a unique occasion for the voicing of common principles and the expression of resentments and prejudices by individuals from the ex-colonial and underdeveloped regions of the globe. Some of the countries at Bandung had never before been represented at a big international forum.

Yet the importance of Bandung has been exaggerated in the minds of many persons. The conference did not represent, as some commentators seem to feel, the consolidation of an Asia-Africa front against the West. It was not, despite the statements of some conference spokesmen, a manifestation of the solidarity and resurgence of the colored peoples of the world against the whites. (Many of the participants, indeed, were white and many who were brown, tan and yellow had few complexes and resentments either about the color of their own skins or the skins of others.)

The conference did bring about an opportunity for the Chinese Communists to promote their influence on a wide, new front. The Chinese peaceful coexistence theme (bolstered by the neutralist idea that the Indians were able to give wider dissemination at the conference) undoubtedly made some headway, and this may well have been the most important aspect of Bandung.

Among the Western observers at Bandung was Richard Wright, who has told in "The Color Curtain" something of what he saw and heard and felt on that occasion. A Mississippi-born Negro, he has already portrayed in several important books, including his autobiographical "Black Boy," the miseries and conflicts of the race problem in this country. He once turned to communism but soon repudiated the ugly realities he encountered. Mr. Wright, therefore, has special qualifications for dealing with a subject such as Bandung. Despite defects, "The Color Curtain" is a vivid and illuminating job of reportage. Mr. Wright brings the scene quickly to life: "We drove past the conference building and saw the flags of the twenty-nine participating nations of Asia and Africa billowing lazily in a weak wind; already the streets were packed with crowds and their black and yellow and brown faces looked eagerly at each passing car, their sleek black hair gleaming in the bright sun, their slanted eyes peering intently, hopefully to catch sight of some Prime Minister, a U Nu, a Chou En-lai, or a Nehru. . . .

"Day in and day out these crowds would stand in this tropic sun, staring, listening applauding; it was the first time in their downtrodden lives that they'd seen so many men of their color, race and nationality arrayed in such aspects of power, their men keeping order, their Asia and their Africa in control of their destinies. . . . They were getting a new sense of themselves, getting used to new roles and new identities. Imperialism was dead here, and as long as they could maintain their unity, organize and conduct international conferences, there would be no return of imperialism."

No sooner had he climbed into the press gallery, Mr. Wright reports, than he sensed that he was witnessing "an important juncture of history in the making. In the early and difficult days of the Russian Revolution, Lenin had dreamed of a gathering like this, a conglomeration of the world's underdogs, coming to the aid of his hard-pressed Soviets, but that dream had been a vain one indeed. And many Western writers . . . had long predicted the inevitable rise of these nations, but in their wildest intuitive flights they had never visualized that they would meet together in a common cause."

This book should provide, for Americans in particular, a further insight into the background and the frightening scope of the problems we face in our relationships with Asian and African peoples. Some of Mr. Wright's fears in this regard seem to me to be exaggerated and therefore tend to create an unbalanced report on the conference.

Mr. Wright, for one thing, overplays the color angle and attributes to Asians and Africans uniformity of attitude on color that does not exist. He does not sufficiently bring out that Western manifestations of racial superiority in Asia and, to a lesser degree, even in Africa are largely a by-product of past Western political domination over the two continents. Superiority and inferiority attitudes have throughout history nearly always marked the relationships between conquerors and conquered, even when they were of the same race.

Mr. Wright properly gives much attention to China Premier Chou En-lai's successful impact on the conference, but he fails to do justice to the strength of the resistance of such countries as Ceylon, Pakistan, the Phillipines, Iran and Turkey to the blandishments of both Chou and India's Prime Minister Nehru. He has no account of the detailed denunciation of communism by Sir John Kotelawala, Prime Minister of Ceylon, that was one of the highlights of the conference.

Mr. Wright's book suffers also from his lack of knowledge of Asian affairs. He portrays, for example, Chou En-lai's offer to let Chinese immigrants in Southeast Asia choose either Chinese or local citizenship as a move well-received by representatives of Southeast Asian nations at Bandung. The opposite is true. Southeast Asian nations, like Western nations, prefer to decide their citizenship laws for themselves and without the negotiations with Peking that Chou's approach involved. It is noteworthy that the Indonesian Parliament has refused to approve the agreement on the citizenship of Chinese in Indonesia negotiated with Peking by the left-oriented Ali Sastroamidjojo Government and announced with much fanfare at Bandung.

In his concluding chapter, however, Mr. Wright correctly poses the crucial question highlighted at Bandung. He asks whether the sensitive and resentful people represented there are to be brought out of their present state of poverty, ignorance and economic backwardness under the aegis of a bloody Communist totalitarianism or through wise and generous aid from the West that will link them with our freer, democratic system.

"It was my belief," he writes, "that the delegates at Bandung, for the most part, though bitter, looked and hoped toward the West. . . . The West, in my opinion, must be big enough, generous enough, to accept and understand that bitterness. The Bandung communique [issued after six days of discussion] was no appeal, in terms of sentiment or ideology, to communism. Instead, it carried exalted overtones of the stern dignity of ancient and proud peoples who yearned to rise and play again a role in human affairs. . . . In sum, Bandung was the last call of westernized Asians to the moral conscience of the West.

". . . Unless the Western world can meet the challenge of the miraculous unity of Bandung openly and selflessly, it faces an Asian-African attempt at pulling itself out of its own mire under the guidance of Chou En-lai and his drastic theories and practices of endless secular sacrifices."

Walter Simmons. "Arrested Case of Communism Looks at Asia." *Chicago Sunday Tribune Magazine of Books,* March 25, 1956, p. 2.

Richard Wright, the famous American Negro author of "Black Boy" and other books, went to the Afro-Asian conference at Bandung last year and came back with some observations that did not jibe with those of most other observers.

He does not feel there is much danger of Indonesia going communist and calls those who fear otherwise "propagandists." He looks on religion as a major force in Asia of the future—a dubious conclusion except as it applies to the Moslem lands.

Wright, a Communist for 12 years but now considered an arrested case, still writes with his old Marxist vocabulary. His views about Asia would be interesting if he would stick around long enough to learn something about the area.

Guy Wint. "Impatience of the East." *The Nation,* 172 (April 14, 1956), 324.

As time goes by, the Bandung Conference may increasingly be regarded as crucial. Few people saw all its significance while it was sitting, even those who were fascinated by it as spectacle. Richard Wright was an exception. He went to the conference believing it to be one of the great events of his generation, and he has now tried to convey his vision. His book is sub-titled Report on the Conference, but it is scarcely that, for he does not give a systematic narrative of its proceedings. Instead he describes the background, the mind of the delegates, their bitter grievances against the West. He is filled with foreboding that all this bitterness may issue in a great assault against the West.

As a Negro, Mr. Wright felt himself able to understand the racial sentiments of Asians, and as a novelist he felt himself able to express them convincingly. He says that Asians confide in a Negro American as they never would in white Americans. His vision may lack balance and urbanity—but that is the nature of visions. He may make errors of fact—but visions transcend fact, and can be true even if some of the details are fictitious. Mr. Wright makes one peculiar judgment. He thinks that the air of Bandung was suffused by religious consciousness as well as by race. Other onlookers at the conference do not seem to have noticed the religion very much.

Mr. Wright's conclusion is that the Bandung Conference exposed, not a yearning toward communism, or egalitarian extremism, but the demand by ancient and proud peoples that they should again play a major part in international affairs. They address this demand to the West, because they feel that the West still restricts their activities and keeps them too much out of the sun. "If the West spurns their call," says Mr. Wright, "what will happen? I don't know. But remember that Mr. Chou En-lai stands there, waiting, patient, with no record of racial practices behind him." To prevent Asia going Communist, Mr. Wright thinks first that the West must abandon all its assumptions of racial superiority. Second an economic levelling-up must be accepted voluntarily by the West. "The white Westerner," says Mr. Wright, "will have to accept, for an unspecified length of time, a much, much lower standard of living, for that is what the de-Occidentalization of present-day mankind will bring about." The long delays in instituting SUNFED do not hold out much hope for this voluntary abnegation.

It is an emotional book. It says little about some of the most important elements of the Asian problem, such as the driving force of the ever-growing populations. But it does one thing very well. It compels the reader to be more aware of the burning racial feelings. A kind of deception has been put on the world by the good humor of the end of British rule in India, and the surprisingly cordial relations which have existed since between Indian political leaders and Britain. But this cordiality may not last, nor are other Asian peoples as tolerant as some Indians of this generation, nor has all colonial power been surrendered in such a satisfactory way as in India. Bandung showed the true feeling, and this book reports it accurately.

A. T. Steele. "Color of Asia." *New York Herald Tribune Book Review,* April 22, 1956, p. 9.

This is an American Negro's appraisal of the Afro-Asian conference at Bandung, Indonesia. Mississippi-born Richard Wright, who had lived in Paris for nine years, went to Bandung not as a delegate but as a reporter. He encountered there representatives from nearly all the non-white nations of the world, among them such utterly diverse personalities as Nehru of India, Chou En-lai of Communist China, Kojo Botslo of the Gold Coast and Nasser of Egypt—to name only a few. Unlike some of his colleagues who could see news only in the fiery clashes between neutralist and anti-communist delegates, Mr. Wright looked for underlying tides. Beneath the choppy surface of controversy he found strong racial and religious currents—currents that could change the shape of the world.

As one who doubtless has suffered many indignities in his lifetime because of the color of his skin, it is natural that Mr. Wright should deplore racism. It is natural, too, that he should derive some satisfaction from the evidence at Bandung of the growing strength and stature of the world's colored peoples. But there were some things he saw that disturbed him. For example:

"I found that many Asians hated the West with an absoluteness that no American Negro could ever muster."

This racial resentment, Mr. Wright points out, is largely a heritage of colonialism and the white man's smug assumption of superiority over brown, yellow and black peoples. It is an attitude that is often colored by irrationalism and emotion, making it all the more unpredictable and dangerous. There were those at Bandung who maintained that the Afro-Asian countries had more to fear from Western imperialism than from communism, though others sharply dissented. Meanwhile, Chou En-lai, the delegate from Peking, almost sprouted wings and a halo from the strain of playing the unfamiliar role of Everybody's Friend. Mr. Wright feels that the final communique at Bandung, with its heavy emphasis on economic independence for Asian and African countries, was in a sense a last call to the moral conscience of the West—a call which the West would be foolish to ignore.

Mr. Wright believes that the path to improved relations between the West and its ex-colonies lies through close economic cooperation. The West, he maintains, should help these countries build up their industries to the point at least of being able to process their own raw materials. And to accomplish this result he proposes collaboration with the elite element in the countries concerned. The elite is usually Western-educated and Westernized in outlook and would, in Mr. Wright's view, provide a strong element of pro-Western stability if given the economic incentive to do so. And if the West fails to respond favorably to the call of Bandung, what then? Mr. Wright admits he doesn't know, but he reminds us that Chou En-lai stands there, waiting.

Mr. Wright was for some years a member of the Communist party, hence he knows whereof he speaks when he warns of the communist danger in Asia and Africa. His conclusions, however, are sometimes vague and unfinished. The book does not pretend to document or detail the proceedings of the Bandung conference: it is a collection, rather, of the author's impressions of those aspects of the conference that interested him particularly. Of special interest are Mr. Wright's observations on the racial issue, which forms one of the main threads of the book.

Ellen Logue. *Books on Trial*, 14 (April-May 1956), 351–52.

Ultimately far more important than the Iron Curtain, the Color Curtain tends to enfold every individual and all the world. The Iron Curtain, as the author points out, often serves as a rallying point against which many diverse forces may unite. The ardent believer, the materialist and the pragmatist can and often do join forces against Communism without raising sharp questions of conscience within themselves. The Color Curtain—differences conditioned merely because of skin color—raises problems in each of us, in our present national politics and, though we hear less about it, most importantly throughout the world.

The problems of all colored persons newly freed from imperialist rule are the main concern of the author in his thought-provoking analysis of the Bandung Conference held in 1955 in the new Republic of Indonesia.

Richard Wright, an outstanding American writer, was intensely interested in this conference, representing well over a billion people of diverse colors, of practically every religion and certainly of every degree of political acumen. Those at the conference were most vitally concerned with a problem of staggering proportions: the relationship of the nonwhite world to the white as represented by the religious, social, economic and political values of the West, particularly of those countries which had colonies or territories or those which are in the process of trying to establish some new relationship with formerly passive subject peoples.

To a problem of such magnitude Mr. Wright brings an amazing clarity in a short book. En route to the conference (at which he was a private citizen observer) the author discussed, with many individuals of different races and beliefs, the points of a questionnaire that he had devised to try to grasp some basic Asian attitudes. At the conference, he noted the main themes which emerged as the talks progressed: the men of color found in the very fact of being nonwhite a basis of unity and, in relation to that fact, the events of history and the problems of the present and of the future were discussed.

Read and reread, those themes can be frightening and they did, indeed, frighten some at the conference. Others pretended not to notice; the thoughtful, including the Communists, pondered. Mr. Wright seems to have judged Chou En lai well in noting his strategy of mixing with the mass and seeing which way the wind blows. By friendliness and sympathy the Red Chinese had nothing to lose and everything to gain for they could easily appear one in aims with the other delegates. As time passes, they can also easily be the ones to supply leadership to the new nations who seem not to know whither they want to go, and thus cannot make positive policy.

The thoughtful are deeply disturbed for there is little time and much to be done against great odds. How can the integrity of a people be preserved, their culture and mores survive and be meaningful when their nation must jump in a few years the span of development which took centuries for the West. The fact is, they *must;* the author is at once rational and imaginative as he suggests how it can be done. This analysis of the Bandung conference and its implications probably will not get the audience it deserves; the questions that it raises merit the attention of us all.

Abner W. Berry. "Richard Wright's Report on Bandung." *New York Daily Worker,* May 15, 1956, p. 5.

A number of readers objected to the brief review by Herbert Aptheker of Richard Wright's book, "The Color Curtain—A Report on the Bandung Conference," in the April 27 issue of the Daily Worker. I have now read Wright's book and find it interesting, informative and containing helpful insights into the relationship between the various countries of Asia and Africa, and between these countries and the major powers. Indeed, Wright's reporting on the actual proceedings of the conference, plus his preparatory interviews with Asians, forming the major portion of "The Color Curtain," constitute the first full, intimate glimpse of the conference for English-speaking readers.

Aptheker, well known for his outstanding contributions to the study of Negro history, was annoyed with Wright's anti-Communism, a brand which is closer to the European variety than to that of McCarthyism in this country. He therefore dismissed, I believe, much that was of value in

Wright's book by concentrating upon the author's erroneous conclusions deriving from his (Wright's) subjectivism and his identification with Western political aims.

Wright makes it clear that he has no love for Communism and wishes that the West would find some way of coming to terms with it in order to prevent an "Asian-African attempt at pulling itself out of its own mire under the guidance of Mr. Chou En-lai." For, Wright adds: ". . . There is no doubt but that Communism can dredge down and rake up the hidden reserves of a people, can shake them, rip them out of the traditional and customary soil in which they have stagnated for centuries."

There are, of course, the loaded words and sentences of the author in this sentence, but I fail to find anything gloomy in it except for the likes of John Foster Dulles and those who still dream of a world neatly ordered and run from Washington, London and Paris through a corps of trained administrators. For why was the Bandung conference held anyway? Wright says the Asian-African nations were frightened out of their wits by the succession of A- and H-bomb threats coming out of Washington. And he describes in his own biased way how the atomic fever engendered solidarity feelings among Asians and Africans. . . .

But Wright does much more than draw generalized conclusions; he gives the reader a peek into the minds of Asians through interviews which he reports with sharp insight. Typical of such interviews is that with Dr. Mohammed Natsir, a former Prime Minister of Indonesia, who answered a question about Communism: "There will be no need for Communism in Moslem countries, Pan-Islam will represent a world force, socialistic in nature, keeping a middle ground between Communism and Capitalism." And Wright comments: "It was obvious to me that, if you tried to make this man choose between Communism and Capitalism, he'd feel that you were pushing him out of his natural mental orbit. He is more pro-Islam than anti-Communist or pro-Capitalist."

Wright identifies himself culturally and politically with the West, and his report can be considered as a warning to the West to mend its ways in Asia and Africa. But he sees no chance of imperialism coming to terms with its former subjects, therefore his doleful tone. Moreover, just as he has no faith in the ability of American Negroes to overcome the racist political overlay in the United States, he similarly emphasizes the "religious" and "irrational" in the Asian-African personality, and cannot affirm their ability to move quickly toward industrialization.

Despite his subjective blinders, Wright saw enough and understood enough to give a factual report of what was done at the conference. In fact, his report is the first where I read of the real role played by Sir John Kotelawala, the Prime Minister of Ceylon; Prince Wan, of Thailand, and Carlos Romulo, of the Phillipines. Most of the newspaper reports had given in full only the portions of their speeches which bowed to the West. The portions of speeches contained in Wright's book emphasize the essential unity with their fellow Asians of these outward partisans of the West in Asia. Indeed, it was Romulo who made out a detailed case against the racism which had been one of the factors impelling the conference participants to gather.

It was, significantly, Romulo who furnished Wright with a thesis. Romulo, an Asian product of Western capitalism pointed out that the West had given Asia and Africa "all our main ideas of political freedom, justice and equity (and it was) Western science which in this generation has exploded the mythology of race."

Wright concludes, and I think correctly, that Western-educated Asians and Africans have added to their local cultures the domestic ideals outlined by Romulo. Less correctly, I believe, he feels that there is possible a unity between "the elite of Asia and Africa," which is "more Western than the West in most cases," and some vague concept which he terms "Western rationalism." This, plus selfless help from the West, aiding Asians and Africans to process their own raw materials, even if this "would necessitate a radical adjustment of the West's systems of society and economics," is Wright's answer to the questions posed at Bandung. The alternatives, he believes, are either a Communist Asia, with science and industry wedded to "mystical notions," launching "vast crusades, armed with modern weapons, to make the world safe for their mystical notions."

I can disagree with Wright's conclusions while being appreciative of his over-all job of reporting Bandung in a way that gives readers a fresh insight into the ideas, cultures and problems of two-thirds of the earth's population. There is much to be gained by reading it.

Charles Wisley. *Masses and Mainstream*, 9 (June 1956), 50–53.

When Richard Wright read press reports that twenty-nine Asian and African countries with more than a billion inhabitants were to meet in Bandung, Indonesia, in April 1955, he forthwith decided that it was worth traveling half way around the world to witness such a gathering.

His experience as an American Negro served him well in the recognition of the importance of the Bandung conference at a time when the United States government looked upon it with a mixture of scorn and apprehension. And unlike certain American observers, he went to Bandung to see and understand, not to defend and explain the rate of progress towards equality in America, which had little to do with the conference.

Such a receptive mind, coupled with considerable literary skill, should have produced a very fine contribution toward a better appreciation in the West of the forces that made the Bandung conference. It is because knowledge and understanding of the role of the new Asian and African powers are so largely lacking even among Western liberals and progressives that Wright's failure to make the greatest possible contribution is most regrettable.

For while Wright went to Bandung to watch and learn, he was unable to shed a highly personal and subjective, preconceived viewpoint. This shows in the very organization of his book. More than half of it is taken up with his own experiences and the reactions of generally unrepresentative Westernized Asians he met.

In a way, the book reveals more about Richard Wright than about the Bandung conference. ". . . I've had a burden of race consciousness. . . . I worked in my youth as a common laborer, and I've a class consciousness. . . . I grew up in the Methodist and Seventh Day Adventist churches and I saw and observed religion in my childhood. . . . I was a member of the Communist Party for twelve years and I know something of the politics and psychology of rebellion." Thus Wright details his qualifications for reporting on Bandung. But he sees and is able to apply only one aspect of these qualifications. "They are emotion . . . I'm conscious of them as emotions."

This is Wright's weakness. On the positive side, his emotional reactions impelled him to go to Bandung. They made him want to identify himself with the upsurge of the colonial and colored peoples of the world. But they did not equip him to analyze fully and objectively the facts of Bandung. Indeed, they hindered him. Class consciousness, after all, is much more than emotion. It is recognition, reason, reality.

Like a tourist who tries to stuff too many souvenirs into the small suitcase he brought with him, Wright seeks to push the many and complicated facts he gathered at Bandung into his own limited framework of feeling. This he does by forcibly compressing the real meaning of Bandung into two dimensions—race and religion.

Again and again, Wright imposes his own *non sequitur* generalizations upon his account of Bandung events. Thus he cites at length from the opening address of Indonesia's President Sukarno, ending with the quotation, "Almost all of us have ties to common experience, the experience of colonialism." Then Wright: "Sukarno was appealing to race and religion; they were the only realities in the lives of the men before him that he could appeal to. . . ."

Bandung did concern itself with racism, particularly its existence in Africa. This was one of the most important issues on which all conference participants agreed. Bandung's opposition to racism is overshadowed in Wright's book, however, by his own concern with what he terms "racism in reverse," namely, discrimination and hostility by colored peoples against whites. There is no doubt that there was such an undercurrent because of the continuing efforts of "white" powers to keep the newly independent countries of Asia and Africa under some form of control.

But basically, Bandung strove to effect the abolition of racism of all kinds. Racism was seen as an instrument and product of imperialism. This is the crux of the matter that Wright misses in emphasizing, explaining, and almost defending "racism in reverse."

In stressing the religious content of the freedom movement of Asia and Africa, Wright again seems to impute to others some of his own outlook. Certainly the prime movers of Bandung—Nehru, Sukarno, Chou, etc.—are very secular leaders. Nor do references to Asia as the continent where all major religions originated necessarily mean that the speakers are religious. They are recalling the ancient glory of their lands in answer to Western slanders of the civilization of Asia.

Wright's estimate of Chou En-lai's role at the conference bears the marks of both his own anti-communism and of the influence of Western propaganda. Wright is surprised and suspicious that Chou did not fulfill the expectations of American commentators by attacking the United States and trying to spread communism at Bandung. But the conference had been called to achieve agreement on issues where agreement was possible, notwithstanding the substantial differences in policies and ideologies among the participants. Chou conducted himself in accordance with the ground rules laid down for the conference and refused to be diverted by Western-oriented delegates who tried to disrupt the gathering with controversial issues. By declining provocations, by concluding a dual nationality treaty with Indonesia, by approaching the delegates of Thailand, Cambodia, Laos and the Philippines with proposals for improving relations, and by suggesting direct talks with the United States on the Formosa situation, Chou in fact contributed greatly to the relaxation of tension in Asia.

Wright's inability to assess the actions of Chou En-lai is perhaps connected with a graver failure. He correctly appreciates Bandung's united demonstration of opposition to colonialism. But he says hardly a word about the main question of our time and one of the most significant aspects of the conference. The architects of Bandung see its contribution to peace as one of its greatest achievements. Bandung, they say, led to the Geneva summit conference. Bandung reduced tensions which were most acute at the time. Bandung broke the iron curtain in Asia.

In short, Bandung was a test of coexistence. As Wright says, it was "beyond left and right." There were most profound issues—like colonialism, racialism and peace—on which both left and right could and did agree. That is a lesson for the world.

Because he does not fully estimate these achievements, Wright sees fear as a motivation for the conference. Further, he believes that the representatives of the non-Communist Asian governments gathered at Bandung did not know what to do with the power they had seized in their countries. Neither assertion is true. One almost suspects that it is Wright who, though welcoming the new power of the colonial peoples, shrinks before the consequences. The conference was a success just because the principal non-Communist leaders had learned how to exert their strength for peace, had overcome many of their fears of the imperialist powers, and were not afraid to sit down to talk with Communists. If anything, it was confidence that inspired Bandung.

The West has sought, since the conference, to foment disunity in the area by such devices as the Baghdad pact. It cannot succeed. As the recent downfall of Sir John Kotelawala in Ceylon shows, the shakiest regimes in Asia are those which pay lip service to Bandung but remain subservient to alien powers. (Incidentally, Wright is mistaken in saying that Communists and Trotskyists supported Sir John's government.)

With all this, Wright's book has something to say to Western readers: "*. . . for centuries Asian and African nations had watched in helpless silence while white powers had gathered, discussed and disposed of the destinies of Asian and African peoples—gatherings in which no Asian or African had ever had any say.*"

To these peoples Bandung marked an earth-shaking change: "*Imperialism was dead here; and, as long as they could maintain their unity, organize and conduct international conferences, there would be no return of imperialism.*"

In bringing this message to the United States, Wright has performed an important service.

Paula Snelling. "Import of Bandung." *The Progressive*, 19 (June 1956), 39–40.

In *The Color Curtain* Richard Wright gives us a good journalistic account of an extraordinary and significant event. Since this is the first reporting of the Bandung Conference available to

Americans in book form, it demands wide reading quite aside from the special insights its author gives.

The book is written in a simple, straightforward manner. The first half, interesting though it is and in which Wright takes on the job of transporting the reader from the psychological background of the West to that of the East, carries considerably less weight than do the last hundred pages. Perhaps the author is justified in leading us slowly through the shallow waters before plunging us with him into the turbulent scenes of the conference itself. By the time he has "oriented" us, we of the West are more nearly ready to give that word the new and deep significance it holds for our common future.

This reviewer, who was in India for five months directly preceding the Bandung Conference, feels that Wright's still briefer visit to Asia gave him insufficient knowledge of the backstage maneuverings which took place among some of the leaders before, during, and after the Conference. Nor does he have adequate background for dealing fully with certain other phases of his subject, which could have come to him only through prolonged study of the philosophical and cultural history of Asia's peoples. Wisely, he does not dwell on these matters. He has something more urgent to tell us. For he is equipped, both as an intellectual and as a colored American (Mississippi-born), to grasp the primary meaning of the sweeping undercurrents from the past and of today's headwinds which combined to create the human tidal wave he witnessed in Indonesia last spring. And as a first-class writer he has been able to convey its basic impact and much of its import.

He gives us a glimpse of the throng outside the conference site: "Day in and day out these crowds would stand in this tropic sun, staring, listening, applauding; it was the first time in their downtrodden lives that they'd seen so many of their color, race, and nationality arrayed in such aspects of power, their men keeping order, their Asia and their Africa in control of their destinies. . . They were getting a new sense of themselves, getting used to new roles and new identities."

Wright shows Chou En-lai shrewd and flexible enough to size up the unanticipated emotional complexities of the conference and discard his short-sighted prepared political speech in favor of extemporized words worthy of a statesman with higher goals than are his own. As Wright views it: "Here was a chance for China to surround herself with men and nations who had suffered at the hands of colony-owning Western states, and, since the United States had not disavowed its support of such states, China then could walk as a fellow guest into an anti-Western house built by a reaction to colonialism and racialism . . . It was a gift from the skies."

Wright sums up his impressions: "I repeat and underline that the document was addressed to the West, to the moral prepossessions of the West. It was my belief that the delegates at Bandung, for the most part, though bitter, looked and hoped toward the West. The West. . . must be big enough, generous enough, to accept and understand that bitterness. . . If the West spurns this call, what will happen? I don't know. But remember that Mr. Chou En-lai stands there, waiting, patient, with no record of racial practices behind him. . . He will listen."

Wright's intentions are to show us the effects of the myth of white superiority upon Asia and Africa. This he does well. And as he does so, he gives us ample evidence that the inhabitants of this globe, from humblest to highest and without regard for geography, are headed toward a future quite different from their past. He makes plain the fateful choice the West must make, and the brevity of the time-span we have to make it in. He does not attempt here to weigh our capacity or our desire to choose wisely and creatively.

For a deeper understanding of the complex forces which have erected barriers so high in the minds of many Westerners that they cannot see the implications of this Asian-African situation, the reader should turn to Lillian Smith's *Killers of the Dream*. These two books, both written by Southerners who are also world citizens, can give us the understanding we need of certain basic facts which the world calendar no longer permits us to evade.

Current History, 21 (July 1956), 44–45.

For Richard Wright, the meaning of the Bandung Conference was. . . urgent. "In sum, Bandung was the last call of Westernized Asians to the moral conscience of the West." A Negro American novelist, Wright is sensitive to the racial implications of the meeting of the colored peoples; he feels that it will not be easy to achieve a "common platform" (Romulo's expression) for the democrats of East and West. Speaking of the first section of the communique, he points out that it "sounds innocent enough," but "When the day comes that Asian and African raw materials are processed in Asia and Africa by labor whose needs are not as inflated as those of Western laborers, the supremacy of the Western world, economic, cultural, and political, will have been broken once and for all on this earth. . . ." Richard Wright's *Report* may be less than objective, but he is a realist. If the average white Westerner accepts the change in the world's economic structure, "he will also have to accept, for an unspecified length of time, a much, much lower standard of living. . . ." This, among other more philosophical problems, is the ultimate meaning of Bandung.

Checklist of Additional Reviews

M. S. Byam. *Library Journal,* 81 (January 15, 1956), 192.

Homer A. Jack. *Saturday Review,* 39 (March 17, 1956), 19-20.

New Yorker, 32 (March 31, 1956), 110-11.

Wisconsin Library Bulletin, 52 (March 1956), 90.

Takashi Oka. *Christian Science Monitor,* April 4, 1956, p. 9.

Richard McLaughlin. *Springfield Republican,* April 8, 1956, p. 10c.

Booklist, 52 (April 15, 1956), 385.

Keith Irvine. *The New Leader,* 39 (April 23, 1956), 24-25.

Herbert Aptheker. *New York Daily Worker,* April 27, 1956, p. 7.

Eugene Gordon. *National Guardian,* July 6, 1956.

Bookmark, 15 (July 1956), 241.

Foreign Affairs, 34 (July 1956), 685.

Hugh Smythe. *The Crisis,* 64 (January 1957), 58-59.

John Lash. *Phylon,* 18 (First Quarter, 1957), 21-22.

RICHARD WRIGHT

PAGAN SPAIN

HARPER & BROTHERS

NEW YORK

Pagan Spain

Milton S. Byam. *Library Journal*, 82 (February 15, 1957), 553.

Back from Bandung, Richard Wright is once again off on a trek to new places to view through peculiar spectacles. The resultant picture, though somewhat awry, is always interesting. This time, the author contends that in spite of its extreme Catholicism, Spain is a pagan nation as demonstrated in its festivals, bull-fights and attitudes toward women. Had Mr. Wright characterized these things as Arabic or even Eastern he might have been more convincing. He has, however, performed a major service in exposing to view the educational techniques of a dictatorship. A textbook used by girls in Spain is quoted from extensively by the author as a kind of backdrop or rhythmic beat to his sightseeing and conversations with people. This results in a more effective portrait of today's Spain—a Spain intent on legislating greatness to itself. Recommended for all current affairs collections in all libraries.

William Hogan. "A Gloomy Report on Present-Day Spain." *San Francisco Chronicle*. February 20, 1957, p. 23.

An American writer who has lived as an expatriate in France for several years, Richard Wright had been advised many times to visit Spain. The consensus among his friends, including the late Gertrude Stein, was that Spain is primitive, romantic and lovely, and that meant the people, too. Wright was held off by a political barrier, his prejudice against Franco's Falangist government. In spite of his onetime U.S. Communist affiliations, since roundly denounced, Wright made a deep foray into the Iberian peninsula in 1955, simply as an American citizen.

"Pagan Spain," his report on this journey, is controversial in the extreme, but he presents a point of view with honesty. Wright reports on no tourist Spain. He attempted, he explains, to examine aspects of life in Spain which he felt hitherto had been unreported.

He expresses himself artfully. Almost in the style of the early Dos Passos, his candid observations, vignettes and snatches of conversation are juxtaposed for dramatic emphasis. Under El Greco skies through a Spain populated by Goya-like figures, he moved from Barcelona to Madrid, Granada, Seville and way-points, talking with intellectuals, flamenco dancers, bartenders, peasants—anyone who would communicate. The more he probed and listened the more obvious it became to him that this voyage was not taking him through precincts of the Western world.

"Totalitarian governments and ways of life were no mysteries to me," he writes. "I had been born under an absolutistic racist regime in Mississippi; I had lived and worked for 12 years under the political dictatorship of the Communist party." But, he insists, he was not prepared for the atmosphere of Falangist Spain.

Among other things, he was disturbed by the overemphasis of sex, by the preponderance of prostitution in this most Catholic of countries. He concluded that Spain's Catholicism is not a true one, but a pagan rite. A holy nation on the surface, he feels Spain is actually as irrational as the sacred state of Akan in the African jungle—in essence a Pagan Spain.

Throughout his report, Wright examines the catechism of the Falange, quoting it for his own purposes. . . . Yet from underneath the tight Falangist thumb Wright heard an occasional anguished cry: "Liberty is finished. . . . Half the people of Spain are hungry."

Controversial? Of course.

Joseph G. Harrison. *Christian Science Monitor*, February 21, 1957, p. 13.

"Pagan Spain" is a book which required courage to write—and even greater courage to publish. For it is a volume which seems certain to call down upon author and publisher a tempest of bitter, resentful, and frightened criticism. Furthermore, a portion, but only a portion, of this criticism will be justified, since this latest work by America's best-known Negro writer clearly includes, along with much truth, just enough exaggeration and bias to give its enemies a legitimate stick with which to beat it.

This volume is the result of a fairly lengthy tour which Mr. Wright took through Spain in the summer of 1954 at the suggestion of authoress Gertrude Stein and of Alva and Gunnar Myrdal, the well-known Swedish sociologists. In general, it is a cry of condemnation against most of what he saw in Spain.

To the author Spain is a country of shameful poverty and pitiless exploitation of human beings; it is a land of confirmed backwardness, hypocrisy, and callousness; it is a nation whose official church is obscurantist and unchristian, and whose government is an anachronism in time, thought, and action.

Seldom, since World War II, has any government and its ruling groups (clerical, aristocratic, military) been subjected to more bitter criticism. That this will result in a virulent counterattack upon Mr. Wright by the supporters of this same government in the United States goes without saying. Although Mr. Wright assures us that his Communist affiliation is a thing of the past and although "Pagan Spain" speaks harshly of Communists' acts in that country during the civil war of 1936-39, many critics of this book will doubtless lay its outlook to left-wing sympathies.

Whether such criticism will be fair is not easy to say. For while "Pagan Spain" is patently written from an outlook that stresses the bad and largely ignores the good, few neutral observers would deny that a great deal of what the author says both is true and urgently needs saying.

Like so many books printed today, "Pagan Spain" may be described as belonging to the "frankly realistic" school; that is, it is filled with situations and freely employs words which would never have passed the censor a generation ago. While this type of writing can be neither supported nor condoned, it is but fair to add that Mr. Wright's purpose is not to titillate but rather to create what he believes is a justifiable mood.

In this book Mr. Wright applies a shrewd device. Having obtained a copy of the political catechism issued by Franco's Falangist Party for the orientation of its female youth organization, the author intersperses numerous selections from it throughout the book, particularly at chapter ends. The purpose is to show what the author feels to be the great gap between official Spain's pretentiously moral position and the life actually led in that country.

From the technical point of view, "Pagan Spain" is powerfully and effectively written. Mr. Wright was deeply stirred by Spain (as favorably in the case of the average citizen and the countryside as he was unfavorably in the case of the privileged groups), and he has been able to transmit this reaction to the reader.

While this is by no means either a complete or wholly fair book on a fascinating and challenging country, it does reveal aspects of Spain which have not been frankly faced in America since Spain became an ally.

"No Castles in Spain." *Charlotte News*, February 23, 1957

As a child Richard Wright suffered the indignities that are the lot of a Mississippi Negro. As an adult he worked for 12 years under the banner of the Communist Party in learning of the evils of that sort of dictatorship.

Freedom and knowledge, then, are two things Richard Wright must hold especially valuable.

In 1954 he made a trip to Spain following the urging of friends who insisted he should see the country. What he saw appalled and sickened him, and when he returned to his home he did not write a book about what he had seen. Instead he let his whirling mind "simmer down." In 1955 he returned to the land to determine if what he had seen still held true, and this book is the result of those two journeys.

To Richard Wright the four horsemen of Spain must be the state, the church, the rich landholder-industrialist, and the degradation of the Spaniard, the last resulting from domination by the other three. The state and the church, charges Richard Wright, by the very nature of their organization foster ignorance, and the industrialist-landholder fosters poverty. With the burden of ignorance and poverty upon it, he believes, "Pagan Spain" is truly that. Africa, long known as the "dark continent" and the greatest enemy of Western civilization has a chance of becoming civilized before Spain does, is Wright's belief.

This opinion was formed during the course of hundreds of conversations with students, workers, beggars, bullfighters, prostitutes, doctors, teachers, farmers, newsmen, intellectuals. From them came verbal attacks upon the Falange, the Catholic Church, and the rich, attacks which explain the prevalence of sin, sex, ignorance and poverty which Wright found to be the earmarks of the country.

Certainly the book will not make him popular with the authorities, and quite possibly may make him persona non grata; it is against these people the attack is directed, these people who are charged with keeping the populace in an ignorance of the "truth which sets men free."

Wright's Spain is not the Spain of the lazy sun, old castles, bullfights and gypsy dances of the tourist. It is the Spain of the ready thumb of the church and the state, the thumb which twists and turns the lives of the poor mortals beneath it, shaping and moving the poor mortals in a way repugnant to much of the world.

Marjorie B. Jones. "Life in Franco's Spain." *Baltimore Morning Sun,* February 24, 1957.

It would be difficult to find two other books whose subject is the same, whose political viewpoint is roughly similar, whose general verdicts approximate each other, and yet are so totally different as these two. Neither is in any sense a where-to-go and what-to-see book; both writers are intensely interested in people and their reactions. But one is a self-portrait, the other a portrait of a nation.

Mr. Brenan, an Englishman, had spent seven years in Andalusia, bought a house near Malaga, was correspondent for the Manchester *Guardian* during the Civil War. Following this, he wrote "The Spanish Labyrinth," sympathetic to the Republican side, and a history of Spanish literature.

Because he has no language barrier, the author could listen to all sorts of people—shopkeepers, peasants, farmers, teachers. Many a Spaniard lives "the life of the addict, whose drug is not sex, or morphia, but politics." Some speak of the paralyzing inflation, of the ever-present black market; most are worn down by the inexorable struggle to keep alive and stifle the pangs of hunger. . . .

Mr. Brenan does not ignore the effects of the horrible blood baths on both sides during the Civil War. Spaniards "live by a tribal or client system, which makes it a moral duty for them to favor their friends at the expense of the state and to penalize their adversaries. That is the first law of this country, and it was as much observed during the rule of the Republic as it is today."

One of the most poignant episodes in "The Face of Spain" deals with the search for the grave of Garcia Lorca near Granada—first at the bone pits, then at the wall where the execution of thousands took place, and then at clay trenches at the foot of barren mountains; here hundreds of small stones are the only markers of graves.

It would be misleading to give the impression that all is politics in "The Face of Spain." Mr. Brenan is often able to transmit his definition of the purpose of travel: "to obtain ecstasy—that delight which one had as a child but lost later." His descriptions, as of "eucalyptus trees, their low branches combed out by the wind, nostalgically dark against the bright, false glitter of the sea" are as eye-rewarding as any painting.

In "Pagan Spain," Mr. Wright does not use one word where three will do the trick, and reports most conversations *in toto* with monotonous results. . . . As his knowledge of Spanish is rather elementary, he was forced to use French or English; this in itself limited the number and types of people he could meet.

There are the usual accounts of the dramatics of the bull fight, of flamenco dancers, of lengthy dinners in Spanish homes. Some readers will be irritated by the undigested Freudian linking of religion and sex; others will be offended by the overemphasis on sexual *mores*.

One would expect this author to be at his best in describing the underdog and the oppressed; he has a haunting and unforgettable chapter which details the sufferings of a Protestant woman who sought only to teach the Bible to children and was put into prison for doing so, without any charge being made publicly against her.

Mr. Wright has wisely chosen to weave the fabric of his narrative together by interspersing excerpts from an official Falangist catechism, which girls aged 9 and upward must know. The dogmatic questions and answers on the origins of the Falange, its leaders, the evils of universal suffrage, etc., ring strangely in our ears, and do more than any analysis to show by what means the present regime holds sway. He concludes that Spain has completely escaped the secularizing process which swept over the Western World. . . .

Mr. Wright's narrative will be the one more talked of; Mr. Brenan's is the one which should receive the accolade of thought and discussion.

Jane A. B. Parker. "Richard Wright Explores a Nation in Candid Report." *Jackson Daily News,* February 24, 1957.

Here is a personal report on Spain today presented by expatriate Richard Wright, taking in Spain's ancient romance, beauty and poverty, its extraordinary brand of Catholicism, its political views, and most of all the way its people feel.

It is vigorous, compassionate and engrossing, it will undoubtedly stir up much controversy, for the Spain reported by Richard Wright is not the Spain that the tourist sees.

The author set out to live, sleep, eat and talk with a cross-section of Spanish people, and he succeeds—there are forty-eight such encounters that include intellectuals, royalty, priests, Protestants, procurers, prostitutes, bullfighters, flamenco dancers, virgins, the old, the young and the hungry.

Throughout he writes with sympathy and there are very dramatic scenes: "Death and Exultation," the chapter concerned with the bullfight, its horrors, its fascinations and its debasement is as moving and dramatic as anything this reviewer has read in a long time.

Perhaps the biggest eye-opener of the book is the chapter that deals with "Sex, Flamenco, and Prostitution." Until you get everything back in perspective, you feel that Spain is but one big brothel; that sex and the restraints imposed upon it by the Church, which actually only increase the morbid interest, is the all-engrossing force in Spain and that Freud must certainly have done his research there.

Wright explains the position of women in Spain, which is certainly not enviable. Virginity before marriage is so highly prized that no good girl goes out unchaperoned, a social habit which makes for many more bad girls than good ones. After marriage, because of the extreme poverty which prevails throughout, even the good and respectable women turn to prostitution in order to provide their children with bread. . . .

This is indeed a controversial book. It is also a very engaging and undoubtedly sincere book. One must certainly read it through to form an opinion. Without any doubt this is not the Spain described in travel brochures. It is not an expose, but it is rather a book designed to take the pulse of a country. This the author has done with candor.

"Volume Destined for Controversy." *Dallas Times-Herald,* February 24, 1957.

A question raised by reading a book of this type, is just how much unpopular truth will the public take before it throws the report away and thus destroys the volume's potential impact.

Put another way, perhaps Mr. Wright has been too graphic, or covered too many facets at one time, so that his report becomes something like a double dose of some types of medicine—the surplus dosage counteracts the values of the first and thus no good is done.

Spain is a delicate subject here; we have not quite reached peace of soul either nationally or individually about our relationships with her. Thus anyone who essays to give "a personal report on Spain today, its ancient romance, beauty and poverty, its unique religion, its politics and people," is leaving the door wide open to all kinds of attack. One has only to recall the relatively recently published report of former Ambassador to Spain Claude Bowers on the last days of the Republic, and the howls of rage hurled at it, to realize that for the sake of peace, silence is the best policy.

But we're not ostrich, as comforting as this might be, in the present instance. Spain is still a very important spot on the globe, so important that our nation has felt it necessary to glaze its eyes to the present condition of Spanish politics and deal with a government whose methods have formed the ideological basis for shooting wars.

And, after all, Americans have the curiosity and the right to know, of the conditions of favor or oppression under which millions of our fellowmen live. How else can we know the best places in which to put forth new or supplement old Marshall aid programs?

It seems strange, does it not, to feel the necessity of defending the right of an author to report on a tour, his conversations with people, his impressions and findings? Yet, Mr. Wright will need defending because the essence of his subject is inseparable from the religious persuasion of the people. Therefore, each negative line in a report filled with jeremiads will be taken as direct criticism of the Church in Spain. This is unavoidable; it is regrettable; but chips must fall not too far from the point of origin.

Viewed for what it is—a report of what one man saw—it is a capable, sensitive, at times heart-rending picture of a people caught in the tentacles of poverty and fear. This is a book and a scene totally devoid of humor. Oppression and hunger, except for the very few at the top, have reduced a whole people to a numbness which can only find release in ecclesiastical pagentry and bullfights. The few "outsiders" who furtively confided in this reporter were either seeking some method of leaving Spain, or had regressed to the level of despair which made even that hope ridiculous.

In the midst of this sea of misery, Wright draws pictures of some of the natural scenery which must be rated as second to none in descriptive literature.

But, in the long run, even for the moment granting any charge against Wright which any critic cares to level, there are portions of this book which speak so loudly that they cannot be shouted down—and these portions are not words of Mr. Wright. They are selections, very generous ones throughout the book, from the political catechism for children. . . .

Destined for controversy, "Pagan Spain" will furnish plenty of ammunition for its critics, as well as providing a worthy line of defense for its friends.

Herbert L. Matthews. "How It Seemed to Him." *New York Times Book Review*, February 24, 1957, p. 7.

This is Richard Wright's Spain, which means that it is fascinating, intense, subjective, emotional. It is not the Spain that anyone else would see, hear or feel. It would never do as a textbook in colleges (for more reasons than accuracy), but for anyone seeking a vivid reading experience it is ideal.

Mr. Wright, it need hardly be said, is one of our most brilliant novelists, a Negro with a deep sense of racial consciousness whose reasons were set forth in his famous autobiography, "Black Boy." In his contribution to "The God that Failed," some years ago, Mr. Wright explained how and why he was a Communist for a short while. This background and these qualities explain the type of book that he has done in "Pagan Spain"—very personal, somewhat naive, bitterly anti-Franco and very anti-Spanish Catholic. Mr. Wright is undoubtedly going to offend profoundly most Roman Catholics who read this book.

He recalls the words of Gertrude Stein. "Dick," she told him, "you ought to go to Spain. You'll see the past there. You'll see what the Western world is made of. And the people! There are no people such as the Spanish anywhere." Clearly, the people and the land of Spain fascinated Mr. Wright, though his report is as individual in its way as the portraits of Goya in theirs.

He did not know Spain or the Spanish language, but since he set out to tell in all honesty and with considerable journalistic talent what he saw and heard in Spain, the limitations are easy to discount. Mr. Wright went to Spain twice, apparently for about three weeks each time, in August, 1954, and the spring of 1955. On his first trip he went to Barcelona, Madrid, Seville and Granada, and on the second to the Basque country and back to Madrid, ending at Seville for the famous Easter "Feria." He kept from the beaten track, stayed with Spanish families, lived in third-class boarding houses and generally got a picture of Spain that was far from the ordinary tourist's and journalist's.

The talent displayed is enormous, as one would expect. Everybody who writes about Spain describes a bullfight, but few can describe one like this author. It is Richard Wright's bullfight, a combination of how he and the bull felt—both very intensely, of course—but there is genuine understanding on Mr. Wright's part, if not approval. Bullfighting is, he acutely says, "a man-made agony to assuage the emotional needs of man."

It is a pity that Mr. Wright did not enlist some expert help to keep his ordinary facts straight. The reader is floored to learn right at the beginning that "I crossed the frontier and entered my first Spanish town. . . Le Perthus," and we get a description of his adventures. As it happens, Le Perthus is a French village in the Pyrénés Orientales just short of the frontier. He faithfully puts down what everybody tells him—some of it true, some of it nonsense, but the reader gets no guidance. No less than sixteen lessons from a Falangist catechism for school-girls are scattered throughout the book in full, the implication being that they are highly significant. In fact, they have little or no significance. El Greco is placed in the Middle Ages although he died in 1614.

The value of "Pagan Spain," therefore, is in Mr. Wright, and it is a high value. Space would not allow here an analysis of why the author considers Spain "pagan." Paradoxically, he concedes that *"all was religion in Spain,"* but *"Spain was not yet even Christian!"* (The italics and exclamation mark are the author's.)

Fortunately, Mr. Wright found that his being a Negro made no difference to Spaniards, who are not race conscious. It was Spanish religion that appalled him, and sex. "Spain seemed one vast brothel," he writes at one point. This is a provocative, disturbing and, at times, sensational book. Spaniards will hate it; Roman Catholics will be dismayed, but other readers will have an exciting time. Mr. Wright does not disappoint his fans.

Ted Holmberg. "Spain and Richard Wright." *Providence Journal*, February 24, 1957.

There can be little question that there is unrest stirring in Spain. From all reports, it would appear that the unrest is of a serious nature and that Franco is concerned about his hold on the nation.

Richard Wright, then, had a most ideal opportunity for a journalistic scoop with his book about Spain and the troubles that afflict that nation. Unfortunately, Mr. Wright has not capitalized on this opportunity, for "Pagan Spain" is a rather superficial examination of a dictatorship.

The author used personal interviews as his basis for reporting and he talked to a wide range of individuals. The conversations and his observations make sprightly and diverting reading. Mr. Wright is never dull.

But he is also never very profound or very original in this book. When he seems to be closing in on the core of the problem, the author flits away to another person, another city, another subject. His conclusions that Spanish Catholicism is pagan in nature because the people worship the trappings and idols and accoutrements without any real understanding or appreciation of their religion, is controversial but it has been said before.

It may be true that the Spanish are not true Christians, but how many nations or individuals in this world worship more than the trappings? Mr. Wright need not have journeyed to Spain to find pagan church-goers.

Mr. Wright explains Spanish character through its relationship to religion and the bullfights, and his examination of the sexual symbols back of bull killing is Hopalong Freud at its most entertaining.

There is no question that a bull fight is loaded with sexual significance, but an alert observer could find symbolic significance in baseball or any other American sport. I don't think that baseball explains America anymore than bullfights explain Spain, and I'm frankly a little tired of psychological examinations by amateurs.

More important than bull fighting are the seeds that grew into the unrest in Spain right now and seldom were we able to find them in Mr. Wright's work. As a matter of fact, he seemed to think that the Spanish people, steeped in pride, would go on taking their lumps from Franco forever. Such may not be the case.

This is an interesting and vastly entertaining travelogue and at another time it could be read for what it is. At this time, we were expecting something more, and, for all his skill in writing, Mr. Wright has not provided it.

"Spain Today." *Washington Star*, February 24, 1957.

"Pagan Spain," by Richard Wright is the American novelist's impressions of Spain today. These impressions are bitter indeed and sure to stir a controversy.

As a Negro brought up in our South, Mr. Wright felt that totalitarian governments were no mystery to him. He was born "under an absolutistic racist regime in Mississippi." He "lived and worked for 12 years under the political dictatorship of the Communist Party in the United States" and he spent a year under "the police terror" of Peron in Buenos Aires.

The author of "Uncle Tom's Children," "Native Son" and other widely sold novels is an able writer. "Pagan Spain" is beautifully written. The content is something else. It is something some who know Spain undoubtedly will answer.

Mr. Wright long ago denounced communism. But he obviously remains a militant left-wing liberal and apparently he went to Spain to find certain things and found them.

He found great poverty. He gathered evidence that the people are oppressed, held down, denied a voice by the Franco government. He blames the Catholic Church for allegedly abetting Franco in his dictatorship.

He quotes a fruit grower, who was not allowed to sell his trees or export his oranges: "And they talk of the evils of communism! This is communism. I live in a religious Communist state."

Mr. Wright insists that prostitution is one of the biggest professions in Spain. He encountered an American white-slaver who was exporting girls to North Africa. He met girls who were eager to go.

Mr. Wright concluded that "the naked African in the bush would make greater progress during the next 50 years than the proud, tradition-bound Spaniard."

Spain's religion, he feels, is largely pagan. "The fact was: Spain was not yet even Christian! It had never been converted, not to Protestantism, not even to Catholicism itself. Somehow the pagan streams of influence flowing from the Goths, the Greeks, the Jews, the Romans, the Iberians and the Moors lingered strongly and vitally on, flourishing under the draperies of the 20th century."

In Spain, he found there was no lay,

no secular life. "Spain was a holy nation, a sacred state—a state as sacred and as irrational as the sacred state of Akan in the African jungle.

"Even the prostitution, the corruption, the politics had about them a sacred aura. All was religion in Spain."

Mr. Wright's patent bias and prejudice weaken all his findings.

Leslie Hanscom. *New York World-Telegram & Sun*, February 25, 1957.

From the first page of Richard Wright's intellectual travelogue, "Pagan Spain," he is indirectly justifying that unexpected title. It is quite near the end of the book when he comes at it explicitly: "For a long time my own Westernness proved a veritable stumbling block to my seeing the truth that stared me in the face. The cold fact was: Spain was not yet even Christian! It had never been converted, not to Protestantism, not even to Catholicism itself."

And yet, "All was religion in Spain. . . there was no lay, no secular life. Spain was a holy nation, a sacred state. . . . Even the prostitution, the corruption, the economics, the politics had about them a sacred aura."

The boundaries of Spanish religiosity, to Mr. Wright's eyes, "went beyond the church." He notes with interest that a minor Vatican official, whom he accompanied on a pilgrimage to the Black Virgin of Montserrat, reacted with a shudder to the decaying body of a bishop, exposed in a glass coffin in a cathedral. "I'm Catholic," the man protested, "but. . . ."

A onetime Communist who long ago recanted, Richard Wright went to Spain involuntarily thinking in the old categories. He planned to observe and analyze in terms of economics and politics. It didn't take long to discover, however, that, "No neat, simple dialectical diagnosis of class relations could clarify the reality that had flooded in upon me."

The class divisions represented such unearthly extremes that they could only be understood by reference to the pagan mystique which the author believes enwraps the whole of Spanish life. . . .

One of Mr. Wright's most interesting finds was an official political catechism for the Spanish people which he uses as a running motif, interspersing large quotations between his observations of the bullfight, flamenco art and the orgiastic religious expression of this people misplaced in time.

In terms of question and answer, the document drivels on about the destiny of the Spanish nation, avoiding the problems of hunger and lack of freedom with an agility that would tax a flamenco dancer.

This summary, based on the author's conclusions rather than on what he saw, may make it sound as though he went to Spain with a chip on his shoulder. This wouldn't be just. Vivid for its sightseeing as well as its thinking, the book makes the Spanish—with all their strange faults—sound like the most alive of people, and their country sound like one of earth's most fascinating. It won't be likely, however, to start an immigration trend.

Granville Hicks. "Richard Wright: Spain the Fossil." *New York Post,* February 29, 1957.

At the beginning of his book Richard Wright tries to explain to the reader why, in spite of the exhortations of Gertrude Stein and other friends, he had avoided Spain. Spain was, he tells us, "the one country of the Western world about which, as though shunning the memory of a bad love affair, I did not want to exercise my mind."

But in the summer of 1954, traveling alone in the south of France, he suddenly decided to cross the Spanish border. He visited Barcelona, Madrid, Granada, and Seville, staying always with Spanish families.

Note that he speaks, in the sentence I have quoted, about exercising his mind. For him Spain was not so much a landscape to be looked at as a problem to be solved.

After he left Spain, he sought in the writings of others for aids to understanding, and he returned a year later to talk with Spanish intellectuals. Having overcome his reluctance to examine the problem of Spain, he would not let it go until he had reached conclusions that satisfied him.

On his first day in Barcelona Wright laid hands on a political catechism, a primer for the instruction of the young, and he scatters through his book long quotations from it about the destiny of Spain and the nature of the Falange.

He quotes, I think, considerably more than is necessary to make his point, but his preoccupation with the turgid little volume is evidence of his determination to get inside the Spanish mind.

His excursion into Spain brought about a dramatic and significant confrontation. "I have no religion in the formal sense of the word," he told a young Spanish woman.

"I have no race except that which is forced upon me. I have no country except that to which I'm obliged to belong. I have no traditions. I'm free. I have only the future."

That is a dramatic enough statement in itself when one thinks of Richard Wright's beginnings as he has described them in "Black Boy." But here was this emancipated cosmopolitan in Spain, a country in which adherence to a particular faith was almost universal, in which a morbid nationalism was systematically cultivated, in which tradition was still, as it had once been for all Europe, the dominant force in almost every life.

Wright used his eyes in Spain, and there are some picturesque passages, but he was chiefly concerned with such matters as poverty, prostitution, the role of the Church, the persecution of Protestants, and the nonsense that passed as political thinking.

He found plenty of evidence of discontent, but he also found that the Spanish way of life retained its validity for many, perhaps for most, Spaniards.

The conclusion that Wright ultimately reached is embodied in his title—"The cold fact was: Spain was not yet even Christian!"

Although he ingeniously develops this theory, I don't believe it holds water. What Toynbee calls fossilization has taken place in Spain, but I suspect that Wright has misdated the fossil.

This doesn't greatly matter. The important thing is that Wright has given an honest and searching account of what happened when two ways of life, representing two extremes of Western culture, were brought face to face.

Roi Ottley. "He Should Stick to Fiction." *Chicago Sunday Tribune Magazine of Books,* March 3, 1957, p. 10.

When a novelist of Richard Wright's stature pauses in his fictional chores to turn journalist and report on a foreign nation's social fabric, one always wonders whether he merely is indulging himself in a writing exercise.

I am an admirer of Wright's novels, but I do not think he has the talents of the skilled reporter, nor indeed has he the developed and subtle understanding necessary accurately to report the social and cultural nuances of the Spanish people.

For example, his description of a bullfight in Barcelona, in which the great Chamaco performs, has depth and emotional content that would do Hemingway proud. But we actually do not see a bullfight. We are only privy to Wright's emotional agonies.

I am embarrassed for him when he reports, with an air of profundity, "I sighed, realizing that, in Spain, all things were Spanish." When he has the Spanish people speak, they are reported in the slangy idioms of Americans who have embraced the Marxist ideology.

To be sure, he talked with intellectuals, peasants, aristocrats, prostitutes, and gypsies. He attempted to examine the complex social system. If he failed to grasp the essence of Spanish life, he was at least unsentimentally compassionate.

This distinguished writer's gifts and insights as a novelist might be better served in reporting such dramas as now unfold in Montgomery, Tallahassee, and Clinton, Tenn. They are tailor made for his talents.

Saunders Redding. *Baltimore Afro-American,* March 9, 1957.

Pagan Spain is Richard Wright's third travel book, the others being *Black Power* and *Color Curtain*—though some may dispute this designation for the last named.

Black Power was his journal of the Gold Coast, and, within its limited frame of political reference, it was percipient.

It was also strangely disturbing, like coming upon a mirrored reflection of oneself in an unexpected place and time and seeing suddenly lines and lineaments one had not seen before.

Though this reviewer thought that Wright marveled and was too much shocked perhaps by his discoveries, the shock may have been proof of a very laudable absence of prejudgment on the part of the author.

Color Curtain was more important than *Black Power,* but it did not have the attention it deserved from the peoples—that is, the Western peoples—to whom it was so obviously addressed.

Clearly, one of its themes was that Western whites, for all their experience with dark peoples in a colonial setting, are not psychologically prepared to deal with dark peoples emerging from a colonial state—or better, dark peoples are determined to emerge from a colonial state.

Color Curtain said plainly that Western observers at the Bandung conference did not realize the dominant role that color-consciousness played in that historic meeting.

Pagan Spain in this reviewer's opinion is more percipient than *Black Power* and just as important as *Color Curtain*.

But its importance is different: its importance is deeply personal to Wright himself. For a long time now this highly articulate writer has been examining the formulae that compose the problem called life.

One by one he has tested them against whatever realities he has chosen to live in; and one by one they have either canceled out or been referred to later consideration.

Communism and existentialism, for instance, canceled out in the novel *The Outsider*. In *Black Power* fascism was referred to later consideration. It gets that consideration only to be canceled out in *Pagan Spain*. And this is well and good.

But it seems to this reviewer that *Pagan Spain* goes a long way also to cancel out that formula called religion. The book is anti-religious, almost bitterly so.

Its very title is a satiric comment, for Spain, Wright shows clearly, the most Catholic and religious of all modern countries, is in fact spiritually and emotionally and culturally rooted in a paganism as gross and a venality as vulgar as the temples of Baal.

Proof surely is needed—in that no one has really seen Wright's Spain before—and he proves his case by relating a series of experiences that range from ironic comedy to bleak tragedy.

It is not the political horror of fascism alone that "the church had had to negate" by making it "the normal lot of men."

There is also the horror of grinding poverty, of blind, crushing ignorance, of degrading prostitution.

Considering all he has rejected, Richard Wright comes close to nihilism, and *Pagan Spain* comes close to documenting and justifying his tragic sense of life.

But it is an interesting—indeed, a fascinating book; for Wright's skill in handling sharp dramatic incident and in portraying people is coupled with a descriptive skill he rarely uses, and both operate to produce the emotional intensity of fiction.

Pagan Spain will be argued about. It will be praised by some and damned by others. It will be read—and this reviewer hopes, widely read.

Francis E. McMahon, S.J. "Spain Through Secularist Spectacles." *America*, 96 (March 9, 1957), 648, 653.

It requires a peculiar kind of daring to attempt to assess the soul of a national culture after a few relatively brief trips into a country and with only a rudimentary knowledge of the language. Richard Wright has tried just that. His limited experience partially accounts for his failure.

A brief word first about the author may not be amiss. He grew up in the (for him) oppressive atmosphere of the U. S. South. A somewhat sensitive and reflective spirit, he acquired an education of sorts despite many handicaps. During the 'thirties, he became a Communist, but broke with the party several years later. He has written a number of works, the best known of which is *Native Son*.

The author undertook this study of

Spain at the urging of friends. He began his journey late in 1954 and for weeks moved about the country, observing, reflecting and recording in his notebook. He conversed with the humble and the mighty. He finally evolved a pattern of explanation which, he is satisfied, authentically accounts for Spanish culture.

The picture he portrays is one of human degradation. Spain, he affirms, is governed by traditions wholly divorced from the main stream of Western European culture. And these traditions are basically of a primitive and primeval character. Spain is essentially pagan, with a paganism akin to that of the primitive tribesmen of Africa. It is a deeply religious country, but its religion is not Christian.

He is frank—brutally so—about Spanish Catholicism. He recognizes that the Church has been the major sociological force in Spain. But the influence of this basically paganized Church, he asserts, has been altogether harmful. The poverty of Spain, the corruption, the sexual immorality, the intolerance toward political and religious dissidents are owing chiefly to the Church. Superstition is rampant. The program of the Falange reflects the Church's desire to make Spain once more a crusading force against Western enlightenment.

It is a formidable indictment. How valid is it? The answer becomes clear by listing the basic assumptions behind the author's criticisms. Richard Wright is a perfect model of the completely secularized mentality. He is committed, more or less consciously, to some modern dogmas; rationalism, sentimental humanitarianism, sociological determinism, Freudian pan-sexualism. It is a motley assortment inhabiting an undisciplined mind. There is a complete lack of awareness of, or appreciation for, anything pertaining to the supernatural. It is difficult to conceive of anyone less equipped to understand Spain.

His observations about the thousand-year-old shrine of Montserrat reveal his unfortunate mentality. Montserrat, for him, can be acounted for according to the categories of Freud's pan-sexual theories. This attempt to explain religious phenomena in the crude terms of sexual sublimation has well been described as a type of Machiavellian denigration. There is no space here to expose the fallacy.

Of pruriency, there is plenty in the book. We do not accuse the author of deliberately striving for the sensational, but he does display a marked talent for allusions to the scatological and the erotic. His vocabulary, moreover, is not innocent of the short Anglo-Saxon words. In the name of "honesty" and "realism," good taste and decency have been sacrificed.

Some of the charges he makes against life in Spain cannot be gainsaid. Spain is poor, corruption is extensive, the traditional Spaniard tends to be intolerant, and the Spaniards can be alarmingly human in their sinning. But the author did find an absence of racial discrimination. If the Church is responsible for everything, why not give it credit for this?

Spanish Catholicism is different, and it has aspects which would be uncongenial to American Catholics. The reverse is likewise true. But one cannot, without falling into absurdity, stigmatize the Church of Teresa of Avila, John of the Cross, Ignatius Loyola, Francisco de Vitoria and a host of other saints and scholars, as inimical to human values.

This work is revelatory more of Richard Wright than it is of Spain. He has abandoned communism, but in its stead he has succumbed to some corroding and corrupting modern dogmas which bode no less ill for the future of Western culture. It is these dogmas which have blinded him to the reality of Spain.

Harry J. Carman. "Richard Wright in Spain." *New York Herald Tribune Book Review,* March 10, 1957, p. 8.

This is a most interesting and informative book. It deals with contemporary Spain and with Spanish people of all classes—aristocrats, intellectuals, gypsies, priests, flamenco dancers, peasants, Protestants, Jews, clerks, bullfighters, Falangists, prostitutes. Mr. Wright is concerned not only with the social-economic status of these various groups but with what they think and feel. His acquaintance with them comes not from weighty tomes of historians and philosophers but from direct contact made possible by travel to practically all parts of the country. In substance, this book is a highly illuminating and provocative report by one of America's liveliest writers.

What are the highlights of this report? They are these: a backward economy characterized by a primitive agriculture, little power and less transport, not enough water and almost no irrigation, concentration of land ownership in the hands of absentee landlords, insufficient manufactures, low wages, widespread unemployment. As a consequence hunger prevails everywhere. Out of hunger flows a stream of mingled results: low standards of living, widespread prostitution, corruption, blackmarketing, illiteracy, the bullfight as an agency to assuage the emotional needs of the masses whose homes are bereft of all things cultural beyond the traditional ecclesiastical—no books, no magazines, no art.

One may well ask why do these conditions continue to prevail in mid-20th century Spain? Richard Wright believes that totalitarianism and the heavy hand of the past—of memories of Spain as a far-flung colonial nation, and the hopes and dreams of the remnant of an aristocracy for the resurrection of Spain to its former pinnacle of power—are the answer. Everywhere in this country the agencies of 20th century totalitarianism are visible: The Falange, the State, the Army, and the Church. These four, in his opinion, are the organs of power that make up the heart of Spanish reality. And because of their domination, the area of the lay or secular life, as thought of in Western terms, never developed in tradition-bound Spain. Indeed, it had no opportunity to develop. New ideas, whether religious, social, economic or political, are abhorred there as being heretical, sinful and dangerous. Any dissent provokes punitive measures. This situation, Mr. Wright thinks, accounts for the large number of soldiers serving in a police capacity, for the relatively small number of Protestants in Spain, for the large number of persons still incarcerated as political prisoners, and the absence in Spain of dynamic pressures that would remold its traditional environment.

Of all repressive agencies in Spain, Mr. Wright believes the Church is the most powerful. But the Church in Spain, in his opinion is pagan. It has never been converted to Catholicism. Let him speak for himself:

> Somehow the pagan streams of influence flowing from the Goths, the Greeks, the Jews, the Romans, the Iberians and the Moors have lingered strongly and vitally on, flourishing under the draperies of the twentieth century.

Mr. Wright's facts are often inaccurate and his point of view is entirely personal. This is the Spain Richard Wright saw. Spaniards undoubtedly will hate the book. Roman Catholics will be distressed by it and many who read it will not agree with many of Mr. Wright's conclusions. Nevertheless, all who read it will find it a challenging report of one man's observations of present-day life in one of the world's most romantic and paradoxical states.

Robert C. Marsh. *Chicago Sun-Times,* March 17, 1957.

Richard Wright went to Spain in August of 1954. He drove from Paris to Barcelona and from there to Madrid, went south to Granada and Seville by train, crossed to Tangier, and returned to France by the same route.

Late in the spring of 1955 he drove from Paris to Madrid by way of San Sebastian and went to Seville, with a stop in Toledo, for Holy Week.

By internal evidence I would estimate his total time in Spain was no more than six weeks.

It is a brave man who writes a book of this sort about a country he has visited only twice for short periods of time. Under the circumstances it is not surprising that we learn as much about the mental and emotional processes of an American expatriate, ex-Communist, agnostic (but a militantly protestant agnostic), Negro intellectual named Richard Wright as we do about Spain.

Wright is angry and dismayed about the condition of the Spanish people under Franco's police state and the economic and emotional poverty he finds in so many of their lives.

He dislikes the sight of guards with machineguns in every place of importance. He is incensed about the denial of freedom to think or worship along lines disapproved by the holders of power.

On the other hand, Wright often selects his material to give a worse impression than is due. . . .

We see in Wright's book too much of Spain's lower elements of society and too little of the devout, self-satisfied, ostensibly pro-Franco middleclass to grasp a sufficiently large view of the complex phenomenon that is modern Spain.

Ellen Gibson. "Mr. Wright's Spain." *Milwaukee Journal,* March 17, 1957.

The Spain that Richard Wright saw on his first visit in 1954 was not the charming, wonderfully inexpensive land that postwar tourists often report.

He took something in—his trepidation about visiting this totalitarian country—and he carried a great deal away. This acquired baggage of thousands of absorbing and conflicting impressions, reflections and experiences is opened in this book.

Spain has a fascination for many, and Wright's book probably will be eagerly read. It is a disturbing book, however. Some of his conclusions about the role of the Catholic church, the oppression of the Protestant minority (whom he compares to the Negroes in America), the flourishing prostitution in a poverty stricken society are bound to cause argument. . . .

Yes, this is not a book that everyone will like to read in the context of the times which made Franco's government an American ally. But, granting his prejudice against the dictatorship and his Protestant origins, Wright does appear to have written what for him is an honest report on Spain. Surely it is intense and dramatic. . . .

It would be difficult and probably unfair to sum up his report too briefly. But one thought does seem to explain many others. Wright believes that Spain, beleaguered by modern ideas and "stormed by the forces of social and political progress" has withdrawn into the past to find an "acceptable form of endurable life" to hold its poetic people together.

Eva J. Ross. *Books on Trial,* 15 (March 1957), 307–8.

Here is a book which must be read with discriminatory care even by those who can separate the wheat from the chaff of the author's active dislike of the externals of the Catholic religion and of Franco's politics, and also his almost pathological pre-occupation with sex and sex symbolism. Undoubtedly the author did not intend to supplant Sacheverell Sitwell's *Spain* with its architectural details, or any comprehensive travel volume or historical account. Instead he tried to understand and to help others understand how the Spanish people live today, economically, politically, and, to some extent, socially. He says that it was suggested that he should do this by the sociologists Alva and Gunnar Myrdal, "whose compassionate hearts have long brooded upon the degradation of human life in Spain."

Now a visitor to Spain may indeed be critical of many things, either because objectively they seem to call for improvement, or because they are so different from his own culture that he has not yet adapted himself to the differences, or is intolerant of them, or just does not understand.

Few Americans really like the Franco regime in all its aspects. Yet this reviewer who also traveled by car alone around Spain in 1953 and 1954 found that although Catalans and Basques want indepdendence, and royalists are to be met in Murcia and elsewhere, the fact remains that the older Spaniards at least merely "want to be governed." The majority seem to desire freedom to dance, or to talk, or to go to their literary circles at ten or eleven at night, after their late dinner (or before a later one). If they are governed well they seem to be content. Apathy if you will, with the fear of another civil war as a possible explanation, but valid for them if they want it that way.

Spanish Catholics, as some of those Wright met, may do things forbidden by their religion and thereafter confess them, but this is a realistic avowal of human frailty provided for by the Catholic religion and shocking only to those who are naive or who misunderstand. It may be because Wright was afraid of how he would be treated, as an American Negro whose earlier communist affiliations are well-known, that he was drawn to such a surprising percentage of prostitutes, pimps and people who showed statues of priests with exposed private parts. Such types are, of course, to be found in any country, but Wright may have been somewhat naive in taking the talk of some such individuals as explaining the Spanish. His knowledge of the language was admittedly poor, and Spaniards have an imagination which is proverbial. His own imagination as regards sex is, too, manifestly overdeveloped.

Yet the poverty of Spanish workers is a fact which worries Spaniards as well as Wright and other visitors. The pride of the poor in their poverty, truly noted by Wright, is not insincerity or brutish acceptance of facts, but a true appreciation of the transiency of human suffering and something Wright cannot understand. Much of the begging is merely due to the relative novelty of tourists in Spain so that they are considered fair bait by all the small fry and some not so small. The moneyed classes in Spain still strive to maintain their vested interests, but the Church, the local and national governments have often worked together to alleviate distress, as shown in the great strides this reviewer could note in Malaga after tidal wave destruction between her visits of October, 1953, and March, 1954. Wright did not meet the people who would tell him of the mission on social justice given in every parish of the Bilbao diocese in November, 1953; of the industrial conference of employers and professors the same month in Barcelona; of the interest in American labor relations and industrial sociology; of the Church's interest in workers' housing in Valencia, Cordoba, Malaga and elsewhere; of the solid work done in the Instituto Leon XIII graduate school in Madrid.

Although one can commend the book's fast pace, the undoubted firsthand descriptions and their frequent beauty, the author is too biased against Spain, too extremely Freudian in his interpretations, too limited in his contacts and in his knowledge of the Spanish language to provide much of value for a real understanding of the country, its people, its religion and its politics.

Current History, 32 (April 1957), 240.

When he writes of himself and of America, Richard Wright is a compelling novelist and a keen observer. When he writes about strangers with a strange language, after visiting them for about six weeks, his work takes on the subjective quality of an introspective novel, or a personal essay. In the first chapter, there is a great deal of information about Richard Wright and some misinformation about Spain. We learn of Wright, in his own words: "I have no religion in the formal sense of the word. . . I have no race except that which is forced upon me. I have no country except that to which I'm obliged to belong. I have no traditions. I'm free. I have only the future." Small wonder that Wright finds tradition-loving, church-loving Spain difficult to understand. As he sees religion, "man senses that if there is anything at all really divine or superhuman in us, it is linked to, allied with, and comes through sex, and is inescapably bound up with sex." Looking at Spain through these Freudian-tinted spectacles, Wright finds a great deal to write about: Spain's poverty, the ignorance of the people, the tyrannical government, the primitive religious ceremonies. He finds it impossible to understand the dedication of the religious, or the patriotism of a young Spanish Jew, or the attitude toward chastity, or what he terms the "sticky maudlinism" of Spanish devotion to children. This is too superficial to be classed as a political or social study, too subjective to be a travel book. Readers will learn more about Richard Wright than they do about Spain, and those who admire him will enjoy his superb writing.

Frederick E. Ellis. *Churchman* (New York), May 15, 1957, p. 13.

Not only is Richard Wright a highly competent writer, he is also a wise traveler who devotes his time and energy to ferreting out the *esprit* or *elan* of a country. The book is a forthright and refreshingly unvarnished statement of what a sensitive, percipient observer found in Spain during a visit in 1954. Surely Spain is a dramatic example of a confessional state at its worst. One leaves the pages of *Pagan Spain* with a keener awareness of the wisdom in the American doctrine of separation of church and state. It is virtually a truism that the marriage of church and state reduces one of the partners to the role of a prostitute. Wright has depicted this tragic dilemma with courage and understanding.

W. Archer Wright, Jr. "Emotional Undertones of Today's Spanish Life." *Richmond Times-Dispatch*, June 9, 1957.

"Pagan Spain" is no mere observer's "inside" analysis. Expatriate Wright makes no attempt to extricate his interpretation from his own emotional eccentricities. The hurts of a black boyhood in Memphis, a sensitive social consicence, disillusionment with institutionalized religion, the artist's sympathetic responsiveness to persons, places and situations, the realist's predilection to earthiness are all frankly unconcealed.

Nor would we have it otherwise, for with his easy, undistinguished style he projects the reader into the midst of the seething emotional undertones of Spanish life. This is notably evident in the uncanny sense of participation one feels at reading the fascinating description of a Barcelona bull fight. . . .

Wright concludes that the partnership of church and dictatorship in Spain is a stifling shadow covering a strange, misplaced medieval paganism. Indicting both Spanish Catholicism and Spanish totalitarianism, the book will move some to anger, some to sympathy. In either case it is a book of moving power and magnetism.

R. P. O. "Titillating Spain." *The National Review*, 3 (August 3, 1957), 141–42.

Mr. Wright's outlook on life will be familiar to everyone who remembers the opening pages of his autobiography, [sic] *Native Son*, which was a best-seller in its day. His new merchandise should be equally profitable. It contains the four-letter words that titillate our intellectuals, and the ritualistic expectorations at General Franco that always warm the cockles of Liberal hearts. Constant reminders that the author as a Negro belongs to a "persecuted racial minority" will silence most critics and jerk tears from old ladies who would otherwise be disgusted by a dirty book.

The author reports that one day he left his apartment in Paris, got into his automobile, and drove to Spain. There he observed mountains, sex, poverty, sex, bullfights, sex, Fascism, and sex. His acute eye discerned phallic symbols in churches, Freudian mysteries in priests, and a profound analogy between the tapers carried in a religious procession and the sperm of a "sexually aroused bull." He also met a large number of Spanish women: the virgins silently yearned to sleep with him, the matrons were waiting to be asked, and the prostitutes clamored eagerly for the privilege.

In the intervals of repose the author automatically discovered that Fascism is a Bad Thing, and that Spain is "trying to turn back the clock of history." But the Liberal line needs to be refurbished now and then. It used to be *de rigueur* to condemn the Spanish for being Catholic. This book will doubtless set the new mode in Liberal *Kaffeeklatsch* with the revelation that "Spain is not yet even Christian!" The religion of Spain, we are told, is the paganism of "the Goths, the Greeks, the Jews, the Romans, the Iberians, and the Moors," and "the nature and function of Catholicism has enabled that paganism to remain intact." This discovery is particularly opportune now that American Liberals have, for some reason, begun to speak respectfully of God.

Mary Ellen Stephenson. "Spain Gets Bitter Barbs from Visitor." *Richmond News Leader*, August 28, 1957.

Richard Wright, the candid author of "Black Boy" and "Native Son," has recently made a trip for observation into Spain. He describes the country in a new volume whose title indicates the point of approach from which he attacks Spain. The word "pagan" refers to the country's religion, but also to her culture, education, government, and to the small emphasis on the human values.

This is a violent book, exciting but at times repulsive, done by a violent man. Only one who has suffered and become bitter could have seen the particular things in Spain which Mr. Wright criticizes or could have reacted to them as he does. He discusses the prevalent display of armed force, the poverty, degradation, and hopelessness of the people, the cheap and yet revealing self-expression of the Spaniards in their leisure-time activities such as bull fighting and flamenco dancing, and their double standard in matters regarding sex. This material and spiritual poverty Mr. Wright attributes to Spain's church and to certain national characteristics of the Spaniards themselves. . . .

Mr. Wright's most bitter barbs are aimed at the Roman Catholic Church, the Franco dictatorship, and at such circumstances as the people's illiteracy and their laxity in sexual matters. His manner of writing is to present a series of sketches from his own actual experiences, and these "slices of life" are more articulate as to his ideas than vast amounts of wordy descriptions could have been.

"Pagan Spain" is not a pleasant book, but it is graphic and arresting. It is not nice to read and it must not have been nice to write, but it probably should have been writtten. Once a reader has picked it up, he will not readily put it down, for it fascinates even as it repels. The author gives his reader bitter, stark facts at the same time that he unwittingly reveals his own bitter, hurt self.

Checklist of Additional Reviews

Booklist, 53 (December 15, 1956), 190; (March 1, 1957), p. 353.

H. M. S. *Wilmington News,* February 10, 1957.

Walter Hackett. *Worcester Sun-Telegram,* February 17, 1957, p. D9.

Springfield Republican, February 17, 1957, p. 15c.

Richard Strout. *New Republic,* 136 (February 18, 1957), 18.

C. L. A. *Labor Daily* (New York), February 20, 1957.

Barc Bowman. *Dayton News,* February 24, 1957.

Grace P. Comans. *Hartford Courant,* February 24, 1957.

Marsh Maslin. *San Francisco Call-Bulletin,* February 24, 1957.

Washington Post, February 24, 1957.

Chicago Daily News, February 25, 1957.

Newsweek, 49 (February 25, 1957), 120, 122.

Paul Manchester. *Nashville Tennessean,* March 3, 1957, p. 5-E.

Winston-Salem Journal, March 10, 1957.

Woodrow Smith. *Chattanooga Times,* March 11, 1957.

Chattanooga News, March 12, 1957.

Thomas G. Bergin. *Saturday Review,* 40 (March 16, 1957), 60–62.

R. E. L. *Albuquerque Tribune,* March 16, 1957.

Hortense Binderup. *Portland Oregonian,* March 17, 1957.

New Yorker, 33 (March 23, 1957), 150–51.

Pittsburgh Courier, March 23, 1957.

F. M. L. *Tacoma Ledger,* March 24, 1957.

Joseph L. Morrison. *Greensboro Daily News,* March 24, 1957.

Rocky Mountain Telegraph (Denver), March 24, 1957.

Elmer Bendiner. *National Guardian,* April 1, 1957.

M. L. *New Bedford Standard-Times,* April 5, 1957.

Patricia Krebs. *St. Louis Post-Dispatch,* April 16, 1957.

Gilbert Cronberg. *Des Moines Register,* April 21, 1957, p. 11-G.

Phyllis Seidkin. *San Francisco Examiner*, April 28, 1957.

James W. Ivy. *The Crisis,* 64 (May 1957), 313–14.

Miami Herald, June 25, 1957.

Wisconsin Library Bulletin, 53 (July 1957), 450.

J. H. Silverman. *The Nation*, 185 (September 7, 1957), 114.

Virginia Quarterly Review, 34 (Winter 1958), p. xxxvi.

Richard Wright

WHITE MAN, LISTEN!

Doubleday & Company, Inc., Garden City, New York
1957

White Man, Listen!

Kirkus Reviews, 25 (August 15, 1957), 614.

The Color Curtain in 1956 revealed Wright as a challenging spokesman for the colored people of Asia and Africa. This new book *White Man, Listen!* specifically takes the psychological reactions of the colored people to the white oppressors—the literature of the Negro as evidence of his thesis—tradition as it is affected by industrialization—and the birth of Ghana on the African Gold Coast. While these chapters are based on lectures he gave in Europe, they are integrated so as to develop his themes. As a white, one cannot but cringe somewhat at the too penetrating uncovering of the cheap superiority of the dominant white, the factors that have kept the colored people feeling down graded. And to be fascinated by the analysis of the false front maintained to "fool" the masters. As for the writing of the Negro in the United States, we have maintained its achievement without sensing the survival of racial feeling, futility, bitterness, despair, only too often inherent. Wright feels that the whites have forced the Negro into a vacuum emotionally, spiritually, even when some have been educated outside their class. The final section on the miracle of nationalism in the African Gold Coast was a succinct presentation of the steps by which that miracle was achieved—perhaps the most exciting achievement in today's world. A valuable book to inform our thinking on a moot subject.

Milton S. Byam. *Library Journal*, 82 (September 15, 1957), 2138.

Some of the speeches of Richard Wright are collected here—speeches which define the area of difference between the world's differing races. These suffer from lack of knowledge in depth, as does most of Mr. Wright's nonfiction which is not straight reporting. Therefore the picture he draws is not always a true one. For instance, he sees the trend toward dictatorship and demagogy in the newly freed colonies as necessary for the rulers of these countries to get support of the masses. Yet any such tools are immoral when applied by a group which is seeking no such support. And he blames the Protestant for slavery while ignoring the role of the Arab, the Portugese and the Spaniard. However Mr. Wright has much of merit to say about the psychology of the world's darker peoples. Awareness of this psychology on the part of Western diplomats and newspapermen should make for the reporting of less nonsense than has been true in the past. Recommended for public, college and university.

Saville R. Davis. "Wright Speaks His Mind." *Christian Science Monitor*, October 17, 1957, p. 11.

White man, you would do well to listen. Richard Wright tells you much that you need to know about the international race problem—not in Little Rock but in Africa and Asia.

A lot of it will be hard to take, some of it extremely so, depending on your point of view. Mr. Wright does not temper words to the white man shorn of his privileged position in the colored parts of the world. He speaks frankly, with what seems like intentional roughness, but it may simply be the Negro who is crusading for colored people and spurns the deceptions which too often go with being polite. He is articulate. What looks like crudity may be the practical realism of today's Negro when he says what he thinks. And what looks at first like a tendency to perfervid language on Mr. Wright's part ceases to obtrude as the book proceeds.

Mr. Wright has the insight of a novelist and poet, so he is not satisfied with the usual sort of comment on race relations. He wants to show the often uncomprehending white man what he has done to hundreds of millions of another color, and what he can do today to redeem the situation. He wants also to explain what happens when a colored people emerges from foreign domination, what are the reasons for their internal struggles, what causes the different attitudes of the simple tribesmen and of the Western-trained elite who are taking over and are wandering between two worlds, Oxford and the bush. His object is not so much to recommend as to help people, demand of them if necessary, to understand. And although many will differ with him on details, few would fail to respect the basic position he sets forth.

Richard Wright is a product, he says, of the Protestant and free United States with all its contradictions and above all its freedoms. He knows learning and it tastes good to him. He respects candor, especially in describing the emotions that bubble and smoke under the surface of the world's racial problems.

"How can the spirit of the Enlightenment and the Reformation be extended now to all men. . . . Can a way be found purged of racism and profits, to swell the rational areas and rational personnel of Europe with those of Asia and Africa?. . . The nations of Asia and Africa and Europe contain too much of the forces of the traditional for anyone to think that the future will take care of itself. . . ."

Mr. Wright speaks of the mental darkness that goes with the old ways of superstition and tribal clericalism. He tells of the fear that the white man, now leaving, will return while the colored man is distracted by the new problems of governing himself in the aftermath of colonialism. He argues that the West must support the western-trained elite in these countries, not by dictating to them, but by trusting them, and giving them the tools for building modern states and leaving them free to wrestle with the task even if their methods sometimes seem offensive to the West.

This smallish book of 190 pages consists of four lectures delivered in Italy, Germany, France and Sweden. Three deal with the problems discussed above, the fourth with the literature (including several indecent folk songs) of the

American Negro. This not a complete discussion of international racial questions by any means and does not pretend to be. But it will break some new ground for the average westerner who can have but little idea of the distorted as well as promising thinking and emotion and political forces in Asia and Africa which have followed an era of preaching the inequality of men.

Oscar Handlin. "Patterns of Prejudice." *New York Times Book Review*, October 20, 1957, p. 3.

This is an indignant book. It is argumentative, belligerent and often wrong-headed. But it deserves to be read with utmost seriousness, for the attitude it expresses has an intrinsic importance in our times.

The novelist, Richard Wright, author of "Native Son," has compounded this volume from four lectures delivered in Europe, where he has spent much of the last decade. One of the essays, "The Literature of the Negro in the United States," is a slight piece and only tangentially related to the central theme. The other three deal with the situation of the Westernized elite who are in the forefront of the nationalist movement of Asia, Africa and the West Indies.

As a Westernized man of color, Wright feels peculiarly competent to speak for these people. Like them, he has absorbed the values of Western civilization; like them he has been excluded by color prejudice from the opportunity to share fully in it. He, too, bears the scars of ambivalence toward societies, attractive through the promise of their ideals, yet hateful through their failure to fulfill those ideals. The overtones of both love and loathing in his warning to the white man express the candor and earnestness with which he writes.

At the heart of our difficulties with the colored folk of the world is the necessity of liquidating the ugly heritage of imperialism. The conquests through which Western culture spread across the earth from Europe destroyed the values of indigenous societies everywhere. The triumphant invaders sometimes carried benevolent intentions with them, but they could envision only one relationship to the natives they encountered—that of dominance and subordination. Color became the mark of inferiority, and patterns of prejudice developed to maintain distance between the master and the servile races.

Now the burdens of oppression have evoked resistance out of which have sprung the nationalist movements of the last ten years. The effort at liberation cannot be confined to Western terms because the West, in the eyes of colored people, bears the responsibility for their degradation. While the new nations intend to adopt the technology of Europe, they insist upon the opportunity to work out their destinies without interference, and they expect in doing so to rediscover their own submerged cultures.

The danger is that in the process they may turn their backs upon the universal values of the West. Mr. Wright sees one hope of avoiding that peril—encouragement of the elite educated in Europe and the United States, to work out a creative accommodation. That will call for more tolerance and understanding than has been shown them in the past.

No one conscious of the plight of the people of the underdeveloped areas of the world will read this plea unsympathetically. Yet the issue is by no means so straightforward as it seems to Mr. Wright. The West, which has the responsibilities as well as the opportunities of power, cannot overlook the tragic fact that it must rid itself of the errors of an earlier imperialism at the same time that it resists the aggressive encroachments of a totalitarian power hostile to the freedom of all peoples.

The leaders of the new states have not always understood this, as the moral obtuseness of the United Nations Afro-Asian bloc in the face of the Hungarian crisis showed. Obsessed by the struggle against the enemies of the past, they have not understood the greater present threat of communism. It would be ironic if the only fruits of liberation from colonialism were to be a new enslavement, even under masters of their own color.

I have no doubt that Mr. Wright understands that danger, too. But a fatal misunderstanding obscures the implications, for him and for those for whom he speaks. He addresses "the white man," as if across the absolute line of color there were but a single type, with the whites all alike in their whiteness. This unhappily was the attitude that permeated the Bandung Conference and it is likely to evoke an exclusive nationalism as unfortunate in its consequences as that of the racism of some white men in the past.

The precise opposite is the truth, if men will but recognize it. The "white man" is no more a fixed category than the "colored." The contact of Europeans with other peoples has not had the disastrous uniformity Mr. Wright ascribes to it. Indeed, a clearer view of the history of that contact would reveal that the forms of prejudice and exploitation that linger with us still are the products of relatively recent and probably transient conditions.

In any case, the future demands an emphasis upon what we all instinctively know, that the lines that divide and the ties that unite are not simply those of color or of nationality. We need more often to be reminded of those common concerns that make freedom, justice and human dignity important to all men without qualification by their yellowness, blackness or whiteness.

Roi Ottley. "Reasoned Passion Against Racism." *Chicago Sunday Tribune Magazine of Books*, November 10, 1957, p. 11.

White men, according to Richard Wright, "buttressed by their belief that their God had entrusted the earth into their keeping, drunk with power and possibility, waxing rich through trade in commodities, human and nonhuman, with awesome naval and merchant marines at their disposal," hurled themselves with "bloody explosion" upon the masses of colored humanity in Asia and Africa.

In the process, he declares, white men plundered Asians and Africans, dehumanized them, destroyed their gods and culture, developed corps of saboteurs and spies within their ranks, and introduced to the world the sordid heresy of racial superiority of white peoples over colored.

The result of all this is apparent today, for black, brown, and yellow men have set off a tide of social, cultural, political, and economic revolution that grips the world. That revolution is assuming many forms—absolutistic, communistic, fascistic and theocratistic—and all marked by "unrest, violence, and an astounding emotional thrashing about."

This book, actually a series of essays originally written for lectures delivered in Europe, is an astringent call to white men of the western world to give sympathetic understanding to the aspirations of colored peoples in Asia and Africa—or else be engulfed and finally swept away in a racial deluge.

Richard Wright unburdens himself of his most trenchant prose. In few works has he risen to such reasoned passion. That this warning to white men is melancholy is to be expected, for when a young woman asked him would the ideas for this book make people happy, he replied bluntly: "My dear, I do not deal in happiness; I deal in meaning."

Joseph F. Maloney. *Best Sellers,* 17 (November 15, 1957), 280.

This is a collection of lectures delivered in Europe in 1950-1956 by the author of *Native Son* and *Black Boy.* Together they form a connected and coherent comment upon white-colored East-West relations in the world today. The chapters are stimulating oratory, valuable for the emotional point of view they present. Although the intellect is aroused, it is left hungry and disappointed.

The dust jacket describes Richard Wright as being spokesman for the American Negro today. I doubt that he is representative of the American Negro if only because he is so rootless and detached. He probably does accurately represent the views of many of the native Asian-African western-educated elite, but surely Langston Hughes and Roy Wilkins, for two, are more representative of the American Negro.

According to Wright the culture of the white world clashed with the culture-worlds of colored mankind resulting in the destruction of traditional beliefs among a billion and a half of black, brown and yellow men, further resulting in a tide of social, cultural, political and economic revolution that grips the world today. The activities of the whites in this encounter are thusly described: "Living in a waking dream, generations of emotionally impoverished colonial European whites wallowed in the quick gratification of greed, reveled in the cheap superiority of racial domination, slaked their sensual thirst in illicit sexuality, draining off the dammed-up libido that European morality had condemned, amassing through trade a vast reservoir of economic fat, thereby establishing vast accumulations of capital which spurred the industrialization of the West. . ." Wright gives slight credit to the activities of the white Christian missionary. ". . . I agree that his boiling down four hundred gods and six hundred devils into one God and one Devil was an advance. But I don't think that the missionaries' efforts went far enough; they should have reduced the whole problem to a psychological project." Wright obviously prefers to abolish the "superstitious" beliefs in even one God in order to facilitate the movement of every human being into a modern industrial age of secularism in the spirit of the Enlightenment.

Wright portrays the Western-educated Asia-African native elite as living in fear that if they do not quickly modernize their countries the white man will return. Hence this elite is engaged in brutally pushing their people into modern industrialization and its benefits without much regard for traditional white-western constitutional niceties. Wright states "I say that the West cannot ask the elite of Asia and Africa, even though educated in the West, to copy or ape what has happened in the West. Why? Because the West has never really been honest with itself about how it overcame its own traditions and blinding customs. . . . Wise Westerners would insist that stern measures be taken by the elite of Asia and Africa to overcome the irrational forces of racism, superstition, etc. . . ." For Wright the valuable contribution of Western heritage is not a particular political or economic system, but freedom of speech, the secular state, the independent personality and the autonomy of science.

There are well-written chapters on the development of American Negro literature and the speedy revolution that resulted in the formation of the new state of Ghana in March, 1957.

This is a valuable book that should be read with care by the educated adult who seeks an understanding of some of the explosive factors influencing the development of our world.

R. J. G. *San Francisco Chronicle*, November 24, 1957, p. 6.

This is a collection of four lectures delivered by Wright in Europe during recent years. One of them is concerned with the role of the Negro in American literature and the other three are powerful, provocative and frightening interpretations of the expanding culture of the Asian and African peoples and what it will, eventually, mean to the Caucasian West.

Wright's interpretation is that the Europeans have sown a powerful harvest of hate and disillusionment in Africa and Asia and unless a new, enlightened and uninhibited view is taken, and its results acted upon, by the West there is no hope for peace upon this planet.

This is a difficult book to read if only because it carries a message so opposite to the traditional. It is hoped that despite this, and other difficulties, it is read and digested by Western leaders on all levels. If Wright's view is the correct one, there have been fewer warnings more timely in history.

James W. Ivy. "Promise and Failure." *The Crisis*, 64 (December 1957), 640.

In his latest book Mr. Wright comes to grips with the realities of color and race as a world issue. He warns the West that international Communism and Russian domination is not the only issue; and, perhaps, for the Asian-African world not the dominant one. He shows in concrete detail that "The Western world has, through sheer selfishness and racial jealousy, lost a vital part of this revolution to Communism, for, when called upon to confess authorship of her own principles, she rejected them and called them forgeries."

Three hundred years of white exploitation and white dominance of colored peoples have created a "psychological distance" between whites and non-whites. It has made full human intercourse between whites and non-whites impossible. There are always reservations, and the black or brown man moves within the shadow of insult. "This useless struggle of having to prove one's humanity, which is a kind of *supra* racism, is the blight that the Western white man has cast upon the colored masses of Asia and Africa," says Mr. Wright.

One of the most revealing chapters in the book deals with "The Psychological Reactions of Oppressed People." They are, the author concludes, "bewildering in their complexity. It simply means that oppression oppresses, that oppression takes its toll, that it leaves a mark behind." It is this psychological reaction of the oppressed, with its soul scars, that Mr. Wright wants the white man to understand, for without understanding on the part of whites there can be no *rapprochement* between the Western and the Asian-African worlds. He points out, too, that the Western-educated leaders of the "newly independent Asian-African states," often bitterly criticized in the West, furnished the only bridge between the Western and non-Western worlds.

"If these few Western-minded leaders are overthrown, it is absolutely certain that their successors will be infinitely more anti-Western than they are. The closer the West approaches the Asian and African masses, the more exclusive, shy, evasive, and militantly racial and nationalistic it will find these masses to be."

White Man, Listen! is a true and revealing book. It consists of four lectures which the author delivered in Europe—Italy, Germany, France, Sweden, Norway, Denmark—during the years 1950-56. One lecture, "The Literature of the Negro in the United States," has only tangential relation to the author's central theme.

Paula Snelling. "Warning Voice." *The Progressive,* 20 (December 1957), 42–43.

It is hard to talk to a deaf man. Especially when he is blind-driving the car we are all riding in, and heading for a precipice. But those with senses intact are going to call out warnings with whatever voices they have.

Richard Wright's is one of the more vibrant and persistent of these voices. He has spoken as cogently and perhaps more persuasively in the past than here. But some who did not listen before may do so now. For the Western white man, despite his self-induced impairment of eyes and ears, knows today that the road he is traveling is not that endless smooth highway he once thought it was.

White Man, Listen! is a collection of speeches the author made in European cities and universities during the past six years. The burden of the book is: First, that East and West, white and black, must find room for each other in their hearts and minds, and in that future whose making and benefits and destructions they will share. Second, that there exists today a group of people, numerically small, precariously poised, but strategically endowed with unique capabilities needed for holding the world together and helping mankind to fuller realization of its human potentialities.

Wright calls these people the tragic elite, men now homeless between two worlds: men of non-Western ancestry, with perhaps enough Western blood in their veins and certainly enough Western ideals and dreams in their hearts to serve as bridge between East and West.

He refers primarily to those political and cultural leaders of Africa and Asia who have been educated in the West and who have accepted those of our goals and methods which seem valid for them also. He pleads for a better understanding from us of their psychological dilemmas (many of which are of our making); for increased aid in meeting their gigantic tasks; and for our realization that emotional and physical needs are propelling the East into accelerated change for which we cannot call the turns.

He says we have to trust these leaders, who share so many of our goals, to find new solutions to the problems they face, which differ radically from the problems the West met or failed to meet as it made its leisurely entrance into the industrial age. He warns that if this "tragic elite" lose their leadership in their own countries, their successors will reject the whole West (its good and its evil) with undiscriminating violence. And he shows the roots of this violence in the arrogance and blindness and greed which characterized so much of the West's penetration of Asia and Africa during recent centuries.

One section of the book is a survey of the literature of Negroes in the United States. Wright evaluates and quotes from the folk-utterances of the semi-literate who gave nameless and poignant voice to the despairs and dreams of oppressed millions who, seeing no hope in their earthly lot, sought consolation where they could find it: in spirituals, blues, and in less publicized leers and jeers of the so-called *Dirty Dozens*. He also quotes many eloquent pleas for freedom and human acceptance which have been wrung from educated, talented, sensitive men and women who have been kept out of the mainstream of America life and letters only because of their skin color. Richard Wright feels that their persisting allegiance to democracy's ideals and their affirmations of human dignity are the real voice of America today, heard, and identified with, by the world's forsaken peoples.

If America can make all its sons, black and white, equally at home here, there will be new hope over the globe that we can progress together to the imperative of our age: a world without arbitrary barriers, freed of old rancors, its energies released for the creative tasks ahead.

Thomas Berry. *The Sign*, 37 (February 1958), 73–74.

Richard Wright is a very confused person, a disturbed prophet, as it were, and fearful lest he be not heard unless he affects a strident tone and writes in the most jagged tradition of contemporary journalism. He presents a repetitious and highly emotional indictment against the White World of the West.

To his charges, we plead guilty. We have done all that he says, although he does not say all that we have done. He obviously feels that he would weaken his cause considerably if he should present a more integral picture of the reality. His one great tribute to the West is that we have originated the first secularist society and have brought this secularist attitude to the entire world.

His creed is very simple. "I feel that man—just sheer brute man, just as he is—has a meaning and value over and above all sanctions or mandates from mystical powers, either on high or from below. I am convinced that the humble, fragile dignity of man, buttressed by a tough-souled pragmatism, implemented by methods of trial and error, can sufficiently sustain and nourish human life, can endow it with ample and durable meaning."

This he has learned from us. Thus the author even more than his book is evidence of the greatest crime of the West. There is the full tragedy for himself and for us all. With naive eighteenth-century trust in "reason," he continues on with his prophetic mission. We read and wonder.

Stanley Plastrik. "Lonely Outsiders." *Dissent,* 5 (Spring 1958), 191–92.

No one knows better than Richard Wright that the white man has not listened for a century, has neither plans nor intention to start listening now and probably couldn't listen if he wanted to. The voices of Asia, Africa and the colonial world are blocked to him by an accumulation of rubbish. Wright's book, as he says himself, is for the "Westernized" elite of the non-European world, the "lonely outsiders" existing on the margins of many cultures. Even though it consists of a collection of speeches delivered before European audiences, this book is the author talking largely to himself, about himself and for himself. It is an important book and the neglect it has met in America only emphasizes the blocking off of communication between the West—all sectors of the West—and as Wright puts it, ". . . a billion and a half colored people in violent political motion."

Richard Wright tells us he is neither perturbed nor unhappy in his chosen state of "alienation"; from his lonely perch in Paris, a Paris swept by waves of "Americanization" and wasting its last energies in a futile colonial war, Wright keeps both his sense of judgment and his passion. He has not forgotten who he is; Bandung was clearly a turning point for him, the crystallization of anti-colonialism into new forms not understood by the white man nor, for that matter, too well understood by those representing the best democratic and socialist traditions of the West. For Wright, Bandung was the first coming together of that "tragic elite" whose thought and mentality, whose very soul he is attempting to explain to us:

> The present-day attitude of the national revolutionary in Asia and Africa has the quality of a man who has been put to sleep for centuries and awakens to find the world of which he was once a functioning part roaring past him. He is bewildered, hurt, stunned, filled with a sense of self-hate. . . The world that such a man sees is devoid of meaning. He looks into this or that theory to find an idea of what has happened to him and his kind. And when he selects a theory, whether it be Marxism or any other revolutionary doctrine, he is not so much concerned emotionally with whether that theory is right or wrong, but whether it fits his feeling and most nearly describes what he sees and feels.

To which might be added: and whether it works, gives results, quick results. Indonesia, India, Egypt, Algeria—these are countries in a hurry, a fact that at least partly explains the bitter clashes that occur between groups within the nationalist movement itself.

The heart of the book is in the two

opening essays: the first, a cataloging of the "psychological reactions of oppressed people," and then the key essay "Tradition and Industrialization." White Europeans freed Asia and Africa from its irrational traditions and customs, but simultaneously created a rootless, westernized elite. This elite, feared and hated by the West, constitutes an island of free men; freer than their most sympathetic supporters of the West since they, at least, are capable of taking action. This elite, says Wright, "must be given its head." Nkrumah, Nasser, Sukarno, Nehru—they are more important to the West than the West itself. This is the only message Wright has to offer; it is a stark one.

Grateful as we must be for Wright's courage in putting things bluntly at a moment when none are listening, does he not tend to be carried away by the starkness of his own thesis? First, it would seem that the central tragedy of his "tragic" elite is that try as it will it cannot lift itself up by its own economic bootstraps; it cannot get around the startling proof recently advanced by Gunnar Myrdal that the gap in wealth between the West and the underdeveloped countries has steadily widened. More important, there is the matter of the vast personal power of men like Nkrumah, Nehru, and Nasser, which Wright tends to gloss over by urging us to believe that the elite seeks power not for itself but for its people. About this, have we not good reason to be skeptical?

Still, the ways of communication must be kept open; and Wright himself is a precious example of what this means.

Nick Aaron Ford. "Blunders and Failures of the White Man." *Phylon*, 19 (First Quarter, 1958), 125–26.

From the beginning of his writing career in 1938 with the publication of *Uncle Tom's Children* down to the present, nine volumes later, Richard Wright has addressed himself continually to the white public. Although the Negro reader has been thrilled by Wright's writings, his enjoyment, especially of the six volumes of non-fiction, has resulted primarily from the pleasure of seeing Wright's arguments against white supremacy expressed so effectively that the opposition appeared to be either downright silly or fantastically unrealistic. *White Man, Listen!* follows the pattern, except that it is more comprehensive in its coverage and more devastating in its technique.

The arguments to which Wright bids the white man listen are organized around four major topics: (1) The Psychological Reactions of Oppressed People, (2) Tradition and Industrialization, (3) The Literature of the Negro in the United States, and (4) The Miracle of Nationalism in the African Gold Coast.

Two-thirds of the book is devoted to the white man's attitudes toward and relations with the colored peoples of Africa and Asia (past, present, and future), especially "those Asians and Africans who, having been partly Westernized, have a quarrel with the West." He says to the white men of the West: "Don't be too proud of how easily you conquered and plundered those Asians and Africans. . . . You must realize it was not your courage or racial superiority that made you win, nor was it the racial inferiority or cowardice of the Asians and Africans that made them lose. . . . Frankly it took you centuries to do a job that could have been done in fifty years!"

Much of the book is concerned with a merciless analysis of the white man's blunders in his efforts to subjugate the colored peoples of Asia and Africa and the white man's failures in his attempt to deny these oppressed peoples their freedom and self-determination. In African-Asian eyes, according to Wright, "a *white man* is a man with blue eyes, a white skin, and blond hair. . . (who) wishes fervently that his eyes remain forever blue, his skin forever white, and his hair forever blond, and (who) wishes this for his children and his children's children." To Europeans colonialism means "the spread of covilization, missions of glory, of service, of destiny even," but to Asians and Africans it means "blood-sucking, murder, butchery, slavery."

Wright blames the church, Catholic and Protestant, for much of the oppression that Asians and Africans have suffered. He contends that the colored peoples of the East have never really accepted Christianity, for it came to them "with fire in its eyes, a sword in its hands, and with the will to conquer and despoil." Although white Western domination in the name of a superior religion has been a reality for five hundred years, the delegates at Bandung (1955) passed a resolution to resurrect their old religions and cultures and modernize them.

Wright believes that the central historic fact of the impact of the white West upon the colored East is the former's influence in weakening the grip of the native religions. This void, which could not be filled by the white man's religion, encouraged the rise of a rational society with freedom at its center. Today the elite in Asia and Africa constitutes islands of free men, "the freest men in all the world today."

In his chapter on The Literature of the Negro in the United States, Wright proposes to interpret some of the important Negro writings, especially poems, by suggesting how they came to be written, how they are related to their time, and what they mean today. For the most part, he has succeeded in accomplishing his purpose. He cites the cases of Alexander Dumas of France and Alexander Pushkin of Russia, both of Negro ancestry, to prove that Negro writing will assume the common themes and burdens of literary expression, which are the heritage of all men, only when the writer is "at one with his culture." Although his theory is sound, his application breaks down when he tries to include Phillis Wheatley, the first Negro in America to publish a book of poems, in this company. Phillis was not at one with her culture (despite Wright's assertion to the contrary); she was only pretending to be. And in that pretense lies a significant part of her tragedy.

He is right when he says, "The voice of the American Negro (writer) is rapidly becoming the most representative voice of America and of oppressed people anywhere in the world today." But his lack of intimate knowledge of some of the latest writings of American Negroes is betrayed by the inference that in the work of Chester Himes, Ralph Ellison, James Baldwin, Ann Petry, Frank Yerby, and Gwendolyn Brooks one finds a drastic reduction of the racial content. This observation can be justified only if he wishes to balance the novels of Yerby against the combined works of the other five.

The most gripping and significant

chapter in the book is the last one, which deals with the rise of nationalism in the African Gold Coast and the birth of Ghana. He gives new insight into the dramatic rise of Nkrumah to political power and world stature. In this chapter alone the artist dominates the philosopher, as he echoes the magnificent literary beauty and power that he revealed in *Pagan Spain* which he published earlier in 1957. In words that cut and bite and sting he pleads for an understanding of what has happened to the Africans. He pleads for a more tolerant appreciation by the West of the statesmanship of Nkrumah, Nehru, Nasser, and Sukarno. He justifies their occasional use of strong arm methods to maintain the continued progress of their nations toward the standards of Western culture which they themselves have embraced. "If these few Westernized leaders are overthrown," he warns, "it is absolutely certain that their successors will be infinitely more anti-Western than they are."

This book is as timely as today's newspaper; yet it has a depth that transcends the journalistic. As I write this review, delegations from forty Asian-African countries are staging a Peoples Solidarity Conference in Cairo and echoing in resolutions to which Europe and America are listening with respectful attention the very arguments which Wright has expressed with power and perspicacity.

This is a bitterly frank book that will not make any reader happy about the past, present, or future. But Wright's answer to an innocent questioner at one of his public lectures suggests reward enough for the writing and the reading: "My dear, I do not deal in happiness; I deal in meaning."

Checklist of Additional Reviews

New Yorker, 33 (October 26, 1957), 203.

Journal of Negro History, 42 (October 1957), 303.

Booklist, 54 (November 1, 1957), 128.

Springfield Republican, November 17, 1957, p. 8c.

Saunders Redding. *Baltimore Afro-American,* November 26, 1957, p. 2.

Ave Maria, 86 (December 28, 1957), 27.

John Pittman. *New York Daily Worker,* January 1, 1958, p. 4.

Nick Aaron Ford, *CLA Journal,* 1 (March 1958), 110–11.

Notes

The Long Dream

A NOVEL BY

Richard Wright

DOUBLEDAY & COMPANY, INC., GARDEN CITY, NEW YORK

1958

The Long Dream

A. N. Barnett. *Library Journal*, 83 (October 15, 1958), 2843.

One of the agonies that may befall a member of an oppressed social minority is that of self-hatred, self-hatred for living in submission to a dominating majority. He loves his people but he may also hate them and himself for an unheroic response to abuse. He hates the majority for its oppression but he tends to identify himself with them because he looks at his people in the way the oppressors do, that is, with scorn for their cringing. The origin, course, consequences, and resolution of this ambivalence in a small-town, middle-class, Mississippi youth, in the years following the Second World War, are the subject of Richard Wright's new novel. The extraordinary candor and wisdom of the author and the genuineness and depth of his characterizations prevail over the defects of a profusion of worn phrases, awkward word formations (I am not referring to the speech of the characters) and a slow, episodic beginning. The reader is brought to the conclusion that if a Negro is not to unman himself, he must either exit from his inferior world of Southern racism, as does the hero who flees to France (a symbol of equality for the American Negro), or, and this point is made by implication, he must fight for equality and dignity in the country of his birth. Recommended strongly for all libraries.

Granville Hicks. "The Power of Richard Wright." *Saturday Review*, 41 (October 18, 1958), 13, 65.

Although Richard Wright has published eleven books over a period of exactly twenty years, "The Long Dream" is only his third novel. His first novel was "Native Son," published in 1940, two years after a collection of short stories, "Uncle Tom's Children." An autobiographical book, "Black Boy," appeared in 1945, but his second novel, "The Outsider," waited until 1953. Since then he has published several volumes of travel description and sociological comment, only now returning to fiction.

"The Outsider" suggested that Wright was moving in a new direction, for, although the leading character was a Negro, the novel was not primarily concerned with race problems, as earlier books had been. On the contrary, Wright deliberately posed the situation of the American Negro as an example of the contemporary predicament, just as Ralph Ellison had done in "Invisible Man." One of the characters says: "Negroes, as they enter our culture, are going to inherit the problems we have, but with a difference. They are outsiders, and they are going to *know* that they have these problems. They are going to be self-conscious; they are going to be gifted with a double vision, for, being Negroes, they are going to be both *inside* and *outside* of our culture at the same time."

But if Wright sees that the race problem is not isolated, he has continued to be preoccupied with it, as demonstrated by such volumes as "Black Power" and "White Man, Listen!" "The Long Dream" returns to that theme, and therefore seems closer to "Native Son" than to "The Outsider." Wright is once more trying to show the world what being a Negro in America is like.

The first part of "The Long Dream" is reminiscent of "Black Boy" in so far as it is an account of a young Negro's experience in Mississippi. The time is some twenty-five years later than that described in "Black Boy," and Fish Tucker is the son of a prosperous undertaker and property owner, whereas Wright grew up in brutal poverty. The lesson Fish learns, however, is essentially the lesson Wright learned, and he learns it in the same harsh way.

In Parts II and III, on the other hand, Fish's life takes a very different course from Wright's, just as Bigger Thomas's did in "Native Son." Like both "Native Son" and "The Outsider," "The Long Dream" turns into melodrama. Fish leaves school at sixteen, and goes to work for his father, Tyree, whose aptitude for making money he seems to have inherited. He not only acquires sexual experience but, at this early age, has a mistress and an apartment to keep her in. When the mistress dies in a dance hall fire, along with some forty others, Fish learns that his father is co-owner of the hall, owner of various other illicit establishments, and an agent of corrupt municipal officials in the exploitation of vice in the Negro section.

Tyree Tucker struggles to save his life and at least some part of his fortunes, but is murdered by the white officials he has served. Fish himself is framed, and is kept in jail, quite illegally, for two years. It is no wonder that, when he is at last released, he flees to France. (Since 1946 Wright has made Paris his home.)

The faults of the novel are obvious. I have spoken of melodrama, and the term is justified, not because the events that unfold are inherently implausible but because Wright works so hard to give them emotional impact. As in his other novels, he displays a preoccupation with scenes of violence that can be understood but cannot be fully defended on literary grounds. His material constantly seems to be getting out of hand, as if he were driven—as I believe he is—by forces beyond his control.

I am also troubled by the characterization of Fish Tucker. Although a boy of sixteen might be as mature as he is supposed to be, he seems to grow up almost overnight. It is true that an acquaintance of his has been lynched and that he himself has had his first encounter with the white man's law and the white man's violence, but one ought to feel more continuity than one does. One ought to feel, as I do not, that the ideas Fish expresses are his ideas and not Richard Wright's.

Finally, there is the question of style. Wright has never been a master of polished prose, and "The Long Dream" is marred by frequent lapses. For one thing, the characters are likely to talk in a fashion that it is hard to accept. Here, for instance, is what the mother of the boy who is lynched says as she looks at his body: "If I had to do it over again, I wouldn't have no child! I'd tear it out of my womb! . . . Gawd, take Your sun out of the sky! Take Your stars away! I don't want Your trees, Your flowers no more! I don't want Your wind to blow on me when my son can die like this." And here, in the last sentence of the book, is another sort of fault, an example of what happens when the prose becomes pretentious: "He peered out of the window and saw vast, wheeling populations of ruled stars swarming in the convened congresses of the skies anchored amidst nations of space and he prayed wordlessly that a bright, bursting tyrant of living sun would soon lay down its golden laws to loosen the locked legions of his heart and cast the shadow of his dream athwart the stretches of time."

Yet it is impossible to deny that this novel, like its predecessors, has power. However one may criticize details, one cannot doubt that in a fundamental way Wright is telling the truth about the situation of the American Negro, and the truth cannot fail to shock us. There is nothing here that we haven't known, but we are compelled to come to terms with what we should like to forget.

When Wright gives us Fish's dreams, as he frequently does, he is not particularly impressive, but he does manage to communicate Fish's sense that his whole life is a nightmare. Wright has always felt that one of the peculiar evils of the Negro's situation is an almost inevitable confusion of values. Bitterly as he rejects the white man's world, Fish can never get rid of a suspicion that the white man may be right. He is not merely alientated from the culture in which he has been born; he is alienated from reality. He can escape, and, like Wright, he can become "relatively free from fear and pressure," but he justly wonders whether he can find himself.

This alienation is what Wright has from the first been able to render. He is not basically a realist, although he probably thinks that he is; he is a man who uses, and perhaps is used by, certain powerful symbols. I am not sure that he always knows what he is doing; at any rate, as I have said, he periodically loses control of his material. For this reason it is not surprising that there are few signs of development in his work, but if he has not grown, he has never lost his ability to touch both the emotions and the consciences of his readers.

Robert Hatch. "Either Weep or Laugh." *The Nation*, 189 (October 25, 1958), 297–98.

Richard Wright's new novel is not a book to be studied from a distance, to gain perspective on a work of art. It should be examined myopically, close to the page, as one reads the chart of a strange and dangerous passage.

> *Lawyer McWilliams, a liberal Southerner:* It's corrupt to *take* bribes and its corrupt to *give* them.
>
> *Tyree Tucker, a proud Negro:* Mr. McWilliams, I ain't corrupt. I'm a *nigger*. Niggers ain't corrupt. Niggers ain't got no rights but them they *buy*. . . . If we niggers didn't buy justice from the white man, we'd never git any.

Tyree Tucker, proud because he has never worked for a white man, buys the justice he needs to operate his undertaking business, his illegal dance hall, his tenements, his bordelloes and gambling games. He is wealthy, even by white standards, and his son Fishbelly, grows up "baffled by the power of dollars to wipe out shame." Tyree greets all whites with a bent back and a self-immolating smile—and drives the dark streets with curses in his throat and a gun across his knees. The two sides of

Tyree, the flashing shift from agonizing clown to contemptuous brigand, is a brilliant study in the art of survival.

Fishbelly hates his father because he cringes and runs and loves him because, though with dirty, humiliating weapons, he fights until he is dead. *The Long Dream* is the story of how the boy learns to reconcile the two feelings. From another viewpoint, it is a tableau of the two races meeting on their only common ground—corruption. In Wright's South, whites and blacks will not eat together or sit together; work together or play together—but they will steal together. And the acrid joke of that for such as Tyree and Fishbelly is that the Negro demoralizes the white by the convenience of his inferiority.

The structure of *The Long Dream* is the step-by-step progress of Fishbelly, a shy black boy, from the safe, warm world of the Negro ghetto into the lawless world between the races where a few Negroes, preying on black and white alike, have the arrogance to live by their wits. It opens up aspects of the South not covered by dictionary words like "segregation" or "miscegenation." Its key words are "rape" and "blood," "lynch" and "hide," "lie" and "scream." And above all, "run." A Negro, says Tyree, must either weep or laugh, and if you can't weep you had better laugh.

But structure is not what you should look at in this book. Richard Wright is a man of considerable literary ability, a man who has made a living for twenty years or more with his writing, but who nevertheless is not primarily a writer. Many literary men have fought crusades; Wright is a crusader who fights with words. It makes a difference and it accounts for the special quality of his fiction. *The Long Dream* is not a badly-made book, as you will discover if you try to pull it to pieces. It is very strong, but its workmanship is careful only where care is needed for Wright's purpose. Elsewhere the book is boldly hammered together—not as a work of art but as the scaffolding for an idea.

Thus, in a given scene, the characters are so vivid that the noise and smell of them come straight to your senses. But how they get from scene to scene, how they develop in understanding and experience from episode to episode, is another matter. The fact is that, having made a point, Wright packs his people up and carts them to where they are needed for the next demonstration. What will throw you off, if you approach *The Long Dream* with the usual instruments of critical measurement, is that the narrative is a palpable machine, but the people are real. You do not often find flesh and blood thus contending on a stage for puppets; it happens this way because Wright spends his talent, not for art, but for an idea.

I do not doubt that if he were a greater artist, he would carry his idea with still greater power. On the other hand, if he concerned himself more with art, he might well fail of the great, rough-hammered platforms he erects.

And he does polish his work as the years pass. He writes now with much more control than he once showed; his ear is wonderfully acute and his judgment of emotional degree and balance is subtle, varied and exciting. Still more he grows in understanding of the problem to which he has devoted his life. Wright is an advocate, not a judge; he sees race from the viewpoint of the Negro, and one does not look to him for any withdrawn, balanced appraisal of issues. But he is not bemused, either, by the sufferings of his people. He does not think that suffering is ennobling or that the Negro is a pure creature in an evil land. Corruption is corruption and Wright exposes it. Tyree does not speak for the author in his outburst to McWilliams—he speaks for his own desperate solution to the problem, and Wright promptly shows where that solution leads.

But if corruption is corruption, so compassion is compassion. Police Chief Cantley represents everything in the white world that Wright most hates. Nevertheless, towards the end of the book he has Cantley scream at Fishbelly:

> Goddam you, you black sonofabitch! I wish to hell I could *believe* you! But you *can't* tell me the truth! . . . I swear to God, I don't know what we can do with you niggers. . . . We make you scared of us and then we ask you to tell us the truth. And you *can't!* Goddamit, you *can't!*

There is real sorrow in this and an approach to love. It is in the poignant vision of the two races locked in terrible, degrading embrace that Wright, a truly proud Negro, has isolated the essence of the tragedy.

Roi Ottley. "Wright's New Novel Isn't for Squeamish." *Chicago Sunday Tribune Magazine of Books*, October 26, 1958, p. 3.

Richard Wright, whose gifts as a novelist were first revealed in his "Native Son," has written a surging, superb new book which closely examines the anatomy of southern racial prejudice and reveals some awful truths. In the process, he has given us a social document of unusual worth.

His portrait of Fishbelly, a Negro boy growing up in the racial crucible of Clintonville, Miss., is a powerfully realized characterization with depth and dimension. Thru this youngster's eyes we see the southern white man, and the Negro too, in postures few writers have been able to portray.

Few will remain untouched by the equally well done portrait of Tyree Tucker, Fishbelly's father, an unlettered undertaker who accommodates himself to prejudice, reaps a harvest from fellow blacks, and in the end is destroyed by the very forces to which he genuflected.

What Wright in essence seeks to show—and does successfully—is that the Negro in the south is a victim of a society that denies him humanity and in the process makes him a caricature of that society. His insights are undeniably valid.

This book is not for the squeamish. Wright's catalog of lynching, police brutality, meanness and emotion running riot in a southern town is calculated to disturb even the most callous.

This story, balanced by Wright's compassion for his people, is an experience of almost nightmarish quality. If someone should ask whether it finally makes people happy, we have only Richard Wright's answer: "My dear," he once told a woman, "I do not deal in happiness; I deal in meaning."

Ted Poston. "Wright: He's Out of Touch." *New York Post*, October 26, 1958.

Richard Wright, one of America's most powerful writers, left his native Mississippi some 30 years ago.

But the memory of that benighted region was still fresh in his mind when he wrote his prize-winning "Uncle Tom's Children" and autobiographical "Black Boy" during the ensuing two decades spent in Chicago and New York.

The author of the even more widely acclaimed "Native Son" has been an expatriate in Paris for the third decade. And it is from there that he returns fictionally to his native Mississippi in his latest and still powerfully-written novel, "The Long Dream."

This time it is the story of young Fishbelly Tucker, son of a crafty and illiterate Negro undertaker, and of others of the 10,000 Negroes who live in a Southern town of 25,000 in the Delta region.

Again he tells a story of brutality, white and black venality created by the system of segregation, lynching, frustration, and—rather oddly for Wright—physical escape and personal hope for his hero.

But somehow, this time it doesn't ring true. Not that the graphic incidents described could not be true. They were probably taken from life as Wright knew it during his long sojourn in America.

For the real tragedy is not in the book. It is in the fact that Wright has lived the most momentous decade in the life of his people far away from the scenes of their tragedies and triumphs.

He shows no awareness of what has happened to America—and even to Mississippi—during this decade.

In brief, Richard Wright sees Mississippi and America in the 1950s through his own intimate knowledge of events and outlook in the 1920s. From his vantage point in Paris, it probably still looks like that.

This is not to intimate that Wright has not told a gripping story in "The Long Dream." It does mean, however, that it is only a gripping tale, but hardly the social document that "Native Son" obviously was.

Wright has travelled and written a lot since he left the U.S. In time and distance he has journeyed through areas of British West Africa, Indonesia, Canada, and South America. And through this, he has, in his own words, developed "an outlook of freedom upon man."

It is unfortunate that the native son didn't return briefly to America or Mississippi before describing them as he thinks they are today.

Saunders Redding. "The Way It Was." *New York Times Book Review*, October 26, 1958, pp. 4, 38.

One day when he was 6 years old and making his first trip downtown alone, Fish Tucker was accosted by a white man. His impulse was to run. Never before had a white man spoken to him, nor he to a white man, and Fish was frightened. "It'll only take a minute," the white man said, gripping the boy's arm and leading him into an alley where three other white men knelt around a heap of crapshooters' money. "This nigger's going to roll my dice," the white man said. "Niggers are born with luck." Gray with fright, Fish rolled the dice, and when he had rolled up a thousand dollars, the white man thrust a dollar into the black boy's hand, and said, "Okay. Run, nigger!" Fish ran.

This is the opening episode in Richard Wright's first novel since "The Outsider," and it sets the tone, which is ironic; establishes the theme, which is the fragmentation of a personality; and, without the author's intending it at all, it foreshadows the major weaknesses. The ironic tone is there, but it is flattened by too much iteration. The theme is valid, but Wright insists that the reader know all and know on and on, until at last knowledge shrinks to that not-caring from which the most errant sensationalism fails to arouse. The major weakness in "The Long Dream" is sensationalism.

The plot moves with spasmodic haste from, but not through, episode after furibund episode. Carefully taught by his father, the wealthy vice lord and funeral director of Negro town, Fish quickly learns the ordinary lessons of his time and place—to associate guile and gain, money and power, lust and love. Then, when he is 12, a man he knows is lynched, and the body brought to Tyree Tucker's funeral home. The victim's nose is gone, an ear sliced off, the neck broken. "Tonight you git your first lesson," Fish's father tells him, "and you got to remember it all your life." The lesson is in shame, terror and abasement, and the boy learns it well. Wright makes his ironic point when he has father say to son, "But I don't want it to keep you from being a man, see?"

At 15, fragmented by his terrible self-hatred, Fish is already a man. (The author makes it clear that it is a lamentable, tragic manhood, but he fails to carry conviction with his basic argument that it is the only kind of manhood possible for a Negro in the South.) He soon has need to be a man; for his father, who has been slowly choking off the flow of vice money to the "white men downtown," is deliberately murdered by the police, and Fish takes over.

The men of the courthouse gang are not satisfied when Fish loosens the flow of graft—they want it all, and the chief of police sets up a frame for Fish: "The white girl's face. . . something that he feared so deeply. . . something toward which he had always been drawn with a sense of dread." He escapes lynching, but not the methodical torture of the police. Thanks to the modicum of justice that can be found even in Clintonville, he escapes the anguish of being prosecuted for a crime he did not commit. The last the reader sees of Fish Tucker, age 18, is on a plane in flight to France, where Richard Wright himself fled a dozen years ago.

"The Long Dream" proves that Wright has been away too long. Severing his cruel intimacy with the American environment, he has cut the emotional umbilical cord through which his art was fed, and all that remains for it to feed on is the memory, fading, of righteous love and anger. Come back, Dick Wright, to life again!

"Tract in Black and White." *Time,* 52 (October 27, 1958), 94, 96.

From his first (1938) book of long short stories to his latest novel, Richard Wright has given proof that anger can sometimes command more attention than art. He has one string to his bow: the shameful plight of the Negro in the white man's world. His writing is graceless, and he uses it with the subtlety of a lynching. It is doubtful for just how many of his fellow Negroes he speaks. But it is impossible to read him without sharing his indignation.

In his autobiographical *Black Boy* Author Wright described how, from a horrible childhood in the South, he fled first to Chicago, then New York, finally to Paris. He was an easy mark for the Communists but eventually saw through them and earned their lasting enmity. In *The Long Dream* the Mississippi Negro boy is called Rex "Fishbelly" Tucker, but so far as the story's essentials are concerned, his name might be Richard Wright. Fishbelly's father, an undertaker, once taught him an important truth as he buried the multilated body of a young Negro who had accepted the sexual invitation of a white woman. Said Tyree Tucker: "One more black dream dead. . . a dream that can't come true." As Fishbelly sees it, growing up in the black belt of a small Mississippi city, every black man can dream, but the white world will see to it that the dream becomes a nightmare. Fish despises his own father for whining and debasing himself when he talks to whites, for becoming rich by running a string of brothels as a sideline. He has also, as undertaker, patched up dead black bodies beaten up by the police and made himself the indispensable Negro contact in the black belt. Gradually Fishbelly sees that the old man is using the white authorities as surely as they are using him. The alliance disgusts him, and when the whole nasty business blows up, Tyree is ruthlessly killed by the police, and Fishbelly spends two years in prison on a trumped-up rape charge. Freed but still fearful, he flees to Paris.

Within the bare outlines of this sordid story, Author Wright hammers away at the brutality, based on fear and hatred, that the white world visits on the Negro. By this time, even Expatriate Wright should know that his picture is too crudely black and white: he writes as if nothing had changed since he grew up in Mississippi. But there is still so much truth in his crude, pounding, wrathful book that no honest reader can remain wholly unmoved.

William Dunlea. "Wright's Continuing Protest." *Commonweal*, 69 (October 31, 1958), 131.

This is a novel throbbing with the same racial traumas that have done much to compel for its author a large interracial audience ever since *Native Son,* the classic Negro novel of social protest. That book appeared in 1940, and, judging by his latest, Richard Wright is angrier than he was then.

The color motif dominates all of Mr. Wright's novels to the extent that the social-historical context outweighs the literary. It is not only because *The Long Dream* is a more uneven work than the poignant *Native Son* that it is so disappointing. Hot with the fumes of an incendiary counterracism, it could not have chosen a less propitious time to be "timely." Certainly it is the most racist of all of this author's anti-racist fiction.

Richard Wright's work has in general been more race-conscious than social-conscious; its crusading timbre has helped to placard him for some as *the* spokesman of the American Negro. For the last ten years he has been in Paris, yet the time of this novel, which is set in the Black Belt of a fictive Clintonville, Mississippi, is exactly this past decade of his absence.

Besides taking Jim Crow in their stride, the Negroes in this story incur virtually every indignity and injustice known to their kind in fact or literature. Yet Wright is not martyrizing them nor exposing their forbearance to easy sympathy; he is deprecating their compliant submission as equivalent to conspiring in their own abasement. As he proceeds to hammer out his thesis, his writing, measured against its earlier attainments, registers loss in narrative sweep, gain in psychological acumen, with these factors operating at cross purposes.

Through the boy "Fishbelly," six when the novel begins, eighteen when it ends, the psyche of the contemporary Deep South Negro is explored; he is the chief medium for the almost incessant editorializing, which all too often entails scrubby prose like: "The emotionally devastating experiences. . . hung suspended in his psychological digestion like stubborn, cold lumps." Mr. Wright means to see that the niceties get home. There is even "aside" comment on dialogue directly following much of it, making it look staged; more is the pity because Wright is very strong on dialogue. Actually the pervading feeling is theatrical: Wright is always on top of his material, always at the top of his voice.

The onus does not wear well on the unfledged hero. Never in his speech and seldom in his behavior does Fishbelly substantiate the restive, questioning, introspective boy of the author's exposition. His "sensitivity" is not projected from himself, rather is imposed through the numerous abuses he suffers at white hands. In effect his white tormentors are the plot's activators, though they are seldom onstage and when so are no more than hypothetical actors. Thus the novel's focus is not the black-white conflict in itself but the divisions it creates within and among the blacks; and this is telescoped by the friction between the boy and his father.

Just as he is being brutally awakened to the ghetto reality in which the Negroes around him live, Fishbelly begins to see Tyree, his father, as he really is: a man desperately trying to buy a cynical respectability and independence from the white folks. An undertaker across the board—the only profession, he instructs his son, in which a "nigger" can be independent, because though they will eagerly lynch him no white will touch a dead nigger—and a trader in live flesh under the table, Tyree has become knowingly a thrall of the most unsavory elements of local white power, who cushion his pride with a wealth and influence unrivaled in black Clintonville, and palliate his conscience by posing as righteously realistic champions of his race.

Tyree has to be a shrewd play-actor to bargain with his partner-owner, the chief of police, and he justifies his cringing and grimacing by observing that the whites can fathom and tolerate but two reactions from the colored: grinning and crying; by the same token the colored man must bend, migrate elsewhere or break, since there is only a white law and he can be hanged for so much as entertaining thoughts of rebellion. Nobody in Clintonville ever heard tell of an N.A.A.C.P. Tyree is an incisive characterization, sympathetically overdrawn. *The Long Dream* would seem to provide little insight on current U.S. interracial realities.

Paul Kiniery. *Best Sellers,* 18 (November 1, 1958), 296–97.

This is strong fare. Richard Wright, the Negro author well known for his *Native Son, Black Boy* and some other half dozen less well known books, now tells us what happened to Fishbelly, the young Negro who grew up in non-existent Clintonville, Mississippi. Fish's (or Fishbelly's) father was a well-to-do undertaker largely because of the rent and profits he received from a house of prostitution which was given police protection by Cantley, the white chief of police. The latter exacted from Fish's father one-half of the profits from the disorderly house. The undertaker and a Negro physician made a good deal of money from a firetrap they operated as a disreputable dance hall openly frequented by prostitutes. Cantley also shared in these profits and therefore allowed the firetrap, known as The Grove, to operate even though fire prevention ordinances were being openly violated. Fish was taken by his father to the disorderly house owned by the father and there made completely familiar with sex. We are given convincing evidence by Mr. Wright that practically all the young Negroes of high school age in Clintonville were sexually promiscuous. That was emphatically true of Fish, Zeke, Tony, Chris, Gloria, Vera, Gladys, Betty, Tillie and the others involved in the story.

The conversation is often slangy, suggestive and profane. The existence of a canine strain is assumed in almost everyone's maternal line of descent. The author makes no effort to present his Negro characters in a favorable light. He portrays them as amoral and as interested in practically nothing but irregular but frequent sexual relations. However, all this is in reality blamed on the white people. The implication is clear. The Negroes of Clintonville were practically forced to become immoral lawbreakers, protected and abetted by the whites. Then tragedy struck when The Grove burned and about forty lives were lost. When it appeared likely that Cantley was to be revealed as the partner of Fish's father, Tyree Tucker, Cantley had his men shoot Tucker. Then Cantley also "framed" young Fish on a charge of raping a white girl because Fish was believed to have secret evidence in the form of cancelled checks that Cantley had received frequent payments from the dead Tyree Tucker. Fish finally became convinced that Negroes could not live in the same community with white people, at least in this country. As Fish sensed it, the Negro

> existed in the bosom of the enemy [the white man], shared his ideals, spoke his tongue, fought with his weapons, and died a death usually of his choosing. Fishbelly wondered if it would always be like that. Black people paid a greater tribute to the white enemy than they did to God, whom they could sometimes forget, but the white man could never be forgotten. God meted out rewards and punishments only after death; you felt the white man's judgments every hour [p. 289].

And why this hatred of the White man for the Negro? Mr. Wright has his characters explain it as a fear upon the part of the white man that if he gave the Negro half a chance, the Negro would surpass the white man. The only way, therefore, for the basically inferior white man to retain his unnatural position of superiority is to keep the Negro intimidated, poverty-stricken and politically helpless. The author clearly implies that Negroes can never live normal and free lives in the American South, perhaps not even in the American North. At the end of the novel, Fish, after having been kept in jail for two years on trumped-up charges, is finally released and leaves America for France because a Negro wrote to him that a colored man could be free in France. Interestingly enough, and possibly not accidentally, Mr. Wright himself left the United States ten years ago and took up residence in France. But is this the only solution to this problem? And is it really a solution? You, the reader, are left with these questions in your mind as you put down this provocative book.

Maxwell Geismar. "Growing Up in Fear's Grip." *New York Herald Tribune Book Review,* November 16, 1958, p. 10.

Richard Wright's "Uncle Tom's Children," "Native Son" and "Black Boy" were solid, bitter, savage, almost terrifying fictional studies of the Negro mind in the United States. But the novel called "The Outsider" was a surrealistic fantasy of paranoid and suicidal impulses, veiled in political terminology. In the present novel, Mr. Wright once again returns to his Mississippi origins. And "the long dream" of Negro aspirations in America is another long nightmare of thwarted power, of obsessive fear and cruelty.

Mr. Wright keeps returning to his early youth and adolescent experiences. The wound, the trauma, is not personal so much as deeply social and deeply racial. The hero of "The Long Dream," Fishbelly, comes from respectable, even rich parents in a Mississippi town. Mr. Wright is a master of life, in this region, whether it is nightmare or reality, and the first half of the novel is a series of brilliant and horrifying episodes of what growing up in Mississippi is like to a talented and sensitive Negro boy.

The boy's father, Tyree Tucker, has built up his wealth and power by working with the corrupt police officials and the corrupt politicians. Officially an undertaker, Tyree has his hand in the brothels, the dance-halls, the tenements of ten thousand Clintonville blacks. When the trap closes in, Tyree's double personality, one for the whites and another for his own people, splits wide open. His is perhaps the best portrait in the novel; his son does not love him, his wife hates him, and he has no friends.

Mr. Wright seems to say that no normal human relationships are possible in this deep southern Negro world which is contingent only upon the white man's pleasure, his greed and sadism. The hero's "salvation" is flight to France, rather like Mr. Wright's own solution. The central emotions of the novel are irony and bitter humor; a continuing fear and hatred of the white man's (and white woman's) world: an acute kind of psychological insight which is unredeemed by human sympathy or compassion. As fiction, "The Long Dream" is uneven and not up to Richard Wright's best work, but one reads the novel with almost a morbid fascination; it is so remarkable, so "true," in the most depressing sense, and so tragic.

Charles Shapiro. "A Slow Burn in the South." *New Republic,* 139 (November 24, 1958), 17–18.

Cross Damon, the lippy hero of Richard Wright's unfortunate novel, *The Outsider,* felt that his life was disastrous, because, "in my heart. . . I'm innocent. . . that's what made the horror." He believed that his problem was one of the relationship of himself to himself, and he drank, not to feel better, but to feel "less." A real, existentialistic cat.

In his latest novel, however, Wright chooses to describe the growth of a less sophisticated Negro, the son of a wealthy, opportunistic businessman in a small Mississippi city. Fishbelly suffers and learns within the framework of his own Southern life, and his talk is fortunately free from either Marxist or existentialist bromides. As a result we have a powerful novel reminiscent of *Native Son,* one that smashes into experience, treating it directly, not by analogy.

Tyree Tucker, Fish's father, runs a colored undertaking establishment while secretly controlling much of the Negro vice in Clintonville. Uneducated but proud, he poses as a crafty conqueror before his son but achieves his business success by giving the whites what they most want. He has mastered the art of Uncle Tomming, putting on public displays of mirth, idiocy, and fawning. Tyree's uneasy relationships with the white powers of Clintonville finally come to a terrifying, self-destructive end, and in the process Fish learns to hate his father's sell-out at the same time gradually coming to understand why Tyree had no other practical alternative. From the age of six, to eighteen, when he flees Mississippi, Fish slowly discovers that it is impossible to be both a successful and sensitive Southern Negro: white women can tease but they may never be touched; the police may be used but they can never be treated as equals; flight is often the best answer to injustice; and, above all, a black man's dreams can never come true, at least not today in the deep South.

Tyree begs his son to play along with his tormentors but to use them. . . . To which Fish can only reply, "But Papa, crying and grinning ain't winning."

As Tyree's submission becomes more acute so does Fish's suffering. It becomes obvious that the Chief of Police is right when he screams out that he can't understand Fish. "You're one of these new kind of niggers. . . . I don't trust you!" And this is the heart of *The Long Dream,* the rise of the new Negro in the South, the rebel who can write, as an army buddy of Fish's did, that "If somebody would prove to me that God's white, I don't think I could ever go to church no more. God just can't be like these goddamned white folks." Exit Amos and Andy and Booker T. Washington.

Wright is in the tradition of the Dreiser of *An American Tragedy* and the Steinbeck of *Grapes of Wrath,* a tradition that is too often patronized. The young and not-so-young literary gents who write professional criticism will have a field day at Wright's expense. Those whose critical arrow points South, who worship peripheral discourse, will laugh at Wright's head-on approach. The sophisticated Northern liberals, whose literary maturity stems from the moment they enrolled in Lionel Trilling's classes and whose political wisdom consists in not having voted for Henry Wallace, will damn *The Long Dream* as naive, and, worst of all, as "innocent."

The novel does have a few rough moments: excessive dream sequences and several pompous speeches. But as we watch Fish develop, as we see him fighting a pal who is always "talking race," and as we watch him loving an almost white girl while he is finding his own courage, the imperfections are carried away by the power of the story, for the writing sins are of excess and not of cowardice.

Nick Aaron Ford. "A Long Way from Home." *Phylon*, 19 (Fourth Quarter, 1958), 435–36.

Richard Wright's latest novel, *The Long Dream,* is the story of the trials and tribulations, the naive dreaming and the rude awakening of Fishbelly (Rex) Tucker, black native of Mississippi. It traces the progress of the hero's physical, mental, and moral growth from the age of six to eighteen. And between those two birthdays the hero is made to witness enough humiliation, debaucheries, brutality, and tragic deaths to crush him completely, drive him insane, or "educate" him. It appears from the final episode that Fishbelly was able to qualify for the third option.

With a father who had sold his soul to the corrupt white rulers of the city for the privilege of preying financially on the ignorance and potential vice of his race, and a mother completely dominated by his father, Fishbelly began life with a hate for the values of his parents but a fondness for the physical comfort those values afforded. Gradually admiration for this father's success at moneymaking as chief undertaker for the Negro population and undisputed sponsor and boss of the vice dens in the black ghetto overcame his antipathy for the sordid values his father lived by. But when his father was murdered by the police chief and he himself incarcerated in the city jail for two years on fabricated charges to prevent an exposé of the corrupt ties between the police chief and the Negro vice boss, Fishbelly was ready to admit (to himself) that financial ease bought with the coin of racial servitude, humiliation, exploitation, and betrayal was not worth the price. The book ends with the eighteen-year-old boy voluntarily renouncing the opportunity to inherit his father's "business" with the police chief's connivance and sneaking out of the country on an airliner bound for Paris.

To the reader who admired the promises of *Uncle Tom's Children* in 1938, felt the extraordinary power of *Native Son* in 1940, and sensed the challenge of a new philosophy in *The Outsider* in 1953, this book is a colossal disappointment. The plot is naively contrived with unconvincing motivation. The characters are wooden puppets whose dilemmas are neither compelling nor natural. For instance, the delicate build up by the chief of police of an intricate trap to lure Fishbelly's father to his death seems very unrealistic, since the entire setting up to that point had presented a community where Negroes had no rights a white man was supposed to respect (not even the right to live) and where questions were never asked by whites or blacks when Negroes were exploited or murdered covertly or openly.

Likewise, on several occasions the police chief, the mayor, and the most distinguished lawyer in the city individually make surreptitious visits to the home of the hero in the late hours of the night, when the reader knows that in a community like that the Negro would be summoned to the city jail or some other rendezvous devoid of such high prestige value for the Negro.

Probably the most disconcerting fact about the book, assuming that the reader is prepared to accept social criticism as a legitimate ingredient of fiction when it is subordinated to an artistic design, is that Wright is fighting a battle that has already been conceded. Although there are still instances of denial to the Negro of the most elemental rights of freedom from gross ridicule and individual humiliation for the amusement of the white man, the battle has moved up to a higher realm. The targets now are equality of job opportunity, the right to vote in the deep South, integrated housing, and integrated schools.

This novel is written largely in the spirit of *Uncle Tom's Children* and *Black Boy*. In fact, some of the incidents are reminiscent of the two earlier volumes. Those books were timely and effective in their day. But that day has passed, and evidently Wright does not know it. His years of residence in France have given him an excellent base for understanding the European, Asian, and African minds; *Black Power, The Color Curtain,* and *Pagan Spain* are ample proof of that. But it has also cut him off from an understanding of the swiftly moving currents of racial attitudes and methods in America. Like the giant Antaeus who needed to touch the ground with his feet to renew his strength, Wright must return to his native land, at least for another brief look, if he wishes to write with strength and insight about the problems of race which still weigh most heavily upon his conscience.

Henry F. Winslow. "Nightmare Experiences." *The Crisis*, 66 (February 1959), 120–22.

Richard Wright' fifth work of fiction since he became a writer to be reckoned with with the publication twenty years ago of *Uncle Tom's Children* puts the nightmare experiences of a middle-class Negro undertaker and his son in terms of a long dream. Born Rex Tucker, but known as "Fishbelly," the tortured protagonist in this novel of terrible truth resurrects the fear-charged atmosphere worked with fresh effectiveness in *Native Son*. Here, however, is greater detail and the progress of a father-son relationship as determined by the racial culture pattern of the Deep South. . . .

Yet, for all the harrowing detail crowded into *The Long Dream,* the crux of this novel stems from two basic contentions. These contentions, moreover, constitute the essential moral structure of all Richard Wright's Americana since he launched his distinguished career in 1938. In fact, they are the upright and crossbeam of a crucifix on which he has nailed the American Negro the better to place it upon the literary lawn of the United States and set it afire time and time again.

As to the crossbeam, he charges, rightly, that the white world of the states has put (for the terrorization of the Negro male) a death premium on the body of the white woman. Thus, much of his writing has been turned against or toned in defiance of this peculiar institution of values. (Fishbelly "knew deep in his heart that there would be no peace in his blood until he had defiantly violated the line that the white world had dared him to cross under the threat of death.") But this crossbeam rests on a more basic upright driven deep into American soil. It is the charge Wright made in the concluding paragraph of his essay explaining the genesis of *Native Son,* "How Bigger Was Born." "We have," he wrote, "only a money-grubbing, industrial civilization."

Thus Canty, Clintonville's police chief whose cut from Tyree's brothels and gambling joints is a hundred ninety dollars weekly (some of which is accepted in the telltale form of checks), personifies this charge. But Wright goes much further than this. He documents the charge by weaving into *The Long Dream* a fictional account of the holocaust of April 24, 1940, in Natchez, Mississippi. So that one wonders where to draw the line between his fact and the fiction. Spanish moss, dry and inflammable, hung on the wall of the Rhythm Nite Club in Natchez when fire gutted it eighteen years ago and took the lives of 215 persons (including that of 33-year-old orchestra leader Walter Barnes), mostly teenagers like Fishbelly. The windows of the club had been boarded against gate-crashers, leaving but one exit. An *Afro-American* newspaper correspondent, Davis Lee, reported seeing 98 bodies at one of two colored undertaking establishments in Natchez, and that a white woman who took flowers to the parlor in memory of her maid dropped the comment that fire officials in Natchez should be sent to the penitentiary for permitting such a fire trap to exist.

With this documented verisimilitude, Wright works Tyree around to the selfsame dramatic focus where Taylor, the horse-whipped Negro minister in "Fire and Cloud," one of the four novellas in *Uncle Tom's Children,* stood his ground on the premise that "Freedom belongs to the strong." . . .

In that bare-knuckled prose beating which Wright (in defense of *Native Son*) administered (in the *Atlantic Monthly* for June, 1940) to David L. Cohn, one of the half dozen or more southern-born journalists and hack writers who attacked the book, the novelist set forth what he yet sees as his mission:

> . . . my task is to weigh the effects of our civilization upon the personality, as it affects it *here* and *now.* If, in my weighing of those effects, I reveal rot, pus, filth, hate, fear, guilt, and degenerate forms of life, must I be consigned to hell?

The Long Dream illustrates that Richard Wright has aged in indignation and developed a more penetrating satire than ever, but it proves most of all that he would quench the violence set off in him by his overriding sense of fire. It will be remembered that *Black Boy,* the record of his childhood and youth, tells of how he set fire to his mother's curtains and that for this she beat him terribly; that a "huge red bed of coals blazed with molten fury" as Bigger brutally prepared the body of Mary for burning; and that Cross Damon (*The Outsider*) set fire to the Seventh Day Adventist church where he obtained a forged draft-board card.

But *The Long Dream* brings Wright to a kind of dead end in the dark night of the troubled soul. It deals not so well with assertion as does John Killens' *Youngblood* and not better with traumatic experience than Chester Himes' *The Third Generation.* It explains him well, but it falls below his own standard.

Dorothy Parker. *Esquire,* 51 (February 1959), 18.

. . . Richard Wright's. . . *The Long Dream* is a grim and stunning report of a little Negro boy, brown and growing up in the South, and of him after that. Certainly it is a novel—no, a real account—to rack with guilt those of us who regard ourselves as supreme because we are inclosed in pink skin. . . .

Phillip Bonosky. "Man Without a People." *Mainstream, 12* (February 1959), 49–51.

There are books which rightly can be considered not so much the bearers of evidence as the evidence themselves, not so much the analysts of the disease as themselves the symptoms. Some books lay bare the problem. Others are merely an aspect of it.

I cannot see this latest book of Wright's, as indeed it was impossible to see his earlier book, *The Outsider*, as a work of art. It lacks objectivity; it is immature—but even worse than that there seems to be such a profound absence of sympathy for his people, of the kind of commitment to his subject without which no serious work of art is possible. It is one of those books that draw the reader's attention away from the subject to the writer himself; and one learns not so much what is true about the locale, Mississippi, in this case, as what happens to a Negro writer who has abandoned his people.

The Long Dream (which the publishers hopefully compare to *Native Son*) is a failure as fiction not because, as some critics have claimed, Wright has been too long away from Mississippi, or any part of the United States, and so has missed the great changes that have presumably taken place. No, there have been exiles before who have known their native land more keenly than the philistines who never left it for a moment.

Wright believes that the Negro people are caught in the tragedy of the "human condition" just as their white oppressors are also helplessly caught; that the ailment goes deep into our unknown bloods, where we are hopelessly poisoned at the source. The Negro is sick because he is an oppressed Negro; the white man is sick, too, and the Negro whom he perversely loves is simultaneously his burden of guilt, which he will hug to him though he perish.

Wright's theories turn their back on social causes, indeed on history itself; he seeks for understanding in psychoanalytical concepts (themselves misunderstood), and in concepts of dark irrational instincts, from which there is really no escape. The white man hates the Negro but loves him, too; and the Negro hates and fears the white man, but since he cannot explain why the white man hates him so irrationally except that he is black—i.e., different—he ends up hating being black, thus finally accepting the white man's judgment on himself. And so from this blackness, this mark of Cain, there is no escape except in flight—not a flight that envisages a later return, better armed, but a flight to the enemy, though now to a "kinder" enemy—the French. That is the solution of Wright's hero, that is his thinking: "Above all, he was ashamed of his world, for the world about him had branded his world as badly inferior. Moreover, he felt no moral strength or compulsion to defend his world. . . ."

Nor does Wright feel any "moral strength" to defend the world he describes—the world of the American Negro caught in the daily hell of life in a Mississippi town. The terror he describes vividly enough. But as each instance is extended into the abnormal the reader discovers, with some horror, that he has been led innocently enough into scenes of torture not to arouse his protest or hatred of cruelty but to engage perversely in its pleasures. Wright's sickness is to love what consumes him. This book therefore is not art; it is a case history.

Wright shows in this book a people whom he apparently believes aren't worth saving, for they possess no characteristics superior to their oppressors, and in actual fact, are inferior if for no other reason than they're not on top. Their only aim is to escape somehow from the accident of birth in order to be free to live like the whites—on no higher moral level, with no greater perspectives. "He sensed in them (the Negro people), a profound lassitude, a sort of lackadaisical aimlessness, a terribly pathetically narrow range of emotional activity veering from sex to religion, from religion to alcohol. He found them too ready to explode over matters devoid of real content and meaning. . . . Grudgingly accepting being classed with his people, he was, deep in him, somewhat afraid of them; there was in him some element that stood aside as though in shame. . . ."

This cannot be taken as the point of view of the character alone, and thus privileged; it is Wright's point of view, which has not changed in almost twenty years. . . .

Having abandoned all respect for his own people, Wright, of course, could not believe in a philosophy which saw in the oppressed Negro people, as in all the oppressed, great horizons of struggle and achievement, great transformations in national character based upon exactly those qualities which Wright cannot find in himself nor in anyone else.

Fish, who is the main character in the book, would like to live "free" like the whites whom he fears and envies. But since he is not white, the pain of oppression does fall on him, and forces a reaction. But how? As a rebel, conscious of the aims and sources of his rebellion? No: he rebels through his glands; through his belly, his sex; by sadism, neuroticism; finally by flight.

Fish is brought up by a man who has learned how to make a go of it in the white world. His father owns an undertaker's establishment, but he also collects rents and has an interest in whore houses. He lives by paying off graft to the white law-enforcers, and because he can't trust them he also sees to it that he keeps some material for blackmail safely in reserve against the day they turn on him. And that day inevitably comes. He loses his life, and Fish almost loses his. But even so, Fish has no real objection to the kind of life his father has handed down to him—blackmail material and whore houses—and leaves it only when the white world catches up with him and threatens to put him underground. Then he runs away, not only out of the state, but out of the country. Sitting in the plane winging over the Atlantic he observes his black hand resting beside the white hand of his fellow passenger, and "unconsciously, stealthily, Fishbelly drew his hand in, covering his right hand with his left black hand, trying vainly to blot out the shameful blackness on him."

What can we understand, then, from such a life? Only that, as he escapes to a "free world," he decides that this flight is a "free gesture of faith welling up out of a yearning to be at last somewhere at home; it was his abject offer of a truce. . . . He was now voluntarily longing to pledge allegiance to a world whose brutal might could never compel him to love it with threats of death."

But the white flag of truce and surrender is not the flag that we have already seen rising on the tall poles in Ghana, Guinea, nor indeed anywhere in the whole colonial world. Nor in Alabama, nor Harlem.

William S. Poster. "The Black Man's Burden." *The New Leader*, 42 (August 31, 1959), 23–24.

Richard Wright may be said to be the possessor of one of those odd talents, which, despite a considerable capacity for adventure or change, never seems to grow much. From *Native Son* to *The Long Dream* is a considerable length of time, but one which has not been productive of any significant alteration in the author's approach to life or art.

Wright's most notable quality is still very much in evidence. Somewhere at the bottom of the most refined and gifted of all novelists there must be the crude, unbaked dough of the storyteller's capacity, the gift for relating human action so that it is not merely believed, but so absorbs the reader that it gives off the quality of real life. Wright has this crude storyteller's quality, this essential narrative gift, to a remarkable extent, to a degree with which he is not usually credited. It redeems numerous faults, especially a chronic carelessness, a lack of either desire or ability to create a unified stylistic surface or to employ a sensibility to make his people not merely believable, but authoritatively and convincingly true to themselves, their place and their time.

Wright often uses extremely young protagonists, either because he has a capacity for vivid, sensation-packed narration, or because his type of novelistic talent naturally gravitates toward youthful experience through a lack of ability to coordinate and unify the complexities of adult existence. "Fishbelly" Tucker, the Mississippi-born young hero of *The Long Dream*, is "Bigger" Thomas with some added dimension of consciousness. He gives the reader the same sensation of having been plunged into human experience like a hot rivet in water.

Wright's youngsters seem to have little or no control of their environment, perhaps because they are colored, and therefore brought up in a hostile, freakish world. They resemble the children and adolescents of Faulkner's novels in their immersion in sensory experience and the lack of any continuous meaning within their minds. But Faulkner's youths react differently—they are at one with their experience, they even help to create the world of which they are a part. Even in their terror, there is a certain sensual savor, the savor of people who belong, a sense of belonging that's transmitted through the adults who command the Southern world. For Bigger and Fishbelly, there is no stake in this world, and its terror is unmitigated except by luck.

One suspects that Wright over-emphasizes the inhumanity of the white world, not merely as it impinges upon the Negro world but as it impinges upon itself. The Southern white, as Wright delineates him, is not only intolerant but intolerable. It is almost impossible to see how the whites put up with each other and the Negroes are able to endure their harsh treatment.

The book tells of one colored boy's adjustment to the white world, and his entire life is told in terms of the race problem. It is by now almost a truism to point out the literary weakness of such an approach: There is no situation or character with a universal dimension and no single character emerges as a full-blown personality. Moreover, the attitudes and ideas about racial minorities are rapidly becoming clichés—in Wright's case, clichés enlivened by an astute intelligence and a sometimes-pleasing-sometimes-mawkish kind of poetry, but clichés nonetheless.

The Long Dream is the story of a well-off member of the Negro community. Fishbelly is the son of Tyree Tucker, an undertaker who also has real estate interests and shares in various illicit enterprises—a brothel among others—which bring him into contact with the Chief of Police, something nebulously called "The Syndicate" and other politicians in their small Mississippi town. A fire in the brothel puts Tyree in the center of an exposé of the graft and corruption by which Southern towns live and, as a Negro, he naturally becomes the victim of the rapacious whites. Fishbelly, now 16 years old, has become involved in his father's schemes and tragedies, and goes to jail for two years, after which he gives up his intention of following in his father's footsteps and joins his former schoolmates in France.

On the plane to France, the climax of the book, he is treated as an equal by white people for the first time in his life. He enters into a discussion with a young white man about conditions in the South and finds himself denying that Negroes are really treated so badly. Thinking things over, he comes to the conclusion that it might be better to lie and declare that the world in which he has existed up to now did not really exist at all. "Above all, he was ashamed of his world, for the world about him had branded his world as bad, inferior. Moreover, he felt no moral strength or compulsion to defend his world. That in him which was always self-conscious was now the bud of a new possible life that was pressing ardently but timidly against the old to shatter it and be free."

The novel as a story is weakened considerably in that one does not quite know what Wright thinks of his protagonist: He shows him, by turns, in his driven life, to be cowardly, heroic, weak, foolish, sensual and intelligent.

But a certain lack of unity in Wright's perspective weakens the novel simply as literature. By now, according to the sociologists, self-hatred has become a dominant feature of the racial picture, but it often tends to subsume more of life than one would have thought possible. Using it as the essential pivot of his character, Wright precipitates him into such a complex dialectic of love and hate of himself and the white world that every principle of identity seems to get lost in a verbal and psychological abstraction.

One feels that Wright fails to give actuality to his Negro characters, that there is something in them that enables them to be more than functions of racial interaction which Wright never reveals. It is not incumbent on Wright to go beyond his hero's consciousness, but it is hard to find anywhere in this novel, or Wright's fiction as a whole, anything beyond the brutal tensions of racialism and the fantastic, burning, quivering life engendered by it.

The only solutions he offers seem to be the gradual succumbing of the Negro to the white man's world or a weak-willed acceptance of a truce. Both a perception of the weakness of the white world and an appreciation of the inner strength of Negro life are absent in Wright's work.

The Long Dream lacks focus and, at times, verisimilitude—despite its erratic power and Wright's quick and easy hand with dialogue—because for Wright there seems to be no sense of any shaping value within the Negro world to give meaning to the Negro's life and to the harsh conflict of interaction with the white. In the end, Wright leaves us dramatically and morally at sea, never knowing whether the grasping, immoral Negroes and whites he portrays are better or worse than the stuffy few who attempt to salvage life through some code of ethics and morals.

Checklist of Additional Reviews

Chicago Daily News, October 29, 1958.

New Yorker, 34 (November 8, 1958), 210.

Hoke Norris. *Chicago Sun Times*, November 11, 1958.

Nick Aaron Ford. *CLA Journal*, 1 (December 1958), 143–44.

Bryan Haislip. *Raleigh News Observer*, May 5, 1959.

John S. Lash. *Phylon*, 20 (Second Quarter 1959), 119–20.

Irving Howe. *Partisan Review*, 26 (Winter 1959), 133–34.

Notes

RICHARD WRIGHT

Eight Men

THE WORLD PUBLISHING COMPANY

Eight Men

Lawrence Lee. "Evident Art Diluted by Uncontrolled Anger." *Chicago Sunday Tribune Magazine of Books*, January 22, 1961, p. 4.

In "The Man Who Went to Chicago," one of the eight stories in this collection by Richard Wright, the author, as the central character, says: "I was persisting in reading my present environment in the light of my old one."

The opening story, "The Man Who Was Almost a Man," tells us again that the old environment is the world in which the white man, economically dominant, is an unchanging agent of evil by whom the Negro is misunderstood, frustrated, and treated with rankling injustice.

Few honest men who have had a significant experience with the world will deny that the judgment is justified; but few men who have written with a passionate hope of doing a good piece of work will believe that such anger as that sustained thru a lifetime by the author of "Uncle Tom's Children," "Native Son," "Black Boy," and "The Outsider" is other than injurious to good art.

That Wright was an artist is evident thru some quality in each of these stories. The fearfully black and looming sailor in the story, "Big Black Good Man," is a characterization of which the Stephen Crane of "The Blue Hotel" might have been proud.

The African who understood too literally what missionaries had taught him about Christianity in "Man, God Ain't Like That. . . ," is a creation of original and affecting worth.

Yet, too often and too incredibly, as in "The Man Who Lived Underground," "Man of All Work," and "The Man Who Killed a Shadow," the white man who was the evil figure of Wright's first works is the unelaborated and unmotivated villain of the last stories.

The writer continued to read all environments in the light of one from which he fled in his youth. Wright had a more painful justification for his passion than have the angry young men or the "beats"; but he, as they, has let an uncontroled self-pity mar his art.

Saunders Redding. *New York Herald Tribune Book Review*, January 22, 1961, p. 33.

Of the eight stories in this posthumous collection, four are bizarre, three are conventional, one is an autobiographical fragment, and all explore the author's favorite theme—rootlessness. "I am a rootless man," Richard Wright once wrote: "but I am neither psychologically distraught nor in any wise particularly perturbed because of it." With no substantial exceptions, his works—including this one—argue otherwise. Indeed, Wright was painfully distressed by his rootlessness, and this anguish was the living substance of his best books, the stuff of which they were made. But after long expatriation from America, where experience fed his anguish, he came to feel it less. Memory alone was not enough to keep the torment vital. This I suppose accounts for the fact that the best of the stories in "Eight Men" were all written before 1945.

"The Man Who Was Almost a Man," "The Man Who Saw the Flood," and the autobiographical piece, "The Man Who Went to Chicago," are recognizably the old Wright who could snare eternal values in a moment of pure sensation, who could dramatize an idea in a rush of earthy dialogue, and who spoke out his supraconsciousness of being Negro in a way that was, as Dorothy Canfield Fisher said, "honest, dreadful, heartbreaking." Of these three, only "The Man Who Was Almost a Man" can properly be called a story. Its hero is a teenage boy who buys a gun his father does not want him to have. The gun is a symbol. It is the symbol but not the substance of manhood, and to get the substance, to "let him know Dave Saunders is a man," he runs away from home. "The Man Who Saw the Flood" is even simpler in outline. A Mississippi sharecropper, who hopes the flood he has lived through has washed away the road, finds that it has not. Literally and figuratively, the road leads nowhere, but it is the road that he must travel all his life. The last of these three pieces is a straight autobiographical account of Wright's Chicago days, and it, too, is marked by the honest simplicity that characterized the author's earliest books; it, too, drives home a point.

The same cannot be said of the five remaining stories, of which two are eccentric experiments in technique, and three are grotesque in subject matter. In "Man of All Work" and "Man, God Ain't Like That" Wright relies exclusively on dialogue. He uses it to establish the mood, to set the scene, to provide dramatic exposition, to advance the narrative, and to delineate character. And dialogue is not enough. It is not enough because it is not good enough nor flexible enough. Wright cannot make dialogue do all that needs to be done to create an illusion of the reality of the farcical circumstance in which a quite ordinary husband and father ("Man of All Work") masquerades so successfully as a woman as to take a housemaid's job and to be sexually assaulted by the woman-chasing master of the house. In "Man, God Ain't Like That," where character is sketchy and plot implausible, it takes more than dialogue to establish a compelling motive for ritual murder, and to explain the failure of the police to solve it, and to drive home the obscure point of it all—if there is a point.

The most impressive story in "Eight Men" is "The Man Who Lived Underground," and it is an impressive failure. It is a fantastic nightmare of guilt, fear and redemption, of sewage filth, of obscene, senseless murder. It has all the dramatic tension of a first-class Gothic tale; there are descriptive passages of extraordinary vividness, and stylistic ornaments of great glitter, but nothing comes to anything: no passion has meaning, no insight is revealed, no idea truly conveyed, no theme made unmistakably plain. It is as if Gabriel, brandishing his trumpet and filling his lungs with air to blow the blast of doom, managed only a penny whistle's pipe.

"Eight Men" is not one of the books by which Richard Wright deserves to be judged. Those who meet the author for the first time through these stories will have but a faulty acquaintance with him. Those who read "Uncle Tom's Children," "Native Son," and "Black Boy" long ago will read "Eight Men" with sad and growing wonder.

Ted Poston. "Wright's Last Book." *New York Post*, January 22, 1961.

As it was in the beginning with "Uncle Tom's Children," so it is in the end with "Eight Men"—another and a final collection of stories by Richard Wright.

The two collections have much in common. Both are harsh, realistic portrayals of Negro life, although the latter ranges wider—from the Deep South through Africa to Scandinavia.

But both are illustrative of the flaming talent which burst on the American scene in 1937 and did more than any other fiction to awaken this country to the cruelties of race discrimination.

There are two tragic aspects in the posthumous publication of this last book by the distinguished author who died in a Paris clinic last Nov. 28. First, of course, is the loss to English literature of a truly eloquent writer.

Second is the fact that Wright, 15 years as an expatriate, probably never knew of the change for the better his native land had achieved in the decade and a half of his absence—a change which his own writings had helped to bring about.

Few people will question the impact that "Native Son," his most successful novel, and the bitterly autobiographical "Black Boy," both Book-of-the-Month selections, had on the American conscience.

Yet his most recent novel, "The Long Dream," while gripping, displayed such ignorance of the current status of his people in his native Mississippi and elsewhere in America that it hardly rang true.

It is probable that Wright's power as a writer shines through in each of these eight stories because most of them were written, and several published, before he became an expatriate.

Two of the stories are told completely in dialogue and the form detracts not at all from the drama. Another, "The Man Who Lived Underground," is reminiscent of Ralph Ellison's "Invisible Man" and is equally powerful. And the same quality, with a touch of "Native Son," is discernible in "The Man Who Killed a Shadow."

The final story, "The Man Who Went to Chicago," might have been taken from "Black Boy."

The concluding story shows why it was almost inevitable that Richard Wright should have joined the Communist Party in his youth, just as his own honesty made it inevitable that he should have left that party when he encountered its opposition to the intellectual freedom which he always sought.

It would have been a good idea to have included in this book his contribution to "The God That Failed," an anthology and disavowal by former Communists.

Richard Sullivan. "Lives of More than Quiet Desperation." *New York Times Book Review,* January 22, 1961, p. 5.

Unhappily, "Eight Men" is a posthumous volume. Richard Wright died in Paris in late November. Still, in his early fifties, he was an American writer of genuine importance, and his best work—some of it contained in this volume—will endure. At times his profound indignation led him into flimsy political philosophizing, which intruded upon his story-telling, understandably, for he was a wounded, sensitive and embattled artist. In "Native Son" and "Black Boy" he illuminated with passion certain aspects of the state of the Negro in this century's American polity. He was a deeply concerned writer, capable of great dramatic intensity, uneven in his achievements, but every instant alive in his awareness of humanity, justice and love, together with their all too frequent negations and denials.

"Eight Men" is a representative book, containing eight stories, some of them published before. Each story centers on a Negro, involved cruelly with his surroundings, beaten down by them; each central figure is in one way or another misunderstood by the world he knows; a few misunderstand and misinterpret that world. Altogether the eight men of these stories have in common a desperate if qualified heroism. They are, at their best and their worst, real men. And the stories are real stories.

A couple of them, rendered largely in dialogue, are technically masterful. One of them, "The Man Who Lived Underground" (the story of a fugitive from justice hiding in a city sewer), is a memorable symbolic piece, worthy of long brooding. Another, "The Man Who Went to Chicago" (which describes the hardships of a migrant worker who comes North), is really a report, half narrative, half essay, the two halves joining impressively. The protagonist in this story says, "I had elected, in my fevered search for honorable adjustment to the American scene, not to submit and in doing so I had embraced the daily horror of anxiety, of tension, of eternal disquiet." Though it is quietly stated, this philosophy of living might be taken from Richard Wright's own experience. One finds it in "Native Son." It is stated, even more explicitly, in the later fragments of autobiography he published in book form. It was a compulsion, a way of living he was destined never to escape entirely, even in his long European exile.

There is not a touch of phoniness or fakery in the book. All eight men and all eight stories stand as beautifully, pitifully, terribly true. Some readers will be shocked by it, for it presents straightforwardly a brilliant American Negro's point of view. Many more readers will be uplifted and encouraged by it; to some it will indeed seem a sign and a token of what is to come and to be welcomed, to be rejoiced at. Because all the way through this is fine, sound, good, honorable writing, rich with insight and understanding, even when occasionally twisted by sorrow.

To a good many readers it will come as an almost inexpressible misery that this book is dedicated to French friends who made the American author "feel at home in an alien land." It is not that those friends are not most estimable and already rewarded; it is that here, in his native land, other friends in the lacking left Richard Wright to perish, like Palinurus, away from a home that must honor him, hereafter, for the sturdy prose he wrote.

Irving Howe. "Richard Wright: A Word of Farewell." *New Republic*, 144 (February 13, 1961), 17–18.

In the two months since the death of Richard Wright there has appeared, to my knowledge, one serious comment about his life or his work: a memoir by James Baldwin in the socialist paper *New America* reflecting with characteristic honesty that mixture of admiration and estrangement most of the younger Negro novelists felt toward Wright. Otherwise, little has been written in tribute or criticism. Our culture seems almost proud of its capacity for not remembering, and is often most cruel toward those figures it was honoring a few decades ago.

When Wright's first novel *Native Son* appeared in the thirties, it seemed important both as an example of literary naturalism and an outcry of Negro protest. A few years later came *Black Boy*, the story of Wright's boyhood and youth in the deep South and perhaps his single best piece of work. Here, one felt, was the American Negro novelist who would speak without hesitation, who for the first time would tell the truth not only about the familiar sufferings of his people but about their buried responses, those inner feelings of anger and hatred which no white man could reach. And this, I think, Wright did succeed in doing. He told us the one thing even the most liberal and well-disposed whites preferred not to hear: that Negroes were far from patient or forgiving, that they were scarred by fear, that they hated every moment of their humiliation even when seeming most acquiescent, and that often enough they hated *us*, the decent and cultivated white men who, from complicity or neglect, shared in the responsibility for their plight. No Negro writer had ever quite said this before, certainly not with so much force or bluntness, and if such younger Negro novelists as James Baldwin and Ralph Ellison were to move beyond Wright's harsh naturalism and toward more subtle modes of fiction, that was possible only because Wright had been there first, courageous enough to release the full weight of his anger.

Before the implications of this fact, it seemed not very important that his image of Negro life in America was becoming historically dated (which is true) or that he occasionally succumbed to black nationalism (also true) or that he wrote badly (sometimes true). The bitterness and rage that poured out of Wright's books form one of the great American testaments, a crushing necessity to our moral life, forever to remind us that moderate analyses of injustice are finally lies.

And now, after fourteen years of voluntary exile in Paris, chosen, as he once told me, because he could no longer bear to live in the United States and see his children suffer the blows of race hatred, Richard Wright is dead. His life was incomplete, as it had to be, and at the end his work as tentative and fumbling as at the beginning. His later years were difficult, for he neither made a true home in Paris nor kept in imaginative touch with the changing life of the United States. He was a writer in limbo, and his best fiction, such as the novelette "The Man Who Lived Underground," is a projection of that condition. His work, so far as I can tell, is hardly read today by serious literary persons; his name barely known by the young.

Eight Men, Wright's most recent and apparently last book, is a collection of stories written over the last 25 years. Though they fail to yield any clear line of chronological development, these stories do give evidence of Wright's literary restlessness, his wish to keep learning and experimenting, his often clumsy efforts to break out of the naturalism which was his first and, I think, necessary mode of expression. The uneveness of his writing is extremely disturbing: one finds it hard to understand how the same man, from paragraph to paragraph, can be at once so brilliant and inept—though the student of American literature soon learns to measure the price which the talented autodidact pays for getting his education too late. Time after time the narrative texture of the stories is broken by a passage of jargon borrowed from sociology or psychology: perhaps the later Wright read too much, tried too hard, failed to remain sufficiently loyal to the limits of his talent.

The best stories are marked by a strong feeling for the compactness of the story as a form, so that even when the language is scraggly or leaden there is a sharply articulated pattern of event. Some of the stories, such as "Big Black Good Man," are enlivened by Wright's sardonic humor, the humor of a man who has known and released the full measure of his despair but finds that neither knowledge nor release matters in a world of despair. In "The Man Who Lived Underground" Wright shows a sense of narrative rhythm, a gift for shaping the links between sentences so as to create a chain of expectation, which is superior to anything in his full-length novels and evidence of the seriousness with which he kept working.

The main literary problem that troubled Wright in recent years was that of rendering his naturalism a more supple and terse instrument. I think he went astray whenever he abandoned naturalism entirely; there are a few embarrassingly bad experiments with stories written entirely in dialogue or self-consciously employing Freudian symbolism. Wright needed the accumulated material of circumstance which naturalistic detail provided his fiction; it was as essential to his ultimate effect of shock and bruise as dialogue to Hemingway's ultimate effect of irony and loss. But Wright was correct in thinking that the problem of detail is the most vexing technical problem the naturalist writer must face, since the accumulation of detail that makes for depth and solidity can also create a pall of tedium. In "The Man Who Lived Underground" Wright came close to solving this problem, for here the naturalistic detail is put at the service of a radical projective image—a Negro trapped in a sewer—and despite some flaws, the story is satisfying both for its tense surface and its elasticity of suggestion.

For some readers, the obsession with violence they detected in Wright's work was more disturbing than any of his technical faults. As Alfred Kazin has written: "If he chose to write the story of Bigger Thomas [in *Native Son*] as a grotesque crime story, it is because his own indignation and the sickness of the age combined to make him dependent on violence and shock, to astonish the reader by torrential scenes of cruelty, hunger, rape, murder, and flight . . . " Apart from the fact that something very similar and quite as damning could be said about the author of *Crime and Punishment*, this judgment rests on the assumption that a critic can readily distinguish between the genuine need of a contemporary writer to cope with ugly realities and the damaging effects these realities may have upon him.

The reality pressing upon all of Wright's work is a nightmare of remembrance, and without the terror of that nightmare it would be impossible to render the truth of the reality—not the only, perhaps not even the deepest truth about American Negroes, but a primary and inescapable one. Both truth and terror depend upon a gross fact which Wright faced more courageously than any American writer: that for the Negro violence forms an inescapable part of his existence.

In a sense, then, Wright was justified in not paying attention to the changes that have been occurring in the South these past few decades. When Negro liberals write that despite the prevalence of bias there has been an improvement in the life of their people down South, such statements are reasonable and necessary. But what have they to do with the way Negroes feel, with the power of the memories they must surely retain? About this we know very little and would be well advised not to nourish preconceptions, for it may well be that their feelings are quite close to Wright's rasping outbursts. *Wright remembered*, and what he remembered other Negroes must also have remembered. Perhaps by now the terror and humiliation that fill his pages are things of the past, even in Mississippi; but men whose lives have been torn by suffering must live with their past, so that it too becomes part of the present reality. And by remembering Wright kept faith with the experience of the boy who had fought his way out of the depths to speak for those who remained there.

The present moment is not a good one for attempting a judicious estimate of Wright's achievement as a novelist. It is hard to suppose that he will ever be regarded as a writer of the first rank, for his faults are grave and obvious. Together with Farrell and Dos Passos, he has suffered from the changes of literary taste which occurred during his lifetime: the naturalist novel is little read these days, though often mocked, and the very idea of a "protest novel" has become a target for graduate students to demolish. The dominant school of criticism has little interest in the kind of work Wright did, and it rejects him less from a particular examination than from a theoretic preconception—or to be more precise, from an inability to realize that the kind of linguistic scrutiny to which it submits lyric poetry has only a limited value in the criticism of fiction.

Now I would not pretend to be writing from any established superiority to current taste, for I too find the murk and awkwardness of most naturalist fiction hard to bear. But I believe that any view of 20th-Century American literature which surmounts critical sectarianism will have to give Wright an honored place, and that any estimate of his role in our cultural life will have to stress his importance as the pioneer Negro writer who in the fullness of his anger made it less possible for American society to continue deceiving itself.

Anger and violence may be present in his work, but the Richard Wright I knew, slightly in person and somewhat more through letters, was a singularly good-hearted and sweet man. When I met him in Paris a few years ago, he was open, vigorous and animated, full of shrewd if not always just estimates of the younger writers, actively concerned with the intellectual life of the African students who clustered about him, and, at a time when it was far from fashionable, still interested in the politics of the democratic left.

Richard Wright died at 52, full of hopes and projects. Like many of us, he had somewhat lost his intellectual way during recent years, but he kept struggling toward a comprehension of the strange and unexpected world coming into birth. In the most fundamental sense, however, he had done his work: he had told his contemporaries a truth so bitter that they paid him the tribute of striving to forget it.

Richard Gilman. "The Immediate Misfortunes of Widespread Literacy." *Commonweal*, 28 (April 1961), 130–31.

One of the misfortunes of an age of widespread literacy is that it inflicts upon us a great deal of literature that in less democratically educated times would not have seen the light of day. Probably the amount of good writing is fairly constant in every epoch, but the percentage is certainly way down. Of the four volumes of short fiction I have just worked my way through, only one seemed to me worth all the trouble it takes (writer, publisher, editor, printer, designer, messenger boy, account executive, book-seller—all those hands in on it, all those skills functioning in air). Another had intermittent virtues, while the third was at best merely unobjectionable and the fourth was embarrassing.

I shall start from the bottom and work up. Richard Wright is dead now and I have no intention of belaboring his memory; but he was simply not a good writer, not even a competent one, and it might be useful to make a notation upon what the sources of his reputation were. I think it clear that he was one of those authors about whom circumstances gather to distill extra-literary excitement and interest, in his case of course the circumstance being the fact that he was Negro and the first of his race to write about what that meant, in full acceptance of its terrors, frustrations and imposed shame.

I haven't read *Native Son* in many years. But if I say that I remember fairly vividly how it jolted me, as it did so many others, it is also true that the jolt was of the sociological order, not the esthetic, impelling me into recognitions that were certainly important, perhaps more important than literary ones, but nevertheless entering a different order of experience and therefore subject to another kind of judgment.

Eight Men has not even the advantage that *Native Son* had. We are long past the stage of shock and recognition; what we need now, if we can ever be said to *need* anything from Negro writers that places them under obligations and pressures different from those of any author, is something in the nature of a merging of images that possess a common base: our reality and their reality, half-identical and half-clashing, seen from their point of view, or point of imagination, and complementing our own, our brother's story, so to speak, told with that kind of fearful intimacy that makes a mockery of our artificial distances.

But *Eight Men*, stories that have been brought together from various periods of Wright's career (a few have not previously been published) is a dismayingly stale and dated book. Its tales of Negroes struggling to survive in a white world or being defeated by it creak with mechanical ineptitude; its attempts at humor, at tragedy, at pathos all fail; its two experiments—stories written entirely in dialogue—are painful to read; and the sensibility at work in it is so self-conscious, so liable to lapses of taste, so unsubtly enamored of literary effects, that all the pain and the earnestness, all the angels that hover over the "right side" cannot rescue it. . . .

Gloria Bramwell. "Articulated Nightmare." *Midstream*, 7 (Spring 1961), 110–12.

The Existentialist, the Outsider, the Kafkaesque man of our time, all find expression in the Negro as we know him in America. Here is a fellow-creature ridden with guilt, maimed by an inferiority complex and tortured into a schizophrenic existence by the accepted mores of his native land. One, moreover, who receives a mortal wound of the psyche in early childhood or very soon thereafter and is expected to spend the remaining years of his existence atoning for the sin of being born black. Further, any attempt on his part to assert his individuality, to deny the stereotype ground into him, may place him in jeopardy.

This is the Negro as seen by Richard Wright, with one important addition—his Negroes do step out of "their place" for one moment and in so doing step into chaos. In thus compulsively fulfilling their stereotype they doom themselves.

Wounded as he was by southern birth and upbringing, Richard Wright fought back blindly with the nearest weapon at hand—in his case, anger. Anger mounting to rage rushes across the pages of his work; too often it overflows and drowns it before it can take shape. And it is the terrible anger of a man who accepts and can see no way out, for his rage is thrust in against himself. That is the greatest irony of all, that a man should be guilty in America by reason of his difference from the majority and acquiesce in his guilt. But Wright is involved in guilt, not irony.

There is a further irony in the fact that the shaping tools he used for his work were first Communism and later, after his self-exile in France, existentialism. Both philosophies had the ultimate effect of weakening his work.

Communism attracted him first and it is easy to see why. The Communist party held out eager arms to Negroes in the depression days of the thirties. It sought to identify the plight of the Negro with that of the downtrodden worker and many Negroes, Wright among them, were seduced by the warm welcome and the chance to mingle with whites on seemingly equal terms. But, as he soon discovered, economics is not all and while a worker whose employment problems are solved may be considered to have arrived at some sort of millenium, a Negro with a steady job working for the kindest of employers at decent wages is still faced with the madness of prejudice in America on every level of his life. Since the Communists had no readier solution to this than any other party, Wright's disillusionment grew and became final.

But the Party had given him a focus and a framework. It came at a time when his work was just beginning and under its tutelage he produced his two most powerful works, *Native Son* and *Black Boy*, and earned an international reputation.

Native Son, the most popular of his novels, has as a protagonist Bigger Thomas, a Chicago slum-dweller. Child-like, illiterate, he has all the faults and virtues of the Negro as seen through white eyes, and like every stereotype he travels the well-worn road which every racist predicts for every Negro down to the murder of a white woman. Wright's intention was to show him as a victim of social injustice, but the Communist philosophy proved to be too much of a straight-jacket for the complex problem and contributed to the stereotyping of the characters. However, the power of the book is not to be denied. In part it derives from the autobiographical nature of much of Wright's best work which gave his documentation of Negro life, its terrors and tragedies, an authority not to be found in sentimentalized accounts presented before him. In part it derives from his Communist training which taught him that a point is most effectively made by example after example hammered home with interlardings of constant reiteration of that point. (This was a lesson he never forgot and even in his posthumous collection of short stories, *Eight Men*, he repeats words and ideas until the mind is saturated with the guilt and fear underlying his picture of Negro life.) And since white America for the most part feels a large measure of guilt on anything pertaining to the Negro, all that was necessary was for someone to speak with the voice of authority and at the same time present a picture which did not deviate too far from certain preconceived notions to be hailed as a classic. This Wright could do brilliantly. But ultimately the difficulty of reconciling his experience with his adopted philosophy forced him to abandon it and seek another.

Just as Wright failed to blend Communism convincingly with his work, so, too, he failed with existentialism. The irony of this lies precisely in the fact that the Negro is an existentialist, living as it were in a perpetual limbo. The Negro is forever outside seeking entry, the intellectual existentialist is inside looking for an exit. Wright, an emotional writer, could paint a stunning picture of the Negro's plight but when he attempted to intellectualize it he embraced it from the wrong angle, from the inside out rather than in terms of his own characters.

A prime example of this occurs in the short story "The Man Who Went to Chicago," an autobiographical study, where he writes:

> Perhaps it would be possible for the Negro to become reconciled to his plight if he could be made to believe that his suffering were for some remote, high, sacrificial end; but sharing the culture that condemns him, and seeing that a lust for trash is what binds the nation to his claims, is what sets storms rolling in his soul.

Now this may be perfectly good existentialist philosophy (as in his Communist days, Wright stuffs his stories with the jargon of his current philosophical beliefs) but it makes no sense emotionally in terms of his character who would be much more inclined to believe that the only chance of reconciliation to his plight is the belief that it will one day end and what sets storms rolling in his soul is not the national lust for trash of which he has his due share, but the terrible knowledge that the lust for a scapegoat seems almost an inherent national characteristic.

While Communism failed him and existentialism provided only a weak adjunct to his writings, he was sustained by an overwhelming sense of guilt, an earlier age would have called it sin. It became increasingly clear to him as he wrote and as we read his work that lying at the bottom of every Negro soul is crushing guilt. For him Negro life took on the proportions of expiation for crimes committed, known and unknown. As he said:

> . . . why was this sense of guilt so seemingly innate, so easy to come by, to think, to feel, so verily physical? It seemed that when one felt this guilt one was retracing in one's feelings a faint pattern designed long before; it seemed that one was always trying to remember a gigantic shock that had left a haunting impression upon one's body which one could not forget or shake off, but which had been forgotten by the conscious mind, creating in one's life a state of eternal anxiety.

Guilt and fear like some crazy quilt pattern themselves through his work. In the story "The Man Who Lived Underground" from which the above quotation is taken, an innocent Negro escapes from the law into the sewers. Fear motivates his flight underground, fear that he may be found guilty of an unknown crime. His miniature odyssey assumes symbolic as well as literal proportions as he views the world from his shelter of invisibility and acquires an anonymous identity paralleling that of Negroes above ground. From his underground vantage point he is able to participate anonymously in a series of social and unsocial acts peculiar to our society. Gradually he moves from fear to self-accusation ending in surrender to the police and death. But even at his death we are no closer to knowing the sort of man he really was. Whether he had family, friends, sweetheart, convictions to sustain him, how he lived till then we have no clue. The protagonist is merely presented as an instrument for the author's ideas moving from a lesser to a greater madness. One does not feel the sharp intelligence, the planned anarchy of Ralph Ellison's *Invisible Man*, a theme of similar dimensions. Ellison's man goes from naivete to wide-eyed awareness and ends as a sniper against the society that made him. He adopts consciously the fate thrust upon him and lives by outsmarting the forces that would keep him down. Wright's man, on the other hand, performs the deeds of theft and murder as a child rebelling against an overstern parent, only to return "home" at the end for the punishment he feels he merits. This inverse paternalism constitutes a major weakness of Wright's as an artist, but at the time of his earlier work it undoubtedly helped his popularity. Today Americans are more sophisticated and more likely to approve Ellison's action as he strips society's pretentions bare, laughs at it himself, and mocks its attempts to destroy him. Wright was never far enough removed to do more than suffer and articulate that suffering incompletely—for without objectivity it must be incomplete—but powerfully enough to touch us. And he is merciless in the presentation of that suffering. Never with all the platitudes uttered about the Negro had one imagined it to be quite like this. It fascinated, it horrified, it aroused, it even repelled, but its force was undeniable. It has the hypnotic force of the most brutal of nightmares from which we cannot wake voluntarily. On waking finally while we lie there sweating and telling ourselves it is only a dream, our heart beats madly as we keep remembering. He articulated as no other an American nightmare. That he could not waken out of it himself is our loss.

Nick Aaron Ford. "Battle of the Books: A Critical Survey of Significant Books by and About Negroes Published in 1960." *Phylon*, 22 (Second Quarter, 1961), 119–20.

The most significant event of 1960 affecting the literature of Negroes throughout the world was the untimely death of Richard Wright in a Paris clinic at the age of fifty-two. Undoubtedly his was the strongest, most listened to (although not necessarily the most heeded), most unchanging, and most uncompromising literary voice that the colored world could claim. He began his writing career with a book of four short stories entitled *Uncle Tom's Children* (1938) and ended it with *Eight Men*, a manuscript of eight short stories sent to the publisher in 1960 and published January 23, 1961. In both books, although twenty-two years apart, the battle is the same: a stinging protest, sometimes subtle and sometimes starkly overt, against the second-class citizenship of colored people throughout the world. The ten books in between have often changed the battleground, but the adversaries have always been the same: the white supremacists wherever they may reside and in whatever guise they may practice their beliefs.

Since 1950 the critics have been saying that the novel (or short story) of social protest is dead and that it could never be revived. Wright, therefore, according to this point of view, had become an anachronism. And any novelist or short story writer who should attempt to revive social protest (especially from a racial standpoint) would never be read. Such a philosophy was expressed by Robert Bone in *The Negro Novel in America* (1958). But it is strangely ironic that in the year that Wright died five of the most significant novels dealing with racial themes, two of them best sellers (one a Book-of-the-Month selection) are in the Wright tradition of social protest (although in two of them, neither likely to be widely read, the protest is largely against the Negro).

It is fitting, therefore, that we dedicate this survey to Richard Wright and begin it with his own posthumous *Eight Men*.

In each of the eight stories in *Eight Men* Richard Wright presents a situation in which a colored man is the victim of the white man's inhumanity. In half of them the white man or the white man's cause suffers because of this inhumanity. In all of them the reader is made aware that the Negro characters are the sensitive ones, the knowing ones, the superior ones, and that appearances are usually wrong, that the strong are never right, and that the prejudiced whites are to be pitied as much as the wronged Negroes.

Half of the stories have been published before, three of them more than fifteen years ago. The new ones are not as good as the old, either in style or content. They vary in types from the purely symbolic such as "The Man Who Lived Underground" and "Man, God Ain't Like That" to the purely biographical such as "The Man Who Went to Chicago." The settings are also varied: the South, the North, Scandinavia, Africa. In style they range from almost pure exposition to almost pure drama entirely dependent upon dialogue. Probably the most logical conclusion one can reach after reading these stories is that they are, with perhaps one or two exceptions, markedly inferior to those in *Uncle Tom's Children* (1938). It appears that this gifted writer had used up the great reserves of his creative power and that he had nothing significant to add to the vision of *Native Son* and *Black Boy*. It may be that the heart attack in the Paris clinic saved this tortured artist from a fate worse than death. . . .

Saunders Redding. "Home Is Where the Heart Is." *The New Leader*, 44 (December 11, 1961), 24–25.

The dedication of Richard Wright's posthumous book, *Eight Men*, to three French friends "whose kindness has made me feel at home in an alien land" is an irony the more poignant because Wright did not intend it. He did not have the ironic cast of mind and heart. Except in intimate privacy, at rare ease with his friends when he was often gay and bright-faced as a child, he indulged no knack for mockery, especially if it was turned against himself, no eye for fun, no ear or tongue for jests. In public—and his books were public—he took the world and all men as he took himself, with deadly seriousness.

The dedication of *Eight Men* was gravely meant as an expression of gratitude, and in this sense it was true. But in a more important sense it was not. If Wright was at home in the "alien land" where he lived for nearly 15 years, how could he have written, near the close of those years, "I am a rootless man"? At home and rootless: could both things be true? "But," he added, "I am neither psychologically distraught nor in any wise particularly perturbed because of it." Without exception, directly or by implication, his published works refute him. No modern writer of comparable great gifts and reputation has been so mistaken in his judgment of himself, nor understood and valued the sources of his spirit so little.

Wright the novelist was not at home in France. He never absorbed, nor ever was absorbed in, the strange environment, the Gallic atmosphere. He saw the *mise en scène*, but did not wholly comprehend it, nor did he have the writer's sense of being in it. France was for him what it had been for Joyce: a friendly lodging and a refuge, a comfortable convenience, a place to hang his hat—but not a home.

Wright never wrote about France. He could not. His passions were not there; they were involved elsewhere. The one thing French that caught him was existentialism (Jean-Paul Sartre, Simone de Beauvoir), but this held him only long enough for him to write his one unqualifiedly bad novel. And even *The Outsider* was an American novel—that is, it was a novel about an American Negro—and in its dedication the word "alien" crops up again: "For Rachel, my daughter who was born on alien soil." When Wright wrote this, he had lived in France for nine years; and in the ninth year, thinking that the "ancestral home of millions of American Negroes," Africa's Gold Coast, would be less alien, he went there. But the Gold Coast was not home, either: The book he wrote about it is a long statement of that fact.

In Spain, Wright was nearer home. There he "felt most keenly . . . the needless, unnatural, and utterly barbarous nature of the psychological suffering . . . [because] I am an American Negro with a background of psychological suffering." What drew his attention was "the undeniable and uncanny psychological affinities that they [Spanish Protestants] held in common with American Negroes." Finally, there is the dedication of *White Man, Listen!* to those "who seek desperately for a home for their hearts."

His heart's home and his mind's tether was in America. It is not the America of the moving pictures, nor of Thomas Wolfe, John P. Marquand and John O'Hara's novels, nor of the histories of Allan Nevins and C. J. H. Hayes. It is the America that only Negroes know: a ghetto of the soul, a boundary of the mind, a confine of the heart. And it was not unusual that Wright should seek escape from it and try to reject it. Other Negro writers have done so, and some are still doing it.

There are various ways to escape. Some pretend there is no such America. Some, like Jean Toomer, fair enough to pass, go into the white race. Countee Cullen and William Braithwaite, both poets, turned to fantasy. Some—William Demby, William Gardner Smith, Chester Himes and James Baldwin—like Wright, expatriate themselves in Italy, Switzerland, Spain or France. But no matter how it is done, escape is a compulsive act of self-abnegation, and the moment the Negro writer begins to do it he begins to flag as a creative artist. He turns precious and "arty"; honesty deserts him; dedication wilts; passion chills.

America has not yet changed to the extent that a Negro writer can deny, effectively suppress or truly escape what Wright himself defined as the "inevitable race consciousness which three hundred years of Jim Crow living has burned into the Negro's heart." He cannot escape the supra-consciousness of what living in America has made him. He can try, as Wright tried, and, failing of Wright's reserve of strength, the effort will reduce him to fatuity or to shadow, while the accomplishment—improbable—would kill him altogether.

Why try to escape? I wish the answer were as simple, as readily explicable and as concrete as it is true. One tries because the supra-consciousness of being Negro in America is a perversion of being a man, of being human. It cripples what one is born to be—equi-souled with other men. It is a cruel, forced alienation from the community of man, a crime against the *natural* self.

If the pathos of man is that he yearns to be whole, hungers for fulfillment and strives for a sense of community with others, it is the particular tragedy of the Negro in America that success (even as an artist) does not gratify the yearning, great fame does not feed the hunger and the wealth of Croesus does not abate the struggle to be free, whole and naturally absorbed in the cultural oneness of his native land. "The fact of separation from the culture of his native land," Wright wrote a few years back, "has . . . sunk into the Negro's heart. The Negro loves his land, but that land rejects him." He is always apart. He is, God help him, always alone. So he seeks a country where he will not be alone. But all such countries are "alien," and only America is home. "I know America"—these are Wright's words —"I know what a great nation and people America could be, but it won't be until there is only *one* American, regardless of his color . . . "

This is the knowledge his creative passions fed on. It is bitter food, and so his books are bitter; but it sustained his great honesty and integrity as a writer. Insofar as he used this knowledge to appeal to the cognitive side of man's being, as he did in *Twelve Million Black Voices*, certain sections of *White Man, Listen!* and in various essays, he followed in the tradition of more provincial Negro writers, whose effort was to destroy the prevailing racial stereotypes.

This is an honorable tradition, and Wright, too, learned from the philosopher-psychologists (especially William James), the sociologists and social activists. But Wright was no one's disciple. He quickened the tradition with his own passionate vitality; he glorified it with his artist's skill for appealing to the connotative and affective side of man's being. He transmuted what he learned into the art of *Uncle Tom's Children, Native Son* and *Black Boy*—art that was, as Dorothy Canfield Fisher said, "honest, dreadful, heartbreaking."

But Wright's art suffered of late. The limitations of mood, the restricted inventiveness and the congeneric characterizations which defined his earlier work became more evident as they became less projective of the small, new realities and the big, new *Weltansicht* of the only place and people that could ever be Wright's home. Angry scorn, alternating with bleak despair, was no longer enough. Violence and brutal physical degradation were still a part of the new reality, but no longer all. Cowardice, self-abasement and unmitigated suffering now fail to highlight the drama and the big dramatic scenes.

It is no wonder, then, that the best stories in *Eight Men* were written before 1946. Fishbelly Tucker in Wright's latest novel, *The Long Dream*, is Big Boy of one of the earliest stories, and Big Boy grew up to be Bigger Thomas in *Native Son*. But *The Long Dream* is less than a shadow of the realities of the decade past and the one just begun. It is simply not true. It is honest, but only to the memory of things past, to passions spent, to moods gone vapid, and sometimes expressed in vaporous language:

"He peered out of his window and saw vast, wheeling populations of ruled stars swarming in the convened congresses of the skies anchored amidst nations of space and he prayed wordlessly that a bright, bursting tyrant of living sun would soon lay down its golden laws to loosen the locked regions of his heart and cast the shadow of his dream athwart the stretches of time."

Wright had forgotten the tough American idiom. He had been gone from home too long. And perhaps in a subliminal, uneasy way he knew this. The rootlessness, which he once boasted did not perturb him, made him restless. He spread himself thin. He could not settle down to the writing of novels, which, when he was at his best, was the thing he could do superbly.

He was no actor, but he went to Argentina and played the lead in the moving picture version of *Native Son*. He went to Africa; he went to Spain; he went to Indonesia for the Afro-Asian Conference, and wrote a book about that too. He wrote radio scripts. He adapted things from the French language. He helped some French Africans, largely Senegalese, organize the international Society of African Culture, but soon broke with the Senegalese and all their works. He went to England on what he hoped would be more than just a visit. He had ambitions to become a critic of jazz. He did everything but the one thing that would make the living, anguished substance of his best books flow again. He did not go home.

But now he is at rest, and he has earned it; has earned, too, the right to be judged by his best. Broadly defined, that best was in the moral stance from which he never wavered, and in his courage and enduring power as a writer. And, for those who knew Dick Wright as a friend, it was in his kindness as a man.

Checklist of Additional Reviews

Kirkus Reviews, 28 (November 15, 1960), 973.

Library Journal, 85 (December 1, 1960), 4394.

Booklist, 57 (January 15, 1961), 294.

W. G. Rogers. *Saturday Review*, 44 (January 21, 1961), 65–66.

James Baldwin. *The Reporter*, 24 (March 16, 1961), 52–55.

Bookmark, 20 (April 1961), 169.

Wisconsin Library Bulletin, 57 (September 1961), 309.

Notes

RICHARD WRIGHT

Lawd Today

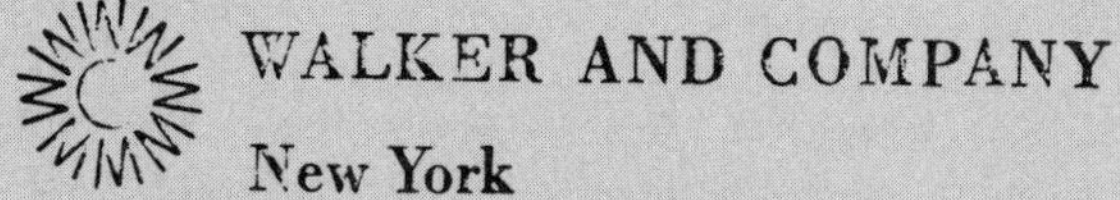

WALKER AND COMPANY
New York

Lawd Today

Granville Hicks. "Dreiser to Farrell to Wright." *Saturday Review*, 46 (March 30, 1963), 37–38.

According to the publisher Richard Wright's *Lawd Today* was written before *Native Son*, which would make it his first novel and contemporary with the stories in *Uncle Tom's Children*. I should like to know more than that. Did Wright himself decide against publication, or, as is more likely, was the novel turned down by a publisher or publishers? And, however that may be, why did he not take up the manuscript again after he had become famous? It is less powerful than either *Native Son* or *Black Boy*, but it has its own kind of interest.

It is the story of one day in the life of Jake Jackson, a Negro post office clerk in Chicago. The day is February 12, 1936, and though the fact that this is Lincoln's Birthday has only minor significance for Jake—"Old Abe Lincoln sure was a smart man"—it has an ironic bearing on the story.

Jake rises sullenly, quarrels with his wife, gives her a slap and a kick, eats a large breakfast, dresses fastidiously, goes out, loses money at policy, has a haircut, joins some of his fellow workers in a game of bridge, eats lunch, and goes to work. At the post office he pleads successfully for his job, which is in jeopardy; borrows a hundred dollars at an exorbitant rate of interest; is bawled out by an inspector for carelessness, and gets through the tedious work day. After work, with the borrowed hundred dollars, which he and his wife need for a dozen purposes, he takes his three friends to a whorehouse. After a brief time of pleasure he finds that his pocket has been picked, and there is a fight. When he gets home, drunk, he has a row with his wife and breaks up the furniture.

The day is described in unsparing detail. More than two pages, for instance, are devoted to Jake's combing of his recalcitrant hair. We are allowed to read the circulars he finds in his mailbox, and we are told how policy is played. Movie posters are described, and the conversation that goes on in Doc Higgins's Tonsorial Palace is reported. The bridge game, with three sample hands, runs to nine pages. A medicine man's spiel takes six. Wright gives a full account of the processes by which mail is sorted, together with pages of the aimless conversation with which the four friends accompany their work.

Growing up in Chicago, and starting out as a writer in the middle Thirties, Wright could scarcely have failed to be influenced by James T. Farrell, who was just beginning to have a strong effect on American fiction. As Farrell had learned something about documentation from Dreiser, so Wright had learned from Farrell. At this point he was clumsier than Farrell, but he had found a way of expressing his vision of life in the Chicago he knew.

What interests me is that, although Wright was a Communist sympathizer and very possibly a member of the Communist Party when he wrote the novel, he did not make it a piece of direct Communist propaganda. Jake is no Communist; on the contrary, he denounces and ridicules the only Communist who appears in the novel. Nor does Wright portray Jake simply as a victim of the capitalist system. He is a victim, to be sure; but of a great complex of forces. Whatever Wright's political opinions may have been, his vision as a creative artist went far beyond them.

If the novel would have been disturbing to most orthodox Communists in the Thirties, it would have been equally distressing to many Negroes. Far from setting an example to members of his race, Jake is a contemptible person. He treats his wife brutally and indulges his appetites with outrageous selfishness. He is improvident, gullible, superstitious, lazy. Although hatred of white discrimination is bred in his bones, he has no sense of racial solidarity—"Yeah, it takes a black sonofabitch to rub it into his own people"—and he regards as fools those Negroes who work for the betterment of their people.

I have used so many negatives that one might get the impression that Jake has no positive qualities, but this is not true. He has a capacity for the enjoyment of life, and even in the dreary day Wright describes there are moments of excitement and satisfaction. At the end, when he is reflecting ruefully on the loss of his hundred dollars, he thinks, "But when I was flying I was a flying fool."

Jake, on this Lincoln's Birthday, is a slave—of an unjust economic system, of racial prejudice, of faulty education—but he is not merely a slave, any more than he is merely a Negro. He is a man, erring but alive.

James Baldwin, in one of the three essays on Wright in *Nobody Knows My Name*, has written: "It is strange to begin to suspect, now, that Richard Wright was never, really, the social and polemical writer he took himself to be. In my own relations with him, I was always exasperated by his notions of society, politics, and history, for they seemed to me utterly fanciful. I never believed that he had any real sense of how a society is put together. It had not occurred to me, and perhaps it had not occurred to him, that his major interests as well as his power lay elsewhere."

Wright, as Baldwin says, was not made to be a political thinker, and it was his misfortune that he lived in a time that cast him in that role. He outgrew his Communism, of course, but he continued to think of himself as a novelist of ideas, and in 1953, under the influence of Jean-Paul Sartre and Simone de Beauvoir, he attempted an existentialist novel, *The Outsider*, which was weak precisely where he wanted it to be strong. (It is interesting to note that the hero of that novel begins as a worker in the Chicago post office, though he has gone a long way by the time the novel ends.) Baldwin observes: "His great forte, it now seems to me, was an ability to convey inward states by means of externals."

Lawd Today was an apprentice work, and Wright soon learned to handle externals more adroitly, but even here what Baldwin says is applicable. Clumsy as the massing of detail sometimes is, we do come to know not only the society in which Jake lives but also Jake himself, and, despicable as he is, we come to feel with and for him.

We often have occasion to wonder why this American writer or that was frustrated and failed to fulfill his promise. With Wright we can make a good guess. It was his misfortune that he became first a Communist and then a self-appointed spokesman for the Negro people of the world. What he was capable of as a writer is evident even in so imperfect a work as *Lawd Today*.

Louise Giles. *Library Journal*, 88 (April 1, 1963), 1549.

A posthumous novel written before "Native Son," this is one day in the life of Jake Jackson, a Negro postal clerk in the Chicago of the Depression. Burdened with debt, an unhappy marriage, and a sharp sense of frustration at being a Negro, Jake, infuriated to find out that his wife, Lil, will have to have an expensive operation soon, picks an argument with her and terminates it by beating her brutally. He borrows $100 and goes with friends to a house of ill-repute to try to forget his troubles, but only succeeds in bringing on more. The atmosphere of "Lawd Today" is just as miserable as that of "Native Son," but it is not nearly so powerful a novel. The characterizations, especially that of Jake, are cruel and brilliant, but the basic implication, as in Wright's other novels, that Negroes are the victims of their environment and there is nothing they themselves can do about the situation, simply does not obtain today. Nevertheless, an important book—one that most libraries should purchase.

"Native Sons." *Time*, 81 (April 5, 1963), 106.

"It is a complex fate to be an American." That this goes double for the American Negro, novelist James Baldwin has made clear. As a spokesman for his generation of U.S. Negroes, Baldwin demonstrates how complicated can be the business of defining what that fate is. Things were simpler for yesterday's generation, which had its voice in the novels of Richard Wright, who died in 1960, aged 52.

Wright's *Lawd Today* was never published during his life, and it predates *Native Son*, which established his reputation. It tells of a dreadful day in the dreadful life of Jake Jackson, a faceless phantom of insulted life from Chicago's black ghetto. Greedy, but with never enough ham hocks and collard greens, lecherous, but always frustrated, aggressive, but always a victim (even to his beaten, tumor-plagued wife, who cuts him up bad at the end of a long, long day), Jake is no left-wing stereotype of a good man. He and society match each other in crude nastiness. The Depression and the code of "The Man" (meaning the white man) press down on him like the lid on a garbage can.

Speaking of Wright today, Baldwin observes: "Today's racial manifestoes are being written very differently." Where is the difference? With Wright, the pain of being a Negro is basically economic—its site is mainly in the pocket. With Baldwin, the pain suffuses the whole man, so that he cannot even stand the white liberals who would "offer" him the equality that is his by right.

Wright today should be judged, Baldwin says, by "how accurately or deeply the life of Chicago's South Side had been conveyed." It is hard to judge. Even if half-true, *Lawd Today* is an appalling document. As an artist, Wright was as crude and humorlessly "sincere" as his Depression-period white twin, James Farrell. The U.S. Negro of Baldwin's generation would not be as credulous as was Wright's Jake Jackson, who was dazzled by a preposterous parade of a mythical black army headed by "The Supreme Undisputed Exalted Commander of the Allied Imperial African War Councils unto the Fourth and Last Generations." Yet Baldwin himself has admitted to having been tempted by less bizarre but more sinister desperado politics of the Black Muslims. If Baldwin's sights are higher than Wright's, it is in part because Wright helped to raise them. Wright and Baldwin had one thing in common: the demand to be treated as men. When this elementary thing is denied, no wonder fantasy comes as an only friend.

Wright saw society as an iron cage for his Jake Jackson. There was no key; the cage must be smashed. Nothing less than revolutionary Communism would do. But the Communists betrayed Wright as badly as Baldwin feels let down by the white liberals. The time came when he saw that colored comrades would denounce a fellow Negro in the presence of white comrades. Wright abandoned the fight and fled to Paris with his white wife.

Baldwin met Wright there. Of course, the meeting was awkward: Baldwin, indeed, was standing on Wright's shoulders. No more books can be written in which the fate of the U.S. Negro is as nasty, brutish, short and hard as it was only yesterday for Jake Jackson. But *Lawd Today* is a thing to remember.

Lewis Gannett. *New York Herald Tribune Books*, May 5, 1963, p. 10.

"Uncle Tom's Children" (1938) stories written by Richard Wright when he was on relief with the Federal Writers Project, gave Wright his first national recognition. "Native Son" (1940), a Book-of-the-Month Club choice, established him as the most powerful Negro novelist in the United States. Before he died, in 1960, he published half a dozen other books. He did not choose to publish "Lawd Today," a story written, by internal evidence, in 1936, and he was wise. It is a kind of apprentice-work, written in the floundering years after Wright had left the Communist Party, before he had formulated his own conception of Bigger Thomas, the "bad nigger" who never had a chance to be good.

Jake Jackson, the hero—if that be the word for it—is another frustrated, hopeless no-good. He begins by beating up his wife, gets drunk on his job at the post-office, is robbed in a cheap joint of the money he borrows to pay his wife's doctor bill, winds up asserting his manhood by shouting obscenities, beating his wife and goading her into cutting him. The essential picture is not unlike that of Bigger, but the tension of "Native Son" is not here, the dialogue is monotonously long drawn out, the overtones are missing. The book's chief interest is as a stage in the development of a writer who, later, made his mark.

Doris Grumbach. *The Critic,* 21 (June-July, 1963), 82.

The late Richard Wright wrote powerful novels dealing with the lives of American city Negroes, the most famous of which was *Native Son*. This posthumous book is like the others in spirit—raw, violent, blasphemous, painfully direct and honest—but perhaps because much of its material had been used by others in fiction, since his first works, it seems less original, forceful and interesting. Compressed into a single day (Lincoln's Birthday) in the life of Jake Jackson, a postal clerk in Chicago in the early thirties, the novel takes us on a hideous and painful odyssey through tonsorial palaces, bedrooms of slum flats, sweatshop-like working places and brothels; we follow Jake along his vengeful, cheated, violent and monomaniac way. The strength of this study lies in the undeviating honesty of this portrait of a social victim; the weakness is in its attempts at excessive realism so that the pages are overloaded with transcriptions of advertising signs, song lyrics, pieces of crackpot religious mail (recreated whole) and lengthy speeches by street-corner orators about hell-fire.

Nick Aaron Ford. "The Fire Next Time?: A Critical Survey of Belles Lettres by and About Negroes Published in 1963." *Phylon*, 25 (Second Quarter, 1964), 129–30.

. . . When Richard Wright died unexpectedly in a Paris clinic, November 28, 1960, at the age of fifty-two, he left two unpublished manuscripts. The first, a collection of short stories entitled *Eight Men*, was published January 23, 1961, two months after his death; the second, *Lawd Today*, which probably was written during his early years, was published in 1963.

Lawd Today is a dull, unimaginative novel concerned with the final twenty hours of the life of Jake Jackson. The setting is Chicago during the depression era when Franklin D. Roosevelt was president. The major characters are Jake's wife, Lil, and his three fellow postal clerks, Bob, Al, and Slim.

The action begins at eight o'clock on February 12 (Lincoln's birthday) and ends about four o'clock the following morning with the death of Jake at the hands of the deeply religious Lil. Between the beginning and the end Jake engages in the following activities: berates and beats his sick wife, who is in desperate need of an operation to remove a tumor; reads his morning newspaper with such headlines as "Roosevelt Strikes at Money Changers," "Hitler Calls on World to Smash Jews," "Einstein Says Space Bends," and "Communists Riot in Streets of New York";

visits the headquarters of a numbers racket and plays the numbers suggested by his dream of the previous night; visits a barber shop where the talk revolves around communism, white women, and the Civil War; goes to Bob's room, where the four friends play cards and talk about Father Divine ("All the folks hates us black people, so Gawd might have done made up His mind to show 'em that everybody's equal. He came as a Jew last time, and how come he won't come as a nigger now? Boy, if that guy *was* Gawd, wouldn't the white folks just die!"); goes to work with his friends on the night shift at the Chicago Post Office, where the Negro clerks complain about the unfair treatment by the white bosses ("Uncle Sam sure mean to his black boys." "Look like white folks don't want us to have nothing."); after working hours accompanies his friends to a brothel where he is beaten, robbed, and ejected; reaches home about four in the morning and immediately begins to beat Lil who is asleep on her knees by the bed; is finally cut to death by broken glass in the hands of his long-suffering wife.

The story is melodramatic, disjointed, padded with a multitude of hackneyed episodes, and supported by conversation reminiscent of *Uncle Tom's Children, Native Son* and *The Outsider*, but devoid of any unified relevance.

It is difficult to believe that *Lawd Today* was written by Richard Wright. The "voice" (style) is the voice of Wright, but the "hands" (techniques, concepts and subject matter) are the hands of a stranger. Unlike Wright's known work, it contains practically every offensive Negro stereotype known to American literature. Furthermore, it is the first book under Wright's name that has not made the white man or the white man's society the predominant villain. If it really is Wright's work, it was probably written before his first published work, *Uncle Tom's Children*, and reveals, therefore, the significant growth of his talent and vision from the beginning to his greatest creation, *Native Son*. It is doubtful that the mature Wright ever would have agreed to its publication. . . .

Checklist of Additional Reviews

Staughton Lynd. "The New Negro Radicalism." *Commentary,* 36 (September 1963), 252–56.

Betty Schneider. *Community,* 23 (January 1964), 14.

Nick Aaron Ford. *CLA Journal,* 7 (March 1964), 269–70.

Notes

AMERICAN HUNGER

Richard Wright

Afterword by Michel Fabre

1817

HARPER & ROW, PUBLISHERS
New York, Hagerstown, San Francisco, London

American Hunger

Roy E. Perry.
Nashville Banner,
May 14, 1977.

A continuation of his classic autobiography *Black Boy*, Richard Wright's *American Hunger* is a record of the author's life after he left the South. Journeying to Chicago, Wright lived a marginal existence as a store clerk, dishwasher, postal worker, and struggling writer.

The heart of the book describes Wright's membership in the Communist Party (1932 to 1944), his efforts to maintain his individuality and integrity as an artist *vis-a-vis* the political demands of the Party, and, finally, his resignation from the CPUSA.

Wright was one of the first members of his race to reject openly the Jim Crow stereotype of Negroes as ignorant, shiftless darkies who shuffle their feet and mumble "Yassuh." He forced us to look "beyond the mask of the smiling Negro" to see a new breed of black man hungry to be treated with dignity as human beings.

The working title of *American Hunger* was "The Horror and the Glory," an ambiguous phrase in that it could be conceived to apply to the Negro's experience in the South, the Negro's experience in America as a whole, or, in Wright's case, the Negro's experience in the Communist Party.

Wright had arrived early at a radical questioning of American society: "Could a Negro ever live halfway like a human being in this g——n country?" Fleeing to the North, he found essentially the same kind of misery he had experienced in the South: "I wondered if a Negro who did not smile and grin was as morally loathsome to whites as a cook who spat into the food."

Pondering the problem of human misery, human dignity, and human unity, Wright moved from his "vision of the disinherited" to a "vision of a communal world." He joined the Communist Party, believing that he saw demonstrated there a new spirit of human worth and dignity, and a remarkable absence of racial discrimination: "How had these people, denying profit and home and God, made that hurdle that even the churches of America had not been able to make?"

The Communist Party, however, became for Wright a "god that failed." He found that the CPUSA could not tolerate "the heritage of free thought—which no man could escape if he read at all." As an artist, an individualist, a thinker, an intellectual, Wright was feared by the Party leadership. Blacklisted as a Trotsky-like intellectual, Wright could only shake his head sadly and uncomprehendingly, and resign from the party.

Ironically, the Communist Party, in revolting against Russian tyranny and in fighting against the Nazi menace, had taken on characteristics of both. The Party had become "fascistic," anti-intellectual, rigidly doctrinaire and authoritarian, and bent upon conducting its own "witch hunts."

Wright comments: "Deep down I

feared their militant ignorance. I had fled men who did not like the color of my skin, and now I was among men who did not like the tone of my thoughts." A radical in the truest sense of the term, Wright resembled Kierkegaard's "Individual" who could not tolerate, or be tolerated by, the herd men of a mass society.

In a brilliantly perceptive "Afterword," Michel Fabre (Professor of American and Afro-American Studies, The Sorbonne) writes: "*American Hunger* takes us far from the hopeful and potentially rosy ending of *Black Boy*. It constitutes a more profound questioning of man's predicament in a mass consumption society whose daily practices negate its humanistic pretenses. It extends his argument into the existential quandary of a politically conscious human being confronted with a barren social and spiritual horizon. (It states that) there is no redemption for human suffering in a culture governed by the 'lust for trash.' "

American Hunger is a "radical" book in the best sense of the term: it grimaces with the horror of social crimes; it glows with the glory of social consciousness; and through it all there speaks the authentic, intelligent voice of a man hungry for truth, for decency, and for human dignity.

Reading this book, I was reminded of Pascal's words: "We are surprised and delighted when we come across the natural style, because we expected to meet an author and instead find a man." Amidst all the works of "trash," this book stands out like a priceless gem. . . .

Jack Conroy. *Kansas City Star*, May 15, 1977, pp. D 1–2. *Panorama-Chicago Daily News*, May 21–22, 1977, pp. 6, 10. *San Francisco Sunday Examiner & Chronicle*, June 26, 1977, "Scene," p. 2.

I first heard of Richard Wright through a young postoffice worker who had sent me a story about workers in a tire factory in Butler, Pa., his home town. It was called "Another Morning" and detailed in rather dreary but graphic terms the start of another day for a tire maker. The author chose "Tom Butler" as a pseudonym, after his home town. Butler wrote me that one of his fellow clerks was a young Negro named Richard Wright, and he too had been doing some writing. I referred both of them to the newly formed John Reed Club, a forum where writers, artists, musicians and others involved in artistic creation could meet and swap ideas.

Both Butler and Wright joined, and Butler soon wrote me of their pleasure and inspiration at finding such a congenial and helpful outfit. "I don't think either of us will ever regret it," Butler wrote, and I don't think Wright did. His difficulties with the Communist Party arose mainly from the efforts of overzealous functionaries to dictate a Marxist ideological matrix into which creative John Reeders were urged to mold their output.

A reading of "American Hunger," the

second half of "Black Boy," is enough to convince one that Wright did enjoy membership in the John Reed Club for some time and that it was of benefit to his writing. Some months after his poems appeared in the Anvil I met him in a national convention of the John Reed Clubs held in a loft on South State Street, opposite the Sears store. In the basement of Sears free samples of a very tasty California wine were being distributed in generous-sized Lily cups. Dick was not taking part in the general jollification but walking about ill at ease or standing alone, rarely speaking to anyone.

Later in the evening at a party thrown in the apartment of the artist Morris Topchevsky, one of the hard-working wheelhorses of the John Reed, I sought him out and in the quieter atmosphere he became somewhat more talkative. On learning that I had contributed to H. L. Mencken's American Mercury, he told how he had by subterfuge obtained some of the Sage of Baltimore's books from the Memphis Public Library. A somewhat enlightened Irish-Catholic who had worked with him at the American Optical Company in Memphis had provided him with his library card and permitted Dick to forge notes saying something like this; "Please give this nigger boy some books by H. L. Mencken." The suspicious librarian, upon being assured that he did not intend to read the books himself, handed him "A Book of Prejudices" and "Prefaces."

The rambunctious Mencken opened up new horizons for the young writer. The first novel he read on Mencken's recommendation was "Main Street." Wright said little of his own writing that evening, though he disparaged slightly the two poems—"Strength" and "Child of the Dead and Forgotten Gods"—that I had just published in the Anvil. It was hard for me, too, to associate the fiery revolutionary verse with the quiet-spoken, mild-mannered author. Fiction, he said, he thought would be his forte, and I asked him to send in a story for the Anvil but he never did.

"American Hunger" in a version including the first part, dealing with Wright's life in the South and ending with his arrival in Chicago, was originally scheduled to be published in March, 1945, as a dual selection of the Book of the Month Club. The upshot was that the first section was published separately as "Black Boy." Part of the last half subsequently appeared here and there in magazines in the 1940s—about early days in Chicago and accounts of various jobs Wright held, his frustrating experience with the Communist Party, his resignation and his subsequent ostracism.

The note of hope that pervades the ending of "Black Boy," as Richard enters the promised land of Chicago soon is muted in "American Hunger." He is astonished at being able to sit beside a white man in a street car, but inasmuch as he had understood the definite boundaries established by "the ethics of living Jim Crow" (as he put it) in the South, a state of ambiguity and a feeling of uncertainty prevailed in Chicago. Acceptable behavior tended to vary with individual and situation. In "Black Boy" Wright recalled an incident where a Negro named Shorty would permit white men to kick him upon payment of a quarter:

"I had stood aghast as Shorty offered himself to be kicked by a white man, but now, while working in Chicago, I was learning that even a kick was better than uncertainty . . . I could now sympathize with—though I could never bring myself to approve—those tortured blacks who had given up and gone to their white tormentors and said: 'Kick me, if that's all there is for me, kick me and let me feel at home, let me have peace.' "

Wright first attended a John Reed Club meeting that was an editorial session for the club's magazine, Left Front. He was surprised to be asked to sit in and even more surprised when he was shortly afterward made a member of the editorial board. I remember sitting with Dick long after midnight as polemical sessions raged at a cultural convention of some sort. He seemed weary and ill-disposed to join the fray and as he left the hall he remarked that radicals ought to talk less and do more.

The latter part of "American Hunger" is so filled with the internecine struggles in the John Reed Club and the Communist Party apparatus in Chicago that it becomes somewhat tedious reading. With the customary (and understandable) caution deemed prudent in the times, Wright has rarely given any real names of the dialectical toreadors, so it is difficult even for a witness to the times to identify some of them.

One of the most grotesque episodes has to do with an escaped madman who terrorized the local comrades and almost succeeded in engineering the expulsion of a painter whose conduct and Marxism actually was above reproach. The lunatic's fluent Marxism, his vague identification as somebody high in the party stood him in stead for some time.

Richard finally found it imperative to resign from the Communist Party, and was thereafter branded as a Trotskyite—in the C.P. lexicon the vilest kind of traitor. Actually, he pointed out, "A Trotskyite or a man bent upon wrecking or disrupting the work of the Communist Party would have remained in the organization so as to better quarrel, obstruct." Nevertheless he felt that the C.P. and its far-reaching and malignant power worked against him first in the Federal Theater Project and then in the Writers Project. A member of the writers' union on the Writers Project, he tried to march with its contingent in the May Day parade of 1936. Wright dramatically relates the denouement as he was forcibly ejected from the line of march by two C.P. musclemen:

"Hands lifted me bodily from the sidewalk. I felt myself being pitched headlong through the air. . . . I could not believe what had happened even though my hands were smarting and bleeding. I had suffered physical assault by two white Communists with black Communists looking on. . . . Suddenly the vast ranks of the Communist Party began to move. Scarlet banners with the hammer and sickle emblem of world revolution lifted, and fluttered in the May breeze. Voices were chanting. The tramp of many feet shook the earth. A long line of set-faced men and women, white and black, flowed past me."

Sitting on a bench in Grant Park, he concluded the marchers had been blinded by their enemies. He recalled the stories in which he "had assigned a role of honor and glory to the Communist Party," and he was glad that he had let them down. Nevertheless he knew in his heart "that I would never be able to write that way again, would never be able to feel with that simple sharpness about life, and never again make so total a commitment of faith."

An afterword by Michel Fabre, professor of American and Afro-American studies at the Sorbonne, provides valuable historical and interpretive light. Dr. Fabre is Wright's literary executor and author of the definitive biography, "The Unfinished Quest of Richard Wright."

Samuel Whitman. *Long Beach* (California) *Independent Press-Telegram*, May 20, 1977.

The average American citizen, most naturally and quite casually, accepts the benefits of his living in this great democracy of ours. The free choices that are his; the many alternatives, advantages, opportunities and freedoms of movements, become part of his taken-for-granted life styles; part of his social, ethnic, economic and personal environment. Like the fishes of the sea, swimming freely in their waters, probably never thinking much about their watery environment because they know no other environment.

So, when this average American hears some other Americans complain about certain lacks of these various liberties, he finds it difficult to relate to these situations. It is not easy for him to give such situations significant attention or sympathy.

This is what I feel the great black novelist Richard Wright, had in mind when he wrote this book. He hoped to "reach" this average American, in this sequel to his famous autobiographical work "Black Boy."

With soul searching language he bared every sensitive nerve in his body to convey what it spiritually means to another human being when the democratic freedoms they treat so cavalierly, are denied him.

In calm dispassionate, every-day terms he portrays what black people are confronted with; why all of us—blacks and whites—should try to understand why certain attitudes and actions of other individuals are different from ours.

Alden Whitman. *Chicago Tribune Book World*, May 22, 1977, Section 7, p. 1.

This is a tantalizing semibook, a severed segment of Richard Wright's "Black Boy," his autobiography published to much acclaim in 1945 and widely distributed among middlebrow whites by the Book-of-the-Month-Club. Wright died in Paris in 1960, a lonely, disoriented exile who had lost his creative powers. And now, 17 years later, the concluding chapters to "Black Boy," excised in 1945, have been exhumed and published.

The precise circumstances of the excision are a mystery, since no one apparently asked Wright about them before he died. It seems likely, however, according to Michel Fabre, that Wright agreed to lopping off these chapters at the suggestion of his editor at Harper's, very probably because such a step would enhance selection of what was left by the Book-of-the-Month Club. The internal evidence of "Black Boy" suggests that this is a safe speculation, for that book as published ends on a comfortably upbeat note, just the sort of thing that BOMC liked to circulate about Negroes in those days. "Black Boy," as some readers will recall, described the narrator's harsh and traumatic early life in the South and concluded with his journey to Chicago at the age of 17, with hope abounding for a happy future.

The rationale for the 1945 autobiography is also cloudy. It is unusual for anyone to sum up his life at the age of 37, which Wright was in that year. He had one major novel to his credit, "Native Son," the story of an atypical angry Negro youth who took out his frustrations against white society by two killings—one of an inoffensive white woman. Appearing in 1940, the novel was a shocker, and in the eyes of many it confirmed the view that Negroes, or blacks we would call them today, were creatures of sadistic impulse. The violent fate of Bigger Thomas, the protagonist of "Native Son"—he was condemned to death—was widely criticized at the time by many black writers.

Perhaps Wright felt their sting, and wanted to make clear that his criticism of American society was cultural, not racial. Indeed, his working title for the autobiography was "American Hunger," later amended to "Black Hunger." Whatever the reasons might have been for the autobiography, the reason for publishing "American Hunger" is bound to perplex many readers, for it is offered with only the sketchiest biographical framework, and one, moreover, that assumes that Wright remains a living presence in American letters. It would have been more useful, in my opinion, to have issued "Black Boy" complete at last, so that the reader could get the full flavor of the autobiography as Wright initially wrote it.

The publisher, however, has chosen otherwise, so what we have to deal with is Richard Wright's Chicago years and, briefly, the start of his New York experience.

What impressed him when he arrived in Chicago from the Deep South was the absence of obvious discrimination. "It was strange," he writes, "to pause before a crowded newsstand and buy a newspaper without having to wait until a white man was served." It was odd, too, to ride in a streetcar and sit beside a white. At the same time he "caught an abiding sense of insecurity in the personalities" of his black acquaintances.

Wright found a job difficult to get, only menial work being available to blacks. He was successively a porter, a kitchen worker, a postal clerk. He lived in the meanest housing, sharing limited space with an aunt, then with his mother and his siblings. He was the while a voracious reader, for he dreamed above all of becoming a writer.

He realized early on the apartness of blacks. "I feel that America's past is too shallow, her national character too superficially optimistic, her morality too suffused with color hate to accomplish so vast and complex a task"—as understanding black suffering. He also soliloquized: "I felt that the Negro could not live a full human life under the conditions imposed upon him by America . . . I felt certain that the Negro could never solve his problems until the deeper problem of American civilization had been faced and solved."

In spite of his instincts, Wright was drawn to the Communist Party, and joined it when he was out of a job and hungry. It seems doubtful that he ever bothered his head with the elements of Marxism; more important to him was the possibility of having his writing published in The Masses. To this end he became active in the John Reed Club of Chicago, and was disenchanted not to be accepted immediately as a writer.

Wright recounts his experiences as a Communist in such a fashion as to cast other blacks in unpleasant light. His membership was contentious, and by 1937 he was out of the party. His break festered, and I get the impression from this book of his protesting too much about his treatment. He was indeed published, but, according to his account, he was asked to heed the party doctrinal line more closely than he was willing to. He sounds both embittered and self-righteous.

His final years in Chicago as a member of the Federal Writers Project were also unhappy, Wright tells us, because of the tensions between him and the Communists. He would go on to New York, eager "to try to build a bridge of words between me and that world outside, that world which was so distant and elusive that it seemed unreal."

I get the distinct impression from this book of Richard Wright as a loner, a seeker in his own way of a better world. He was obviously in those years a man of invincible ego, who believed that only the beat of his own heart was worth listening to. And he was a romantic, thinking lofty thoughts about cultural unity, human wholeness, and wisdom.

Does "American Hunger" stand up by itself? Readers who come to it afresh without a rather detailed knowledge of the author are likely to be baffled. Those who know his work will find it important and interesting. I realize that these comments constitute a copout, but I do not see the book as of more than casual interest to most readers. It is essentially a sensitive vignette of Chicago life as experienced by a struggling black writer 50 years ago, but it lacks texture and context.

Michael Harrington. *Chicago Sun-Times Book Week*, May 29, 1977, p. 7. *Newark Sunday Star-Ledger*, June 26, 1977. *New Orleans Times-Picayune*, July 17, 1977.

Richard Wright was one of the two or three most talented blacks of his generation and his books "Native Son" and "Black Boy," are an important part of American literature. Now, almost 20 years after he died as an expatriate in Paris, there is a brief, but moving, coda to his autobiography. It was originally written as part of "Black Boy," but Wright decided to take it out of that volume.

"American Hunger" focuses on Wright's experiences in Chicago, and particularly upon his relationships with the Communist Party. Yet, it is not an essentially political document. What led Wright to break with the Communists was not a disagreement over their positions but rather his comrades' inability to understand him as a writer. They wanted him to concentrate on routine committee work focused on the cost of living; he rightly understood that the development of his talent required privacy, loneliness, introspection.

In his economic philosophical manuscripts Marx had commented that a genius working alone in his or her room was engaged in a social act.

Thus I read "American Hunger" as a sensitive work of an artist and psychologist who was political; not as a political tract. There are, for example, marvelous images of the shock which came to a Southern black when he entered the theoretically free, yet racially treacherous North: "While working in Memphis I had stood aghast as Shorty had offered himself to be kicked by white men; but now, while working in Chicago, I was learning that perhaps even a kick was better than uncertainty." And so he came to "a dim notion of what life meant to a Negro in America . . . not in terms of external events, lynchings, Jim Crowism and the endless brutalities, but in terms of crossed-up feeling, of psyche pain. I sensed that Negro life was a sprawling land of unconscious suffering, and there were but few Negroes who knew the meaning of their lives, who could tell their story."

In trying to tell that story, Wright came into conflict with the Communists, a group he had resisted in his early days in Chicago and then joined during the Depression. At first it had to do with a shift in cultural policy when the Party moved from its "Third Period" radicalism to the liberal alliances of the Popular Front period. But more basically, the problem arose because the Party did not, and could not, understand Wright as an artist. He was excluded, slandered, put in Coventry by his former comrades. In an unforgettable scene—Wright described it, as I remember, in the contribution to the God That Failed—he was even bodily tossed out of a May Day parade even as the marchers were singing the Internationale, the hymn to the "wretched of the earth."

And yet, if "American Hunger" shows Wright as hurt and angry and perplexed, he does not turn on the Communists and hate them in return. He tells of a party "trial" of a friend of his and is even understanding when the accused breaks down and confesses to his party crimes out of fear of being put outside the community of the oppressed. To the great and good fortune of the American people—the blacks foremost—these experiences made Wright want to speak to the common humanity of the "underpaid, bewildered black men and women" and the whites "as miserable as their black victims." In short, this is a moving memoir of the process which led to the emergence of a major writer, not simply for blacks, or for America, but for the world.

Jay Thiemeyer. *Richmond News Leader Book Page*, June 1, 1977.

This brief book is the continuation of Richard Wright's autobiographical *Black Boy*. It is actually the original conclusion to *Black Boy*, but Wright's editors cut it for "later publication," owing to its somewhat touchy contents. That was 30 years ago.

I suppose the implication of this book is that things have changed for the better since 1940, when the stunning *Native Son* came out, and 1945, when *Black Boy* was published. So, the time is ripe—really, overripe—for Wright's heretofore unpublished work. *American Hunger* is the first fruit of a project to prepare never-before-published material gleaned from his collected papers.

The book reveals a great deal about Richard Wright. It contains some writing both very good and very bad. When he indulges himself and quietly constructs his remarkably delicate psychological insights, he is at his best. When he attempts to be didactic he is dry and vapid.

He writes of the phenomenon of his life—as Richard Wright, the writer with blind faith and dedication; as a young, black American struggling out of the seemingly unbreachable containment of Southern poverty, ignorance, and racism; and as an uneasy member of the Communist Party.

Richard Wright, in the original conclusion to his autobiography, emerges as a machine-like man, steeled to his adversities—which, as much as he plays them down, are incredible. He fits nowhere, but he wants to fit, wants to contribute, and to be recognized as good.

Most of all, he wants to be understood. His voice as represented in *Black Boy*, and especially in *American Hunger*, is the voice of a courageous individual attempting some kind of nobility in an unpromising environment.

Wright seems to have sensed that not only had he never known satisfaction or an unshifting identity, but that he also probably would never know either. One of the contributions of this new material certainly will be the light shed on Wright's continuing efforts to deal with what was known in the 1940s as "the American dilemma." There is reason to believe that even this eminent series of exhibits will prove inadequate. Where *could* Wright really feel like a whole man, having been as attuned to his native land and so casually disavowed by it?

He remarks early in the book: "I sensed that Negro life was a sprawling land of unconscious suffering, and there were but few Negroes who knew the meaning of their lives, who could tell their stories."

That was Wright's burden and contribution. It is good to see this elusive figure of American letters further revealed.

Kenneth Walker. *Washington Star*, June 5, 1977, p. F-19.

For all the literary and historical achievement of Richard Wright's "Black Boy," the book has simply never fullfilled its autobiographical promise.

Providing, as it did, one of the earliest and most seering accounts of the pervasive violence that regulated 20th century race relations in the American South, "Black Boy" was easy enough to evaluate by its successes.

Even the book's depiction of the personal violence on Wright's childhood—from his literal starvation to the many deadly childhood scraps—provided a rare glimpse into the dynamics of the southern black family.

The feast in the book is so abundant that many readers are distracted from the fact that the book ends with a 19-year-old hopeful, northward looking Wright—full of an optimism his book doesn't justify.

As a result of that ending, the book leaves not only an incomplete account of Wright's personal life—which certainly did not end at 19, where the book leaves off. But the book's historical contribution was stopped cold in its tracks. The mass black exodus from the American south, as well as the reception encountered by those refugees was certainly deserving of Wright's autobiographical attention.

Wright fans troubled by that enigma will welcome the recent release of the 16 chapters Wright originally intended to serve as the ending to the book.

The chapters, released under the title "American Hunger," are *not* just commercial attempts to exploit an increasingly popular literary name. "American Hunger" is so substantive that it changes the very emphasis and direction of "Black Boy"—if, as Wright originally intended, the two books are read as one.

The same precision with which Wright depicted the brutal details of southern racial protocol is obvious in the author's account of the reception fleeing blacks encountered in the promised land of the north, where they were met by the full assault of urban ills—from massive poverty and crime to municipal corruption.

While "Black Boy" held out the promise of success and redemption in the American North, "American Hunger" ends with Wright firmly dashing his idealism for a cynicism more appropriate for a black American Communist with a ninth grade education in Chicago during the Great Depression.

The book also gives a much broader and more balanced view of Wright's overall development—as a writer, which he was foremost, a man, and a member of the American Communist party.

While "Black Boy" demonstrated well enough that Wright could write, "American Hunger" reveals just how badly the author yearned to practice his art. It was that yearning—an obsession, really—that led Wright and many other black artists at the time into Communist Party organizations.

Wright's attraction to Marxist theory—based as it is in the liberation of the oppressed classes, of which Wright was consciously a member—was real enough. But it becomes clear that the young author first cultivated his contacts with the Communists because pamphleteers were needed to write in party organs. All of which is not to suggest that the party had no influence in northern black city neighborhoods.

"American Hunger" serves as a reminder of the intense activism of the communist party in black communities. The communists, not unlike other messianic groups that flourished in black neighborhoods during the Depression, seized every issue from the economy to the Scottsboro Boys case, to garner black support. With masterful propaganda techniques—the communists had plenty to work with—the Reds led some of the largest black demonstrations at the time.

Wright provides an insider's account to why the communists' mission failed.

"American Hunger" was dropped from the book after the full two-part autobiography was set in page proofs in 1944, according to Wright biographer Michel Fabre.

It is unclear whether the Book-of-the-Month Club, which was considering the work, insisted on a book only to include Wright's experience in the south, or if Wright's editor, Edward Aswell did. But Fabre insists the author approved the change.

Whatever the genesis of that decision, the release of "American Hunger," however late, should be commended.

Herb Marynell. *Evansville* (Indiana) *Press* June 9, 1977.

The publishing firm of Harper and Row has released the first of possibly six previously unpublished books by Richard Wright, one of the most notable angry young black writers of America. Wright died in 1960.

"American Hunger" was originally planned as the second half of Wright's impressive autobiography "Black Boy," published in 1945 and recalling his childhood as a black growing up in the South.

"American Hunger" takes us from Wright's arrival in Chicago in 1927, through his struggle to survive in menial jobs and his days in the Communist party. He broke with the party in the mid-1930's and was ostracized by its members.

"American Hunger" may not be as powerful as "Black Boy" and Wright's novel-masterpiece "Native Son," published in 1940. But the concise clarity of Wright's style in "American Hunger" can still make one angry at racism, materialism and our insensitivity to our fellow man.

In fact, Wright's struggle was really more than a black trying to survive in a white-dominated existence. It's more a story of a human trying to survive among ignorance, hatred and a system impervious to humanistic needs and rights.

Wright was out-of-step from the outset. As a black dishwasher in Chicago he was suspect because he read magazines and books. Later, when he viewed communism as a possible solution to his race's and the country's woes, he was suspect, this time because he preferred to use his writing talents to aid the party. He went only to grammar school, but was an intellectual threat to the party.

Wright doesn't tell us anything new in "American Hunger." Over the past 30 years the world's failings have been pointed out many times over. It's just that Wright, as usual, says it so well.

Joseph Benson. *Greensboro Daily News.* June 12, 1977.

American Hunger is a continuation of Richard Wright's early record of childhood and youth, *Black Boy*, first published in 1945.

It deserves attention for several reasons. It is an honest autobiographical study by a major American writer. It reveals new and expansive elements of Wright's personality which shed light on his later expatriate writing. And it distinctly alters the intent and impression of *Black Boy*, long considered one of the most revealing and influential autobiographies in American literature *American Hunger* will exert considerable influence on Wright's canon.

There are three Wright autobiographies: The first never appeared—a work comprising both *Black Boy* and *American Hunger*, originally intended for publication in one volume in 1945. The second is the *Black Boy* we know, published in 1945, covering Wright through his Chicago years to 1927. The third is *American Hunger*, just published, which covers an additional ten years (1927-1937) including Wright's years in New York, his association with the Federal Writers Project of the WPA, and his affiliation with the Communist Party.

American Hunger consists of 146 pages, some of them previously published without impact, containing anecdotes and humorous episodes which make for enlightening reading. Wright's description of his employment as a store clerk, dishwasher, and other menial jobs clearly indicates the depth of racism in America and the massive pressure placed on him simply because he was black. In order to survive psychologically and succeed financially, he became a writer.

The sections on his early days with the Communist Party are especially revealing and painfully described. If nothing else, this confessional should lay to rest the myth that Wright was thoroughly indoctrinated in Marxist ideology and felt its influence the rest of his life. It is generally known that Wright attempted to remove the stigma of having once been a Communist when in 1945 he published "I Tried to be a Communist." The stigma remained. In *American Hunger* Wright describes how his function in the Communist Party developed, how it became distorted and how he was bodily removed by his comrades when attempting to march in a May Day parade.

The following passages reveal the

force of *American Hunger*. The words, spoken between Wright and a chance acquaintance, speak for themselves.

> "I got it," he said.
> "You've got what? I asked.
> "This old race problem you keep talking about," he said.
> "What about it?"
> "Well, it's this way," he explained seriously. "Let the government give every man a gun and five bullets, then let us all start over again. Make it just like it was in the beginning. The ones who come out on top, white or black, let them rule."
> His simplicity terrified me. I had never met a Negro who was so irredeemably brutalized.

The brief afterword by Michel Fabre, although it assumes a good deal of knowledge about Wright, is most helpful in describing the circumstances surrounding the publication of both *Black Boy* and *American Hunger*. Professor Fabre also includes a page of the original manuscript of *American Hunger*, bearing Wright's editing.

It is now apparent that *American Hunger* alters our view of Wright's intentions for the early joint autobiography. *Black Boy* is generally taught and discussed as an American rags-to-riches success story. Wright made it to the top through hard work and intensity. In point of fact, *American Hunger* concludes on a note of pessimism instead of promoting the American dream. Wright describes his growing distrust of all systems and ideologies. It is a personal, philosophical sense of aloneness, moving far beyond racial and political lines to discuss the human condition. Wright ended *American Hunger* still searching. The book he left behind when he died in 1960 is a remarkable testament to the power of an honest, committed writer.

Jerome W. Mondesire. *Philadelphia Inquirer*, June 12, 1977, p. 14-H.

Richard Wright's autobiographical classic "Black Boy" concluded with the very spiritual, upbeat dreams of a teenage Negro fleeing the wicked South of 1925 for a Northern dreamland. The North, to naive young Wright, was more than merely the land of opportunity; it was supposed to be the place where a black male could express his real identity—a sinful act in the South punishable by lynching or worse.

But as the recently published second part of Wright's autobiography clearly shows, "Black Boy" was only half of his story.

All migrations have two parts, a departure and an arrival. But it took 32 years for "American Hunger" to appear so we could find out what happened when Wright arrived on Chicago's South Side full of youth's expectant anxiety.

Gone was the psychological terror of his fanatically strict family; gone was the physical brutality of the Mississippi white power structure; gone was the sense of dread that shadowed Wright as he tried to avoid any situation that might force him to reveal his true feelings about whites and thus make himself vulnerable to their retribution.

But despite these differences, Wright found that Northern urban life for a black during the thirties and forties was largely a continuation of his inferior status, minus some of the more overt brutalizations.

This work, written while the late Rev. Dr. Martin Luther King, Jr. was in high school, powerfully projects Wright's struggle to find meaning in his life and his search for a white, just one, to whom he could reveal his true self.

Comfortable in a job as porter-errand boy in an optical plant, Wright thinks he can at last end his search when his white boss helpfully warns him that another black errand boy in a nearby plant is lying in wait for him, switch-blade in hand. But acting on a kernel of doubt, a kernel planted long ago by the white natives of Natchez, Miss., Wright confronts his alleged attacker and finds that his boss has lied. The white boss thought it sporting to place bets on which one of them would win the knife duel.

The depth and starkness of "Black Boy" overshadow the early pages of "American Hunger." It is not until Wright relates his tortuous love-hate relationship with the Communist Party that the book finds its own individual character.

Wright's efforts to convince his comrades of the wisdom of building a common strength upon sturdy individual contributions put him on a collision course with the party leaders. But his naive belief that he can persuade them to his point of view, against the gloomiest of odds, leads him on. This commitment to ideals, in the face of certain disaster, is convincing evidence that Black Boy has indeed matured. The dream of a racism-free haven above the Mason-Dixon line may not have come true, but this human being who once felt that he was a "non-man" in an alien white world, found through his kamikaze-like assault on the communist tide that indeed there was marrow in his soul.

It is an utter shame that this work comes 32 years after "Black Boy." The impact of the first part of the autobiography, which the afterword explains was edited to contain a conclusion of toned rejoicing, is undeniably ripened by the appearance of "American Hunger."

The appearance of "American Hunger" also helps explaim the full meaning of Wright's decision to become an expatriate. Unlike white Americans who may leave, knowing that they have a country, a black has to fight hard for many years to find his place here, knowing that America's bosom often holds only bile for so many poor young blacks. So when a black, who has toiled so hard, finally relinquishes the struggle as Wright did when he fled to Paris (where he died in 1960), it is with the full realization that he has indeed sentenced himself to this hazy, limbo-like existence because no other alternative was attainable.

"All my life I had been full of a hunger for a new way to live . . . " says Wright, still seeking meaning for his having left the South, and explaining his failure to find salvation in Chicago—but certain that his hunger was in fact shared by a world of the dispossessed, which perhaps is the majority of the world.

Bob Greenlee. *New Haven Register*, June 19, 1977, p. D-3.

For those who've read Richard Wright's "Black Boy," an internationally renowned autobiography of one of America's greatest black writers, "American Hunger," is perhaps the best of six unpublished works that will be published by Harper & Row of Wright's work.

I say this because I have read "Black Boy," and while it was internationally acclaimed, "American Hunger," which

Wright is reported to have not wanted published at the time because it was "too controversial," cuts to the quick as a literary masterpiece . . . it is something of a tragedy that it wasn't published when intended, because if it had then there is no doubt in my mind that Wright's star would have risen much faster than it did.

"American Hunger" is about Wright's years in Chicago, shortly after he left the South, and in it he probably sets the tone for a book that was to come later by another black author, Ralph Ellison, whose "Invisible Man" has been described in much the same way as Wright's "Black Boy," a literary masterpiece by a black writer.

In each of these two books, "American Hunger" and "Invisible Man," the authors—Wright and Ellison—capture the intense feeling of what it is like to be black in a nation that rarely, if ever, recognizes that non-whites have something to contribute (in this case the literary talents of the two aforementioned authors) that cuts across racial and ethnic lines to become universally accepted.

There are several moving situations in "American Hunger" that give substance to Wright's book.

One such moving passage is when he lands a job as a porter in a Jewish delicatessen and has to lie about taking time off to take his civil service examination for a better paying job in the Post Office.

So unnerved was Wright about having to take the time off and how his boss would feel about such an act that he told one lie after another, when he finally came back to work, never realizing that his employers—Mr. and Mrs. Hoffman—were treating him as an equal, something that was unheard of in his native South.

Yet Wright continued to tell one lie upon another in an attempt not to incur their anger. Little did he know that the one thing they hated was a "liar."

The lesson was a painful one, but one that taught Wright about his new situation in the North—that he did not have to cower to white people, as he did in Tennessee.

Another was an experience he had, working in a cafe, where he caught the beloved cook spitting in the food that was being prepared.

His Southern experience had taught him that if he told the Boss Lady of the cafe about the cook, who was white, he wouldn't be believed.

In this episode, it took the courage of a new employee, a black girl hired as a waitress, to push Wright into telling the boss about the cook. The girl, after she learned of what Wright knew about the cook, finally confronted the boss about what she'd seen. Then, and only then, did the boss fire the cook.

True, these are only slices of life views of Wright's experiences in Chicago; they, nevertheless, capture the spirit of the time and the feelings about his being that the then young writer was trying to come to grips with, as he experienced life in the North.

Theodore Rosengarten. *Washington Post Book World,* June 19, 1977, p. K 1. *New York Post,* June 25, 1977. *Rocky Mountain News* (Denver), July 10, 1977.

Richard Wright was a lonely man. Hunger for food set him apart from the boys and girls of his childhood. Hunger for explanations divided him from the people he worked and lived with. From his birth in Natchez, Mississippi, in 1908, until his death in Paris, in 1960, hunger of one sort or another was his constant companion.

American Hunger is the continuation of Wright's autobiography. The first volume, *Black Boy*, appeared in 1945, five years after the publication of his great novel, *Native Son*. At the end of *Black Boy*, Wright stands poised to leave the South, to follow his cravings free from the stunting racial laws and customs he never learned to tolerate. *American Hunger*—written with *Black Boy* as one work but withheld until now—picks up his story in Chicago, in 1927.

This poignant, bewildering book covers seven years in Wright's maturation as a writer and as a person with a coherent political outlook. At the center of the drama is Wright's romance with the Communist Party. It was not love at first sight. In fact, Wright was repulsed by the style of Negro Communist orators who mimicked the dialect of white Communists and wore caps on their heads "because Lenin had worn caps."

But the Party appealed to Wright's nature. He was hungry for insight and found in the Party "an organized search for the truth in the lives of the oppressed and isolated." His life as a Negro in America had led him to feel "that the problem of human unity was more important than bread, more important than physical living itself." The Communists were saying the same thing. Furthermore, they practiced what they preached when it came to race: at all visible levels the Party was integrated. Wright's cynicism melted, his hopes brightened. Through the Party he had his first sustained human relationships. And for the first time in his life he had a clear purpose—to bridge the gulf between Communist agitators and common people, to reveal the one to the other through his writing.

Wright was fooled by appearances. He learned to his dismay that the Party valued discipline over truth, that the truth was handed down from the top and members were expected to adopt it without criticism. Though racism was conquered within the Party, factional hatreds took its place. Wright himself was accused of corrupting majority opinion. All he had done was to speak against the majority opinion. It was inconceivable to him "that a man could not have his say." After all, he had come North "just to talk freely."

The Party did not want him to talk at all, at least not in his own language, or in his own form. Party officials demanded that he cease writing fiction and turn out pamphlets instead. Wright responded by defending the long-term impact of artistic works. The Party wouldn't listen, and Wright had no choice. A hunger to learn and convey the ways of the world had brought him to the Party; now it compelled him to leave.

Wright had known rejection before—by his father, his educators, his employers, by his fellow artists—but this was the most painful rejection of all. The people among whom he had made "the first total emotional commitment of my life" now ostracized and assaulted him.

Other enemies from the ranks were placed on trial, allowed to admit their guilt, and embraced back into the Party. Wright was not given the chance. His comrades could not try him because "they did not know how to give names to what they feared in me." They could not understand a man who craved human unity and loneliness, who was most productive in isolation. "Writing had to be done in loneliness," he says, "and Communism had declared war on human loneliness."

American Hunger is the testimony Wright would have given in defense of himself. Brilliant in its indictment of racism and of white America's "lust for trash," it would have been a proof of the organizing power of imaginative works. Most likely he would have been stopped from giving it. As a person who tried to think for himself, Wright presented a danger everywhere he went. At the spellbinding trial of a former comrade, Wright "whispered" to himself his whole dilemma: "God, I love these people, but I'm glad they're not in power, or they'd shoot me."

How did Wright get into this position? Because in repudiating racism he repudiated all kinds of oppression, which his comrades could not yet do. He took two steps where they took one. That makes his voice more durable than theirs. It makes his concerns current concerns. Though written more than 30 years ago, *American Hunger* opens still another chapter in American Negro heartbreak.

Frank Campenni. *Milwaukee Journal*, July 3, 1977, Part 5, p. 5.

Much of this small book was previously published in sections, yet it is a major literary event. "American Hunger," in fact, is the second half of "Black Boy" and drastically affects our early readings of Richard Wright's so-called autobiography, published more than 30 years ago.

Even read jointly, these two slender volumes leave the reader with a 28 year old author in embryo, two years short of "Uncle Tom's Children" and four years prior to his powerful first novel, "Native Son."

"Black Boy" had apparently "ended" on an optimistic note as 19 year old Richard left the South forever. But Wright had hastily added a five page conclusion to the middle of a dismal book. The publisher then dropped all of what now appears as "American Hunger," the story of Wright's 10 years in Chicago.

The publishing history of this truncated autobiography will probably never be unraveled. Apparently, the published version, called "Black Boy," modeled on the slave narratives, was to trace Richard's life from an oppressed Southern boyhood to his adolescent journey northward to freedom. Published in 1945 when Wright was an international literary celebrity, the book scored as a black Horatio Alger story and eased Northern consciences.

The two volumes complement each other in several ways. "Black Boy" was concerned mainly with external signs of oppression, the codes and rules of the South designed to blight the hopes of a bright but black child. In "American Hunger," Wright depicts the most scarring marks of oppression, the lack of trust of blacks for each other and their lack of faith in themselves. "Black Boy" threw the shadow of Southern tyranny—and it was a form of fascism to blacks—over Richard's life, while "American Hunger" moves on to the subtler tyranny of the radical left. For Wright, like many black intellectuals of the 1930s was drawn into the orbit of American Communism, and he remained longer than most.

The publishers may have withheld "American Hunger" because 80% of the book deals with Wright's years in the Communist Party. Although Wright's version here suggests that he jumped, fell or was pushed from the party in 1936, he actually lingered in its environs for another half dozen years.

And here is the last interesting parallel between the two parts of his autobiography. Earlier, Wright had rebelled against the authoritarian ways of his conservative, religious family and the hierarchy of the South. He was to find Communist suppression of dissidence just as repulsive, and the party's attempts to control his writings intolerable. Years later, he would frame the story of these clashes with commissars in Richard Crossman's compendium, "The God That Failed," but that account is more self-serving than these honest, humiliating pages. The story is dated but still moving and informative.

We wish there were more of the story. In "American Hunger," as the title suggests, Wright soon moves beyond the story of racial oppression to cultural criticism as he tells of his pity for the white waitresses with whom he worked:

"They were an eager, restless, talkative, ignorant bunch, but casually kind and impersonal for all that. They knew nothing of hate and fear, and strove instinctively to avoid all passion."

Ten years after this volume leaves off, Wright was to leave the United States forever. His Parisian days trailed off into paranoid bitterness when he died at 52, convinced that the FBI and CIA were opening his mail and smearing his name.

Since "American Hunger" is part of a project to publish his private papers, we can only wait and hope for the third volume of Wright's own life story.

David Bradley. "Soul on Ice," *Quest/77*, 1 (July-August 1977), 80–81.

Beginning this year, a series of as many as six books assembled from the papers of Richard Wright will be released by Wright's original publisher. The first in the series, a thin volume entitled *American Hunger*, was intended to be the final segment of Wright's autobiography. The portion that was published in 1945 under the title *Black Boy* covered Wright's youth in the South, ending with his departure in search of the Promised Land—in Chicago. The omitted portion would have exposed Paradise by telling of Wright's life in a North that merely substituted subtle bigotry for the blatant Southern version. The picture was at variance with the North's liberal self-image; it would hardly have been popular. Perhaps for this reason either Wright's publisher (then called Harper & Brothers) or the Book of the Month Club gently suggested that the book might end "more logically" with the traditional escape from the South—never mind to what. Wright acquiesced.

I have always had problems in dealing with Wright. I read him because I was black and ambitious to become a writer and he was, in the words of more than one authority, the greatest writer black America had ever produced. I opened *Black Boy* expecting to find, if not sublime resonance, at least harmonics of my own artistic and spiritual vibrations. What I found was hardly that, hardly even subtle discord; Wright was in a different key altogether, to my mind a minor one. I read with disbelief and dismay his ideas on the souls of black folk; me. And himself. Those ideas struck me as . . . racist. One passage lingered in my mind, almost verbatim: "I used to mull over the strange absence of real kindness in Negroes, how unstable was our tenderness, how lacking in genuine passion we were, how void of great hope, how timid our joy, how bare our traditions, how hollow our memories, how lacking those intangible sentiments that bind man to man, and how shallow was even our despair." Reading that, I found myself wondering what They had done to him to make him feel that way, write that way. (And worrying if, somehow, They would manage to do it to me—whoever They were.)

American Hunger does not do much to answer the question. It is simply the story of Wright's struggle for survival in Depression Chicago and of his Kafkaesque confrontations with the Communist party. It is powerful; it is all but impossible to read of Wright's doomed efforts to surmount the effects of chronic malnutrition and gain 15 pounds, so that he could weigh 125 and meet the minimum requirement for a job in the post office, without feeling sympathy and rage rising in the gut like a spring tide drawn by a massive moon. This is protest literature written by a master, perhaps *the* master. But it is not autobiography.

It is not personal. It does not cleave into the meaty emotions that fleshed Wright's life; it does not tell how it felt to be solvent at 32 after 31 years of near starvation; to be the author of *Native Son*, a runaway best-seller, suspecting—as he must have—that the success was due less to the acceptance of one's meaning than to the sensational nature of one's vehicle. It does not tell how it felt to be the "esteemed Negro author" whom one's agent could not take out to lunch for fear of encountering Jim Crow in his Northern incarnation, and whom even a wartime army would not take as a gift. It does not reveal an author who allowed the story of his own life to be truncated so that the ending might be "more logical"; or who—after two decades of international fame and two best-sellers—hesitated to use the surnames of his editor and his agent in a dedication, feeling that being so closely identified with a Negro might prove an embarrassment to them.

And yet *American Hunger*, in the white spaces between the cold type, does reveal Wright—as something of a cold-blooded intellectual, friendless, alone, prone to perceiving people, even himself, as perfect prototypes rather than human beings. *Black Boy's* troublesome reduction of blacks is ruthlessly extended here, first to a group of white waitresses with whom Wright worked: "I learned about their tawdry dreams . . . They knew nothing of hate and fear, and strove instinctively to avoid all passion"; then even to a black woman with whom Wright often made love: "Sex relations were the only relations she ever had; no others were possible with her, so limited was her intelligence."

These observations seem to reflect more than they illuminate; to me they reveal a man horribly crippled, uneasy with emotion, unaccustomed to warmth.

The causes of that crippling are not totally clear. *Black Boy* suggests that it derived from the brutality of the South, *American Hunger* that it resulted from the privation of the North, and Wright notes: "My readings in sociology had enabled me to discern many strange types of Negro characters . . . " thus suggesting another possible cause. A black reading about blacks in the sociological literature of the twenties is a bit like a man with an ulcer drinking sulfuric acid.

But these possible causes do not seem enough, and one can only speculate on the deeper origins of Wright's coldness. Knowing of it, though, one can understand a bit more why he wrote and acted as he did; can comprehend, for example, why he was attracted to communism, can see him gamboling amidst its icy absolutes and congealed perceptions. One can also see him freezing to death, and ultimately this is the power and value of *American Hunger*. It is as if Wright, sensing what had happened, was happening to him, were offering himself up as a case study, the archetype of protest novel; as if he were possessed by a great frigid fatalism, a belief that there was no way to come in from the cold, that there was nothing to do but protest and, in the end, to flee, suspecting, knowing, that there was no real escape.

George Breitman. *International Socialist Review*, 38 (supplement to *The Militant*) (August 5, 1977), 12.

Prospective buyers of *American Hunger* should be warned that the Harper and Row book jacket makes a false and highly misleading claim about its contents. (I leave aside errors of fact such as the assertion, made twice, that Richard Wright moved from the South to Chicago in 1934; as Wright wrote in the first paragraph of the first page in this book, "The year was 1927.")

Wright was one of the best American writers of his time (1908-60). Nobody wrote novels, stories, or essays so vividly depicting the reality of racism in the United States and its effects on Blacks and whites. He was also a severe critic of the inhumanity, brutality, and spiritual barrenness of capitalism. His *Black Boy* remains one of the great American autobiographies.

American Hunger is published seventeen years after his death as an expatriate in Paris. It was written originally as the last six chapters of *Black Boy*. Wright agreed before its publication in 1945 to omit these six chapters and to restrict *Black Boy* to the story of his life in the South, which he left at the age of nineteen when he moved to Chicago. The omitted chapters were about Wright's life in Chicago from 1927 to 1936.

Of these six chapters, the book jacket says that "the bulk of it has, until now, remained unpublished. . . . Any find relating to Richard Wright is exciting. The reappearance of this absorbing work is more than that; it is very much an event."

Responding to such cues, Gwendolyn Brooks, the poet, agrees: "It *is* an event, this discovery." Irving Howe, the literary critic who has written much about Wright, including a famous controversy with Ralph Ellison, cannot understand how a "personal history by one of our most important writers" could have been "lost" or "forgotten," and notes peevishly that the publisher does not explain "why we have had to wait so long" *(New York Times Book Review*, June 26); but he accepts the publisher's contention that we have had to wait. Darryl Pinckney, another critic, not only accepts it but takes it a notch further by quoting a speculation that Wright may have considered it too "sensitive to publish during his lifetime" (*Village Voice*, July 14).

But the facts are that "the bulk" of *American Hunger* was published quite a while ago, and while Wright was alive. The last three of the six chapters, dealing with Wright's experiences in the Communist Party, were published in 1950 in a book edited by Richard Crossman, *The God That Failed*, with only a few minor and insignificant changes. These three chapters make up 76 of the 135 pages by Wright in *American Hunger*, or 56 percent of the total. Before that, in 1944, this material had been published in the *Atlantic Monthly*. The Crossman book, by the way, was published by Harper.

That is not all, Virtually all of the material in the first three chapters has also been published before: first as an essay in a book edited by Edwin Seaver, *Cross Section, 1945*, and then as an essay in Wright's *Eight Men*, published in 1961 after his death. Adding this to the material from *The God That Failed* enables us to say that well over 90 percent of *American Hunger* was published before. (So long ago that Howe, who read *The God That Failed* and *Eight Men*, has forgotten that he read it before; so long ago that the younger Pinckney may never have heard of these other books.)

The publisher, however, is well aware of the facts; he has to be, to avoid suits for infringement of copyright. His awareness is shown in a publisher's note inside the book stating that "portions . . . saw scattered publication in the 1940's." This note discreetly avoids mention of the number and size of the "portions." How else are you going to gull critics, poets, and more credulous people? How else are you going to make "an event" out of the prosaic publication for the third time of articles that were first published in the 1940s and then published a second time in the 1950s and 1960s?

As for the book itself, it adds little to Wright's stature, and it is not hard to see why he chose not to publish it as a separate work. It has some excellent episodes, especially about his jobs as dishwasher in a cafe, agent for a Black insurance company, and orderly at a medical research institute in a large hospital, and about his alienation from his fellow workers as well as his employers. But I don't think that the force of these passages about Wright's lonely life in the urban North can be fully appreciated unless you have first read about his preceding years in the South. Standing by itself, *American Hunger* is insubstantial.

The major part of the book is about Wright's experiences as a member of the Communist Party in Chicago. This will be of interest to people who are concerned with U.S. radical history, the relation between politics and art, the role of intellectuals in workers parties, and similar topics. But a word of caution is needed here too; the author does not display much political insight, and he is not completely candid.

In a later book, *Black Power*, published in 1954, Wright says that he was a member of the CP from 1932 until 1944. For reasons that he does not explain, at the end of *American Hunger* he deliberately makes it appear that he left the CP in 1936. He did have a rift with the CP that year, but it was temporary and must have been healed by 1937 when he was in New York and was writing for the *Daily Worker* as its Harlem correspondent.

The real break did not take place until 1944, when he was completing his autobiography. Meanwhile, he served on the board of *New Masses* and numerous CP front organizations and faithfully supported its political line, whatever that might be—for the "People's Front" and support of Roosevelt until 1939, then against the war and against Roosevelt until Hitler invaded the Soviet Union in 1941, then for the war and for Roosevelt, and so forth. This means he was for a separate state in the "Black Belt" of the South when the CP advocated it in the early 1930s and against it when the CP shelved it during the "People's Front" period; for Black militancy during the Stalin-Hitler pact and against it during the Stalin-Roosevelt alliance.

Although the book is very short, it suffers from many anachronisms. Wright says that during a writers' conference in Chicago in the summer of 1934 there was discussion about the CP's "new People's Front Policy," but this policy was not introduced into the United States until 1935 and had not yet been christened with that name when it first appeared in France in mid-1934. He says that at a CP inquisition trial where a Black CP member confessed his "deviations" some time before May 1936, " I knew as I sat there, that there were many people . . . who had been skeptical of the Moscow trials." However, he couldn't have known or thought that because the first of the Moscow trials was not staged until August 1936.

Such anachronisms are bound to happen when people rely on their memory rather than more objective evidence. Wright's deliberate obfuscation about when he left the CP is a different and more serious defect because it tends to undermine the credibility of his narrative for anyone who reads the facts elsewhere.

Wright's conversion to communism as he understood it was a very important stage in his development. It broadened his horizons immensely and led him to the themes of his best writing. But most of his story is about the unsatisfactory side of his relations with his comrades in Chicago, especially his Black comrades on the South Side. He is very critical sometimes even contemptuous, about their mannerisms, pronunciation, modes of speech, dress; about their suspiciousness, intolerance, anti-intellectualism, and "militant ignorance."

What Wright is describing here is a style that pervaded the whole CP at that time, and not only the American CP but all the other affiliates of the Stalinized Communist International. It was the style of the "third period," which lasted from 1928 to 1934. Third-period politics were ultraleft, sectarian, adventurist, often seemingly insane, and based on the delusion that revolution was around the corner, or nearer; the bizarre style of the period (when Wright first approached the CP) merely reflected the bizarre politics. At first it seems strange that Wright castigates the style of the third-period Black members but has nothing to say about the same style of the white members. It seems less strange when you realize that he has nothing whatever to say about third-period politics, even after they were abandoned and replaced by the new "People's Front" politics, which led to a new and "more respectable" style. Wright did not have much understanding of, or real interest in, politics.

Wright had a prickly personality, and the frictions between him and the CP could not have come all from one side. Relations became bitter at some points—for example when two CP leaders physically assaulted and ejected him from the May Day parade in 1936. But, as he says, he never had any political differences with the CP leadership, whatever policy it was pursuing. The CP leaders knew this was true, despite their occasional slanders against him. That was why they never expelled him, despite his long stretches of inactivity. Wright did not know the difference between revolutionary Leninism and counterrevolutionary Stalinism when he joined the CP, he never grasped the difference while he was in the CP, and he continued to equate these opposites after he left the CP. That is why there is not much to be learned politically from this book.

Checklist of Additional Reviews

Kirkus Reviews, 45 (March 15, 1977), 341.

Publishers Weekly, 211 (April 4, 1977), 88.

David Isaacson. *Library Journal*, 102 (May 1, 1977), 1011.

John E. Cooney. *Wall Street Journal*, May 5, 1977, p. 20.

Mark Stevens. *Christian Science Monitor*, May 12, 1977, p. 23.

Booklist, 73 (May 15, 1977), 1390.

Earl J. Dias. *New Bedford Standard Times*, May 15, 1977.

Stephen A. Monroe. *Rochester Democrat and Chronicle*, May 15, 1977.

Paul Pintarich. *Portland Oregonian*, May 15, 1977.

Abe C. Ravitz. *Cleveland Plain Dealer*, May 15, 1977.

Les Payne. *Houston Chronicle*, May 22, 1977.

Geoffrey Wolff. "The Lion in the Path." *New Times* 8 (May 27, 1977), 57–62.

Marc Galvin. *South Bend Tribune*, May 29, 1977.

Robert Kirsch. *Los Angeles Times*, May 29, 1977, pp. 1, 71.

William Hogan. *San Francisco Chronicle*, May 30, 1977.

Margo Jefferson. *Newsweek*, 89 (May 30, 1977), 81.

Edwin Warner. *Time*, 109 (May 30, 1977), 74.

Terry Pluto. *Cleveland Press*, June 3, 1977.

Pamela Moreland. *Pasadena Star News*, June 5, 1977.

New Yorker, 53 (June 6, 1977), 138.

Peter McNally. *Hartford Courant,* June 9, 1977, p. 48.

William Murchison. *New Rochelle Standard-Star*, June 11, 1977.

L. M. C. *Asheville Citizen Times*, June 12, 1977.

Carol Felsenthal. Newspaper Enterprise Association, June 17, 1977. Reprinted *Bremerton Sun* (Washington), June 24, 1977, p. 3.

Lesley Crosson. *Camden Courier-Post* (N. J.), June 23, 1977.

Gregg Thomas Weinlein. *Schenectady Kite*, June 23, 1977.

Irving Howe. *New York Times Book Review*, June 26, 1977, pp. 1, 34.

The Atlantic, 239 (June 1977), 93–94.

Phil Thomas. AP Newsfeatures, July 1, 1977. Reprinted: *Gardner News* (Mass.), July 6, 1977; *Champaign*

News-Gazette, July 8, 1977; *Poughkeepsie Journal*, July 10, 1977; *Vallejo Times Herald*, July 10, 1977; *Hazleton Standard-Speaker*, July 12, 1977; *Gary Post-Tribune*, July 17, 1977; *Fitchburg-Leminster Sentinel & Enterprise* (MA), July 19, 1977; *Decatur Daily*, July 22, 1977; *Nogales Herald* (Ariz.), July 25, 1977, etc.

Thomas A. Johnson. *New York Times*, July 2, 1977, p. 15.

Darryl Pinckney, "Richard Wright: The Unnatural." *Village Voice*, July 4, 1977, pp. 80–82.

Human Events, 37 (July 9, 1977), 12.

William Harrington. *Columbus Sunday Dispatch*, July 10, 1977.

L. M. Collins. *Nashville Tennessean*, July 10, 1977.

Rolling Stone (July 14, 1977), 72.

Sylvia Rothchild. *Jewish Advocate* (Boston), July 14, 1977.

Jay Vanleer. *Cleveland Call and Post*, July 23, 1977.

Best Sellers, 37 (August 1977), 152.

American Poetry Review, 6 (September 1977), 40.

School Library Journal, 24 (September 1977), 156.

The Progressive, 41 (September 1977), 44.

Index